EQUITY, TRUSTS AND COMMERCE

This collection of essays, written by leading commentators from across the common law world, examines a range of topics concerning Equity and Trusts in the commercial context. The essays investigate the way in which doctrines derived from the equitable jurisdiction interact with and shape various areas of the law, including company law, commercial law and agency law. Subjects considered include the difficulties in identifying trust assets in the commercial context; the court's role in supervising the trust; and the remedies available in cases of fiduciary or trustee wrongdoing. This book will be of interest to both academics and practitioners working in these difficult areas of equity and commercial law.

Volume 24 in the series Hart Studies in Private Law

Equity, Trusts and Commerce

Edited by
Paul S Davies and James Penner

• HART •
PUBLISHING
OXFORD AND PORTLAND, OREGON
2017

Hart Publishing
An imprint of Bloomsbury Publishing Plc

Hart Publishing Ltd
Kemp House
Chawley Park
Cumnor Hill
Oxford OX2 9PH
UK

Bloomsbury Publishing Plc
50 Bedford Square
London
WC1B 3DP
UK

www.hartpub.co.uk
www.bloomsbury.com

Published in North America (US and Canada) by
Hart Publishing
c/o International Specialized Book Services
920 NE 58th Avenue, Suite 300
Portland, OR 97213-3786
USA

www.isbs.com

HART PUBLISHING, the Hart/Stag logo, BLOOMSBURY and the Diana logo are trademarks of Bloomsbury Publishing Plc

First published 2017

British Library Cataloguing-in-Publication Data
A catalogue record for this book is available from the British Library.

ISBN: HB: 978-1-50990-729-8
ePDF: 978-1-50990-731-1
ePub: 978-1-50990-730-4

Library of Congress Cataloging-in-Publication Data

Names: Davies, Paul S. (Law teacher), editor. | Penner, J. E. (James E.), editor.

Title: Equity, trust, and commerce / edited by Paul S. Davies and James Penner.

Description: Oxford [UK] ; Portland, Oregon : Hart Publishing, 2017. | Series: Hart studies in private law ; v. 24 | Includes bibliographical references and index.

Identifiers: LCCN 2016057787 (print) | LCCN 2016058886 (ebook) | ISBN 9781509907298 (hardback : alk. paper) | ISBN 9781509907304 (Epub)

Subjects: LCSH: Equity. | Trusts and trustees. | Commercial law.

Classification: LCC K795 .E68 2017 (print) | LCC K795 (ebook) | DDC 346/.004—dc23

LC record available at https://lccn.loc.gov/2016057787

Typeset by Compuscript Ltd, Shannon
Printed and bound in Great Britain by Lightning Source UK Ltd

PREFACE

In the first line of his judgment in *AIB Group (UK) Plc v Mark Redler & Co*,[1] Lord Toulson said: '140 years after the Judicature Act 1873, the stitching together of equity and the common law continues to cause problems at the seams'. In many ways, the essays in this collection work at these 'seams', investigating the way in which doctrines derived from the equitable jurisdiction interact with and shape areas of the law, such as company, commercial law and agency law, which reflect not only common law doctrines of long standing, but significant statutory innovation. The topics encompassed by 'equity', 'trusts' and 'commerce' are, to say the least, many and varied, as this collection attests.

Our first essay by Tan Cheng-Han and Wee Meng-Seng, 'Equity, Shareholders and Company Law', explores from a historical perspective the influence of equitable doctrine on the relationships of shareholders. The authors consider this issue through the prism of the 'just and equitable winding-up doctrine', examining the way in which it constrained the power of majority shareholders and its relation to the modern concept of unfair prejudice. In 'Some Aspects of the Intersection of the Law of Agency with the Law of Trusts', Peter Watts considers the case of agents who are also trustees, and deftly raises a host of questions concerning how the authority of agents interacts with the authority of trustees. Tang Hang Wu examines a different aspect of the way that equity may impinge upon commercial transactions in 'Equity in the Marketplace: Reviewing the Use of Unconscionability to Restrain Calls on Performance Bonds'. Tang investigates the Singaporean departure from the orthodox rule as applied in England, namely that there is no room for considerations of unconscionability when commercial parties initiate calls on performance bonds; restraints are only allowed on the very limited basis of fraud. Tang argues that the exceptional Singapore experience represents a conscious policy choice of the courts which, on the basis of local imperatives, will act to restrain calls that they regard as abusive.

Our next three essays revolve around the issue of intention and 'certainty of subject matter' for the purposes of identifying trust assets in the commercial context. Michael Bridge's essay, 'Certainty, Identification and Intention in Personal Property Law', explores the difficulties the law has encountered in identifying specific personal property interests, ranging over future property, property in sales of goods cases, trust interests in the commercial context, and in the law of charges.

[1] *AIB Group (UK) Plc v Mark Redler & Co* [2014] UKSC 58 , [2015] AC 1503 [1].

Robert Stevens's focus in 'Floating Trusts' is narrower, interrogating in detail the finding of trust interests in mixed funds in the complex 'repo' securities transactions examined by the courts following the collapse of Lehman Brothers. James Penner's essay, '"Sort of" Backwards Tracing' raises issues about intention and the subject matter of a trust in a different way. In the Privy Council decision in *Brazil v Durant International*[2] a Commonwealth court explicitly recognised for the first time the claimant's entitlement to an asset on the basis of 'backwards' tracing, but Penner convincingly argues that a host of questions remain to be resolved before the impact of that decision can properly be assessed.

Our next three essays take us back to more traditional issues in trusts, all of which concern the special relationship that trusts as a legal device have with the courts. Richard Nolan, in 'Invoking the Administrative Jurisdiction: The Enforcement of Modern Trust Structures', shows that, whilst modern trusts often include a wide range of trustee discretions, the traditional, well-established power of the courts to ensure that a trustee complies with the trust terms can be adapted flexibly and sensibly to modern trust structures, in particular in cases of breach of trust. In 'Trusts, Objectivity and Rectification', Simon Douglas explores in detail the relationship between a settlor's intention in creating a trust and the power of a court to intervene by rectifying the trust instruments. Douglas argues that, despite some cases in which the court appeared to base its decision to rectify on the settlor's 'subjective' intention, the true and correct rule is that primacy is given to the objective meaning of the settlor's declaration of trust. Raising the issue of the court's special relationship to the administration of trusts from a very different angle in 'The Arbitrability of Trust Instruments: Why Not?', Elaine Chew weighs the various arguments in favour of—and against—the law allowing settlors to require trustee–beneficiary disputes to be determined by arbitration, rather than only through invocation of the court process.

Our last five essays all concern the best way in which to understand the remedies available in cases of fiduciary or trustee wrongdoing. In 'Bribery', Paul Davies points out that whilst much attention has been paid to the liability of the recipient of a bribe, the liability of the person making the bribe has been insufficiently explored, and in this essay he makes up for that deficiency. Deborah DeMott, in 'Accessory Disloyalty: Comparative Perspectives on Substantial Assistance to Fiduciary Breach', compares American and English approaches towards accessory liability. In the US, both breach of fiduciary duty and culpably assisting in the fiduciary's breach are characterised as tortious, and such characterisation is important when determining the elements of accessory liability. Jamie Glister's 'Equitable

[2] *Brazil v Durant International* [2015] UKPC 35.

Liability of Corporate Accessories' explores two models for understanding the liability of a corporate entity that assists in the misapplication of another's funds: on the first, the wrongdoing fiduciary and the corporate accessory are so close, that the two are treated as the same actor for the purposes of liability; on the second, the corporate entity is regarded as a distinct 'third-party' accessory. In 'The Nature of "Knowing Receipt"', William Swadling examines one by one the different justifications for the liability of the recipient. Swadling concludes that the only viable explanation is a liability occasioned by the defendant's equitable wrong, and argues that the fault requirement should be pitched high in terms of the defendant's knowledge, given the availability of a strict liability proprietary claim against him as well as a strict liability personal claim against the defaulting trustees. Sarah Worthington, in 'Exposing Third-Party Liability in Equity: Lessons from the Limitation Rules', takes as her starting point the treatment of recipients and accessories by the UK Supreme Court in *Williams v Central Bank of Nigeria*, which involved the application of the Limitation Act 1980 to cases of breach of trust.[3] Worthington's central claim is that anyone who, for whatever reason, has property-holding and/or property-managing duties with respect to the property of another is a true trustee, and so the need to resort to 'constructive' trusteeship formulations in this area of doctrine obscures the real issues at stake, not least for the law of limitations.

These essays were all first presented at the National University of Singapore on 12 and 13 April 2016. Each essay was presented by another contributor, and discussed for up to an hour. The debate was lively, and we are very grateful to all the authors for making the workshop so enjoyable and for providing such thoughtful comments on all the essays. We conclude by expressing our immense gratitude to the National University of Singapore Centre for Law & Business and the Faculty of Law, University of Oxford, for their generous support of that event without which this publication would not have been possible. We are also very grateful to Jia Wei Lee for his assistance in preparing the manuscript for publication, and to Bill Asquith and the team at Hart Publishing for supporting this project so enthusiastically. Finally, we would like to thank Tan Cheng-Han who came up with the idea of a conference in the first place, and without whose persistent encouragement this book would never have been produced.

Paul S Davies and James Penner
September 2016

[3] *Williams v Central Bank of Nigeria* [2014] UKSC 10; [2014] AC 1189 (SC).

CONTENTS

LIST OF CONTRIBUTORS

Michael Bridge is Professor of Law, National University of Singapore and Cassel Professor of Commercial Law, London School of Economics and Political Science.

Elaine Chew is Lecturer in Law, National University of Singapore.

Paul S Davies is Associate Professor of Law, University of Oxford and Fellow of St Catherine's College.

Deborah A DeMott is David F Cavers Professor of Law, Duke University School of Law.

Simon Douglas is Associate Professor of Law, University of Oxford and Peter Clarke Fellow of Jesus College.

Jamie Glister is Associate Professor of Law, University of Sydney.

Richard Nolan is Anniversary Professor of Law, University of York.

James Penner is Professor of Law, National University of Singapore.

Robert Stevens is Herbert Smith Freehills Professor of Private Law, University of Oxford and Fellow of Lady Margaret Hall.

William Swadling is Reader in the Law of Property, University of Oxford and Fellow of Brasenose College.

Tan Cheng Han SC is Professor of Law, National University of Singapore.

Tang Hang Wu is Professor and Director, Centre for Cross-Border Commercial Law in Asia, Singapore Management University.

Peter Watts QC is Professor of Law, University of Auckland.

Wee Meng-Seng is Associate Professor of Law, National University of Singapore.

Sarah Worthington QC is Downing Professor of the Laws of England, University of Cambridge and Fellow of Trinity College.

1

Equity, Shareholders and Company Law

TAN CHENG-HAN AND WEE MENG-SENG*

I. Introduction

Equity has played an important role in company law from its modern inception when the Joint Stock Companies Act 1844 was enacted. This is unsurprising given that prior to the Act of 1844, most joint stock companies were unincorporated associations to which the law of partnership and trust law principally applied. The only incorporated associations at the time were established by Royal Charter or by a private Act of Parliament. These were not easily obtained. Accordingly, a substitute developed as, by the end of the seventeenth century, some idea had been gleaned of one of the primary functions of the company concept, namely the possibility of combining the capitalist with the entrepreneur.[1] This was effected through the formation of large quasi-partnerships known as joint stock companies.[2]

The term 'company' in this context was of course a misnomer by modern standards as it simply meant association, and joint stock companies were unincorporated associations,[3] many of which were originally formed as partnerships by agreement under seal, providing for the division of the undertaking into shares which were transferable by the original partners.[4] In essence they continued to be partnerships and what distinguished them from a typical partnership was that they generally consisted of many members, and the articles of agreement between

* We are grateful to Professor Hans Tjio, Professor James Penner and Professor Paul L Davies for comments on an earlier draft, and to the participants at the conference, April 2016. The usual caveats apply.

[1] PL Davies, *Gower's Principles of Modern Company Law*, 6th edn (London, Sweet & Maxwell, 1997) 23.

[2] *Re Agriculturist Cattle Insurance Co, Baird's Case* (1870) LR 5 Ch App 725, 733–34.

[3] R Austin, I Ramsay and HAJ Ford, *Ford, Austin & Ramsay's Principles of Corporations Law*, vol 1, 16th edn (Sydney, LexisNexis Butterworths, 2014) para 2.110.

[4] Davies (n 1) 21.

the parties were therefore usually very different.[5] This structure was not without its problems as partnership law was not well suited for a large association. For example, each of the investors was liable for the joint stock company's debts; each investor had power to bind the others to a contract with outsiders; and if the joint stock company wanted to sue a debtor, all investors had to be joined as plaintiffs.[6] The converse was also true if the joint stock company was to be sued; all investors had to be joined as defendants.

The transferability of shares allowed speculative activity to take place and the early part of the eighteenth century saw a boom in company flotations and a great bull market in joint stock trading. The English Parliament decided to intervene to curb the gambling mania that ensued which led to the so-called 'Bubble Act' of 1720.[7] It was intended to prevent persons from acting as if they were corporate bodies, or to have transferable shares without any authority from Parliament.[8] At the same time, the Act was also likely a piece of special interest legislation that was intended to benefit the infamous South Sea Company which had drawn up an ambitious scheme to acquire the national debt. Though the intention behind the legislation failed and indeed backfired on the South Sea Company, it was the prime force behind the passage of the Act.[9] It has been said that throughout the eighteenth century (and beyond) the shadow of 1720 retarded the development of incorporated companies.[10]

Nevertheless, notwithstanding the Bubble Act, unincorporated joint stock companies continued to exist. An important provision in the Act was to be found in section 25 that exempted 'trade in partnership' that 'may be lawfully done'. Given that joint stock companies were in essence partnerships, there was considerable scope to work around the Bubble Act. This manifested itself in the 'deed of settlement company' which was linked to the two equitable forms of group association, the partnership and the trust.[11] Many such 'companies' were established during the period the Bubble Act was in force.[12] In this incarnation, the 'company' would be formed under a deed of settlement (something approximating to a cross

[5] W Watson, *A Treatise of the Law of Partnership*, 2nd edn (London, Butterworth, 1807) 3; see also N Lindley, *A Treatise on the Law of Companies, Considered as a Branch of the Law of Partnership*, 5th edn (London, Sweet & Maxwell, 1889) 608–09.

[6] Austin et al (n 3) para 2.110.

[7] 6 Geo 1 c 18 (this is sometimes referred to as the Royal Exchange and London Assurance Corporation Act 1719 because the Royal Exchange Assurance Corporation and the London Assurance Corporation were incorporated under it).

[8] CA Cooke, *Corporation, Trust and Company: An Essay in Legal History* (Manchester, Manchester University Press, 1950) 80–82.

[9] R Harris, 'The Bubble Act: Its Passage and Its Effects on Business Organization' (1994) 54 *Journal of Economic History* 610, 623.

[10] Davies (n 1) 28; see also WR Scott, *The Constitution and Finance of English, Scottish and Irish Joint-Stock Companies to 1720*, vol 1 (Cambridge, CUP, 1912) 438; HAL Fisher (ed), *The Collected Papers of Frederic William Maitland*, vol III (Cambridge, CUP, 1911) 390; *cf* Harris (n 9) 623–26.

[11] Cooke (n 8) 85.

[12] Davies (n 1) 30; R McQueen, *A Social History of Company Law: Great Britain and the Australian Colonies 1854–1920* (Farnham, Ashgate Publishing, 2009) 20.

between a modern corporate constitution and a trust deed for debentures or unit trusts) whereby the subscribers would agree to be associated in an enterprise with a prescribed joint stock divided into a specified number of shares; the provisions of the deed would be variable with the consent of a specified majority of the proprietors; management would be delegated to a committee of directors; and the company's property would be vested in a separate body of trustees, some of whom would be directors also.[13] The deed of settlement would also provide that the trustees could sue or be sued on behalf of the company to get around the difficulty of claims by or against an unincorporated body with a potentially large membership. As James LJ described in *Re Agriculturist Cattle Insurance Co*:

> A joint stock company ... is an agreement between the owners of shares, or the owners of stock, that they or their duly recognized assigns, the owners of the shares for the time being, whoever they may be, shall be and continue an association together, sharing profits and bearing losses. No shareholder in a joint stock company is, in the legal sense of the word, any more a partner than the owner of bank stock is; he may not have the same limit of liability, but in every other respect he is the same; he has the same right to take part in public meetings of the body, he has the same right to elect or remove directors, he has the same right to vote for or against the resolutions of the body, he has the same right to such dividends as may be declared, and he has the same right to dispose of his share as a separate and distinct piece of property, and no other rights in or over the association, its assets, or its transactions, and if he is liable under any contracts or obligation, or in respect of any act of the body, it is ... because they are the contracts, obligations, and acts of the quasi body corporate ... by its properly constituted agents. It may be, and generally is, no doubt, that the agents, the directors, are shareholders, and in that sense partners, but it is certain that there may be a board of directors perfectly competent to bind the whole body, although every one of them may have disqualified himself by parting with every share.[14]

In addition, the deed would provide that each shareholder was to be liable only to the extent of his share in the capital stock. Although such a provision could only apply to the shareholders inter se and not be binding on third parties dealing with the company,[15] limited liability could be achieved if contracts between the company and third parties stipulated that the other party to the contract could only look to the common stock of the company and not the assets of individual shareholders.[16] A number of cases in the insurance context held that policyholders were bound by the terms of the deed of settlement of the insurance company if such terms were incorporated into the insurance contract.[17]

[13] Davies (n 1) 29. See also Cooke (n 8) 86–87.
[14] *Re Agriculturist Cattle Insurance Co* (n 2) 734–35.
[15] *Hallett v Dowdall* (1852) 18 QB 2, 118 ER 1.
[16] Austin et al (n 3) para 2.120; Cooke (n 8) 87.
[17] *Hallett v Dowdall* (n 15); *Re Waterloo Life Assurance Co, Carr's Case* (1864) 33 Beav 542, 55 ER 479; *Re Family Endowment Society* (1869–70) LR 5 Ch App 118; *Re European Assurance Society, Hort's Case* (1875) 1 Ch D 307.

Given the ineffectiveness of the Bubble Act in preventing persons from acting as if they were corporate bodies, or such bodies having transferable shares without any authority from Parliament, the Act was eventually repealed. Deed of settlement companies continued to flourish after the repeal and even after the enactment of the Joint Stock Companies Act 1844 which may be taken as the beginning of modern company law in England. The Act of 1844 provided, inter alia, for incorporation by registration without the need for a Royal Charter or Act of Parliament, and required all new deed of settlement companies with more than 25 members, or which had transferable shares, to be registered as incorporated companies. The Act of 1844 did not, however, provide for limited liability. This only came about through the Limited Liability Act 1855.

Notwithstanding these legislative developments, the unincorporated joint stock company formed by a deed of settlement prior to the Act of 1844 continued to coexist for many years after. In fact, the incorporated form did not take off initially as by 1885 limited companies accounted for at most 5 per cent and 10 per cent of the total number of important business organisations.[18] It was only from the 1870s that the corporate form came to be adopted by a growing number of unincorporated firms.[19] Even so, by the mid-1880s the company as a legal organisational form was very much subordinate to the partnership.[20]

In this brief historical introduction, it can be seen that at its outset modern company law was heavily influenced by what had gone before. The unincorporated joint stock company with a deed of settlement was essentially the business organisation that was adopted by the Act of 1844, though as a body corporate. The deed of settlement used by corporate bodies did not differ greatly from that which had evolved prior to the 1844 Act. It was still the repository of the rules for the internal governance of the company. Although the Joint Stock Companies Act 1856 introduced the memorandum and articles of association in place of the deed of settlement, the articles of association originated from deeds of settlement and the model articles which were found in the Act were based on widely used precedents.[21] Furthermore, as the business organisation that was adopted in early company law was based on a fusion of partnership and trust law, together with the law of agency,[22] which were all heavily infused by equitable doctrines, company law was susceptible to the influence of the law of equity. An instance of this was the introduction very early on of the 'just and equitable' winding up ground in the

[18] PL Payne, 'The Emergence of the Large-scale Company in Great Britain, 1870–1914' (1967) 20 *Economic History Review* 519, 520.

[19] WJ Reader, 'Versatility Unlimited: Reflections on the History and Nature of the Limited Liability Company' in T Orhnial (ed), *Limited Liability and the Corporation* (London, Croom Helm, 1982) 192.

[20] P Ireland, 'The Rise of the Limited Liability Company' (1984) 12 *International Journal of the Sociology of Law* 239, 244.

[21] R Tomasic, S Bottomley and R McQueen, *Corporations Law in Australia*, 2nd edn (Sydney, Federation Press, 2002) para 1.3.5.

[22] Agency law was relevant because it was intended that the acts of the directors of the joint stock company should be binding on the body of shareholders.

Joint Stock Companies Winding Up Act of 1848 which was influenced by the then uncodified law of partnership.[23]

It is suggested that a further major impetus to equity playing a significant role in company law was the use of the corporate vehicle by small businesses that resembled partnerships. These are sometimes referred to as 'quasi-partnerships' or 'incorporated partnerships'. While they are incorporated entities, they resemble partnerships in that they were formed on the basis of trust and confidence between the shareholders who all expected to be involved in management, and there were restrictive limits to the transferability of shares. It is the somewhat ironic converse of the unincorporated joint stock company that sought to escape the shackles of partnership law; these were corporate bodies that sought the benefits of limited liability but wanted to retain many features of a partnership structure. By the 1890s, two-thirds of existing company registrations were of small 'one-man' type companies.[24] Such 'private companies' partially accounted for the eventual meteoric rise of the company as the predominant business vehicle.[25] The early legislation relating to companies was not originally envisaged for such small companies.[26] This necessitated developments in company law that were generally not appropriate for large corporate enterprises with freely transferable shares. Equity, as an instrument to mitigate the rigours of the common law, was well suited to this gap-filling role, particularly given how the corporate form evolved in England.

One of the areas in which equity played an important role was to ameliorate the position of minority shareholders against majority rule. This is the subject that will be explored here and specific aspects that will be discussed are the just and equitable ground in winding up; the modern unfair prejudice remedy; the limitations placed on members when altering the corporate constitution; and other non-statutory constraints on the majority. It will be suggested that there is a common element in all these areas that give rise to the intervention of equity. This common element is an agreement or understanding between the shareholders of the company, whether express or implied, and whether enforceable or not as a matter of law.

II. Statutory Remedies: Just and Equitable Winding Up and Unfair Prejudice

Although the 'just and equitable' ground for winding up was influenced by the law of partnership, it was not at the time it was introduced in 1848 a discrete ground

[23] PL Davies and S Worthington, *Gower & Davies' Principles of Modern Company Law*, 9th edn (London, Sweet & Maxwell, 2012) para 20-40.

[24] McQueen, *A Social History of Company Law* (n 12) 273–74.

[25] Ireland (n 20) 245.

[26] ibid 241–44; McQueen, *A Social History of Company Law* (n 12) 274.

on which partnerships might be dissolved. No mention of such a ground is mentioned in an early treatise on partnership law though a breakdown in relations between the partners, and the inability of the partnership to attain the purposes for which it was entered into, are mentioned as grounds on which a partnership might be dissolved.[27] Today, these are regarded as falling within the just and equitable ground for partnership dissolution.[28] Similarly, prior to 1890, Lord Lindley makes no reference to just and equitable dissolution of partnerships in his well-known work.[29] This appeared for the first time in 1891 as a supplement to a revised fifth edition[30] in the context of the Partnership Act 1890 which introduced the just and equitable ground for dissolution.[31]

It is therefore curious how the just and equitable ground was inserted into the Act of 1848 which allowed a contributory to petition for dissolution or winding up where 'any other matter or thing shall be shown which in the opinion of the court shall render it just and equitable that the company should be dissolved'.[32]

It is suggested that this came about because the Act was intended to apply to both incorporated and unincorporated businesses. The preamble to the Act states that it 'shall apply to all companies, corporate or unincorporated', and the word 'company' in the Act meant 'any partnership, association, or company, corporate or unincorporated, to which this act applies'. Given that company law was in its infancy, and an incorporated company was regarded as little more than an extended form of partnership,[33] it is likely that the 'just and equitable' phrase was thought to express sufficiently the basis on which both incorporated and unincorporated joint stock companies might be dissolved or wound up as the case may be, with the applicable principles being drawn from the law of partnership.

While the just and equitable ground in the context of company law has been held by the courts to encompass a number of different circumstances,[34] it has been well observed that in the course of the twentieth century the ground has been moulded by the courts into a means of subjecting small private companies to equitable principles derived from partnership.[35] Such a result can be regarded

[27] Watson (n 5) 379–82.

[28] See R Banks, *Lindley & Banks on Partnership*, 19th edn (London, Sweet & Maxwell, 2010) paras 24-89–24-90; G Morse, *Partnership Law*, 7th edn (Oxford, OUP, 2010) para 7.14.

[29] N Lindley, *A Treatise on the Law of Partnership*, 5th edn (London, Sweet & Maxwell, 1888). The grounds that are mentioned at 570 of volume II are fraud; the will of any partner; the impossibility of going on in consequence of the hopeless state of the partnership business, insanity or misconduct; illegality, death and bankruptcy. On misconduct, Lindley stated at 580 that the misconduct must have led to some partners being excluded from the concern, or was such as to destroy the mutual confidence that must exist between partners.

[30] N Lindley, *A Treatise on the Law of Partnership, With a Supplement Consisting of the Partnership Act, 1890*, 5th edn (London, Sweet & Maxwell, 1891).

[31] Partnership Act 1890, s 35(f).

[32] Joint Stock Companies Winding Up Act 1848, s 5(8).

[33] BH McPherson, 'Winding Up on the "Just and Equitable" Ground' (1964) 27 *MLR* 282, 283.

[34] See S Girvin, S Frisby and A Hudson, *Charlesworth's Company Law*, 18th edn (London, Sweet & Maxwell, 2010) paras 22.023–22.024; CH Tan (ed), *Walter Woon on Company Law*, 3rd rev edn (Singapore, Sweet & Maxwell, 2009) paras 17.52–17.76.

[35] Davies and Worthington (n 23) para 20-40.

as serendipitous given that company legislation had for a long period not otherwise provided for any means by which minorities may be protected from unfair conduct that could not have been reasonably contemplated at the time the company was established or when they became shareholders. Two cases have been particularly influential. The first is *Re Yenidje Tobacco Co Ltd*,[36] a case that involved a private company that was described as being in substance a partnership.[37] There was a complete deadlock between the only two shareholders and directors and the court ordered that the company be wound up on the just and equitable ground even though the company was highly profitable. Lord Cozens-Hardy MR said that circumstances which would justify the winding up of a partnership were circumstances that should justify the court in exercising its discretion to wind up the company. More importantly, the court ought to apply 'the analogy of the partnership law and to say that this company is now in a state which could not have been contemplated by the parties when the company was formed and which ought to be terminated as soon as possible'.[38]

The second case is *Ebrahimi v Westbourne Galleries Ltd*[39] which also involved a company that was in substance a partnership. The appellant and N were partners in a business that was subsequently taken over by a private company in which the appellant and N were shareholders and directors. Soon after the incorporation of the company, N's son also became a director and shareholder with N and his son holding 60 per cent of the company's issued capital. Sometime later, they caused the appellant to be removed as a director, whereupon he commenced a petition based on section 210 of the Companies Act 1948 or alternatively that the company be wound up. The petition based on section 210 was dismissed but the company was ordered to be wound up on the just and equitable ground. The Court of Appeal set aside the order for winding up and the appellant appealed to the House of Lords.

The House of Lords allowed the appeal. Lord Wilberforce, who delivered the leading judgment, said that the respondents 'were not entitled, in justice and equity, to make use of their legal powers of expulsion' and the just and equitable course was to wind up the company.[40] In an important passage, his Lordship said:

> The words [just and equitable] are a recognition of the fact that a limited company is more than a mere legal entity, with a personality in law of its own: that there is room

[36] *Re Yenidje Tobacco Co Ltd* [1916] 2 Ch 426.

[37] ibid 432.

[38] ibid, and see also *Re Wondoflex Textiles Pty Ltd* [1951] VLR 458, 467. Singapore courts have cited *Re Yenidje Tobacco Co Ltd* with approval, eg, *Chua Kien How v Goodwealth Trading Pte Ltd* [1992] SGCA 29, [1992] 1 SLR(R) 870; *Sim Yong Kim v Evenstar Investments Pte Ltd* [2006] SGCA 23, [2006] 3 SLR(R) 827 [36].

[39] *Ebrahimi v Westbourne Galleries Ltd* [1973] 1 AC 360. *Ebrahimi* has been cited by numerous Singapore cases, including *Sim Yong Kim* (n 38); *Lim Swee Khiang v Borden Co (Pte) Ltd* [2006] SGCA 33, [2006] 4 SLR(R) 745; *Over & Over Ltd v Bonvests Holdings Ltd* [2010] SGCA 7, [2010] 2 SLR 776; *Lim Kok Wah v Lim Boh Yong* [2015] SGHC 211, [2015] 5 SLR 307.

[40] *Ebrahimi* (n 39) 381.

> in company law for recognition of the fact that behind it, or amongst it, there are individuals, with rights, expectations and obligations inter se which are not necessarily submerged in the company structure. That structure is defined by the Companies Act and by the articles of association by which shareholders agree to be bound. In most companies and in most contexts, this definition is sufficient and exhaustive, equally so whether the company is large or small. The 'just and equitable' provision does not, as the respondents suggest, entitle one party to disregard the obligation he assumes by entering a company, nor the court to dispense him from it. It does, as equity always does, enable the court to subject the exercise of legal rights to equitable considerations; considerations, that is, of a personal character arising between one individual and another, which may make it unjust, or inequitable, to insist on legal rights, or to exercise them in a particular way.[41]

Although the respondent could be removed under legislation relating to companies and the company's articles of association, and must normally accept such removal, the just and equitable ground would come to his rescue if he could point to, and prove, some special underlying obligation of his fellow members in good faith, or confidence, that he was entitled to participate in management as long as the business continued, such that if this basic obligation was broken, the association had to be dissolved, consistent with the principles that have been worked out in partnership cases.[42]

While both the above cases involved quasi-partnerships, the just and equitable ground of winding up is not limited to such companies.[43]

Although it is clear that equity is invoked to justify the court's intervention, the principle(s) of equity that is relied upon is not clearly stated. Perhaps this was deemed unnecessary given that legislation has explicitly provided for recourse to equitable principles,[44] and all that the court perhaps needs to do is to set out the considerations it will take into consideration in determining whether to intervene to put an end to unjust, or inequitable, or unfair conduct through the mechanism of winding up. Nevertheless, it is suggested that to ensure that the notion of injustice or unfairness is not altogether too indefinite, vague or subjective,[45] the basis of equity's intervention should be more clearly articulated.

It is suggested that the court's discretion to wind up a company under the just and equitable ground is grounded on the concept of fraud in equity. One example of such equitable fraud is where a party improperly relies on his or her legal rights[46] as equity will not allow statute and common law to be used as an instrument of fraud, in the sense that it will act *in personam* against the conscience of a

[41] ibid 379.

[42] ibid 380.

[43] *Loch v John Blackwood Ltd* [1924] AC 783; *Re Wondoflex Textiles Pty Ltd* (n 38) 465; *Chow Kwok Chuen v Chow Kwok Chi* [2008] SGCA 37, [2008] 4 SLR(R) 362.

[44] Generally, see HW Tang, 'Equity in the Age of Statutes' (2015) 9 *Journal of Equity* 214.

[45] Lord Hoffmann's caution in *O'Neill v Phillips* [1999] 1 WLR 1092, 1098–99 in the context of the UK unfair prejudice remedy.

[46] JD Heydon, MJ Leeming and PG Turner, *Meagher, Gummow and Lehane's Equity: Doctrines and Remedies*, 5th edn (Chatswood, NSW, LexisNexis Butterworths, 2015) para 12-050.

defendant to prevent that person from taking inequitable advantage of another.[47] Fraud in the context of equity is a broader notion than that at common law and does not necessarily connote dishonesty.[48]

In cases where the courts order the winding up of a company because the court considers it just and equitable to do so even though there has been compliance by the defendant shareholder(s) with the companies legislation or the corporate constitution, it does so because it will not allow such shareholder(s) to rely on his strict legal rights to take inequitable advantage of the plaintiff(s). What makes the conduct of the defendant subject to the scrutiny of equity is that there is an underlying obligation or expectation between the shareholders that a court of equity will uphold. To allow the Companies Act and the corporate constitution to override such an obligation would be to allow the law to be used in an unjust fashion.[49]

In *Asseinagon Asset Management SA v Irish Bank Resolution Corp Ltd*,[50] Briggs J expressed the view that the principle of equity applicable in just and equitable winding up[51] was that which constrained all exercises of majority power,[52] such as when a majority of shareholders or debenture holders respectively attempt to alter the corporate constitution or modify the terms of the debenture issue. He cited *Blisset v Daniel* where Page Wood V-C had said:

> It must be plain that you can neither exercise a power of this description by dissolving the partnership, nor do any other act for purposes contrary to the plain general meaning of the deed, which must be this—that this power is inserted, not for the benefit of any particular parties holding two-thirds of the shares, but for the benefit of the whole society and partnership.[53]

It is submitted respectfully that if the stated basis is that shareholder power must be exercised not for the benefit of the shareholder but for others, this is not the correct principle that operates in a shareholder dispute (or that involving debenture holders). This is because there is a fundamental difference in the relationship between partners inter se and between partners and the partnership (which is fiduciary), and between shareholders inter se or between shareholders and the

[47] A Hudson, *Equity and Trusts*, 8th edn (Oxford, Routledge, 2015) para 1.4.13 and para 1.4.18. See also Heydon, Leeming and Turner (n 46) para 12-100 on equity not allowing statutes as cloaks for frauds.

[48] Heydon, Leeming and Turner (n 46) para 12-005; Hudson (n 47) para 1.4.18.

[49] This does not necessarily entail any wrongdoing at the corporate level. A deadlock might occur because of a reasonable difference of opinion as to the strategic direction the company should take. Where such a state of affairs is outside the expectations of the parties when the company was incorporated, the equitable fraud lies not in the different views of the shareholders per se, but in the desire of one or more of the shareholders to keep the enterprise alive despite the deadlock being inconsistent with the initial common understanding of the shareholders.

[50] *Asseinagon Asset Management SA v Irish Bank Resolution Corp Ltd* [2012] EWHC 2090, [2013] 1 All ER 495.

[51] And the unfair prejudice remedy which will be discussed below.

[52] *Asseinagon Asset Management SA* (n 50) [41]–[45].

[53] *Blisset v Daniel* [1853] 10 Hare 493, 523–24; 68 ER 1022, 1035.

company (which is not). Accordingly, and this will be discussed in greater detail later when considering alterations of the corporate constitution, the test of a power that must be exercised for the benefit of another is not an appropriate test where shareholders are concerned. Furthermore, as explained in the immediately following paragraphs, the key consideration in the just and equitable ground of winding up is the existence of an agreement or understanding between the shareholders even where such agreement or understanding does not give rise to any legal rights.[54] While Lord Wilberforce in *Ebrahimi*[55] had referred to the principles in *Blisset v Daniel*, it is suggested that his Lordship did so simply to illustrate how an explicit power to expel could not be invoked where this was contrary to an underlying obligation or expectation.

Taking as the starting point that the defendant shareholders have acted within their strict legal rights, and given the drastic nature of the winding up remedy, any power to wind up a company must not be exercised expansively and there should be clear limits. It is suggested that a fundamental consideration is that the state of the company is not what could reasonably have been contemplated by the parties when the company was incorporated, or in appropriate cases when the complainant became a shareholder, or because 'there was a settled and accepted course of conduct between the parties'.[56] Or to put it slightly differently, the parties contemplated a very different state of affairs from that which subsisted at the time of the complaint.[57] This is what gives rise to the underlying obligations between shareholders. The obligations or expectations came about either because of an express agreement or understanding between the parties outside the corporate constitution, regardless of whether the agreement is enforceable,[58] or the circumstances are such that the law would usually regard such an obligation or expectation as implicitly arising between the parties. An example of the latter is where a partnership becomes incorporated. If the previous partners were all actively engaged in the partnership, the courts will generally consider that each of them was entitled to expect that he or she would be involved in the management of the corporate entity.[59] Similarly, where persons with a close personal relationship incorporate a business, the courts are likely to regard the existence of mutual trust and

[54] In *Asseinagon Asset Management SA* (n 50) [46] Briggs J expressed the view that when such a constraint is imposed on the majority debenture holders, it is because the limitation is an implied term of the facility agreement. In this context no equitable principle is required because the implied term is binding on the parties as a matter of contract. It is suggested that reliance on implied terms may not be necessary if there is a general principle of law that constrains the exercise of majority power, perhaps based on the proper purposes doctrine, as to which see the discussion below in the context of alterations of the corporate constitution.

[55] *Ebrahimi* (n 39) 380–81; see also *O'Neill* (n 45) 1100–01, where Lord Hoffmann states, inter alia, that there is more than one theoretical basis on which *Blisset v Daniel* (n 53) can be explained.

[56] *Re Fildes Brothers Ltd* [1970] 1 WLR 592, 596.

[57] See also *O'Neill* (n 45) 1101–02.

[58] *Re Fildes Brothers Ltd* (n 56) 596; *O'Neill* (n 45) 1101; *Kam Leung Sui Kwan v Kam Kwan Lai* (2015) 18 HKCFAR 501 [46].

[59] eg *Ebrahimi* (n 39) 380; *Re a Company (No 002567 of 1982)* [1983] 1 WLR 927; *Re Guidezone Ltd* [2000] 2 BCLC 321, 355–56.

confidence as an element of the business relationship notwithstanding the separateness of the corporate entity.[60] These arise even though there was no agreement or discussion between the shareholders.[61] Thus, in *Ebrahimi*, Lord Wilberforce said when the appellant and N incorporated their partnership business, the 'inference must have been indisputable' that they did so on the basis that the character of the association remained the same.[62] It is suggested that such an 'inference' arises in a manner analogous to what was described as 'a term which the law will imply as a necessary incident of a definable category of contractual relationship'.[63] While the court is not in the corporate context implying a term in law as a matter of contract, the court does form a view that certain types of associations or relationships within the corporate context generally give rise to certain obligations or expectations as a necessary incident of such an association or relationship. This is because some types of company have 'peculiar characteristics' and such characteristics are relevant to the issue of whether a company may attract equitable considerations.[64] On the other hand, a large publicly listed company is not likely to attract any such considerations as the general position for such companies must be that the sum total of the shareholders' rights are set out in the corporate constitution and perhaps some of the rules of the stock exchange.[65]

This explains why, for example, winding up is justified where the purposes for which the company was established cannot be fulfilled or where the company engages in acts which are entirely outside what can fairly be regarded as having been within the general intention and common understanding of the members when they became members;[66] where there is deadlock, exclusion from management and generally a loss of mutual confidence and trust in companies where the shareholders had envisaged a close working relationship based on trust;[67] where the company's business has been carried on in a fraudulent manner contrary to the expectations of shareholders;[68] where the company's capital has been spent and there is nothing left with which the company can be resuscitated;[69] or where there has been misconduct or oppressive conduct.[70] These examples of the

[60] eg *Re RA Noble & Sons (Clothing) Ltd* [1983] BCLC 273; *Re Bird Precision Bellows Ltd* [1984] Ch 419, 429–30 (affd [1986] Ch 658); *Re London School of Electronics Ltd* [1986] Ch 211; *Re Citybranch Group Ltd* [2004] EWCA Civ 815, [2004] 4 All ER 735.

[61] Though their subsequent conduct may give rise to an informal agreement, see *O'Neill* (n 45) 1101.

[62] *Ebrahimi* (n 39) 380.

[63] *Scally v Southern Health and Social Services Board* [1992] 1 AC 294, 307.

[64] *Kam Leung Sui Kwan* (n 58) [46].

[65] This is in part because the shareholder composition of public listed companies changes frequently and it is therefore unlikely that there will be any agreement or understanding common to all shareholders (but see *Luck Continent Ltd v Cheng Chee Tock Theodore* [2013] 4 HKLRD 181 for a case where there was such a common understanding). It would be wrong to regard some members only as being entitled to certain expectations that other members do not share.

[66] *Re German Date Coffee Co* (1882) 20 Ch D 169; *Re Tivoli Freeholds Ltd* [1972] VR 445.

[67] *Re Yenidje* (n 36); *Ebrahimi* (n 39); *Chow Kwok Chuen* (n 43).

[68] *Re Thomas Edward Brinsmead & Sons Ltd* [1897] 1 Ch 406.

[69] *Re Diamond Fuel Co* (1879) 13 Ch D 400, 410.

[70] *Loch* (n 43); *Re Wondoflex Textiles Pty Ltd* (n 38).

scope of the remedy potentially overlap, for example, a variety of conduct such as oppression of minority shareholders or carrying out the business in a fraudulent manner can lead to a loss of mutual trust and confidence. The common thread running through them is that reasonable shareholders would not generally contemplate the occurrence of such circumstances within companies of which they are members (even though there was no express discussion or agreement between them on such matters) and equity will therefore not allow the exercise of strict legal rights to maintain this uncontemplated status quo. Winding up brings such a state of affairs to an end if it is sought by a shareholder.

The just and equitable ground of winding up was for a long period the only statutory remedy available to shareholders. Its weakness was that the remedy was a drastic one. In Singapore, a recent legislative amendment has sought to provide the court with an alternative outcome, namely that instead of winding up the company when it has been established that it would be just and equitable to do so,[71]

> the Court may if it is of the opinion that it is just and equitable to do so, make an order for the interests in shares of one or more members to be purchased by the company or one or more other members on terms to the satisfaction of the Court.[72]

The Singapore High Court has cautioned against seeing this provision as a means for a shareholder to exit at will. If this was the intention for commencing a winding-up petition, and there was no real interest in the company being wound up, it may amount to an abuse of process.[73] In the UK, section 125(2) of the Insolvency Act 1986 provides that a court need not wind up a company on such ground if it is of the opinion that some other remedy is available to the petitioners and they are acting unreasonably in seeking to have the company wound up instead of pursuing that other remedy.[74]

An obvious alternative remedy in the UK is the statutory unfair prejudice remedy in the Companies Act 2006, section 994(1)[75] which provides that a member may petition to the court for relief where 'the company's affairs are being or have been conducted in a manner that is unfairly prejudicial to the interests of

[71] Companies Act (Cap 50, 2006 Rev Ed) (Singapore), s 254(1)(i).

[72] ibid s 254(2A). Even in the absence of such a provision, a court may order a stay of the winding-up order for a specified period to allow the parties to consider if they can come to an arrangement that would avoid the winding up of the company, see *Sim Yong Kim* (n 38) [50]; *Kam Leung Sui Kwan* (n 58) [64].

[73] *Ting Shwu Ping v Autopack Pte Ltd* [2016] SGHC 7, [2016] 2 SLR 152 [17].

[74] No such provision exists in Singapore and the Court of Appeal in *Sim Yong Kim* (n 38) [38] has said that a court would not be precluded from ordering winding up on the just and equitable ground simply because a s 216 remedy would otherwise be available. Nevertheless, the Court also said at [39] that a shareholder who prefers the just and equitable winding-up remedy in order to harass the company will risk having his application struck out as being vexatious. Given that there are more moderate remedies available under s 216, a court may take the view that a claimant is motivated by spite where such claimant seeks winding up even though the relief the claimant seeks can be satisfied by some other remedy.

[75] The predecessor provision was the Companies Act 1985, s 459.

members generally or of some part of its members (including at least himself)' or 'that an actual or proposed act or omission of the company (including an act or omission on its behalf) is or would be so prejudicial'. In Singapore the equivalent is section 216(1) of the Companies Act which allows a member to seek relief where the affairs of the company are being conducted or the powers of the directors are being exercised in a manner oppressive to one or more of the members in disregard of his or their interests as members, or that some act of the company has been done or is threatened or that some resolution has been passed or is proposed which unfairly discriminates against or is otherwise prejudicial to one or more of the members or holders of debentures (including himself).[76]

In the context of the UK unfair prejudice remedy, Lord Hoffmann has in *O'Neill v Phillips*[77] held that the basis for the remedy is equitable and moreover is similar to that underlying just and equitable winding up.[78] His Lordship said that one of the traditional roles of equity was to restrain the exercise of strict legal rights in certain relationships in which it considered that this would be contrary to good faith. Such a principle has been carried over into company law as a result of the influence of the law of partnership, and would lead to the conclusion that there will be cases in which equitable considerations make it unfair for those conducting the affairs of the company to rely on their strict legal powers.[79] Lord Hoffmann agreed[80] with the statement in another case that,

> in order to give rise to an equitable constraint ... what is required is a personal relationship or personal dealings of some kind between the party seeking to exercise the legal right and the party seeking to restrain such exercise, such as will affect the conscience of the former.[81]

A useful cross-check according to his Lordship was to ask whether the exercise of the power in question would be contrary to what the parties, by words or conduct, have actually agreed.[82] This more 'contractual' approach[83] lends support to the earlier proposition in the context of just and equitable winding up that the court can in appropriate circumstances imply an agreement or understanding between

[76] The Singapore courts have held that the four individual limbs of oppression, disregard of a member's interest, unfair discrimination or otherwise prejudicial conduct are not to be read disjunctively. The common thread underpinning the entire provision is the element of unfairness, see *Over & Over Ltd* (n 39); *Lim Kok Wah* (n 39) [97].

[77] *O'Neill* (n 45).

[78] ibid 1099.

[79] ibid 1098–99; see also *Kam Leung Sui Kwan* (n 58) [43]–[44].

[80] *O'Neill* (n 45) 1101.

[81] *Re Astec (BSR) Plc* [1998] 2 BCLC 556, 588; see also *Grace v Biagioli* [2005] EWCA Civ 1222, [2006] 2 BCLC 70 [61] where Patten J in the Court of Appeal said that the rights and obligations of members that are usually enshrined in the articles of association and any collateral agreements between them 'are subject to established equitable principles which may moderate the exercise of strict legal rights when insistence on the enforcement of such rights would be unconscionable'.

[82] See also *Grace v Biagioli*, ibid.

[83] Davies and Worthington (n 23) para 20-13.

shareholders,[84] for example, that certain obligations or expectations are generally a necessary incident of particular types of company which have 'peculiar characteristics'. Lord Hoffmann was at pains to make it clear that unfair prejudice did not only arise out of a breach of promise or undertaking. He gave an example, being an event which puts an end to the basis on which the parties entered into the association, likening it to contractual frustration.[85] It is also possible to understand this as being outside the implied understanding of the parties given the association in question that was contemplated by them. That this is consistent with the analogy of contractual frustration mentioned by Lord Hoffmann is clear from the factors to be taken into account in determining if a contract has been frustrated:

> Among the factors which have to be considered are the terms of the contract itself, its matrix or context, the parties' knowledge, expectations, assumptions and contemplations … as at the time of contract, at any rate so far as these can be ascribed mutually and objectively, and then the nature of the supervening event, and the parties' reasonable and objectively ascertainable calculations as to the possibilities of future performance in the new circumstances.[86]

Lord Hoffmann's adoption of the reasoning in *Ebrahimi* on just and equitable winding up for the unfair prejudice remedy has given rise to the interesting and difficult question of the relative scope of the two provisions. Judicial opinion has been divided. In *Re Guidezone Ltd*,[87] a case decided shortly after *O'Neill v Phillips*, Jonathan Parker J rejected the submission that the just and equitable winding-up jurisdiction is wider than the unfair prejudice jurisdiction. But in *Re Neath Rugby Ltd (No 2)*,[88] the Court of Appeal overruled *Re Guidezone Ltd* on this point for two reasons. It held that Jonathan Parker J had misinterpreted Lord Hoffmann's brief remarks in *O'Neill v Phillips* on the relationship between the two jurisdictions, and it gave two examples of circumstances, viz, deadlock between the shareholders and loss of substratum, which in appropriate cases would fall within the just and equitable winding-up jurisdiction but may not without more amount to unfairly prejudicial conduct. Earlier, in *Sim Yong Kim v Evenstar Investments Ltd*,[89] the Singapore Court of Appeal was of the same view. The Singapore Court of Appeal has also expressed agreement with Lord Hoffman's view that the basis for the section 216 remedy is equitable and similar to that underlying just and equitable winding up.[90] This is not the place to discuss this issue fully, which has

[84] See also *Re a Company (No 002015 of 1996)* [1997] 2 BCLC 1, 18 (the existence of complex written agreements between the members did not exclude the possibility of some other express or implied arrangements or understanding between them); *Lim Kok Wah* (n 39) where the court in dismissing an action under s 216 found that there was neither any express or implied agreement or understanding that would justify relief.

[85] *O'Neill* (n 45) 1101.

[86] *Edwinton Commercial Corp v Tsavliris Russ (Worldwide Salvage & Towage) Ltd (The Sea Angel)* [2007] EWCA Civ 547, [2007] 2 Lloyd's Rep 517 [111].

[87] *Re Guidezone Ltd* (n 59).

[88] *Re Neath Rugby Ltd (No 2)* [2009] EWCA Civ 291, [2009] EWCA Civ 261, [2009] 2 BCLC 427.

[89] *Sim Yong Kim* (n 38) [85].

[90] *Lim Swee Khiang* (n 39) [82].

surprisingly attracted little commentary,[91] but three observations are in order. First, although deadlock and loss of substratum have traditionally been expressed as distinct instances of the just and equitable jurisdiction, they may readily be seen as illustrations of the principle expressed in *Ebrahimi*, ie, the situation that has arisen is outside what the parties contemplated by the arrangement they entered into, or what has been done is contrary to the assumptions which are the foundation of their agreement. Indeed, writing in 1964, in an age when the profession and the courts were more familiar with the just and equitable winding-up jurisdiction, McPherson (who became McPherson JA of the Queensland Court of Appeal) suggested that, if the principle expressed in *Re Wondoflex Textiles Ltd*,[92] which was approved and adopted in *Ebrahimi*

> is, indeed, the underlying principle which governs the making of orders on the just and equitable ground, then it may be that it amounts to little more than the application, in the field of company law, of the contractual doctrines of discharge by frustration and discharge by breach.[93]

Although a contractual approach has judicial support, it operates only by analogy and it must not be forgotten that the basis of the court's jurisdiction lies in equity. Any contractual analysis must ultimately be able to support relief in equity.

Second, while it may be thought that some element of blameworthiness in bringing about the underlying disagreement between the parties should be an important distinguishing factor between the statutory remedies, an issue which overlaps with the third point, Lord Hoffmann expressed in dicta in *O'Neill v Phillips* that unfair prejudice could be established where some event puts an end to the basis on which the parties entered into association with each other, the unfairness arising from one party insisting on maintaining the association in circumstances contrary to the original understanding of the parties.[94] If this is correct, there is no reason why a deadlock situation or loss of substratum cannot equally fall within unfair prejudice. Thus, even if it is correct to recognise a distinction between both remedies, the distinction is a relatively thin one with the additional element of blameworthiness potentially arising from the desire to continue the uncontemplated situation the shareholders now find themselves in. Third, there is the issue which has been termed 'no fault divorce', ie, a minority shareholder is entitled to exit at will where the relationship of trust and confidence between the shareholders in an incorporated partnership has broken down. In *O'Neill v Phillips*, Lord Hoffmann rejected the argument that unfair prejudice encompasses the notion of no fault divorce. However, the just and equitable winding-up jurisdiction, as stated in *Ebrahimi*, is broad enough to encompass such no fault divorce. Moreover, it is

[91] eg B Clark 'Just and Equitable Winding Up: Wound Up?' (2001) 12 *Scots Law Times* 108; S Acton, 'Just and Equitable Winding Up: The Strange Case of the Disappearing Jurisdiction' (2001) 22 *Company Lawyer* 134.

[92] *Re Wondoflex Textiles Ltd* (n 38) 467.

[93] McPherson (n 33) 305.

[94] *O'Neill* (n 45) 1101–02.

also arguable that as the distinction between both remedies is a thin one, and the insistence of the majority on maintaining the association when the relationship of trust and confidence between the parties has broken down could constitute unfair conduct, it would take very little for unfair prejudice to come close to encompassing no fault divorce.

From the foregoing, it seems clear that generally, in determining if just and equitable winding up is potentially applicable, or if relief should be granted for unfair prejudice, the circumstances faced by the complainants must be contrary to some express or implied agreement or understanding between the parties (bearing in mind the type of company) and this includes a state of affairs that an objective and reasonable shareholder would not have contemplated at the time the company was established. This is what lies at the heart of the statutory equitable jurisdiction of the courts to prevent shareholders of companies from taking advantage of their strict legal rights. This approach is also consistent with good economic theory. Companies enhance investment and entrepreneurship by allowing the easy pooling of resources, asset partitioning and limited liability. However, this is conditional on company law as a whole providing a proper framework of rules that do not allow majorities to take unfair advantage of minorities thereby providing a degree of confidence that investments will not be easily diminished by sharp practice. If the law does not place any constraints on majority rule when such constraints can be said from an objective standpoint to have been agreed upon either expressly or by implication, it would ultimately undermine the utility of the corporate vehicle as an instrument for enterprise and diminish its social value.[95]

One final point can be made. The courts have variously used phrases such as 'legitimate expectations'[96] or 'commercial unfairness'[97] to denote when the unfair prejudice and section 216 remedy will be granted. In an early case on section 181(1) of the Malaysian Companies Act 1965, which is *in pari materia* with section 216, Lord Wilberforce speaking for the Privy Council used the phrase 'visible departure from the standards of fair dealing and a violation of the conditions of fair play which a shareholder is entitled to expect' as the test to be applied. Such terms are vague and of second order relevance, as they do not in themselves provide explanations for why certain expectations are legitimate, or the reasons for why conduct has been commercially unfair or a visible departure from standards that a shareholder can expect. As Lord Hoffmann said in *O'Neill v Phillips*,[98] it may not be ideal to use the term 'legitimate expectation' (and by extension other terms such as 'commercial unfairness') to describe a concept which is sufficiently defined

[95] See also DD Prentice, 'The Theory of the Firm: Minority Shareholder Oppression: Sections 459–461' (1988) 8 *OJLS* 55.

[96] eg *Re Saul D Harrison & Sons plc* [1995] 1 BCLC 14, 19; *Ng Sing King v PSA International Pte Ltd (No 2)* [2005] SGHC 5, [2005] 2 SLR(R) 56; *Sim Yong Kim* (n 38) [40]; *Over & Over Ltd* (n 39) [78]; *Lim Kok Wah* (n 39) [103].

[97] eg *Over & Over Ltd* (n 39) [81]; *Ng Kek Wee v Sim City Technology Ltd* [2014] SGCA 47, [2014] 4 SLR 723 [34].

[98] *O'Neill* (n 45) 1102.

in other terms. It is suggested that it would be better for the courts to explicitly develop the law along the equitable principles discussed here and use such terms only where they are useful catchphrases for circumstances giving rise to equitable intervention.[99] As an example, the term 'legitimate expectations' could be a convenient reference to agreements or understandings that have arisen informally or implicitly.[100]

III. Altering the Corporate Constitution

Moving beyond statutory provisions that expressly incorporate equitable concepts, we may now consider how the courts have brought equitable principles into company law. An early example relates to alterations of the corporate constitution. Legislation relating to companies typically allows the corporate constitution to be altered subject to the proposed alteration being approved by a super-majority present and voting at the shareholders' meeting. This super-majority is often set at 75 per cent.[101] Given that alterations of the constitution are made more onerous than normal resolutions, it might be thought that if shareholders can overcome the threshold the alteration will be conclusive. This is not the position as the courts have retained the discretion to set aside changes to the constitution even when there has been compliance with the requirements for alteration.[102]

The first case that must be considered is *Allen v Gold Reefs of West Africa Ltd*[103] where the articles were altered to allow the company to have a lien on fully paid shares for any indebtedness by a member to the company. Prior to such amendment the company only had a lien on shares that were not fully paid up. The executors of a deceased insolvent member who held both fully paid-up shares (he was the only such holder) and shares not fully paid up brought an action to set aside the amendment. Lindley MR (with whom Romer LJ agreed) expressed the view that the power to alter was subject to certain conditions beyond those found in the Act:[104]

> The power thus conferred on companies to alter the regulations contained in their articles is limited only by the provisions contained in the statute and the conditions contained in the company's memorandum of association. Wide, however, as the language of s 50 is [providing for alteration by special resolution], the power conferred by it must,

[99] See also *Lim Kok Wah* (n 39) [102] where Coomaraswamy J said that the starting point in a s 216 action was not to show unfairness but to show that the company was subject to equitable considerations which has thereby made it unfair for the majority to rely on their strict legal rights.

[100] eg *Sim Yong Kim* (n 38); *Over & Over Ltd* (n 39).

[101] Companies Act 2006, s 21(1) read with s 283; Companies Act (Cap 50, 2006 Rev Ed) (Singapore), s 26(1) read with s 184(1).

[102] Note also s 33 of the Companies Act (Cap 50, 2006 Rev Ed) (Singapore) which allows alterations of the company's objects clauses (if any) to be challenged in court.

[103] *Allen v Gold Reefs of West Africa Ltd* [1900] 1 Ch 656.

[104] ibid 671.

> like all other powers, be exercised subject to those general principles of law and equity which are applicable to all powers conferred on majorities and enabling them to bind minorities. It must be exercised, not only in the manner required by law, but also bona fide for the benefit of the company as a whole, and it must not be exceeded. These conditions are always implied, and are seldom, if ever, expressed.[105]

In upholding the alteration in *Allen*, although the fact that only the complaining member was affected and this might raise questions as to the bona fides of the company, the court held there was no bad faith on the part of the directors[106] as the altered articles would apply to all shareholders even if practically the deceased member was the only holder of fully paid-up shares who at the time was in arrear of calls.[107]

What is noteworthy about the approach is that the court in *Allen* subjected the power to alter to equitable principles, in particular that the power must be exercised 'bona fide for the benefit of the company as a whole'.[108] It is non-controversial that where a majority genuinely believes that they are acting to advance the interests of the company, it is unlikely that such decision can be challenged. What is controversial is why there should be any restraint on the power of alteration given the clear statutory language. Should a shareholder not be entitled to vote in favour of an alteration even if such shareholder did not have the interests of the company in mind? Additionally, by requiring the power to be exercised bona fide for the benefit of the company, the court appears to have imposed fiduciary obligations on shareholders when exercising their voting rights in cases involving alterations to the constitution. Not only do members almost never owe fiduciary obligations to the company, given that a member's vote is an incident of such person's property in the shares he owns, it is not clear how a fiduciary obligation can arise when exercising one's property rights. It is well established that shareholders are entitled to vote in their personal interests.[109] The test also does not appear helpful if the alteration is one that only affects shareholders but has no impact on the company.[110] For example, a resolution that affects the pre-emptive rights of members might cause unhappiness to certain members but is not a matter that

[105] Such a constraint on majority power has been applied in other contexts, eg, in *British America Nickel Corporation v O'Brien* [1927] 1 AC 369 and *Asseinagon Asset Management SA* (n 50) where the issue was whether resolutions passed by the requisite majority of debenture holders were binding on the dissenting minority.

[106] This is likely a reference to the directors putting the alteration to the shareholders in a general meeting.

[107] *Allen* (n 103) 675.

[108] Cases citing this test include *Brown v British Abrasive Wheel Co* [1919] 1 Ch 290; *Sidebottom v Kershaw, Leese and Co* [1920] 1 Ch 154; *Dafen Tinplate Co Ltd v Llanelly Steel Company* [1920] 2 Ch 124; *Shuttleworth v Cox Bros & Co (Maidenhead) Ltd* [1927] 2 KB 9; *Southern Foundries (1926) Ltd v Shirlaw* [1940] 1 AC 701, 713; *Greenhalgh v Arderne Cinemas Ltd* [1951] 1 Ch 286; *Smith v Croft (No 2)* [1988] 1 Ch 114; *Citco Banking Corp NV v Pusser's Ltd* [2007] UKPC 13, [2007] BCC 205; *Re Charterhouse Capital Ltd* [2015] EWCA Civ 536, [2015] 2 BCLC 627.

[109] *North-West Transportation Co Ltd v Beatty* (1887) 12 App Cas 589.

[110] *Peters' American Delicacy Co Ltd v Heath* (1939) 61 CLR 457, 481; *Citco Banking Corp NV* (n 108) [18]; *Re Charterhouse Capital Ltd* (n 108).

particularly affects the company as a separate entity.[111] The same point may be made in relation to the payment of dividends or the power to dispose of shares.[112] Nor is the issue rendered clearer by equating the company with the body of shareholders[113] as shareholders do not generally owe fiduciary duties to each other.

This may explain Evershed MR's attempt in *Greenhalgh v Arderne Cinemas Ltd* to reformulate, in the context of a dispute over the rights of shareholders only, what is meant by 'the company as a whole', when he said:

> [T]he phrase … does not (at any rate in such a case as the present) mean the company as a commercial entity, distinct from the corporators: it means the corporators as a general body. That is to say, the case may be taken of an individual hypothetical member and it may be asked whether what is proposed is, in the honest opinion of those who voted in its favour, for that person's benefit.[114]

This is so vague that it is singularly unhelpful. It must generally be the case that the majority voting in favour of an alteration are themselves individual hypothetical members who no doubt voted in favour of the constitutional amendment because they considered it to be for their benefit. Perhaps realising this Evershed MR added a further gloss which will be discussed in the following paragraph.

In *Shuttleworth v Cox Bros & Co (Maidenhead) Ltd*,[115] an important gloss was added to Lindley MR's test. In that case, the articles of association provided that the plaintiff and four others were to be 'permanent' directors. The articles were altered to add an additional ground for the removal of directors, after which the plaintiff was removed and he brought an action claiming that the dismissal was wrongful. Atkin LJ framed the limitation in the following terms: 'whether or not the shareholders, in considering whether they shall alter articles, honestly intend to exercise their powers for the benefit of the company'.[116] He then went on to say that the 'circumstances may be such as to lead to one conclusion only, that the majority of the shareholders are acting so oppressively that they cannot be acting in good faith'.[117] Similarly, Bankes LJ said that 'the test is whether the alteration of the articles was in the opinion of the shareholders for the benefit of the company' and the 'alteration may be so oppressive as to cast suspicion on the honesty of the persons responsible for it, or so extravagant that no reasonable men could really consider it for the benefit of the company'.[118] Similarly, Evershed MR in *Greenhalgh* stated that the issue was whether the effect of the amendment caused discrimination in that it offered to majority shareholders an advantage denied to the minority. When the cases were examined, this was the ground on which resolutions have been successfully attacked. Persons voting for a special (or indeed

[111] eg *Greenhalgh* (n 108).
[112] See *Peters' American Delicacy Co Ltd* (n 110); *Citco Banking Corp NV* (n 108) [18].
[113] As in *Re Imperial Chemicals Ltd* [1936] 1 Ch 587, 619–20.
[114] *Greenhalgh* (n 108) 291.
[115] *Shuttleworth* (n 108).
[116] ibid 26.
[117] ibid 27.
[118] ibid 18.

ordinary) resolution need not dissociate themselves altogether from the prospect of personal benefit.[119] Thus, the effect of the alteration becomes relevant as it may cast doubt on the good faith of the majority. Nevertheless, the key issue is still whether reasonable shareholders could have considered that the amendment was for the benefit of the company[120] and if this is the case the alteration is valid.

This test has rightly met with scepticism in Australia where the alteration relates only to conflicting interests between shareholders.[121] It is suggested respectfully that while the courts in England rightly saw any limitation on the power to alter as being founded on equitable principles, it was incorrect to regard such limitation as being founded on, or analogous to, fiduciary obligations. Indeed the basis for reliance on fiduciary duty is unclear. It is speculated that given the history of corporate law, the underlying rationale may have come about by analogy with articles of partnership.[122] For example, where the articles of partnership allowed a partner to be expelled upon a vote of two-thirds of the partnership shares, such a power 'is inserted, not for the benefit of any particular parties holding two-thirds of the shares, but for the benefit of the whole society and partnership, it being considered to be an advantage to all that there should be this particular power'.[123] And where a power to alter the partnership agreement is subject to terms, the power must be exercised in good faith.[124] This is unsurprising given that the relationship between partners is a fiduciary one.

As the relationship between shareholders is not fiduciary, in the context of alterations of the corporate constitution it is suggested that the better basis in equity when an alteration is regarded as objectionable is to regard the particular alteration as an improper exercise of power. This rule is well recognised as being applicable to the exercise of powers by directors.[125] The rule, as Lord Sumption (with whom Lord Hodge agreed) put it in the context of directors' duties, has its origin in the equitable doctrine of 'fraud on a power',[126] which simply meant that the power had been 'exercised for a purpose, or with an intention, beyond the scope of or not justified by the instrument creating the power'.[127] As the scope of the proper purpose rule is concerned with abuse of power, the test is subjective and the state of mind and motive of those who acted are important.[128]

[119] *Greenhalgh* (n 108) 291. See also *Peters' American Delicacy Co Ltd* (n 110).

[120] As reiterated in *Citco Banking Corp NV* (n 108) [24]–[25].

[121] *Peters' American Delicacy Co Ltd* (n 110); *Gambotto v WCP Ltd* (1995) 182 CLR 432, and this has been acknowledged in *Re Charterhouse Capital Ltd* (n 108) [90], [96].

[122] See also *Peters'American Delicacy Co Ltd* (n 110) 502–03 (Dixon J).

[123] *Blisset v Daniel* (n 53) 524; 1035; see also *Asseinagon Asset Management SA* (n 50).

[124] Banks (n 28) para 10-13.

[125] For a recent case discussing this, see *Eclairs Group Ltd v JKX Oil & Gas plc* [2015] UKSC 71, [2016] 1 BCLC 1; noted H Tjio, 'The Proper Purpose Rule' [2016] *Lloyd's Maritime and Commercial Law Quarterly* 176.

[126] *Eclairs Group Ltd* (n 125) [15].

[127] *Vatcher v Paull* [1915] AC 372, 378.

[128] *Eclairs Group Ltd* (n 125) [15]. There is an objective aspect as well in the sense of the court having to identify the purpose(s) underlying the power, see [30] and [32] (Lord Sumption SCJ); and *Howard Smith Ltd v Ampol Petroleum Ltd* [1974] 1 AC 821, 835.

There is some authority that the proper purpose rule applies to alterations of the corporate constitution. In *Dafen Tinplate Co v Llanelly Steel Co*, Petersen J, while setting out the bona fide test, also said that the alteration 'must not exceed the limits of the power conferred by the statute'.[129] Dixon J in *Peters' American Delicacy Co Ltd v Heath* has expressed the principle as follows:

> The chief reason for denying an unlimited effect to widely expressed powers such as that of altering a company's articles is the fear or knowledge that an apparently regular exercise of the power may in truth be but a means of securing some personal or particular gain, whether pecuniary or otherwise, which does not fairly arise out of the subjects dealt with by the power and is outside and even inconsistent with the contemplated objects of the power. It is to exclude the purpose of securing such ulterior special and particular advantages that Lord Lindley used the phrase 'bona fide for the benefit of the company as a whole'.[130]

Further Australian authority can be found in *Gambotto v WCP Ltd* where the court said that in relation to alterations that gave rise to a conflict of interests and advantages between shareholders, the bona fide in the best interests of the company test was inappropriate. In such cases, the general approach was that an alteration was valid unless it was, inter alia, 'beyond any purpose contemplated by the articles'.[131] A power to alter had to be exercised for a proper purpose and its exercise should not operate oppressively in relation to minority shareholders.[132]

The decision in *Redwood Master Fund Ltd v TD Bank Europe*[133] is also instructive, involving as it does a group that did not owe fiduciary responsibilities to each other, though in this case the proper purpose rule was implied as a term of the contract. The case involved a group of lenders and the claimants brought an action to set aside a variation to the facility agreement that had been passed by a sufficient majority of the lenders. The claimants' case was that the majority lenders abused their position and breached their duty to act bona fide in the interests of the lenders as a whole. Rimer J accepted that while the case did not involve a company, the principles outlined by Evershed MR in *Greenhalgh* applied to a case where a class of lenders conducts itself in relation to matters that affected the entire class.[134] However, taking reference from Dixon J in *Peters' American Delicacy Co Ltd* as well as *Howard Smith Ltd v Ampol Petroleum Ltd* (where it was held that directors had exercised the power to issue shares for improper purposes),[135] Rimer J said that where there were conflicting interests between the different classes of lenders, it was misplaced to apply the bona fide test (in this instance to the lenders as a whole). Instead, the vice against which control on the exercise of majority power

129 *Dafen Tinplate Co Ltd* (n 108) 139.
130 *Peters'American Delicacy Co Ltd* (n 110) 511.
131 *Gambotto* (n 121) 444.
132 ibid [445]; see also McHugh J [453].
133 *Redwood Master Fund Ltd v TD Bank Europe Ltd* [2002] EWHC 2703 (Ch), [2006] 1 BCLC 149; see also *Asseinagon Asset Management SA* (n 50).
134 *Redwood Master Fund Ltd* (n 133) [84].
135 *Howard Smith Ltd* (n 128).

was directed is 'the potential for a dishonest abuse of that power. The starting point in assessing the validity of its exercise must be to assess … whether the power is being exercised in good faith for the purpose for which it was conferred'.[136]

In *Re Charterhouse Capital Ltd* the Chancellor expressed the view that the limitations on the exercise of the power to amend a company's articles arise because, as in the case of all powers, the manner of their exercise is constrained by the purpose of the power and because the framers of the power of a majority to bind a minority will not, in the absence of clear words, have intended the power to be completely without limitation. These principles may be characterised as principles of law and equity or as implied terms.[137] *Allen*[138] and *Asseinagon Asset Management SA*[139] were cited in support. It is suggested that implied terms in this context does not mean terms implied as a matter of contract. While *Asseinagon Asset Management SA* was a case involving the implication of such a limitation as a matter of contract, constitutional alterations are about a power conferred by statute. Thus, when Lindley MR in *Allen* said that the limitation on a majority to alter the articles of association was a condition that was always implied and seldom, if ever, expressed,[140] he simply meant that the limitation was not one that had been expressly recognised by the Act. The limitation is implied within the terms of a legislative provision and is not a matter of contractual implication. It was as Lord Watson observed:

> In a Court of Law or Equity, what the Legislature intended to be done or not to be done can only be legitimately ascertained from that which it has chosen to enact, either in express words or by reasonable and necessary implication.[141]

If the proper purpose rule is the real basis for the restriction on the right of shareholders to alter the corporate constitution, the cases immediately assume greater coherence. First, as the power to alter is very widely expressed in legislation, and shareholders are not under a fiduciary duty when exercising their vote, the starting point must be that it will be difficult to argue that a particular exercise of the power is for an improper purpose.

Second, the power to amend is subject to an implied limitation and any exercise of the power beyond such limitation constitutes an abuse of such power. What then is the scope of the limitation that will cause equity to restrain a particular exercise of the power? It is suggested that the particular mischief that the limitation is directed at is discriminatory treatment between shareholders. An alteration that will cause a differentiation in the rights and obligations of members post-amendment will therefore generally not be permitted. Majorities should not make

[136] *Redwood Master Fund Ltd* (n 133) [105].
[137] *Re Charterhouse Capital Ltd* (n 108) [90].
[138] *Allen* (n 103).
[139] *Asseinagon Asset Management SA* (n 50).
[140] *Allen* (n 103) 671.
[141] *Salomon v Salomon* [1897] AC 22, 38.

presents of the company's assets to themselves,[142] or expropriate the shares of the minority.[143]

Third, it is suggested that discriminatory treatment will not be an improper exercise of the power where the interests of the company are clearly served, ie, where the harm to the minority is clearly outweighed by the benefit to,[144] or the harm avoided by, the company. Accordingly, in *Sidebottom v Kershaw, Leese & Co Ltd*,[145] an alteration allowing the directors the power to buy out at a fair price any member who competed with the company's business was upheld. As Warrington LJ put it: '[T]he fact that there was this competitor, and probably the knowledge that he was doing harm to the company, awoke the directors to the disadvantage in which they were placed by having such a man as one of their shareholders'.[146] By contrast, in *Gambotto*,[147] although there were tax and administrative savings, and the basis for expropriation was to be on fair terms, the amendment to insert a compulsory acquisition clause into the constitution was rejected. In the court's view, an expropriation may be justified where it is reasonably apprehended that the continued shareholding of the minority is significantly detrimental to the company, its undertaking or the conduct of its affairs—resulting in detriment to the interests of the existing shareholders generally—and expropriation is a reasonable means of eliminating or mitigating that detriment.[148] It was not sufficient that there was a benefit to the company given the proprietary nature of a share; that the benefit of it would only inure to the remaining shareholders; and it would deprive minorities of the protection offered to them in resisting compromises, reconstructions, schemes of arrangement, etc.[149]

Since the majority in *Gambotto* made it clear that the benefit-detriment distinction was made in the context of determining whether an expropriation was valid, the distinction should not be taken to be of general application. Having said this, it is suggested that the benefit-detriment dichotomy is difficult to justify.[150] The avoidance of a detriment also confers a benefit on a company. *Gambotto* therefore stands at the highest for the proposition that expropriation is so drastic an action that any benefit to the company that might justify such an act must be very significant. The benefit of avoiding material harm to the company crosses the threshold but not if the benefit merely leads to a different corporate structure that gives rise to commercial advantages.[151]

142 *Peters' American Delicacy Co Ltd* (n 110) 504.

143 *Dafen Tinplate Co Ltd* (n 108); *Brown* (n 108); *Gambotto* (n 121).

144 Though see the discussion in text to n 147 on *Gambotto*, where the court was of the view that only the avoidance of significant detriment to the company would justify compulsory acquisition; benefit to the company alone would not suffice.

145 *Sidebottom* (n 108).

146 ibid 171–72.

147 *Gambotto* (n 121). *Gambotto* has attracted various criticisms, which are outlined in H Tjio, P Koh and PW Lee, *Corporate Law* (Singapore, Academy Publishing, 2015) para 05.071.

148 *Gambotto* (n 121) [26]–[27].

149 ibid [28].

150 In *Gambotto* (n 121), McHugh J demurred forcefully on this point: [14].

151 ibid [27].

Finally, it is suggested further that the above glosses to a seemingly untrammelled power is rooted, similarly with the statutory remedies discussed earlier, in the implicit understanding among shareholders that there are expectations and obligations that are not submerged in the company structure. All these are instances of equity intervening where there is fraud in the equitable sense. It is readily understandable that while shareholders appreciate fully that the corporate constitution is not writ in stone, it is at the same time implicitly understood that alterations will not be effected so as to discriminate between shareholders unless a significant benefit is conferred on the company that clearly outweighs any harm to dissenting shareholders and such shareholders are treated as fairly as possible.

IV. Constraining Shareholder Action beyond Alterations of the Corporate Constitution

The general rule in company law is that where a wrong is done to a company the company is the proper plaintiff and a shareholder of a company may not sue to enforce rights belonging to the company.[152] This 'proper plaintiff rule' is a manifestation of the broader principle that a company is a legal entity separate from its shareholders. As such, the decision whether to bring a claim against a wrongdoer is one that should be resolved internally, usually by the board and sometimes the shareholders.[153] One important exception to this general rule is where there has been a 'fraud on the minority'. Essentially, where the wrongdoers are in control of the company and therefore in a position to prevent the company from asserting its rights, the court will in certain circumstances allow a shareholder to bring an action on behalf of the company against such wrongdoers. A usual example of such a situation is where the majority has attempted to appropriate to themselves money, property, or advantages which belong to the company, or in which the other shareholders are entitled to participate.[154] Such actions by the minority are commonly referred to as 'derivative actions' as they are derived from the company.[155]

The juristic basis for this exception is in equity. In *Nurcombe v Nurcombe* Browne-Wilkinson LJ said that where the technicality of the proper plaintiff rule

[152] *Foss v Harbottle* (1843) 2 Hare 461, (1843) 67 ER 189.

[153] It seems that under the common law, where the board refuses to act, the shareholders may in some circumstances by ordinary resolution decide to take action. See Davies and Worthington (n 23) para 17-3. For Singapore, see *Chan Siew Lee v TYC Investment Pte Ltd* [2015] SGCA 40, [2015] 5 SLR 409.

[154] *Burland v Earle* [1902] AC 83, 93; *Wallersteiner v Moir (No 2)* [1975] 1 QB 373, 390; *Sinwa SS (HK) Co Ltd v Morten Innhaug* [2010] SGHC 157, [2010] 4 SLR 1.

[155] This remedy has now been put into statutory form in the UK and replaces the 'common law derivative action' (see Companies Act 2006, ss 260–64), unless the matter relates to a 'multiple' or 'double' derivative action, see *Universal Project Management Services Ltd v Fort Gilkicker Ltd* [2013] EWHC 348 (Ch), [2013] Ch 551. In other jurisdictions such as Singapore, the common law derivative action coexists with the newer statutory derivative action (Companies Act (Cap 50, 2006 Rev Ed), s 216A).

would lead to manifest injustice, the courts of equity permitted a person interested to bring an action to enforce the company's claims.[156] Again, 'fraud' in this context is to be understood in the equitable sense and not in the more limited common law meaning of the word.[157] Templeman J said the principle is that a minority shareholder who has no other remedy may sue where directors use their powers, intentionally or unintentionally, fraudulently or negligently, in a manner which benefits themselves at the expense of the company.[158] In *Estmanco (Kilner House) Ltd v Greater London Council* Megarry VC explained the basis of the exception as such:

> [T]he essence of the matter seems to be an abuse or misuse of power. 'Fraud' in the phrase 'fraud on a minority' seems to be being used as comprising not only fraud at common law but also fraud in the wider equitable sense of that term, as in the equitable concept of a fraud on a power.[159]

Under the 'fraud on a minority' exception, equity does not allow majority shareholders to prevent an action by a minority shareholder where a wrong has been done to the company and the majority stand to benefit from preventing such an action being brought. The law will also regard any attempt by the majority to ratify the wrongdoing as being improper. Any such attempt by the majority to exercise their voting rights will be regarded as an improper exercise of power.[160] On the other hand, there will be no improper exercise of such power if a majority of independent shareholders who do not stand in any way to benefit from the absence of an action vote in favour of ratifying the wrongful act, or where it is abundantly clear that such an independent majority are against the bringing of an action. Accordingly, where a general meeting has been called, and a majority of all shareholders (including the wrongdoers) with full disclosure vote in favour of ratifying the wrong, and after disregarding the votes of the wrongdoers (and those associated with them), it is clear that a majority of the remaining (independent) votes were in favour of ratification, the resolution to ratify or waive the wrongdoing must be taken to have been carried. The approach taken in *Smith v Croft (No 2)* was therefore correct.[161]

It can be seen that two interrelated factors are at play here. The law is constraining majority power because of the need to prevent opportunistic conduct and a

[156] *Nurcombe v Nurcombe* [1985] 1 WLR 370, 378. See also *Roberts v Gill & Co* [2010] UKSC 22, [2011] 1 AC 240 [56], [110]; *Sinwa SS (HK) Co Ltd* (n 154) [69].

[157] *Daniels v Daniels* [1978] Ch 406; *Estmanco (Kilner House) Ltd v Greater London Council* [1982] 1 WLR 2; *Konamaneni v Rolls Royce Industrial Power (India) Ltd* [2002] 1 WLR 1269.

[158] *Daniels v Daniels*, ibid, 414; cited in *Ting Sing Ning v Ting Chek Swee* [2007] SGCA 49, [2008] 1 SLR(R) 197 [13].

[159] *Estmanco (Kilner House) Ltd* (n 157) 12.

[160] Similarly with the limitation imposed on the power to alter the corporate constitution, it must be the implicit understanding of all shareholders that they are entitled to be treated equally and not be discriminated against. This is the objective standard by which the actions of the majority in preventing a claim being brought, or ratifying the wrongful act, are judged.

[161] *Smith v Croft (No 2)* (n 108) 185. See also *Ting Sing Ning* (n 158).

conflict of interest. It would seem though that the disqualification of the majority shareholder-directors from voting at the shareholder meeting is principally premised on opportunistic conduct, namely that it would otherwise result in their unfair appropriation of an item of property (including corporate opportunities) belonging to the company which other shareholders have an indirect interest in. In other circumstances, shareholders who are directors may fully participate in shareholder resolutions that seek to waive breaches of fiduciary duty.[162] In *North-West Transportation Co Ltd v Beatty*,[163] the Privy Council held that a director was entitled to use his votes as a shareholder to ratify a sale of property to the company. It was accepted that the purchase of the steamer from the director was essential to the company's business, it was not possible to purchase any other steamer that was as well suited to the business, and the price was not excessive or unreasonable.

Beyond the foregoing non-statutory instances of limits on majority shareholder action, might there be a more general rule constraining majorities? If the foregoing instances are manifestations of the fraud on a power principle, there is no reason why limits on majority rule cannot be imposed in other instances. For example, where legislation relating to companies requires shareholder approval for the issue of shares,[164] and approval is given with a view to preventing a takeover or to dilute certain shareholders, it would not be difficult in principle to consider this an improper exercise of the power.[165] An attempt to fashion a more general approach was made in *Clemens v Clemens Bros Ltd*[166] which involved an attempt to issue additional shares which would have had the effect of diluting the plaintiff's interest in the company to below 25 per cent. Foster J found that while the majority shareholder would genuinely like to see the other directors of the company have shares and have a trust set up for long-service employees, the resolutions were framed so as to give her and her fellow directors complete control of the company at the expense of the plaintiff who was the only other shareholder. After referring to cases involving fraud on the minority, cases where the articles of association were being altered, and *Ebrahimi*, Foster J said that the defendant was not entitled to exercise her majority vote in whatever way she pleased. The difficulty was in finding a suitable principle that underpinned this. He ultimately said it would be unwise to try to do so as the circumstances of each case are infinitely varied. Quoting Lord Wilberforce in *Ebrahimi*, Foster J said that the defendant's exercise of her votes was subject to 'equitable considerations'.[167] The resolutions to, inter alia, allot more shares were therefore set aside.

[162] In *Sinwa SS (HK) Co Ltd* (n 154) [52], Andrew Ang J considered that the scope of fraud on the minority was amenable to further consideration.

[163] *North-West Transportation Co Ltd v Beatty* (n 109). See also *Burland* (n 154) 93–94.

[164] Companies Act 2006, s 551; Companies Act (Cap 50, 2006 Rev Ed) (Singapore) s 161.

[165] This has been held to be the case in the context of directors exercising such a power: see *Hogg v Cramphorn Ltd* [1967] 1 Ch 254; *Howard Smith Ltd* (n 128).

[166] *Clemens v Clemens Bros Ltd* [1976] 2 All ER 268.

[167] ibid 282.

Foster J's decision does not appear to have been adopted in the UK or Singapore. Although it is respectfully suggested that his intuition was correct, the failure to articulate a principled basis for the broader application of equitable considerations represented a weakness in the authoritativeness of the case. In addition, the apparent inability or unwillingness of the courts to fashion a broader remedy at common law to protect minorities led to the statutory unfair prejudice remedy which in turn appears to have relieved the courts of the need to further do so.[168] Nevertheless, it is submitted that there is a strong basis for the courts outside the unfair prejudice remedy to fashion additional remedies for minority shareholders should there be a need to do so in future.

V. Conclusion

The overlap between just and equitable winding up and the unfair prejudice remedy has already been noted. Similarly, where the constitution has been amended in a discriminatory fashion, or there has been fraud on a minority, the statutory remedies may be engaged. This should not be surprising if the element common to them is that of an express or implied agreement or understanding even though as framed they have different purposes.

One of the objectives of company law is to provide a set of default rules that can conveniently and with relatively little cost be adopted by parties seeking the benefits of incorporation. To this end, model constitutions have been a feature of corporate legislation. As these are default rules, it is open to parties to modify or exclude them. This is often done, particularly where the parties are sophisticated commercial organisations seeking to use the corporate vehicle to pursue joint ventures with others. In the great majority of instances though, this is not done because the corporate vehicle is also used by small businesses that will often incorporate without the benefit of legal advice.[169] Indeed, in Singapore the desire to reduce business costs and allow quick incorporation has led to most company registrations being done online in accordance with default provisions. Given this, it is understandable that the corporate constitution will not truly reflect the intentions or expectations of the incorporators or all shareholders. At law such intentions or expectations where not reduced to an enforceable agreement have no effect. Equity is not similarly constrained, for example, in promissory

[168] The predecessor of the unfair prejudice remedy was enacted on the recommendation of the Cohen Committee, which wanted to strengthen the position of minority shareholders of a private company in resisting oppression by the majority shareholders or the controllers of a company: *Report of the Committee on Company Law Amendment* (Cmnd 6659, 1945) [60].

[169] To this extent, at least in Singapore, it is not true that persons who incorporate companies do so 'with legal advice and some degree of formality': *O'Neill* (n 45) 1098 (Lord Hoffman).

estoppel.[170] Accordingly, equity constrains shareholders from acting within their strict legal rights to the inequitable disadvantage of other shareholders, and prevents powers from being used for improper purposes. Equity does so to prevent a fraud on such powers. As these constraints on the majority flow from this principle, it is not surprising that there is a common element in their application. In essence, the scope of these constraints depends on what the courts regard as being within the reasonable contemplation of shareholders in the type of company in question.

[170] Indeed, the Alabama Supreme Court in *Mazer v Jackson Insurance Agency*, 340 So 2d 770, 772 (Ala 1976) stated that the 'purpose of equitable estoppel and promissory estoppel is to promote equity and justice in an individual case by preventing a party from asserting rights under a general technical rule of law when his own conduct renders the assertion of such rights contrary to equity and good conscience', thereby seeing estoppel as having roots in equitable fraud which similarly underlies the corporate statutory remedies discussed in this chapter. If this is correct, it is another aspect of the contractual approach that can be employed to determine the operation of the statutory remedies.

2

Some Aspects of the Intersection of the Law of Agency with the Law of Trusts

PETER WATTS*

I. Introduction

Lawyers are regularly charged with making the law unnecessarily complex. This charge is most commonly levelled at the diction of those documents routinely drafted by lawyers, to wit statutes and other legal instruments.[1] But judge-made rules can also attract such criticism. A legal system that acquires, like England did, more than one set of judges, each set following in varying degrees its own lines of thought, creates a recipe for complexity, certainly, and for incoherence, potentially.

One subject that, in parts, descends into incoherence is the English law relating to group decisions. This has quite a lot to do with the fact that *three* sets of courts generated rules in this area that were not fully co-ordinated. A small corner of this topic takes up three-quarters of this chapter, but the most incoherent aspects have been sketched then avoided. This has been possible by limiting the scope of the chapter to the intersections between the law of agency and the law of trusts. This is a topic more complex than incoherent. One would expect a reasonable degree of coherence because the law of trusts was designed to work *with* the rules of the common law. While the trust was the brainchild of those working outside the common law, its creators were at least conscious that they were adding a layer on top of the law's basic rules. In this aspect of equity, to seek to *fuse* the two existing

* The author is grateful to the Leverhulme Trust and to the NUS and Oxford Law Faculties for their support to write this chapter, and to Richard Nolan, Matthew Conaglen and Jamie Glister for their helpful comments on a draft of it.

[1] *cf* the 'purgatorial complexity' of the documents before the Supreme Court in *Belmont Park Investments PTY Ltd v BNY Corporate Trustee Services Ltd* [2011] UKSC 38, [2012] 1 AC 383 [138] (Lord Mance).

bodies of law would not work: the one is parasitic on the other. A reformer would perhaps do better to create an entirely new set of rules.

The body of law that deals with disputes that arise out of the deployment of intermediaries (generally 'agents') has been predominantly developed at common law. Although equity's fiduciary law has had a large role to play as between principal and agent, it is possible for agencies to operate without engaging with the law of trusts. Equally, it is possible for trusts to operate without engaging the law of agency. Sometimes the courts have allowed themselves to confuse the two sets of rules in ways that are illegitimate. We will see examples of this in section IV of this chapter. Another recent example that will not be pursued in this chapter has involved a court wrongly treating trustees as if they were agents of their beneficiaries.[2]

But the two bodies of law do sometimes quite legitimately come into contact with one another, and from opposite directions. On the one hand, trustees may on occasions find it necessary, or convenient, to delegate tasks to agents.[3] This chapter is mostly absorbed with the consequences of delegations that exceed permissible bounds. On the other hand, principals sometimes require their agents to hold moneys provided to them (either by the principals themselves or by a third party) on trust for the relevant principal. These situations too give rise to particular legal problems. These issues will be more briefly addressed in the last section of the chapter.

II. Three Models of Decision-Making Amongst Groups

As indicated, the rules for decision-making by groups in their dealings with outside parties are derived historically from three different sets of courts—common law, equitable and ecclesiastical. Usually such groups will have powers of disposition over property, either as co-owners, or as co-agents on behalf of an owner or owners. But the group may also be running a business together that may or may not deal in tangible property. In general, the rules, at least where one is concerned with authorised decision-making, are presumptions only. They are therefore subject to contrary arrangement so long as designated mechanisms for deviation are met. Each of the three major models has subcategories, but the principal features of the models are as follows.

[2] See *Wishart v Credit and Mercantile Plc* [2015] EWCA Civ 655, [2015] 2 P & CR 15, criticised by J Sampson, 'Estoppel and the Land Registration Act 2002' (2016) 75 *CLJ* 21; M Dixon, 'The *Boland* Requiem' [2016] *Conveyancer and Property Lawyer* 284; A Televantos, 'Trusteeship, Ostensible Authority, and Land Registration: the Category Error in *Wishart*' [2016] *Conveyancer and Property Lawyer* 181.

[3] Where the trustee is an incorporation the trustee, on a traditional analysis anyway, is going to *have* to operate through agents. Nothing more is said on this topic in this chapter.

First, the species making up the common law genus are characterised by: (a) majority decision-making; and (b) subject to context, the ability to delegate. Members of the group may be liable to their colleagues, or where they are co-agents to their principal, for carelessness in their decisions or in their choice of delegates, but they and their delegates would usually have actual or, where the standard requirements of agency law are met, apparent authority to effect a disposition of property under their charge. They may also have such authority to bind themselves or their common principal to the terms of a contract extending beyond any disposition of property. A good example of a group which is made up of co-principals is the partnership, and of a group that is made up of co-agents is the board of a company. Both operate on a presumption of majority rule.[4]

Second, the equity genus largely comprises the trust. Here, in contrast to the common law model, the decision-makers are: (a) supposed to act unanimously; and (b) may not delegate, except in respect of the implementation of decisions they have already made.[5] The position is different with charitable trusts, where majority rule is the presumption,[6] and majority rule is the norm for trusts in general in Scottish law.[7] There may be some variation too in powers of delegation both by type of trust, and by virtue of statute, by jurisdiction.[8]

The third genus, that derived from ecclesiastical law,[9] comprises executors and administrators (though there is some doubt whether the rules of dealing were exactly the same for both categories). In this genus, decision-makers can act *unilaterally* to bind their colleagues in relation to a relevant disposition of personalty, including leases of land. By statute in some jurisdictions, this rule can extend to dispositions of other interests in land.

If one places the three models on a spectrum, one gets the remarkable result that in respect of dispositions of many types of property: (a) single executors can bind their colleagues without consulting them; (b) partners and other co-agents, such as company directors, can usually make decisions by majority rule, and a delegate from them might have actual or apparent authority to bind; but (c) trustees must act unanimously and may not, in general, delegate.

[4] eg Partnership Act 1893 (UK), s 24(8); Partnership Act 1908 (NZ), s 27(h); Companies (Model Articles) Regulations 2008 (UK), sch 1, cl 17 and sch 3, cl 13; Companies Act 1993 (NZ), sch 3, cl 5.

[5] D Hayton, P Matthews and C Mitchell, *Underhill and Hayton: Law of Trusts and Trustees*, 18th edn (London, LexisNexis, 2010) Arts 51 and 52; *cf* J Getzler, 'Duty of Care' in P Birks and A Pretto (eds), *Breach of Trust* (Oxford, Hart Publishing, 2002) 60–67.

[6] See *Re Whiteley* [1910] 1 Ch 600. Presumably, this reflects the fact that charitable trusts have traditionally had larger numbers of trustees than private trusts.

[7] See Trusts (Scotland) Act 1921, s 3(c). For a fuller picture, see Scottish Law Commission, *Report on Trust Law* (Law Com No 239, 2014) Part 5.

[8] An open-ended unqualified power of appointment can be tantamount to ownership, and in which case the power can be delegated: *Fonu v Merrill Lynch Bank and Trust Company (Cayman) Ltd* [2011] UKPC 17, [2012] 1 WLR 1721 [53]. See also *Clayton v Clayton* [2016] NZSC 29, [2016] 1 NZLR 551.

[9] For a useful overview, see E Haertle, 'The History of the Probate Court' (1962) 45 *Marquette Law Review* 546.

The foregoing account is only the starting point of the complexity. There are other layers to it. There are two main types of complication at the next level. First, as already noted, the trust works as an attachment to common law ownership, and though the courts have sometimes lost sight of the point, the two sets of rules operate in tandem. Second, it is not only possible for an executor to also be a trustee in some respects, but it can be difficult too to tell when someone has ceased to be an executor and become solely a trustee.[10] Hence, there have been cases where an act has been held invalid in equity because not all trustees concurred in it, when it might have been valid if the same personnel had effected it while still executors.[11]

Below this, there is yet further complexity. This chapter does not propose to address the regime for executors, but the complexity there borders on the diabolical, and cries out for statutory simplification.[12] Just by way of an example, a leading case explains that while executors can generally ride solo, if they expressly purport to act with the consent of their colleagues but do not have that consent, then they will not bind their colleagues, though they may be personally liable for breach of warranty of authority.[13]

At the same time, it would be wrong to suggest that all the divergence in the various approaches to group decision-making is the accident of history. In particular, the non-delegation principle in the law of trusts is not irrational, and probably derives from the family context of the traditional trust where a settlor personally selected the trustees, knowing that one might need to act as a brake on the others.

With this background, we can turn to look in more detail at the role of agency law in the making of contracts and dispositions by trustees.

III. Trustees: Their Contracts and Dispositions

The main argument being made in this chapter in relation to contracts and dispositions by trustees is that whether co-trustees become bound to a contract, and to any transaction that effects a disposition of property of a type that is recognised by the common law, is prima facie governed by common law rules, not equitable ones.[14] It follows that if some trustees wrongly delegate decision-making to

[10] See C Sherrin, 'Aut Ovis Aut Capra: Personal Representative or Trustee?' (1995) 25 *Hong Kong Law Journal* 239; see also *Re King's WT* [1964] Ch 542; *Porteous v Rinehart* [1998] WASC 270.

[11] eg *Attenborough v Solomon* [1913] AC 76 (pledge of chattels).

[12] eg Succession Act 1981 (Qld), s 49.

[13] See *Fountain Forestry Ltd v Edwards* [1975] Ch 1; and *Birdseye v Roythorne & Co* [2015] EWHC 1003 (Ch) [33]. Joshua Getzler has suggested to the writer that the rules developed to reflect the need often to dispose quickly of the chattels of estates, especially in rural areas when formerly communication was not easy.

[14] See too M Conaglen and R Nolan, 'Contracts and Knowing Receipt: Principles and Application' (2013) 129 *LQR* 359, 360, who argue (at least in relation to a trust of legal property) that a trustee's powers all come from the common law, and that the deployment of them consistently with the trust simply gives the trustee an immunity.

the remaining trustees or if the trustees delegate to some other agent, they will commit a breach of trust but they will have conferred actual authority on those delegates. Any resulting contract or disposition of trust property will be effective at law as a result of the ordinary operation of the (common) law of agency. The starting point of the common law is that whatever can be done personally can be done by an agent: this is one of the renditions, admittedly loose, of the expression *qui facit per alium, facit per se.*[15] The common law does, presumptively, inhibit the power of an agent to sub-delegate,[16] but trustees are principals, not agents.

If the outside party knows that its counterparties are trustees and knows that there has been a breach of the delegation rules, the contract will still impose obligations on the trustees personally, but equity will permit neither the trustees nor the outside party to have recourse to any trust assets in execution of the contract.[17] An injunction would issue (usually at the behest of a beneficiary) to prevent any trust assets being transferred, and any property already transferred is likely to be held by the outside party on constructive trust. The fact that the transaction is defective only at equity, and not at law, is in such circumstances not going to matter much to that party. Either way, that party is in difficulty,[18] save as to rights to damages it may have in contract against the trustees. But, absent that knowledge, the outside party would be safe. The breach of trust would sound only against the relevant trustees themselves.

Trustees may also become bound by the conduct of some of their number, or by the conduct of other agents, through the operation of the common law rules of apparent authority. The position is relatively straightforward where the outside party is unaware that its counterparties are trustees. Where the trustees are simple co-owners of the trust assets, the outside party would usually need to show some fact-specific holding out, because there is no usual authority of one co-owner at law to bind the others.[19] But where, as is not uncommon, trustees are running a business they will often be partners at common law. In such circumstances, there will be usual apparent authority at common law for one partner to bind the others in relation to 'any act for carrying on in the usual way business of the kind carried on by the firm'.[20]

[15] See P Watts and F Reynolds (eds), *Bowstead & Reynolds on Agency*, 20th edn (London, Sweet & Maxwell, 2014) para 2-017; G Dal Pont, *Law of Agency*, 2nd edn (London, LexisNexis 2008) paras 3.16–3.19.

[16] See Watts and Reynolds (n 15) Art 44.

[17] As to whether a breach of trust makes a disposition under a contract void or voidable at equity, see R Nolan, 'Controlling Fiduciary Power' (2009) 68(2) *CLJ* 293; Watts and Reynolds (eds) (n 15) paras 8-219–8-220.

[18] An outside party who knows that its counterparties are asking for a contract to be performed in a way that would involve a breach of trust may be justified in declining to meet the directions of the counterparty: see *Re Flower and Metropolitan Board of Works* (1884) 27 Ch D 592.

[19] See *Kennedy v De Trafford* [1897] AC 180, 188; as to an estoppel, see *Doueihi v Construction Technologies Australia Pty Ltd* [2016] NSWCA 105 [222].

[20] Partnership Act 1890 (UK), s 5; Partnership Act 1908 (NZ) s 8.

The position becomes more complex if the outside party needs to rely on apparent authority because there has been no actual delegation, and knows there is a trust but does not know there has been a breach. Does the outsider's knowledge that the counterparties are trustees hinder, or even foreclose, a plea of apparent authority? To put the matter another way, would it be reasonable for an outsider to assume that putative promisors would willingly have exposed themselves to an action for breach of trust by forgoing their deliberative role? The main reason for resisting the automatic integration of the common law and equity in relation to the making of contracts is that trusts are designed to operate 'under the radar', and for that reason it would be unjust to have unknowing parties affected by their (express or implied) terms. That rationale ceases to apply, or at least is not so compelling, where the outside party is aware of the trust. The relationship between the common law and equity is not absolutely one of oil and water. Given that there is nothing that precludes the express terms of a contract from recognising equitable rights and duties, it may not be inappropriate when determining whether a representation of conferral of authority to contract has been made by a putative principal to consider whether it is likely that the principal would have put him or herself in a position of breach of trust.

However, the question is not made simpler by the fact that equity's own position in relation to third parties who do not have actual knowledge of a breach of trust is unstable around the Commonwealth. There may be more than one test to be applied, depending on whether the third party still has possession of the relevant trust property. And it is unclear just what those tests are; is the test one of dishonesty, or unconscionable conduct, or one of unreasonable failure to perceive the breach of trust?[21] It would be surprising if the concept of apparent authority at law operated more restrictively than equity itself.[22] There is a lot to be said for both law and equity applying a commercial reasonableness standard in this context,[23] but these difficult issues need not be pursued here.

IV. Modern Case Law, Much of it Problematic

Perhaps because the above thesis as to the interrelationship of law and equity is widely shared by lawyers, there has until recently been little case law in leading Commonwealth jurisdictions addressing the effect on outside parties of wrongful

[21] On the last of these tests, see *Westpac Banking Corp v Savin* [1985] 2 NZLR 41, where a good discussion of older English authority can be found.

[22] See also Conaglen and Nolan (n 14).

[23] The author has written on this subject elsewhere: as to reasonableness within apparent authority, see P Watts, 'Some Wear and Tear on *Armagas v Mundogas*: The Tension Between Having and Wanting in the Law of Agency' [2015] *Lloyd's Maritime and Commercial Law Quarterly* 36, 48–56; and within equity, P Watts, 'Tests of Knowledge in the Receipt of Misapplied Funds' (2015) 131 *LQR* 511.

delegations by trustees.[24] In this regard, one should note that some jurisdictions have enacted legislation permitting (unless the trust deed otherwise provides) delegations by trustees of some types of decision-making either to some of their number or to other agents. However, such legislation rarely cauterises the issues covered in this chapter, because qualifications are usually attached to the powers. Hence, Part IV of the Trustee Act 2000 that applies in England and Wales permits broad delegations of 'asset management powers' but only where the delegation is in writing and the trustees have created a 'policy statement' guiding the exercise of the delegation. In many cases, these requirements will not have been complied with.[25]

The relatively sparse case law on the subject has over the last 15 years or so been added to by a swathe of New Zealand cases. Unfortunately, the New Zealand courts have in many instances lost sight of the fact that the law of trusts works in combination with the common law, not as a substitute for it. Since it is not inconceivable that these errors might be repeated elsewhere, this chapter takes this case law as its focus.

Before turning to the New Zealand cases, one can note one older case where the court got the general principles correct. In *McLellan Properties Ltd v Roberge*,[26] a decision of the Supreme Court of Canada, a trustee granted a power of attorney in relation to his trust powers. The attorney purported to exercise the power by entering into a contract of sale of some trust land. The Court accepted that the delegation was a breach of trust but held that it was not void at law. On the facts, however, there had also been a ratification of the contract by the trustee, which would have been effective both at law and equity.[27]

As to New Zealand, signs of misunderstanding can be found in earlier cases,[28] but the principal source of confusion has been the decision of the Court of Appeal in 2001 in *Niak v Macdonald*.[29] Before outlining the facts, we can note that the Court may have been beguiled into eliding law and equity by the fact that a separation of the two sets of rules may not have made a difference to the outcome on the facts of the case. The dangers are still there.

In *Niak*, the relevant trust had three trustees: M, his wife S and W, a solicitor. The principal assets on settlement of the trust were derived from an inheritance by S. She was also the principal beneficiary of the trust, but one infers from the way the case was argued that she was not the only beneficiary. A yacht was purchased by M using trust funds. M intended to take title to the yacht in his personal

[24] Perhaps too in some jurisdictions it has been more routine for trust deeds to provide for majority rule and to permit delegation.

[25] s 24 of the Act provides that failure to meet the Act's requirements does not invalidate the delegation, but at the same time the Act does not generally validate improper delegations at equity.

[26] *McLellan Properties Ltd v Roberge* [1947] SCR 561.

[27] See further text to n 40.

[28] eg *Rodney Aero Club Inc v Moore* [1998] 2 NZLR 192.

[29] *Niak v Macdonald* [2001] 3 NZLR 334.

capacity. At the time, S and W appear to have generally condoned M's using the funds of the trust for private purposes, but they did not specifically authorise the purchase of the yacht (though S certainly knew that M was buying it). M and S separated some six months later, and it appears that the wife at some stage thereafter asserted that the yacht belonged to the trust. More than two years after that, M mortgaged the yacht to a bank to secure a loan to him. Very shortly thereafter, M was removed as a trustee, and the new trustees ('the plaintiffs') asserted that their claim to the yacht was superior to the bank's.

The Court held that the free hand S and W had given M was in breach of the unanimity and non-delegation rules, and that therefore M had no authority at *law* to purchase the yacht.[30] Thus, the seeds of future misunderstanding were sown. But on the facts of the case itself this conclusion, if argued for by the plaintiffs, did not suit them because they still wanted to treat the yacht as a trust asset. They proceeded to concede that if the yacht was to be subject to the trust, they could then defeat the bank's mortgage only if the bank was aware of the wrongful delegation.

This concession was probably inevitable, because even if the Court was right that the purchase of the yacht was unauthorised at law, that would not have prevented legal title in the yacht passing to M as a result of the intention of the seller, who was completely unaware of the trust. The husband as legal owner was then able to give a legal mortgage to the bank,[31] and did so before the other trustees had taken any stance, by ratification, or by asserting rights to trace at law (assuming those mechanisms of the law would have achieved anything). The Court proceeded to hold that the plaintiffs had failed to show that the bank knew of the plaintiffs' rights.

As it happens, this last conclusion was another controversial feature of *Niak*. The evidence was that the bank's solicitor had gained knowledge of the plaintiffs' claim to the yacht before the mortgage took place, albeit in his capacity of acting for M in his matrimonial property dispute with S. The Court held that this knowledge was not imputable to the bank,[32] but this conclusion may not be consistent with older case law. This issue will not be pursued here, but it should be noted that the broad statutory protection against imputation of an agent's knowledge conferred in England by the Law of Property Act 1925, section 199, has a much narrower equivalent in New Zealand.

[30] See especially, ibid [18].

[31] See *Lipkin Gorman v Karpnale Ltd* [1991] 2 AC 548, 573; *Foskett v McKeown* [2001] 1 AC 102. See further, P Birks, *Unjust Enrichment*, 2nd edn (Oxford, OUP, 2005) 198; R Chambers, 'Tracing and Unjust Enrichment' in J Neyers, M McInnes and S Pitel (eds), *Understanding Unjust Enrichment* (Oxford, Hart Publishing, 2004) 302–05; *cf Branwhite v Worcester Works Finance Ltd* [1969] AC 552; *Smith v Cunningham* (1915) 34 NZLR 392; *Spangaro v Corporate Investment Australia Funds Management Ltd* [2003] FCA 1025, 47 ACSR 285.

[32] It is beyond the scope of this chapter to address this point, but the writer considers that principle would support the imputation of knowledge on the facts of the case. See P Watts, 'Imputed Knowledge in Restitutionary Claims: Rationales and Rationes' in S Degeling and J Edelman (eds), *Unjust Enrichment in Commercial Law* (Sydney, Lawbook Co, 2008).

The thesis of this chapter would have provided a cleaner solution to *Niak* than the one adopted. The consent of the trustees would have put pay to any claims based on lack of authority, leaving the matter to be solved solely at equity.[33]

The potential difficulties with the reasoning in *Niak* would have been much more acute had the husband purported to *sell* a chattel belonging to the trust, say a yacht, rather than buying one. On the Court's reasoning that the relevant delegations were invalid at law, the buyer of the yacht would not have obtained legal title, under the principle *nemo dat quod non habet*. In contrast, on the thesis of this chapter the buyer would have obtained legal title and could have been subject to a trust claim only if sufficiently aware of a breach of trust.

In *ASB Bank Ltd v Davidson*,[34] another decision of the New Zealand Court of Appeal, the reasoning in *Niak* was assumed to be correct, but the case was decided on the particular wording of a contract that all trustees had signed with the claimant bank. Nonetheless, the decision should be noted for a brief dictum of Glazebrook J,[35] who gave the lead judgment, that the bank could not rely on allegations of a holding out of authority by two trustees of a delegation to the third, in a way which would affect the trust assets, when the bank knew they were all trustees. This dictum did not result from deliberation on the point, but nonetheless does suggest that a deemed knowledge of equity might undermine a holding out, at least insofar as the putative contract was held to affect trust assets.

The Court of Appeal returned to the issue in *Ponniah v Palmer*.[36] Here two trustees who owned three apartments in a complex afflicted with 'leaky building syndrome' instructed a firm of solicitors to conduct litigation against the builder and a local authority in relation to the defects in the apartments. They delegated to the settlor of the trust, S, the management of the litigation and it was he who had the day-to-day dealings with the solicitors. Some three years later, the solicitors became concerned about receiving payment for their work in conducting the litigation and therefore procured from S, purportedly on behalf of the owners, agreement to give a mortgage to the firm over the apartments. The trustees then denied S's authority to give the mortgage, a denial which provoked these proceedings. It was held at first instance that no actual authority was given by the trustees to mortgage the trust property. This was probably all that needed to be decided. Moreover, it appears that the solicitors knew that the owners were trustees. However, the judge went on to find that the trustees had no power at law to delegate under the trust deed and that fact would also have prevented the firm obtaining a mortgage. These findings were upheld by the Court of Appeal, relying on *Niak*. The Court also used *Niak* to rule that a plea by the solicitors against the trustees in estoppel could not succeed. This cause of action was essentially one

[33] *Pilcher v Rawling* (1872) LR 7 Ch App 259.
[34] *ASB Bank Ltd v Davidson* (2005) 8 NZBLC 101, 597.
[35] ibid [33]; see also *Thorpe v Hannam* (2010) 11 NZCPR 471 [24].
[36] *Ponniah v Palmer* [2012] NZCA 490.

based on apparent authority. The Court peremptorily ruled it out on the basis that 'no assumption of powers by [S] which are ultra vires can be validated by raising an estoppel'.[37]

It is respectfully submitted that again the Court mixed up questions of authority at common law with breach of trust. It is one thing to say that courts should not lightly find a holding out of authority by trustees when that would involve them in breach of trust. It is another to disempower them at law from estopping themselves. It is clear from the leading text on estoppel—*Spencer Bower on Estoppel*[38]—that the principle that one cannot raise an estoppel in respect of what would be ultra vires action on the part of the person estopped is concerned with cases where the assertion is being made against a person (usually a public authority or a corporation) that lacks *legal* capacity to do the thing asserted. The trustees here did not lack legal capacity.

Again, it is not that the result in *Ponniah* was wrong. S lacked authority at common law to give the mortgage, and that was the short answer. Even if there had been a finding that carte blanche had been given to S, including to give security to the solicitors, the solicitors' knowledge of the existence of the trust was likely to have made the mortgage subject to challenge in equity. The correct parties to raise such a plea would ordinarily have been the beneficiaries of the trust, but there is also authority that would support permitting trustees to disown their own conduct or, more usually, that of their predecessors, by seeking a declaration that they or their predecessors acted in breach of trust.[39]

Another case applying *Niak*, and eliding law and equity, is *Finnigan v Butcher (No 2)*.[40] Here the issue was the validity of a resolution to liquidate a company, X Ltd, most of the shares in which were divided between the trustees of two family trusts. Both trusts had three trustees, and they shared one of their trustees in common (a trustee company, Y Ltd, the shares in which were held by a solicitor who advised both trusts). Only two of the three trustees of each trust signed the written resolution, Y Ltd not being involved. The liquidators whose appointment was now being challenged argued that the solicitor had on behalf of Y Ltd given his clients a general authority to act on behalf of the trusts in the affairs of the company. This argument was peremptorily rejected by the judge on the basis of the non-delegation principle. He went on to hold, nonetheless, that the solicitor on behalf of Y Ltd had subsequently ratified the decision to liquidate X Ltd, referring both to ratification within the common law of agency and to the principle

[37] ibid [28].

[38] P Feltham, D Hochberg and T Leech, *Spencer Bower's The Law Relating to Estoppel by Representation*, 4th edn (London, LexisNexis, 2004) ch VII 6.1.

[39] The leading case, much discussed, is *Young v Murphy* [1996] 1 VR 279; see also *Equiticorp Industries Group Ltd v The Crown (No 47)* [1998] 2 NZLR 481, 545–46; *Agricultural Land Management Ltd v Jackson (No 2)* [2014] WASC 102, (2014) 285 FLR 121 [331]; *Dalriada Trustees Ltd v Woodward* [2012] EWHC 21626 (Ch) [37].

[40] *Finnigan v Butcher (No 2)* [2012] NZHC 2463.

that allows a trustee to ratify in equity decisions of his or her co-trustees that they made without consultation.[41]

The judge, it is respectfully suggested, was wrong to conclude that the resolution was prima facie invalid because of the non-delegation principle. If there had indeed been a general delegation, then subject to one argument, that delegation would have been effective at law, even though a breach of trust would have been involved. Under New Zealand law, as in many other jurisdictions, companies are generally interested in the rights of legal owners of shares only, and are not concerned with the equitable duties of those owners. So, section 89(2) of the Companies Act 1993 provides that a company may treat the registered holder of a share as the only person entitled to exercise the rights attaching to the share. Section 92 forbids the entry on the share register of notice of a trust in respect of shares. Moreover, clause 11 of Schedule 1 to the 1993 Act provides that:

> where 2 or more persons are registered as the holder of a share, the vote of the person named first in the share register and voting on a matter must be accepted to the exclusion of the votes of the other joint holders.

While this clause is designed to provide a solution for cases where joint holders have differing views as to how a vote should be cast, it would seem to apply just as much to cases where more junior co-shareholders are not consulted at all or are in agreement as to how to vote.

This leaves to be considered the counter-argument foreshadowed in the last paragraph. There is, in fact, a long-standing presumption of company law (arguably an unfortunate one) that a shareholder cannot at *law* delegate his or her power to vote, in the absence of constitutional provision for proxies.[42] This presumption, however, does not apply in relation to voting by co-shareholders, because then clause 11, above, applies.

None of the foregoing argumentation would be determinative of a dispute amongst trustees, or between beneficiaries and the trustees, as to how the legal powers attached to shares held by the trust should be, or have been, exercised. In such contexts, the unanimity and non-delegation rules would be applicable. Such a dispute can be found in *Radich v Brown*,[43] a case concerned with local authority trustees holding shares in an electricity company.

With some reluctance, mention should now be made of the decision of the Victorian Court of Appeal in *Australasian Annuities Pty Ltd (in liq) v Rowley Super Fund Pty Ltd*.[44] The case is rather inaccessible for a number of reasons. Aspects

[41] See too *Visini v Cadman* [2012] NZCA 122, (2012) 21 PRNZ 70 [17]; *Hansard v Hansard* [2014] NZCA 433, [2015] 2 NZLR 158 [51].

[42] See *Harben v Phillips* (1883) 23 Ch D 14 (CA). It is common for constitutions to provide for proxy voting. See, more generally, R Nolan, 'The Continuing Evolution of Shareholder Governance' (2006) 65 *CLJ* 92.

[43] *Radich v Brown* HC Blenheim, CP4/01, 13 August 2001 (Doogue J). See also *Tisdale v Ballanday Pty Ltd* [2006] NSWSC 909; *New Zealand Maori Council v Foulkes* [2014] NZHC 1777 (Issues 4–6).

[44] *Australasian Annuities Pty Ltd (in liq) v Rowley Super Fund Pty Ltd* [2015] VSCA 9.

of the pleadings were inadequate, which led at least one member of the Court to rule out certain key arguments. Second, the case was affected by the rather narrow approach to imputation of knowledge that the High Court of Australia took in *Farah Constructions Pty Ltd v Say-Dee Pty Ltd*.[45] Third, the judges confused the imputed knowledge of agents with the different concept of constructive knowledge.[46] The High Court of Australia declined leave for a further appeal.[47] Nonetheless, it is an appellate decision raising potentially interesting issues.

The claimant was a trustee company of what were nominally superannuation funds, but which funds had been sourced as a result of a series of commercially dubious transactions promoted by the then controller of the claimant, 'S'. S proceeded to arrange for the transfer of the funds to four individual trustees of whom he was one and his wife and sons the others. This transfer was held to involve a breach of fiduciary duty by S in relation to the claimant. These individual trustees were then replaced by a new trustee company, X Ltd, of which S was again found by the majority of the Court (Neave JA and Garde AJA) to be the controller. The claimant went into receivership and liquidation and commenced these proceedings to recover the funds in knowing receipt, suing the individual trustees and X Ltd. The majority of the Court held that X Ltd was liable in knowing receipt. But none of the judges found that the individual trustees, other than S, were liable in knowing receipt.

For present purposes, it was the position of the individual trustees that was the most interesting. There was insufficient evidence to show that those trustees, other than S, had personal knowledge of S's breach of duty. Though imputation of knowledge to them through the agency of S had not been properly pleaded by the claimant, all members of the Court considered that there was no place for imputation in any event. The duty on trustees not to delegate was one factor that was found by Warren CJ, with whom Neave JA agreed on this issue, to militate against S being an agent for the other trustees.[48]

It is suggested here that it is doubtful whether the unanimity rule carried much weight on these facts, even when the cause of action being considered was equitable rather than legal. It is true that in ordinary circumstances the duty to act unanimously might furnish a ground for thinking that trustees would not lightly delegate decisions to one of their number, assuming they know the rules of equity. However, it could not do more than that. On the facts, the individual trustees were not disowning their beneficial receipt of the funds, and to get to that position they needed to rely on the contract made on their behalf by S. In these circumstances, it is hard to understand how that contract was made without S acting as their agent.

[45] *Farah Constructions Pty Ltd v Say-Dee Pty Ltd* [2007] HCA 22, (2007) 230 CLR 89; see Watts, 'Imputed Knowledge in Restitutionary Claims' (n 32) 434–36.
[46] *Australasian Annuities* (n 44) [98].
[47] [2015] HCATrans 235.
[48] ibid [99] (Warren CJ).

The Court's conclusion that none of the trustees other than S could be liable in knowing receipt (without even needing to consider any defences that they might have had) also leaves something of a puzzle as to how the majority could then hold that X Ltd could be made liable in knowing receipt having received a transfer of the funds from those innocent trustees. The Court imputed S's knowledge to X Ltd, but X Ltd was acquiring the funds from persons who had been held to be bona fide purchasers for value,[49] so it is arguable that the imputation of S's wrongdoing came too late. It may be that if S was the sole beneficial owner of X Ltd, he might be compelled by equity to cause X Ltd to return the funds to the claimants, on the basis that equity will not allow a dishonest trustee to purchase, even from an honest seller, former trust assets free of the trust.[50]

In contrast to the foregoing decisions is the decision of the New Zealand Court of Appeal in *Murrell v Hamilton*.[51] Here the defendants were the trustees of Mr Hamilton's family trust, Mr Hamilton being one of the trustees. The trust owned a property on which, during Mr Hamilton's de facto relationship with the claimant, a house was completed and in which the parties then lived. When some eight years later the parties separated, the claimant sought an interest in the property based on New Zealand's constructive trust principles. Having convinced the judge at first instance that she deserved an interest in the property, she faced the hurdle that the independent trustee of the trust was a solicitor who lived in a different city and had only very limited knowledge of what had happened on the property and the contributions the claimant had made. The Court of Appeal, reversing the first instance judge on this issue, concluded that the inactive trustee had delegated all affairs relating to the trust assets to the active trustee, and must be bound by his actions and omissions.

On its face, this robust reasoning fits better with the argumentation of this chapter than the other decisions that have been discussed.[52] However, the focus of the reasoning in this chapter is on the enforceability of *common law* rights, namely the contracts in question and dispositions of *legal* interests under them. The claim being made in *Murrell* was an *equitable* one, which meant that the contest was ultimately one between equitable interests, that of the claimant and those of the beneficiaries of the trust. Priority contests in equity are governed by their own sets of rules. How these ought to have played out in *Murrell* will not be pursued here, other than to note that equity's basic priority rule, the first-in-time rule, may not be applicable to parties asserting rights under a discretionary trust.

Similar complexities attend one of the few potentially relevant English cases, *Fielden v Christie-Miller*.[53] The claimant brought a proprietary estoppel claim

[49] *cf Re Stapleford Colliery Co, Barrow's Case* (1880) 14 Ch D 432; *Kettlewell v Watson* (1882) 21 Ch D 685, 712 (reversed on other issues, (1884) 26 Ch D 501 (CA)).

[50] See *Re Stapleford* (n 49) 445.

[51] *Murrell v Hamilton* [2014] NZCA 377 (leave to appeal to SC declined: [2014] NZSC 162); see also *Lang v Southen* [2001] NZHC 666; *cf Vervoort v Spears* [2016] NZCA 375.

[52] See also *FAI Money Ltd v Crawley* [2016] NZCA 219.

[53] *Fielden v Christie-Miller* [2015] EWHC 87 (Ch).

against the owners of land who were trustees of it. He was aware that the legal owners of the land were trustees, but he was not aware that the rights he was claiming were inconsistent with the owners' trust duties, or at least what were alleged by a beneficiary of the trust to be the trustees' duties. The present hearing was concerned merely with the sufficiency of the pleadings. The defendant trustees argued that the claimant was up against the unanimity principle, and given that not all trustees had directly sanctioned the rights claimed by the claimant, his claim must fail. The judge, Sir William Blackburne, recognised the principle but plainly considered that the trustees' position was to be determined by the law of agency. As it happens, the pleadings in their current form fell short of establishing authority at common law, so the claimant was in difficulty on any basis. But the judge accepted that the claimant might be able to re-plead and prove that the other co-owners had given authority to the representing party to make the relevant representations on which he was relying.

It is of some interest that the claimant also relied on a dictum of Scarman LJ in *Crabb v Arun DC* which seems to suggest that the appearance of authority in an agent needed to create a proprietary estoppel against an owner of land might be less than that needed to establish a contract.[54] In particular, the dictum can be read as allowing an agent with some actual authority to extend that authority by self-authorisation. Sir William Blackburne was plainly not attracted to this dictum. He stated:

> Elementary fairness requires that before a person can be bound by the acts of another purporting to act on his behalf, that other must have his authority to bind him in the matter. Whether he has will depend on the usual principles of agency. This applies, in my judgment, as much in the field of estoppel as it does in other contexts.[55]

It may be that a claimant will receive a more sympathetic hearing when the acts on which a plea of proprietary estoppel are based have demonstrably raised the market value of the defendant's land.[56]

Fielden has since been followed in *Preedy v Dunne*,[57] on very similar facts. Again, the defendants pleaded the unanimity rule as an answer to any estoppel. Master Matthews appears to have been attracted to that argument,[58] but then concluded that any estoppel depended on whether the active trustee had authority 'actual, implied or ostensible' to bind the other trustee.[59] On the facts, such authority could not be shown.

[54] *Crabb v Arun DC* [1976] 1 Ch 179, 193.

[55] *Fielden* (n 53) [26]; *cf Doueihi* (n 19) [223].

[56] *cf Blue Haven Enterprises Ltd v Tully* [1996] UKPC 17; noted P Watts, 'Unrequested Improvements to Land' (1996) 122 *LQR* 553; B McFarlane, 'Unjust Enrichment and Proprietary Estoppel: Two Sides of the Same Coin?' [2007] *Lloyd's Maritime and Commercial Law Quarterly* 14.

[57] *Preedy v Dunne* [2015] EWHC 2713 (Ch).

[58] ibid [42].

[59] ibid [43].

Going a long way back in time, potential issues as to the effect at common law of a delegation by a trustee arose in *Sneesby v Thorne*.[60] In this case two executors held some land in Sussex. One of them, Y, who was living in Dorset, expressed a view to the other, X, that the land should be sold, but gave no particular authority to sell. Y then went off to Canada. X, taking Y's advice to heart, purported to sell the land to the claimant. Y on his return objected that he had not approved *this* sale. The Lords Justices held that Y was not bound by X's conduct (the rule that one executor could bind the estate did not apply to land), and hence the claimant's proceeding for specific performance must fail. Although they did not expressly use the language of agency, the evident conclusion of the judges was that X had neither actual nor apparent authority.

But Knight Bruce LJ clearly considered that the claimant would have had a remedy at law against X on these facts, presumably on a breach of warranty of authority.[61] It was the position at law that determined whether there was a contract, and for that purpose it was the law of agency that did the work. The claimant having lost its claim, costs were also awarded in favour of Y, but significantly not in favour of X. In this period, when the courts of equity and common law were still separate in every sense, the judges would have been unlikely to coalesce the two systems as occurred in *Niak*. It was indeed normal practice for a court of equity to withhold specific performance even where there was a valid contract at law if there was a breach of trust on the part of the vendor such that enforcing the sale would be prejudicial to the beneficiaries. But this was without prejudice to the purchaser's rights at common law against the vendor.[62]

It is surely not too much to hope that a party who is justifiably ignorant of a breach of a merely equitable duty should be expected in dealing with multiple legal owners of assets to be affected only by the rules of the common law, which in relation to such dealings are perilous enough anyway. But, it is not just due consideration for the interests of innocent third parties that is at issue. There is coherence too. In particular, the *Niak* approach requires one to speculate whether it is only wrongful delegations that are treated as removing a trustee's powers of disposition. Would not any stepping outside trust powers by a trustee, even when the sole trustee, result in the conduct being a nullity? Certainly, an outright misappropriation by a trustee, which is morally much worse than a careless delegation, would have to be treated the same. Yet, the case law dealing with dispositions of legal title that are knowingly inconsistent with a claimant's equitable rights, instances of which are far more numerous in the law reports than improper delegations, make it plain that a third party who acquires the legal title is protected if that party was

[60] *Sneesby v Thorne* (1855) 7 De GM & G 399, (1855) 44 ER 156.

[61] ibid 157.

[62] See the cases in F White and O Tudor, *A Selection of Leading Cases in Equity*, vol 2, 5th edn (London, Maxwell & Son 1877) 497; see also Conaglen and Nolan (n 14) 360–61.

in good faith and gave value without notice of the breach.[63] To obtain legal title one has only to meet the *common law's* requirements for the transfer of ownership.

V. Importation of Trusts into Agency Relationships: Two Issues

It is time now to turn to the other side of the coin, the intrusion of trusts into agency relationships. There are two topics addressed here. First is the issue of when parties have succeeded in stitching trust duties into what would otherwise be a purely contractual relationship. And the other is what difference such stitching might make to the personal obligations between principal and agent. The treatment of these two issues can be brief, because the first is largely a factual question, and the second is more complex but the writer has developed a detailed argument on this topic elsewhere.

A. The Limits of Stitching a Trust Duty onto the Agency Relationship

Principals frequently have to put their agents in funds before the services the agents are to perform for them have been carried out. They worry about the agent becoming insolvent, and given modern banking mechanisms the trust is the most convenient, if not the only practicable, way in which those funds can be ring-fenced against the agent's general creditors. Similarly, it is frequently convenient to have agents collecting in payments from customers, and the same concern arises as to the possible intervention of the agent's insolvency.

It is remarkable how often principals fail to spell out whether moneys in the agent's hands are to be held on trust for the principal. It is unlikely that a trust requirement would meet the standard test, to the extent that there is now such a thing,[64] for an implied term in the contract of agency. Nonetheless, in settling what is in essence a question of fact courts have often found an intention to create a collateral trust even though the parties have not expressly used the phrase 'on

[63] See JD Heydon, MJ Leeming and PG Turner, *Meagher, Gummow and Lehane's Equity: Doctrines and Remedies*, 5th edn (Chatswood, NSW, LexisNexis Butterworths, 2015) para 8-225 ff; see also *MCC Proceeds Inc v Lehman Brothers International (Europe)* [1998] 4 All ER 675.

[64] See *Marks and Spencer Plc v BNP Paribas Securities Services Trust Company (Jersey) Limited* [2015] UKSC 72, [2016] AC 742; see also D McLauchlan, 'Construction and Implication: In Defence of *Belize Telecom*' [2014] *Lloyd's Maritime and Commercial Law Quarterly* 203; *cf* J Carter and W Courtney, '*Belize Telecom*: A Reply to Professor McLauchlan' [2015] *Lloyd's Maritime and Commercial Law Quarterly* 245. Still less will courts impose a constructive trust in such circumstances: see *Angove's Pty Ltd v Bailey* [2016] UKSC 47, [2016] 1 WLR 3179; noted P Watts, 'The Insolvency of Agents' (2017) 133 *LQR* 11.

trust'. A clear expectation that the agent is to keep the principal's money separate from the agent's personal funds may be sufficient. A collection of cases falling either side of the line can be found in *Bowstead & Reynolds on Agency*.[65]

It is worth noting here a recent New Zealand decision, *Bambury v Jensen*,[66] that 'pushes the envelope' in terms of both contractual implication and furnishing the essential elements of a trust. This was a case where the impetus to allege a trust was not the usual one of the agent's insolvency, but the operation of limitation periods. In many jurisdictions, limitation periods do not apply to actions for failure to account brought against an express trustee.[67]

The litigation arose out of the breakdown of a long and successful relationship between a New Zealand contemporary artist and his agent. Because their relationship had been so close and trusting, in the lay sense, the legal arrangements between them were largely oral. The artist now claimed that the agent had over a long period failed properly to account for the proceeds of sales of some 60 artworks. While the judge was able to group some of the claims, he was required to make a long series of factual findings. A number of interesting legal issues arose, most of which, however, are not pertinent here. The artist was successful in only a fraction of his claims. The trust point was seen as important because the great majority of claims fell outside the standard six-year limitation period. Whether this really mattered is briefly discussed at the end of this section.

There was no evidence that the agent had been expressly required to bank the proceeds of paintings and other artworks into a separate account tagged for the principal. Such a duty is often the most important marker of a trust relationship. The duty frequently supplies both the evidence of the requisite intention to create a trust and the certainty of subject matter necessary for a trust to exist. However, Fogarty J held that the duty to keep the proceeds separate is not absolutely crucial to there being a trust interest.[68] He concluded that it was wrong to read Millett LJ's well-known dicta in *Paragon Finance Plc v DB Thakerar & Co* as saying otherwise.[69]

In *Paragon*, Millett LJ stated that: 'It is fundamental to the existence of a trust that the trustee is bound to keep the trust property separate from his own and apply it exclusively for the benefit of his beneficiary'.[70] But Fogarty J pointed out that that sentence was preceded by one that was directed at a situation (the one in *Nelson v Rye*)[71] where the agent was not only able to pay the relevant moneys into his own account but was able to use them for his own cash flow and had to account only at the end of the year. He also pointed out that the sentence which followed the one quoted spoke of its being fatal to a trust for the agent to be able to mix the money received with his own *and* be able to use it for his cash flow.

[65] See Watts and Reynolds (eds) (n 15) para 6-041.

[66] *Bambury v Jensen* [2015] NZHC 2384.

[67] See the discussion in *Williams v Central Bank of Nigeria* [2014] UKSC 10, [2014] AC 1189.

[68] *Bambury* (n 66) [119].

[69] *Paragon Finance Plc v DB Thakerar & Co (A Firm)* [1999] 1 All ER 400, 415 (CA).

[70] ibid.

[71] *Nelson v Rye* [1996] 1 WLR 1378.

On the facts of *Bambury*, the evidence both as between the parties and within the 'industry' was that payment out to the artist was expected to be very prompt and frequently took place within two days of receipt of the sale proceeds by the agent. The judge concluded that, although each transaction had to be considered on its own facts, where the agent was not entitled to use the funds, even when in a bank account in his own name, for his own purposes, the proceeds of sales of artworks were held on trust.

There are a number of criticisms that might be made in relation to the judge's reasoning. He was not as clear as he might have been on the difference between fiduciary obligations and trust obligations. Nor did he spell out that where the funds permissibly went into the agent's bank account, in order for a trust to have arisen the artist must have had a beneficial interest in the chose in action between the agent and his bank. In other words, in order to meet the tests for trust certainty, it would have been necessary that the artist and the agent have been joint beneficial owners of the bank account, even though the agent was the only party to the contract with the bank.

Those criticisms apart, it would be difficult to argue that it is legally *impossible* for there to be a trust on a fact pattern such as that in *Bambury*. The law of trusts has made itself very flexible and accommodating. Hence, equity does not preclude a trustee from being one of the beneficiaries of the trust. The only ultimate rule is that the sole trustee cannot also be the sole beneficiary.[72] Nonetheless, if the trustee is free to apply all the money in his or her own favour the trust would be a discretionary one, and the interest of a creditor-beneficiary would in such circumstances probably be worthless in an insolvency. To guard against that possibility in the present context, the trustee's right to have recourse to the 'mixed' account would need to be made subject to there being enough other moneys in the account at all times to meet the rights of the client or clients.[73]

On the basis of the analysis just given, the dictum of Keane J in a recent decision of the High Court of Australia, *Korda v Australian Executor Trustees (SA) Ltd*,[74] that 'absence of a contractual intention that money be held in a separate fund must surely be fatal to the imputation of a contractual intention to create a trust over that money' should be regarded as an oversimplification. The dictum can be contrasted with some remarks of Lord Collins in *Lehman Brothers International (Europe) Ltd v CRC Credit Fund Ltd*:

> There is no doubt that money in a mixed fund may be held on trust, and that a trust of money can be created without an obligation to keep it in a separate account: *In Re Kayford Ltd* [1975] 1 WLR 279, 282, per Megarry J.[75]

[72] *Goodright v Wells* (1781) 2 Doug 771, 778, 99 ER 491, 495; *DKLR Holding Co (No 2) Pty Ltd v Commissioner of Stamp Duties* [1980] 1 NSWLR 510, 519; and on appeal (1982) 149 CLR 431, 464, 473.

[73] See further, R Stevens, 'Floating Trusts' ch 5; and M Bridge, 'Certainty, Identification and Intention in Personal Property Law' ch 4, in this volume.

[74] *Korda v Australian Executor Trustees (SA) Ltd* [2015] HCA 6, (2015) 255 CLR 62 [111].

[75] *Lehman Brothers International (Europe) Ltd v CRC Credit Fund Ltd* [2012] UKSC 6, [2012] 3 All ER 1 [194].

At the same time, the *Korda* decision and a decision of the English Court of Appeal a month before on similar facts, *Juliet Bellis & Co v Challinor*,[76] could be used to mount an argument that Fogarty J was too generous to the claimant in *Bambury*. Courts will, it is suggested, be alive to the fact that Fogarty J's approach is calculated to lead to multiple trust claims on the one account, and will wish to avoid that complexity if they can. Moreover, they are unlikely to want to encourage the 'double-dipping' that trust claims lead to in insolvencies; trust claimants want to stay outside the insolvency while they can still identify their moneys, but if those moneys cease to be identifiable, they still want to share in the residual assets derived from the insolvent's dealings with the unsecured creditors.

It is possible to conjecture that it was the different context of the limitation period that led to Fogarty J's being more open to inferring a trust interest. It is one thing, in cases such as *Korda* and *Bellis*, to foresee insolvency and provide for it. But it might be harder to detect that one's agent has not accounted properly for sales made on one's behalf. There is in fact a long, if rather old, body of case law that suggests that independently of a trust, any accounting between agent and principal can be reopened back through an indefinite period if there is evidence of fraud or even only unconscionable dealing (ie, equitable fraud).[77]

B. What Liability when the Agent Accidentally Releases Trust Funds?

The other topical issue in this area has been the effect the stitching of a trust onto the agency relationship might have for the personal obligations between principal and agent. There can be no doubt that the main purpose of requiring an agent to hold onto trust money received from (or for) the principal is to protect the principal vis-à-vis third parties, particularly external administrators who might be appointed in respect of the agent's affairs should the agent become insolvent. But most conspicuously, it had been argued in *Target Holdings Ltd v Redferns*,[78] and again in *AIB Group (UK) Plc v Mark Redler & Co Solicitors*,[79] that imposing such trust obligations also created more stringent personal obligations on the agent than would arise under the simple contract of agency.

Target and *AIB Group* were both concerned with the release by the defendant solicitors in breach of instructions of funds they held on trust for their client, in each case a finance company. Both the House of Lords in *Target* and the United Kingdom Supreme Court in *AIB Group* accepted that the liabilities that arise at equity in such circumstances might not be precisely the same as those of the common law. However, the Courts also held, *Target* more ambiguously than *AIB Group*,

[76] *Juliet Bellis & Co v Challinor* [2015] EWCA Civ 59.

[77] See Watts and Reynolds (eds) (n 15) para 6-098. In general, however, it appears that a failure to account is governed by limitation periods: *Paragon Finance* (n 69) 415.

[78] *Target Holdings Ltd v Redferns* [1996] AC 421.

[79] *AIB Group (UK) Plc v Mark Redler & Co Solicitors* [2014] UKSC 58, [2015] AC 1503.

that equity's remedies are ultimately hedged in, like those of the common law, by a requirement that the breach of duty cause the principal's loss. So, if agents can show that, even had they studiously complied with their instructions, the principal would have suffered a loss at least equal to that resulting from the breach, then there will be no recovery. On the facts of the two cases, the solicitors were, in substance, able to show just that. The real cause of the loss in each case was the fact that the security required by the finance company of the borrower was never going to cover the loan, not the failure by the solicitors to follow instructions.

The writer has argued elsewhere that the introduction of trust obligations into the agency relationship is not intended to add significant new personal obligations to that relationship.[80] Equity's obligations inter partes are likely to mimic the common law's. This much is consistent with the reasoning in *Target* and *AIB Group*. But what seems equally incontrovertible as a matter of general contract principle, let alone true of the agency relationship, is that it is not the case, as was the premise of the reasoning at least in *AIB Group*, that a promisee who finds that its promisor has not done what was promised is confined to expectation damages. In particular, this ignores restitutionary, or refund, remedies, which permit a promisee simply to demand the return of moneys paid the promisor upon the latter's failure to do what was required in respect of that money. It is, in general, no defence to such claims for promisors to argue that had they done as asked the promisee would have lost money.

Nor is the restitutionary remedy at common law confined to recovery of the *remuneration* paid to procure performance. It extends to money paid (or even goods) to be used by the recipient in executing the promise. So, where the money paid over includes sufficient funds to allow the promisor to procure materials needed to perform the contract, those funds too will be recoverable. Nor, prima facie, does it matter that the promisor has embarked on performance. If the promisor makes a botched job of the set task, sufficient at least to cause 'a total failure of consideration', the promisee is entitled to cancel the contract and call for a refund.[81]

These common law principles seem straightforwardly to apply to cases where an agent disburses funds in breach of instructions. Indeed, they have been held to apply to an agent who has acted without reward.[82] One would expect equity to have taken a similar approach, and it is possible to show that it did,[83] before *Target*

[80] P Watts, 'Agents' Disbursal of Funds in Breach of Instructions' [2016] *Lloyd's Maritime and Commercial Law Quarterly* 118.

[81] See *Gartell & Son (a firm) v Yeovil Town Football & Athletic Club Ltd* [2016] EWCA Civ 62; *Head v Tattersall* (1870) LR 7 Ex 7; *Heywood v Wellers* [1976] QB 446, 458, citing *Hill v Featherstonhaugh* (1831) 7 Bing 569 (CP), 131 ER 220.

[82] See *Martin v Pont* [1993] 3 NZLR 25.

[83] See A Shaw-Mellors, 'Equitable Compensation for Breach of Trust: Still Missing the Target?' [2015] *Journal of Business Law* 165; J Penner, 'Distinguishing Fiduciary, Trust, and Accounting Relationships' (2014) 8 *Journal of Equity* 202, 223–25; M Conaglen, 'Equitable Compensation for Breach of Trust: Off *Target*' (2016) 40(1) *Melbourne University Law Review* 126.

and *AIB Group* came along. Not that it matters much, but it is arguable that the common law remedies should arguably be the first port of call. In disbursing the funds in cases such as these, the solicitor is exercising agency functions, changing the client's legal status from that of promisor to that of creditor, rather than trustee functions. After all, the borrower is not a beneficiary of the trust.[84] Disbursing the funds correctly certainly terminates the trust duties, but it is less clear that that process involves their *performance*.

So, in *Target* and *AIB Group* what happened with the client funds was in each case a serious breach of contract that would have justified termination of the contract, and a call by the client for a return of the moneys at common law. In this regard, the Court of Appeal in *AIB Group* was correct to conclude that solicitors who get only a second mortgage for their client when their instructions required a first mortgage commit a breach justifying cancellation of the mandate, small though the amount owing on the first mortgage might be. After all, the client may itself have raised the funds from the public on an undertaking that the funds would be on-lent only on first mortgage.

As it is, the logic of the reasoning of the Supreme Court in *AIB Group* would have given the client no remedy had the solicitors sent the funds to a totally wrong person, so long as the solicitors could show that the *intended* recipient was also worthless. Arguments of that sort would be irrelevant to a restitutionary claim elsewhere in the law of contract, and they should not be permitted in respect of a deviation from mandate by an agent. The agent has simply not done what was asked. The promisee is entitled to its restitutionary remedy, tout court, and is not required to give the defendant the opportunity to show at trial that the promisee would have lost money had the contract been performed.

Yet, it is crucial to understand that the restitutionary remedy is quite brittle. The victim of non-performance who becomes aware that the promisor has failed to do what was asked cannot stand by to see how things turn out. Such claimants must take a stance promptly, cancel the contract and ask for restitution of all money paid to the promisor. They will otherwise be taken to have affirmed the contract, albeit without prejudice to rights to damages.[85] Even were the law to develop to allow post-affirmation refunds, it would be very rare that total refunds would be available once a contract had been affirmed.

That is the best explanation why the Court was right to conclude that the client should not succeed in *AIB Group*. Having learned what had happened, the client did not cancel and assert its restitutionary remedy.

Target is more complex because there the client could not be accused of standing by, since it did not become aware that the solicitors had released the moneys prematurely until a long time later. The claimant should still have lost. The reason

[84] See *Barclays Bank Ltd v Quistclose Investments Ltd* [1970] AC 567.

[85] See *Weston v Downes* (1778) 1 Doug 23, 99 ER 19; *Kwei Tek Chao v British Traders and Shippers Ltd* [1954] 2 QB 459, 475; *Yeoman Credit Ltd v App* [1962] 2 QB 508, 520–21, 523–24.

is that while the solicitors' action was a repudiatory breach of contract that in itself did not terminate the contract. The repudiation needed to be accepted. More than that, the breach did not necessarily terminate the solicitors' mandate to continue to perform the contract. By still getting in the required mortgage, albeit tardily, the agent acted within authority, and thereby cured the breach. Cure will not always be possible (getting in a second mortgage instead of a first, as happened in *AIB Group*, would not be cure, for instance), but where it operates it forecloses subsequent cancellation of the contract and at the same time forecloses the restitutionary remedy. Again, one would expect law and equity to be in step on such matters.

One should not close without accepting that for all the criticisms that were made in the writer's fuller discussion of *Target*,[86] it was overlooked that in two short passages Lord Browne-Wilkinson did accept that there had been an unqualified obligation on the relevant solicitors to restore to the client's account moneys wrongly paid away but he concluded that that obligation ceased once the underlying instructions had been completed.[87] Those passages are indeed consistent with the restitutionary arguments made here, and by others. For this oversight an apology is owed.

[86] Watts, 'Agents' Disbursal of Funds in Breach of Instructions' (n 80).
[87] *Target Holdings Ltd* (n 78) 436 D–E. Thanks to Rob Stevens for pointing this out.

3

Equity in the Marketplace: Reviewing the Use of Unconscionability to Restrain Calls on Performance Bonds

TANG HANG WU*

I. Introduction

In describing the role of equitable jurisprudence in the market place with its emphasis on open-ended concepts like conscience, Lord Millett famously observed in an extrajudicial essay that:

> Even twenty years ago there was still a widely held belief, by no means confined to common lawyers, that equity had no place in the world of commerce. Businessmen need speed and certainty; these do not permit a detailed and leisurely examination of the parties' conduct. Commerce needs the kind of bright line rules which the common law provides and which equity abhors. Resistance to the intrusion of equity into the business world is justified by concern for the certainty and security of commercial transactions.[1]

Writing in relation to fiduciary law, Lord Millett dismissed the anti-equity sentiment in the first sentence of his essay by stating that: 'Equity's place in the law of commerce, long resisted by commercial lawyers, can no longer be denied'.[2]

This tension, described by Lord Millett, between bright line rules which promote certainty in commercial dealings as compared to equitable jurisprudence based on a detailed examination of parties' conduct is played out acutely in the debate

* I am grateful to James Penner, Dora Neo, Robert Stevens, Paul S Davies, Kelry Loi, Lau Kwan Ho and the participants of the survey for their help. The usual caveats apply.

[1] PJ Millett, 'Equity's Place in the Law of Commerce' (1998) 114 *LQR* 214, 214.

[2] ibid.

on the role of unconscionability in restraining performance bonds. English law which subscribes to the philosophy of promoting certainty in relation to performance bonds restrains a call on performance bonds on the very limited basis of fraud.[3] This is because English law subscribes to the principle that a performance bond, like a letter of credit, should be considered to be autonomous from the underlying contract between the parties. Or to put it in another way, a performance bond is treated as cash in hand and the beneficiary of the bond should be allowed to avail himself or herself of the bond. In contrast, Singapore's jurisprudence on performance bonds is noteworthy because it represents a conscious and significant departure from English law. The Singapore Court of Appeal confirmed in *GHL Pte Ltd v Unitrack Building Construction Pte Ltd & Anor*[4] after a period of some uncertainty[5] that unconscionability is a separate and distinct ground from fraud to restrain a call on performance bonds. This has resulted in a robust debate found in the banking literature on whether this development in Singapore is desirable and should be adopted by other jurisdictions.[6]

This conscious divergence from English law may be seen as a major development in the history of Singapore's commercial law. With regard to contract and commercial law, Singapore has always endeavoured to mirror English law. True to its status as an international commercial hub, Singapore has since its earliest days sought to retain the purest form of English commercial law.[7] As Voules J explained in *Seng Djit Hin v Nagurdas Purshotumdas & Co*,[8] this pragmatic policy was 'to inspire confidence amongst merchants by assuring them that any questions arising in regard to their commercial transactions will be decided in the like case at the corresponding period in England'. Although the formal reception of English commercial law was discontinued in 1993, English contract and commercial decisions are still today invariably cited by counsel in court, often accepted as persuasive and routinely applied by the Singapore courts. In other words, while English decisions are not binding in a stare decisis sense on the Singapore courts,

[3] *United City Merchants (Investments) Ltd v Royal Bank of Canada* [1983] 1 AC 168 (HL).

[4] *GHL Pte Ltd v Unitrack Building Construction Pte Ltd & Anor* [1999] 3 SLR(R) 44.

[5] The developments are traced in L Hsu, 'Autonomy of Performance Bonds in Singapore' (1992) *Lloyd's Maritime and Commercial Law Quarterly* 297; A Loke, 'Injunctions and Performance Bonds—A Return to English Orthodoxy' (1995) *Singapore Journal of Legal Studies* 682; L Hsu, 'Performance Bonds in Singapore: An Update' (1996) *Lloyd's Maritime and Commercial Law Quarterly* 35; A Wong, 'Restraining a Call on a Performance Bond—Should "Fraud or Unconscionability" be the New Orthodoxy?' (2000) 12 *Singapore Academy of Law Journal* 132; Q Loh and HW Tang, 'Injunctions Restraining Calls on Performance Bonds—Is Fraud the Only Ground in Singapore?' [2000] *Lloyd's Maritime and Commercial Law Quarterly* 353.

[6] There is some evidence that the unconscionability exception jurisprudence has taken root in Malaysia. See *Sumatec Engineering and Construction Sdn Bhd v Malaysian Refining Company Sdn Bhd* [2012] 4 MLJ 1.

[7] See Civil Law Act (Cap 43, 1985 Rev Ed) s 5, which provides questions and issues with respect to mercantile law generally shall be the same as that which would be administered in England. This section was repealed in 1993. See A Phang, 'Reception of English Law in Singapore: Problems and Proposed Solutions' (1990) 2 *Singapore Academy of Law Journal* 20.

[8] *Seng Djit Hin v Nagurdas Purshotumdas & Co* [1923] AC 444 (PC).

they are nevertheless regarded as highly persuasive authority.[9] Hence, this divergence from English law on the law on performance bonds heralds a new age where Singapore judges are increasingly confident of developing their own jurisprudence in commercial law.[10]

At the start, it is important to set out what this chapter does not purport to do. The present author resists the temptation to seek to demonstrate which position is the better approach to performance bonds, ie, English or Singapore law. It is suggested that there is no way to reach a firm conclusion one way or the other. This is because the arguments for each position are well known and firmly entrenched. In favour of the English position of a bright line rule that the courts may not intervene save for fraud is that this promotes certainty in relation to performance bonds. As opposed to an emphasis on the value of certainty, the Singapore courts adopt a fact-sensitive approach to protect the obligor of a performance bond from abusive calls on performance bonds. The obvious drawback to the Singapore jurisprudence on performance bonds is the lack of certainty as to when the courts would intervene. But that is the price to pay for adopting a fact-sensitive test to protect the weaker contracting party in the relationship. However, this is not to say that the English position is perfect and wholly free from criticism. In order to achieve the bright line rule of certainty, the English position is essentially a blunt tool. English law is only capable of dealing with fraudulent calls on performance bonds; it is unable to deal with the problem of abusive calls on performance bonds which does not reach the threshold of fraud. Viewed in this context, it is not possible, in my view, to say that one position is 'better' than the other position. Rather, the divergence in the law represents a conscious policy choice which each jurisdiction has adopted to achieve a particular goal.

Instead of embarking on an inconclusive enquiry as to which is the better approach, this chapter surveys every single reported and unreported Singapore decision at every level since *GHL Pte Ltd v Unitrack Building Construction Pte Ltd & Anor*[11] where a call on a performance bond was challenged on the ground of unconscionability. Hence, this review provides a case study as to how unconscionability operates as a legal doctrine on the ground. Further, most academic work has tended to focus on decisions by the High Court and Court of Appeal while ignoring the unreported decisions in the District Court. By surveying and analysing the District Court's decisions, it is hoped that this chapter would provide a more accurate insight as to how unconscionability is applied. On a more

[9] Although in recent times the Singapore courts are increasingly developing their own jurisprudence. See S Menon, 'The Somewhat Uncommon Law of Commerce' (2014) 26 *Singapore Academy of Law Journal* 23 which traces the development of Singapore's jurisprudence on implied terms in contract.

[10] eg the Singapore Court of Appeal refused to follow the English approach as found in *The Achilleas* [2008] UKHL 48, [2009] 1 AC 61 (HL) on remoteness in contractual damages. See *Out of the Box Pte Ltd v Wanin Industries Pte Ltd* [2013] 2 SLR 363; noted Y Goh, 'Contractual Remoteness in England and Singapore Compared: Orthodoxy Preferable?' (2013) 30 *Journal of Contract Law* 233.

[11] *GHL Pte Ltd* (n 4).

granular level, there are several aims to this survey of the cases. First, a survey of these cases will show, to a certain extent, the number of challenges that have been brought to court. This will then either confirm or refute the fear that the adoption of the ground of unconscionability would result in an intolerable floodgate of applications before the court. Second, the survey of cases will seek to determine the percentage of successful restraints and the grounds on which unconscionability has been made out. Thus, the analysis of the cases will essentially map out the ambit of unconscionability in the context of performance bonds. Third, a study of the cases will also reveal that some contracting parties have begun to choose foreign law to govern the performance bond or exclude unconscionability as a distinct ground for restraint from the terms of the performance bond. This is an interesting development because it provides some evidence that when the law is uncertain, sophisticated parties with a stronger bargaining power may draft their contracts to exclude these uncertain default rules.

A well-known criticism of the use of unconscionability as a legal doctrine in the market place is that it is too uncertain and prevents practising lawyers from advising their clients properly.[12] Essentially, this argument is an empirical assertion. In order to assess this argument in the context of performance bonds, a survey of leading practitioners in the construction industry in Singapore was undertaken to ascertain their views and practices in relation to performance bonds. More specifically, questions as to their clients' contracting behaviour were posed to these lawyers. Other questions included whether they have experienced calls on performance bonds which were tactical and abusive, whether their clients were concerned with performance bonds being restrained on the ground of unconscionability and whether they were frequently asked by their clients to restrain performance bonds. The survey also delved into the number of hearing days such applications would take and the legal costs involved. In this survey, the lawyers were also asked whether they thought the law was certain enough for them to advise their clients and whether they thought that unconscionability in this context was a positive or negative development. The results of their responses will demonstrate how practising lawyers in Singapore cope with the uncertainty inherent in the law of unconscionability in relation to performance bonds. An enquiry about the choice of foreign law to govern performance bonds and clauses which exclude unconscionability was also pursued in this survey.

The data from the survey of the cases and practitioners' responses may prove useful to any jurisdiction which is confronted with the policy choice of whether to adopt a separate ground of unconscionability with regard to restraints on performance bonds. Ultimately, the overarching theme which emerges from this chapter is that while unconscionability is undoubtedly a fact-sensitive enquiry and not capable of being stated in the form of bright line rules, it can still operate in this

[12] eg P Birks, 'Equity in the Modern Law: An Exercise in Taxonomy' (1996) 26 *Western Australia Law Review* 1.

field where commercial certainty is said to be of paramount importance. The survey of the practitioners' responses also indicated that more sophisticated parties who have the bargaining power are now contractually excluding unconscionability from the terms of the performance bond. If this trend continues, this may spell the demise of the unconscionability exception to calls on performance bonds. As a commentator recently noted, the unconscionability exception may 'possibly [be] rendered moot by the power of private law and the freedom to contract'.[13]

II. Unconscionability as a Ground for Relief: Rationale, Doctrinal Underpinnings and Standard of Proof

The policy rationale for adopting unconscionability as a separate ground to restrain performance bonds as compared to the more stringent standard of fraud which is the sole ground for restraint for letters of credit has been traversed extensively in the Singapore cases[14] and academic literature.[15] Essentially, there are two main explanations for this. First, the Singapore judges have pointed out that the apparent symmetry between letters of credit and performance bonds is flawed.[16] LP Thean JA makes the point in *GHL Pte Ltd v Unitrack Building Construction Pte Ltd & Anor*[17] that

> it should not be forgotten that a performance bond is basically a security for the performance of the main contract, and as such we see no reason, in principle, why it is should be so sacrosanct and inviolate as not to be subject to the court's intervention except on the ground of fraud.

Chan Sek Keong JA reiterated this point in *JBE Properties Pte Ltd v Gammon Pte Ltd:*

> [A] performance bond is merely security for the *secondary* obligation of the obligor to pay damages *if* it breaches its primary contractual obligations to the beneficiary. A performance bond is not the lifeblood of commerce, whether generally or in the context of the construction industry specifically.[18]

[13] G Wooler, 'The New "Asplenium Clause"—Unconscionability Unwound' [2016] *Singapore Journal of Legal Studies* 169, 179.

[14] See *GHL Pte Ltd* (n 4); *JBE Properties Pte Ltd v Gammon Pte Ltd* [2011] 2 SLR 47; *BS Mount Sophia Pte Ltd v Join-Aim Pte Ltd* [2012] 3 SLR 352.

[15] eg LP Thean, The 12th *Singapore Law Review* Lecture: 'The Enforcement of A Performance Bond: The Perspective of the Underlying Contract' (1998) 19 *Singapore Law Review* 389; A Lee, 'Injuncting Calls on Performance Bonds: Reconstructing Unconscionability' (2003) 15 *Singapore Academy of Law Journal* 30.

[16] An argument made by C Debattista, 'Performance Bonds and Letters of Credit: A Cracked Mirror Image' (1997) 7 *Journal of Business Law* 289, 304.

[17] *GHL Pte Ltd* (n 4).

[18] *JBE Properties Pte Ltd* (n 14) [10].

Second, the recognition of the unconscionability exception was to counter abusive calls on performance bonds. In *GHL Pte Ltd v Unitrack Building Construction Pte Ltd & Anor*,[19] LP Thean JA observed that a performance bond may operate as an oppressive instrument if it is misused. The Court of Appeal in *BS Mount Sophia Pte Ltd v Join-Aim Pte Ltd*[20] accepted the observation by commentators who argue '[i]n certain cases, it is not unforeseeable that an abusive call may effectively cripple the principal financially … An abusive call may render the principal insolvent or incapable financially to proceed to arbitration or litigation'.[21]

However, it would be a mistake to think that the Singapore courts approach the issue of restraining a performance bond lightly. The judges are acutely aware of the arguments against the unconscionability exception. Andrew Phang JA described this area as posing a 'perennial tension' in *BS Mount Sophia Pte Ltd v Join-Aim Pte Ltd*[22] and acknowledged that liquidity concerns would also affect the beneficiary of the bond. In other words, 'the deprivation of *the beneficiary's* right to call on the performance bond could *equally well* be as detrimental to its liquidity' (emphasis in the original). Due to this 'perennial tension', the learned judge said a balance needs to be struck and as such, Phang JA said that 'the *actual grant* of such injunctions should be kept within a *very narrow compass*' (emphasis in the original).[23]

While the Singapore judges have articulated the policy reasons, they have thus far not explained the doctrinal basis for the unconscionability exception. This point is important because it would impact on the issue of whether the unconscionability exception may be contractually excluded by the parties. There are several competing possibilities to justify the doctrinal underpinning for the unconscionability exception. First, the unconscionability exception may be justified as an extension of equity's rule against penalties and relief against forfeiture. Second, the doctrinal basis is premised on the notion of inequality of bargaining power between the parties. Finally, the unconscionability exception in relation to performance bonds is truly a new doctrine created by the judges as a response to the policy reasons given above.

It is interesting to note that penalty rule developed from the equitable jurisprudence to provide relief against defeasible penal bonds.[24] Such penal bonds are promises to pay a certain sum of money subject to the satisfaction of a condition, for example, the performance of a primary obligation. In other words, once the obligation is performed, the penal bonds cease to be payable. While it is tempting to equate the unconscionability exception with equity's rule against penalties and relief against forfeiture, there is a major difference between these doctrines.

[19] *GHL Pte Ltd* (n 4).

[20] *BS Mount Sophia Pte Ltd* (n 14) [27].

[21] Loh and Tang (n 5).

[22] *BS Mount Sophia Pte Ltd* (n 14).

[23] ibid [31].

[24] The history of the rule against penalties was traced recently in *Cavendish Square Holding BV v Makdessi* [2015] UKSC 67, [2015] 3 WLR 1373 (HL).

In relation to penalties and forfeiture of monies, the claimant invokes equity's jurisdiction to prevent a defendant from keeping the entire sum of money. However, the unconscionability exception with respect to performance bonds is merely a temporary restraint on the fund. If it can be demonstrated after the dispute resolution process between the parties that the damages are indeed far less than the sum called on the performance bond, the defendant must account to the claimant.[25] Thus, it could be argued that the rule against penalties and relief against forfeiture deals with a more draconian situation whereby the defendant is attempting to keep the monies regardless of his or her damages. It is therefore understandable that the law would be more hesitant in letting parties contract out of these rules.

The second possible doctrinal explanation for the unconscionability doctrine need not detain us for too long. Like other parts of the Commonwealth, Singapore does not have a free-standing doctrine of inequality of bargaining power. Thus, the most persuasive account of the unconscionability exception in this context is that it is a new doctrine in the face of pressing policy considerations. Indeed, this explanation is consistent with the case law as the judges have not been concerned to look at similar doctrines in developing the unconscionability exception.

Initially, there was some confusion as to the standard of proof required to establish unconscionability. Thean JA had said in *GHL Pte Ltd v Unitrack Building Construction Pte Ltd & Anor*[26] that 'where there is prima facie evidence of fraud or unconscionability, the court should step in to intervene'. However, the Court of Appeal subsequently clarified in *Dauphin v The Private Office of HRH Sheik Sultan bin Khalifa bin Zahed Nahyan*[27] that the standard of proof required was a strong prima facie case of unconscionability. The reason for requiring a high threshold for unconscionability has been rationalised as 'the need to strike the appropriate balance between the conflicting positions of the obligor and beneficiary of a performance bond'.[28] It is also important to note that the Singapore courts do not approach a restraint on the ground of unconscionability from an 'all or nothing' perspective. In *Eltraco International Pte Ltd v CGH Development Pte Ltd*,[29] the Court of Appeal ordered a partial restraint of the bond after examining the facts of the case.

Arguably, a further gloss to the standard of proof was added in *BS Mount Sophia Pte Ltd v Join-Aim Pte Ltd*.[30] Justice Phang after affirming the strong prima

[25] See *Cargill International SA and Another v Bangladesh Sugar and Food Industries Corporation* [1998] 1 WLR 461 (CA). Such relationships are not uncommon in other banking contexts. See S Booysen, '"Pay Now—Argue Later": Conclusive Evidence Clauses in Commercial Loan Contracts' (2014) 1 *Journal of Business Law* 31.

[26] *GHL Pte Ltd* (n 4).

[27] *Dauphin v The Private Office of HRH Sheik Sultan bin Khalifa bin Zahed Nahyan* [2000] 1 SLR(R) 117 [57].

[28] *BS Mount Sophia Pte Ltd* (n 14) [24].

[29] *Eltraco International Pte Ltd v CGH Development Pte Ltd* [2000] 3 SLR(R) 198.

[30] *BS Mount Sophia Pte Ltd* (n 14).

facie case of unconscionability test emphatically said '[w]e must emphasise that the courts' discretion to grant such injunctions must be sparingly exercised and it should not be an easy thing for an applicant to establish a strong *prima facie* case'.[31] It is anticipated that these words would have an impact on the future success rate of injunctions to restrain performance bonds.

III. Negative Academic Reactions to Unconscionability and the Singapore Court of Appeal's Response

Generally, overseas academic reactions to the Singaporean jurisprudence on unconscionability and performance bonds have been largely negative. The first objection to unconscionability as a separate ground for restraining a performance bond is that such an additional ground would erode the integrity of performance bonds which are treated as equivalent to cash. As Professor Nelson Enonchong writes: 'that easy availability of injunctions would destroy confidence in [performance] bonds as the equivalent of cash in hand and undermine their utility as the lifeblood of commerce'.[32] In a similar vein the learned editors of *Jack: Documentary Credits* state that such an exception 'would tend to reduce confidence in the system of credits'.[33] Second, detractors of unconscionability point out that this exception will lead the court to become entangled in the underlying contractual dispute. Enonchong argues that the 'recognition of the unconscionability exception may lead to the courts getting involved in disputes arising from the underlying contract when such disputes should be resolved in separate proceedings and in accordance with any arbitration or jurisdiction clause in the underlying contract'.[34] Horowitz pursues this theme as well in her monograph by contending that the unconscionability exception forces the court to probe too deeply into circumstances surrounding performance of the underlying contract.[35] Third, commentators point out that unconscionability as a ground for restraint is imprecise, vague and difficult to define. It is argued that accepting unconscionability as a ground for restraining performance bonds would inject intolerable uncertainty in an area where clarity

[31] ibid [21]. The distinction between unconscionability and fraud will be dealt with in section V below.

[32] N Enonchong, The Problem of Abusive Calls on Demand Guarantees' [2007] *Lloyd's Maritime and Commercial Law Quarterly* 83, 104 and N Enonchong, *The Independence Principle of Letters of Credit and Demand Guarantees* (Oxford, OUP, 2011) para 7.34.

[33] A Malek and D Quest, *Jack: Documentary Credits* (London, Tottel Publishing, 2009) para 9.30.

[34] Enonchong, The Problem of Abusive Calls on Demand Guarantees' (n 32) 105 and Enonchong, *The Independence Principle of Letters of Credit and Demand Guarantees* (n 32) para 7.35.

[35] D Horowitz, *Letters of Credit and Demand Guarantees: Defences to Payment* (Oxford, OUP, 2010) 169.

and certainty are highly prized.[36] Finally, Horowitz argues that many of the Singapore cases decided on unconscionability may be determined in a similar fashion based on the fraud exception. She argues that these cases may be restrained on the ground of fraud because the beneficiary had 'no honest belief' that the beneficiary was entitled to call on the performance bond. Horowitz's point will be considered in the section on the survey of cases.

Two well-known Singapore banking scholars, Peter Ellinger and Dora Neo, have also expressed scepticism about the unconscionability exception. They argue that an independent guarantee serves the function where the beneficiary 'can be paid first and talk later'.[37] Ellinger and Neo also point out that the beneficiary may have sacrificed a stronger position by not insisting on retention money and accepting a bond. In these circumstances, they argue that the autonomy principle is as equally important in performance bonds as in a letter of credit.

Interestingly, the Singapore Court of Appeal responded to these academic critiques on two occasions in *JBE Properties Pte Ltd v Gammon Pte Ltd*[38] and *BS Mount Sophia Pte Ltd v Join-Aim Pte Ltd.*[39] Chan Sek Keong CJ disagreed with Ellinger's and Neo's argument that the autonomy principle should apply with equal force to a performance bond. The Chief Justice thought that if parties had agreed to the provision of a performance bond instead of cash, the parties must have accepted the risk that a call on the performance bond might be restrained. According to Chan CJ, the fact that performance bonds may be restrained 'is a factor which the employer-beneficiary must be taken to have considered and accepted in preferring a performance bond to a cash deposit'.[40] In relation to the point of the potential ease of obtaining an injunction, Andrew Phang JA in *BS Mount Sophia Pte Ltd* accepted that this was a valid concern. The key consideration according to Justice Phang is that unconscionability must be applied in a nuanced manner and applied 'in *a principled manner, having regard to the facts of the case at hand*' (emphasis in original).[41] However, the learned judge repudiated the assertion that it was easy to obtain an injunction based on unconscionability. In this regard, Phang JA cited Kelry Loi's work where Loi pointed out that such an injunction may only be obtained where there is unconscionable behaviour and it is provable on strong evidence.[42] The learned judge also responded to the argument that the recognition of unconscionability would lead the court to getting involved in disputes arising from the underlying contract. Again, the Court cited

[36] Enonchong, 'The Problem of Abusive Calls on Demand Guarantees' (n 32) 105 and Enonchong, *The Independence Principle of Letters of Credit and Demand Guarantees* (n 32) para 7.33; see also Malek and Quest (n 33) para 9.30.

[37] P Ellinger and D Neo, *The Law and Practice of Documentary Credits* (Oxford, Hart Publishing, 2010) 325–26.

[38] *JBE Properties Pte Ltd* (n 14) [10].

[39] *BS Mount Sophia Pte Ltd* (n 14).

[40] *JBE Properties Pte Ltd* (n 14) [11].

[41] ibid [33].

[42] K Loi, 'Two Decades of Restraining Unconscionable Calls on Performance Guarantees—From *Royal Design* to *JBE Properties*' (2011) 23 *Singapore Academy of Law Journal* 504, 508–09.

Loi, who argues that the autonomy principle has already been comprised by the fraud principle. Loi says rhetorically that 'the courts will … not allow the law or its offices to become instruments of unconscionable conduct'.[43] With regard to the point that the concept of unconscionability is too vague, Phang JA thought that this was a far too pessimistic view. The learned judge said that while crisp definitions of legal doctrines are generally preferable, 'we do not think that relief for unconscionable conduct should be categorically rejected simply because a neat and tidy definition of the same is not forthcoming'.[44] Thus, while Phang JA alluded to general principles associated with the unconscionability exception, it would seem that the jurisprudence in this area is to be decided incrementally with reference to a multi-factorial approach. This multi-factorial approach will be explored below.

IV. Contracting Out of Unconscionability: Choosing Foreign Law and Excluding Unconscionability

Predictably, it was a matter of time before a contracting party with the stronger bargaining power sought to mitigate the uncertainty surrounding the concept of unconscionability by attempting to contract out of unconscionability.[45] However, the option of contracting out of unconscionability raises its own potential uncertainty. Would the court respect such clauses? Or more fundamentally, are parties able to agree amongst themselves to contract out of unconscionable behaviour? Prima facie, it seems counterintuitive that parties may agree that one party may act in an unconscionable behaviour in a contractual setting. The inherent uncertainty associated with such clauses may explain the reason why they only surfaced in the reported decisions many years after *GHL Pte Ltd v Unitrack Building Construction Pte Ltd & Anor*.[46]

An obvious method to try to disapply the unconscionability exception would be to choose English law as the choice of law for the performance bond. This would potentially get round the ambiguity of whether parties may contract out of unconscionable behaviour. Instead, the problem could be presented to the court as a simple choice of law problem where the parties chose a foreign law. But choosing a foreign law in this regard raises a conflict of laws issue: is the law governing injunctive relief in this context a procedural or substantive law? If it is the former, then the *lex fori* would apply. In contrast, if the matter is regarded as a substantive

[43] ibid 510–511.

[44] *BS Mount Sophia Pte Ltd* (n 14) [35].

[45] *cf JBE Properties Pte Ltd* (n 14) [15] where the terms of the performance bond expressly stipulate that the exceptions to payment is fraud or unconscionability.

[46] *GHL Pte Ltd* (n 4).

law, then the choice of the law of the performance bond would apply. Andrews and Millett thought, albeit without citation of any authorities, that this was probably a matter of procedural law of the forum.[47] Hence, on their analysis, the unconscionability exception would still apply. On the other hand, Professor Yeo argues that the injunction here is to protect substantive legal rights and hence should be governed by the choice of law. In other words, where an injunction is issued to protect legal rights, these rights are established by choice of law rules. Yeo, relying on the English Court of Appeal's decision in *Wahda Bank v Arab Bank plc*,[48] argues that '[w]here the issuer of a performance bond is refusing to pay the beneficiary because of the beneficiary's fraud, the proper law of the performance bond has been applied to determine the issue of fraud'.[49] He concludes that this is a sensible conclusion because parties reasonably expect the proper law to apply to this question subject always to the fundamental public policy of the law of the forum.

Lee Seiu Kin JC (as he then was) foresaw this in *Marinteknik Shipbuilders (S) Pte Ltd v SNC Passion*[50] where he speculated that if parties chose English law to govern the relevant contract and bond, there is the question as to whether a contracting party may rely on unconscionability as an additional ground to restrain the bond. However, this was not a live issue in that case and he did not have to make a final decision. Many years later, the issue of a foreign choice of law governing the performance bond came to be considered before the same judge in *Shanghai Electric Group Co Ltd v PT Merak Energi Indonesia and another*.[51] In this case, the plaintiff was hired by the defendant to construct a power plant in Indonesia. The contract provided for the defendant to pay the plaintiff an advance payment of 10 per cent of the contract price which amounted to US$ 10.8 million by way of a performance bond. The contract and performance bond were both governed by English law. However, the Singapore Court was given a non-exclusive jurisdiction to hear proceedings arising out of the bond. Lee J thought that a restraint on the beneficiary's right to receive immediate payment on the bond would deprive the defendant of a substantive right envisaged by the bond. Since a substantive right was engaged, the choice of law would govern the relationship. It followed that English law would govern the restraint on a call on the bond. This holding is consistent with the position advocated by Professor Yeo as opposed to Andrews' and Millett's view.

Quite apart from choosing English law, another possibility would be to expressly exclude unconscionability as a ground for restraint from the terms of the performance bond. The first case in which contracting parties sought to exclude unconscionability as a ground of restraint is *Scan-Bilt Pte Ltd v Umar Abdul Hamid*.[52]

[47] GM Andrews and R Millett, *Law of Guarantees* (London, Thomson Reuters, 2015) 656–57.
[48] *Wahda Bank v Arab Bank plc* [1999] EWCA Civ 1599.
[49] TM Yeo, *Choice of Law for Equitable Doctrines* (Oxford, OUP, 2004) para 4.34.
[50] *Marinteknik Shipbuilders (S) Pte Ltd v SNC Passion* [2001] SGHC 140.
[51] *Shanghai Electric Group Co Ltd v PT Merak Energi Indonesia and another* [2010] 2 SLR 329.
[52] *Scan-Bilt Pte Ltd v Umar Abdul Hamid* [2004] SGDC 274.

This is a little noticed case at the District Court level involving a performance bond for the value of S$125,000. In this case, the performance bond contained the following terms:

> Except only in the clear case of fraud, the Contractor shall not be entitled to enjoin or restrain the Employer from making any call or demand on the performance bond or receiving monies under the performance bond, on any other ground including the ground of unconscionability.

This clause was not disclosed to the Court when the plaintiff obtained an ex parte injunction to restrain the performance bond. The defendant applied to discharge the injunction on the ground of a failure to make full and frank disclosure. Eugene Teo DJ thought that the plaintiff had failed to make full disclosure of this clause to the Court and discharged the injunction.

The issue of contracting out of unconscionability came to the fore recently in *CKR Contract Services Pte Ltd v Asplenium Land Pte Ltd*.[53] In this case, the developer, Asplenium, employed CKR as a main contractor for the construction of a condominium in Singapore. The contract sum was S$88 million and CKR had to furnish Asplenium with an S$8.8 million performance bond. It was provided in the terms of the performance bond that CKR agreed that except in the case of fraud not to enjoin or restrain a call on the performance bond. Specifically, the terms of the bond mentioned that this prohibition against restraining a call on the performance bond included the ground of unconscionability. Subsequently, disagreement arose and Asplenium called on the bond. CKR retaliated by applying for an injunction to restrain the call on the performance bond. The issue that is relevant is whether the clause excluding a restrain based on unconscionability was unenforceable. At first instance, Edmund Leow JC held that this clause was unenforceable for three reasons. First, the clause was an attempt to oust the jurisdiction of the Court. Second, the power to grant injunctions emanated from the Court's equitable jurisdiction which could not be limited by contract. Third, the unconscionability exception was premised on policy considerations which could not be excluded by contract.

On appeal, Andrew Phang JA, delivering the judgment of the Court of Appeal, held that the clause excluding unconscionability was enforceable. As a starting point, Phang JA observed that while freedom of contract is the norm, the courts may override the contractual rights of the parties on public policy concerns such as an ouster of the jurisdiction of the courts. However, the countervailing consideration is that courts should be careful not to apply this policy concern to situations where contracting parties place limitations on their rights and remedies. Such limitations on rights and remedies such as a limitation of damages have not been treated as an ouster of the court's jurisdiction. The learned judge thought that the present clause 'was more in the nature of an *exclusion or exception clause* (*as opposed to* a clause seeking to *oust the jurisdiction of the court*)' (emphasis in original).[54]

[53] *CKR Contract Services Pte Ltd v Asplenium Land Pte Ltd* [2015] 3 SLR 1041.
[54] ibid [22].

In other words, the present clause is one which sought to limit the right to an equitable remedy and not a clause which sought to oust the jurisdiction of the court. Phang JA said that this clause is potentially subject to the Unfair Contract Terms Act and might be unenforceable if it was regarded as unreasonable.[55] However, this was not an argument that was run and Justice Phang did not state a conclusive view on this issue.

With regard to the argument that a contractual clause excluding unconscionability was unenforceable on public policy grounds, the learned judge observed as follows:

> The particular conception of policy that formed the basis for the unconscionability doctrine is *quite different from* the concept of *public policy* which underpins the category of contracts which are void and unenforceable as being contrary to public policy as such contracts seek to *oust the jurisdiction of the court* (emphasis in original).[56]

CKR Contract Services Pte Ltd v Asplenium Land Pte Ltd has drawn some disquiet from commentators. For example, Dora Neo comments that 'one might feel slightly uncomfortable that the "bad guys", that is, beneficiaries who call on performance bonds in unconscionable circumstances, should be allowed to have their way'.[57] However, Neo rationalised that it is ultimately up to the obligor of the performance bond to decide if it is willing to forego equity's protection in this context. Lau Kwan Ho has also subjected this decision to an extensive critique in a *Modern Law Review* piece.[58] Lau has three major criticisms of the position that parties may exclude injunctive relief premised on unconscionable conduct. First, he stresses that there is a difference between primary and secondary obligations pursuant to the contract. A primary obligation is an obligation to perform the contract whereas a secondary obligation arises to pay damages in the event of a breach. He argues that the court when deciding to order an injunction is essentially seeking to enforce primary obligations under the contract. In other words, '[t]he right to expect contractual performance is generally allied to a right to seek equitable relief to compel such performance'.[59] While it is relatively uncontroversial for parties to contractually limit their liabilities under a secondary obligation, it is questionable whether parties may contractually amend the content and the performance of their primary obligations. Second, parties should not be able to exclude the unconscionability exception due to its underlying policy. According to Lau, '[t]he true policy at work here is that of ensuring that parties do not contract themselves out of the law'.[60] Third, unconscionability like fraud should

[55] It is likely that the Unfair Contract Terms Act does not apply in most cases because these contracts are not consumer contracts nor written standard form contracts.

[56] *CKR Contract Services Pte Ltd* (n 53) [41].

[57] D Neo, 'Banking Law' (2014) 15 *Singapore Academy of Law Annual Review of Singapore Cases* 73, 94.

[58] KH Ho, 'Injunctive Relief: But Let's Agree Not to Have It?' (2016) 79 *MLR* 468.

[59] ibid 472.

[60] ibid 473.

fall within 'the sphere of general immunity from contractual manipulation'.[61] He cites *Regus (UK) Ltd v Epcot Solutions Ltd*[62] as support for the proposition that it is not possible to exclude liability for fraud or wilful damage. Lau concludes 'that people expect and are entitled to nothing less than honest dealing in their relationships'.[63]

Implicit in Lau's analysis is the assumption that the primary contractual obligation contained in a performance bond is that the beneficiary is only entitled to make genuine calls on the bond if the beneficiary has suffered damage under the underlying contract. As such, the beneficiary is under a primary obligation not to make an unconscionable call on the bond which is abusive and tactical. While I see some merit in this characterisation, it is ultimately question begging and circular. Lau's thesis starts with the premise that parties may not limit the primary obligations inherent in the contract. In order to reach the conclusion that unconscionability may not be excluded contractually he assumes that the obligation not to make unconscionable calls on the bond is within the primary obligation of the parties. In my view, the debate on whether it is possible to contractually exclude the unconscionability exception in relation to a performance bond cannot be resolved by dividing the contractual obligations undertaken by the parties into a neat dichotomy of primary and secondary obligations. In contrast to Lau, the Court of Appeal noted that performance bond in this particular context was provided in lieu of a cash deposit. Thus, if we proceed with this line of analysis, the primary obligation of the parties is that the bond is to function as a cash deposit and the beneficiary is entitled to call on the bond save for the fraud exception. Or to put this in another way, it could be argued that the primary obligation on the obligor is not to apply for an injunction restraining payment save for fraud. In other words, the contractual exclusion of the unconscionability exception restores the cracked image (using Debattista's imagery)[64] between the performance bond and letter of credit. Another way of putting the argument in support of the Court of Appeal's decision is that the parties have by contract incorporated the autonomy principle inherent in letters of credit within their obligations under the performance bond.

It is suggested that the most pertinent issue inherent in the Court of Appeal's decision in *CKR Contract Services Pte Ltd v Asplenium Land Pte Ltd* is whether there is a public policy objection to allow a contracting party to exclude liability for one own's unconscionable conduct. This is a distinct policy consideration from the public policy of ousting the court's jurisdiction which was considered extensively by the Court of Appeal. Unfortunately, the Court of Appeal did not deal with this issue squarely in their judgment. Instead, the judgment of the Court of Appeal concentrates solely on the question whether an exclusion of

[61] ibid 475.
[62] *Regus (UK) Ltd v Epcot Solutions Ltd* [2008] EWCA Civ 36, [2009] 1 All ER (Comm) 586 (CA).
[63] Ho (n 58) 476.
[64] Debattista (n 16) 304.

unconscionability is an ouster of the court's jurisdiction. Perhaps this was because of the manner in which arguments developed before the Court of Appeal. As Lau correctly points out, there is English authority which suggest that it is not possible to contractually exclude liability for fraudulent conduct. Similarly, it is not possible to contract out for liability for a person's fraudulent misrepresentation.[65] However, Andrew Burrows points out that 'the question of whether, as a matter of public policy, one can exclude other forms of conduct somewhat analogous to fraud, such as duress and undue influence, appears not to have been decided or discussed'.[66] Ultimately, this is a policy choice which the courts have to make, ie, between freedom of contract between the parties and the court's ability to intervene where one party is exercising his or her legal rights in an unconscionable manner. The Court of Appeal in Singapore seems to have made the choice in preference of the former policy, ie, respecting the contractual bargain struck by the parties. However, the counter argument against this is that the rationale of unconscionability doctrine in relation to performance bonds is that it was developed to prevent abusive calls and mitigate the unequal bargaining power of the parties.[67] If so, then a case may be made for holding that unconscionability like the fraud exception is not a ground which may be excluded by the parties. This is because large contracting parties may now insist on such clauses being included in their contracts. Be that as it may, this is not the position adopted by the Court of Appeal. The issue of the contracting parties' behaviour will be explored in the empirical part of the chapter.

V. Analysis of the Survey of the Cases

A comprehensive review of the reported and unreported Singapore case law was conducted using the database *Lawnet*[68] to survey all the cases which have discussed the unconscionability exception post *GHL Pte Ltd v Unitrack Building Construction Pte Ltd & Anor*.[69] The present author reviewed all the cases which came up with the relevant search terms and identified the decisions directly relevant to applications restraining performance bonds. The author then read the cases while taking note of the subject matter of the suit, the quantum of the performance bond and whether the application to restrain the performance bond was ultimately successful. Where the case was appealed to the Court of Appeal, the author only took note

[65] *HIH Casualty General Insurance Ltd v Chase Manhattan Bank* [2003] UKHL 6, [2003] 2 Lloyd's Rep 61, [16], [24], [76] and [121]–[122] (HL).

[66] A Burrows, *A Restatement of the English Law of Contract* (Oxford, OUP, 2016) 238–39.

[67] Wooler (n 13).

[68] The terms 'unconscionable' and 'performance bond' were entered into *Lawnet*. The cases were surveyed between 2000 and 2015.

[69] *GHL Pte Ltd* (n 4).

and reviewed the appellate court's decision to prevent a double counting of cases. While reviewing the grounds of decision, the author also took note of the judges' reasons in allowing or dismissing such applications. The data is summarised in a table marked Appendix A to this chapter.

The survey of the cases reveals that there were 31 reported and unreported cases between 2000 and 2015. Over a span of 15 years, this averages to two cases per year which suggests that there were not many applications to restrain calls on performance bonds. Prima facie, these figures suggest that the number of attempts to restrain performance bonds is at a tolerable level. However, these figures are not conclusive because the practice is that judges in Singapore would only write the grounds of decision when a party lodges a notice of appeal. It may be that there were many applications to restrain performance bonds where the losing party did not lodge a notice of appeal. Thus, this survey is inconclusive as to the actual number of challenges filed by contracting parties in Singapore to restrain calls on performance bonds. The limited conclusion which may be reached with the data is that the number of appeals resulting from applications to restrain a performance bond does not happen frequently in Singapore.

A summary of the number of cases broken down in the five-year period and the success rate is found in the table below.

Table 3.1: Summary of the Number of Cases

Time period	Number of cases	Percentage	Number of cases which were successful	Remark
2000–05	14	45.2	6	11 of the challenges were between 2000 and 2002
2005–10	6	19.4	3	
2010–15	11	35.5	4	9 cases between 2013 and 2015

It is also interesting that out of 31 reported and unreported decisions, 11 of these cases were dated between 2000 and 2002. This represented 35 per cent of all the reported and unreported decisions. This could potentially be explained on the fact that when the unconscionability exception was first recognised, the contours of the doctrine were not fully mapped out. As a result, there were frequent challenges. As the case law developed and more guidance was given by the courts, the challenges become less frequent. However, this hypothesis does not explain the spike of cases which happened subsequently, ie, 35.5 per cent which occurred between 2010 and 2015. Out of 11 cases between 2010 and 2015, nine of the cases were reported between 2013 and 2015. This is rather surprising considering this period was after the Court of Appeal's decision in *BS Mount Sophia*

Pte Ltd v Join-Aim Pte Ltd[70] where Andrew Phang JA said that the decision to restrain a performance bond should be exercised sparingly and that it would be difficult for a party to show a strong prima facie case of unconscionability. Perhaps, the only way to explain the data is that the number of applications to restrain performance bonds closely mirrors the construction industry and state of the economy of Singapore. Recall that Singapore suffered a prolonged economic slump which affected the property market between 2001 and 2006 due to global events like the 'September 11' attacks on the New York World Trade Center and the SARs crisis that affected Asia. Therefore, it is unsurprising that there were only two cases between 2002 and 2005 because it is likely that the construction industry in Singapore suffered a slowdown due to the economy. Subsequently, the property market in Singapore experienced a sharp rise which led to more construction projects. Thus, this could explain the spike of cases between 2010 and 2015 as more construction projects were completed and the performance bonds in relation to these projects were engaged.

In terms of successful applications to restrain calls on performance bonds, we see 13 successful challenges out of 31 of the reported and unreported cases. These figures include partial restraints on calls of performance bonds. This represents a 41 per cent success rate out of the reported and unreported cases. Again, this figure is not indicative of the overall success rate of all applications. As mentioned above, there would not be any grounds of decision if parties did not file a notice of appeal. It could be that parties were more inclined to file a notice of appeal in situations where the application to restrain a performance bond is successful.

The quantum value of the performance bonds in the cases is summarised as follows in the table below.

Table 3.2: Value of the Performance Bonds

Quantum (in Singapore dollars)	Number of cases
≤250,000	11
≥250,000 ≤750,000	6
≥750,000 ≤1,000,000	2
≥1,000,000	10
Not stated	2

The most number of challenges from the reported and unreported cases comes from the lower tier in terms of the quantum of performance bond, ie, below S$250,000. There are several possible explanations for this. First, it could simply be that there are more small-scale construction projects which are valued at S$2.5 million and below (the bond is usually 10 per cent of the project price). Second,

[70] *BS Mount Sophia Pte Ltd* (n 14).

abusive and tactical calls are more common in smaller scale projects. It should also be noted that there are 10 applications to restrain bonds which are worth more than S$1 million. Again, this could tentatively be explained on the number of projects and unconscionable calls on performance bonds within this band. These explanations are only tentative hypotheses.

Although Andrew Phang JA in *BS Mount Sophia Pte Ltd v Join-Aim Pte Ltd*[71] disavowed a formulaic approach to unconscionability and counselled that the whole broad set of facts must be analysed, the present author attempted to isolate the factors in which the judges have regarded as significant in holding that a call was unconscionable. In terms of mapping out unconscionable calls on performance bonds, the following are factors which the courts have taken into account:

(i) The delay in the works was contributed by the beneficiary of the bond.[72]
(ii) There is independent evidence such as evidence from the architect that there was no delay/defect in the works.[73]
(iii) The beneficiary did not assert that it had suffered damage.[74]
(iv) The alleged damages/rectification works were based on arbitrary figures or grossly inflated.[75]
(v) The claim for damages was already time barred.[76]
(vi) There was a partial restraint of the bond because the contract sum had been reduced.[77]
(vii) No performance was due because the defendant's main contract had been terminated.[78]
(viii) The call on the bond was not due to the plaintiff's poor performance but based on an ulterior motive to attempt to force the plaintiff to take over a contract.[79]

The judges have not placed much emphasis on the knowledge of the obligee in calling on the bond. Instead, the judges rely on written documentation such as letters and architects' certificates in establishing the factors listed above. Unfortunately, there does not seem to be a hierarchy of the factors and thus there is some uncertainty inherent in the application of these factors. It is hoped that by listing

[71] *BS Mount Sophia Pte Ltd* (n 14).

[72] *A1 Design & Build Pte Ltd v Neo Choon Seng* [2015] SGDC 86; *BS Mount Sophia Pte Ltd* (n 14); *Global Facade (S) Pte Ltd v Eng Lim Construction Company Private Limited* [2001] SGDC 325.

[73] *A1 Design & Build Pte Ltd* (n 72); *Polink Engineering Pte Ltd v Chen Hwei Lai & Ors* [2010] SGDC 36.

[74] *York International Pte Ltd v Voltas Limited* [2013] 3 SLR 1142.

[75] *Scada Solutions Pte Ltd v Anderco Pte Ltd* [2013] SGDC 237; *JBE Properties Pte Ltd* (n 14); *Newtech Engineering Construction Pte Ltd v BKB Engineering Constructions Pte Ltd and others* [2003] 4 SLR(R) 73; *Eltraco International Pte Ltd* (n 29) 198.

[76] *Econ Piling Pte Ltd v Aviva General Insurance Pte Ltd and another* [2006] 4 SLR(R) 501.

[77] *Hiap Tian Soon Construction Pte Ltd and another v Hola Development Pte Ltd and another* [2003] 1 SLR(R) 667.

[78] *Prolian M&E Services Pte Ltd v Loh Lin Kett* [2001] SGDC 322.

[79] *Samwoh Asphalt Premix Pte Ltd v Sum Cheong Piling Private Limited and Another* [2002] 1 SLR 1.

down these various factors, this would assist practitioners and judges in determining when it is regarded as unconscionable to call on a performance bond. In analysing the jurisprudence from Singapore, Deborah Horowitz suggested that many of the instances could be analysed as coming within the fraud exception on the grounds that the beneficiary had no honest belief that the beneficiary was entitled to call on the bond. Horowitz writes:

> One chief difficulty with the Singaporean cases on unconscionable conduct in relation to abstract payment instruments is that the courts seem to have forgotten about the fraud defence—or, rather, the applicant in the cases frequently does not plead it. It is true that there are risks for a party (or its counsel) who pleads fraud: one must genuinely believe in, and have sufficient proof of, the fraud allegation. Nonetheless, given the potential fraud and unconscionable conduct, it is still surprising that parties have chosen to plead the latter defence, but not the former, in many of the cases.[80]

With respect, there are several problems with the passage above. On a descriptive level, this statement is wrong because the multiple factors the courts have considered show quite conclusively that the unconscionability exception goes beyond the no honest belief analysis. The underlying thread running through most of the factors identified above is that the beneficiary of the bond is not entitled to the damages pursuant to the underlying contract between the parties. In order to determine this enquiry, the courts would have to assess the underlying dispute between the parties. If the court is of the view that there is a genuine contractual dispute between the parties, the court would not restrain the call on the performance bond but ask the parties to proceed to arbitration or litigation. However, if there is strong evidence that the damages are not due, the courts would regard this as a case of an unconscionable call on the performance bond. Horowitz's criticism that the Singapore judges and practitioners have forgotten about the fraud defence is both condescending and wrong. As she rightly notes, in many cases, this ground is not asserted by counsel. Therefore, it is perplexing for Horowitz to criticise the Singapore courts as having forgotten about the fraud exception. Further, there is an obvious and practical reason why fraud is not pursued by counsel—the standard of proof associated with fraud is almost impossible to make out at the interlocutory stage. This is a frequent refrain from the survey of the practitioners and it is to this part that we now turn in the next section.

VI. Survey of Construction Law Practitioners Based in Singapore

Since most of the cases on performance bonds arose from construction disputes, the present author embarked on a survey of leading building and construction

[80] Horowitz (n 35) 163.

lawyers to attempt to get the practitioners' insight into various problems associated with the unconscionability exception. The questions used in the survey are found in Appendix B. In particular, the survey asks, inter alia, the following questions:

(i) Are clients concerned about a potential restraint on performance bonds at the contract formation stage?
(ii) If they are concerned, do clients factor this into the contract price?
(iii) Do clients choose a foreign law to govern the performance bond?
(iv) Do clients seek to exclude unconscionability as a ground for restraint from the words of the performance bond?
(v) How often do you see calls on performance bonds which are tactical and abusive?
(vi) Is the law in Singapore clear enough for you to advise your client on restraining a call on a performance bond?
(vii) What is a ballpark figure as to hearing days and costs for restraining a call on a performance bond?
(viii) How often do parties appeal a court's decision to allow or deny a restrain a call on a performance bond?
(ix) Do parties attempt to settle disputes on a restraint on a call on a performance bond? What are the impediments to settlement, if any?
(x) In your personal opinion, is unconscionability as a separate ground for restraining performance bonds a positive or negative development?

In order to carry out the survey, the author used two leading online legal guides to practitioners—*Chambers and Partners*[81] and *Legal 500*.[82] *Chambers and Partners* listed the following as the leading firms in construction law.

Band 1	**Band 2**	**Band 3**
Pinsent Masons MPillay LLP	Allen & Gledhill LLP	Rajah & Tann Singapore LLP
WongPartnership LLP	Clifford Chance	Rodyk & Davidson LLP
	Hogan Lovells Lee & Lee	TSMP Law Corporation

The author emailed the survey questions to a construction partner in the firms listed above. Some partners were happy to fill out the survey and others who were busy preferred a short telephone interview. The present author managed to get survey responses from lawyers from all these firms listed in *Chambers and Partners*. Care was also taken not to speak to multiple lawyers from the same firm in order to prevent a particular firm's practice from the skewing the data. The only exception was one firm on this list where the author spoke to both the construction partner and also a partner with a commercial arbitration/shipping practice.

81 www.chambersandpartners.com/guide/asia/8/188/1.
82 www.legal500.com/c/singapore/.

This was because the latter partner was counsel in a major case on the restraint of a performance bond in the High Court and Court of Appeal. In order to enlarge on the sample size, the author also consulted the online version *Legal 500* directory. Unlike *Chambers and Partners*, *Legal 500* does not have a discrete construction law section but lists the lawyers within a combined category of Real Estate and Construction. The author went through the list and found three lawyers on the *Legal 500* list with a construction practice focus who were willing to complete the survey. There was also the fear that both the *Chambers and Partners* and *Legal 500* list of lawyers would be lawyers who advise on big deals and the response would not accurately reflect the views of the smaller players. To counter this potential bias in the data, the present author managed to speak to three lawyers in small law firm practice who identified their practice as mainly in the construction field. Overall, the author managed to obtain 15 survey responses.

In relation to whether clients are concerned with a restraint on a call of a performance bond at the contract formation stage, the responses were almost evenly split. Seven of the lawyers surveyed said that their clients were not concerned with such a risk at the contracting stage. Several lawyers said that their clients were more concerned at this stage about the details and profitability of the project rather than worrying about the performance bond. Also, at the contracting stage, parties were typically very optimistic about the project and did not think that the performance bond would have to be engaged in the future. Two lawyers gave a qualified answer to this issue, ie, that some of their clients were now aware of the possibility that unconscionability as a ground for restraint may be excluded by the contractual provisions post the decision in *CKR Contract Services Pte Ltd v Asplenium Land Pte Ltd*.[83] The remaining six lawyers surveyed said their clients were concerned with the risk of injunctive relief against a call on a performance bond at contracting stage. These responses suggest a high level of sophistication in terms of clients' awareness of the law in this area. Furthermore, most of the respondents who said that their clients were concerned about restraints on performance bonds thought that their clients would have factored this risk into the contract pricing, although it is difficult to tell precisely how this risk was priced.

The survey responses also showed that there are practical reasons for parties not choosing a foreign law to govern the performance bond if the construction project is in Singapore. The main reason seems to be that for such contracts the entity which issues the performance bond would either be a Singapore bank or insurer. Singapore banks and insurers have certain regulatory concerns about issuing an English law governed bond. In addition, Singapore banks and insurers were less comfortable with issuing bonds governed by English law because they would usually not have English qualified in-house legal counsel on their staff. A very significant development from the survey results is that lawyers from three law firms considered the 'Big Four' law firms in Singapore indicated that they are receiving

[83] *CKR Contract Services Pte Ltd* (n 53).

many enquiries about excluding unconscionability as a ground for restraint in their contracts after the case of *CKR Contract Services Pte Ltd v Asplenium Land Pte Ltd*.[84] In fact, one of these lawyers who is the construction head of a Big Four law firm said that this is done '[i]n almost every construction contract that we assist clients on'. Another construction lawyer in a Big Four law firm said that this is a trend in 50 per cent of the cases because the clients' quantity surveyors are now aware that the law allows parties to contract out of unconscionability. This lawyer said that he expected an upward trend in the practice of excluding unconscionability in the future. The practice of excluding unconscionability from the terms of the bond is not confined to local Singapore law firms. At least two partners in international law firms have reported the same phenomenon of excluding unconscionability in the terms of the performance bond. If this practice spreads across all the law firms, this could potentially spell the demise of the ground of unconscionability as a separate ground of restraint for performance bonds because parties would have excluded this ground from the terms of the bond.

The responses were mixed in terms of the number of calls on performance bonds that the lawyers have encountered in their practice which they considered to be tactical and abusive. Seven of the respondents said that they often see calls on bonds which are abusive and tactical. In contrast, the remaining eight lawyers thought that abusive calls on performance were relatively rare. Several lawyers who said that abusive calls were rare were sanguine and observed that this question was very subjective and really depended on the profile of their client. Obviously, those who were acting for owners/employers thought they were entitled to call on the bond. With regard to lawyers who said they often see abusive calls, a respondent wrote:

> We see calls that are obviously aimed at putting contractors under financial pressure to compromise and settle claims, or to accept the employer's demands. There are P[erformance] Bond calls which seem to be aimed at causing insolvency so that the contractor cannot pursue its claims in Court/Arbitration.

Another common tactic is to inflate the alleged damages suffered or to unjustifiably assert that the contractor had delayed the works. A senior construction lawyer in a Big Four law firm said:

> Calls which are tactical and abusive are calls for amounts which do not reflect the amount of losses which the Employer has suffered. Usually these losses are inflated as a result of large amounts of liquidated damages which are, in turn, based on delays for which the Contractors have not been given adequate extensions of time.

Some lawyers also explained that calls on performance bonds are used in the contractual power play between the parties to obtain leverage against the other side. One scenario mentioned by three respondents is that the bond may be called by the employer when the contractor asks for payment pursuant to the adjudication

[84] ibid.

process enacted under the Security of Payment Act.[85] By way of background, the adjudication process was set up to speed up payment in the building and construction industry. Viewed in this context, the call is usually aimed at retaliating at the contractor for seeking out the adjudication process. As one respondent from a small practice observed, sub-contractors are very concerned that if they take out an application under the adjudication process, their main contractor will call on their bond.

All the lawyers unanimously said that their clients have asked them to restrain calls on performance bonds. This is an unsurprising result and suggests that applications to restrain performance bonds are far more common than the 31 reported and unreported cases surveyed in the earlier part. What is interesting is that the lawyers are again divided on the clarity of the law on unconscionability. Eight lawyers thought that the law was clear enough for them to advise their clients on applications to restrain performance bonds. However, the remaining seven respondents disagreed. As a construction partner in an international law firm points out:

> What remains for counsel like us is to survey precedent decisions in which restraint had been ordered for conduct amounting to 'unconscionability' and to try to align our clients' case accordingly. Even so, results may vary from case to case, and although these are largely facts-dependent, we also suggest that to a lesser degree, it can also be tribunal-dependent.

Another construction lawyer gave the following ambivalent answer and referred to unconscionability as an oxymoronic 'known unknown'. He said:

> Yes and no in that the law is clearly unclear. The courts have deliberately left the test for unconscionability quite fluid with no pre-determined categories of unconscionability. So it is a known unknown, except perhaps where the facts are close to those in previously decided cases of unconscionability.

The responses which said that the law was unclear all pointed out that unconscionability is very fact-sensitive and would depend on the judge hearing the case.

In terms of hearing dates and ballpark figures as to cost, 13 of the 15 lawyers provided information on this. All 13 lawyers said that a hearing date could be held within one to two days. The costs estimate involved ranged between $8,000 and $100,000 depending on the size of the bond and the complexity of the matter. However, the average costs provided by the lawyers were between $30,000 and $50,000. With regard to settlement of disputes on calls on performance bond, the respondents pointed out the parties usually do not regard the performance bond issue as a discrete dispute. Instead, there are usually multiple disputes between the parties at the material time. If a settlement was to be reached, it would be a global settlement with regard to the entire myriad of issues between the parties. Some lawyers pointed out that the performance bond is often used as a form of leverage in these negotiations. If the owner/employer has successfully called on the bond,

[85] Security of Payment Act (Cap 30B, 2006 Rev Ed).

then the owner/employer is regarded as having the upper hand. However, if the obligor has successfully restrained a call on the performance bond, then the bargaining position is equalised somewhat.

The responses to the final question as to whether unconscionability is a positive or negative development saw a majority of the lawyers (10 out of 15) saying that this was a positive development in the law. Several reasons were proffered in support of the position that this was a positive development. First, several lawyers pointed out that the threshold of establishing fraud as a ground of restraint was almost impossible to achieve in practice. Second, the lawyers supportive of the unconscionability exception said that this ground deals effectively with abusive calls on performance bonds. Third, some lawyers pointed out that the unconscionability doctrine evens out (to a certain extent) the unequal bargaining position between parties in the building construction contract. Otherwise, contractors are powerless in the face of an abusive call on a performance bond. In contrast to the positive responses, two lawyers said that this was a negative development pointing out that unconscionability is an uncertain concept. The remaining three lawyers were ambivalent about the unconscionability exception—they said they understood what the courts were trying to do but raised the uncertainty of the ambit of the unconscionability exception.

Several tentative conclusions may be drawn from this limited survey of practitioners' responses. First, from the responses from three of the Big Four law firms, clients (or their legal advisers) who have the upper hand in terms of the bargaining power were uncomfortable with the inherent uncertainty associated with the unconscionability exception to calls on performance bonds. These clients are now actively excluding unconscionability from the terms of the bond. In fact, one of these Big Four law firms is advising *all* their clients to exclude unconscionability. If this trend becomes common place, it is surmised that this will herald the death of unconscionability as a separate ground of restraint. Second, while some lawyers complain about the uncertainty which unconscionability entails, others are perfectly comfortable with the open-ended nature of the law. This may be explained by lawyers who may have differing philosophies, ie, those who prefer certainty to lawyers who are happy to leave the courts with the residual guided discretion to determine which situations are regarded as unconscionable. Third, some lawyers report that abusive calls on performance bonds are unfortunately common in Singapore's construction industry. Fourth, the hearing days and costs of resolving performance bond issues are not excessive in Singapore, typically taking one or two days and costing between S$30,000 and S$50,000. Finally, two-thirds of the lawyers surveyed thought that was a positive development in the law. There could be several explanations for this. It could be that all these lawyers saw the policy reasons for adopting the unconscionability doctrine in relation to performance bonds and could tolerate a degree of uncertainty inherent in its application in advising their clients. Next, another potential explanation is local pride in the Singapore court developing its own jurisprudence. Of course there is the more cynical explanation that the inherent uncertainty of the concept of unconscionability meant that this would generate more legal work for the practitioners, and hence they viewed this development of the law as a positive one.

VII. Conclusion

Singapore's experiment with unconscionability presents an interesting case study of equity's jurisprudence operating in the market place. While there have been high level calls that it is desirable for common law courts to reach similar conclusions in matters pertaining to the commercial law,[86] Singapore's divergence represents a conscious policy choice in the face of local imperatives, ie, abusive calls on performance bonds. The aim of this chapter has been to sketch out the developments in the law since the recognition of the unconscionability exception by surveying all the case law and leading construction law practitioners' perspectives on the operation of the unconscionability exception. As an overarching theme, the conclusion reached by the present author is that although the concept of unconscionability does entail a degree of uncertainty, it has worked in Singapore in this context. In terms of the number of reported and unreported cases, the survey of the cases shows that it is at a low level, ie, an average of two cases per year. Hearing days on unconscionability do not seem to be protracted (one or two days) and the costs of hearings were not too astronomical. Furthermore, while some practitioners lamented on the inherent uncertainty associated with unconscionability, others thought the law was clear enough for them to advise their clients. It is also telling that 10 out of the 15 practitioners surveyed thought that the unconscionability exception was a positive development. But the survey results also show that we may be at the beginning stage of the ultimate demise of the unconscionability exception. Since the Court of Appeal's holding that unconscionability may be excluded from the terms of the bond, the largest law firms in Singapore are seeing their clients contracting out of unconscionability. If this trend persists, we may find unconscionability in relation to performance bonds as merely a legal historical footnote in Singapore's jurisprudence.

[86] See S Menon, 'Transnational Commercial Law: Realities, Challenges and a Call for Meaningful Convergence' [2013] *Singapore Journal of Legal Studies* 231; *FHR European Ventures LLP & Ors v Cedar Capital Partners LLC* [2014] UKSC 45, [2015] AC 250 (HL) [45] (Lord Neuberger).

Appendix A

S/No	Date reported	Name of case	Subject matter of suit	Quantum involved	Successful application?	Reasons/interesting features
1.	4 March 2015	*JK Integrated (Pte Ltd) v 50 Robinson Pte Ltd and another* [2015] SGHC 57	Building and construction	$4.7 million	✗	— No under certification of payment. — Owner did not delay the works.
2.	22 April 2015	*A1 Design & Build Pte Ltd v Neo Choon Seng* [2015] SGDC 86	Building and construction	$159,600	✓	— No delay in the work as the work was certified by the architect. — Alleged delay was contributed by the beneficiary of the bond. — There's evidence that the owner confirmed that there is no defect.
3.	16 Jan 2014	*CAA Technologies Pte Ltd v BHCC Construction Pte Ltd and ABN Amro Bank NV* [2014] SGDC 25	Building and construction	$534,080	✗	— This was an advance payment bond. — Genuine dispute as between the parties on performance and amount due.
4.	27 Feb 2014	*Builders Designers Engineers (Bde) Pte Ltd v Sin Chew Woodpaq Pte Ltd* [2014] SGDC 78	Building and construction	$199,900	✗	— Allegation that progressive payment was not paid rejected: payment not endorsed by the professional engineer. — Evidence by quantity surveyor that the owner had overpaid the contractor.

5.	16 April 2014	*CCM Industrial Pte Ltd v 70 Shenton Pte Ltd and another* [2014] SGHC 75	Building and construction	$4,728,250	×	— Evidence of delay in the works.
6.	31 March 2014	*Tech-System Design & Contract (S) Pte Ltd v WYWY Investments Pte Ltd* [2014] SGHC 57	Building and construction	$988,888	×	— Architect has not certified an extension of time: owner prima facie entitled to claim liquidated damages.
7.	24 April 2013	*Ryobi-Kiso (S) Pte Ltd v Lum Chang Building Contractors Pte Ltd and another* [2013] SGHC 86	Building and construction	$1.88 m	×	— There was clear evidence of breaches of contract. — Plaintiff was in delay of the contract. — Genuine construction disputes between the parties.
8.	1 July 2013	*York International Pte Ltd v Voltas Limited* [2013] 3 SLR 1142	Supply, deliver, test and commission chillers	Not stated: 10% of the purchase price	✓ (on the grounds that this is a conditional bond)	— Bond was interpreted to be conditional. — Ambiguity should be construed against the beneficiary. — Deliberate omission of the word 'unconditional'. — Beneficiary did not assert damage due to breach of contract.

(continued)

S/No	Date reported	Name of case	Subject matter of suit	Quantum involved	Successful application?	Reasons/interesting features
9.	5 August 2013	*Scada Solutions Pte Ltd v Anderco Pte Ltd* [2013] SGDC 237	Building and construction	$188,000	✓(restrained for $156,616.08)	— Call on performance bond based on an arbitrary figure of alleged damages. — Set off not quantified with details and particulars as required by the set off provisions in the contract. — No delay certificate or certificate of practical completion relied in quantifying the liquidated damages. — The Defendant had written to the Plaintiff prior to the call on the performance bond saying that the Plaintiff owes the Defendant $47,583.92.
10.	18 April 2012	*Master Marine AS v Labroy Offshore Ltd and others* [2012] 3 SLR 125	International shipbuilding contract: offshore elevating rig	Five instalments: not stated in the report	✗	— Doctrine of strict compliance applied.
11.	9 May 2012	*BS Mount Sophia Pte Ltd v Join-Aim Pte Ltd* [2012] 3 SLR 352	Building and construction	$484,440	✓	— There was evidence that the completion date had been pushed back. — There was evidence that the beneficiary of the bond did not genuinely believe that the Plaintiff was responsible for the delay.

12.	6 January 2010	*Shanghai Electric Group Co Ltd v PT Merak Energi Indonesia and another* [2010] 2 SLR 329	Building and construction	$10.8 m	×	— Bond governed by English law. — Genuine disputes of contract. — The bond was given to secure advanced payment.
13.	27 January 2010	*Polink Engineering Pte Ltd v Chen Hwei Lai & Ors* [2010] SGDC 36	Building and construction	$123,800	✓	— The Defendant had interfered with the previous architect. — Changed an architect and found a 'compliant' architect who certified on the calling of the performance bond.
14.	3 December 2010	*JBE Properties Pte Ltd v Gammon Pte Ltd* [2011] 4 SLR 47	Building and construction	$1,151,500	✓	— The terms of the performance bond mentioned unconscionability as reason for non-payment. — Quotation for rectification works obtained by the owners was grossly inflated. — Owner never gave the contractor a chance to rectify the alleged defects. — Cost of alleged rectification works is less than amount owed.

(continued)

S/No	Date reported	Name of case	Subject matter of suit	Quantum involved	Successful application?	Reasons/interesting features
15.	26 August 2010	*Astrata (Singapore) Pte Ltd v Tridex Technologies Pte Ltd and another and other matters* [2011] 1 SLR 449	Building and construction	$490,000	×	— Strong prima facie case of unconscionability not made out. — Genuine disputes of contracts which should be referred to arbitration.
16.	12 January 2009	*Leighton Contractors (Singapore) Pte Ltd v J-Power Systems Corp and Another* [2009] SGHC 7	Building and construction	$956,395	×	— Genuine disputes of contract.
17.	12 September 2006	*Econ Piling Pte Ltd v Aviva General Insurance Pte Ltd and another* [2006] 4 SLR(R) 501	Building and construction	$173,400	✓	— Claim was already time barred.
18.	4 November 2004	*Scan-Bilt Pte Ltd v Umar Abdul Hamid* [2004] SGDC 274	Building and construction	$125,000	×	— Clause in Performance Bond specifically excluded unconscionability as a ground to restrain payment.

19.	26 June 2003	*Newtech Engineering Construction Pte Ltd v BKB Engineering Constructions Pte Ltd and others* [2003] 4 SLR(R) 73	Building and construction	$200,000 $43,150	✓	— Defendant had 37 legal actions against it. — Discrepancy in the final statement of account: the damages claimed had ballooned in five months.
20.	15 January 2002	*McConnell Dowell Constructors (Aust) Pty Ltd v Sembcorp Engineers and Constructors Pte Ltd (formerly known as SembCorp Construction Pte Ltd)* [2002] 1 SLR(R) 60	Building and construction	$125 m	✗	— Bank guarantee was provided to be called if the proposed funder failed to procure financing. — It was clear that the proposed funder had failed to procure financing.
21.	17 July 2002	*Seng Hock Heng Contractor Pte Ltd v Hup Seng Bee Construction Pte Ltd and another* [2002] 2 SLR(R) 486	Building and construction	$1,295,000	✗	— 'The evidence before me is inconclusive and difficult to evaluate although, if pressed, my sympathy inclines towards the plaintiff'.

(continued)

S/No	Date reported	Name of case	Subject matter of suit	Quantum involved	Successful application?	Reasons/interesting features
22.	31 October 2002	*Hiap Tian Soon Construction Pte Ltd and another v Hola Development Pte Ltd and another* [2003] 1 SLR(R) 667	Building and construction	$1,009,000	✓ (only entitled to call for $ 790,000	— Contract sum had been reduced from $10 m to $7.9 m.
23.	25 November 2002	*Anwar Siraj and another v Teo Hee Lai Building Construction Pte Ltd* [2003] 1 SLR(R) 394	Building and construction	$120,000	✗	— Owner was an extremely difficult person. — Owner interfered with architect. — Owner denied Plaintiff the opportunity to remedy the work. — Not sufficient to be regarded as unconscionable.
24.	20 June 2001	*Marinteknik Shipbuilders (S) Pte Ltd v SNC Passion* [2001] SGHC 140	Shipbuilding	€666,000	✗	— Genuine disputes as to the defects.
25.	8 October 2001	*Prolian M&E Services Pte Ltd v Loh Lin Kett* [2001] SGDC 322	Building and construction	$74,000	✓	— The Defendant's main contract had been terminated. — No performance due from the Plaintiff. — There was no basis for the Defendant to call on the performance bond.

26.	10 October 2001	*Global Facade (S) Pte Ltd v Eng Lim Construction Company Private Limited* [2001] SGDC 325	Building and construction	$93,000	✓	— Project was certified by the architect as completed. — Call was two years after completion. — Defendant has not filed any legal proceedings to pursue its alleged claims.
27.	20 October 2001	*WW Welding & Construction Pte Ltd v Multiplex Construction Pty Ltd* [2001] SGDC 332	Building and construction	$218,500	×	— Plaintiff claimed that Defendant owed it money. — Defendant claimed that Plaintiff owed it money. — Burden of proof of strong prima facie case of unconscionability not discharged.
28.	8 November 2001	*Liang Huat Aluminium Industries Pte Ltd v Hi-Tek Construction Pte Ltd* [2001] SGHC 334	Building and construction	$538,000	×	— Not possible to determine at interlocutory stage whether Defendant's claims against Plaintiff are justifiable.

(*continued*)

S/No	Date reported	Name of case	Subject matter of suit	Quantum involved	Successful application?	Reasons/interesting features
29.	5 Dec 2001	*Samwoh Asphalt Premix Pte Ltd v Sum Cheong Piling Private Limited and Another* [2002] 1 SLR 1	Building and construction	$500,000	✓	— Ulterior motive for calling on the bond. — The Defendant wanted the Plaintiff to take over the main contract when they were only the nominated sub-contractor. — The call on the performance bond was a bargaining chip in the negotiations.
30.	17 January 2000	*Dauphin Offshore Engineering & Trading Pte Ltd v The Private Office of HRH Sheikh Sultan bin Khalifa bin Zayed Al Nahyan* [2000] 1 SLR(R) 117	Building of a yacht	$877,500	×	— No unconscionability because there were genuine disputes. — Some hesitation because Plaintiff has done substantial work but has not been paid.
31.	18 September 2000	*Eltraco International Pte Ltd v CGH Development Pte Ltd* [2000] 3 SLR(R) 198	Building and construction	$2,438,800	✓(partial restraint—only entitled to call on $600,000)	— Damages not to the extent of the full bond value. — Contrasted with the English case of *Cargill.*

Appendix B

Personal Information

1. Please state your number of years with Post Qualification Experience.
2. Please elaborate on your practice (eg, do you work in a local or international law firm, size of firm, area of practice).
3. Please elaborate on the profile of your clients (eg, owners, main contractors, sub-contractors, paid up capital etc).

Formation of Contract Stage

4. Are clients concerned about a potential restraint on performance bonds at the contract formation stage?
5. If clients are concerned about a potential restraint on performance at the contract formation stage:
   a) Who is the person (eg, legal counsel, quantity surveyor, engineer etc) typically concerned about this?
   b) Do clients factor this into the contract price?
   c) Do clients choose a foreign law to govern the performance bond?
   d) Do they seek to exclude unconscionability as a ground for restraint from the words of the performance bond?
6. If the answer to question 4 is no, please elaborate why your clients are not concerned.

Calls and Restraint on Performance Bonds

7. How often do you see calls on performance bonds which are tactical and abusive? Please elaborate on your answer as to what you consider to be tactical and abusive calls.
8. Do your clients often ask you to consider a restraint on a call on performance bond?
9. Is the law in Singapore clear enough for you to advise your client on restraining a call on a performance bond?
10. Please give a ballpark figure as to hearing days and costs for restraining a call on a performance bond?
11. How often do parties appeal a court's decision to allow or deny a restrain a call on a performance bond? Do they appeal all the way to the Court of Appeal? Can you give a ballpark figure on the costs and hearing days involved?

12. Do parties attempt to settle disputes on a restraint on a call on a performance bond? What are the impediments to settlement, if any?
13. In your personal opinion, is unconscionability as a separate ground for restraining performance bonds a positive or negative development? Please elaborate on your answer.

4

Certainty, Identification and Intention in Personal Property Law

MICHAEL BRIDGE

I. Introduction

A key indicator of a property right is whether that right is exigible against a thing. If there is no identified thing against which a right may be exacted, whether that thing is a tangible ship or an intangible balance in a bank account, it therefore follows that the claim of a property right fails *in limine*. As Lord Blackburn once remarked: 'The [rule] that the parties must be agreed as to the specific goods on which the contract is to attach before there can be a bargain and sale, is one that is founded on the very nature of things'.[1]

This exigibility requirement may therefore be regarded as demanding a sufficient degree of certainty in the subject matter of any grant or encumbrance or other proprietary disposition before the law will recognise a proprietary interest in it arising out of that disposition. We may be considering the creation of a beneficial interest by way of trust, or the assignment of a thing in action, or the passing of property in goods under a contract of sale, or the taking of security in the assets of a company or individual. Whatever the transaction, and whether we are acting at law or in equity, the certainty requirement embedded in 'the nature of things' imposes itself.

Two fundamental questions present themselves in property enquiries. First, what is it about a right that makes it a property right? Second, when can it be said that a property right comes into existence? The concern of this chapter is with the second of these questions, though it cannot be said that there is a completely clean separation between the two. In answering this second question, it is not merely a

[1] C Blackburn, *A Treatise on the Effect of the Contract of Sale* (London, William Benning & Co, 1845) 122, a passage approved by the Privy Council in *Re Goldcorp Exchange Ltd* [1995] 1 AC 74, 90. In his capacity as Blackburn J and later Lord Blackburn, the author's views on the matter appear distinctly more favourable to the claimant of a part interest in an identified bulk: see *Martineau v Kitching* (1872) LR 7 QB 436 and *Inglis v Stock* (1885) 10 App Cas 263. This may not have been fully appreciated in *Re Goldcorp*, 93, discussed below.

matter of observable fact whether the requirement of certainty permits a property right to be created. There is also the matter of intention, more importantly the grantor's or disponor's intention, to consider, together with any statutory imperative or even an estoppel. In distinguishing certainty and intention, it is important to determine whether a supposed requirement is essential in establishing the requisite degree of certainty, or is of a lesser intensity in supplying evidence of an intention to create a type of property right. The distinction here made is a vital one. One reason why this is important is that it is not always straightforward whether a claim for property rights fails because of the lack of an identified source of property rights. To anticipate the case of *Re Goldcorp Exchange Ltd*,[2] discussed below, did the unallocated claimants fail because there was no bulk from which their claimed share could be extracted, or because such goods of the type claimed and held by the exchange were never intended by the exchange to be the subject matter of property rights held by those claimants?

In taking further the 'when' question, I shall examine the various consensual dispositions mentioned above[3] with a view, in part, to seeing whether and for what reason the certainty requirement, even the intention requirement too, is compromised. Before doing so, however, I shall consider the extent to which property that does not yet exist is by anticipation treated for certain purposes as having a present existence.

II. Future Property

It is a truism to say that future property has no present existence, so that unless and until it comes into existence no proprietary right over it can be created,[4] irrespective of any disponor's intention to that effect. '[A] mere expectancy or possibility of becoming entitled in the future to a proprietary right is not an existing chose in action.'[5] Consequently, the object of a discretionary trust or of a power

[2] *Re Goldcorp Exchange Ltd* [1995] 1 AC 74.

[3] Hence, I shall not be dealing with constructive trusts.

[4] *Belding v Read* (1865) 3 H&C 955, 961, 159 ER 812 (Pollock CB): 'there cannot be a prophetic conveyance'; *Re Count D'Epineul (No 2)* (1882) 20 Ch D 758; *Re Clarke* (1887) 36 Ch D 348 (CA); *Glegg v Bromley* [1912] 3 KB 474 (CA); *Raiffeisen Zentralbank Österreich AG v Five Star General Trading LLC* [2001] EWCA Civ 68, [2001] QB 825 [60], [80]; *Mac-Jordan Construction Ltd v Brookmount Erostin Ltd* [1992] BCLC 350.

[5] *Norman v Federal Commissioner of Taxation* (1965) 109 CLR 9 (Windeyer J). As to what constitutes an expectancy as opposed to a vested right where a power of appointment exists, see *Re Brooks' Settlement Trusts* [1939] Ch 993, holding that no such right existed if the power could be exercised so as to remove the beneficiary's entitlement. Similarly, see *Campbell Connelly & Co Ltd v Noble* [1963] 1 WLR 252, 261, holding that an assignment of renewal copyright, conditional upon the assignor surviving 28 years from the date of the assignment, a matter that he could not control, amounted to an assignment of future property and thus a contract to assign.

of appointment has nothing to assign.[6] And yet the matter is not quite so simple, in that the law in some circumstances recognises a transaction concerning future property as having a type of proprietary effect even before the property comes into existence. Suppose, for example, that a disponor creates two competing assignments over future debts. Under the rule in *Dearle v Hall*,[7] priority between them will be accorded to the first assignment of which notice is given, even if this assignment is the second in time, except that a second assignment cannot be promoted in this way if the assignee was aware at the time of the assignment of the existence of the earlier assignment.[8] Even though these two assignments may not have attached to any extant property at the time they were created, the priority between them will in this example be partly dependent upon events that have occurred before the property came into existence. There is no question of a type of dead heat between them, occurring as and when the two assignments bite simultaneously on the property at the moment it comes into existence.

The rule regarding competing assignments applies also in the case where one of them is an assignment by way of charge, more particularly a fixed charge. An assignment by way of charge has a suspensive character in that it is completed only when the chargee takes steps to enforce the charge.[9] Despite this, the charge is treated as concluded for the purpose of establishing priority between the two under the priority rule in *Dearle v Hall*.[10]

Another case of what might be called fictitious proprietary effect concerns the assignment by way of charge of future property that is required to be registered as a present charge under the Companies Act if it is to prevail against liquidators, administrators and other secured creditors of the chargor.[11] Registration must be effected by filing the requisite documents within 21 days of the creation of the charge. A difficult distinction has to be taken between contingent charges and present charges over future property, with the 21-day period tolling from the grant of the charge only in the latter case. Hence, a purported charge over moneys received by an assured under an indemnity insurance policy is not treated as a present charge at the time of its creation: the claim under the policy may never have to be made.[12] On the other hand, a charge over hire purchase debts falling due under hire purchase agreements yet to be made will be treated as a present

[6] *Schmidt v Rosewood Trust Co* [2003] UKPC 26, [2003] 2 AC 709 [40]; *Gartside v Inland Revenue Commissioners* [1968] AC 553 (HL) 607: '[A] right to require trustees to consider whether they will pay you something does not enable you to claim anything'.

[7] *Dearle v Hall* (1828) 3 Russ 1.

[8] *Ward v Duncombe* [1893] AC 369.

[9] M Bridge, L Gullifer, G McMeel and S Worthington, *The Law of Personal Property* (London, Sweet & Maxwell, 2013) paras 27-011–27-012.

[10] *Colonial General Mutual Insurance Co Ltd v ANZ Banking Group (New Zealand) Ltd* [1995] 1 WLR 1140.

[11] Companies Act 2006, ss 859A *et seq* (UK); Companies Act, ss 131 *et seq* (Singapore).

[12] *Paul & Frank Ltd v Discount Bank (Overseas) Ltd* [1967] Ch 348.

charge for the purposes of the legislation,[13] even though it is possible, though perhaps unlikely, that those agreements will not be concluded. The hire purchase debts are predictable and striven for in the chargor's ordinary course of business; a policy of indemnity insurance gives financial protection against an event that is not sought. Once the registration requirement does apply in a given case, however, this does not amount to an overt recognition that the charge has a proprietary effect in respect of future property at the time it is granted. This is because any failure to register has the negative effect of preventing the chargee at a later date from asserting its rights under the charge and as granted by the charge. A different view would have to be taken if our law were to go down the path of Article 9 and similar Commonwealth legislation, where registration (or filing) serves a positive purpose in that priority derives from the fact of registration rather than from the instrument of charge itself.

A further case of fictitious proprietary effect concerns the so-called lightweight floating charge which made an appearance in *Re Croftbell Ltd*.[14] A company was contesting the right of a debenture holder to appoint an administrative receiver which the legislation in force at the time permitted if the debenture holder's security, over the whole or substantially the whole of the company's assets, contained at least one floating charge. The company was part of a corporate group. It was a non-trading company and engaged only in intra-group dealings. Its sole asset was the entire shareholding in another company in the same group; that company in turn owned only one asset (a valuable site). The company granted the debenture holder a floating charge covering the whole of its undertaking in the usual way, as well as a pledge of the shares.[15] Although it was plain that the floating charge captured nothing after the pledge was taken into consideration, the debenture holder's claim that it had the power to appoint an administrative receiver,[16] so as to block the appointment by the court of an administrator, prevailed. In addressing the argument that the pledge was but a device to lock out a court-appointed administrator, the court declined to consider the pledgee's motive. It was also unimpressed by the fact that at the time of its execution the floating charge was an empty vessel—noting that this is commonly the case where a charge finances the commencement of a business—and, in response to the argument that the company never intended to acquire assets that might be captured by the charge, simply observed that the company's intentions might change. The case leaves us therefore with a floating charge that could not be said 'to have no operation at all'.

[13] *Independent Automatic Sales Ltd v Knowles & Foster* [1962] 1 WLR 974.

[14] *Re Croftbell Ltd* [1990] BCC 781.

[15] The company also granted a second-ranking fixed charge over the shares to another creditor.

[16] Further to the Insolvency Act 1986, s 29(2), which applies where a floating charge, or a floating charge in combination with another security, captures the whole or substantially the whole of a company's property.

Another case of a charge being given by anticipation a proprietary effect in respect of property that has not yet come into existence is *Foamcrete (UK) Ltd v Thrust Engineering Ltd*,[17] where a clause in a joint venture agreement provided that rights and obligations under the agreement between FTE and Thrust could not be assigned without the other party's written approval. Two years previously, FTE had granted to its bank a debenture containing a floating charge over its undertaking present and future. An assignee of the bank's rights made a claim against Thrust for non-payment of certain moneys owed to FTE, which Thrust resisted on the basis of the non-assignment clause. One of the grounds on which the assignee's claim was upheld was that the bank's rights derived not from the prohibited assignment but from the antecedent floating charge. The floating charge gave the bank an immediate beneficial interest in all the property of the chargor, present and future, including the future debt. Yet it is plainly a fiction to say that the bank has a present interest in moneys not yet due under a contract not yet concluded. Since the non-assignment clause spoke in future terms about what the parties might not do, the same conclusion might have been reached by construing in restrictive terms the non-assignment clause.[18]

It has been said in other circumstances that a charge has a proprietary character even before the property in question comes into existence. The purported charge will be recharacterised as a promise to grant a charge, binding if consideration has been given for the promise. In *Re Lind*,[19] the debtor, next of kin to his mother, mortgaged his future inheritance from her on two occasions in favour of separate creditors in return for advances. Between the grant of the mortgages and the death of his mother he was adjudicated bankrupt and then discharged. Neither creditor put in a proof in his bankruptcy. Lind's argument now was that the discharge freed him from the mortgage debts, but it was held instead that the mortgages were not merely a matter of contract during Lind's bankruptcy. Rather, they survived the discharge and captured the share of his mother's estate when he inherited it. They did so even though they were bereft of content up to that point in time. Although Phillimore LJ observed that '[a]ssignments of property not then in existence pass, as such, nothing', he went on to say that the mortgagees' entitlement was more than a matter of specific performance in that, prior to the inheritance falling in, the mortgagees had 'something more than a mere right in contract, something in the nature of an estate or interest'.[20] The trial judge had stated that the charges had

[17] *Foamcrete (UK) Ltd v Thrust Engineering Ltd* [2000] EWCA Civ 351, [2002] BCC 221.

[18] ibid [8]: 'Provided that neither of the parties to this agreement *shall be* entitled to assign this agreement or any of its rights and obligations under this agreement' (emphasis added).

[19] *Re Lind* [1915] 2 Ch 345.

[20] Ibid 363. Bankes LJ ascribes to the mortgagees an extant security that became enforceable when the property came into existence (ibid 373–74) and Swinfen Eady LJ refers to the mortgage security remaining in force and becoming effective when the expectancy vested (ibid 357). See also *Performing Right Society v B4U Network (Europe) Ltd* [2013] EWCA Civ 1236, [2014] Bus LR 207 [26]; *PK Airfinance SARL v Alpstream AG* [2015] EWCA Civ 1318, [2016] 2 P&CR 2 [138]–[141]; *cf Collyer v Isaacs* (1881) 19 Ch D 342.

'a prospective interest in the distributive share in question'.[21] The appeal of this quasi-proprietary feature of mortgages and charges over future assets, no doubt, owes much to the smooth way in which equity allows future assets to be captured by a charge as soon as they come into existence. In Maitland's words:

> And so lawyers easily slipped into the way of saying that in equity one could make an assignment of goods hereafter to be acquired though one could not do so at law. This was a compendious way of putting the matter and was not likely to deceive any equity lawyer.[22]

There is no need for a separate transfer as each one becomes extant for that would have spelt the death of future assets financing. Instead, using the doctrine of specific performance in an instrumental, rather than discretionary, way, equity deems the asset to be captured automatically by the charge. Value having previously been given by the creditor, no more needs to be done to fill out the charge.[23] In equity, a promise to give a charge is as good as a charge provided consideration is given for it,[24] so that in a plausible sense the charge is anticipated from the moment of the binding promise. Binding promises, automatically enforced, collapse the future into the present.[25]

It is not always clear whether property is extant or future in character.[26] A debt payable in the future is a present right,[27] even if it is subject to possible deductions that have yet to be calculated.[28] Share dividends yet to be declared are not present property—the directors have a discretion in the matter, not curtailed by company policy in declaring dividends in the past—and interest on a loan payable in the future is also future property in those cases where the debtor may have the right to accelerate payment and thus foreclose the accrual of interest.[29] It is arguable, nevertheless, that the right to a dividend could not be said to have vested but that the right to interest was in existence though liable to be divested.[30] Finally, any difficulties we might still have in respect of charges over future property can be disposed

[21] *Re Lind* [1915] 1 Ch 744, 758.

[22] FW Maitland (eds AH Chaytor and WJ Whittaker) *Equity* (Cambridge, CUP, 1910) 153.

[23] *Tailby v Official Receiver* (1888) 13 App Cas 523; *Re Clarke* (n 4) 352: 'In the present case the contract is not wholly executory. The mortgagee has performed his part of it by advancing his money on the faith of it, and the principle that damages are a sufficient remedy does not apply'. See also *Holroyd v Marshall* (1862) 10 HLC 191; *Palette's Shoes Pty Ltd v Krohn* (1937) 58 CLR 1, 26–27 (Dixon J); *Norman* (n 5) (Windeyer J).

[24] See *Re Ellenborough* [1903] 1 Ch 697.

[25] In a similar way, it has been said that there can be a statutory assignment under the Law of Property Act 1925 s 136 when written notice of the assignment is given, even though the notice refers to debts not yet due and can therefore only be notice of a contract to assign: see *Jones v Humphreys* [1910] 1 KB 10, 13: 'I think there is no doubt that an absolute assignment of future debts may be a good assignment for the purposes of the section'; *Cottage Club Estates Ltd v Woodside Estates (Amersham) Ltd* [1928] 2 KB 463, 467.

[26] See also n 5.

[27] And is treated as such for the purpose of legal set-off.

[28] *G&T Earle (1926) Ltd v Hemsworth Rural District Council* (1928) 44 TLR 758.

[29] *Norman* (n 5).

[30] There was a bare majority in the court in *Norman* (n 5) on the interest point.

of, almost by sleight of hand, by taking a different view of what constitutes the subject matter of a disposition. It is one thing to assign future royalty payments; it is another to assign a share of a present right to receive royalty payments in the future. The former is future property; the latter is existing property. The right to receive royalties is the tree and the royalty payments themselves, dependent upon the contingent extent to which a licence to exploit an invention might be taken up, the fruits of that tree.[31]

III. Portions and Quantities: Legal Interests

A correct identification of what constitutes the subject matter of a disposition has proven also to be important when it comes to sale of goods transactions and declarations of trust, though in different ways.[32] In the case of sale of goods, the fundamental rule for the passing of property is that the joint intention of the parties is the paramount consideration.[33] This intention is presumptively found for unascertained goods when goods are unconditionally appropriated to the contract by one party (usually the seller) with the assent of the other.[34] Sale and trust diverge here in that a seller's manifest intention or even promise to pass the property, unilaterally evidenced or expressed, does not have proprietary effect, whereas a unilateral declaration of trust does. The governing rule of intention in sale of goods law cannot however prevail if the goods that are the subject matter of the sale have never been ascertained.[35] Until the reforms of the mid-1990s,[36] this rule captured all unascertained goods, whether they were generic goods of no stated source or provenance, or stipulated but unseparated quantities of goods contained in a larger, identified bulk. The property, therefore, in six bottles to be drawn from a specified case could not pass before the particular six bottles had been ascertained in the sense of being identified, typically by a physical act that amounted to earmarking (labelling or setting aside) the six bottles.[37] No intention on the part

[31] *Shepherd v Federal Commissioner of Taxation* (1965) 113 CLR 385.

[32] Nevertheless, a case failing as a declaration of trust may equally be cited as concerning goods that were never ascertained for the purpose of the passing property: *Re London Wine Co Ltd* [1986] PCC 121.

[33] Sale of Goods Act 1979, s 17 (Sale of Goods Act).

[34] ibid s 18, Rule 5.

[35] ibid s 16.

[36] Inserting Sale of Goods Act ss 20A-B and introducing and amending definitions in s 61(1).

[37] In a case involving the sale of metals stored in warehouses, lot numbers in warehouse receipts were held to be insufficient to amount to a system of identification that constituted ascertainment of the goods: *RBG Resources Plc v Banque Cantonale Vaudoise* [2004] 3 SLR(R) 421. It was not enough, moreover, that the warehouse manager had indicated to the buyer the places in the warehouse where the metals were stored given that the manager was aware that the seller did not have sufficient metals to carry out all of its transactions. There is some evidence that the warehouse manager was acting in collusion with the seller and without authority from the warehouse.

of seller and buyer to contrary effect could allow for the passing of property in unascertained goods, which is why legislation was required to alter the position, though such legislation went on to say that it was subject to any contrary agreement between buyer and seller.[38]

Although the sale of a share of goods has been characterised as the sale of intangible property,[39] it was never entirely clear prior to the 1990s reforms that a sale of a share of goods fell outside the Sale of Goods Act. Indeed, the Act made provision for sales between one part owner and another.[40] Whether a contract for the sale of a share was otherwise in or outside the Act prior to the reforms, the ascertainment bar to the passing of property seems not to have prevented the property in that share from passing once the goods had been identified to the contract. The position is clearer now because the Act has been amended to include in the definition of goods 'an undivided share in goods'.[41] Moreover, specific goods are now defined so as to include 'an undivided share, specified as a fraction or percentage, of goods identified and agreed upon'.[42] This means that the ascertainment bar to the passing of property cannot apply to the sale of a share of specific goods, because that bar applies only where the contract is for the sale of unascertained goods. Oddly, however, the Act in its present form may have imposed a permanent bar to the passing of property where the contract is for a share in future goods, for example, a ship yet to be built,[43] if something that has no physical existence at the contract date cannot be described as goods 'identified and agreed on at the time [the] contract of sale is made': a contract for the sale of the first 20 widgets to come off a manufacturing seller's production line next Monday may for this reason not be a contract for specific goods. The contract for the sale of a share in a future ship is now clearly a sale of goods contract and so may be subject to the bar on the passing of property in unascertained goods. This surely is not what Parliament intended.

As for a contract for the sale of a specified quantity of goods, there have occurred in the past numerous failed attempts to overcome the rule that the property in unascertained goods was incapable of passing, even where the source of such goods could be identified with a degree of precision. One such failed attempt concerned rights arising by way of tenancy in common. As a general proposition, it seems correct to say that outside legislative intervention to which we shall soon turn, tenancy in common has proved less effective in the creation of property

[38] But the legislation, in providing for contrary intention, is concerned with a disapplying intention, and not with an intention to give a proprietary right in a bulk where the terms of the legislation themselves do not capture the case (eg, where the buyer has not paid).

[39] *Re Sugar Properties (Derisley Wood) Ltd* [1988] BCLC 146.

[40] Sale of Goods Act, s 2(2).

[41] ibid s 61(1).

[42] ibid.

[43] This is because a contract of this type can no longer be claimed to fall outside the Sale of Goods Act and because the provisions enacted for the passing of a part interest in a specified bulk of unascertained goods apply only if the contract is for a specified *quantity* of goods.

rights[44] than it has when it comes to the survival of pre-existing property rights.[45] As a result of statutory reforms dating from the mid-1990s, the position now is that, provided such goods are to come from an 'identified bulk', the contract is in effect recharacterised as a contract for the sale of a share (or part interest) in that bulk. The buyer acquires, commensurately with any payment made for the goods, an interest in common (as opposed to a joint interest) with other parties.[46] The starting point is that the normal rules concerning tenancy in common at common law should apply,[47] but this is subject to the following two qualifications. The first concerns a measure of doubt about whether and to what extent those rules are modified for a seller who retains an interest in the bulk. The question here is whether, in cases where the bulk shrinks, that seller's interest should abate first before the same process begins to affect the buyers.[48] For reasons largely to do with risk, falling outside the scope of that paper, the normal rule of rateable abatement between co-owners should apply.[49] The second qualification concerns an extraordinary provision, for which no justification apart from a yearning for legal simplicity has ever been advanced, that would allow a co-owner to recover his contractual share in full from a bailee, without sanction, even though this exceeds his shrunken proprietary share.[50]

Just as exigibility demands that property must be identified as the source of a property right, so the Sale of Goods Act as amended requires that the bulk be identified. The Act defines a bulk as 'a mass or collection of goods of the same kind … contained in a defined space or area' and requires also that the bulk consist of fungible goods, so that 'any goods in the bulk are interchangeable with any other good therein of the same number or quantity'. That bulk, moreover, must be

[44] eg *Laurie and Morewood v Dudin and Sons* [1926] 1 KB 223.

[45] *Re Stapylton Fletcher Ltd* [1994] 1 WLR 1181 and mixture cases such as *Spence v Union Marine Insurance Co Ltd* (1868) LR 3 CP 427. A particularly interesting case is *Mercer v Craven Grain Storage Ltd* [1994] CLC 28, an interlocutory appeal in the House of Lords. On what looked like the physical equivalent of a 'repo' transaction, the deposit of grain in bulk, where one possible outcome was that an equivalent quantity would be redelivered to the depositor, was held to give rise to a tenancy in common right of the depositor in that bulk.

[46] Sale of Goods Act, s 20A.

[47] One difference between a share in a bulk of say, grain, and a share in a ship or a racehorse is that the former may be partitioned, with each co-owner extracting his share, whereas the latter cannot be broken up in this way.

[48] Sale of Goods Act, s 20A(4): 'Where the aggregate of the undivided shares of buyers in a bulk … would at any time exceed the whole of the bulk at that time, the undivided share in the bulk of each buyer shall be reduced proportionately so that the aggregate of the undivided shares is equal to the whole bulk'.

[49] Another reading of s 20A(4), which jars with established rules of transfer of risk, would have the seller's interest abate first, on the ground that abatement of buyers' interest only begins once their combined proprietary shares amount to less than the bulk. But the seller may also be a buyer from a seller further up the chain, which complicates matters. Furthermore, if s 20A(4) is supposed to have the seller's interest abate first, it is not clear in its purport: legislation should have to pass a high standard of clarity if it is to be given expropriatory effect. See further M Bridge, *The Sale of Goods*, 3rd edn (Oxford, OUP, 2014) para 3.56.

[50] Sale of Goods Act, s 20B.

'identified either in the contract or by subsequent agreement between the parties'. The only reported case on an identified bulk under this legislation is the Singapore case of *RBG Resources Plc v Banque Cantonale Vaudoise*,[51] where a representative of the buyer visited the offices of the Singapore warehouse company that the seller had named as the warehouse keeper. Bearing warehouse receipts (for delivery 'In warehouse Singapore') for the metals that were the subject of the sale contract, he was then directed to the particular warehouse in Singapore said to contain the metals. The manager of the third-party warehouse indicated to the representative the places in the warehouse where these metals were being stored. There was an overt issue in the case that concerned the honesty of the manager, and a less clear issue about whether the manager had the authority to make statements that bound his employer or even the seller, apart from which the court's conclusion that the bulk had not been identified by agreement seems doubtful. The court was on surer ground when it concluded that an identified bulk could not simply be equated with a seller's general trading stock, though that stock surely could constitute a bulk if sufficiently identified as the source of the buyer's goods by reference to a defined place or area where the totality of the stock is kept. If there is a difficulty with this conclusion, it is because trading stock on land is dynamic and shifting, whereas a quantity of goods locked into a dry bulk carrier at sea is fixed.

The conclusion we arrive at is that a buyer cannot claim property rights in goods unless there has occurred a sufficient identification of the goods, or of the source of the goods, to the contract. As for the source, it must be a 'defined space or area', such as a specific ship[52] or warehouse. A contract for soya beans shipped in a given month from a port or ports in the Gulf of Mexico will not satisfy the requirement of a defined space or area. There will be many such shipments and nothing yet to identify the particular shipment from which the buyer will receive its goods. Even if the seller were to make or adopt only one shipment in the stated month, the maxim *id certum est quod certum reddi potest* would not avail the buyer, if only because of the absence of any agreement identifying that particular shipment as the sole source of the goods. A final point concerns whether any constraint in the contract on the source from which the seller might supply the goods should be material in determining whether there is an identified bulk. In *Re London Wine Co Ltd*,[53] Oliver J, in a case predating the above statutory changes, was not prepared to interpret a contract for the sale of wine 'lying in bond' as 'providing an identifying label for the mass from which the goods were to be selected', since the seller 'remained free to fulfil the contracts to its various purchasers from any source'. This is surely too narrow a reading of the contract and hence far enough from the spirit of the statutory changes that it ought to play no part in their interpretation.

[51] *RBG Resources Plc v Banque Cantonale Vaudoise* [2004] 3 SLR(R) 421 (applying identical Singapore statutory provisions).

[52] There may be some difficulty in determining whether large bulk carrier with more than one hold is a sufficiently defined space or area: Bridge (n 49) para 3.53.

[53] *Re London Wine* (n 32).

IV. Portions and Quantities: Trust Interests

The issue of identification is expressed in different language when it comes to a declaration of trust. Here, the question is whether the subject matter of the trust is sufficiently certain for the trust to be properly constituted. *Re Goldcorp Exchange Ltd*[54] is one of a series of cases where a buyer who had paid for goods found that there were no goods available for delivery.[55] In that case, one category of claimants had purchased unascertained bullion from a seller which the seller then undertook to store on their behalf on an unallocated basis. The claimants were assured that 'your' bullion was being stored on 'your' behalf free of charge and that they could withdraw it on giving seven days' notice. They each received a certificate of ownership. Had the seller declared a trust of such bullion answering the description that it possessed at the time it made these statements or that later came into its possession? In the court's view, the statements of the seller did not amount to a declaration of trust of their existing stock for that would have inhibited any dealings with that stock. Apart from its question-begging character, the difficulty presented by this conclusion is that it bears on the inward state of the seller's mind and not on the way that the seller's words might have been interpreted by the claimants. There is no good reason why a declaration of trust should be determined by subjective means when a statement of contractual intent is objectively interpreted.[56] Nevertheless, in holding that the various sales were not ex-bulk, the court added that each claimant could not have contemplated that his rights would be defined according to whatever bullion of the contract description the seller had in stock at the relevant time, in combination with the numbers of other claimants with a similar claim to that same stock. One response here is to ask why this could not have been contemplated by the claimants: at the time of the litigation they were adamantly of the view that they did. The rhetoric of the court tends towards the case having an inevitable outcome when a cold appreciation of the facts yields considerably less certainty. The court went on to hold that no trust could attach to incoming stock since there would have had to be a separated bulk as the sole source from which the buyers' claims should be satisfied. The mixing of trading stock and

[54] *Re Goldcorp* (n 2).

[55] The issue had presented itself in *Re Wait* [1927] 1 Ch 606, where the buyer of 500 tons of grain on board a named ship paid before the 500 tons were separated from bulk. The core of the buyer's claim was that the buyer had by operation of law an equitable lien over a quantity of 530 tons on that ship remaining with the seller and previously represented by a bill of lading for 1,000 tons to the order of the seller.

[56] 'A settlor must, of course, possess the necessary intention to create a trust, but his subjective intentions are irrelevant. If he enters into arrangements which have the effect of creating a trust, it is not necessary that he should appreciate that they do so; it is sufficient that he intends to enter into them': *Twinsectra Ltd v Yardley* [2002] UKHL 12, [2002] 2 AC 164, 185 (Lord Millett); see also *Byrnes v Kendle* [2011] HCA 26, 243 CLR 253, [54]–[59].

stored bullion was fatal to the trust claim and there is even some suggestion in the case that there should have been individual storages of each claimant's entitlement for the trust argument to succeed.[57] I shall return to this issue of segregation which, it is submitted, is concerned more with an intention to create a trust than with a requirement of certainty of subject matter.

In *Re London Wine Co*, the trust argument of wine investors also failed notwithstanding statements made by the seller acknowledging investors' ownership of wines in the seller's possession and the issue of certificates of ownership, together with the levying of storage charges. It was fatal to the investors' claims that these were based on the numbers of bottles purchased rather than upon a percentage of the type of stock consisting of those bottles. There had to be a 'homogeneous *whole*'[58] and what constituted a homogeneous whole depended upon the nature of the property. In explaining why there was no trust of individual investors' wines, Oliver J said:

> I appreciate the point taken that the subject matter is a part of a homogeneous mass so that specific identity is of as little as importance as it is, for instance, in the case of money. Nevertheless, as it seems to me, to create a trust it must be possible to ascertain with certainty not only what the interest of the beneficiary is to be but to what property it is to attach.[59]

The judge went on to cite the example of a farmer declaring himself a trustee of two unidentified sheep, concluding that this would not amount to an effective declaration of trust even if there were a flock of sheep out of which the trust interest could be satisfied. But he also went on to say that the farmer might declare himself a trustee of 'a specified proportion of his whole flock', giving rise in this way to an equitable tenancy in common between himself and the named beneficiary. Such an intention would not, however, be inferred from a declaration that a number of sheep were to be held on trust.[60]

The distinction made by Oliver J and the question of identification presented themselves again in controversial circumstances in *Hunter v Moss*.[61] This case began with a finding of fact that a settlor had informally constituted himself trustee of 5 per cent in the issued share capital of a company (which consisted of 1,000 certificated shares of which the settlor held 950). When a motion was entertained by the trial judge to raise a point not mentioned at trial, namely, the issue of certainty of the subject matter of the trust, the issue somehow was transformed into something rather different, namely, whether the settlor had succeeded in creating

57 *Re Goldcorp* (n 2) 90. This would have grave implications for investors in securities held in a pooled account.

58 *Re London Wine* (n 32) 136 (original emphasis).

59 ibid 137.

60 ibid.

61 *Hunter v Moss* [1993] 1 WLR 934; [1994] 1 WLR 452. See *White v Shortall* [2006] NSWSC 1379 for a similar conclusion, noting that the point had been left open in *Herdegen v Federal Commissioner of Taxation* (1988) 84 ALR 271, and also at [153] *et seq* for a lengthy treatment of responses to *Hunter*.

a trust over 50 of his 950 shares. The distinction between these two cases was further blurred in the Court of Appeal:

> The first issue that arises in this appeal is that the conclusion that the defendant had declared himself trustee for the plaintiff of 50 shares in [the company], being 5 per cent of the share capital of that company, is challenged.[62]

The reforms to the Sale of Goods Act discussed above were founded on a fundamental distinction drawn between the sale of an unseparated share or percentage of an identified bulk and the sale of a stated quantity of goods contained in a larger, identified bulk, a distinction not clearly taken in *Hunter v Moss*. Treating it, as the courts did, as a case of a trust of 50 shares, the question raised is how the case can be distinguished from *Re London Wine Co Ltd*.

The judge at first instance made much of the difference between chattels and shares, the latter having a fungible character denied to chattels, and distinguished *Re London Wine Co Ltd* so far as it concerned the creation of a tenancy in common of a bulk of bottles of wine.[63] The distinction is proper enough when it comes to a flock of sheep—some are male and some female, some young and some old, and so on—but it surely overstates the individuality of bottles of wine, say, a 2001 Cornas produced by a pre-eminent named grower. For the purposes of the amendments to the Sale of Goods Act, it is highly unlikely that the idiosyncratic character of individual bottles would prevent there from existing an identified bulk consisting of 'a mass or collection of goods of the same kind which … is such that any goods in the bulk are interchangeable with any other goods therein of the same number or quantity'. There is nothing in the individual aspect of a bottle of such wine to show that it is corked when another bottle is not, or has cellared better than another bottle, and so on. The person making the selection has nothing to go on in determining whether to pick up one bottle as opposed to another. Individual bottles of the same wine are fungible when individual sheep, unless cloned, are not.[64] A court in another case had no difficulty in finding a legal tenancy in common when ascertained investors' wines were pooled in a common stock,[65] so there is no good reason why an equitable tenancy in common should be any different, nor any reason why tenancy in common principles should be applied differently according to whether an interest is being created or instead preserved out of an earlier, plenary property entitlement.

[62] [1994] 1 WLR 452, 454 (Dillon LJ). This carries through into *Re Harvard Securities Ltd* [1997] 2 BCLC 369, 383, a case dealing with a claimed entitlement to a stipulated number of shares, where reference is made to a 'part of a holding of chattels and [a] part of a debt or fund', no distinction being drawn between number and proportion.

[63] The same justification is used in *Re Harvard* (ibid 383) to distinguish that part of Oliver J's judgment in *Re London Wine* (n 32).

[64] This is a reason to doubt Oliver J's conclusion in *Re London Wine* (n 32) that there can be a trust of a proportion of a flock of sheep.

[65] *Re Stapylton* (n 45).

The cursory judgment of the Court of Appeal in *Hunter v Moss*[66] stated briefly, and without explaining why, that a distinction existed between an appropriation of chattels and the passing of property therein, and a declaration of trust, but rather more needs to be said to define the fields of the distinction and to justify that distinction. To start with, appropriation is a word of doubtful import in sale of goods transactions. It may mean simply ascertainment or identification,[67] or it might mean the type of physical conduct that puts it out of the seller's power to change his mind and thus presumptively passes the property in goods,[68] usually an event that follows on from ascertainment. The Court seems, however, to be treating appropriation to mean identification, the latter being a more proper word for dealing with bulks. It is the very fact that something has not yet been extracted from a bulk—that is, appropriated from it—that gives rise to the question whether a transaction can nevertheless have proprietary effect. When it comes to the identification of property to a transaction, this is a matter of observable fact that ought not to call for any difference in principle between equitable and common law powers of observation. Either there is a fungible bulk or there is not. A similar unexplained distinction is made in the briefest of terms in the case between a trust and a charge.[69] Given that a charge is an encumbrance and not a transfer, so that it extends to the whole of a bulk or fund and not to an unseparated part, this is correct but it should have been said why this was the case. There is, however, a persuasive way in which the outcome can be justified, though it comes close to obliterating the distinction between a share and a quantity. A trust of 50 out of 950 shares in effect gives rise to a trust for two beneficiaries, the intended disponee and the settlor himself, beneficially sharing the bulk in different proportions. In the words of an Australian judge, guided by the notion of a fund:

> It is because the trust is construed of the entire shareholding of the company that it is not necessary for the [disponee] to be able to point to some particular share and be able to say, '*That share is mine*'.[70]

Hunter v Moss has been criticised too on the ground that it creates difficulties for the application of trust principles, such as liability for breach of trust, when it can hardly be known which precisely are the assets held on trust for the declared beneficiary.[71] It creates difficulties too when the trustee comes to dispose of other

[66] Rather, the judgment of Dillon LJ in which Mann and Hirst LJJ concurred. See D Hayton, 'Uncertainty of Subject-Matter of Trusts' (1994) 110 *LQR* 335 and the searching criticism of the reasoning in the case in *White* (n 61) [166]–[192].

[67] See *Wait v Baker* (1848) 2 Ex 1.

[68] *Carlos Federspiel & Co SA v Charles Twigg & Co Ltd* [1957] 1 Lloyd's Rep 240.

[69] See the criticism of this passage in *White* (n 61) [190].

[70] *White* (n 61) [212] (Campbell J). But the Court also notes at [216] that fund-based reasoning cannot apply in the case of something, like a horse, that cannot be partitioned.

[71] A problem that can be overstated. See *Re International Contract Co, Ind's Case* (1872) 7 Ch App 485, a case concerning a share transfer where the wrong identifying numbers had been inserted in the transfer but the transfer was not vitiated by the error. According to Mellish LJ at 487: 'I think the numbers of the shares are simply directory for the purposes of enabling the title of the particular persons to be traced; but that one share, an incorporeal right to a certain portion of the profits of the company, is the same as the other, and that share No 1 is not distinguishable from share No 2 in the same way as a grey horse is distinguishable from a black horse'.

parts of the same bulk. Is the trustee selling out of the remainder or selling the same part again?[72] Just as it is important to distinguish between the application of trusts to commercial and to family cases, so too should it be remembered that there are different types of trust cutting across this contextual distinction. A bare trust would not carry responsibility for the management and investment of trust assets that would exist in the case of a more intensive trust. Furthermore, it is perfectly possible for the bare legal interest and the entire equitable interest to be vested in different persons, without there being a trust relationship between them.[73] The problem of whether an unseparated quantity out of a bulk satisfies the certainty requirement of a trust goes away when a share of the bulk is substituted for a number. Even though the distinction between these two was blurred in *Hunter v Moss*, and even though a disposition of a share of chattels may make commercial sense in only a limited number of cases,[74] it is a vital distinction to draw, even though the issues concerning a trustee's responsibilities and repeat dispositions out of the bulk still remain to be solved. Had the decision been expressed in terms of an agreed portion of the 950-share holding of the settlor, as the initial finding of fact accepted, the case should not have come in for the criticism that it received for recognising a trust of 50 unidentified shares in that larger holding.[75]

A final point presented by *Hunter v Moss* concerns again the distinction between number and portion. So far as the beneficiary was claiming 50 shares, what did this mean? Even given the character of the shares as certificated, share certificates are not negotiable documents[76] and are merely evidence of ownership of the shares. They are presented to the company along with transfer forms in order that changes in the legal ownership might be recorded on the register of members. It is a difficult matter to discern what ownership of shares means, but a share as its very name signifies is a share in something else, and the argument has been pressed that shares in multiple numbers are but a multiple share of the company itself.[77] Even if those share certificates are numbered, the characterisation of their nature is not affected. By this reasoning, the owner of 500 shares in a company with 10,000

[72] See S Worthington, 'Sorting Out Ownership Interests in a Bulk: Gifts, Sales and Trusts' [1999] *Journal of Business Law* 1. In *White* (n 61) [220], the court saw a trustee as being free to deal with the surplus in excess of the quantity of unnumbered shares in the larger bulk.

[73] *Westdeutsche Landesbank Girozentrale v Islington London Borough Council* [1996] AC 669, 706–07 (Lord Browne-Wilkinson, citing the examples of the acquisition of title to land by estoppel and the action for the redemption of mortgaged property by a mortgagee (*scil* mortgagor) who has repaid the mortgage debt.

[74] A contract to sell a share in a ship or a racehorse is one thing, but an unlikely commercial proposition is a contract to sell a share in a bulk shipment of soya beans. Given the changes inaugurated by the Sale of Goods Act s 20A, the buyer of goods who has paid for, say, 10,000 tonnes of soya beans in an identified bulk, will under a sub-sale contract for the same quantity transfer an interest in common to a paying sub-buyer.

[75] In fact, all the shares were sold by the time of the action, hence the would-be beneficiary was claiming only a share of the money proceeds.

[76] *Colonial Bank v Cady* (1890) 15 App Cas 267; *MCC Proceeds Inc v Lehman Brothers International (Europe)* [1998] 4 All ER 675.

[77] A point made firmly in R Goode, 'Are Intangible Assets Fungible?' [2003] *Lloyd's Maritime and Commercial Law Quarterly* 379.

issued shares owns 5 per cent of the company and a disponee of 500 shares does not receive 500 shares as such—for that confuses the property interest with the evidential paper—but a divisible, intangible interest in the company measured as 5 per cent.

Identification has been held to play a very diminished role in what we might call statutory trusts. A court minded to do so can ride roughshod over the identification requirement, finding a trust when there is no more than a promise or a duty to appropriate property to a trust, if the legislation is thought to require it. This is what occurred in *Lehman Brothers International (Europe) Ltd v CRC Credit Fund Ltd*.[78] A prime broker, acting in breach of its statutory duty by retaining client moneys and securities in its general trading account instead of transferring them to a pooled client account,[79] was treated for the purpose of an insolvency distribution as having done what it ought to have done, so that clients whose assets had not been so treated were held entitled to participate in the pooled account.[80] The legislative provisions in question were generously interpreted in favour of the wronged clients by reference to EU Directives striving for a high degree of client protection in the financial markets. The strains of the Lehman Brothers insolvency and the perceived need to prop up the financial system amounted to a significant stress test for proprietary principles.[81] The ability of a court in common law systems to treat legislation as an excrescence rather than an integral part of a legal system permits a case of this sort to be dealt with in the non-principled way that it was, secure from any fears that the reasoning in the case will infect non-statutory trusts.

The identification of trust property, as stated above, and the intention to create a trust, are separate matters. Nevertheless, this is often more a matter of analytical than practical separation since the two issues in fact will often run into each other.[82] It is well known that, in order to declare a trust, it is not necessary to use explicit trust language. Commercial imperatives may persuade a court to infer a trust from language that does not obviously bespeak trust.[83] This has been demonstrated in a particular way in other Lehman's litigation[84] not concerning the

[78] *Lehman Brothers International (Europe) Ltd v CRC Credit Fund Ltd* [2012] UKSC 6, [2012] 3 All ER 1.

[79] The rules required the firm either to put client moneys directly into a segregated client account or, having first put them into a house account, to transfer them to a segregated client account on a daily basis. The prime broker took neither of these actions.

[80] *cf Vintage Bullion DMCC v Chay Fook Yuen* [2016] SGCA 49 [55]–[56] (Singapore statutory trust arising only when client moneys had been segregated).

[81] See M Bridge and J Braithwaite, 'Private Law and Financial Crises' (2013) 13 *Journal of Corporate Law Studies* 361.

[82] See the discussion above of *Re Goldcorp* (nn 2, 54).

[83] eg *Don King Productions Inc v Warren* [2000] Ch 291.

[84] A broad label since other financial institutions were involved in the welter of case law following the financial crisis of 2008.

statutory trust of client assets. Acting as prime brokers and as lenders, a Lehman's (or other) entity from time to time managed client assets, converting them to cash and replacing them with other assets at intervals. The arrangement between the entity and its clients made no explicit mention of a trust but referred instead to 'custody' and 'custodian' and to assets that 'belong to the Counterparty [client]'. Under the terms of a security collateral arrangement, the entity in question was granted a right of hypothecation (or use) so that it might for its own purposes remove assets from an account and replace them at a subsequent date. These purposes were personal to the entity: it might use them to manage a short position, or to provide margin for a clearing house, or to transfer them on under a stock lending agreement. In so doing, it was not required to seek the prior permission of its client or to account to the client for the gains resulting from its activities. Despite this wide-ranging freedom,[85] as well as the possibility that an account might be emptied in this way from time to time, courts were prepared to conclude that the arrangement in question amounted to a trust and satisfied the requirements of a trust.[86] This conclusion comes close to a proposition that, in extreme financial circumstances, a court will be prepared to conjure a trust out of thin air and prompts the following question: does the arrogation to a trustee of an extreme freedom to deal beneficially with trust assets tend towards negativing any intention to create a trust, or is it so inconsistent with a trust that a trust cannot be constituted whatever the intention of the parties may be? Are assets really identified to a trust as trust property if the so-called trustee is given such a wide-ranging personal freedom? Can a trust be said to exist when it is fully depleted at intervals? If the Lehman's litigation testifies to anything, it is that 'diseases desperate grown by desperate appliance are relieved or not at all'. At the very least, it has to be asked whether these cases should be used as a guide in the application of trust principles, not merely in domestic arrangements but also in less esoteric commercial matters.

The next question under this heading concerns the segregation of trust property. This is more than just a matter of identification: it concerns whether the trust property should not merely be part of an identified bulk but should actually be isolated, that is, be separated from any bulk. Here again, the boundary between identification and intention falls to be considered. In *Henry v Hammond*, Channell J said:

> It is clear that if the terms upon which the person receives the money are that he is bound to keep it separate, either in a bank or elsewhere, and to hand that money so kept as a separate fund to the person entitled to it, then he is a trustee of that money and must hand it over to the person who is his cestui que trust. If, on the other hand, he is not

[85] See *Lomas v RAB Market Cycles (Master) Fund Ltd* [2009] EWHC 2914 (Ch).

[86] *Re Lehman Brothers International (Europe)* [2011] EWCA Civ 1544 [68], [2012] BCLC 151. *cf* Slade J in *Re Bond Worth Ltd* [1980] Ch 228, 261: 'W]here an alleged trustee has the right to mix tangible assets or moneys with his own other assets or moneys and to deal with them as he pleases, this is incompatible with the existence of a presently subsisting fiduciary relationship in regard to such particular assets or moneys'.

> bound to keep the money separate, but is entitled to mix it with his own money and deal with it as he pleases, and when called upon to hand over an equivalent sum of money, … he is not a trustee of the money, but merely a debtor.[87]

Apart from the modern orthodoxy that a relationship of trust and debt can coexist between two persons,[88] this dictum shows how far the Lehman's cases have strained the boundaries of trust. Subject to the qualification of the payee being free to deal with the money as he pleases, the passage comes close to requiring an agreed segregation of assets if a trust is to be properly constituted. This, however, is not the case.[89] If a trust is supposedly created, by agreement or otherwise, the absence of a segregation requirement goes to the question of intention to create a trust,[90] always provided that a bulk containing the trust assets can be identified.[91] If no countervailing factors are present, the absence of a prohibition against mixing tends towards a finding that no trust is created[92] but it will not negative explicit trust language.[93] Nor should it necessarily negative the clear implication of a trust if the relationship between the parties points strongly towards a trust.[94] That it is a matter of intention rather than identification may be tested according to 'whether, immediately after the purported declaration of trust, the court could, if asked, make an order for the execution of the purported trust'.[95] There is no prohibition on a trustee being also one of the beneficiaries of a trust,[96] so long as the trustee is not the sole beneficiary, for in that case there would be a merger of legal and beneficial interests.[97]

[87] *Henry v Hammond* [1913] 2 KB 515, 521 (Channell J).

[88] *Barclays Bank Ltd v Quistclose Investments Ltd* [1970] AC 567. This applies to secured creditors and trustees too: *Re Lehman Brothers* (n 86).

[89] See *White* (n 61).

[90] *Re Nanwa Gold Mines* [1955] 1 WLR 1080; *Hinckley Singapore Trading Pte Ltd v Sogo Department Stores (S) Pte Ltd* [2001] 4 SLR 154. But see *Vintage Bullion* (n 80) [61]–[62] (segregation, though not sufficient for the inference of an express trust, was in this case necessary for the trust to be properly constituted since intention alone was not sufficient).

[91] A trust of segregated assets would not be vitiated by a later admixture of the trustee's own assets: *Vintage Bullion* (n 80) [52] (trustee adding its own assets to client accounts to avert the risk of client undermargining).

[92] *Re Clowes (No 2)* [1994] 2 All ER 316, 325. The trial judge in *Hunter* (n 61) 941, restrictively interpreting certain language in *Re Andrabell Ltd* [1984] 3 All ER 407, 415, was firmly of the view that the absence of a segregation requirement did not mean that a trust failed for uncertainty. Similarly, in respect of payment into a bank account, see also *Re Kayford Ltd* [1975] 1 WLR 279, 282.

[93] *Re Lewis's of Leicester Ltd* [1995] 1 BCLC 428; *Associated Alloys Pty Ltd v CAN 001 452 106 Pty Ltd* [2000] HCA 25 [34].

[94] See *Re Fleet Disposal Services Ltd* [1995] BCC 605 (agent entitled to deduct commission and expenses from a trust account into which sale receipts had been paid); *cf Paragon Finance Plc v DB Thakerar & Co* [1999] 1 All ER 400, 416 (where the agent used moneys received as cash flow and was required to account at annual intervals, compared with the five days in *Fleet Disposal*).

[95] *Hunter* (n 61) 945.

[96] See, eg *White* (n 61).

[97] P Watts, 'Some Aspects of the Intersection of the Law of Agency with the Law of Trusts' (ch 2 in this volume), citing *Goodright v Wells* (1781) 2 Doug 771, 778, 99 ER 491; *DKLR Holding Co (No 2) Pty Ltd v Commissioner of Stamp Duties* (1982) 149 CLR 431, 464, 473.

V. Portions and Quantities: Charges

It was stated above that the failure of a claim of property rights could be laid either at the door of an insufficiently defined subject matter of the claim, or attributed instead to the absence of any intention to create property rights. It is understandable in the case of sale of goods and declarations of trust that the emphasis should have been placed on the former approach. In the case of equitable charges, however, which tolerate a degree of vagueness about the day-to-day depth of a chargee's interest in charged property, the main difficulties that have arisen have been due to a lack of clarity in the requisite intention. That said, when the Court of Appeal in *Re Wait*[98] dismissed the claim of a pre-paying buyer to the lion's share of goods (wheat) still in the seller's possession at the critical date, it treated indifferently two proprietary claims made by the buyer: one was that there had occurred an equitable assignment of the 500 tons of wheat claimed by the buyer, where the language of equitable assignment of goods, as opposed to things in action, makes sense only if it is translated into the language of express trust; and the other was that the goods remaining with the seller were subject to an equitable charge or lien (the only difference between the two for present purposes being that the former is consensual and the latter, where it exists, arises by operation of law).

The question whether a transaction amounts to a declaration of trust or instead to an equitable charge has proved to be notoriously vexing, especially in those cases involving unpaid sellers who have by contractual means purportedly succeeded in having the buyer declare itself the trustee of the proceeds of resale or of a part of the proceeds. The practical issue here is whether a court should recharacterise a purported trust as but a charge under another name, so that a failure in the case of a corporate buyer to see to the registration of the charge results in the charge being struck down as void against liquidators, administrators and secured creditors of the buyer.[99] Even if a court were otherwise persuaded to view a transaction as giving rise to a charge and not to a trust, and even though the company charges legislation defines a charge skeletally as including a mortgage,[100] there is no reason why a court might not consider a trust to be a charge for the purposes of the Act, in view of the purposes served by the requirement that charges be registered.[101] This, however, is not a course of action suggested in the case law. English courts have routinely concluded that proceeds trusts of this kind are charges rather than trusts, essentially because of the absence of any true intention that the seller shall have the whole of the proceeds, or because the period of credit under the sale contract

[98] *Re Wait* (n 55).

[99] Companies Act 2006, ss 859A *et seq.*

[100] ibid s 859A(7).

[101] The majority judgment in the Australian High Court in *Associated Alloys* (n 93) assumes that once a transaction has been classified as a trust it therefore cannot be a charge under company charges legislation.

containing the clause does not match the period of credit allowed by the buyer to the sub-buyer in the follow-on sale, or because the buyer is at liberty to pay the seller from a source other than the sub-sale proceeds, in which last case the buyer's supposed duty to account for the proceeds as trustee falls away.[102]

Nevertheless, in *Associated Alloys Pty Ltd v CAN 001 452 106 Pty Ltd*,[103] a majority of the Australian High Court concluded that a contractual clause, according to which a buyer declared itself trustee of such share of the money proceeds of a sub-sale as represented the indebtedness of buyer to seller at the date of their receipt, gave rise to a trust and not a charge. As a matter of construction, the difference between a charge and a trust can be difficult to draw, but there was no ambiguity in the language in this case, which spoke explicitly of a trust.[104] Consequently, resort did not have to be made to any implied intention that a trust arise, which might have presented difficulties for the seller given the absence of any requirement that the proceeds be segregated. The presence of express language meant that the question depended squarely on whether the certainty of subject matter condition, required of a trust, had been met, more particularly, whether the defined part of the proceeds of the sub-sale had been in part sufficiently identified to pay the debt owed by the buyer. And this was an issue that simply was not addressed by the majority judgment, since no reference at all was made to the payment cycle or to the defeasance of the trust on payment being made from a non-trust source.[105] Moreover, the need to identify a source, even a mixed source, identified to the trust for payment should have been fatal: the trust settled on the 'undifferentiated finances' of the buyer.[106] A provision in a construction contract that a site owner will hold a percentage of the agreed price for the works on trust for the contractor in a retention fund will not give rise to a trust of unpaid moneys if no fund is ever created into which the sum in question is paid. In the absence of identifiable trust assets, the supposed trust is but a contractual obligation to set up a trust.[107]

[102] The second point is essentially a different way of stating the third.

[103] *Associated Alloys* (n 93).

[104] ibid [9]: 'In the event that the [Buyer] uses the goods/product in some manufacturing or construction process, then the [Buyer] shall hold such part of the proceeds of such manufacturing or construction process as relates to the goods/product in trust for the [Seller]. Such part shall be deemed to equal in dollar terms the amount owing by the [Buyer] to the [Seller] at the time of the receipt of such proceeds'.

[105] This issue is addressed in the dissenting judgment of Kirby J, who refers to the defeasibility of the trust, the absence of a requirement that the buyer pay as soon as payment under the sub-sale was received and the absence of any obligation on the buyer to pay out of a particular fund. Kirby J concludes at [91] by saying that the clause in question was a charge for registration purposes because in 'substance and reality' it operated as a charge to secure a debt. He also makes a segregation point by referring to the absence of 'a particular identifiable fund'.

[106] A point made by Kirby J (ibid [94]).

[107] *Mac-Jordan* (n 4). Even the concession of the competing bank, which had a floating charge (which later crystallised) over the site owner's assets, that the site owner's contractual obligation was specifically enforceable could not give rise to a proprietary right in property yet to be identified.

Apart from such cases, the question whether a transaction gives rise to a charge, as opposed to no proprietary interest at all, has presented itself in a number of cases where directions or restrictions have been set up that affect a fund or other money source. A good starting point is *Palmer v Carey*,[108] which inverts the segregation question as previously discussed in relation to declarations of trust. It concerned an arrangement between debtor and creditor under which the debtor was put in funds to acquire trading stock. When the stock was sold, the debtor was to pay the moneys received into an account of the creditor at the creditor's bank. The creditor would then deduct the amount he had advanced together with one-third of the debtor's gross profits. When the debtor failed, he still had stock in his hands as well as money proceeds not yet paid into the creditor's bank account. The Privy Council firmly and economically held that the stock purchased with the creditor's funds belonged to the debtor and that the money proceeds belonged to the debtor too. Even though there was an obligation on the debtor's part to pay those proceeds into the creditor's account—and even though in an appropriate case an injunction might issue to prevent the debtor applying the proceeds in any other way—there was no charge on the proceeds in the debtor's possession, but merely a contract to pay them into the creditor's account.

In so holding, the court cited with approval a well-known dictum of Lord Truro in *Rodick v Gandell* that an agreement to pay a debt out of a specific fund coming to the debtor creates a valid equitable charge on the fund.[109] Why then were the moneys in the debtor's hands not a specific fund, given that he was required to pay them into a designated account? And could it not be said that the debtor was to pay the debt out of those funds, albeit in the form of proceeds arising from the payment of those moneys into an account giving rise to a credit balance in favour of the creditor? If the debtor had been required to hand over the money proceeds to the creditor as and when received, it would not have been easy to see what more would have been required, in the absence of express language, to give rise to a charge. Where control of the proceeds is as closely defined as it was in *Palmer v Carey*, it is surely unnecessary to require additional language. The court provides no guidance as to whether the creditor's pitfall was a matter of identification of the assets or of intention; it is unclear which of the two posed the greater difficulty for the creditor. This is one of those cases where they are hard to separate since either or both of the following might be said: there was a lack of clear intention that payment should be made out of the fund, and the subject matter of the purported charge had not been sufficiently identified.

A case more clearly demonstrating the absence of an intention to create a charge is *Flightline Ltd v Edwards*,[110] where an action for damages leading to a worldwide freezing injunction had been commenced against an airline. Pending the

[108] *Palmer v Carey* [1926] AC 703.
[109] *Rodick v Gandell* (1852) 1 De GM & G 763, 777–78.
[110] *Flightline Ltd v Edwards* [2003] EWCA Civ 63, [2003] 1 WLR 1200.

resolution of the case, the injunction was discharged when the airline agreed to pay a stipulated sum into a designated bank account in the joint names of the parties' solicitors. The airline undertook not to withdraw, dispose of, deal with, or encumber the balance in the account by letting it fall below an agreed amount.[111] It was held to be fatal to the existence of a charge for any damages awarded against the airline that there was no positive obligation to discharge the airline's indebtedness out of the account.[112] The problem here for the claimant was more a matter of identification than of intention: no fund had been sufficiently identified as the source of payment. Had the issue been one of trusts, the argument would have been one for a trust of an uncertain amount from a bulk suggestively but not clearly identified.

VI. Estoppel and Property

Suppose that the actions of a disponor fall short of transferring a property interest to a disponee. This may be for various reasons. The property in question might not have been separated from a larger mass so as to give it the necessary identity of a subject of transfer, or a contractually agreed condition for the transfer might not yet have occurred. Notwithstanding this, the disponor gives the disponee to understand that a transfer has successfully occurred. In what circumstances might the disponor be estopped from denying that the transfer has been successfully completed, and how effective in proprietary terms will any such estoppel be?

Let us begin with a striking example of estoppel at work. It arose in the so-called RASCALS case,[113] which concerned a 'repo' scheme for the continuous selling of securities back and forth between a Lehman's hub company in Europe and its various European affiliates. The current litigation concerned the Swiss affiliate with which there was both a manual and an automatic system conducted at frequent intervals between the two companies. In the case of the automatic system, which concerned fixed-income securities, the hub company first purchased securities for the affiliate from the marketplace, extending credit to the affiliate in the form of paying the purchase price for those securities on behalf of the affiliate. An equitable title to those securities vested in the affiliate. At that point, the repo scheme, operating at daily intervals, would come into play with the affiliate selling the

[111] The report does not make it clear how the company could have dealt with the account in the joint names of the parties' solicitors in any of these prohibited ways.

[112] On the question whether an order going beyond the terms of that made in *Flightline* amounted to a security over an account in joint names, see *Ready Rentals Ltd v Ahmed* [2016] EWCH 1996 (Ch) [34]–[39].

[113] *Re Lehman Brothers* (n 86). See also R Stevens, 'Floating Trusts' (ch 5 in this volume). The acronym stands for the Regulation and Administration of Safe Custody and Global Settlement and may be thought to take colour from the type of working environment in which the scheme was conceived.

securities to the hub company under the first leg of the transaction. The price paid by the hub company took the form of a set-off of the amount owed by the affiliate for the initial purchase of the securities from the marketplace. When the securities were sold back to the affiliate, a debit entry was made against the affiliate, which was settled by the first leg of the next repo and so on indefinitely. The problem in this case was that the sale price for the repo transactions was calculated on a mark-to-market basis, with the consequence that the price paid by the hub company for their initial purchase did not match the sale price under the first leg of the repo transactions. Consequently, the offsetting of that initial purchase price against the amount due under the first leg of the repo transaction did not discharge the debt owed to the affiliate under the first leg, so the property in the securities at no point passed to the hub company.[114] Yet, throughout the process, both parties believed that it had done. When the hub company and the affiliate then entered into insolvency proceedings, there was a contest between the creditors of both companies, with no secured creditors present to complicate the outcome.

Had the court stopped at the point where title to the securities never passed to the hub company, the decision would have gone in favour of the Swiss affiliate. This was not due to any uncertainty concerning the subject matter of the various transactions but because the agreed condition for vesting title in the hub company had never occurred. Nevertheless, throughout the process both companies believed that it had and this was sufficient to give rise to an estoppel by active acquiescence so that the affiliate could not deny that title had vested in the hub company. That estoppel bound the liquidator of the affiliate, standing in the shoes of the affiliate itself. The conclusion was surely a generous one. Although it was Swiss, the affiliate had only three directors, all non-executive, and 12 full-time employees, who worked mainly in the London offices of the hub company. Without going so far as to pierce the corporate veil, it is fair to ask whether such an unbalanced relationship involving a captive affiliate can support the estoppel found in the case.

A similar estoppel argument failed in *Re Goldcorp Exchange Ltd*.[115] Given the seller's assertion that it was storing bullion belonging to the claimants, the claimants now maintained that the seller could not now be heard to deny that it had claimants' bullion in its vaults. This argument would of course serve no purpose unless there was indeed bullion in the seller's vaults. But even the existence of such a stock would not have been sufficient since, as the Privy Council observed, a 'bulk [cannot] be conjured into existence ... simply through the chance that the vendor happens to have some goods answering the description of the res vendita in its trading stock at the time of the sale'. Earlier, the court had dismissed the argument that the seller had declared a trust over the bullion in its possession, one reason for this being that the seller could not have intended to create a trust over its general trading stock so as to inhibit any dealings with it. Its business plan

[114] For a fuller account of the transaction, see Bridge and Braithwaite (n 81).
[115] *Re Goldcorp* (n 2).

being to retain only so much bullion as predictably might be needed by investors calling for delivery, the seller throughout behaved more like a bank than a bailee. In the quoted passage, the court merely implies that the seller had not in the first place agreed to appropriate bullion from its existing stock, so that any promise or representation made thereafter to the claimants could not be referenced to an identified bulk.[116] This is confirmed in the court below.[117] If the sales to unallocated claimants had been expressed to come from existing stock, their estoppel argument would have possessed much greater, even compelling, force. And if, on top of that, the seller had unconditionally appropriated separated bullion to each contract, with the presumed assent of the claimants, then the claimants would have had more than an estoppel claim: they would have had rights at law as tenants in common of the commingled mass of bullion.

Supposing, however, that the claimants had succeeded in establishing a proprietary estoppel binding on the seller, they would still have failed against the chargee bank whose floating charge later crystallised. This is because the estoppel does not succeed in passing any property interest.[118] The chargee bank is not in the position of a liquidator or trustee in bankruptcy acting as a 'universal successor' of the insolvent seller. As much as a floating charge sanctions a broad form of activity under the banner of acting in the ordinary course of business,[119] which on one reasonable view of the matter might be taken to include incurring liability in the form of an estoppel with proprietary effect,[120] the court was firm in its conviction that this did not extend to circumscribing the assets available to the chargee bank as a result of incurring a personal liability.

VII. Summary

A number of the issues dealt with in this chapter are common to both equity and the common law. There is, for example, no reason to suppose there is any difference

[116] *Knights v Wiffen* (1870) LR 5 QB 660 was distinguished on dubious grounds as the case of 'a sale ex bulk, or at least it must have been seen as such, for otherwise Lord Blackburn's judgment would have contradicted his treatise' (see fn 1 and accompanying text). In *Knights v Wiffen*, the estoppel in question was between a seller and a sub-buyer, where the buyer never made payment to the seller. No sacks of barley were ever appropriated to the contract of sale and the seller's statement to the sub-buyer made no reference to any identified bulk.

[117] *Sub nom Liggett v Kensington* [1993] 1 NZLR 257, 267: 'Nothing is said about the source of the bullion sold to the customer, so Exchange would be free to draw on its own existing stock or buy'.

[118] See *Re London Wine* (n 32); *cf Eastern Distributors Ltd v Goldring* [1957] 2 QB 600.

[119] Extreme examples are *Re Borax Ltd* [1901] 1 Ch 326 and *Willmott v London Celluloid Co* (1886) 34 Ch D 147.

[120] One reason why an execution creditor defeats a floating chargee is that the latter authorises the chargor to enter into ordinary course transactions that are subject to the normal consequences arising from a failure to perform those transactions: *Evans v Rival Granite Co* [1910] 2 KB 979, 995 (Fletcher Moulton LJ).

in the treatment of property according to whether it is subject to a common law tenancy in common or an equitable tenancy in common. Issues of identification also present themselves in broadly the same way. The trust of 50 undifferentiated shares in *Hunter v Moss* finds its common law counterpart in section 16 of the Sale of Goods Act, which, if the subject matter had been a sale of 50 sheep or 50 bottles of wine in an identified bulk, would not have recognised the passing of the legal property prior to ascertainment of the 50 items. It took legislation to change the Sale of Goods approach, but that legislation did not pass the property in the 50 sheep or the 50 bottles of wine. Instead, it recharacterised the contract as one for the sale of a share in the bulk. When the Court of Appeal dealt with a similar problem in *Hunter v Moss*, it failed fully to appreciate the difference between a trust of a quantity in a bulk and a trust of a share of the bulk. Even had it done so, the Court, in the absence of any ambiguity in the expressed intention of the settlor, would not have had the power to recalibrate the settlor's intention to salvage a trust that might otherwise have failed for lack of certainty.

Further points raised in this chapter point to the lack of clarity separating property and no-property, instrumental reasons sometimes requiring an anticipatory recognition of something as property, for one or more purposes, when it has not truly matriculated as an item of property. Finally, the law in this area turns upon a fine balance between identification of an item as capable of being the subject matter of a proprietary disposition and the intention of a disponor that a property right therein be created or transferred. The line between the two is not always as clearly drawn in the case law as it should be.

5

Floating Trusts

ROBERT STEVENS

I. The Problem

It's an ill wind that blows no good whatsoever. The collapse of Lehman Brothers has generated some interesting cases concerning the law of trusts.

It was Lehman Brothers' practice for one company in the group, in each time zone, to act as a hub company for the acquisition and sale of all securities in that zone. Lehman Brothers International Europe (LBIE) was the hub for Europe. The RASCALS decision concerned whether securities acquired from third parties (annoyingly called 'the street') for the account of affiliate companies in the same group were held on trust. To understand the decision, it is necessary to read both Briggs J at first instance and that of the Court of Appeal (the judgment of the Court delivered by Lloyd LJ) which largely concurs with it.[1]

LBIE itself did not acquire the underlying securities, but rather acquired rights against a depository (sometimes through one or more further intermediaries) which had the relevant rights vested in it. The use of a hub company for buying and selling in this way had advantages in terms of efficiency of scale. The economic risks and rewards of ownership were to fall on those for whom the securities were acquired, but the right to the rights to the securities held by the depository was vested centrally in LBIE.

In the 1990s three problems were perceived to arise.

First, LBIE paid for the securities and had a right to reimbursement from the affiliate for whom they were acquired. This unsecured debt gave rise to a concern that regulators would require LBIE to have sufficient capital to secure it against the risk of non-payment of these debts.

Second, that LBIE would be required to segregate its securities for the accounts of third parties (affiliates and others). LBIE's practice was to hold all securities in unsegregated house accounts.

[1] *Re Lehman Brothers International (Europe) (in administration)* [2010] EWHC 2914 (Ch) (Briggs J), [2011] EWCA Civ 1544.

Third, that LBIE had unencumbered title to the rights it sold such that third parties who acquired securities from it would not be prejudiced by any interests of affiliates or others.

These perceived problems led Lehman Brothers to adopt from 1996 a process of Regulation and Administration of Safe Custody and Global Settlement (RASCALS). Under this Byzantine arrangement, once LBIE acquired the securities for the affiliate, they would enter into a repo contract, providing for the sale of the securities to LBIE by the affiliates, followed by a sale back to the affiliates of equivalent securities (plus a fee). LBIE would have the use of securities in the meantime between sale from affiliate and purchase back. These purchases and repurchases were not effected through the payment of cash, but rather through a series of book entries with LBIE's initial obligation to buy being offset against the affiliate's obligation to pay the purchase price. Some of these repo transactions took place automatically each day, with LBIE the unencumbered owner of the securities during each day (so-called 'automatic' RASCALS). These transactions were all done by computer. Other repo transactions took place manually, rather than automatically daily, with a sale by the affiliate to LBIE with a right in the affiliate to reacquire equivalent security upon payment at some point in the future.

Once LBIE acquired securities it would deal with them freely as part of its business assets. If there was a dividend paid this would be credited to the affiliate, but if LBIE made profits from short-term dealings in the securities, this would accrue to LBIE. At any given time LBIE may have had none of the securities originally acquired for the affiliate but merely other rights that traceably represented those securities.

When the music stopped in 2008 with the collapse of Lehman Brothers a new question arose: who in the group was entitled to the securities? The affiliates claimed that the securities were held on trust for them. LBIE claimed that they were not.

II. How Do Intermediated Securities Work?

If A, the owner of Blackacre, declares himself a trustee of the right to his land in B's favour, the law (by which is meant here law and equity together) does 'not say that [B is] the owner of the land, it says that the trustee was the owner of the land, but adds that he is bound to hold the land for the benefit of [B]'.[2] This may be illustrated by the fact that B has no standing to sue for violation of the right to the land

[2] FW Maitland (eds AH Chaytor and WJ Whittaker) *Equity: A Course of Lectures, revised by J Brunyate* (Cambridge, CUP, 1936) 17–18.

itself: only A may sue a trespasser or the creator of a private nuisance.[3] B has no right in relation to the land exigible against the rest of the world, but only one as against the person with title to Blackacre from time to time. B does not, therefore, acquire in the narrow sense employed by the Romans, a right *in rem*.

B's right that A hold the title to the land for his benefit (which is simply the converse of A's duty to hold the title to the land for B's benefit) is not simply a right against A personally, a right *in personam* in the traditional sense. Rather, the subject matter of B's right is A's *right* to the land.[4] If, therefore, A gives the (right to) Blackacre to his son, C, B's right will bind C because B's right is in relation to the right C has acquired. Similarly, if A goes into bankruptcy, B's right against A's right will bind A's trustee in bankruptcy and hence will be protected in this event.[5] Because of these characteristics, we are content to describe B's right as proprietary, although it is not of the same kind as a right *in rem* strictly so called.

Whenever one party is obliged to hold a right for the benefit of another a trust arises, because that is, as a matter of definition, what a trust is. So, if A makes a binding contract to transfer specific shares, or receivables, or title to land, or an intellectual property right, or an equitable interest that he owns to B, A becomes a trustee of this right even though the requisites of transfer have not been fulfilled.

It is vital to note that this equitable property right is not a mere personal right against the trustee. Such a view would be inconsistent with the additional protection against certain third parties enjoyed by a holder of an equitable property right. An equitable property right is not a right against a thing, nor simply a right against a person, it is rather a right to another right. So, if A holds a right (whether it be a personal right or a right to a thing) on trust for B, then B has a right to A's right. This means that, if B can follow that right into the hands of a third party, C,

[3] The decision of the Court of Appeal in *Shell UK v Total UK* [2010] EWCA Civ 180, [2011] QB 86 is, in part, inconsistent with this proposition as beneficiaries under a trust of the title to an oil refinery were allowed to claim for consequential loss they suffered as a result of the defendant's negligent damage of the refinery, provided that the trustee was joined as a party to the proceedings. The prior authorities do not support this proposition and the dismissal of arguments to the contrary as 'legalistic' (at [132]) is not a high point in English jurisprudence. The better view is that the case is rightly decided because the claimants were in joint possession of the land (and therefore had title) through the agency of those who operated the refinery on their behalf. If the claimants had unanimously instructed the operator to destroy the refinery, the operator would have had to do so.

[4] See also R Chambers, *An Introduction to Property Law in Australia*, 3rd edn (Sydney, Thomson Reuters, 2008) para 13.90; L Smith, 'Unravelling Proprietary Restitution' (2004) 40 *Canadian Business Law Journal* 317; L Smith, 'Philosophical Foundations of Proprietary Remedies' in R Chambers, C Mitchell and J Penner (eds), *Philosophical Foundations of the Law of Unjust Enrichment* (Oxford, OUP, 2009) 281; L Smith, 'Trust and Patrimony' (2008) 38 *Revue générale de droit* 379; L Smith, 'Trust and Patrimony' (2009) 28 *Estates, Trusts and Pensions Journal* 332; W Swadling in A Burrows (ed), *English Private Law*, 2nd edn (Oxford, OUP, 2007) paras 4.140–4.153; B McFarlane and R Stevens, 'The Nature of Equitable Property' (2010) 4 *Journal of Equity* 1; *cf* R Nolan, 'Equitable Property' (2006) 122 *LQR* 232.

[5] For bankrupt individuals this is expressly stated in the Insolvency Act 1986, s 283(3)(b). It is also true of insolvent companies despite the absence of expression in legislation: see eg, *Barclays Bank Ltd v Quistclose Investments Ltd* [1970] AC 567.

it may also be possible for B to show that C is under a duty to B. In particular, it means that B receives some protection in A's insolvency: if the right held by A on trust were to pass to A's trustee in bankruptcy, B could prevent the trustee in bankruptcy using that right for the benefit of A's general creditors.

Analysing equitable property rights as rights to other rights has many advantages. It can explain the fact that B can have such a right in relation to a personal right held by A; it can explain why B can make a claim against a third party, such as C, who acquires a right that depends on A's right, but not against X, who acquires no such right. In addition, it can assist in explaining why equitable property rights arise: if B can show that A is under a duty to B in relation to a specific right held by A, B necessarily acquires an equitable property right—a right to A's right. That core right, capable of having an effect on third parties and thus giving B protection in A's insolvency, thus combines with any additional personal duties that A may be under to B. In addition, the analysis, unlike one which sees the separation of legal and equitable title as constitutive of an equitable property right, can account for cases in which A holds an equitable right on trust for B. For example, if Z holds a right on trust for A, it is clear that A can then hold that right on trust for B. Such a sub-trust arises because A holds a particular right (A's right under the head trust) and is under a duty to B in relation to that right.

This analysis can be applied without difficulty to the phenomenon of intermediated securities. The holder of the underlying right (eg, a depository) may come under a duty to Intermediary 1 to hold that underlying right for the benefit of Intermediary 1. No transfer of the underlying right is required; indeed, the very essence of the arrangement is that the holder keeps the right and comes under a duty to Intermediary 1 in relation to that right. Nonetheless, Intermediary 1 acquires more than a mere personal right against the holder of the right. As the holder's duty relates to the underlying right, Intermediary 1 has the ability to make a claim against a third party who acquires a right from the holder and is therefore protected in the insolvency of the holder. Depending on the terms of his contract with the holder, Intermediary 1 may have additional personal rights against the holder: those rights arise from duties binding the holder but which do not relate to specific rights of the holder.

Having thus acquired a right to the holder's right, Intermediary 1 may also deal with his right. This may be done through a transfer of that right: in that case, Intermediary 1 loses his right and that right is acquired by the transferee. In such a case, there is no new link in the chain. Alternatively, Intermediary 1 may retain his right, and give Intermediary 2 a right to that right. As well as acquiring that core right to a right, Intermediary 2 may acquire personal rights against Intermediary 1, as a result of duties assumed by Intermediary 1 that do not relate to any specific rights held by Intermediary 1. Intermediary 2, having thus acquired a right to Intermediary 1's right then has the same power to either transfer his right or to retain it and give another party a right to it.

What is thereby created is a chain of trusts which in principle can be of any length (sub-trusts, sub-sub-trusts, sub-sub-sub-trusts etc). What is essential however is the right that the investor has to the right of the intermediary, or put synonymously, the duty that the intermediary has in relation to the right of the investor.

III. What Was RASCALS Intended to Do?

When an affiliate 'sold' its interest in the securities to LBIE what happened? If A holds a right to a car on trust for B, if B 'sells' his beneficial interest to A, nothing is transferred to A. Rather A is no longer under a duty to B, so that the right to the car is no longer held on trust. If it were the case that B's equitable interest were transferred back to A, then writing would be required every time there was a 'sale' by B to A,[6] but fortunately this is incorrect.[7] There is a release and not a transfer. A's right to the car is a single right, he does not have separate rights at law and in equity any more than I do in the computer on which I am currently typing. Whilst it is possible to speak of the 'beneficial title being passed to'[8] the trustee from the beneficiary in such a case, this is only true in economic not legal terms. It is not possible to hold an asset on trust for oneself as there cannot at law be any duty to oneself.

The assumption underlying the introduction of RASCALS was that the affiliate was selling, or more accurately releasing, its interest under the trust to LBIE as trustee. When LBIE 'sold' its interest back to the affiliate, it transferred nothing but instead created a new right under a trust in the affiliate's favour.

However, Briggs J concluded that, absent the RASCALS procedure, LBIE did not initially hold securities acquired on trust for the affiliates. This finding was rightly not challenged on appeal. LBIE was free to deal with the securities in the ordinary course of business. Commercially there was no need for anything more than a personal obligation on LBIE to account for the value of the securities and their fruits.[9]

The result of this (clearly correct) conclusion was that the entire basis of the RASCALS procedure was misconceived, proceeding as it had done on the assumption that the affiliate had some kind of proprietary interest it needed to 'sell' to LBIE. The concern that LBIE did not have an unencumbered title to the securities was similarly incorrect. LBIE was not merely an unsecured creditor for capital adequacy purposes as it did not hold the rights which related to the securities by way of trust for the affiliates.

However, with the introduction of RASCALS it clearly was intended that when the affiliate 'bought back' their interest in the securities (which on the first occasion

[6] Law of Property Act 1925, s 53(1)(c).

[7] *Vandervell v Inland Revenue Commissioners* [1966] UKHL 3, [1967] 2 AC 291, 311 (Lord Upjohn); *cf Re Paradise Motor Co* [1968] 1 WLR 1125 (a disclaimer not a release).

[8] *Re Lehman Brothers* (n 1) [2011] EWCA Civ 1544 [127] (Lloyd LJ).

[9] *Re Lehman Brothers* (n 1) [2010] EWHC 2914 (Ch) [275]–[276] (Briggs J).

of such a purchase was in fact an initial acquisition) that they would thereby acquire such a beneficial interest.[10] Briggs J and the Court of Appeal concluded that this intention sufficed in order to create a trust in favour of the affiliates. This conclusion is problematic.

IV. Was there Certainty of Subject Matter?

It has been a source of some concern that the holding of securities through intermediaries may sometimes or indeed usually fail for want of certainty of subject matter.[11] One of the benefits of the RASCALS decision is that it clarifies both that this is not so and, in the judgment of Briggs J, why it is not so.

If B has a right under a trust, he has right to a right of the trustee. To have such a right, B needs to show that the trustee is under a duty to B and that A's duty relates to a specific right (or set of rights) held by A. For example, if A owns 20 sheep and declares that he holds (his title to) two of those sheep on trust for B, it is clear that A intends to come under a duty in relation to his title to two specific sheep. However, A can only come under such a duty if those specific sheep have been identified; some form of segregation is therefore necessary. There is in principle exactly the same need for segregation if A instead attempts to sell (his title to) two of his sheep to B: a sale is a transfer of rights, and no such transfer can occur until the identification of the specific rights to be transferred has occurred. This explains why recourse to the law of trusts provides no consolation to B where he has a contract with a now insolvent A for the sale of unascertained goods. The very reason that prevents B acquiring A's title to any specific goods also prevents B acquiring a right to A's right to such goods.

The Court of Appeal in *Hunter v Moss*[12] confirmed the validity of A's declaration of a trust, in favour of B, of 50 of 950 shares held by A. A trust was created without the need for A to segregate 50 specific shares which he was to hold on trust for B. Clearly, the reasoning behind the decision means that if, for example, A holds an interest in 100 shares in X Co, then an investor (B) can acquire an equitable property right if A states that it holds 50 of those shares for B: there is no need for any particular shares to be segregated from the 100 in which A has an interest.

The decision in *Hunter v Moss* attracted a great deal of academic disapproval[13] and how the result is capable of being squared with general principles is obscure in

[10] ibid [2011] EWCA Civ 1544 [68] (Lloyd LJ).

[11] Financial Markets Law Committee, 'Property Interests in Investment Securities: Analysis of the Need for and Nature of Legislation relating to Property Interests in Indirectly Held Investment Securities, with a Statement of Principles for an Investment Securities Statute' (FMLC Papers, Issue 3, 2004): www.fmlc.org/papers/fmlc1_3_july04.pdf, para 6.10.

[12] *Hunter v Moss* [1994] 1 WLR 452.

[13] eg D Hayton, 'Uncertainty of Subject-Matter of Trusts' (1994) 110 *LQR* 335.

the case itself.[14] The explanation for the result, if not the reasoning, was provided by Professor Goode. A requirement of segregation may be justified in relation to sheep, but is irrelevant when considering shares or other securities.[15] Separating out an individual share, unlike the notion of separating an individual sheep from the flock, makes no sense. A share is simply that: a proportionate right against the company and other shareholders. If a company issues 200 shares of which A owns 100, A does not have 100 separate rights. Rather he has a half share in the company. As a result, dealings with shares, unlike dealings with sheep, are always dealings with co-ownership. This means that, in practice, there is no need for A to segregate any specific shares before declaring a trust in B's favour or making a transfer to B. Indeed he could not do so. If A declares a trust of his freehold under which B has a 50 per cent beneficial interest, no one would suggest that the trust fails because A has not segregated a specific half of his land. Similarly, if A declares that he holds 50 of 100 shares for B, there is no difficulty in finding that B has not only a personal right against A, but also a right to half of A's shares. The subject matter of B's right is A's entire holding of shares of that kind, not any right to any individual 50 shares as A has no separable right to such shares.

Precisely the same reasoning applies to debts. If A is owed £1,000 by C, A has one right against C. Any trust over this debt which A declares in B's favour must have as its subject matter the entire debt. A does not have one thousand claims for £1 against C (or 100,000 claims for one penny) which can be separately identified, but rather one claim for £1,000. If, therefore, the beneficiary's claim is not to the full £1,000 but to some lesser figure the trust should not fail for want of certainty of subject matter as the subject matter of the trust is and could only be, the entire debt, of which the beneficiary acquires a right to an appropriate share.

RASCALS goes further than *Hunter v Moss* however because LBIE remained free to deal with all of the assets it acquired as it saw fit. They may have had none of the relevant securities at all at any given time but merely a right to call for equivalent from third parties. Briggs J concluded however that '[a] trust does not fail for want of certainty merely because its subject matter is at present uncertain, if the terms of the trust are sufficient to identify its subject matter in the future'.[16] For this proposition he cited *Tailby v Official Receiver*,[17] a case of an equitable assignment of future property where the subject matter of the assignee's rights was initially unascertained (because in the future) but became certain as they were acquired.

If we are to conclude that the trust does not fail for want of certainty of subject matter, what was the subject matter of each individual affiliate's right? Because LBIE traded freely in the securities it bought for the affiliates, the subject matter

[14] *Re Lehman Brothers* (n 1) [2010] EWHC 2914 (Ch) [232] (Briggs J).

[15] R Goode, 'Are Intangible Assets Fungible?' [2003] *Lloyd's Maritime and Commercial Law Quarterly* 379.

[16] *Re Lehman Brothers* (n 1) [2010] EWHC 2914 (Ch) [225] (Briggs J).

[17] *Tailby v Official Receiver* (1888) 13 App Cas 523.

of the trust was clearly more complex than in *Hunter v Moss*. What was held on trust included 'LBIE's right to recover equivalent securities from street lending counterparties, and its rights as against affiliates to make good short positions'.[18] However, it may be wondered whether this is a possible stopping point. An affiliate who demanded from LBIE that it account for the securities acquired on its behalf would have no cause for complaint if LBIE held no such securities at any given time or anything representing them, but instead went out into the market and acquired them for cash upon demand.

Rather, the central difficulty in RASCALS is in identifying any specific rights, save perhaps LBIE's entire corpus of assets, that it was required to hold for individual affiliates. Unlike in *Tailby v Official Receiver* no future event ever cured this uncertainty.

V. What Needs to be Intended?

Clearly the intention of the parties arising under the RASCALS procedure was that the affiliates, once they had purchased back, should acquire a beneficial interest under a trust. Once the problem of uncertainty of subject matter was overcome, both Briggs J and the Court of Appeal took this to be dispositive.[19] Clearly the common law is not generally in the business of frustrating the intentions of commercial parties, but it may be that the consideration of the necessary intention was too compressed.

If the parties to an agreement intend to create a licence to use land, but the agreement grants exclusive possession for a term at a rent, it is a lease regardless of whether that is what they intended to create.[20] A still closer analogy to the present case is the distinction between a fixed and floating charge. The parties to the agreement in *National Westminster Bank plc v Spectrum Plus Limited*[21] intended to create a fixed charge, but because the agreement allowed the borrower freedom to deal with the assets in the ordinary course of business, it was a floating charge.

Similarly the mere fact that the parties intended to create a trust, and the subject matter is sufficiently certain, should not suffice.

As we have seen, Briggs J considered that for the pre-RASCALS period the fact that LBIE remained free to deal with the assets in the ordinary course of business was strongly indicative of there being no trust.[22] It should have been seen as fatal,

[18] *Re Lehman Brothers* [2010] EWHC 2914 (Ch) (n 1) [239] (Briggs J); *cf Re Lehman Brothers* (n 1) [2011] EWCA Civ 1544 [54] (Lloyd LJ).
[19] ibid [245] (Briggs J); [68] (Lloyd LJ).
[20] *Street v Mountford* [1985] AC 809.
[21] *National Westminster Bank plc v Spectrum Plus Limited* [2005] UKHL 41, [2005] 2 AC 680.
[22] *Re Lehman Brothers* (n 1) [2010] EWHC 2914 (Ch) [275] (Briggs J).

just as the freedom of the borrower to deal with assets in the ordinary course of business in the House of Lords in *Spectrum Plus* was fatal to the existence of a fixed charge.[23]

As we have seen, the nature of a trust is that one party is under a duty to hold particular rights for another. What is the minimum content of this duty?[24] At a minimum the trustee must be under a duty not to use the right for his own benefit (save to the extent that he is also a beneficiary under the trust). A trust is not a fixed charge because the trustee is obliged to hold the right absolutely for the beneficiary, and not merely by way of security. However, trusts and fixed charges have in common the need for a minimum duty in relation to the rights which are the subject matter of the equitable property right. It is difficult to identify any duty in relation to specific rights that LBIE was under to the affiliates.

In the realm of secured transactions we permit floating charges. The security holder has the power to crystallise the charge, and from that point subject the debtor to the obligation to hold the assets which are the subject matter of the charge for him by way of security (ie, to create a fixed charge). The power that the charge holder has prior to crystallisation has proprietary effects, if the assets are given away to a third party outside the ordinary course of business the charge holder may follow the rights so transferred into the hands of the recipient. Could the RASCALS case similarly be seen as recognising a power in the affiliates to create a full-blown trust at some point in the future over the assets which are the subject matter of their claim, whilst leaving LBIE free to deal with the assets in the ordinary course of business prior to doing so: a floating trust? Powers to create trusts (such as the equity to rescind of a party induced by an innocent misrepresentation to sell his land) are recognised by our law and similarly have proprietary effects. The difficulty would seem to remain, however, that the affiliates would have no cause for complaint after exercising an option to require LBIE to account for the shares acquired on the affiliate's behalf, if LBIE used any source to acquire equivalent securities to those it was obliged to account to the affiliates for. If this is so, the recognition of the affiliate's proprietary rights still seems problematic. Put colloquially, the affiliates needed to be able to assert 'that is mine', and they could not. If we say that the subject matter of the affiliate's rights was all the securities from time to time held by LBIE, this interest was defeasible upon payment of a sum equivalent to the value of specific shares bought for the affiliate. That looks like a floating charge, and they are void for want of registration upon a debtor's insolvency.

[23] See also *Henry v Hammond* [1913] 2 KB 515, 521 (Channell J); *Paragon Finance Plc v DB Thakerar & Co* [1999] 1 All ER 400, 416 (Millett LJ).

[24] *cf Armitage v Nurse* [1998] Ch 241, 253 (Millett LJ); *Citibank v MBIA* [2007] EWCA Civ 11, [2008] 1 BCLC 376.

VI. Conclusion

The conclusion of Briggs J was that LBIE had (in effect) paid to buy from the affiliates their interests in the securities, leaving the affiliates with no proprietary rights. Any trust had therefore come to an end. In other words, the conclusion was identical to that which would have been reached if the entire RASCALS procedure had never been mistakenly entered into in the first place. This conclusion is consistent with the view that there was never any trust at all. The Court of Appeal agreed, save to the extent that they disagreed as to whether LBIE had in fact paid for all of the securities subject to the manual RASCALS process.[25]

The first case to unequivocally recognise the existence of the floating charge in England is usually taken to be the decision of the Court of Appeal in *Re Panama, New Zealand and Australian Royal Mail Company*.[26] Since then academics have had a great deal of entertainment seeking to explain the legal nature of the floating charge. If nothing else, the RASCALS decision should similarly add to the gaiety of nations.

[25] *Re Lehman Brothers* (n 1) [2011] EWCA Civ 1544 [150], [162] (Lloyd LJ).

[26] *Re Panama, New Zealand and Australian Royal Mail Company* (1870) 5 Ch App 318.

6

'Sort of' Backwards Tracing

JAMES PENNER*

I. Introduction

In the UK Court of Appeal (CA) decision in *Relfo v Varsani*[1] the CA implicitly acknowledged that a claimant could 'backwards trace' in order to found a proprietary claim. In *Brazil v Durant International*[2] the Privy Council (PC) explicitly allowed a claimant to do so. But the PC's approval of the ability to backwards trace was tentative, and issues of principle were not really discussed, so the effect of the decisions is not clear. Much remains open.

One 'backwards traces' when one traces into property acquired by the recipient before he receives the money that is traced. If, for example, a rogue trustee buys an antique table worth £3,000 on credit, by taking a loan from a bank, or by using his overdraft facility, or with his credit card, and then later discharges the debt with trust money, the antique table is the 'backwardly' traceable proceeds of the trust money.

In a moment we shall look at Smith's elaboration of this idea, but first it is necessary to say a word about terminology. In the passage below Smith says that what is traced is the value of what is exchanged into the thing it is exchanged for. Lord Millett says the same thing in *Foskett v McKeown*.[3] That is, one traces the value of one's car into the cash one receives upon selling it. For reasons I have explored at length elsewhere,[4] I think this terminology is misleading. I should rather say that one *realises* the value of one's car by exchanging it for money. There is no 'transfer' or 'flow' of the value of the car into the money one receives in exchange. What one

* I am grateful to Michael Bridge, Joe Campbell, Robert Chambers, Matthew Conaglen, Lionel Smith and participants at the conference, April 2016, for conversations, comments and criticisms. Any remaining faults, which I suppose to be many, lie with the author.

[1] *Relfo v Varsani* [2014] EWCA Civ 360.

[2] *Brazil v Durant International* [2015] UKPC 35.

[3] *Foskett v McKeown* [2001] 1 AC 102, 127C.

[4] JE Penner, 'Value, Property, and Unjust Enrichment: Trusts of Traceable Proceeds' in R Chambers, C Mitchell and J Penner (eds), *Philosophical Foundations of the Law of Unjust Enrichment* (Oxford, OUP, 2009) 306.

traces is the *ownership* of one right into the right one receives in exchange. Because I hold title to the car I can use one of the powers that go with having that title to exchange it. The money I receive in exchange is the 'exchange product' of my exercising my power to sell it. Thus, my ownership of the money is mine—I acquire title to the money—because I was the one who owned the car and exercised the power of exchange going with that ownership, or title, to exchange it.

Smith elaborates the nature of backwards tracing as follows:

> Suppose that D buys a car from C with some money. If we were tracing the value inherent in ownership of the money, we could trace it into ownership of the car. Now change the facts slightly, so that D buys the car on credit; he takes ownership of the car, but he is C's debtor in respect of the purchase price. A day later, D pays the debt with the money being traced. Can we trace from the money into the car as before? It is difficult to see why not. There is no substantial change in the transaction; the period of credit might be reduced to a minute or a second to better make this point. If that is right, then when money is used to pay a debt, it is traceable into what was acquired for the incurring of the debt … [I]nstead of tracing through substitutions in D's hands, we could trace through substitutions in C's hands. When the car is bought for cash, the car is the traceable proceeds of the money; that is the substitution in D's hands. Clearly, from the other perspective the money is the traceable proceeds of the car; that is the substitution in C's hands. It is easy to show that adding a period of credit does not change this conclusion … C gave up ownership of the car in exchange for a debt; that debt asset is therefore the traceable proceeds of the car. Later, the debt is paid with the money in question. This money is therefore the traceable proceeds of the debt; but since the debt was the proceeds of the car, therefore the money is the proceeds of the car, via an intermediate step.[5]

When money is paid into a bank account, there is no difficulty on 'forwards tracing' principles in determining the exchange of rights that has occurred. The bank takes title to the money and gives value in exchange in the form of the increased bank balance. The increased bank balance is, of course, the traceable proceeds of the payment in of the money. Where, however, £500 is paid into an account that is £500 in overdraft, resulting in a balance of zero, there are no forwardly traceable proceeds. In exchange for the title to the money, the bank gives, in return, a reduction of the debt that it is owed by the customer, to zero in this case. No debt now exists between the bank and the customer, and therefore no rights between them that can be the forwardly traceable proceeds of the £500 payment. Whilst it is true that nothing now *in the account* is traceable by the claimant, because there is no existing right between the bank and customer, this does not mean that the tracing exercise must end when the rights between the bank and its customer 'run out'; if you stop there, so backwards tracing reasoning goes, you have merely given up the tracing exercise prematurely; the tracing exercise has not come to a 'natural' or 'logical' conclusion by itself. The overdraft was incurred, after all, by withdrawing funds, and the payment of the overdraft is backwardly traceable into those funds, and into whatever those funds were spent on.

[5] L Smith, *The Law of Tracing* (Oxford, OUP, 1997) 146.

Conaglen raises the objection that this way of looking at things depends upon a conceptual confusion. Forgive the long quotation:

> It is useful to have in mind the example that Smith posits, of a car being bought on credit, and the debt subsequently being paid with money that has been stolen (or paid away in breach of trust). Smith argues that tracing the money backwards through payment of the debt into the car is a natural corollary of the fact that the vendor of the car can trace the car into the debt and thence into the money that is accepted in payment of the debt. Smith describes the debt as a 'red herring in the tracing exercise'.
>
> Beguilingly simple as it is, the difficulty with this argument is that it is not the case, to use Smith's words, that
>
>> 'if from one perspective the money is the proceeds of the car, it follows that from the other perspective, the car is the proceeds of the money'.
>
> The trust beneficiaries' rights to the car (if any) derive from those of the buyer, rather than the seller, and there is no reason why a transaction of this sort must have symmetrical effects for buyer and seller alike. There is no doubt that, on the seller's side, the car can easily be traced into the asset that the seller acquires in return for parting with title to the car (viz the debt), which in turn can be traced into the money that is paid to satisfy the debt. But that is because 'tracing is a process whereby assets are identified' and, at each stage, there is an asset that the seller can claim as the substitute for the asset that he or she had at the outset of the process. The same cannot be said of the buyer's side of the transaction. The buyer begins with an original asset (for example, trust money) but that money is retained by the buyer when he acquires the car. Thus, the buyer acquires a new asset (the car) but the buyer also assumes a liability (the debt). It is that liability that is later discharged by payment of the money to the seller, at which stage the buyer is left with the new asset (the car).
>
> The reason the two sides of the transaction are not simply mirror images of one another is that the debt has a different juristic characteristic on each side of the transaction: the debt is an asset in the hands of the creditor (the seller), and so it can provide a basis for traditional tracing, but the debt is a liability—the opposite of an asset—in the hands of the debtor (the buyer). As Smith says, 'the thief parts with money in exchange for a release from a liability'. That is not the same thing as the acquisition of an asset. Indeed, an important part of the point of debt finance, from the borrower's perspective, is to enable him or her to make money by acquiring assets without paying for them until later, so that the assets can in turn be used to generate funds with which to pay the debt, ordinarily because the borrower does not, at the time of acquisition, either have or want to lay out sufficient funds to pay for the assets. Thus, in a credit sale transaction, the seller gives up an asset in return for another asset (the benefit of the debt) whereas the buyer acquires an asset alongside a liability (the burden of the debt). The two sides of the transaction are different, and so there is no reason why the same rules must apply to each side …
>
> [T]he acquisition and extinguishment of debts are two very different things. There is no doubt that a debt can be acquired from the creditor, who holds it as an asset. But when the debt is paid, the debt is not being acquired from the creditor—it is being destroyed.[6]

[6] M Conaglen, 'Difficulties with Tracing Backwards' (2011) 127 *LQR* 432, 446–48.

Conaglen's point is well taken, but depending upon how stringently one follows its logic, it may lead to a very drastic reduction in the ability of a beneficiary to trace at all.

We can consider three cases: (1) over-the-counter shop sales, where I should say that it is indisputable that the transfer of title to the money paid over to the vendor is consideration for the transfer of title to the purchased goods. Case (2) has two components: (i) the contract of sale is executory, ie, made on the basis that the purchaser, under the contract, incurs a duty to pay the price, and the vendor the duty to transfer title to the goods—in other words, the consideration is an exchange of *voluntarily undertaken obligations* (colloquially, an 'exchange of promises'), the purchaser to discharge a debt, and the vendor to transfer title to the goods; (ii) the second component is one of timing: title to the goods passes to the purchaser *after* the purchaser discharges his duty to pay the price. Case (3) is identical to case (2) as to (i), the contract's being executory, but in this case (iii), the title to the goods passes from vendor to purchaser *prior* to the latter's paying the price, ie, prior to the time he discharges his debt under the contract of sale.

Regarding (1), as I have set out in detail elsewhere,[7] barter transactions and over-the-counter cash sales in shops do not involve executory obligations. Rather than an exchange of executory obligations, one to transfer title to the goods, one to pay the price, these sales involve an exchange of performances, ie, the passing by the vender of title to the goods by delivery, the passing of title to the money likewise by the purchaser. If these actions are not more or less simultaneous, but one party goes second, and before performing changes his mind and decides not to proceed ('Oh, sorry, I see this has already been sold. Here's your money back'. 'Oh, sorry, it seems I have come out without my wallet') then that, legally, is the end of the matter; there is no breach of contract because neither side undertook an obligation to perform. The underlying idea is that it is no good, especially here, to try to squeeze every legally valid exchange into the straitjacket of an *exchange of executory obligations*. The terms of exchange must be agreed,[8] but not necessarily as obligations to do something in the future.[9] There is no question that in case (1) sales the goods are the traceable proceeds of the money, and vice versa, each being the consideration given respectively by the vendor and the purchaser under the contract of sale.

The trouble begins with case (2) and case (3). In *each* case, the money the purchaser pays goes to discharge a debt. On Conaglen's logic, if payment to discharge a debt merely extinguishes the debtor's liability, just 'destroys the debt', then it is difficult to see how the receipt of title to the goods, either *before and after* the debt

[7] JE Penner, *The Idea of Property in Law* (Oxford, Clarendon, 1997) 154–64.

[8] And these are quite properly understood as sales, to which all the normal sale of goods law applies regarding warranties, conditions, limitation periods, etc.

[9] I draw some sustenance for this view from the maritime law consideration of 'Himalaya' clauses, which have been found effective in terms of 'mutuality of performance', as opposed to 'mutuality of obligation': see *The Eurymedon* [1974] UKPC 1, [1974] 1 Lloyd's Rep 534, 539 (Lord Wilberforce); *The New York Star* [1979] 1 Lloyd's Law Reports 298, 304–05 (Barwick CJ).

under the contract of sale is actually paid, is the traceable proceeds of the payment of the money: the goods are not the traceable proceeds of the money used to pay the debt, but rather the traceable proceeds of the vendor's executory promise to deliver them; and the consideration for that was the debtor's liability to pay the price, ie, the contractual debt the purchaser incurred. My suspicion is that this point has not been sufficiently noticed before because in type (2) cases, where the payment is made and then title to the goods transferred, ie, where there is no 'intervening period of credit', the payment to discharge the contractual debt is treated like the *performance of payment* in type (1) cases ('Suppose that D buys a car from C *with some money*'; 'When the car is bought *for cash*, the car is the traceable proceeds of the money'),[10] even when, on the strict logic Conaglen employs, it is plainly incorrect to do so. Happily, as we shall see,[11] the law on the sale of goods seems to treat both cases (2) and (3) as ones where tracing should be allowed, given its treatment of the concept of 'price' and 'consideration'.

II. Authority on Backwards Tracing Prior to *Brazil*

Prior to *Brazil*, authority for the proposition that a claimant could backwards trace was spotty and never explicitly framed as cases where backwards tracing was allowed. Nevertheless, it is clear that the courts have actually backwards traced in particular cases: in *Agip (Africa) Ltd v Jackson*[12] the court allowed the plaintiff to treat a payment by Lloyds Bank in London to the defendant as the transfer of his money, even though the payment from the plaintiff to Lloyds' correspondent bank in New York was made later. Thus, Lloyds had made the payment to the defendant before, and in expectation of, receiving a corresponding amount from the plaintiff via a New York bank. Furthermore, backwards tracing necessarily underlies the ability of equity to trace through bank cheque clearing systems generally, since the settlement between banks is not simultaneous with the crediting and debiting of accounts.

There is also the Canadian case of *Agricultural Credit Corporation of Saskatchewan v Pettyjohn*.[13] Farmers purchased cattle using an overdraft facility, and then discharged the overdraft with money acquired from ACCS. ACCS was entitled to claim that the cattle were the proceeds of the money then advanced. In giving the judgment of the PC in *Brazil*, Lord Toulson had this to say about *Pettyjohn*:

> 37 On those facts the court was right in the view of the Board not to divide minutely the connected steps by which, on any sensible commercial view, the purchase of the cattle

[10] Taken from the quotation from Smith above, my italics.

[11] Text to n 49 below, discussing the Sale of Goods Act 1979 (as amended).

[12] *Agip (Africa) Ltd v Jackson* [1990] EWCA Civ 2, [1990] Ch 265; affirmed on appeal [1991] Ch 547; see also the tracing through credit facilities in *El Ajou v Dollar Land Holdings plc* [1993] 3 All ER 717.

[13] *Agricultural Credit Corporation of Saskatchewan v Pettyjohn* (1991) 79 DLR (4th) 22 (Sask CA).

> was financed by the credit corporation, but to look at the transaction overall. The interposition of the bank was purely to provide bridging finance to cover the gap in time between the purchase and the credit corporation's funds coming through as previously arranged.

This looking at the 'transaction overall' is a point to which we shall have to return.

The House of Lords conducted a backwards tracing exercise in the most important review of the law of tracing in a century, *Foskett v McKeown*,[14] without explicitly stating that that was what they were doing. Trust money was used to pay the last two premiums on an insurance policy. The trust beneficiaries were able to trace into the policy proceeds when the insured committed suicide and claim a co-ownership share in the proceeds, a share proportionate to the premiums the trust money paid for out of all the premiums paid. Giving the leading judgment for the majority, Lord Millett was explicit in finding that the chose in action, that is, the right to receive the death benefit, was acquired under the contract of insurance upon the payment of the first premium, and that single right remained in existence throughout. No new right arose as each subsequent payment was made:

> In the case of an ordinary whole life policy the insurance company undertakes to pay a stated sum on the death of the assured in return for fixed annual premiums payable throughout his life. *Such a policy is an entire contract, not a contract for a year with a right of renewal.* It is not a series of single premium policies for one year term assurance. It is not like an indemnity policy where each premium buys cover for a year after which the policyholder must renew or the cover expires. The fact that the policy will lapse if the premiums are not paid makes no difference. The amounts of the annual premiums and of the sum assured are fixed in advance at the outset and assume the payment of annual premiums throughout the term of the policy …
>
> In the present case the benefits specified in the policy are expressed to be payable 'in consideration of the payment of the first premium already made *and of the further premiums payable*' … It is beyond argument that the death benefit of £1m paid on Mr Murphy's death was paid in consideration for all the premiums which had been paid before that date, including those paid with the plaintiffs' money, and not just some of them. Part of that sum, therefore, represented the traceable proceeds of the plaintiffs' money.[15]

And further on:

> Why should the proceeds of the policy be attributed to the first premium when the policy itself is expressed to be in consideration of all the premiums? There is no analogy with the case where trust money is used to maintain or improve property of a third party. *The nearest analogy is with an instalment purchase.*[16]

An instalment purchase, of course, is a purchase on credit, where title passes at the outset in consideration of the discharge of a debt paid in instalments. In this case, if later premiums were not paid, the initially acquired chose in action *lapses*.[17]

[14] *Foskett* (n 3).
[15] ibid 133E–H (emphasis added); see also 110E (Lord Browne-Wilkinson),116B (Lord Hoffmann).
[16] ibid 137E (emphasis added).
[17] ibid 137C, 137G.

Conaglen suggests that the result in *Foskett* can be explained without reference to backwards tracing. Conaglen first discusses the case of *Primeau v Granfield*, which Smith explains as a case of backwards tracing. Primeau was allowed to trace money of his expended by Granfield to pay the rent on a lease into the lease itself. Conaglen says:[18]

> [W]hile the decision can be interpreted as depending on tracing Primeau's money into the payment of obligations owed by Granfield under the lease, H and J seemed to think of the payments as being in the nature of rent. As the Privy Council has said, 'the rent is equivalent to the purchase money'[19] for a lease—in other words, 'the monetary compensation payable by the tenant in consideration for the grant'.[20] The lease entitled Granfield to mine for gold, but that right was dependent on his payment of a price for the right (the rent) and Primeau's money had been used to pay that price. In substance, Primeau's money had been used to acquire the rights that the lease gave to Granfield ...
>
> It is not suggested that this interpretation of *Primeau v Granfield* is categorically inconsistent with Smith's interpretation of the case: although it was not the case historically, the modern cases have treated rent as a contractual obligation, so that payment of rent can be considered payment of a debt and *Primeau v Granfield* can thus be interpreted as supporting Smith's thesis. But that support is weak given that the facts of the case are also consistent with Primeau's money having been used to procure the asset that Granfield held, *at least in terms of his continued holding of that asset* ... Treating the use of Primeau's money as payment of the rent for the goldmine lease makes *Primeau v Granfield* similar to the House of Lords' decision in *Foskett v McKeown*, where trust beneficiaries were able to trace into an insurance policy after the premiums were paid with trust funds.

In a footnote[21] to the last sentence, Conaglen says:

> Penner argues that *Foskett* itself involved backwards tracing, for this reason ... But that does not accurately reflect the Lords' reasoning: Lord Millett, in particular, identified substituted assets (rather than the payment of a debt) at each stage of his analysis of the facts (see [2001] 1 AC 102 at 134).

With respect, it is not clear how these thoughts undermine the claim that *Foskett* was a case of backwards tracing. It is immaterial how 'rent' is characterised so long as it is understood to be *consideration*, 'purchase money', for an asset (the lease) *already* acquired. Indeed, treating rent in this way seems to affirm that the law has recognised later consideration as transactionally linked to the prior acquisition of an asset. As to whether the preceding discussion of *Foskett* accurately reflects the court's reasoning, I regret that I cannot find anything on page 134 which unsettles what I have said above. Of course I do not claim that either Lord Millett or the other two of their Lordships in the majority, Lord Browne-Wilkinson or Lord

[18] Conaglen (n 6) (emphasis added).

[19] *Malayan Credit Ltd v Jack Chia-MPH Ltd* [1986] 1 AC 549, 560.

[20] *Property Holding Co v Clark* [1948] 1 KB 630, 648.

[21] Conaglen (n 6) fn 38.

Hoffmann, explicitly endorsed the result as one of backwards tracing.[22] It is their characterisation of the chose in action under the policy as one acquired at the outset into which later premiums could be traced which makes irresistible the conclusion that backwards tracing was allowed. True, later on in his judgment Millett, unlike Browne-Wilkinson and Hoffmann, would have treated the premiums as going first to buy units under the policy's formula for allocating part of the premiums to the investment element of the policy, and part to the life insurance element.[23] But as to the latter, which generated the sought-after proceeds, it is still clear on Millett's reasoning that that allocation resulted in the relevant fraction of the premiums in question serving as consideration for the chose in action which he emphasised was acquired at the outset.[24]

Then we have the case of *Law Society v Haider*.[25] Judge Richards QC allowed the claimant to trace from a payment discharging a mortgage into the house that was purchased with the mortgage loan, and thence into the proceeds of the sale of that house and into another house purchased with those proceeds. Conaglen argues that the result in the case can be explained by way of treating the claimant

[22] They did not, in their judgments, address the defendant counsel's argument that this was a case of backwards tracing, and thus not to be allowed, but neither did this argument succeed: *Foskett* (n 3) 105G–H, 106A.

[23] ibid 140H–145D.

[24] Joe Campbell has suggested to me an alternative analysis of *Foskett* that does not turn on backwards tracing. He asks us to consider a bank account. Upon entering into the banker–client contract, the client acquires a chose in action, a right to be paid the current balance of the cleared funds in the account upon demand. So in a way the contract provides the client with a single chose in action at the outset of the contract. But the value of that chose in action fluctuates with payments in and withdrawals out. Thus, it seems to be the case that the various payments in can be traced 'forward' into the later balance in the account. By parity of reasoning, whilst the chose in action represented by the complex of rights under the insurance policy was acquired at the outset of the contract of insurance, the payments of the policy premiums can be traced forwards into the complex of rights making up that chose in action, the value of which fluctuated as further premiums were paid. At any particular time, the precise rights that the policyholder had would not be identical to the rights the day the policy was taken out. In the insurance contract in *Foskett*, premiums were allocated under a formula (expressed in terms of 'units') whereby part of any premium was allocated to the 'investment' component of the policy, part to the 'insurance' component. But, with respect, this bank balance analogy does not justify the actual result in *Foskett*. On the facts it was clear that the 4th and 5th premiums paid with trust money did not contribute, or contribute much, to the 'insurance' component of the policy, into the proceeds of which the court allowed the beneficiaries to trace. The payments of trust money marginally enhanced the surrender value of the policy, by contributing to the policy's investment component which, at the time of the policyholder's death five years after its inception, would have had investment contributions of somewhat less than £50,000 (part of each premium going to sustain the 'insurance' component). It was clear on the facts that even had the 4th and 5th premiums not been paid, the result would have been a significant decline in the surrender value of the policy, as money from the 'investment' side would have been 'cancelled' to keep the 'insurance' side on foot. So on principles analagous to the banker–client accounting, the beneficiaries would have at most had a claim to the enhanced surrender value of the policy immediately prior to the death of the policyholder; at most (assuming that the insurance company was not a fantastically good investor) this would have been in the region of somewhat less (again accounting for the fact that part of each premium went to keeping the 'insurance' component on foot) than £20,000 plus investment returns. Perhaps £20,000 or thereabouts. But the beneficiaries received two-fifths of the £1 million payout.

[25] *Law Society v Haider* [2003] EWHC 2486.

as subrogated to the mortgagee whose loan was initially discharged with the trust money.[26] That may be so,[27] but it was not how the court reasoned. The judge explicitly treated the case as a 'tracing exercise',[28] and there is no mention whatsoever of a subrogation claim.

Bishopsgate Investment Management Ltd v Homan[29] is the first case where backwards tracing was explicitly considered. At first instance Vinelott J was willing to allow backwards tracing in limited circumstances, ie,

> where an asset was acquired by [the defendant] with moneys borrowed from an overdrawn or loan account and there was an inference that when the borrowing was incurred it was the intention that it should be repaid by misappropriation of [the plaintiff's] money. Another possibility was that moneys misappropriated from [the plaintiff] were paid into an overdrawn account of [the defendant] in order to reduce the overdraft and so make finance available within the overdraft limits for [the defendant] to purchase some particular asset.[30]

Dillon LJ accepted elements of Vinelott's reasoning, but Leggatt LJ found the contention utterly wrong on the basis that it was simply impossible for a claim to be made in respect of an asset acquired before the misappropriation took place.[31] Henry LJ simply agreed with both judgments, so the case is frail authority on the status of backwards tracing.

We now come to *Relfo* and *Brazil*. Schematically, both cases involved payments of the following kind: A caused B to make a payment to C; A then afterwards paid B with funds, which payment was equivalent to a misapplication of trust moneys; in both cases, the court held that the claimant could trace the second payment to B into the first, prior payment from B to C, so that C held those funds as a recipient of trust property.

In *Relfo* the payment of Relfo's funds was made to Mirren Ltd. On the same day a payment in like amount was made from Intertrade Group LLC to the defendant. On the facts it was clear that 'there was no transfer out of Mirren's account in advance of the Intertrade payment which could have funded it'.[32] Nevertheless, Arden LJ, giving the leading judgment, held that Relfo could trace its money into the payment received by the defendant. One feature of the case is that whilst Arden LJ briefly referred to Leggatt's judgment in *Bishopsgate*,[33] there was no

[26] Conaglen (n 6) 441–42.

[27] The problem is that the report of the case does not disclose the content of the order agreed upon by the parties. A subrogation claim will not provide the same valuation of the charge on the final traceable asset as would a backwards tracing claim. See the discussion of the different results arising from subrogation as against a backwards tracing in the last section, examples (1) and (2) below.

[28] *Haider* (n 25) [39]–[42].

[29] *Bishopsgate Investment Management Ltd v Homan* [1995] Ch 211.

[30] *Bishopsgate Investment Management Ltd v Homan* [1994] Pens LR 179 [156] (Vinelott J at first instance).

[31] *Bishopsgate* (n 29) 221F–G.

[32] *Relfo* (n 1) [14].

[33] ibid [31].

discussion of that case which was presumably binding upon a subsequent Court of Appeal. The court held that the trial judge was right to infer that money from the Mirren account was subsequently paid over to Intertrade to fund, ex post facto, Intertrade's payment to the defendant.[34] In so holding, Arden J said the following:

> 61 The inference that the judge made means that he found that what had happened was on the following lines. At the start of the chain of transactions, Relfo had money on deposit with its bank, ie it had the benefit of a debt owed to it by its bank. It exchanged this right for a debt owed to it by Mirren. The value of this debt lay in the credit balance on this account. Mirren agrees to transfer this balance to another person or person at some future date in exchange for Intertrade making the Intertrade payment.
>
> 62 I therefore accept Mr Shaw's submission that the fact that Mirren did not reimburse anyone for the Intertrade payment until after the Intertrade payment had been made does not matter. On the judge's findings, the Intertrade payment and the other payments made throughout the chain of substitutions *was made on the faith of the arrangement that Mirren would provide reimbursement.* By making that arrangement, Mirren exploited and used the value inherent in Relfo's money that had been paid into Mirren's account (my italics).
>
> 63 In my judgment, Mr Shaw is correct in his submission that Agip is authority for the proposition that monies held on trust can be traced into other assets even if those other assets are passed on before the trust monies are paid to the person transferring them, provided that that person acted on the basis that he would receive reimbursement for the monies he transferred *out of the trust funds*. The decision in Agip demonstrates that in order to trace money into substitutes it is not necessary that the payments should occur in any particular order, let alone chronological order. As Mr Shaw submits, a person may agree to provide a substitute for a sum of money even before he receives that sum of money. In those circumstances the receipt would postdate the provision of the substitute. *What the court has to do is establish whether the likelihood is that monies could have been paid at any relevant point in the chain in exchange for such a promise. I see no reason in logic or principle why this particular way of proving a substitution should be limited to payments to or by correspondent banks* (my italics).

The passages I have italicised throw up a difficulty in interpreting the ratio of the case. In order for the payment from Intertrade to the defendant to be the backwardly traceable proceeds of the payment (whenever it came) to Intertrade, that payment must have discharged a debt owed to Intertrade incurred when Intertrade made the payment to the defendant. So that was one inference, that the rogue director of Relfo had promised Intertrade to reimburse it for the payment to the defendant. But the first passage in [63] that I have italicised suggests that the court made a further inference, that the arrangement between the rogue director and Intertrade was *also* that the money to discharge the debt to Intertrade for making the payment to the defendant was to come from Relfo. Call this the 'second inference'. It is not clear why such a finding was either necessary or even relevant.

[34] ibid [57]–[58].

Consider Smith's criticism of Vinelott's version of backwards tracing in *Bishopsgate*.[35] It seems to violate the general principle of tracing to require that the defendant intends in advance to use the trust property that was in fact misappropriated to purchase the asset. All that is generally required is that he actually acquires the asset in exchange for passing title to the trust assets to the other party to the exchange—his prior intentions are entirely irrelevant. Test the matter this way. Let us assume the court held that making the second inference was essential to the success of Relfo's claim. Thus, if the rogue director had merely promised to reimburse Intertrade, but did not disclose the source of the funds, then Relfo would not have been successful. But this seems to impose an irrelevant requirement, since *ex hypothesi* it was Relfo's funds which were actually used. Or weaken the requirement to this: that an essential element of Relfo's claim was that the rogue director himself *intended* to reimburse Intertrade with Relfo's funds at the time he agreed to reimburse Intertrade for making the payment to the defendant. Again, why should this matter? Imagine that he did thus intend, but when the time for reimbursing Intertrade came along, he reimbursed them instead with money from another company, Delfo, of which he was also a director. Why should Delfo not have a claim in these circumstances? Because their being a source of funds did not *cause* the rogue director to make the arrangment with Intertrade, whereas Relfo's being a source of funds did? Should this reasoning entitle Relfo to trace into the payment made with Delfo's funds? Another way of putting this objection is that tracing is normally regarded as *transactional*, not *causal*. As Lord Millett put it in *Foskett* in criticising the judgment in the Court of Appeal in that case:

> [That] argument is based on causation and as I have explained is a category mistake derived from the law of unjust enrichment. It is an example of the same fallacy that gives rise to the idea that the proceeds of an ordinary life policy belong to the party who paid the last premium without which the policy would have lapsed. But the question is one of attribution not causation.[36]

Turning to *Brazil*, in his judgment for the Board Lord Toulson reviewed the authorities and the arguments of both Smith and Conaglen. He said:

> 33 More particularly the plaintiffs submit, as Professor Smith argues, that money used to pay a debt can in principle be traced into whatever was acquired in return for the debt. That is a very broad proposition and it would take the doctrine of tracing far beyond its limits in the case law to date. As a statement of general application, the Board would reject it. The courts should be very cautious before expanding equitable proprietary remedies in a way which may have an adverse effect on other innocent parties. If a trustee on the verge of bankruptcy uses trust funds to pay off an unsecured creditor to whom he is personally indebted, in the absence of special circumstances it is hard to see why the beneficiaries' claim should take precedence over those of the general body of unsecured creditors.

[35] L Smith, 'Tracing, 'Swollen Assets' and the Lowest Intermediate Balance: *Bishopsgate Management Ltd v Homan*' (1994) 8 *Trusts Law International* 102.

[36] *Foskett* (n 3) 137G.

In context, the last sentence seems to be an endorsement of Conaglen's view,[37] cited by his Lordship at [31], viz:

> When the already precarious position of unsecured creditors is weighed against the concomitantly far better protected position of trust beneficiaries, it is suggested that the law ought not to recognise the possibility of tracing backwards. The unsecured creditors should not have their position worsened further by effectively making them insurers for the beneficiaries against trustee defalcations. Trust beneficiaries whose money has been wrongly applied in satisfaction of a debt can stand in the position of the satisfied creditor (by subrogation), but it is a step too far, in policy terms, to allow them to stand in the position of the debtor and act as owners of property the trustee acquired before the debt was paid.

However his Lordship went on to allow backwards tracing in this case, on the following basis:

> 38 The development of increasingly sophisticated and elaborate methods of money laundering, often involving a web of credits and debits between intermediaries, makes it particularly important that a court should not allow a camouflage of *interconnected transactions* to obscure its vision of their true overall purpose and effect. If the court is satisfied that the various steps *are part of a co-ordinated scheme*, it should not matter that, either as a deliberate part of the choreography or possibly because of the incidents of the banking system, a debit appears in the bank account of an intermediary before a reciprocal credit entry. The Board agrees with Sir Richard Scott V-C's observation in *Foskett v McKeown* [1998] Ch 265 that the availability of equitable remedies ought to depend on the *substance of the transaction* in question and not on the strict order in which associated events occur.
>
> …
>
> 40 The Board therefore rejects the argument that there can never be backward tracing, or that the court can never trace the value of an asset whose proceeds are paid into an overdrawn account. But the claimant has to establish a *co-ordination between the depletion of the trust fund and the acquisition of the asset which is the subject of the tracing claim, looking at the whole transaction*, such as to warrant the court attributing the value of the interest acquired to the misuse of the trust fund. This is likely to depend on inference from the proved facts, particularly since in many cases the testimony of the trustee, if available, will be of little value.
>
> 41 The Board does not doubt the correctness of the decisions in *James Roscoe (Bolton) Ltd v Winder* [1915] 1 Ch 62 and *In re Goldcorp Exchange Ltd* [1995] 1 AC 74, but in neither case was there evidence of *an overall transaction embracing the co-ordinated outward and inward movement of assets* (my italics).

Apparently, then, the Privy Council has adopted a restricted application of backwards tracing, restricted that is to cases where the debt and the payment with which it is discharged are in substance part of the same overall transaction, such that there is some sort of co-ordination between the depletion of the trust fund and the acquisition of the asset. Such a requirement, though not identical to the

[37] Conaglen (n 6) 455.

'second inference' requirement canvassed above, would presumably treat such an inference as relevant for determining that the separate transactions were in substance part of an overall scheme of co-ordination.

Perhaps, but only perhaps, some illumination of the concept of a 'composite transaction' can be gleaned from the more or less contemporaneous UK Supreme Court decision in *Menalaou v Bank of Cyprus UK Ltd*.[38] The parents of the claimant, M, were indebted to the defendant, 'the Bank', to the tune of £2.2 million, secured by two charges on their family home. In order to reduce their indebtedness and free up some money for other purposes, they decided to sell the home and buy a less valuable property for £785,000, which they intended to put in the name of M to be held on trust for herself and two of her siblings. It was proposed that following the sale of the old family home, the Bank would receive £750,000 to reduce the parents' indebtedness and would release its charges over that property, but would acquire a charge over the property put in the name of M. The Bank agreed to this plan of action. The proceeds of the sale of the old family home were received by the parents' solicitors and applied at their instructions according to the agreement, that is, they were disbursed to the right persons under the parents' agreement with the Bank. The Bank received its £750,000, and the purchase price of £785,000 for the property in M's name went to its vendor. Moreover, the solicitors secured a charge over M's property in favour of the Bank. However, as events later transpired, it became clear that M was unaware that the property in her name was to be subject to a charge and did not consent to it, and in consequence, the charge was improperly obtained and was void. Not aware that the charge was void, the Bank released its charges over the old family home about a month after the new property was purchased in M's name.

The Bank claimed that, although the charge over M's property was void, it was entitled to be subrogated to an unpaid vendor's lien over that property, and it succeeded in this claim in the UK Supreme Court. In deciding in favour of the Bank, the UK Supreme Court did so on the basis that the Bank had no proprietary interest in the money received from the purchase of the old family home; in other words, the parents received the proceeds of the sale of the old family home beneficially (although through the receipt of their solicitors), though they were contractually bound to spend it according to their agreement with the Bank.[39] This raised the problem that M could be characterised as at most an 'indirect' recipient of value from the Bank, that is, M was not enriched by a direct transfer of value from the Bank to her, but in some other way.

Both Lord Clarke and Lord Neuberger, endorsing in broad respects the reasoning of the Court of Appeal, held that there was sufficient connection between the Bank, the parents, and M to hold that M's acquistion of the uncharged freehold to the new property was an enrichment at the expense of the Bank, and that it

[38] *Menalaou v Bank of Cyprus UK Ltd* [2015] UKSC 66, [2015] 3 WLR 1334.
[39] ibid [13], [53] (Lord Clarke), [85] (Lord Neuberger).

was unjust.[40] It is difficult to discern in quite what way M's enrichment was at the expense of the Bank, but Lord Clarke reasoned that '[t]he bank was central to the scheme from start to finish', and '[i]t was thus thanks to the bank that [M] became owner of [the property], but only subject to that charge'.[41] The sale of the old family home and the purchase of property in M's name 'were not separate but part of one scheme, which involved the bank throughout':[42]

> The question in each case is whether there is a *sufficient causal connection*, in the sense of a sufficient nexus or link, between the loss to the bank and the benefit received by the defendant, here [M].[43]

For his part Lord Neuberger found that it was 'appropriate' to treat the sale of the old family home and the purchase of a new property in M's name as 'part of one scheme, at least for present purposes'.[44] He also said:

> There was in reality a single transaction, and it was from that transaction that [M] directly benefitted, even though the benefit was effected at the direction of [M's] parents. The benefit to [M] was direct because *it arose as the immediate and inevitable result of the very transaction to which she was party* and which gave rise to the unjust enrichment … I should add that, even if [M] could be characterised as an indirect recipient of any enrichment, I do not consider that that would assist her: she would still properly be liable on the facts of this case, essentially for the same reasons.[45]

> Standing back, any fair-minded person would say that, as a matter of fairness and common sense, by acquiring the freehold [free] from any charge [M] was unjustly enriched at the expense of the bank, albeit not because of any fault of hers.[46]

It is difficult to find any precise characterisation of the transaction in these passages which provides much in the way of guidance. The two passages I have italicised seem to insist on some kind of causal connection between one transaction and another, ie, that had the bank not agreed to the parents' scheme then the parents would never have received the money to buy the house in M's name. It is worthwhile pointing out that this seems to be a notion of 'but for' causation in the strong sense that in the absence of 1, 2 could simply not have taken place. This is to be distinguished from a weaker sense of 'but for' causation operating in the realm of the defence of change of position. There the defendant must show that his receipt of the money, say mistakenly transferred to her, prompted her to make

[40] The reasoning of the Court of Appeal and Lord Clarke and Lord Neuberger can be criticised, and was by Lord Carnwath: [107]-[40]. According to Lord Carnwath, the orthodox application of '*Quistclose*' trust principles would entail that the bank *was* beneficially interested in the money the solicitors received from the sale of the old family home, and given that, the purchase of the house in M's name with that money made available to them a right to be subrogated to an unpaid vendor's lien.

[41] *Menalaou*(n 38) [24].

[42] ibid [25].

[43] ibid [27] (emphasis added), [33].

[44] ibid [67].

[45] ibid [73] (emphasis added).

[46] ibid [77].

an expenditure that she otherwise *would* not have made, not necessarily one she *could* not have made. Perhaps the most that can be gleaned from *Menelaou* and *Brazil* is that the UK Supreme Court will be sensitive to treating linked transactions, especially if an earlier one is a 'but for' cause of a later one in the strong sense just identified, as a composite transaction if that reflects some sense of 'economic reality', or 'fairness and common sense'.

III. 'Composite Transactions' and Bona Fide Purchase

There are two axes upon which the acquisition of an asset and a payment to discharge a debt can be treated as co-ordinate, or composite, so as to form, in substance, part of an overall transaction: (1) the relation of the incurring of the debt to the asset into which one traces; and (2) the intentions of the defalcating trustee or fiduciary. Regarding (1), we can make a distinction between two sorts of case.[47] The first sort of case concerns what I shall dub 'D-claims', for *direct backwards tracing claims*, those in which the debt arises under the same agreement under which the asset is acquired. The obvious cases are sales of goods, and credits and debits through the banking system (*Agip*, etc). Mortgage loans, and perhaps credit card purchases, are a little trickier. The second sort of case is where the debt obligation arises independently of any asset acquisition. In these cases, such as the grant of overdraft facilities, the debt arises when the facility is made use of, but the debt is not incurred in respect of any particular acquisition of an asset *as a matter of the contract in which the party in question incurred the debt*. This is so even if the reason for which the debtor acquired the loan facility was because a particular asset acquisition was in mind. I shall call these IND-claims, short for *indirect backwards tracing claims*. This brings us to (2). It is arguable, in the case of IND-claims, that only where the defalcating trustee or fiduciary in charge of the property of others, such as a company director (whose misapplications of his principal's property is treated as equivalent to a breach of trust,[48] as in *Relfo*), incurred the debt with the intention to acquire a specific asset and discharge the debt with trust moneys/the money of his principal that the beneficiary/principal should be able to trace into that asset. The idea is that the trustee/fiduciary's intention makes the case more or less equivalent to a D-claim. But let us begin with D-claims before tackling this thorny issue.

My suggestion regarding D-claims is that they seem suited to satisfy Lord Toulson's concern about the transaction being 'in substance' an overall transaction or a co-ordinated scheme. The easiest case, it is submitted, is the case of a sale

[47] My recognition of this distinction owes a lot to conversations with Rob Chambers. I am not sure he would be willing to take much if any credit for the passages that follow.

[48] *Re Lands Allotment Co* (1894) 1 Ch 616; JE Penner, *The Law of Trusts*, 10th edn (Oxford, OUP, 2016) para 11.15.

of goods, and we can also draw some assistance here from the doctrine of bona fide purchase.

The Sale of Goods Act 1979, which is well known as a statutory embodiment for the most part of the pre-existing common law, treats the price paid by the buyer as consideration for title to the goods acquired whether or not the price is paid prior to or after title to the goods passes to the buyer.[49] The important point to note is that if one can trace into the payment of the price in a case where title to goods passes in advance, this is essentially a case of backwards tracing through the discharge of a debt, yet it is clear that whenever the price is paid, it counts as *consideration* for acquiring title to the goods. The Act leads us to comprehend a more capacious definition of 'consideration' than those purchases of property which, for tracing purposes, would only entitle a beneficiary to trace where title to the goods passed at the time of or following the payment of the price. But, as we saw earlier in attending to Conaglen's conceptual objection to backwards tracing[50] even here we must be circumspect: on strict forward-tracing principles, tracing into the goods acquired would not be allowed in so far as the money is used to discharge a debt, here the debt incurred on entering into the contract of sale; strictly speaking, only simultaneous shop counter transactions would count because only in these cases would it seem that the payment of the price would not amount to the discharge of a pre-existing contractually incurred debt. What the sale of goods example illustrates is that the common law has never had such a restricted understanding of consideration. The sale of goods case also seems to diminish in respect of D claims the worry expressed by Conaglen, and apparently endorsed by Lord Toulson, about the trustee's creditors. Why should not the beneficiary be entitled to trace into the actual goods his money was used to acquire, as long as his money was used to pay the price, ie, his money was the consideration in law for the trustee acquiring title to the goods?

One last thought about sales cases, concerning causal and transactional links. Consider the very common 'all moneys' version of retention of title provisions in sales of raw materials. Such provisions prevent title passing under each individual sale agreement until all outstanding debts owed to the supplier under any contract of sale are discharged. Thus, in a simple case, A orders 100 gallons of orange paint, incurring an obligation to pay his supplier, B, $1,000 on 1 May, and a month later orders 100 gallons of green paint, the price of $1,200 falling due on 1 June. A pays B on time under both contracts, and it would seem unremarkable to say that if A paid B $1,000 on time under the first contract with trust money, the beneficiaries should be able to claim that any remaining orange paint in A's hand was the traceable proceeds of trust money. Yet, notice, A's payment of $1,000 was not the cause of title to the paint passing to A—rather, as a matter of causation, it was the

[49] This seems to be the clear effect of s 2(1), which defines the 'price' as the money consideration for the goods, s 17, which would allow the property in the goods to pass prior to the price being paid, and s 39 (unpaid seller's rights), s 41 (seller's lien), s 49 (action for price), and s 57(2) (auction sales).

[50] Text to n 6.

second payment of $1,200 which did so. Such an example reinforces the point that tracing is a transactional, not a causal, enquiry, that is an enquiry of determining which rights served as consideration for other rights acquired by exchange.

The key here is to focus on the idea of consideration, and we can learn something from the doctrine of bona fide purchase in trusts law and the holder in due course rule in the case of money and negotiable instruments. The receiver of trust money is entitled to the defence[51] of bona fide purchase if he accepts the money he receives in discharge of a debt the trustee owes to him[52] and, as Smith points out, 'For the purposes of the [defence of holder in due course], the value which must be given includes *any consideration* which would support a contract'.[53]

In each of the D-claims, the debt arises under the same agreement as that under which title passes or in pursuance of which contract title can be acquired. This was the case in *Foskett* (the contract of life insurance) and, arguably, in *Relfo*, in the sense that the court inferred that the rogue director 'purchased' the Intertrade payment to the defendant. Mortgage loans, as in *Haider*, or credit card purchases are not strictly speaking D-claims because the debt is incurred to a different party, through a contract of finance, from the person, the vendor, from whom title is acquired. However, in purchases of land the two contracts, one of sale and one of finance, are so closely linked—for instance the amount borrowed is used in the mortgage loan case to pay part of the purchase price of the land and is immediately secured by a mortgage on the land—that they would appear to meet any sensible 'composite' transaction test. With credit card purchases, each debt under the finance agreement arises simultaneously with the card holder's purchase, so again it is difficult not to see the transaction as an 'overall' one.

More difficult are IND-claims, where the debt discharged was undertaken without any clear purchase in mind, and where the discharge of the obligation may take place some substantial amount of time, perhaps many years, after the acquisition of title to the sought-after proceeds. So, for example, consider the case of someone who gets a loan of $10,000 secured by a second mortgage over his house in 2001, which he then uses to purchase shares. In 2015, he discharges the debt and accrued interest with money from the bank account of the company of which he is a director, and the shares are now worth $35,000. It is in this sort of case, one presumes, that Conaglen and Lord Toulson would not extend to the company the facility to backwards trace, removing the shares from the director's estate. I can see

[51] Michael Bridge raises an interesting point about whether, pleading points aside, it is right to treat bona fide purchase as a defence. For example, if someone brings a wholly unwarranted claim in conversion against me, I might equally say that my acquisition of the goods from the true owner constitutes a defence to the conversion claim. Where I have to rely upon the bona fide purchase doctrine in defending an action, I am equally relying upon the good title I acquired, albeit in this case from a non-owner. At the point when the property in goods passed from the non-owner to me, the former true owner ceased to have a good title that could be asserted against me so that I did not commit, as it were, the actus reus of conversion when taking delivery from the non-owner.

[52] *Taylor v Blakelock* (1885) 23 Ch D 560.

[53] L Smith, 'Security' in A Burrows (ed), *English Private Law*, 3rd edn (Oxford, OUP, 2013) para 5.119 (emphasis added).

something of the force of this, but I would also say that I do not see that one can turn such an IND-claim into an allowable composite IND-claim just because, for example, the director always harboured an intention to pay off the mortgage with money from his company or some other illegitimate source of funds. This seems to me to be an illicit introduction of a causal consideration, something like 'but for his intention to pay off the loan with his company's money, he would never have taken out the loan in the first place and hence wouldn't have acquired the shares'.

IV. Backwards Tracing and Subrogation

This last section concerns the interaction between backwards tracing and 'reviving subrogation'. In certain circumstances, if X pays off Y's debt to Z, X will, by operation of law, be subrogated to Z's right as a creditor. In other words, by paying off Z, X will in effect 'purchase' Z's right to the payment of the debt against Y. Notice that unlike in the case of an indemnity insurer being subrogated to the claim of the insured against a third-party tortfeasor, where the insurer takes over rights that the insured continues to have against his tortfeasor, in the case of reviving subrogation, by paying off Y's debt, X extinguishes the debt and thus Z's right as a creditor. The right against Y that X acquires by subrogation is a new right that arises by operation of law; in essence Y's debt is revived in favour of X, hence the label 'reviving' subrogation.[54]

The right to be subrogated to the creditor's rights in this way has been explained as a remedy which reverses the unjust enrichment of the original debtor,[55] and was most prominently applied in a breach of trust context in *Boscawen v Bajwa*[56] by Millett LJ. Bajwa intended to sell his mortgaged land for a price roughly equal to what he owed under the mortgage to the Halifax Building Society. On the sale Bajwa would be required to use the purchase money to pay off the mortgage, which would leave him with little if any proceeds for himself. The purchasers raised £140,000 on a mortgage loan from Abbey National, and the money was transferred to solicitors in advance of the completion of the sale. In breach of trust the money was advanced before completion and was applied to pay off the mortgage loan to Halifax. The sale never occurred; because the contract of sale was not in writing it was void, so there was no possibility of a decree of specific performance or a vendor–purchaser constructive trust in favour of the intending purchaser. As a result Bajwa ended up with an unmortgaged property, whilst Abbey National had advanced funds and received no mortgage on the property in return. Giving the judgment of the Court of Appeal, Millett LJ held that Abbey National was entitled to be subrogated to Halifax's mortgage on the land, thus entitling them to priority

[54] C Mitchell, *The Law of Subrogation* (Oxford, OUP, 1994) 4.
[55] *Banque Financière de la Cite v Park (Battersea) Ltd* [1998] UKHL 7, [1999] 1 AC 221.
[56] *Boscawen v Bajwa* [1995] EWCA Civ 15, [1996] 1 WLR 328.

over a charge on the land that had been subsequently granted by the court to Bajwa's judgment creditors. The court clearly distinguished between the process of tracing, which allowed Abbey National to show that its value was received by Bajwa, and the claim to be subrogated.

In the course of so deciding Millett LJ said:

> If the plaintiff succeeds in tracing his property, whether in its original or in some changed form, into the hands of the defendant and overcomes any defences which are put forward on the defendant's behalf, he is entitled to a remedy. The remedy will be fashioned to the circumstances ... [I]f the plaintiff's money has been used to discharge a mortgage on the defendant's land, then the court may achieve a similar result by treating the land as subject to a charge by way of subrogation in favour of the plaintiff ... Tracing was the process by which the Abbey National sought to establish that its money was applied in the discharge of the Halifax's charge; subrogation was the remedy which it sought in order to deprive Mr Bajwa ... of the unjust enrichment which he would otherwise obtain at the Abbey National's expense.[57]

For reasons which I shall now explore, I do not find the result or reasoning in this case easy. The main difficulty is that the right to be subrogated here is understood to be a remedy the beneficiary of a trust has to reverse the defendant's unjust enrichment, but the interaction between the rights of the beneficiary when the trust has been breached and the law of unjust enrichment was not really explored. Note first that subrogation, whilst achieving a similar result in the case of a secured loan, is the opposite of backwards tracing. In backwards-tracing, one traces into items purchased with the borrowed funds. In contrast, a subrogation claim allows the beneficiary claimant to stand in the shoes of the paid-off creditor; in the case of an unsecured debt, for example a credit card debt that is paid off with trust money, the beneficiary will acquire by subrogation nothing more than a personal claim for money against the defendant, because that is all the credit card company had. In the case of a purchase-money mortgage, however, subrogation provides a result similar to backwards tracing. A backwards tracing claim would allow the beneficiary to trace his value into the property purchased with the credit given, and in the case of a first mortgage of land, that will be the land itself, of course. The beneficiary might then claim a proportionate share of the value of the land or, if the recipient is a trustee or wrongdoer, elect for a lien over the property securing the amount of trust money expended. By subrogation, the claimant will necessarily acquire a proprietary right in the land too, since the loan is a secured one, and the charge forms part of the right to which he is subrogated. But the claimant cannot acquire by subrogation an ownership or co-ownership share. So the first thing to note is that, if backwards tracing had been recognised and applied in this case, whether explicitly or implicitly, the issue of subrogation might never have arisen.

But the real difficulty is that if the beneficiary is entitled to make a claim reversing the defendant recipient's unjust enrichment by way of subrogation, the question is why the beneficiary should not have a restitutionary remedy for 'subtractive'

[57] ibid 335.

unjust enrichment in all cases where trust property (or its equivalent, eg, company funds) is misapplied. I am still convinced that there should be no such general remedy for the reasons given by Lionel Smith some 15 years ago:

> It has been said that the claim in knowing receipt belongs to the law of unjust enrichment, and since claims in unjust enrichment do not depend on fault, therefore it cannot be right that the knowing receipt claim should depend on fault. The startling consequence is that not some but all of the cases on the subject are wrong. More recently, another line has been taken, to the effect that even if the claim in knowing receipt is based on wrongdoing rather than unjust enrichment, nonetheless there is no reason that a plaintiff cannot put to one side the claim based on wrongdoing, and sue instead in unjust enrichment. The consequences of this view are only slightly less startling: the cases may be right, but all of the lawyers and judges involved failed to notice that there was another claim available to the plaintiff, and moreover one which renders otiose any inquiry into cognition. That of course is the inquiry with which the cases are most concerned. It is important to stress that no defendant appears ever to have been made strictly liable for the receipt of trust property …
>
> Writing on this subject, [Lord Nicholls (1998)] deploys the following example. A defendant innocently receives some money, trust property, as a gift from the trustee. He spends it on something which he would have bought anyway, and which leaves no traceable product. If fault is required, there is no claim; if fault is not, then there probably is, because the facts are intended to imply that the defendant cannot use the defence of change of position. Lord Nicholls takes the view that this defendant should repay; he has been made better off out of the claimant's trust fund, and if the defendant is required to repay, he will only be back to where he started. But of course the fact that someone is only back to where he started does not justify liability. Otherwise all gifts would be recoverable, subject only to a defence of change of position. Presumably Lord Nicholls would say, this is not a gift; the plaintiff never intended the defendant to be enriched. But in another sense, it was a gift; it was a gift from the trustee. Ignoring that amounts to ignoring that there is a trust. This defendant might reasonably ask why he should be required to account in court for what he has done over the preceding several years with money that was legally his own (subject only to the [plaintiff's] undiscoverable equitable interest), failing which he will have to dig into his pocket to repay. He might ask why the plaintiff should not instead look for relief to his trustee, the one to whom the money was entrusted in the first place. But the argument for strict liability consistently ignores the essential fact that there is a trust, and seeks to treat the trust beneficiary like a legal owner.[58]

The underlying idea here is that the beneficiary is only entitled to a personal claim when he can falsify the account, essentially claiming that the payment did not come from the trust funds, but from the trustee himself, whether the original trustee or a third-party recipient whose knowledge of the trust makes any disposition of the assets which is inconsistent with the beneficiary's beneficial interest in the assets similarly 'falsifiable'. In such a case the trustee is personally liable to restore the misapplied funds. On the other hand, where the beneficiary chooses to trace

[58] L Smith, 'Unjust Enrichment, Property and the Structure of Trusts' (2000) 116 *LQR* 412, 412–13, 432–33.

into the proceeds of the misapplied trust assets, whether against the trustee himself or a non-bona fide purchaser third-party recipient, the trustee or third party have not been enriched; the beneficial interest in the assets is that of the beneficiary. This way of seeing things flows from the very nature of the trust: (i) from the fact that the trust is a fund in which one asset can serve as the substitute for another; (ii) from the fact that non-bona fide third-party recipients of trust property are bound by the beneficiary's continuing trust interest in the assets received and in any traceable proceeds that arise when those assets are exchanged; and from the fact that the beneficiary's personal remedy is always against someone conceived of as a trustee, ie, as one whose dissipation of the trust assets in a way that fails to comply with the beneficiary's trust interest, ie, in breach of trust, entitles the beneficiary to falsify the account, ie 'disown' the misapplication of the trust assets, treating them as an expenditure by the trustee of his own funds. To repeat, on this logic, either the recipient is enriched by a transfer from *the trustee's own assets*, or he is not enriched at all, for the beneficial interest in the property remains with the beneficiary. If there is anything that seems 'artificial' about this, that is because the trust itself is a creature of artifice, legal artifice.

In view of these considerations, *Boscawen* amounts either to a revolutionary case in which the nature of the beneficiary's claim against third-party recipients has been affirmed as falling within the law of unjust enrichment, or a case that mistakenly imports unjust enrichment principles into the property rules and fault-based rules which govern liability for receipt of trust property.[59]

In *Farah Constructions Pty Ltd v Say-Dee Pty Ltd*[60] the unanimous decision of the High Court of Australia gave voice to concerns similar to those of Smith:

> [T]he restitution basis is unhistorical. There is no sign of it in clear terms in any but the most recent authorities. It is inherent in the Court of Appeal's conclusion that for many decades the courts have misunderstood the tests for satisfying [personal recipient liability]: that is improbable. It is inherent in the conclusion advocated by Say-Dee that for many decades the courts have failed to notice the existence of a form of liability co-existing with [it]: that is equally improbable.[61]

Perhaps more importantly, the Court also rejected the theoretical approach of the proponents of the restitutionary approach:

> The restitution basis reflects a mentality in which considerations of ideal taxonomy prevail over a pragmatic approach to legal development. As Gummow J said [in Roxborough v Rothmans of Pall Mall Australia Ltd (2001) at 544 [72]]:
>
> > 'To the lawyer whose mind has been moulded by civilian influences, the theory may come first, and the source of the theory may be the writings of jurists not the decisions

[59] In *Primlake Ltd (in liquidation) v Matthews Associates* [2006] EWHC 1227 Lawrence Collins J held that a company was entitled to be subrogated to a mortgage loan owed by a dishonest de facto company director and his innocent wife following its discharge by the latter using misappropriated company funds. Backwards tracing was not considered, and *Boscawen* was not cited by the court.

[60] *Farah Constructions Pty Ltd v Say-Dee Pty Ltd* [2007] HCA 22.

[61] ibid [154].

of judges. However, that is not the way in which a system based on case law develops; over time, general principle is derived from judicial decisions upon particular instances, not the other way around.'

The restitution basis was imposed as a supposedly inevitable offshoot of an all-embracing theory. To do that was to bring about an abrupt and violent collision with received principles without any assigned justification.

Of course the decision has been criticised,[62] although Hayton concludes his analysis of the case by stating:

> It would not be surprising if, when the unjust enrichment point is crucial to a dispute, so that detailed argument from counsel on both sides is directed to the point, the House of Lords refuses to strengthen equitable rights through developing unjust enrichment principles so as to wholly undermine the knowledge requirements that restrict personal liability [of the recipient]. Possession and the right to possession are at the core of the notion of legal ownership of land and chattels, meriting protection in their own right irrespective of any fault on the defendant's part. That is not the case for equitable interests in property, lower down the hierarchy of property.[63]

This raises other issues of policy to which we must now turn. Lord Toulson and Matthew Conaglen express sympathy for the plight of the trustee's creditors if backwards tracing were generally available. Yet Conaglen does not evince any similar sympathy for the plight of innocent third-party recipients of misapplied funds who face a beneficiary's subrogation claim.

Notice that the subrogation claim does not turn on whether the debt that was discharged with trust money is a secured debt.[64] The right to be subrogated applies prima facie to the payment of any debt the recipient makes with trust property.

[62] R Chambers, 'Knowing Receipt: Frozen in Australia' (2007) 2 *Journal of Equity* 40.

[63] D Hayton, 'Lessons from Knowing Receipt, Liability and Unjust Enrichment from Australia' (2007) 21 *Trusts Law International* 55, 61.

[64] Historically, subrogation to an unsecured debt has occurred in a number of instances; see JD Heydon, MJ Leeming and PG Turner, *Meagher, Gummow and Lehane's Equity: Doctrines and Remedies*, 5th edn (Chatswood, NSW, LexisNexis Butterworths, 2015) paras 9-005, 9-295 (where a surety or guarantor has discharged the debt of the primary obligor); 9-035 (the right of an employer's insurer to be subrogated to an employer's indemnity against an employee where the employer has been found vicariously liable for the employee's tort); 9-125 (in the case of borrowings unenforceable owing to incapacity). Mitchell, however, seems to doubt the availability of a right to be subrogated to the creditor in the case of an unsecured debt: '[The courts] have forgotten that a claimant cannot be entitled to subrogation in this sort of case unless he also has a direct personal claim in unjust enrichment deriving from the fact that he has discharged the defendant's debt. Hence the fictional "acquisition" of the creditor's rights is redundant unless these rights were secured. The courts have sometimes failed to recognise this, or have chosen to ignore it, and have awarded a personal remedy in the form of a subrogation order while simultaneously denying the claimant a direct personal claim. This is self-contradictory': C Mitchell, 'Subrogation' in A Burrows (ed), *English Private Law*, 3rd edn (Oxford, OUP, 2013) (n 53) para 18.280. Mitchell's position seems to be based on the idea that the principle of unjust enrichment provides a direct personal remedy against B where A pays B's debts, so the right to be subrogated to the personal debts of others is redundant. This reasoning will not apply in jurisdictions, such as Australia, where subrogation is awarded on the basis of equitable principles not analysed in terms of a general liability for unjust enrichment.

Of course, this right to be subrogated to the payment of an unsecured debt will only give the beneficiary a personal right against the recipient to repay the money expended on the debt, and where the recipient is a trustee this will be a pointless, additional right, because the trustee is strictly personally liable to restore the trust anyway; the same applies to the case of a third-party recipient who knows that the property in his hands is trust property; he will be strictly personally liable as well; but an innocent recipient, whilst liable to hold the trust property or traceable proceeds in his hands as trust property—ie, the beneficiary can specifically enforce the trust over this property against him—on conventional knowing receipt/knowing dealing principles[65] is not personally liable to dig into his own pocket to restore the trust. But if the subrogation claim is generally available, then it is likely that the innocent recipient will be personally liable to restore the trust to a large extent, because if you think of the way people spend money, they almost always do so in the discharge of debts. As we have seen, except for gifts and over-the-counter shop sales,[66] most expenditures of money pay off contractually incurred debts of one kind or another. When you pay your restaurant bill at the end of dinner, you pay off a contractual debt incurred when you ordered the meal; when you pay for your vacation you pay off the debt incurred when you booked the holiday. Everything you ever buy on a credit card, ie, on credit, creates a debt that you must ultimately discharge. Thus, if a beneficiary can be subrogated to the rights of all the debtors whom a recipient pays off with trust money and, as we have just seen, most payments a person makes discharge debts, then the beneficiary is subrogated to an array of personal claims against this innocent recipient, with the result that, contrary to what the traditional law teaches us, the innocent recipient is largely personally liable to restore the trust out of his own pocket. Although those in favour of an unjust enrichment analysis of liability for receipt of trust property would be happy with, perhaps exult in, this result, it cannot be the case that this general right of subrogation can stand alongside the conventional law under which an innocent recipient of trust property is not personally liable to restore the value of any trust property or traceable proceeds he receives. It is perhaps worth noting that Lord Millett, when giving the leading decision in *Foskett*, the most important tracing and claiming decision in a century, specifically denied that tracing had anything to do with unjust enrichment and, further, when discussing the claims available to a beneficiary when he traces his equitable interest into the hands of a recipient, did not even mention the *Boscawen* subrogation claim. (To the extent subrogation was raised, it was in respect of the CA holding that Mr Murphy, the insured who applied trust moneys to pay the premiums under the policy of insurance, would be entitled to a lien over the proceeds for repayment of the premiums, a lien to which the trust beneficiaries would be subrogated. We will return to Lord Millett's holding on this point below.)

[65] Penner, *The Law of Trusts* (n 48) para 11.162.
[66] See text to n 7.

Rob Chambers has recently argued that the *trustee* (or equivalent fiduciary in charge of his principal's funds), not the beneficiary, should have a restitutionary claim against the third-party recipient in cases where the trustee misapplied trust property. He states:

> There are three different potential claims against a recipient of assets transferred in breach of trust: (i) an equitable property claim to the assets or their traceable proceeds (which might be regarded as restitution of unjust enrichment); (ii) an equitable personal claim for knowing receipt (which might be regarded as the equitable equivalent to damages for breach of duty); and (iii) a common law personal claim for restitution of unjust enrichment. The first two belong to the beneficiaries and the third to the trustees. There is no need to give the beneficiaries a new equitable claim for restitution of unjust enrichment, since they can compel the trustees to assert their common law claim.[67]

Now of course the trustee of a trust has all the common law rights available to him. If the trustee makes a mistaken payment, say mistakenly pays a second time a brokerage fee to a broker who sells trust shares, then he is entitled to a personal claim against the broker for return of the same amount, and of course he holds that claim on trust for the beneficiaries. So far, so conventional. The further question is whether his second payment can be treated as a misapplication of trust property. Arguably, the broker is not a bona fide purchaser of the funds since, *ex hypothesi*, he provided no consideration for the second mistaken payment. But I, for one, would hesitate to so characterise the situation with the consequence that the broker holds the received funds on trust, exposing him to liability as a knowing recipient/knowing dealer. Assuming for the sake of discussion that not all recipients of mistaken payments hold the amounts they receive on some sort of unjust enrichment trust,[68] there seems no reason that the beneficiaries should have a different, better claim than the trustee's own when this sort of claim arises in the course of the trustee properly, albeit mistakenly, pursuing trust business. I should say the same sort of reasoning should apply when a trustee is defrauded, say selling a trust painting for a worthless cheque. The trustee would be entitled to rescind the transaction, both in law and equity,[69] and that right would be held for the beneficiaries' benefit; it is not clear why these rights should be enhanced by further allowing the beneficiaries to claim that the painting remains beneficially theirs, ie, trust property, throughout.

But Chambers' suggestion is that the trustee has a claim for restitution of unjust enrichment in cases where it is definite that the beneficiary can rightly claim the beneficial, equitable ownership of the funds received by the third-party recipient.

Consider two cases: (1) the trustee innocently overpays a trust beneficiary, say because he miscalculates the money representing the income and overpays the

[67] R Chambers, 'The End of Knowing Receipt' (2016) 2 *Canadian Journal of Comparative and Contemporary Law* 1, 24–25.

[68] The position favoured by Rob Chambers; for discussion see Penner, *The Law of Trusts* (n 48) paras 5.22–5.24.

[69] eg Heydon, Leeming and Turner (n 64) ch 25.

income beneficiary by $10,000; the beneficiary spends the property on shares which fall in value to $7,000; (2) the trustee *mala fide* transfers trust property to a non-beneficiary, giving, for example, his niece a gift of $10,000 from trust funds to celebrate her graduation; the niece uses the funds to discharge a mortgage loan incurred in the usual way, the loaned funds used to pay the vendor of the land acquired. Let us also say that the value of the land purchased has fallen by half.

As to (1), it would not seem right that the trustee should just have a restitutionary claim for the value received, of $10,000, unconnected to the beneificaries' continuing rights in the traceable proceeds. If that were right, both the trustee would have this personal claim, and the beneficiaries would have a proprietary claim to the shares. Whilst it might be said that the trustee would have to hold any money received under the personal, restitutionary claim on trust for the beneficiaries, the income beneficiary in this example would be ill-advised to pay it, for it is not clear how the trustee's enforcing his claim in this way would extinguish the beneficiaries' interest in the shares. It is also not clear how the trustee's enforcing his claim is to be understood on falsification/adoption principles according to the conventional way of understanding the trustee's liability to account. Let us say the beneficiaries falsify the account. The restitutionary claim he is supposed to hold for the beneficiaries would then be unburdened by the trust interest. His liability to the beneficiaries would then be a personal one to restore the account from his own pocket, and so the nature of his claim against the overpaid income beneficiary would be that he paid *his own funds* to the income beneficiary. Why should this payment, a gift, be reversible? The 'mistake' he wishes to rely upon is no longer relevant, since his payment is now not to be conceived of as a mistaken application of trust funds. But neither does any claim for restitution of an unjust enrichment, whether held by the trustee or the beneficiaries, make sense if the beneficiaries choose to 'adopt' the payment to the income beneficiary, in the sense of claiming that trust money did go to the income beneficiary, who received it bound by their trust interests, and traceable into the shares; on that way of seeing the transaction, the income beneficiary is not unjustly enriched, for she is not enriched at all. Assets held on trust for another, or held subject to the beneficial equitable interests of another, are not part of one's own wealth. Of course, on conventional rules for assessing recipient liability, the income beneficiary is not personally liable at all for any innocent dissipation of the traceable proceeds.

Three more points on this case: in conversation Robert Chambers has suggested to me that the trustee's personal restitutionary claim would be reduced to $7,000 because the income beneficiary could claim a change of position defence. But that is not straightforward. One would need to show that the share purchase was an extraordinary expenditure, ie, but for the overpayment the shares would not have been purchased. If the income beneficiary had planned to purchase the shares anyway and just happened to use the trust fund overpayment, no change of position defence would be allowed. Unjust enrichment reasoning is causal, not transactional. Consider also the case where the shares rose in value to $14,000. It can hardly be right that the income beneficiary could escape her proprietary liability to the beneficiaries as a group for the shares by discharging her restitutionary liability to the trustee. But if not on the unjust enrichment perspective, why not? How is her ability to invest well *causative* of an *unjust* enrichment *at the expense of the* beneficiaries? Finally, consider the case if the beneficiaries have a right to be subrogated to the debt that the income beneficiary discharged under her share transfer contract with the vendor of the shares. Why should the innocent income beneficiary, willing and able to return the traceable proceeds of the money she received, be subject to a superior personal liability to the beneficiaries. Is the change of position defence supposed to reduce the 'value' of the *debt* she discharged to $7,000?

Now consider (2). The restitutionary claim Chambers proposes is supposed to be held by the trustee on trust for the beneficiaries. In this case the 'unjust factor' in which the trustee would ground his personal claim for restitution against his niece would be his own (intentional) wrong; there is no mistake in such a case. It is not clear why the court should allow him to proceed, and surely the *ex turpi causa* principle would apply here.[70] Relevantly, Lord Millett said in *Foskett*, dismissing the reasoning of the Court of Appeal:

> I do not for my own part see how [Mr Murphy's] intention to make further advancements into the settlement [by paying money to the trustees to fund the later premiums on the life insurance policy] can be rebutted by showing that he was not using his own money; as between himself and his children the source of the funds is immaterial. *He could not demand repayment from the trustees by saying: 'I used stolen money; now that I have been found out you must pay me back so that I can repay the money'.* Moreover, even if the presumption of advancement were rebutted, there would be no resulting trust. Mr Murphy was either (as I would hold) a father using stolen money to make further gifts to his children or a stranger paying a premium on another's policy without request: see *Falcke v Scottish Imperial Insurance* Co 34 Ch D 234.[71]

As to the subrogation claim, in this case giving the beneficiaries an election between pursuing the backwards tracing claim and being subrogated to the mortgage lender would place the niece at a serious disadvantage; to adapt Conaglen's concern about the trustee's creditors, it would seem to make her an insurer of the value of the trust assets. Clearly, tracing backwards through the loan into the land will give rise to a beneficial co-ownership share in the land the value of which will be significantly less than the $10,000 used to discharge the mortgage loan because of the decline in the value of the land. On conventional principles, in such a case the alternatives which present themselves to the beneficiaries would be to falsify the account to make the trustee personally liable or to claim the co-ownership interest in the land. For the reasons canvassed above, I do not see the justice in a third claim, either held by the trustee or by the beneficiaries, sourced in the law of subtractive unjust enrichment.

70 *Patel v Mirza* [2016] UKSC 42, [2016] 3 WLR 399.
71 *Foskett* (n 3) 140E–F (emphasis added).

V. Conclusion

Any conclusion at this stage of the development of the law of backwards tracing is necessarily inconclusive. It is good that the Privy Council, at least, is discussing the issue in terms and is willing to recognise backwards tracing in at least some cases. But neither the scope of the beneficiary's rights to backwards trace, nor the 'opposite' remedy of subrogation where trust money is used to discharge a debt, has been explored in sufficient detail. This chapter is merely a first step in that direction.[72]

[72] I must draw the reader's attention to JC Campbell, '*Republic of Brazil v Durant* and the equities justifying tracing' (2016) 42 *Australian Bar Review* 32, in which the author takes an entirely different line from the one taken here, in essence denying that 'backwards tracing' is a concept doing meaningful work. It is well beyond the scope of this chapter to address all the intricate matters the author raises there.

7

Invoking the Administrative Jurisdiction: The Enforcement of Modern Trust Structures

RICHARD NOLAN*

I. Introduction

Modern settlements are very often discretionary in form. This means that they generally consist in various, often very wide form, discretionary dispositive powers, with some final default trust or trusts. The powers might be powers of appointment over capital or income or both, or powers of advancement, or a combination of these. A particular power might be vested in the trustees, a named appointor or a protector or, again, a combination of them, such as where trustees may appoint an interest in the trust fund but only with the prior (often written) consent of the protector. There might be powers to add or subtract beneficiaries. The variety is nigh on limitless.

Yet the width of the discretions in these settlements has led some to raise questions about their enforceability, and hence their validity. The first purpose of this chapter is to address those concerns, and to demonstrate just how such settlements are enforceable. This involves a clear focus on the fundamental mechanisms for the enforcement of trusts. A proper appreciation of basic, but often overlooked, principles provides the answers. The key is the inherent administrative jurisdiction of the court, which works in a manner fundamentally different from the paradigm common law bipartite right-remedy form of action. The chapter shows how, and to what extent, the objects of a dispositive fiduciary power may invoke the administrative jurisdiction of the court in order to enforce the obligations of a trustee to replenish the trust fund. Next, it briefly considers whether the objects

* The author is grateful to Professor Matthew Conaglen, Dr David Fox, Professor Jenny Steele, Dr Peter Turner and Professor Peter Watts for comments on earlier drafts of this chapter. The views expressed in the chapter should not necessarily be attributed to anyone other than the author. The errors are his alone.

of a mere (non-fiduciary) power may do likewise, before considering the same question in relation to protectors. The chapter then goes on to consider the practical and theoretical implications of this body of law. Before that, however, some historical background to the questions is useful.

II. History

Discretionary dispositive powers in settlements have a long history and were used first to allow trustees (and others) to react to changing circumstances.[1] The importance of these powers in this regard has not diminished. Indeed, the present author, when an articled clerk in private client practice over 25 years ago, was advised never to create a settlement whose funds could not be distributed fully at a moment's notice by the use of powers. But it was the introduction of Estate Duty in the Finance Act 1894 that really brought discretionary settlements into vogue.

Estate Duty was imposed on the full capital value of land, and all other property, real or personal, settled or free, which passed or was deemed to pass on the death of an individual. As part of that scheme, the 1894 Act contemplated, and taxed, strict settlements.[2] Indeed, while Estate Duty was originally introduced as a source of revenue, it later was used as a deliberate instrument for the redistribution of wealth, particularly the break-up of large aristocratic, often settled, estates. A feature of the duty, controversial at the time of its introduction, was its progressive nature with a rate of 1 per cent for estates between £100 and £500 rising to a maximum of 8 per cent for estates exceeding £1 million.[3]

It comes as no surprise that those who, today, would be called 'wealth management advisors'—lawyers, accountants and the like—immediately set out to devise means of mitigating the new tax. One of these was to create discretionary settlements, under which the trustees had power to distribute the income at their discretion amongst a named group of beneficiaries, but no beneficiary had any right to any part of the income, and thus no interest in the settled property terminated on death to trigger a charge to tax: discretionary settlements were simply outside the scope of the charging provisions in the 1894 Act, as originally enacted. Income tax considerations also drove the growing use of discretionary settlements and offshore discretionary settlements.[4]

[1] See generally, JS Vaizey, *Vaizey on Settlements*, vol 1 (London, H Sweet & Sons, 1887) ch VIII.

[2] See Finance Act 1894, ss 2(1)(b) and 5.

[3] See generally UK Valuation Office Agency, *Inheritance Tax Manual*, section 2: manuals.voa.gov.uk/corporate/publications/Manuals/InheritanceTaxManual/sections/b-section_2/b-iht-man-s2.html.

[4] eg the affairs of the Vestey family as disclosed in *Lord Vestey's Executor v Inland Revenue Comrs* [1949] 1 All ER 1108 and *Vestey v IRC* [1980] AC 1148.

Lord Walker usefully summarised the increasing use of discretionary settlements, and the fiscal reasons for that, in *Schmidt v Rosewood Trust Ltd*. As he noted:

> Counsel have very properly referred the Board to a considerable number of authorities, some of them going back to the early years of the 19th century. It is appropriate to reflect that during the long period covered by these authorities (but especially during the second half of the 20th century) the forms and functions of settlements have changed to a degree which would have astonished Lord Eldon. By the 1930s high rates of personal taxation led some wealthy individuals to make settlements which enabled funds to be accumulated in the hands of overseas trustees or companies: see for instance *Lord Vestey's Executor v Inland Revenue Comrs* [1949] 1 All ER 1108. This practice increased enormously with the introduction of capital gains tax in 1965...
>
> There is another element, also linked (though less directly) to taxation, which has encouraged the inclusion in settlements of very widely defined classes of beneficiaries. After the Second World War estate duty was charged in the United Kingdom at very high rates, with much less generous reliefs for agricultural and business property than those now available. A wealthy landowner or businessman might be advised that the safest way to preserve his fortune was to give most of it away, while he was still in the prime of life, to trustees of an irrevocable settlement in discretionary form under which the settlor himself was not a beneficiary. It is not surprising that a settlor in such a position should wish to cover as comprehensively as he could all possible current and future claims on his bounty, since he was being asked to make an immediate, irrevocable disposition of much of his wealth, rather than being able to review from time to time the ambulatory dispositions in his will and codicils. But his lawyers might also advise him that the most natural expressions for defining discretionary objects of his bounty (such as 'relatives', 'old friends', 'dependants' or 'persons with moral claims') were of doubtful legal efficacy. So there was a tendency to define the class in the widest possible terms. The process can be seen in a long line of cases starting with *In re Gestetner Settlement* [1953] Ch 672. It led to *In re Manisty's Settlement* [1974] Ch 17, upholding the validity of an 'intermediate' power comparable to that in clause 3.3 of the Everest Trust [at issue in the case] (that is, a power to add as beneficiaries anyone in the world apart from a very small class of excluded persons).[5]

In all these contexts, the state had imposed tax—income tax or estate duty—by reference to fixed entitlements, and settlors, and their advisers, sought to avoid that tax by creating settlements in which there were no fixed entitlements in possession, that is, settlements which were very largely discretionary in form, with only remote fixed entitlements in remainder: '[r]arely did a beneficiary take an indefeasibly vested interest with an ascertainable market value'.[6] But the state, as is only to be expected, reacted with ever stricter tax legislation.

Two Acts of Parliament deserve mention as major factors in bringing to an end the 'glory days' of discretionary settlements. These were the Finance Act 1965, which, in Part III, introduced Capital Gains Tax,[7] and the Finance Act 1975, which,

[5] *Schmidt v Rosewood Trust Ltd* [2003] UKPC 26, [2003] 2 AC 709 [34]–[35].
[6] ibid [34] (Lord Walker).
[7] See now Taxation of Chargeable Gains Act 1992, as amended.

also in Part III, introduced Capital Transfer Tax, that later became Inheritance Tax.[8] Capital Gains Tax was charged on trustees as a single continuing body of persons. This taxation of the trustees made it much harder to avoid tax through the creation of ever more refined beneficial interests under the settlement.[9] Capital Transfer Tax simply devised a special regime for discretionary settlements—or, as the 1984 Act more precisely calls them, 'settlements without interests in possession'.[10] Of course, that is not to say the legislation was perfect in its aim of taxing trusts; and much amending legislation has since been passed. But the basic principles of the two new taxes did make discretionary settlements much less effective as devices for tax planning.

Still, discretionary settlements held their enduring attraction for some settlors, as witness *Schmidt v Rosewood Trust Ltd* itself, and there are still many such settlements in existence which were created before the tax regime became as strict as it is today. So the question of how such settlements are enforced retains its importance.

The rights, if any, of protectors to enforce an obligation of the trustees to replenish the trust fund are also important. Again, some background is useful in order to appreciate this. The use of 'protectors' in settlements has become much more common, particularly in offshore settlements. To quote Lord Walker once more:

> It has become common for wealthy individuals in many parts of the world (including countries which have no indigenous law of trusts) to place funds at their disposition into trusts (often with a network of underlying companies) regulated by the law of, and managed by trustees resident in, territories with which the settlor (who may be also a beneficiary) has no substantial connection. These territories (sometimes called tax havens) are chosen not for their geographical convenience ... but because they are supposed to offer special advantages in terms of confidentiality and protection from fiscal demands (and, sometimes from problems under the insolvency laws, or laws restricting freedom of testamentary disposition, in the country of the settlor's domicile). The trusts and powers contained in a settlement established in such circumstances may give no reliable indication of who will in the event benefit from the settlement. Typically it will contain very wide discretions exercisable by the trustees (sometimes only with the consent of a so-called protector) in favour of a widely-defined class of beneficiaries. The exercise of those discretions may depend on the settlor's wishes as confidentially imparted to the trustees and the protector ...
>
> All these considerations may encourage a settlor to entrust substantial funds to an apparently secure and confidential off-shore shelter.[11]

A recent text on protectors puts the point as follows:

> For at least 40 years instruments establishing international trusts in many relevant jurisdictions have often appointed a protector of the trust, as well as a trustee. Protectors

[8] See now Inheritance Tax Act 1984, as amended.

[9] See Finance Act 1965, s 25, now reflected in Taxation of Chargeable Gains Act 1992, s 69.

[10] Finance Act 1975, s 21 and Schedule 5, paras 12–13, now reflected in Inheritance Tax Act 1984, Part III, Chapter III.

[11] *Schmidt* (n 5) [1]–[2].

> of trusts governed by English law have also been appointed, but their use in domestic contexts has not as yet become commonplace.
>
> ...
>
> The modern use of protectors of trusts can be argued to have arisen as an alternative to the reservation of powers by the settlor and as a way of extending the idea of the reservation of powers beyond the settlor's lifetime ... The idea being that the appointee would not have the trust assets vested in him and hence would not be a trustee. This was understood to mean that there would normally be no fiscal or other reason why the protector would need to be resident offshore. The appointee would be, or would appear to be, independent of the settlor, so the latter could not be said to be retaining control over the trust assets.[12]

In other words, the appointment of a protector was a means of squaring the circle. The settlor could appoint offshore trustees, with the fiscal benefits, and protection from creditors and forced heirship laws, that comes from vesting assets in residents of a jurisdiction that is generally sympathetic to trustees. Yet by appointing a protector, the settlor could solve the problem that he does not know or necessarily trust (in the colloquial sense) the trustee he has appointed, without endangering the advantages which flow from appointing offshore trustees. Equally, the settlor would not retain such control himself because of anti-avoidance provisions in the tax legislation: were he to do so, he would put in jeopardy the very tax benefits prima facie associated with appointing offshore trustees.[13] So custody of the trust assets could be vested in offshore trustees, but at the same time control over the trust assets could be given to someone whom the settlor actually trusts—a protector.

When discussing protectors, however, it is important to remember that the word 'protector' is not an unvarying term of art, though it is occasionally defined in the trust legislation of some (often offshore) jurisdictions.[14] But all it means, essentially, is a person who is not acting as a trustee but who nevertheless has certain powers in relation to the administration and/or distribution of a trust fund, and may or may not be acting as a fiduciary in relation to those powers.[15] Other words are sometimes used to describe a person in this situation, such as 'supervisor', 'special appointor' or such like; nothing, however, turns on nomenclature for present purposes.

Still, for reasons outlined above, the use of protectors in offshore settlements has grown. And it has become correspondingly important to understand the rights of the protector under the settlement.

[12] M Hubbard, *Protectors of Trusts* (Oxford, OUP, 2013) paras 1.1 and 1.15.

[13] For examples of such anti-avoidance laws in the context of UK taxation, see Finance Act 1986, ss 102–102C (inheritance tax); Taxation of Chargeable Gains Act 1992, s 86 (capital gains tax); and Income Tax (Trading and Other Income) Act 2005, ss 624–25 (income tax).

[14] eg Trustee Act 1998 (Bahamas), ss 3, 81.

[15] See *Kan v Poon* [2014] HKCFA 65, (2014) 17 HKCFAR 414 [67] (Ribeiro PJ), citing with approval M Conaglen and E Weaver, 'Protectors as Fiduciaries: Theory and Practice' (2012) 18 *Trusts & Trustees* 17. The other Justices agreed with Ribeiro PJ.

III. The Enforcement of Trusts: Basic Principles of Enduring Significance

The inherent jurisdiction of the Court of Chancery, and all its successor courts in common law jurisdictions across the world, to supervise, and if necessary intervene in, the administration of trusts is an ancient and well-established jurisdiction of such courts. It is a jurisdiction that marks a radical distinction between the law of trusts and the wider law of obligations. Lord Eldon LC referred to the jurisdiction as long ago as 1805, though it is older than that by far:

> As it is a maxim, that the execution of a trust shall be under the controul [*sic*] of the court, it must be of such a nature, that it can be under that control; so that the administration of it can be reviewed by the court; or, if the trustee dies, the court itself can execute the trust: a trust therefore, which, in case of maladministration could be reformed; and a due administration directed; and then, unless the subject and the objects can be ascertained, upon principles, familiar in other cases, it must be decided, that the court can neither reform maladministration, nor direct a due administration.[16]

More recently, Lord Browne-Wilkinson stated in *Target Holdings Ltd v Redferns* that:

> The basic right of a beneficiary is to have the trust duly administered in accordance with the provisions of the trust instruments, if any, and the general law … Accordingly, in the case of a breach of such a trust involving the wrongful paying away of trust assets, the liability of the trustee is to restore to the trust fund, often called 'the trust estate', what ought to have been there.[17]

In the context of beneficiaries' rights to information about a trust, Lord Walker supplemented these statements with a dictum that has become highly influential, as will be seen:

> The right to seek the court's intervention does not depend on entitlement to a fixed and transmissible beneficial interest. The object of a discretion (including a mere power) may also be entitled to protection from a court of equity, although the circumstances in which he may seek protection, and the nature of the protection he may expect to obtain, will depend on the court's discretion: see Lord Wilberforce in *Gartside v Inland Revenue Comrs* [1968] AC 553, 617–618 and in *In re Baden* [1971] AC 424, 456–457, Templeman J in *In re Manisty's Settlement* [1974] Ch 17, 27–28 and Warner J in *Mettoy Pension Trustees Ltd v Evans* [1990] 1 WLR 1587, 1617–1618.[18]

Lord Walker's views have since been cited with approval by the High Court of Australia.[19]

[16] *Morice v Bishop of Durham* (1805) 10 Ves 522, 539–40; 32 ER 947, 954.

[17] *Target Holdings Ltd v Redferns* [1996] AC 421, 434.

[18] *Schmidt* (n 5) [51].

[19] *CPT Custodian Pty Ltd v Commissioner of State Revenue* [2005] HCA 53, (2005) 224 CLR 98 [17].

The inherent jurisdiction of the court in relation to trusts is wide and extends to much more than simply enforcing the obligations of the trustee.[20] But for present purposes, what is important to understand is that it is this inherent jurisdiction of the court to secure the performance and execution of trusts that lies at the root of enforcing trustees' obligations. A beneficiary had, and has, standing to invoke that jurisdiction, and to have the administration of the trust reformed: the beneficiary's powers extend to more than merely recovery of compensation for harm done to him.

Where trustees' liabilities are concerned, the beneficiary's power was given effect through the process of accounting, and the orders made consequent on the account. Professor Conaglen puts it thus:

> Equity traditionally approached a trustee's liability for a breach of trust through the mechanism of taking an account of the trust: '[t]he taking of an account is the means by which a beneficiary requires a trustee to justify his stewardship of trust property. The trustee must show what he has done with that property'.[21]

The account might be in common form, or on the footing of wilful default.[22] In either case, if the claimant beneficiary was successful, the account would show that the state of the trust fund as it ought to be, if the trustee's unjustified action(s) were ignored. This would very likely be more than the trust fund actually comprised.[23] Consequently, there would be an order for reinstatement of the trust fund, usually by the payment of a sum of money by the trustee personally into the trust fund, perhaps from funds realised by the sale of an asset found to be subject to an equitable lien, but occasionally by means of the transfer of an asset *in specie*.

Lord Millett NPJ put the point as follows. It is worth quoting his judgment at some length:

> [A]n order for an account does not in itself provide the plaintiff with a remedy; it is merely the first step in a process which enables him to identify and quantify any deficit in the trust fund and seek the appropriate means by which it may be made good. Once the plaintiff has been provided with an account he can falsify and surcharge it. If the account discloses an unauthorised disbursement the plaintiff may falsify it, that is to say ask for the disbursement to be disallowed. This will produce a deficit which the defendant must make good, either in specie or in money. Where the defendant is ordered to make good the deficit by the payment of money, the award is sometimes described as the payment of equitable compensation; but it is not compensation for loss but restitutionary or restorative. The amount of the award is measured by the objective value of the property lost determined at the date when the account is taken and with the full benefit of hindsight.

[20] See generally R Nolan, '"The Execution of a Trust shall be under the Controul of the Court": A Maxim in Modern Times' (2016) 2 *Canadian Journal of Comparative and Contemporary Law* 469, and the authorities cited there.

[21] M Conaglen, 'Equitable Compensation for Breach of Trust: Off *Target*' (2016) 40(1) *Melbourne University Law Review* 126, 128, citing *Ultraframe (UK) Ltd v Fielding* [2005] EWHC 1638 (Ch) [1513] (Lewison J).

[22] Conaglen, 'Equitable Compensation for Breach of Trust: Off *Target*' (n 21) 132–35.

[23] Occasionally there may be no loss: eg *Blades v Isaac* [2016] EWHC 601 (Ch).

> But the plaintiff is not bound to ask for the disbursement to be disallowed. He is entitled to ask for an inquiry to discover what the defendant did with the trust money which he misappropriated and whether he dissipated it or invested it, and if he invested it whether he did so at a profit or a loss. If he dissipated it or invested it at a loss, the plaintiff will naturally have the disbursement disallowed and disclaim any interest in the property in which it was invested by treating it as bought with the defendant's own money. If, however, the defendant invested the money at a profit, the plaintiff is not bound to ask for the disbursement to be disallowed. He can treat it as an authorised disbursement, treat the property in which it has been invested as acquired with trust money, and follow or trace the property and demand that it or its traceable proceeds be restored to the trust in specie.
>
> If on the other hand the account is shown to be defective because it does not include property which the defendant in breach of his duty failed to obtain for the benefit of the trust, the plaintiff can surcharge the account by asking for it to be taken on the basis of 'wilful default', that is to say on the basis that the property should be treated as if the defendant had performed his duty and obtained it for the benefit of the trust. Since *ex hypothesi* the property has not been acquired, the defendant will be ordered to make good the deficiency by the payment of money, and in this case the payment of 'equitable compensation' is akin to the payment of damages as compensation for loss.
>
> In an appropriate case the defendant will be charged, not merely with the value of the property at the date when it ought to have been acquired or at the date when the account is taken, but at its highest intermediate value. This is on the footing either that the defendant was a trustee with power to sell the property or that he was a fiduciary who ought to have kept his principal informed and sought his instructions.
>
> At every stage the plaintiff can elect whether or not to seek a further account or inquiry. The amount of any unauthorised disbursement is often established by evidence at the trial, so that the plaintiff does not need an account but can ask for an award of the appropriate amount of compensation. Or he may be content with a monetary award rather than attempt to follow or trace the money, in which case he will not ask for an inquiry as to what has become of the trust property. In short, he may elect not to call for an account or further inquiry if it is unnecessary or unlikely to be fruitful, though the court will always have the last word.[24]

As Lord Millett notes, sometimes the process of accounting can be short-circuited by an application for an award of equitable compensation. Professor Conaglen has provided a fuller account of the evolution of a direct award of equitable compensation for breach of trust out of the process of accounting.[25] In the case of a breach of trust:

> It is not a question of concurrent liabilities under different causes of action generated by the same conduct. There is only one claim and the only question is whether the remedy

[24] *Libertarian Investments Ltd v Hall* [2013] HKCFA 93, (2013) 16 HKCFAR 681 [168]–[172].

[25] Conaglen, 'Equitable Compensation for Breach of Trust: Off *Target*' (n 21) 146–50; see also JD Heydon, MJ Leeming and PG Turner, *Meagher, Gummow and Lehane's Equity: Doctrines & Remedies*, 5th edn (Chatswood, NSW, LexisNexis Butterworths, 2015) para 23-030.

> for that claim differs depending on how it is brought. It is suggested that there is no reason why the result should differ simply because the plaintiff seeks equitable compensation directly rather than following the taking of an account.[26]

Notwithstanding the evolution of a direct claim by a beneficiary for equitable compensation to be paid into the trust fund, or occasionally to himself personally if he is or was solely entitled to the fund, the right to an account, and the right to orders made in consequence of the state of the account, remain the fundamental means of enforcing trustees' obligations. To put the point in more general terms, notwithstanding the evolution of direct actions for equitable compensation, the invocation and utilisation of the administrative jurisdiction of the court is and remains fundamental to the enforcement of trusts.

It follows that the ability to invoke the administrative jurisdiction is the key to the enforcement of a trust. Standing to invoke the administrative jurisdiction in connection with a trust is a necessary (but, as will be seen, possibly not sufficient) condition to enforce the trust. The question of just who may invoke that jurisdiction for the purpose of enforcing the trustees' obligations is, therefore, crucial to understanding the enforcement of trusts.

IV. Claims for Breach of Trust: Claims by Fixed Beneficiaries and by Objects of Dispositive Fiduciary Powers

It is axiomatic that a trust may be enforced by a beneficiary who has some positive claim to benefit from the trust fund, whether income or capital or both, which does not depend on the exercise of any discretion. Trusts are, *ex hypothesi*, matters of enforceable obligation, unless and until validly revoked or else set aside on the basis of some recognised vitiating factor. As Sir William Grant MR said in *Morice v Bishop of Durham*: 'There can be no trust, over the exercise of which this Court will not assume a control; for an uncontrollable power of disposition would be ownership, and not trust'.[27] Cases also clearly establish that a trust providing that some members of a class must receive benefit, though there is discretion as to which members of the class and how much benefit, are also valid if the class is expressed with sufficient certainty.[28] Given that such an arrangement constitutes

[26] Conaglen, 'Equitable Compensation for Breach of Trust: Off *Target*' (n 21) 150; see also PG Turner, 'The New Fundamental Norm of Recovery for Losses to Express Trusts' (2015) 74 *CLJ* 188, 190.

[27] *Morice v Bishop of Durham* (1804) 9 Ves Jun 399, 404–05; 32 ER 656, 658; see also *Armitage v Nurse* [1998] Ch 241 (CA).

[28] *McPhail v Doulton* [1974] AC 421, supplemented by *Re Baden's Deed Trusts (No 2)* [1973] Ch 9 (CA).

a trust in favour of such persons, it necessarily follows that they are beneficiaries with standing to enforce the trust.

But what of a person who is simply the object of a power to benefit him (and likely others as well)? Modern trusts make enormous use of such powers, and the objects of the powers are very often intended to take the benefit of the trust fund to the exclusion of the (fixed) default beneficiaries. Again, to quote Lord Walker:

> [I]ncreasingly stringent anti-avoidance measures encouraged legal advisers to devise forms of settlement under which the true intended beneficiaries were not clearly identified in the settlement. Indeed their interests or expectations were often barely perceptible. Rarely did a beneficiary take an indefeasibly vested interest with an ascertainable market value.[29]

In these circumstances, it is vital to understand the rights of the object of such a power to enforce the trustees' duties. Three recent cases have addressed this issue, one quite directly. All three cases concerned the objects of dispositive fiduciary powers; so the position of the object(s) of a mere personal power will be examined separately in the next section.

The first of the recent cases is *Lemos v Coutts (Cayman) Ltd*.[30] The issue of interest to the present enquiry was raised only obliquely; but the case is still important in its impact on later decisions.

In 1984, Captain Lemos, a wealthy Greek shipowner, had established a discretionary settlement known as the Trofos Foundation: both income and capital were subject to discretionary powers of appointment and trusts in default of appointment. The principal beneficiaries of the trust were the four children of Captain Lemos and their issue. Captain Lemos died on 3 December 1989, and subsequently a rift developed between his sons and daughters. This resulted in litigation which was settled by compromise in early 1994. The compromise involved a substantial rewriting of the trusts, with the court supplying approval of the compromise on behalf of unborn beneficiaries and beneficiaries incapable of giving their own consent. The capital of the settlement comprised, inter alia, substantial shipping assets and investments. By 1998, the first and second plaintiffs, who were beneficiaries of the trust, had become very concerned about the performance of the shipping investments. On 29 July 1998, the plaintiffs issued the present proceedings in the Grand Court of the Cayman Islands, alleging negligence by the trustees in their management of the trust fund, which had caused it loss.

The proceedings were slow to progress. In part at least, this was because there was another action, commenced in October 1998, originally seeking the Court's directions for the management of the settlement, and the replacement of its trustees, but resulting in the division of the settlement into four new settlements,

[29] *Schmidt* (n 5) [34].
[30] *Lemos v Coutts (Cayman) Ltd* (2005) 8 ITELR 153.

one for each of the families of Captain Lemos's children. This was achieved by appointments out of the original settlement to create the four new settlements.

Eventually the July 1998 action progressed to the stage of discovery. At that point, further facts came to light which led the plaintiffs to seek leave to re-amend the statement of claim to include allegations of wilful misconduct by the trustees. It is this application for leave that is of present interest.

The trustees sought to resist the application on grounds of limitation. They alleged that if the new allegations had been made in a new action begun by a separate writ, they would be time barred. Therefore, they argued, any such action should not be allowed to proceed by way of amendment to an existing statement of claim, because that would amount to an end-run around the protection of the statute of limitation. However, section 27(3) of the Limitation Law (Laws of the Cayman Islands, 1996 Revision) provided:

> For the purposes of this subsection [dealing with limitation periods applicable to an action for breach of trust], the right of action shall not be treated as having accrued to any beneficiary entitled to a future interest in the trust property until the interest fell into possession.[31]

This could be read so as to mean that the plaintiffs' claims were not yet time barred: if the plaintiffs had 'a future interest in the trust fund', the limitation period applicable to their claims would not run until the later date contemplated by the section. In response, the trustees alleged that the plaintiffs, as mere objects of fiduciary dispositive powers, did not have a 'future interest in the trust property' within the meaning of the statute, so it could not apply to extend the limitation period applicable to their claims.

Levers J was ultimately able to avoid this question and allow the plaintiffs' application. He held that:

> [T]he facts relevant to this particular amendment are substantially the same facts as those that founded the original cause of action albeit cast in a different light after the specificity which only discovery can expose came to light. Accordingly, these amendments are expressly permitted by the Rules of Court.[32]

Levers J went on to say, in the alternative, that:

> Even if I am wrong in that [above] assessment of the facts forming the basis of these amendments, it can only be because they are sufficiently distinct from the original facts to be considered entirely new facts in which event, these facts having come to light as a result of discovery by the defendants must be presumed to have been entirely within the defendants' purview prior to discovery and, as such, deemed to have been deliberately concealed. In that event … the time for limitation purposes did not start to run until the plaintiffs obtained discovery.[33]

[31] This text follows exactly the equivalent text of the Limitation Act 1980 (UK), s 21(3).
[32] *Lemos* (n 30) [50].
[33] ibid [51].

Nevertheless, Levers J, while not ruling on the point, appears to prefer the view taken by the English Court of Appeal in *Armitage v Nurse*,[34] and by the New Zealand Court of Appeal in *Johns v Johns*,[35] that the object of a discretionary, dispositive power did not have a 'future interest' in the trust fund within the meaning of the Limitation Law.

However, the key point to remember is Lord Wilberforce's admonition in *Leedale (Inspector of Taxes) v Lewis*,[36] repeated by Millett LJ in *Armitage v Nurse*,[37] that, 'The word "interest" is one of uncertain meaning and it remains to be decided on the terms of the applicable statute which, or possibly what other, meaning the word may bear'.[38] While the object of a discretionary dispositive power may not have a 'future interest' within the meaning of the Cayman, English and New Zealand statutes of limitation, that is a matter of the proper construction of the statutory language in context: it does not necessarily follow that the object of such a power has no rights at all to enforce the trustees' duties.

This was explicitly recognised in *Lemos v Coutts (Cayman) Ltd*. After considering the implications of *Target Holdings Ltd v Redferns*[39] and *Schmidt v Rosewood Trust Ltd*,[40] noted above, Levers J said:

> The cases state the principle very clearly that a discretionary beneficiary has the right to invoke the court's power to ensure that the trust fund is properly administered. However, does that then give them a future interest in the trust fund? Mr Briggs argues that it does not. He concedes that a discretionary beneficiary, the object of a mere power, has the right to invoke the court's inherent jurisdiction to seek the proper administration of the trust fund and the relief claimed can be the reconstitution of the trust fund. However, he submits, that since the discretionary beneficiary has no proprietary interest, then it cannot be said that he has a future interest in the trust fund. He further submits that the discretionary beneficiaries in this case do not have a future interest. What they have is an immediate interest to ensure that the breach is rectified forthwith by invoking the court's jurisdiction here and now.[41]

The clear view of the judge, albeit obiter—and the considered concession of counsel for the trustees, Michael Briggs QC, now Briggs LJ—was that the object of a fiduciary dispositive power may enforce obligations of the trustees. Which of the trustees' obligations he may enforce is another matter, of course.

[34] *Armitage* (n 27), considering the Limitation Act 1980 (UK), s 21(3).

[35] *Johns v Johns* [2004] NZCA 42, [2004] 3 NZLR 202, considering the Limitation Act 1950 (NZ), s 21(2).

[36] *Leedale (Inspector of Taxes) v Lewis* [1982] 1 WLR 1319, 1329.

[37] *Armitage* (n 27) 261.

[38] See also *Gartside v IRC* [1968] AC 553; *Martin v Martin* [1988] 1 NZLR 722; *Commissioner of Taxation v Linter Textiles Australia Ltd* (2005) 220 CLR 592; *CPT Custodian Pty Ltd* (n 19).

[39] *Target Holdings Ltd* (n 17).

[40] *Schmidt* (n 5).

[41] *Lemos* (n 30) [47].

The views of Levers J and Briggs QC are entirely consistent with earlier learning. In *Gartside v IRC*, Lord Wilberforce said:

> No doubt in a certain sense a beneficiary under a discretionary trust has an 'interest': the nature of it may, sufficiently for the purpose, be spelt out by saying that he has a right to be considered as a potential recipient of benefit by the trustees and a right to have his interest protected by a court of equity. Certainly that is so, and when it is said that he has a right to have the trustees exercise their discretion 'fairly' or 'reasonably' or 'properly' that indicates clearly enough that some objective consideration (not stated explicitly in declaring the discretionary trust, but latent in it) must be applied by the trustees and that the right is more than a mere *spes*. But that does not mean that he has an interest which is capable of being taxed by reference to its extent in the trust fund's income: it may be a right, with some degree of concreteness or solidity, one which attracts the protection of a court of equity, yet it may still lack the necessary quality of definable extent which must exist before it can be taxed'.[42]

More recently, in *Johns v Johns*, Tipping J, delivered the judgment of the New Zealand Court of Appeal that the object of a discretionary power did not have a 'future interest' within the meaning of section 21(2) of the Limitation Act 1950 (NZ), but said (again obiter) that:

> Nevertheless a discretionary beneficiary may well be able to bring proceedings to compel proper administration of the trust. In this respect we note that in *Jacobs' Law of Trusts in Australia* (6th ed, 1997) at para 317 (p 68) the learned authors, Justices Meagher and Gummow, state that although a discretionary beneficiary has no proprietary interest in the trust assets he has sufficient standing to compel proper administration of the trust.[43]

The point actually arose for decision in the second of the recent cases to be considered, *Freeman v Ansbacher Trustees (Jersey) Ltd*.[44] This case involved three claims against Ansbacher, the former trustee of a settlement, for breaches of its duties of care and skill in managing the trust fund during its tenure as trustee of the fund. The claims arose out of facts which were complex but for present purposes need no further explanation. The law applicable to the claims was Jersey law, and the proceedings in respect of them were brought before the Jersey Royal Court (Samedi Division).

Ansbacher applied to have the claims struck out before trial. It put forward five grounds in support of its application, four applicable to all the claims, the fifth applicable only to one of them. Just one of those grounds is of present interest: Ansbacher alleged that the plaintiffs in the action lacked 'the necessary standing to bring the claims, being simply the objects of a mere power'.[45] (Later in its

42 *Gartside* (n 38) 617–18.
43 *Johns* (n 35) [34].
44 *Freeman v Ansbacher Trustees (Jersey) Ltd* [2009] JRC 003, [2010] WTLR 569.
45 Ibid [27(ii)].

judgment, the Court made it clear that the relevant power was a *fiduciary* power vested in the trustee—the words '*mere* power' simply indicated that there was no duty to distribute trust property.)[46] The Court emphatically rejected Ansbacher's allegation. And it did so on the explicit basis that the applicable Jersey law was the same as English law.[47]

The Court could have chosen simply to rule that the claimant's *locus standi* was at least arguable and therefore should be considered at trial. But it thought the point was one of pure law, on which full argument had been heard, and Deputy Bailiff Birt therefore made a definitive ruling on the point:

> I am in no doubt that I should declare Jersey law to be ... that the object of a fiduciary power (whether a trust power or a mere power) has *locus standi* to apply to the Court for relief and that such relief can include the reconstitution of the trust fund where loss has been caused by a trustee's breach of trust.[48]

The view taken obiter by Levers J in *Lemos*, and conceded by counsel, was upheld.

The main argument put by Ansbacher against that conclusion was that it was contrary to the traditional' position:

> The traditional approach of the court was to draw a line between discretionary trusts and fiduciary powers. Objects of discretionary trusts had *locus standi* to bring an action to secure the trust fund and their right in it, while objects of fiduciary powers had *locus standi* to seek a removal of trustees who failed to give due consideration to an exercise of their fiduciary powers, but none to seek any other kind of relief, with the possible exception of a claim to enforce an exercise of the power in special circumstances.[49]

This position was said to be illustrated by *dicta* of Templeman J in *Re Manisty's Settlement Trusts*:

> If a person within the ambit of the power is aware of its existence he can require the trustees to consider exercising the power and in particular to consider a request on his part for the power to be exercised in his favour. The trustees must consider this request, and if they decline to do so or can be proved to have omitted to do so, then the aggrieved person may apply to the court which may remove the trustees and appoint others in their place. This, as I understand it, is the only right and only remedy of any object of the power.[50]

Deputy Bailiff Birt, following the learned authors of *Lewin*, considered that this position could not survive the decision of the Privy Council in *Schmidt v Rosewood Trustees Ltd*.[51] He gave four reasons for this conclusion.

[46] ibid [34]–[36].
[47] ibid [38], [42], [44].
[48] ibid [42].
[49] See L Tucker, N Le Poidevin and J Brightwell (eds), *Lewin on Trusts*, 19th edn (London, Sweet & Maxwell, 2015) para 39-073, repeating text from L Tucker, N Le Poidevin and J Brightwell (eds), *Lewin on Trusts*, 18th edn (London, Sweet & Maxwell, 2014) para 39-069, cited with approval in *Freeman* (n 44) [39].
[50] *Re Manisty's Settlement Trusts* [1974] Ch 17, 25.
[51] *Schmidt* (n 5).

First, the dicta of Templeman J needed to be understood in context: the *Manisty* case was concerned with what, if anything, the object of a dispositive power might do to remedy failure by the holder of the power to consider exercising it. It was not concerned with, and did not even address, what the object of such a power might do in response to a breach of trust which had depleted the trust fund. The dicta should therefore not necessarily be taken as a comprehensive statement of the rights of an object of a fiduciary dispositive power.

Second, even if *Manisty* were to be read widely—too widely—as suggesting that the object of a fiduciary dispositive power has no standing to bring proceedings to remedy a breach of trust that has depleted the trust fund, such a reading of *Manisty* could not survive *Schmidt*.[52] Lord Walker, in *Schmidt*, asserted the court's general jurisdiction to secure the due administration of a trust, and to reform its maladministration; and he did so in terms that did not draw a dividing line between the holders of fixed interests or discretionary interests and those who were merely the object of a dispositive fiduciary power.

Third, the practicalities of the situation—which should never be forgotten, particularly in a case where there is argument about the correct view of the law—spoke strongly in favour of acknowledging that the object of a dispositive fiduciary power had *locus standi* to bring proceedings to have the trust fund which is subject to that power restored to its proper state. As Deputy Bailiff Birt said:

> It would in my judgment be a highly unsatisfactory situation if such beneficiaries [*ie* objects of a fiduciary power, who are often those realistically expected to benefit from the trust fund] were held not to have standing to sue the trustees for breach of trust where, for example, the trustees had made speculative investments which had resulted in devastating loss to the trust fund.[53]

Finally, Deputy Bailiff Birt noted that: 'As was made clear in *Schmidt* (see para [66]) the differences in this context between trusts and powers are a good deal less significant than the similarities'.[54] He also noted for completeness that none of the foregoing reasoning based on English law was precluded by, or inconsistent with, the written provisions of the Jersey Trusts Law.

Support for this conclusion, albeit obiter, can be found in the third of the trio of recent cases considered in this part, the English case of *Blades v Isaac*.[55]

[52] *Schmidt*, of course, is Isle of Man authority. But it has been accepted as representing English law in *Breakspear v Ackland* [2008] EWHC 220 (Ch), [2009] Ch 32. So Deputy Bailiff Birt was correct to treat *Schmidt* as representing English law, and justified in using the case in reasoning explicitly based on English law (see text to n 47). New Zealand law also follows *Schmidt* and allows a discretionary beneficiary standing to seek disclosure of trust documents and information: *Foreman v Kingstone* [2004] 1 NZLR 841; *Re Maguire (dec'd)* [2010] 2 NZLR 845; *Erceg v Erceg* [2016] NZCA 7. Australian law is in more of a state of flux on this point: see JD Heydon and MJ Leeming (eds), *Jacobs' Law of Trusts in Australia*, 7th edn (Chatswood, NSW, LexisNexis Butterworths, 2006), para 1716, criticising *Schmidt*; and *Deutsch v Trumble* [2016] VSC 263 [71]–[72] (Hargrave J).

[53] *Freeman* (n 44) [43(iii)].

[54] ibid [43(iv)].

[55] *Blades* (n 23).

The case concerned a discretionary trust established by will. The trustees were legatees under the will and held their gift upon trust and, inter alia, subject to a dispositive fiduciary power of which the claimant was an object. When considering the extent to which the claimant could obtain information about the estate, of which she was not a direct beneficiary, Master Matthews noted that:

> [T]the Claimant could hold the trustees to account, for what the trustees had received and for what they had done with it: see *Schmidt v Rosewood Trust Co Ltd* [2003] 2 AC 709. But what she could not claim to be was a legatee of the estate, and therefore directly to enjoy the information rights of a legatee …
>
> Nevertheless, in my judgment the rights of the trustees as legatees to information about the estate (whatever they were) were properly part of the trust estate in which she was interested as a trust beneficiary. If need be, therefore, she could claim as against the trustees that they as trustees should exercise those rights, or, if they could not or unreasonably would not do so, claim to exercise them herself, though in that case on behalf of the trust: *Parker-Tweedale v Dunbar Bank plc* [1991] Ch 12.[56]

The clear doctrinal conclusion is that the object of a fiduciary dispositive power has standing to invoke the jurisdiction of the court to remedy a breach of trust, though that does not mean the court has to grant his claim, as will be seen. And the practical conclusion implicit in that doctrinal position is that settlements which make great use of dispositive fiduciary powers, and which, in practical terms, contemplate that the objects of those powers are to be the economically and socially significant beneficiaries of the settlement (rather than the default beneficiaries, who usually have fixed interests), are trust structures that can perfectly well be enforced. They are not beyond control. Their widespread use is entirely consistent with the axiomatic proposition that 'the execution of a trust shall be under the controul [*sic*] of the court, [so] it must be of such a nature, that it can be under that control'.[57] There may be practical risks in the use of such settlements—for example, trustees who do not properly understand or properly use their powers, or objects of those powers who decide that they have no practical motivation to use their standing to enforce obligations of the trustees, because the objects believe they stand to gain little or nothing personally by taking such action. But those are practical, not legal, risks.

There is one further issue to consider in relation to enforcement of a trust by the object of a dispositive fiduciary power. It is one thing to establish that such an object has standing to invoke the court's jurisdiction to administer trusts and remedy their maladministration. What the court does in response to that invocation is another matter. This is because the claim to enforce a trust is not conceptualised as an absolute right in the fashion of the common law. It is worth remembering here words of Lord Millett, cited earlier, that in remedying a breach of trust, 'the

[56] ibid [53]–[54].
[57] See text to n 16.

court will always have the last word'.[58] As in the case of all equitable remedies, the court retains its own discretion whether or not to allow the remedy;[59] and, if it allows the remedy, the discretion to mould it.[60] The existence and importance of this discretion is evidenced very clearly in *Schmidt v Rosewood Trust Ltd* itself, in the court's attitude to applications for the disclosure of documents or information relating to a trust.[61]

So any object of a dispositive fiduciary power should have standing to invoke the jurisdiction of the court. But it does not follow that the court must accede to every such invocation. If the object can demonstrate that he or she has a significant claim on the trustees' consideration, it might well be appropriate to allow the case to proceed. But if the object only has a very remote chance of benefit—for example, he is a member of a very widely drafted class but there is nothing to show the settlor had any intention that the power should be used to benefit him—then the court could dismiss the case. Again, the point has been made in the context of access to documents and information concerning a trust:

> Evaluation of the claims of a beneficiary (and especially of a discretionary object) may be an important part of the balancing exercise which the court has to perform on the materials placed before it. In many cases the court may have no difficulty in concluding that an applicant with no more than a theoretical possibility of benefit ought not to be granted any relief.[62]

So in practical terms, recognising that objects of dispositive fiduciary powers, even very wide powers, all have prima facie standing to apply to court to remedy the maladministration of a trust certainly does not mean that the court will have to accede to claims by those with very little expectation of benefit under the trust. The court can limit the claims it hears to those made by an object who has a substantial possibility of seeing benefit from the trust, or other good reason for bringing the proceedings—one of 'the true intended beneficiaries' of the settlement.[63] And even if it hears a claim, it does not have to accede to it, or do so in full. But the court need not even entertain claims brought by those who have no substantial expectation of benefit. Who are the 'true intended beneficiaries', and who are not, simply

[58] See text to n 24.

[59] eg *British Steel v Granada Television Ltd* [1981] AC 1096, 1114 (Megarry VC in the High Court) 1174 (Lord Wilberforce in the House of Lords); *Warman International v Dwyer* [1995] HCA 18, (1995) 182 CLR 544, 559 (Mason CJ, Brennan, Deane, Dawson and Gaudron JJ); *Westdeutsche Landesbank Girozentrale v Islington LBC* [1996] AC 669, 722 (Lord Woolf); *Sempra Metals Ltd v IRC* [2007] UKHL 34, [2008] 1 AC 561 [150] (Lord Scott), [186] (Lord Walker). See generally, WMC Gummow, 'Equity: Too Successful?' (2003) 77 *Australian Law Journal* 30, 39–42.

[60] eg *Warman* (n 59).

[61] *Schmidt* (n 5) [67]–[68] (Lord Walker).

[62] ibid [67]; see also *Hartigan Nominees Pty Ltd v Rydge* (1992) 29 NSWLR 405, 432; *SAS Trustee Corp v Cox* [2011] NSWCA 408, (2011) 285 ALR 623 [148]; *Segelov v Ernst & Young Service Pty Ltd* [2015] NSWCA 156 [130]; *Erceg* (n 52).

[63] See *Schmidt* (n 5) [34] (Lord Walker); see also *Murphy v Murphy* [1999] 1 WLR 282, 293 (Neuberger J).

turns on the evidence, and the court's evaluation of that evidence. And there will often be a letter of wishes which makes the distinction clear, something that the court can always demand to see.

If the object of a fiduciary power succeeds in his application to remedy a breach of trust, his remedy is not confined to a sum that reflects only the infringements of his rights personally. His remedy is to compel the trustees to restore the trust fund to its proper state.[64] Of course, the object, like any beneficiary, can only complain in respect of a fund, or part of a fund, from which he might see benefit.[65]

In normative terms, the rights of an object of a fiduciary dispositive power warrant his standing to sue to remedy a breach of trust. A fund exists in respect of which they have claims. The claims may be weak claims in legal theory, though perhaps more significant in reality where they are 'the true intended beneficiaries': interesting as that contrast is, it is not relevant for present purposes. These objects have claims in relation to a fund and should therefore be prima facie entitled to complain if the integrity of that fund has been jeopardised or compromised. In short, the beneficiary principle, to which English law still adheres,[66] gives standing to enforce a trust to those who have some claims on or in respect of the trust property.

V. Claims for Breach of Trust: Claims by Objects of Personal, Non-Fiduciary Powers

Personal, non-fiduciary powers are much less commonly encountered in settlements than fiduciary dispositive powers. And it is unlikely that the objects of personal powers have rights of enforcement similar to those just outlined in the context of fiduciary powers.[67]

The holder of a fiduciary dispositive power owes positive duties to the objects of that power. The holder must consider whether to exercise the power, consider the range of objects of the power, and consider the appropriateness of individual (proposed) exercises of the power.[68]

By contrast, the holder of a merely personal power does not owe duties to the donor or the objects of the power.[69] So the holder can ignore the power if

[64] *Target Holdings Ltd* (n 17) 434, cited in text to n 17.

[65] See Tucker, Le Poidevin and Brightwell (n 49) para 39-076.

[66] *Morice* (n 16); see generally Tucker, Le Poidevin and Brightwell (n 49) para 39-076 and paras 4-043–4-046.

[67] ibid para 39-074.

[68] *Re Gulbenkian's Settlement* [1970] AC 508, 518 (Lord Reid); *Re Hay's Settlement Trusts* [1982] 1 WLR 202, 210 (Megarry VC).

[69] See, eg, *Re Somes* [1896] 1 Ch 250, 255 (Chitty J); *Re Gulbenkian's* (n 68) 518 (Lord Reid); *Re Wills' Trust Deeds* [1961] Ch 219, 227–29 (Buckley J); *Re Hay's Settlement Trusts* (n 68) 208–09 (Megarry VC).

he chooses; and he does not have to consider the objects of the power or their interests. He can release the power at will.[70] The only constraint on the holder of the power is that he must stay within its bounds—both its express terms, and the implicit limitations which apply even to personal powers, such as the requirements to act in good faith and for proper purposes.[71] However, those constraints on the holder of the power exist for the benefit of those who take in default of any exercise of the power: they are to be benefited by the fund in question save to the extent that benefit is validly deflected away from them by proper exercise of the power. The constraints do not entitle the objects of the power to anything; they merely delimit the extent to which benefit can be taken away from the default beneficiaries. Thus, any infringement of the constraints is solely the concern of the default beneficiaries: they can claim their interests have been prejudiced if the constraints are infringed. The objects of the power never had any interest in the fund, nor any claim on the holder of the power; so any misbehaviour of the holder is of no *legal* significance to them, whatever their practical disappointment or concern.

So while the rights of an object of a fiduciary dispositive power warrant his standing to sue to remedy a breach of trust, as noted above, the objects of a mere power, by contrast, have no such rights and correspondingly no foundation for any complaint. The beneficiary principle gives standing to enforce a trust to those who have some claims on or in respect of the trust property, but not others.

VI. Claims for Breach of Trust: Claims by Protectors

Any general statements about protectors are necessarily tentative. Protectors are all creatures of the specific terms of their appointment. Their powers are various both in form and function. Each such power may or may not be fiduciary in nature. As Ribeiro PJ noted in *Kan v Poon*:

> The position is explained in an article by Matthew Conaglen and Elizabeth Weaver entitled 'Protectors as fiduciaries: theory and practice'. As the learned authors point out, the term 'protector' is not a term of art and generally 'signifies little more than that a person who is not the (or a) trustee has been granted a power affecting the operation of the trust'. One cannot assume that such a power is held in a fiduciary capacity requiring it to be exercised only in the interests of others to the exclusion of the donee of the power.[72]

[70] See Law of Property Act 1925, s 155 and *Re Wills' Trust Deeds* (n 69) 227 (Buckley J).

[71] eg *Aleyn v Belchier* (1758) 1 Eden 132, 28 ER 634; *Lady Wellesley v Earl of Mornington* (1855) 2 K & J 143, 69 ER 728; *Redwood Master Fund Ltd v TD Bank Europe Ltd* [2002] EWHC 2703 (Ch), [2006] 1 BCLC 149; *Citibank NA v MBIA Assurance SA* [2006] EWHC 3215 (Ch), [2007] EWCA Civ 11; *Assénagon Asset Management SA v Irish Bank Resolution Corporation Ltd (formerly Anglo Irish Bank Corporation Ltd)* [2012] EWHC 2090 (Ch), [2013] 1 All ER 495.

[72] *Kan* (n 15) [67], citing M Conaglen and Weaver (n 15).

Consequently, general statements about someone in the position of a protector must be made and read with caution.

It is undoubtedly true, however, that a protector who holds fiduciary powers is subject to the inherent jurisdiction of the court to administer a trust and reform its maladministration. For example, in *Steele v Paz Ltd*,[73] a Manx appellate court held that the position of protector in the settlement at issue was a fiduciary position, and that the court could accordingly appoint a new protector to fill a gap in tenure of the office, in the same way that it could appoint a trustee in order to prevent a trust from failing for want of a trustee. In *Re Freiburg Trust*,[74] the Jersey Royal Court held that the protector of the trust, whose consent was required for the exercise by the trustees of a number of their powers, including payments of income or capital, was in the position of a fiduciary. The Court, accordingly, could remove him pursuant to its inherent jurisdiction, and did so, because he had been convicted of offences of fraud in Belgium (including misappropriation of monies from the Freiburg Trust itself). In the Jersey case of *In the Matter of the A and B Trusts*,[75] the court again ordered removal of a protector in exercise of its inherent jurisdiction. Much of the factual background of the case was not reported publicly for reasons of confidentiality. Briefly, relations had broken down completely between the protector and the adult beneficiaries of two Jersey settlements and the protector of the settlements, who misconceived his role as ensuring that the wishes of the settlors were carried out, rather than upholding the interests of the beneficiaries at all times. The court made it clear that its jurisdiction could be exercised well beyond the extreme circumstances of a case such as *Re Freiburg Trust*: the protector's mistaken view of his role, the breakdown in relations with so many beneficiaries, and the prejudice that caused to the administration of the trust, warranted his removal from office.

In the cases outlined above, the application was made by beneficiaries and the subject matter of the application was the protector or his office. But there are other cases indicating that a protector himself may make applications to court in connection with the exercise of his powers, for example, an application for a declaration as to the validity of his own action,[76] or an application to invoke (what was then) the *Hastings–Bass* jurisdiction to set aside an exercise of his powers.[77] A protector may bring an application to determine the legitimacy of action by the trustees where the trustees' action is (at least alleged to be) an infringement of the protector's powers.[78]

[73] *Steele v Paz Ltd* [1993–95] Manx LR 426.

[74] *Re Freiburg Trust* [2004] JRC 56.

[75] *In the Matter of the A and B Trusts* [2012] JRC 169A.

[76] See, eg, *Re Omar Family Trust* [2000] WTLR 713 (Cayman); *Virani v Guernsey International Trustees (No 1)* [2004] WTLR 1007 (Guernsey); *Re Papadimitriou* [2004] WTLR 1141 (Isle of Man); *Alhamrani v Russa Management* [2010] WTLR 443 (Jersey).

[77] *Re L* [2011] JLR 085.

[78] *Re the Hare Trust* (2001) 4 ITELR 288 (Jersey).

However, none of these cases goes so far as to suggest that a protector, even a protector holding fiduciary powers (and a fortiori a protector who holds personal powers), can sue to restore the trust fund, assuming of course that the protector is not a beneficiary of the trust in question. And the rationale of the beneficiary principle, noted above,[79] that standing to ask a court to compel reconstitution of a trust fund is given to those who have some claim under the trust on, or in respect of, the fund, would strongly suggest that protectors have no such standing by virtue of their office or powers.

This conclusion is strongly supported by the recent decision of Henderson J in *Davidson v Selig*.[80] In that case, the judge noted that two joint protectors had:

> [F]our principal functions to perform in relation to the administration of the trusts. First, they have power to give or withhold consent to any exercise by the Trustees of their beneficial powers of appointment, or revocation of earlier appointments, from time to time. Secondly, they have power to remove any trustee from office, with or without cause, provided that there will still remain a minimum number of trustees. Thirdly, they have a contingent power to appoint new trustees which will be exercisable only after the death or incapacity of both Settlors. Finally, the protectors may together appoint new protectors. These powers are fiduciary, and they must be exercised in the interests of the beneficiaries. *The protectors do not, however, have a general power or duty to supervise the administration of the Settlements, and they may only apply to the court for relief which relates to the proper exercise of their own powers.*
>
> I would provisionally accept these submissions, which appear to me firmly based on general principles of trust law and to reflect the limited nature of the powers conferred on the Protector by the 2003 Deeds.[81]

Henderson J went on to deny the relief sought by one of the two joint protectors.[82] His judgment was framed in narrower terms than the dicta cited above. In the context of two claims, protectors as such had no standing under the relevant statutory provisions,[83] let alone a single protector acting on his own who should have acted, if at all, jointly with his co-protector. In the third claim, for information about the trust, Henderson J declined to make any order while the claimant protector's own status was under challenge. In the other claim, the judge held that the claimant protector could not, in the circumstances, seek replacement of his co-protector. Strictly, therefore, Henderson J's comments on the general powers and duties of protectors to procure the due administration of a trust were obiter; but they are quite clear and, with respect, entirely consistent with principle.

[79] See text to n 66.
[80] *Davidson v Selig* [2016] EWHC 549 (Ch).
[81] ibid [55]–[56] (emphasis added).
[82] ibid [57]–[64].
[83] One claim was for the appointment of new trustees by the court (Trustee Act 1925, ss 41, 58), and the other for an order to authorise dealings with trust property (Trustee Act 1925, s 57).

Of course, where the law concerning the enforcement of trusts has been changed by statute, a different result may obtain. So, for example, a protector might well be considered a person sufficiently interested in a Bermudian purpose trust as to be able to enforce the trust under section 12B(1)(d) of the Trusts (Special Provisions) Act 1989 (Bermuda). Equally, a protector might well be the sort of person a Cayman court might appoint to enforce a special trust under section 100 of the Cayman Trusts Law (2011 revision). But these possibilities are purely a function of local legislation: they have no wider significance.

Still, a protector might still be of use where the trustees have committed a breach of trust that necessitates the reinstatement of the trust fund. If the beneficiaries are in no position practically to take the necessary action themselves, the court might allow the protector, as a suitably interested person, to take the proceedings on behalf of the beneficiaries. The court has such a jurisdiction to depart from the proper plaintiff rule—the rule that prima facie the correct person to bring proceedings is the person whose interests are at issue which, for present purposes, is prima facie a beneficiary affected by the breach of trust in question.

This equitable jurisdiction is the origin of the 'fraud on the minority' exception to the rule in *Foss v Harbottle*,[84] that is, the exception where a member of a corporation may sue to remedy a wrong done to the separate legal person of the corporation.[85] However, the equitable learning concerning a fraud on a minority has now been replaced, with regard to companies registered under the Companies Acts, by Part 11 of the Companies Act 2006.

Courts of equity have also departed from the proper plaintiff rule in allowing a trustee to sue on behalf of beneficiaries in respect of a breach of trust.[86] While it is true that a trustee has a duty to protect and where necessary take action to restore the trust fund,[87] and these duties clearly have bearing on the readiness of the courts to give the trustee standing to sue to remedy a breach of trust, cases of this nature do illustrate the ability of the court to allow departure from the proper plaintiff rule in an appropriate case—and, for present purposes, an appropriate case of breach of trust. A protector might be an appropriate person for the court to appoint as nominal claimant in an action for breach of trust, whether

[84] *Foss v Harbottle* (1843) 2 Hare 461, (1843) 67 ER 189.

[85] See eg, *Foss* (n 84) 490–92, 202–03 (Wigram VC), citing the general principle stated in *Wallworth v Holt* (1840) 4 My & C 619, 635–36; 41 ER 238, 244–45 (Lord Cottenham LC); *Atwool v Merryweather* (1867) LR 5 Eq 464; *Russell v Wakefield Waterworks* (1875) LR 20 Eq 474, 480–81 (Jessel MR), again citing *Wallworth*; *Burland v Earle* [1902] AC 83, 93–94 (Lord Davey).

[86] This is a well-established jurisdiction, fully and usefully discussed in *Young v Murphy* [1996] 1 VR 279 (see especially the judgment of Brooking J). Note also the result, but rather sparse reasons, in *Montrose Investment Ltd v Orion Nominees Ltd (No 2)* [2004] EWCA Civ 1032, [2004] WTLR 1133 [23]–[26]. There is further discussion in *Nicholson Street Pty Ltd (Receivers & Managers Appointed) (in Liquidation) v Letten* [2015] VSC 583.

[87] *Re Brogden* (1888) 38 Ch D 546; *Young* (n 86) and the cases discussed there.

under its equitable jurisdiction considered above, or under its statutory rules of procedure.[88]

But in any such case, whether arising under the court's equitable jurisdiction or its rules of procedure, the position of a protector as claimant in an action for breach of trust would be a representative position, enforcing beneficiaries' rights on behalf of those beneficiaries who, for whatever reason, are not practically able to vindicate their own rights. Protectors still would not have standing to sue in their own right to put a trust fund back into its proper state.

VII. Practical Implications

Those who create settlements that make significant use of dispositive fiduciary powers should be reassured: these structures are enforceable. This accords with a trend in trust law that sees the courts generally try to accommodate new developments devised by legal practitioners in response to the requirements of their clients. The widespread use of such settlements, and the main reasons for that, are examined above. A series of cases, most of them in the 1960s and 1970s, established the boundaries within which such powers are valid; and those boundaries are very widely drawn, as has been seen. While logically the courts could have conceded the validity of such powers, but left enforcement of the trustees' duties under such a settlement to beneficiaries with some more doctrinally substantial entitlement, that would fly in the face of the courts' generally pragmatic approach to the law of trusts. If such powers are valid and widely used, it is surely much more natural for a pragmatically inclined judiciary to develop the law so that the trustees' duties are enforceable by those who may—and in many cases, very likely will—take benefit under the powers.

This can still leave some practical problems. Allowing the object of a fiduciary power standing to enforce duties of trustees does not, and cannot, ensure that any such object has the motivation or incentive to hold the trustees to account. At first sight, it might therefore seem that settlements which make much use of dispositive fiduciary powers will be largely unenforced in practical terms, even if enforceable in doctrinal terms. But again, this may be too simplistic. The object of a power who is (very) likely to benefit under the power—one of the 'true intended beneficiaries'—may well have the motivation to see the trust fund from which he stands to benefit restored to its rightful condition, especially when proceedings against the trustees to procure restoration of the trust fund are combined with an application for the removal of the miscreant trustees (if still in office) and the appointment of new trustees whose attitudes to a discretion vested in them will

[88] eg Civil Procedure Rules, r 19.7.

not be tainted by any hostility the miscreant trustees might harbour towards some object of that discretion who has had the temerity to sue them.

Also, any person with standing to sue the trustees may do so whatever others with similar standing may think of the action, unless the terms of the trust limit those rights, for example, to circumstances where a majority of the beneficiaries concur. Trust law does not have the problem of default majority rule which makes it difficult for individual shareholders to take action in respect of a wrong done to the company.[89] If there is an analogy in corporate law, the better analogy is with claims under section 994 of the Companies Act 2006 (remedying of unfair prejudice to a member's interests): proceedings founded on breach of a fiduciary's duties are often brought under the Act by those with a minority stake in a company who have the necessary standing under the section, irrespective of their status as a minority, as long as they have sufficient personal motivation to bring the proceedings.

A practical implication which concerns protectors is that they are not functionally equivalent to the non-beneficiary 'enforcers' of trustees' duties which exist under the legislation of many offshore jurisdictions, for example, section 12B(1) of the Trusts (Special Provisions) Act 1989 (Bermuda) or section 84A of the Trustee Act 1961 (British Virgin Islands) or Part VIII of the Trusts Law (Cayman, 2011 revision). Nor does there seem any doctrinal basis upon which to develop the office of protector into such a role. Developments of that sort require a direct reformulation of the beneficiary principle, whether by statute or, possibly, judicial decision.

VIII. Theoretical Implications

The most important theoretical implications from the law surveyed above are the nature of the parties' rights and the court's role in the enforcement of trusts. Another key theme is the continuing importance of practitioners in the development of trusts, and the courts' response to the practitioners' efforts.

The invocation and utilisation of the administrative jurisdiction of the court is and remains fundamental to the enforcement of trusts: the ability to invoke the administrative jurisdiction is the key to the enforcement of a trust. This means that litigation to enforce trustees' duties to restore the trust fund is not, at root, a simple matter of remedying the infringement of the claimant's own interest. The claimant is seeking to do something else, to restore a fund in which he has an interest but not necessarily the only interest. The claimant is seeking a remedy for the benefit of himself and all others interested in the fund. While in form his action is an action in his own right, in substance it is neither purely personal nor purely representative. The aim of his action is not to repair harm done to him, in

[89] See Companies Act 2006, s 263(2)(c), (3)(c) and (d).

the manner of an action for damages at common law, but to restore the proper functioning—the due administration—of an organisation from which he may or will see benefit. Harm done to a person, even from the functioning of an organisation, can be remedied by an award of money to that person alone. By contrast, due administration of a trust necessarily benefits all those interested in the trust: due administration by definition involves administration of the trust for all those to benefit from it.

The primacy of securing the due administration of the trust as the aim of remedies for breach of trust has consequences in the scope of those remedies, which are not limited to reversing harm done to the trust fund but allow remedies, including money remedies, equivalent to performance rather than loss. This phenomenon has been described as the 'good man theory of trusts', where a trustee in breach of duty must do his duty or pay the money equivalent of performance, as opposed to the to the 'bad man theory of contract', where a contract-breaker can breach contract, pay damages for harm done to the other party, but then take advantage of his breach.[90] (Restitutionary damages for breach of contract are exceptional,[91] even in jurisdictions such as England where they are available.)

But as well as informing the scope of remedies for breach of trust, the primacy of securing due administration of the trust informs the identification of those who may sue to remedy a breach of trust: those to whom the trustees owe obligations in respect of their application of the trust fund, rather than those who can show their property or chances have been devalued or lost. To focus on those who have lost property is too narrow: this category does not include those to whom the trustees owe obligations in respect of their dispositive discretions. To focus on those who lose chances by the trustees' actions is too wide: that category could include those to whom the trustees owe no obligations, such as objects of a non-fiduciary power of appointment, whose chances of benefit from the trust are nevertheless factually diminished by a breach of trust. Trust law is a matter, inter alia, of obligations in respect of the application of the trust fund: correspondingly, those to whom such obligations are owed are the people who should be eligible to procure due administration of the trust.

Of course, as noted before, standing does not guarantee the court will entertain the allegations made, even if they are factually justified: an object of a wide fiduciary power who is far from one of the 'true intended beneficiaries' might technically have standing to sue to remedy a breach of trust; but the court, in exercise of its discretion in its administrative jurisdiction may decline to hear the case, for example, because in substance it amounts to officious meddling. And this is entirely acceptable in terms of the rule of law. The court, in such a case, is not capriciously refusing to remedy a wrong—harm—done to that claimant, in a way

[90] See DJ Hayton, 'The Development of Equity and the "Good Person" Philosophy in Common Law Systems' [2012] *Conveyancer and Property Lawyer* 263.
[91] *Attorney General v Blake* [2001] 1 AC 268.

that might raise concern about equal protection under the law. It is refusing to allow someone to become embroiled in the affairs of an institution when he has no significant interest in the management of the institution and has himself suffered no loss.

The law surveyed also shows the importance of the interaction of the legal profession and the judiciary in developing the law. As seen above, practitioners pioneered the widespread use of fiduciary dispositive powers in response to their clients' needs. Once the judges had accepted the validity of such powers; once they had clothed their tenure with obligations; once they had realised that the objects of such powers were more important to the settlor than the beneficiaries who took in default of any exercise of those powers, it was hardly surprising that the judges should accord standing to those objects. The judges, after all, are former practitioners: judges such as Lord Wilberforce, Lord Templeman and Lord Walker had careers at the Bar involved in the creation of settlements which made great use of such powers, and they brought that perspective to the bench. The practitioner perspective is important: it is clearly recognised by the judiciary, and so it needs to be recognised in the theoretical perspective, not just in a socio-legal perspective.

Finally, as noted earlier, the process of securing due administration of a trust through taking accounts can be short-circuited by an application for an award of equitable compensation. However, focusing on compensation alone, and a failure to examine thoroughly the process of accounting, can be the cause of considerable confusion, as witness two cases of high authority in the last 20 years, *Target Holdings Ltd v Redferns*,[92] and *AIB Group (UK) plc v Mark Redler & Co Solicitors*.[93] Yet both cases can be accommodated and explained perfectly well within the framework of the inherent jurisdiction to hold trustees to account.

Lord Millett first provided an elegant solution to the problems of *Target*.[94] In that case, the defendant solicitors' unauthorised disbursement of the £1.49 million was a clear breach of the trusts on which they held those (client) monies: the monies had been released without obtaining a mortgage in exchange. So that action could be falsified in the trust accounts, leaving the solicitors liable, *at that time*, to pay £1.49 million to reconstitute the trust fund. But by the time of action, the solicitors had received the relevant mortgage charges, and when they did so, their authority to execute the trust by paying out the trust funds on receipt of the mortgage still subsisted. So the receipt of the mortgage had to be taken into the account as a credit entry, balancing the disbursement of the £1.49 million. So the trust accounts as they should appear would thus match the actual state of the trust fund, and therefore no compensation was payable.

[92] *Target Holdings Ltd* (n 17).

[93] *AIB Group (UK) Plc v Mark Redler & Co Solicitors* [2014] UKSC 58, [2015] AC 1503.

[94] PJ Millett, 'Equity's Place in the Law of Commerce' (1998) 114 *LQR* 214; see also M Conaglen, 'Explaining *Target Holdings v Redferns*' (2010) 4 *Journal of Equity* 288.

There is much more debate about whether the second of two cases, *AIB v Redler*, can be equally elegantly explained by remembering and applying the principles of trust accounting. Professor Conaglen has suggested not.[95] However, accounting can perfectly well explain the result in that case.

AIB agreed to lend £3.3 million against the security of a property valued at £4.5 million, but the lender insisted on securing its loan by a first charge. The existing mortgages on the property had to be redeemed so that could happen. The loan funds were advanced to solicitors, who released them without obtaining a first charge over the property. As a result of negligence, £1.2 million was paid to the prior mortgagee to redeem its mortgage, but this was too little by £0.3 million. So the prior mortgage continued on foot, albeit to secure just £0.3 million. The £0.3 million was instead paid to the borrower. In subsequent attempts to rectify the situation, it proved impossible for AIB to obtain a first mortgage. So the breach was never rectified, in contrast to *Target*. The borrower defaulted, the property was sold and the first £0.3 million of the realisation was paid to the prior mortgagee, as was proper. But that meant AIB only received approximately £0.87 million. The solicitors admitted negligence, but the claim in contract was limited to the £0.3 million which AIB had lost as a result of not having had a first charge. AIB therefore sued for breach of trust, arguing that the entire £3.3 million had been disbursed in breach of trust, as no valid first charge had been received, and thus needed to be replaced. It failed: its claim was limited to the £0.3 million extra that it would have received had it been the first mortgagee. The reasoning of the Supreme Court was couched in terms of equitable compensation. This has led some to question the result, as it is seen to be inconsistent with the process accounting. However, it is suggested that the result is in fact perfectly consistent with accounting as the primary remedy for breach of trust.

In brief, the process of accounting would begin with falsifying the disbursement of the £3.3 million. The acquisition of a second mortgage did not cure the breach of trust, and so would not be taken into account. But what must be taken into account are the solicitors' duties. It is true that, on taking an account, the defendant trustee is not allowed to speculate that he would have used his powers in a certain way and thereby mitigated to the breach of trust. This rule is justified on the basis that the trustee should not be allowed to give self-serving, and very likely untrue, evidence in his defence. But what was at issue in *AIB* was not the trustee's *powers*, but its *duties*. Once in possession of the £3.3 million, it was the trustee's duty to acquire a first mortgage, and so what should show in the account is the first mortgage, not £3.3 million. It was clearly the *duty* of the trustee to acquire that mortgage, not merely its *power*: the trustee could hardly be heard to say that it might or might not choose to expend the monies on the mortgage; it had to do so. This duty was originally revocable, of course. AIB could have called off the whole transaction at least until it took the benefit of the second mortgage, though

[95] Conaglen, 'Equitable Compensation for Breach of Trust: Off *Target*' (n 21).

it is hard to see how AIB could resile once it had voluntarily taken benefit (the second mortgage) from the acquisition of the property: taking such a benefit and yet denying authority for the very transactions which generated that benefit would be inconsistent. So, on the assumption that AIB did not countermand acquisition of the mortgage, this mortgage is what should show in the accounts, not a sum of cash. On that basis, when the borrower defaulted, the trust fund would contain a second mortgage when it should contain a first mortgage; and the loss to the fund would be the difference between realisation of a first mortgage and realisation of the second mortgage, in other words, £0.3 million.

The trustee's liability is a function of its duty; and there is no reason why the trustee cannot point to its *duty* (rather than its *powers*) in order to establish the scope of its liability. The trustee is not taking advantage of his own misconduct: it is open to a defendant who is liable, even a trustee who is liable, nevertheless to ask the court to pay attention to the basis and extent of its liability, that is, to pay attention to the nature of its duties.

So in both *Target* and *AIB*, the courts intuitively reached a justifiable result. But explaining the result in the correct terms is still useful in itself.

IX. Conclusion

The inherent jurisdiction is flexible, innovative and vitally important. It allows for flexible and innovative trust structures and provides for their enforcement. It provides answers to the questions of who may enforce a trustee's duties and in what circumstances. Modern trust structures which make great use of dispositive fiduciary powers do not present significant legal risk and their enforcement. There may be practical issues related to enforcement, but these go to the motivation, rather than the availability, of a beneficiary with standing to enforce the trustees' duties.

Enforcement of a trustee's obligations by a beneficiary is in principle different from a typical common law claim and remedy as between two parties, though sometimes and, in some simple cases, it may bear some superficial similarity. The court's inherent jurisdiction provides the mechanism for one member of a group of beneficiaries to secure enforcement of obligations owed to the entire group for the benefit of the whole group. And it is this principle that underlies cases that are litigated as claims for equitable compensation against a trustee. There is no harm in such form of action as long as it is remembered that it is a way of achieving more quickly what is provided by an account of the trustee's stewardship of the trust fund. The confusion surrounding some recent cases emphasises the importance of this point. But what cannot be overemphasised is the importance of understanding the flexible and innovative inherent jurisdiction of the court to secure the due administration of a trust.

8

Trusts, Objectivity and Rectification

SIMON DOUGLAS*

I. Introduction

In order to establish the existence of an express trust a basic requirement is that the settlor's intention to create a trust on particular terms be certain.[1] It is commonly said that a court must adopt an 'objective' enquiry when it approaches this question. Perhaps the strongest statement to this effect comes from the recent Australian case of *Byrnes v Kendle*[2] where French CJ said: 'The relevant intention in such a case is that manifested by the declaration of trust. Such a case does not require any further inquiry into the subjective or "real" intention of the settler'.[3] In this respect, as the High Court noted, there is no difference between how the court ascertains the relevant intention of the parties to a contract and how it ascertains a settlor's intention to create a trust: in both cases the subjective intention of the parties is irrelevant.[4]

The High Court also noted in the case that there are some exceptions to the objective approach.[5] One apparent exception, which is considered in this chapter, is that of rectification. Rectification is generally said to be available in cases where a document, such as a contract[6] or a trust deed,[7] has been executed but there has been some error in the recording of the parties' intentions.[8] The remedy of rectification,

* I am very grateful to Paul Davies, James Penner, Joshua Getzler, Rob Stevens and Peter Watts QC for their comments on an earlier draft of this chapter.

[1] *Knight v Knight* (1840) 49 ER 58.

[2] *Byrnes v Kendle* [2011] HCA 26, 243 CLR 253.

[3] ibid [17].

[4] ibid [59]–[65] (Gummow and Hayne JJ).

[5] ibid [100]–[101] (Heydon and Crennan JJ).

[6] There has been much academic interest of late in rectification owing, in part, to the controversial speech of Lord Hoffmann in *Chartbrook Ltd v Persimmon Homes Ltd* [2009] UKHL 38, [2009] 1 AC 1101, which held that rectification, in the context of contract law at least, involves an objective enquiry into the intention of the parties.

[7] The case of *Walker v Armstrong* (1856) 8 De GM & G 531, 44 ER 495 provides an early example of the jurisdiction of the Chancery Court to reform a trust deed.

[8] See generally D Hodge, *Rectification: The Modern Law and Practice Governing Claims for Rectification for Mistake*, 2nd edn (London, Sweet & Maxwell, 2016) ch 1.

as Mummery LJ notes, 'involves bringing the trust document into line with the true intentions of the settlor as held by him at the date when he executed the document'.[9] When a court is asked to rectify a trust deed it is commonly said that the enquiry becomes a subjective one, with a court rectifying a document if it does not reflect what the settlor 'meant to say'. For instance, in the recent case of *Day v Day* Etherton LJ said:

> What is relevant in such a case is the subjective intention of the settlor. It is not a legal requirement for the rectification of a voluntary settlement that there is any outward expression or objective communication of the settlor's intention.[10]

The notion that rectification provides an exceptional case, where the court should eschew its normal objective approach, and enquire into the 'true' or 'actual' intention of the settlor, is problematic. If a settlor can obtain rectification if, subject to certain conditions,[11] his subjective intention is at odds with the objective meaning of his words then, arguably, rectification, far from being a mere exception to the objective approach, wholly undermines it.

This purpose of this chapter is to examine this apparent contradiction in the law of trusts. In the first section of the chapter it will be asked whether courts do, in fact, assess a settlor's intention objectively. It is often remarked that the rules governing the assessment of a settlor's intention to declare a trust are largely under-theorised.[12] The English[13] law of trusts does not appear to have any authoritative leading cases, such as those found in contract law,[14] where objective principles are put on a clear footing. One must carefully review the English authorities in order to reach a firm conclusion on this issue. The second section of the chapter asks whether rectification of trust instruments is, as suggested in the above quote, a subjective process, and whether this undermines the objective approach to interpretation.

II. Objectivity in Trusts

The rules governing the objective interpretation of contracts are well known and the subject of much scholarly attention. The corresponding rules in trusts law, by contrast, have attracted little by way of comment and analysis. Most textbooks will, as a matter of course, say that the rules governing the interpretation of trusts are, like their contractual counterparts, objective. Yet there are important differences

[9] *Allnutt v Wilding* [2007] EWCA Civ 412 [11].
[10] *Day v Day* [2013] EWCA Civ 280, [2014] Ch 114 [22]; noted F Dawson (2014) 130 *LQR* 356.
[11] Specifically, that none of the bars to rectification apply. The principal bars are laches, acquiescence and the impact on a third party. See Hodge (n 8) chs 6 and 7.
[12] *Byrnes* (n 2) [59] (Gummow and Hayne JJ).
[13] As opposed to the Australian law of trusts, where *Byrnes* (n 2) is the leading case.
[14] eg *Smith v Hughes* (1871) LR 6 QB 597.

between contracts and trusts, in particular the voluntary nature of most trusts. So, what evidence is there of an objective approach? In order to answer this question it may be helpful to begin by considering the meaning of 'objectivity'.

A. What is Objectivity?

Most attempts to define objectivity draw some distinction between the meaning attached to a statement by the speaker, and the meaning conveyed to the addressee, or a reasonable person in the addressee's position. For instance, Spencer, in explaining the objective approach to contractual interpretation said: 'Words are to be interpreted as they are reasonably understood by the *man to whom they were spoken*, not as they were understood by the *man who spoke them*'.[15] When a speaker encodes his thoughts in words, he may mean one thing by them, but the addressee may understand those words to mean something quite different. In such cases, the objective and subjective enquiries point in different directions. The distinction between speaker meaning and addressee meaning can be applied outside the contractual context. For instance, in *Norton on Deeds*, in a quote cited with approval in *Byrnes v Kendle*,[16] we see support for an objective approach to the interpretation of deeds:

> The word 'intention' may be understood in two senses, as descriptive either (1) of that which the parties intended to do, or (2) of the meaning of the words that they have employed; here it is used in the latter sense ... In other words, the question to be answered always is, 'What is the meaning of what the parties have said?', not, 'What did the parties mean to say?'.[17]

The facts of *Byrnes v Kendle* provide a neat illustration of the difference. The defendant in the case, using both his own and his then wife's savings, had acquired freehold title to a house. He then executed a trust deed, which stated, amongst other things, that he held the title 'on trust' for the benefit of himself and his then wife. Following his separation from his wife, and her assigning her interest to her son (the claimant), a dispute arose as to the payment of rent, as the defendant had permitted his own son to live at the premises rent free. If there was a trust of the freehold, with the claimant holding a beneficial interest, then it was clear that he was entitled to the receipt of rent. The defendant attempted to introduce evidence that he believed, in executing the deed, that he was merely undertaking to share the sale value of the land should he ever sell it in the future, and hence no trust

[15] JR Spencer, 'Signature, Consent and the Rule in L'Estrange v Graucob' (1973) 32 *CLJ* 104, 106. For discussion of the extent of the objective theory on contract law, and whether there is any room for a subjective enquiry, see D McLauchlan, 'Objectivity in Contract' (2005) 24 *University of Queensland Law Journal* 479, 484 and D McLauchlan, 'The Contract that Neither Party Intends' (2012) 29 *Journal of Contract Law* 26.

[16] *Byrnes* (n 2) [53].

[17] R Morrison and H Goodman (eds), *Norton on Deeds*, 2nd edn (London, Sweet & Maxwell, 1928) 50.

was ever created. The dispute in the case, therefore, was whether the 'certainty of intention' requirement for the establishment of a trust had been satisfied.

In most cases it does not matter whether a court adopts an objective or a subjective approach to the certainty of intention requirement, as both enquiries will yield the same result. Parties preparing legal documents, who have had time to consider their choice of words, are usually good at encoding their thoughts in language, so that their meaning is successfully conveyed to the addressee. Yet this is not always true, Mr Kendle providing a case in point. A subjective approach—what did Mr Kendle mean by his words 'on trust'?—would result in there being no trust as Mr Kendle meant no more than a promise to split the proceeds of sale in the future. An objective approach—what would the reasonable addressee understand the words 'on trust' to mean?—would result in a trust, those words clearly conveying an intention to settle the title in this way. It is important to determine, therefore, which question the courts ask when they deal with the certainty of intention requirement. In *Byrnes v Kendle* the court was of the view that an objective enquiry was appropriate, with Heydon and Crennan JJ holding that

> the 'intention' referred to is an intention to be extracted from the words used, not a subjective intention which may have existed but which cannot be extracted from those words. This is as true of unilateral declarations of alleged trust as it is of bilateral covenants to create an alleged trust.[18]

Whilst this makes the position in Australian law clear, we must ask whether it reflects the approach of the English courts to the certainty of intention requirement.

B. Is Intention Assessed Objectively in the Law of Trusts?

The High Court of Australia's adoption of an objective approach in the context of trusts was influenced, in part, by the corresponding contractual rules of interpretation. These rules, as noted by Gummow and Hayne JJ, were in 'command of the field'[19] and provide an obvious starting point in any analysis of a trusts dispute. Further, as Heydon and Crennan JJ noted, contracts provide a common base for the establishment of some trusts, and the fact that the two enquiries are similar is 'not surprising'.[20] Yet, some may be reluctant to push the analogy with contract too far. Trusts, it must be noted, are often unilateral in the sense that their creation depends entirely on the settlor's exercise of his power to create a trust.

[18] *Byrnes* (n 2) [114].

[19] *Byrnes* (n 2) [59], citing Mason ACJ, Murphy and Deane JJ in *Taylor v Johnson* (1983) 151 CLR 422, 429.

[20] ibid. The notion that 'what goes for contract goes for trusts' is further supported by the line of cases where a declaration of trust has been inferred from the terms of a contract. The leading example is that of *Re Sigma Finance Corporation* [2009] UKHL 2, [2010] 1 All ER 571. Dyson Heydon expressed some concerns over the contractualisation of trusts principles: JD Heydon, 'Implications of *Chartbrook Ltd v Persimmon Homes Ltd* for the Law of Trusts' (paper at the STEP Annual Trusts Symposium, Adelaide, 18 February 2011).

The resulting focus on the settlor's intention, to the exclusion of any other party such as the trustee or beneficiary, may lead some to favour a subjective approach. This tendency may be particularly strong where the settlor is acting gratuitously: if Mr Kendle, for instance, was under no obligation to divest himself of the value of his title, then why should he be bound by a construction that he never intended? There is an obvious temptation to favour a subjective approach in the context of trusts law. This is perhaps encouraged, as Heydon and Crennan JJ note, by the 'constant repetition of the need to search for an "intention to create a trust"'.[21]

There is some evidence of a subjective approach to interpretation in trusts law. The best example is the problematic Australian case of *Commissioner of Stamp Duties (QD) v Jolliffe*.[22] Under a statute, it was illegal for an account holder to hold a second account at a bank, except where the second account is held on trust for another. The defendant, already holding an account, deposited money in a second account and made a declaration to the bank that he held it on trust for his sisters. The defendant subsequently denied the existence of a trust. His argument succeeded as the court permitted him to introduce evidence that, notwithstanding his declaration of trust, his real intention was to retain title to the fund and earn interest on it. As this intention was never disclosed (until the legal proceedings), it could only be ascertained by conducting a subjective enquiry into the defendant's mental state; an objective enquiry—what meaning did the defendant convey to a reasonable person?—would yield nothing other than an intention to create a trust as that is all that was communicated.

The question has often been raised of whether *Jolliffe*, which has now been overruled in Australia by *Byrnes v Kendle*, ever represented the legal position in England. Citations of the case in successive editions of *Lewin on Trusts*[23] posed this question, and one can certainly find some support for it in the old case law. In the nineteenth-century case of *Field v Lonsdale*,[24] which involved facts almost identical to those found in *Jolliffe*, the Master of the Rolls, Lord Langdale, refused to give effect to the obvious (objective) meaning of the defendant's declaration of trust over the second bank account: 'the only intention was to evade the provisions of the Act of Parliament [prohibiting a second account], and not to create a trust. The declaration is, therefore, ineffectual, and the claim must be dismissed'.[25]

Yet *Jolliffe*, and similar cases like *Field v Lonsdale* despite never being expressly rejected in the English courts, are clearly inconsistent with principles developed in relation to the certainty of intention requirement. Specifically, the cases do not square with the traditional exclusion of evidence of an undisclosed or secret intention. It is not mental states per se which constitute trusts, but the communication

[21] *Byrnes* (n 2) [114].
[22] *Commissioner of Stamp Duties (QD) v Jolliffe* (1920) 28 CLR 178.
[23] WJ Mowbray (ed), *Lewin on* Trusts, 16th edn (London, Sweet & Maxwell, 1964).
[24] *Field v Lonsdale* (1850) 13 Beavan 78, 51 ER 30.
[25] ibid 81.

of them. Indeed, this was pointed out in *Jolliffe* in the strong dissenting judgment of Isaacs J:

> It is just as improper morally to permit a man who has openly undertaken such a trust to escape his conscientious obligation by reason merely of a secret mental reservation not to fulfil what he has openly undertaken. An open declaration of trust is therefore an expression of intention that is final and beyond recall.[26]

The irrelevance of uncommunicated or secret intentions, which can only be discovered by conducting a subjective enquiry, is evident from the need for a 'declaration' in order to establish an express trust.[27] To 'declare' a trust a settlor must 'manifest',[28] or communicate, his intention to another. This was emphasised by French CJ in *Byrnes v Kendle* where he said, 'the relevant intention in such a case is that manifested by a declaration of trust'.[29] Secret intentions do not pass this threshold, and hence are irrelevant to the question of whether or not a trust has been constituted. As Megarry J said in *Re Vandervell (No 2)*, 'To yearn is not to transfer'.[30] One area of law in which this has been stressed in recent years is that of 'sham trusts' (of which *Jolliffe* could be said to belong), where a settlor 'declares' a trust in order to take assets out of his estate (to avoid, for instance, the effects of bankruptcy), but secretly intends to retain ownership of the assets. If the settlor does not communicate his 'shamming' intention with the trustee, but keeps it to himself, then he is precluded from denying the existence of a trust. An example is *Shalson v Russo*[31] where the defendant, who had defrauded the claimant of money, settled much of the money on trusts for his family. In response to the allegation that the defendant secretly intended to keep the money for himself, Rimer J said:

> The settlor may well have an unspoken intention that the assets are in fact to be treated as his own … But unless that intention is from the outset shared by the trustee … I fail to see how the settlement can be regarded as a sham.[32]

What we have established so far is that a basic requirement for the creation of an express trust is the communication of intention by the settlor. We may now ask

[26] *Jolliffe* (n 22) 187.

[27] The classic statement of the need for a declaration is found in Lord Nottingham's judgment in *Cook v Fountain* (1676) 3 Swan 585, 591, 36 ER 984, 987, where he said: '[E]xpress trusts are declared either by word or writing; and these declarations appear either by direct or manifest proof, or violent and necessary presumption'.

[28] WJ Mowbray et al (eds), *Lewin on Trusts*, 18th edn (London, Sweet & Maxwell, 2008) para 4-01. The need for a 'declaration' does not require the settlor to use, orally or in writing, the specific words 'I declare'. For instance, in *Paul v Constance* [1976] EWCA Civ 2, [1977] 1 WLR 527, the settlor was held to have constituted a trust over a sum of money merely by saying that the money 'is as much yours as mine'. An interesting question is whether this can be done by conduct. See, for instance, *Re Kayford Ltd* [1975] 1 WLR 279 where a company was held to have declared itself a trustee without it expressly saying or writing anything.

[29] *Byrnes* (n 2) [17].

[30] *Re Vandervell (No 2)* [1974] Ch 269, 294.

[31] See also *Grant v Edwards* [1986] 1 Ch 63; and *Rowe v Prance* [1999] 2 FLR 787.

[32] *Shalson v Russo* [2003] EWHC 1637 (Ch), [2005] Ch 281, 342; see also *In re Esteem Settlement* [2003] JLR 188.

how these acts of communication are interpreted by the courts: do courts attempt to ascertain what the settlor meant by his words, or do they ask what a reasonable person would understand those words to mean? Whilst the law of trusts does not have the same body of case law on this issue as that found in contract law, there is more than enough evidence to show that the courts ask the latter question, ie, the enquiry is an objective one.

Perhaps the leading case on this issue is the House of Lords' decision in *Commissioners of Inland Revenue v Raphael*.[33] A testator had left money to his son on the condition that the son settled it on a trust with specific terms. The son attempted to follow his father's instructions. However, the wording he used when settling the trust was clearly incompatible with the conditions set out in the will and, consequently, the gift failed. The son attempted to save the gift by arguing that the terms of the trust that he had settled should be interpreted subjectively, so that the words carried the meaning he had hoped for, namely a meaning consistent with the conditions set out in the will. Rejecting the argument, Lord Wright said:

> It must be remembered at the outset that the court, while it seeks to give effect to the intention of the parties, must give effect to that as expressed, that is, it must ascertain the meaning of the words actually used.[34]

What the son desired the words to mean, therefore, was wholly irrelevant. Similar statements can be seen in the House of Lords' decision in *Twinsectra Ltd v Yardley*[35] where the claimant had transferred money to the defendant's solicitor to finance the defendant's purchase of land. The terms of the loan provided, amongst other things, that when the money was paid to the solicitor it was to be retained by the solicitor until it was required for the acquisition of the property and that it could not be used for any purpose other than the acquisition of property.[36] The judge at first instance held that these words did not constitute a transfer on trust[37] because the claimant had not meant by those words to create a trust, finding that he 'set no store' by them.[38] Overturning this finding, the House of Lords held that what the claimant actually meant by those words was not important. Lord Millet said:

> A settlor must, of course, possess the necessary intention to create a trust, but his subjective intentions are irrelevant. If he enters into arrangements which have the effect of creating a trust, it is not necessary that he should appreciate that they do so; it is sufficient that he intends to enter into them.[39]

As such, it was not the claimant's intention that was relevant, but what the reasonable person would understand the claimant to have intended.

[33] *Commissioners of Inland Revenue v Raphael* [1935] AC 96.
[34] ibid 142.
[35] *Twinsectra Ltd v Yardley* [2002] 2 AC 164.
[36] ibid [9].
[37] The allegation is that it constituted a form of Quistclose trust; see also *Swiss Bank v Lloyd's Bank* [1982] AC 584, 595–96 and *Cooper v PRG Powerhouse Ltd (in liq)* [2008] EWHC 498 (Ch), BCC 588 [71].
[38] *Twinsectra* (n 35) [2002] UKHL 12, [2002] 2 AC 164, [14].
[39] ibid [71].

Aside from these general statements from the House of Lords, the objective approach can be found in various pockets of trusts law. One area is the interpretation of wills. It is well established that when a court construes a will it does not ask what the settlor intended, but what a reasonable person would understand them to have intended.[40] This approach applies equally to trusts created by will. So in *Charles v Barzey*,[41] where a testatrix left a freehold to the claimant, but provided that the defendant could 'use the garage as long as he liked', on the question of whether this created a trust, Lord Hoffmann said:

> The interpretation of a will is in principle no different from that of any other communication. The question is what a reasonable person, possessed of all the background knowledge which the testatrix might reasonably have been expected to have, would have understood the testatrix to have meant by the words which she used.[42]

This objective approach can also be seen in the old line of cases where courts were called upon to construe marriage settlements, typically where a spouse found that the terms of the settlement gave them less control over the fund than was desired by the settlor.[43] In one such case, Jessel MR said that although the terms of the settlement had a meaning which 'I cannot help thinking was never intended by the framer', the court still had to 'consider the meaning of the words, [and] not what one may guess to be the intention of the parties'.[44] A more recent line of cases, where courts have continued to approach the certainty of intention requirement objectively, is that of constructive trusts in the family home. In these cases, one of the partners typically has a freehold title and makes representations to the other partner which suggest that they are to share the value of the land. In *Gissing v Gissing*, Lord Diplock said that in asking whether an intention to create a trust is present in such cases,

> the relevant intention of each party is the intention which was reasonably understood by the other party to be manifested by that party's words or conduct notwithstanding that he did not consciously formulate that intention in his own mind or even acted with some different intention which he did not communicate to the other party.[45]

The objective approach in the family homes context is particularly important in cases where the party with freehold title gives an 'excuse' for not making their partner a joint tenant of the legal estate.[46] We may suspect that the freeholder in such cases is being deceitful and has no desire to share the value of their home. Yet, a secret intention to keep the freehold absolutely can only be disclosed by

[40] *Grey v Pearson* (1857) 6 HLC 61, 10 ER 1216.

[41] *Charles v Barzey* [2002] UKPC 68, [2003] 1 WLR 437.

[42] ibid 439.

[43] *Constantinidi v Ralli* [1935] 1 Ch D 427.

[44] *Smith v Lucas* (1881) 18 Ch D 531, 542.

[45] *Gissing v Gissing* [1971] AC 886, 906. This was cited with approval in *Jones v Kernott* [2011] UKSC 53, [2012] 1 AC 776 [51(3)]: 'the relevant intention of each party is the intention which was reasonably understood by the other party to be manifested by that party's words and conduct notwithstanding that he did not consciously formulate that intention in his own mind or even acted with some other intention which he did not communicate to the other'.

[46] *Grant* (n 31) and *Rowe* (n 31).

an enquiry into the subjective intention of the freeholder and, as such, is of no relevance.

C. What Type of Objectivity?

Before turning to the issue of rectification, we can take our analysis of objectivity further, and ask what *type* of objective approach is being employed by the courts. We have seen that an objective approach enquires into what meaning was reasonably conveyed by the settlor's words. The difficulty in asking this question, however, is that a settlor's words can reasonably convey different meanings to different persons. Take the nineteenth-century charitable trust case of *Shore v Wilson*[47] where a testatrix left a sum of money on trust for 'poor and Godly preachers of Christ's holy gospel'. To a detached observer, who shares the testatrix's language but little else, the words can reasonably be understood to mean that any person of the Christian faith is a potential beneficiary. However, to the persons to whom the will was addressed (the trustees), who were aware that the testatrix was a strict Calvinist, the words could reasonably be understood to refer to a much narrower group of people, namely those belonging to the non-conformist group. Tindal CJ, in a much cited speech, said that evidence could be introduced to show that 'besides their general common meaning, [the words] have acquired, by custom or otherwise, a well-known peculiar idiomatic meaning … in the particular society of which [the testatrix was] a former member'.[48]

Declarations of trust are acts of communication. Let us say that a purported settlor, alone in his living room, says 'I declare myself trustee'. Aside from the difficulties of proving this, it is unlikely, as a matter of law, whether this can constitute a trust.[49] The settlor's intention must, at some point, be communicated to the relevant parties, namely the trustee and beneficiary. As declarations of trust are acts of communication addressed to specific persons, then it logically follows that the court, when interpreting the declaration, should ask what meaning is reasonably conveyed to the addressee (ie, the trustee or beneficiary). This is sometimes referred to as 'promisee objectivity', or 'addressee objectivity'.[50] It simply means that words are interpreted, as Spencer explains, 'as they are reasonably understood by the *man to whom they were spoken*'.[51] It is sometimes contrasted with the 'fly on the wall' or 'detached objectivity' approach which, as Howarth notes, requires the

[47] *Shore v Wilson* (1842) 9 Cl & Finn 355, 8 ER 450.
[48] ibid 567.
[49] *cf Middleton v Pollock* (1876) 2 ChD 104 CA.
[50] W Howarth, 'The Meaning of Objectivity in Contract' (1984) 100 *LQR* 265, 267.
[51] Spencer (n 15) 106, emphasis added A possible example of promisee objectivity is *Hartog v Colin Shields* [1939] 3 All ER 566 where the defendant was aware that the claimant had made a mistake in offering the defendant a number of hare skins at a certain price 'per lb', when all of the preceding negotiation had been been conducted in terms of price 'per skin'. To a reasonable person in the position of the purchaser, who is aware of previous communications and the market practice, it would be obvious what the vendor intended.

reasonable man 'to adopt a stance apart from that of either promisor or promisee, a viewpoint which is independent of the perspectives of either of the parties or even a reasonable person in their position'.[52] The choice between these approaches is essentially one of how much background context the court is willing to supply to the putative reasonable man who hears the settlor's communication: the purported addressee, of course, has a much better sense of the context of the statement than the detached observer, as *Shore v Wilson* illustrates.[53]

The courts, when construing purported declarations of trust, must adopt the stance of the person to whom the declaration was addressed, namely the trustee (or beneficiary, in cases of self-declarations of trust).[54] This becomes further evident when we consider that in some cases a settlor will communicate certain things to a purported trustee but conceal these communications from third parties. An example is that of sham trusts. As noted above, the allegation of a sham trust is often made in cases where the settlor has attempted to give the impression that he has taken assets out of his estate by transferring them to a trustee on certain declared trusts.[55] The specific allegation made in these cases is that although the settlor has declared a trust (usually in writing), he has simultaneously told the trustee (usually orally) that the declaration is designed to give a false impression, and that he has no desire to divest himself of his assets. Where parties have successfully proved this allegation of 'sham', the courts have held that the certainty of intention requirement for a trust has not been satisfied.[56]

If the courts in these cases were to apply a 'detached objectivity' enquiry, then it would be difficult to reach the conclusion that there was no trust in these cases. To a detached observer standing apart from the parties (such as, for instance, a potential creditor or revenue authority) who sees only the formal 'declaration of trust', the settlor's words are reasonably to be understood as a straightforward declaration of trust. However, to a person in the position of the trustee, to whom not only is the 'declaration of trust' addressed, but other communications which inform him of the settlor's desire to retain his assets, a different view is formed: to such a person the settlor is reasonably understood *not to intend* the creation of a trust.[57]

[52] Howarth (n 50) 267. An example of the detached objectivity approach in contract law is often said to be found in Lord Denning's decision in *Solle v Butcher* [1950] 1 KB 671.

[53] For other possible examples of 'promissee objectivity', see *Doe d Cox v Roe* (1803) 4 Esp 185 and *Mannai Investment Co Ltd v Eagle Star Life Assurance Co Ltd* [1997] 2 WLR 945. An example of a case that may involve an application of 'detached objectivity' is *re Goods of Peel* (1870) LR 2 P & D 46.

[54] Aside from *Shore* (n 47), which clearly illustrates this, we can see an express endorsement of this approach in the case of *Gissing* (n 45) 906, where Lord Diplock said that 'the relevant intention of each party is the intention which was reasonably understood *by the other party*' (emphasis added).

[55] See *Shalson* (n 32); *Re Esteem Settlement* (n 32); *Gaskell v Gaskell* (1828) 2 Y & J 502.

[56] eg *Raftland Pty Ltd v Federal Commissioner of Taxation* [2008] HCA 21.

[57] A similar example is that of fully secret trusts, of the kind discussed in *McCormick v Grogan* (1869) LR 4 HL 82, where a testator purports, in his will, to make an absolute gift to another; however, the testator privately communicates to the donee that he wishes the donee to hold the gift on certain trusts. A detached observer, who sees nothing but the public documents (ie the will) may interpret the

It has been argued that sham trusts are an exception to the general objective approach to the certainty of intention enquiry so that when a litigant makes an allegation of sham the court will be permitted to inquire into the subjective intention of the settlor.[58] Conaglen, in an influential article, argues that in sham cases

> courts are faced with situations where the objective interpretation of the parties' documentation or conduct is at variance with the substance of their agreement, and so the courts look behind the objective appearance to get at the truth of the matter.[59]

However, just because the court is 'looking behind' the written declaration of trust does not mean that it is adopting a subjective approach. As we have seen, the objective approach employed in trusts law requires the court to ask what the settlor's words meant *to a reasonable person in the position of the addressee*. Such a person in sham cases (usually the trustee) is privy not just to the 'declaration of trust', but to other communications which inform the 'trustee' of the settlor's desire to keep hold of his assets.[60] To ask—what would a reasonable person in the position of the trustee have understood the settlor to mean?—therefore, naturally forces the court to 'look behind' the declaration of trust as the trustee was privy to other communications.

Indeed, far from being an exception to the general objective approach to the certainty of intention requirement, the 'sham trust' line of cases have consistently rejected a truly subjective approach. The reason for this is that it is well established that if the settlor does not communicate his 'shamming intent' to the trustee, but keeps it a secret, then the 'sham' allegation will fail.[61] If the approach of the courts in such cases was 'subjective' then this would make little sense, as an uncommunicated secret intention can still be discovered by a subjective enquiry, as happened in the case of *Jolliffe*.[62] The need for communication to the trustee, therefore, only makes sense if the courts are adopting an objective approach.[63]

To conclude this section, when asking the 'certainty of intention' question, the court's approach is an objective one. It asks what the settlor's words mean to a reasonable person in the position of the addressee, usually the trustee.

settlor's intention as a desire to make a gift. Yet, a reasonable person standing in the position of the donee, who has been privy to other communications, would reasonably understand it to be a transfer on trust, not a gift.

[58] M Conaglen, 'Sham Trusts' (2008) 67 *CLJ* 176.

[59] ibid 183.

[60] For the difficulty in applying this reasoning to self-declared trusts, see: *Painter v Hutchison* [2007] EWHC 758 (Ch), [2007] All ER (D) 45.

[61] *Shalson* (n 32); *Re Esteem Settlement* (n 32).

[62] *Jolliffe* (n 22).

[63] It may be argued that the 'subjective approach' is still present, but that it just has the proviso that the subjective intention must be 'common' or 'shared' between the settlor and trustee. However, a shamming intention will only ever be 'common' to the settlor and trustee if the former has communicated it to the latter, which leads us back into the objective enquiry. See S Douglas and B McFarlane, 'Sham Trusts' in R Hickey and H Conway (eds), *Modern Studies in Property Law* (forthcoming, 2017).

II. Rectification

When a settlor declares a trust, although there is no general legal requirement for him to do so in writing,[64] committing a declaration to writing is standard practice.[65] Yet when a settlor's intentions are recorded in this way, errors are sometimes made. To give an example, take the case *of Re Farepak Food and Gifts Ltd*[66] where a company, about to go bankrupt, told its solicitor that it desired to protect customers paying funds into their customer account by declaring a trust over the account. However, when the trust deed was drafted by the solicitor the wrong account number, which referred to an empty account, was recorded. This mistake in the recording of the settlor's intention needed to be remedied by rectifying the document so as to make it reflect the settlor's prior communication. As Mummery LJ said in *Allnutt v Wilding*, 'rectification involves bringing the trust document into line with the true intentions of the settlor as held by him at the date when he executed the document'.[67] The remedy is available, he continued, when 'owing to a mistake in the drafting of the document, it fails to record the settlor's true intentions'.[68]

The jurisdiction to rectify clerical errors, slips and other mistakes may not seem promising material for a discussion about basics concepts in trusts law. Yet the remedy has attracted much academic and judicial interest of late. This is due to the fact that some have argued that the purpose of rectification is to give effect to the subjective intentions of the settlor. We will consider this 'subjective model' of rectification, before looking at an alternative 'objective model' advocated in this chapter. We will review the case law to see if support can be drawn for either model.

A. Two Models of Rectification

i. The Subjective Model

The objective approach to interpretation can result in a settlor being bound by a declaration of trust even though he never desired or appreciated that his words would have that effect. This was the case in *Byrnes v Kendle* where the defendant, in declaring his freehold title on trust, argued that he meant no more than a promise to share the proceeds of the sale of the land should he ever sell it. Given that the transaction was purely voluntary, it may seem unfair to hold him to the effect of

[64] Even trusts declared over land need not be put in writing to take effect; rather they must be 'manifested and proved' by some writing: Law of Property Act 1925, s 53(1)(b).

[65] *Re Kayford* (n 28) where Megarry J was able to infer a declaration of trust from the company's conduct, the judge lamented the lack of writing which would have made things much clearer.

[66] *Re Farepak Food and Gifts Ltd* [2006] EWHC 3272, [2008] BCC 22.

[67] *Allnut* (n 9) [11].

[68] ibid.

his words if he never desired that effect. Perhaps to mitigate the asperity of this objective approach, it was suggested that a rectification claim could be brought to bring the deed into line with Mr Kendle's subjective intentions.[69] A similar point was made in *Commissioners of Inland Revenue v Raphael*.[70] It will be recalled that the court interpreted the defendant's declaration of trust objectively which had harsh results for the defendant as it caused a gift to him to fail. Yet, Lord Wright suggested that this could be avoided by rectifying the trust deed: 'If in some cases hardship or injustice may be effected by this rule [of objective interpretation], such hardship or injustice can generally be obviated by the power of equity to reform the contract'.[71] Again, this is a suggestion that rectification can be used to make the trust deed consistent with the settlor's subjective intentions. The clearest endorsement of this approach comes from the recent case of *Day v Day* where, it will be recalled, Etherton LJ said:

> What is relevant in such a case is the subjective intention of the settlor. It is not a legal requirement for rectification of a voluntary settlement that there be an outward expression or objective communication of the settlor's intention.[72]

This view has also found favour amongst some academics. Although writing in the context of contract law, Paul Davies provides a similar justification for the (more limited) jurisdiction to rectify a contract: 'It is entirely appropriate that rectification should operate as a *subjective* "safety-valve" from the objectivity of the common law rules of interpretation. This is how equity can *complement* the common law'.[73]

This 'safety-valve' view of rectification is problematic for a number of reasons. First, it should be noted that there is little need for rectification to fulfil this role: protecting settlors from the unintended effects of their words is already done by the remedy of rescission. Rescission permits the court to set aside a transaction if the parties to the transaction were mistaken in some way. Although the remedy can be difficult to obtain in the contractual context where the interests of two parties must be considered, the remedy is available on a more liberal basis when it comes to unilateral transactions, such as trusts.[74] Courts have held that a transaction can be set aside when there has been a mistake,[75] which can include a mistake as to the effect of the terms of a trust, ie, where a settlor believes that the words mean something different from what they actually do. For instance, in *Phillips v Mullings*[76] the settlor mistakenly believed that the trust deed he executed provided a power of revocation; but on an objective reading of the document it was

[69] *Byrnes* (n 2) [101].
[70] *Raphael* (n 33).
[71] ibid 143.
[72] *Day* (n 10) [22].
[73] P Davies, 'Rectifying the Course of Rectification' (2012) 75 *MLR* 412, 421.
[74] For a discussion of the type of mistake required for rescission, see B Häcker, 'Mistaken Gifts after Pitt v Holt' (2014) 67 *Current Legal Problems* 333.
[75] The leading case is *Pitt v Holt* [2013] UKSC 26, [2013] 2 AC 108.
[76] *Phillips v Mullings* (1871) LR 7 Ch App 244.

clear that no such power existed. This mistake, which was no more than a mismatch between the subjective and objective meaning of the trust deed, was a sufficient ground for rescission. It is clear, therefore, that there is some protection for settlors when their 'declarations' have unintended effects. There is no necessity for rectification to fill this gap.

A second problem is that it is doubtful whether the jurisdiction to rectify actually gives courts the power to give effect to the settlor's subjective intention. This is because the court's power to rectify a trust deed is merely a power to correct a mistake, not a power to make or improve a transaction. As the authors of Meagher, Gummow and Lehane write:

> It is of the utmost importance to appreciate that the court, by its decree, merely reforms the instrument in which the parties have mistakenly expressed their intention. The basis of the equitable jurisdiction is to rectify mistaken expressions to effectuate the relevant intention, it is not to manufacture intention for someone who intends nothing.[77]

Another way of putting this is that the court must give effect to the trust that would have been declared but for the error in the trust deed. As Turner LJ said in *Walker v Armstrong*: 'The very principle of this Court in correcting instruments is that the parties are to be placed in the same situation as they would have stood in if the error to be corrected had not been committed'.[78] Importantly, but for the mistake, the trust could not have taken effect according to the settlor's subjective intention because, as we have seen, the settlor's subjective intention is irrelevant when one applies the certainty of intention requirement. If a court, when rectifying a document, cannot make or improve upon a transaction, then it can only give effect to communications that would (but for the mistake) have satisfied the substantive rules for the constitution of trusts. These rules ignore the settlor's subjective intentions.

Third, the subjective view of rectification cannot account for an important limitation in the scope of the doctrine, namely that it is limited to written documents. There is no jurisdiction to rectify an oral declaration of trust or contract. This is difficult to explain. Take, for instance, Paul Davies' recent defence of the subjective model. The doctrine is best understood, he argues, as being based on unconscionable conduct:

> The objective intentions of the parties do bind the parties together, and the courts must decide whether the written document accurately reflects the parties' bargain. If the written instrument does not accord with both parties' subjective intentions then the court has a good reason to alter the document; it cannot simply stand by safe in the knowledge that no performance can be demanded under the contract … Moreover, the principles underpinning rectification do not need to rest upon the same basis as interpretation. It has already been argued that too much objectivity in this area is simply unhelpful,

[77] JD Heydon, MJ Leeming and PG Turner, *Meagher, Gummow and Lehane's Equity: Doctrine and Remedies*, 5th edn (Sydney, LexisNexis, 2016) para 27–15.

[78] *Walker* (n 7).

> and the courts of equity have long recognised that rectification rests upon a different rationale: unconscionable conduct.[79]

For Davies, whilst interpretation may be an objective matter, courts will rectify a document in order to prevent a party unfairly holding someone to a bargain that they did not subjectively intend. Whilst this may seem compelling in its own terms, it is difficult to explain why it should not apply to oral contracts and declarations of trust. Take the example of a settlor who *orally* declares a trust on terms *xyz*, but subjectively believed that he was creating a trust on terms *abc*. As there is no written declaration, there is no scope for the doctrine of rectification to apply. This is difficult to explain for Davies: it should make no difference that the declaration is oral rather than written as it is equally unfair for the settlor to be bound by a trust that he did not subjectively intend. The limitation of rectification to written instruments makes no sense on the subjective model. However, as we will see below, it does make sense for the objective model of the doctrine where, as argued, rectification is best seen as an exception to the parol evidence rule—a rule which only applies to written instruments.

A final problem with the subjective view of rectification is that it would result in a contradiction in the law. Let us say that a settlor executes a trust deed believing the words in the deed to mean *abc*, yet when construed objectively they mean *xyz*. The rules of construction state that the trust should take effect on terms *xyz*. However, if the settlor is able to reform the trust so that it takes effect on terms *abc*, simply by adding a rectification claim to his pleadings, then it may be asked what point is there in conducting an objective enquiry in the first place?[80] This conflict has been noted in the contractual context by Marcus Smith who explains that given that 'the subjective and objective tests for intention will, in many cases, point in different directions', it would be odd for the court to give primacy to the objective approach except for when litigants tag a 'rectification' claim on to their pleadings.[81] The House of Lords was receptive to this argument in *Chartbrook Ltd v Persimmon Homes Ltd*[82] where Lord Hoffmann said that rectification, in the context of contracts, still requires the parties' intention to be 'objectively determined'.[83] There is no reason why a different rule should prevail in the context of trusts.

[79] P Davies, 'Rectification Versus Interpretation: The Nature and Scope of the Equitable Jurisdiction' (2016) 75 *CLJ* 62, 80.

[80] The bars to rectification may prevent this contradiction arising in a small number of cases, but they do not avoid the more general problem of the rules of interpretation coming into conflict with the rules of rectification.

[81] M Smith, 'Rectification of Contracts for Common Mistake, *Joscelyne v Nissen*, and Subjective States of Mind' (2007) 123 *LQR* 116, 127.

[82] *Chartbrook* (n 6).

[83] ibid [59]. Some senior members of the judiciary have expressed some caution when applying Lord Hoffmann's approach to interpretation and rectification. See, in particular, Lord Neuberger's comments in *Arnold v Britton* [2015] UKSC 3, [2015] 2 WLR 1593. However, at least at the time of writing, *Chartbrook* appears to remain good law.

ii. The Objective Model

Where there has been a mistake in the trust deed, an objective approach to rectification is one that seeks to give effect to the settlor's prior communication of intention. Let us say that a settlor communicates an intention to a trustee to settle a trust on terms *xyz*, but subsequently executes a trust deed which contains terms *abc*. If the court is satisfied that the expression of intention in the trust deed is a mistake, then it can reform the trust so that it gives effect to the terms communicated earlier, namely *xyz*. In so doing, the court does not need to give effect to the settlor's subjective state of mind; rather, it can give effect to the objective construction of the settlor's earlier communication. An example can be found in *Re Farepak Food and Gifts Ltd* where, it will be recalled, the settlor communicated an intention to declare a trust over its customer account in a conversation with its solicitor, but the subsequent trust deed referred to a different account. In rectifying the trust deed, the court was not giving effect to the company's subjective intentions: there was no enquiry into what was passing through the mind of the company's officers, and no reference was made to internal memos that may provide evidence of a subjective intention. Rather, the court gave effect to a prior communication of intention, a communication that still fell to be interpreted in the normal objective way.

This conception of rectification raises a difficult question. A reasonable person, who is aware of Farepak's oral communication with its solicitor, as well as the terms of the subsequent trust deed, would clearly recognise that there had been a mistake in the trust deed. The alternative, that Farepak, by the time it declared the trust, had changed its mind and wanted the trust to take effect over a different (and empty) account, is highly unlikely. A reasonable observer, aware that Farepak's purpose was to protect customers, would clearly see that Farepak's intention was to create a trust over the account containing the customers' monies, meaning that the written declaration was a mere mistake.[84] This conclusion raises a difficulty. If interpretation is the ascertainment of the meaning conveyed to the reasonable person, then why not just interpret Farepak's trust in this way, ie, a trust over its current account? In other words, why is there a need to rectify the trust deed at all? Indeed, the claimant in Farepak made this argument, suggesting that the trust should simply take effect according to the prior statement of intention. The reason why this argument failed, as Robert Stevens has recently demonstrated,[85] is due to the parol evidence rule which prevents us from taking into consideration earlier communications by Farepak.

To explain Stevens' argument we must first understand the significance of a settlor committing his intention to create a trust to writing.[86] Whilst there is no legal requirement for a settlor to do this, should he decide to, then the normal

[84] *cf* Davies, 'Rectifying the Course of Rectification' (n 73) 421: 'the best evidence of what the parties objectively intended can be found in the final written contract. Why should an objective prior accord trump the later, more formal, agreement reached by the parties?'.

[85] R Stevens, 'Objectivity, Mistake and the Parol Evidence Rule' in E Peel and A Burrows (eds), *Contract Terms* (Oxford, OUP, 2007).

[86] ibid.

inference to be drawn is that the settlor has intended the trust to be constituted according to the terms expressed in the writing. This is best illustrated by the leading case on parol evidence in the context of trusts, *Rabin v Gerson*,[87] where the claimant, after seeking an opinion from counsel, expressed the wish to advance money to a Jewish educational association upon a charitable trust. However, the trust deed subsequently drafted by counsel and executed by the claimant did not properly reflect this, and the words used in the deed were held to mean that there was an absolute transfer to the association. The claimant wished to introduce into court the opinion that they had received from counsel in order to demonstrate that their intention had been to transfer the money upon trust. Rejecting the argument, Fox LJ said: 'Such evidence, I think, is simply parol evidence of the intention of the grantor … The result, in my view, is that the opinions cannot be referred to generally for the assistance that their contents may give'.[88] It is worth pausing to consider this. Given that the claimant, prior to the execution of the deed, may well have expressed an intention to transfer funds on trust rather than absolutely, and given that the counsel's opinion may be evidence of this, why would the court exclude it when it conducts the certainty of intention enquiry? The trust deed was not a formal requirement, in that there was no need to execute it in order to constitute the trust. Why then, in searching for the settlor's intention, are we not permitted to consider, in addition to the trust deed, prior communications statements that shed light on the settlor's intention? The answer to this is that the claimant, in executing the trust deed, clearly intended the transfer to take effect on the terms *contained in the deed*. This is what Fox LJ alluded to when he described the opinion as 'parol evidence'. Although a trust deed may not be a formal requirement in most cases, when a settlor executes one the normal inference is that the settlor intends to be bound on the terms of the deed and, consequently, previous expressions of intention are substituted by the written terms. We would not be giving effect to the settlor's intention, therefore, if we were to look behind the trust deed to other communications.[89] By contrast, where a settlor has not intended the trust to take effect on the terms contained in the trust deed, then there is logically no reason why extrinsic evidence of other communications cannot be admitted in order to ascertain his intention.[90] An example of this would be sham trusts, where the essence of the allegation is precisely that the settlor did not intend to be bound by the terms of the trust deed that he executed.[91]

This description of the parol evidence rule helps explain the role of rectification. Let us say that a settlor orally states to a trustee that he wishes to create a trust on terms *xyz*, and then executes a trust deed which contains terms *abc*. If the settlor has intended the trust to take effect on the terms communicated in the trust

[87] *Rabin v Gerson* [1986] 1 WLR 526.
[88] ibid 531.
[89] Stevens (n 85) 107.
[90] *Hawke v Edwards* (1947) 48 SR (NSW) 21; *Walker Property Investments v Walker* (1947) 177 LT 204.
[91] *Antle v Canada* [2010] FCA 280.

deed then we are prohibited, by the parol evidence rule, from considering his earlier communication when ascertaining his intention. What rectification does, as Stevens explains, is that it rescinds the settlor's intention to be bound by the terms contained in the document; the error in the recording of the settlor's intention in the document allows the court to ignore the settlor's wish that the trust take effect subject to those written terms only.[92] The consequence of this is that, in our example, when attempting to ascertain the settlor's intention, the court is not confined to examining the words contained in the deed (which point to terms *abc*), but can also examine the earlier oral communication (which point to terms *xyz*). As Stevens states, 'The effect of rectification is to give rise to the contract there would have been if it had not been agreed that the document was to constitute the parties' entire agreement'.[93] So in *Re Farepak* the court, in rescinding the claimant's intention that the trust take effect only on the terms contained in the deed, was then able to consider earlier communications made by the claimant which pointed to a different intention.

The crucial point for present purposes is that it does not follow, from this description of rectification, that the court must switch from an objective enquiry to a subjective one. If rectification merely permits the court when conducting the certainty of intention enquiry to look at communications of intention prior to those contained in the trust deed, then there is no reason why it should not construe those earlier communications in the normal objective way.

B. The Case Law

The majority of cases where rectification has been successfully pleaded are entirely consistent with the objective model. Courts frequently rectify trust deeds to bring them into line with prior communications of intention. *Re Farepak* is an example of this, where the court reformed the trust deed so that it gave effect to a prior oral communication. In the recent case of *Industrial Acoustics Co Ltd v Crowhurst*[94] pension trustees published a resolution (which was communicated to members of the pension fund) which stated that women were to be able to retire from age 65 (rather than 60). However, when the rules of the scheme were subsequently updated the old reference to women being able to retire at 60 was maintained. In rectifying the document, the court brought it into line with a prior expression of intention. Indeed, Vos J specifically noted that he was not giving effect to the subjective intention of the trustees:

> It is not good enough for the parties simply inwardly to think something without giving effect to it in a way that is discernable to the objective observer, knowing all of the facts as they relate to the position of the parties.[95]

[92] Stevens (n 85) 119.
[93] ibid.
[94] *Industrial Acoustics Co Ltd v Crowhurst* [2012] EWHC 1614 (Ch), [2012] Pens LR 371.
[95] ibid [54].

Of course, it has been suggested that the only reason why the law requires a prior objective communication of intention is that such a communication is evidence of the settlor's subjective state of mind, leading us back to the subjective view.[96] If this were correct, then it should follow that any evidence of the settlor's subjective intention, not just his prior statements, should be admissible. This does not appear to be the case. Consider the decision of *Constantinidi v Ralli*.[97] Before getting married, a widow had instructed her solicitor to draft a marriage settlement which provided that, should her husband predecease her, she could deal with the assets in the settlement 'by will'. Importantly, the widow in giving instructions to her solicitor had gone so far as to provide a suggested draft herself, so that the words 'by will' were included at her behest. When her husband died she discovered that the words 'by will' did not, as she believed, mean that she had absolute discretion to deal with the estate during her lifetime, but merely gave her testamentary freedom over it. The court held that this did not disclose a claim for rectification as the terms of the settlement were not at variance with her prior communications. Eve J said that there was nothing to show 'that the settlement did not as it stood carry out her intentions'.[98] Of course, the words 'by will' did not mean what the widow intended them to mean and as such she was able to show that the written settlement did not give effect to her subjective intention. Yet the court considered this to be irrelevant. The court was clearly of the view that a document could only be reformed to bring it into line—a prior, objectively expressed, intent.

Can any cases be found that support the subjective approach? The obvious place to start is the case commonly cited as clear evidence of the subjective approach,[99] *Re Butlin's Settlement Trust*.[100] The settlor transferred funds on trust for the benefit of family members. There were five trustees. When counsel was drafting the trust deed, the settlor gave instructions that the trustees should be able to act by a majority decision, writing in a letter, 'Would it not be wise to give the trustees power to decide matters … by a majority decision?'[101] When the deed was drafted, however, it provided that the trustees could only act by majority decision in the case of a trustee being ill or abroad. In ordering rectification of the settlement, Brightman J certainly made comments that could be interpreted as a search for the settlor's subjective intention. He said, 'a settlor may seek rectification by proving that the settlement does not express his true intention … [and] it is not essential for him to prove that the settlement fails to express the true intention of the trustees'.[102] Despite this, there is nothing in the case which suggests that the court conducted a subjective enquiry into the settlor's intention. It is important to stress that the settlor's intention that the trustees can act by a majority was objectively

[96] For discussion of the status of the 'common accord' requirement, see Hodge (n 8) paras 4-31–4-48.
[97] *Constantinidi* (n 43).
[98] ibid 434.
[99] See Smith (n 81) 129.
[100] *Re Butlin's Settlement Trust* [1976] 1 Ch 251.
[101] ibid 259.
[102] ibid 262.

expressed in his written instructions to counsel which, as we have seen, posed the question of whether trustees should be able to act 'by a majority decision'. At no point did the court ask what the settlor meant by these words, but simply adopted their ordinary objective meaning. *Re Butlin's Settlement Trust* provides a standard example of a rectification case, where an earlier objective expression of the settlor's intention replaces that found in the trust deed.

The next case to consider is that of *Day v Day* where, it will be recalled, Etherton LJ expressly endorsed the subjective model of rectification.[103] A mother, who had a freehold title to land, instructed a solicitor to draft a deed that would make her son, the defendant, a joint tenant of the legal estate. The solicitor, probably acting under the influence of the defendant, went beyond these instructions and also included a declaration of trust in the deed, with the son as a beneficiary. The court rectified the deed with the reference to the trust in favour of the son being expunged and being replaced with a trust for the benefit of the mother. The case cannot support the objective model of rectification: prior to the execution of the deed, the mother did not express an intention that the freehold title be held on trust for her; as such the court cannot be said to be giving effect to a prior objective communication of intention. Yet, it is difficult to see how the case supports the subjective model either. There is no suggestion in the case that the mother, in instructing the solicitor to make her son a legal joint tenant, thought that the effect of her words was to declare a trust over the land in her favour. The rectified document, therefore, cannot be said to be giving effect to her subjective state of mind. The case is a straightforward example of an agent, the solicitor, exceeding his authority. The proper remedy was to have the conveyance rescinded and set aside.

There are a number of cases that, like *Day v Day*, appear to offer support for the subjective model, but are better understood as rescission cases. Take the recent case of *Ashcroft v Barnsdale*[104] where beneficiaries under a trust instructed their solicitor to draft a deed that would change the proportions of their respective shares, as they believed that this would create inheritance tax savings. When changes did not produce the desired tax savings, the beneficiaries sought to have the deed rectified. Hodge QC permitted the claim, saying 'the function of rectification is to enable the court to put the record straight by correcting a mistake in the way in which the parties have chosen to record their transactions'.[105] The case does not support the objective model as there was no disparity between the terms of the deed and prior statements of intention, as the deed accurately reflected the instructions given to the solicitor. Yet, neither does the case support the subjective view of rectification as there is no suggestion that the deed did not mean exactly what the beneficiaries intended it to mean. Their mistake was not as to the meaning of their words,

[103] *Day* (n 10).
[104] *Ashcroft v Barnsdale* [2010] EWHC 1948 (Ch).
[105] ibid [15].

but as to a background factor (the operation of inheritance tax rules). Rescission, not rectification, is the appropriate remedy in such a case. As much was held in the similar case of *Allnutt v Wilding*[106] where a settlor, also desirous of reducing inheritance tax, discussed with his solicitor the possibility of transferring his assets on a discretionary trust for his children. A trust deed was drawn up which accurately reflected these instructions. It was subsequently discovered that the settlor (who had since died) needed to make the children's interests in the trusts absolute, rather than discretionary, to achieve the desired tax savings. Rejecting the children's claim for rectification, Mummery LJ said:

> The settlement correctly records [the settlor's] intention to benefit [the children] through the medium of a trust rather than the alternative of making direct gifts in their favour. I am unable to see any mistake by the settlor in the recording of his intentions in the settlement.[107]

This conclusion is entirely correct. Neither the subjective nor objective model of rectification could assist the children as the deed meant exactly what the settlor intended it to mean. The mistake was not as to the terms of the trust, but the effect of some background tax factor. Such cases are appropriate for rescission, not rectification.

The only cases that the author can find which lend clear support to the subjective approach is a small number of first instance pension cases, of which *MNOPF v Watkins*[108] is representative. The case concerned an industry-wide pension scheme for retired members of the merchant navy. It had two sections, one for benefits accrued before 1978, and one for benefits accrued after that date. The scheme had been run in the past in such a way that there was no guaranteed revaluation of benefits accrued pre-1978, but there was guaranteed revaluation for benefits accrued after that date. However, in 1999, the trustees of the scheme executed a new trust deed which stated that both sections of the scheme would be subject to automatic revaluation. This substantially increased the costs of the scheme, and the trustees applied to have it rectified. In allowing the claim, John Martin QC took into consideration the minutes of the pension trustee meeting. This clearly showed that when the draft deed was being discussed, the trustees believed that it referred to post-1978 benefits only. The minutes of the trustee meeting are evidence of subjective intention only; they record an internal discussion that is not communicated to the members of the pension scheme or anyone else. To reform the deed so that it gives effect to the intention found in these minutes, therefore, is to give effect to the subjective intention of the trustees.Whilst *MNOPF v Watkins* does provide support for the subjective approach, there are several pensions cases

[106] *Allnutt* (n 9). See also *Lady Hood of Avalon v Mackinnon* [1909] 1 Ch 476; *Phillips* (n 76); *Tucker v Bennett* (1887) 38 Ch D 1; *Gibbon v Mitchell* [1990] 1 WLR 1304; *cf Ashcroft* (n 104); *Farmer v Sloan* [2004] EWHC 606 (Ch); *AMP v Barker* [2001] Pens LR 77.

[107] *Allnutt* (n 9) [19].

[108] *MNOPF v Watkins* [2013] EWHC 4741; see also *Gallaher v Gallaher* [2005] Pens LR 103 and *Lawie v Lawie* [2012] EWHC 2940, [2013] WTLR 85.

that cohere with the objective approach. For instance, in *AMP v Barker*[109] which involved similar facts to *MNOPF v Watkins* (pension trustees had executed a deed that was far more generous than had been intended), Lawrence Collins J stressed the need for some prior 'outward accord' as a condition for rectification.[110] A first instance decision, which is inconsistent with well-established authority, is a weak plank upon which to erect an argument for a subjective approach to rectification in trusts law.

III. Conclusion

Although there is some slight evidence of a subjective approach in a small number of rectification cases, most cases support the objective model advocated in this chapter. Were this otherwise, the law surrounding the constitution of trusts would be radically different. Take the High Court of Australia's view in *Byrnes v Kendle* that primacy ought to be given to the objective meaning of a settlor's declaration. If rectification were to involve a subjective enquiry then there would be nothing to stop defendants from simply adding rectification to their pleadings and bring their declarations into line with their actual mental states. The High Court's unimpeachable statement of principle would become largely meaningless. Another odd result would be how we view sham trusts. As noted above, a settlor will be bound by his declaration of trust even though he has a secret uncommunicated intention to retain control of his assets. Again, if rectification were a subjective process, then what would there be to stop such settlors having the trust deed rectified to bring it into line with their uncommunicated intention? The objective principle that underpins the certainty of intention enquiry in trust law would be largely undermined if rectification were to involve a subjective test. This is wrong in principle and not supported by authority.

[109] *AMP* (n 106).
[110] ibid [66].

9

The Arbitrability of Trust Instruments: Why Not?

ELAINE CHEW

I. Introduction

Jurisdictions such as the Bahamas, Guernsey, Malta, Arizona and Florida, have already legislated to expressly allow for the arbitration of trust disputes.[1] However, a question remains as to whether a settlor can put in place an enforceable arbitration provision, governing trust disputes, even in a jurisdiction which has not expressly allowed for such. To date, the few courts before which the question has been placed have mostly answered in the negative, with the Texas Supreme Court decision in *Rachel v Reitz*[2] forming a notable exception. But why should that be so?

Consider this scenario—a settlor (S) creates a fixed trust over his property, Blackacre, requiring the trustee (T) to apply the income from the property for the benefit of one beneficiary (B1) for the duration of her life, and to pay over the capital to a second beneficiary (B2) at the end of 10 years. All the protagonists named are of legal age and sound mind. S expressly stipulates in the trust deed that arbitration should be resorted to in respect of issues regarding:

(i) The reasonableness of the trustee's fees.
(ii) The prudence of the investments entered into by the trustee.
(iii) The interpretation of the trust instrument.
(iv) The appointment and removal of the trustee in favour of an agreed replacement.
(v) The dissolution of the trust.
(vi) Accounting disputes.
(vii) Variation of the terms of the trust.
(viii) The seeking of declaratory or advisory relief in general (clause 1).

[1] See the Annex for a list of the relevant legislative provisions of the jurisdictions cited.
[2] *Rachel v Reitz* No 11-0708, 3 May 2013, Supreme Court, Texas (LexisNexis).

S expressly provides that questions that are to be excluded from the scope of arbitration include:

(i) Whether the trust is validly constituted.
(ii) Any matters that the court declares to be unarbitrable (clause 2).

S further provides that as a precondition to the appointment of T as trustee, T must agree to arbitrate all disputes arising out of clause 1. T is additionally under an obligation to ensure that all successive trustees similarly agree to arbitrate all disputes arising out of clause 1 (clause 3). S also provides that the vesting of the beneficial interest in B1 and B2 respectively is conditional upon their agreement to arbitrate all disputes arising out of clause 1 (cl 4). S chooses Singapore as the law of the trust and the seat of arbitration (clause 5). S designates that the rules of the Singapore International Arbitration Centre shall apply (clause 6). In the event of dispute, the Singapore courts are expressly empowered to rule on whether any given matter should proceed to arbitration or be tried in court (clause 7). Before any arbitration of the trust is to be commenced, notice has to be given to all parties interested in the trust, namely, T, B1 and B2 (clause 8).[3]

Is there any reason why the settlor's intention, that disputes arising out of the trust be arbitrated, ought not to be given effect? In particular, is there any reason why the settlor's intentions ought not to be given effect under instruments such as the New York Convention on the Recognition and Enforcement of Foreign Arbitral Awards (New York Convention) or the UNCITRAL Model Law on

[3] For other examples of arbitral clauses in trust disputes, see the ICC Model Clause in Trust Disputes, discussed in CP Koch, 'A Tale of Two Cities!—Arbitrating Trust Disputes and the ICC's Arbitration Clause for Trust Disputes' [2012] *Yearbook of International Arbitration* 179; and BW Boesch, 'The ICC Initiative' (2012) 18 *Trusts & Trustees* 316, as well as the clause in the settlement deed in *Rinehart v Welker* [2012] NSWCA 95. Another sample, kindly provided by Richard Nolan, as drawn from an English law deed with US style drafting reads:

> **XVIII Dispute resolution:** Any dispute of whatsoever nature between the trustee and any beneficiary or person claiming through any beneficiary (as defined in Article IV above) regarding this settlement generally and in particular the effect of this settlement or the exercise or purported [sic] by the trustee of any of its powers or any act or omission of the trustee, or the exercise or purported [sic] by the Protector of any of his powers or any act or omission of the Protector, may at the sole and absolute discretion of the trustee be referred in the first instance to a mediator selected by the trustee who shall be such independent person as the trustee may in its sole and absolute discretion consider to be appropriate and if after reasonable efforts to resolve any such dispute by mediation have failed (of which the trustee shall be the sole and undisputed judge) the dispute may at the sole and absolute discretion of the trustee be referred to a single arbitrator agreed between the parties for resolution by arbitration under the Rules of the London Court of International Arbitration and the English Arbitration Act 1996 (both of which as for the time being in force being deemed to be incorporated into this clause) such arbitrator to be a barrister of not less than 20 years standing or a Queens Counsel qualified in either case to practice before the Courts of England and Wales and nominated in the event of the parties' inability to agree by the Chairman for the time being of the Chancery Bar Association of London. I intend that this clause shall be binding on myself, the trustee, all beneficiaries under this settlement and any other person including any beneficiary deriving title through myself, the trustee, and any beneficiary.

International Commercial Arbitration (Model Law)?[4] Granted, certain disputes, which are inherently going to entail the participation of non-parties to the trust, such as questions as to validity, are not suitable for arbitration. Also, there may be situations, for example, when the beneficiaries are minors, legally incompetent, unborn or unascertained, where it may be strategically more viable to litigate in order to obtain a result that is binding on all relevant parties. However, with careful drafting, a settlor ought, in principle, to be able to create an enforceable agreement to arbitrate the majority of disputes arising out of a trust, even in jurisdictions which have not expressly legislated to allow for such.

II. Advantages of Arbitrating Trust Disputes

Attempts by settlors to provide for the alternative dispute resolution (ADR) of trust disputes are not new. One of the most famous examples is that of George Washington, who prior to his death in 1799, had provided in his will that

> all disputes (if unhappily any should arise) shall be decided by three impartial and intelligent men, known for their probity and good understanding; two to be chosen by the disputants—each having the choice of one—and the third by those two. Which three men thus chosen, shall, unfettered by Law, or legal constructions, declare their sense of the Testator's intention; and such decision is, to all intents and purposes, to be as binding on the Parties as if it had been given in the Supreme Court of the United States.[5]

A more modest example is that of *Re Tuck's Settlement Trusts*,[6] where the settlor had conferred on the Chief Rabbi the power to decide the single question of whether the intended wife of a potential beneficiary of the trust was 'an approved wife' of Jewish blood, which was a condition of the disposition. These attempts to remove issues arising out of the trust from the ambit of the courts and into the hands of alternative decision-makers point to the existence of 'powerful commercial or domestic reasons for parties to have disputes between a trustee and beneficiary settled privately'.[7]

[4] The New York Convention requires its more than 150 contracting states to recognise and enforce arbitral awards made in other contracting states and is widely regarded as a foundational instrument for the practice of international commercial arbitration. Both the 1985 and 2006 version of the Model Law were designed by UNCITRAL to assist adopting states to reform and modernise their laws on arbitration to create a uniform practice that takes into account the needs of international commercial arbitration and its particular features.

[5] George Washington's Last Will and Testament, 9 July 1799: gwpapers.virginia.edu/documents/george-washingtons-last-will-and-testament/.

[6] *Re Tuck's Settlement Trusts* [1977] EWCA Civ 11, [1978] Ch 49. Granted, Lord Russell and Eveleigh LJ upheld the settlement on different bases from Lord Denning but the point remains that if Lord Denning is correct, the settlor can effectively be seen as having removed the question of who was 'an approved wife' from the ambit of the courts.

[7] *Rinehart* (n 3) [175].

Given the wealth of literature that already exists on the advantages of arbitration, both generally, and specific to trust disputes,[8] it is necessary to point briefly to only the three most compelling in favour of the arbitration of trust disputes. First, arbitration is a private process, unlike litigation, which is a matter of public record unless the court directs otherwise. The confidentiality of arbitration proceedings may appeal to settlors who do not wish to have the extent of their wealth or the dirty linen of their personal affairs aired in public. Second, unlike litigation, which procedures are constrained by the specific rules of the jurisdiction in which the matter is being heard, the procedures adopted in arbitration can be customised by agreement to meet the needs of parties. If wielded effectively, this can translate into both time efficiency and cost savings.[9] Third, subject to very narrow exceptions, the New York Convention allows arbitral awards to be enforced in over a hundred signatory states,[10] through a process far less arduous and more certain than the usual methods of enforcing court judgments. This can be particularly helpful where a settlor anticipates that the assets of the trust and its beneficiaries may be spread out over several jurisdictions.

Even taking a step back and considering the issue from the viewpoint of the state, the arbitration of trust disputes may potentially be an attractive proposition from an economic perspective, if overseas settlors can be attracted to create trusts within the domestic regime. Further, given that there are already jurisdictions that have legislated to allow for the arbitration of trusts, states may not have the indefinite luxury of sitting on the fence on this issue. As the UK Trust Law Committee noted, there is a danger that overseas jurisdictions may eventually take over, or seek to take over, trust work that would or could more appropriately be done domestically. Such an outcome would be harmful to the development of domestic trust law and potentially harmful to the economy, not to mention the legal professions and those other professions with an interest in trust.[11]

III. Arbitrability

The question of whether or not an arbitration clause in a trust instrument has any effect ought to start with the basic question of arbitrability. The 'non-arbitrability'

[8] eg G von Segesser, 'A Step Forward: Addressing Real and Perceived Obstacles to the Arbitration of Trust Disputes' (2014) 20 *Trusts & Trustees* 37, 38–41; A Holden, 'The Arbitration of Trust Disputes: Theoretical Problems and Practical Possibilities' (2015) 21 *Trusts & Trustees* 546, 555–56; Trust Law Committee, 'Arbitration of Trust Disputes' (2012) 18 *Trusts & Trustees* 296, 298–99; A Cremona, 'Successful Arbitration of Internal Trust Disputes the Maltese Way' (2012) 18 *Trusts & Trustees* 363, 364–65.

[9] There has been much ink split on whether arbitration is actually more cost and time efficient than litigation, with no definitive landing either way. However, the growing number of arbitrations around the world attest to client satisfaction that arbitration can have advantages over the litigation process.

[10] See Arts III and V.

[11] Trust Law Committee (n 8) 299.

doctrine applies to subjects or disputes that are deemed by the domestic law to be incapable of resolution by arbitration, even if the parties have otherwise validly agreed to arbitrate such matters.[12] Generally the law of the seat of the arbitration, which will govern the procedural aspects of the process, governs the question of arbitrability. However, as Article V(2)(a) of the New York Convention permits a court to refuse enforcement of an arbitral award where the 'subject matter … is not capable of settlement by arbitration under the law of that country',[13] the law of the states in which the award is likely to be enforced ought to be taken into account as well.[14] The matter is further complicated because, as Strong notes, although national and international laws on arbitration contemplate the possibility that certain issues are non-arbitrable, seldom are the parameters of arbitrability firmly and clearly drawn.[15] In this respect, most jurisdictions have not taken a clear position in their legislation as to whether trust disputes are arbitrable, but seem content to leave the matter to the discretion of the courts as and when such issues arise.

Arbitrability may be described as the 'quality of the subject-matter in dispute'.[16] This is distinct from the separate question of whether the dispute falls within the ambit of the scope of arbitration agreed between parties. The former requires an examination of whether arbitration of the subject matter in dispute would be at odds with any mandatory rules or public policy of the relevant jurisdiction.[17] Common examples of non-arbitrable disputes are those concerning criminal matters, bankruptcy or insolvency, trade sanctions, consumer claims and intellectual property matters. While on balance, commentators that have considered the issue at length have generally concluded that internal trust disputes, ie, those involving only trustees and beneficiaries, are for the most part arbitrable,[18] the usual objections by the doubting Thomas tend to be that:

(a) Arbitration would 'effectively extinguish the trustee's obligation to account to the beneficiaries, which obligation is a necessary precondition for the existence of a valid trust'.[19]
(b) '[T]he trust concept is itself the creature of the courts (historically the courts of equity) … so that the legal rights of beneficiaries and trustees can be validly determined only by the courts'.[20]

[12] G Born, *International Commercial Arbitration*, vol 1, 2nd edn (Amsterdam, Kluwer Law International, 2015) 944.
[13] Similarly, Art 34 of the Model Law allows the award to be set aside if the subject matter of the dispute was not arbitrable, or if the award conflicts with the public policy of the state.
[14] Koch (n 3) 187.
[15] SI Strong, 'Arbitration of Trust Disputes: Two Bodies of Law Collide' (2012) 45 *Vanderbilt Journal of Transnational Law* 1157.
[16] BGE 118 II 193 (28 April 1992), Swiss Federal Court BG.
[17] Segesser (n 8) 45.
[18] SI Strong, 'Mandatory Arbitration of Internal Trust Disputes: Improving Arbitrability and Enforceability through Proper Procedural Choices' (2012) 28 *Arbitration International* 591, 612.
[19] Holden (n 8) 547.
[20] Trust Law Committee (n 8) 300.

(c) The arbitration of trust disputes would amount to an ouster of the court's inherent jurisdiction to supervise the trust.[21]
(d) The remedies required for the resolution of trust disputes are not available in the arbitration context.[22]

None of the above points form a valid basis for coming to the conclusion that trusts ought, in principle, to be non-arbitrable.[23]

The first objection traces back to a number of cases such as *Re Raven*,[24] *Rhodes v Muswell Hill Land Company*[25] and *Re Wynn*,[26] which, when read in context, are scenarios where the trustees were empowered by the terms of the trust to make determinations on disputes between themselves as to entitlements under the trust. Obviously, in those instances, the offices of the trustee and the dispute resolution decision-maker having been conflated, the interests of the beneficiaries would be compromised[27] and have been described as being repugnant to public policy.[28] However, provided that the arbitrator and the trustee are separate persons, the first objection ought not to form a basis for concern given that the trustee could be called to account before the arbitrator, just as he would have to before a judge in a state court.

The second and third objections can be taken together—they are invalid if one accepts that there is simply no magic in having a court as opposed to an arbitral tribunal decide the issue.[29] Granted, there are numerous judicial pronouncements that a cardinal principle of trust law is that the court has an inherent jurisdiction to supervise the administration of the trust. Indeed, as the Privy Council noted in *Schmidt v Rosewood Trust Ltd*, '[i]t is fundamental to the law of trusts that the court has jurisdiction to supervise and if appropriate intervene in the administration of a trust'.[30] However, it is worthwhile noting, as John Langbein and SI Strong have, that the creation of the exclusive jurisdiction of the courts of equity was

[21] Holden (n 8) 547.
[22] *Rinehart* (n 3) [226]–[227] (Young JA).
[23] It may also be apposite here to refer to the speech of the Lord Chief Justice of England and Wales, Lord Thomas of Cwmgiedd, at the Bailii Lecture 2016, where at para 5, he pointed out that 'far fewer developments of the law are made in areas where the probability is that the case has had to begin in arbitration': www.judiciary.gov.uk/wp-content/uploads/2016/03/lcj-speech-bailli-lecture-20160309.pdf. However, this ought not to constitute a reason for denying the arbitrability of trust disputes as a matter of public policy, given that similar arguments in respect of contractual disputes have not been accepted. In any event, some arbitral institutes do publish the awards made under their umbrella and that may go some way towards ameliorating the effects arbitration might have on common law development.
[24] *Re Raven* [1915] 1 Ch 673.
[25] *Rhodes v Muswell Hill Land Company* (1861) 29 Beav 560.
[26] *Re Wynn* [1952] Ch 271.
[27] But see the comments of Lord Denning MR in *Re Tuck's Settlement Trusts* (n 6), in light of *Dundee General Hospital Board of Management v Walker* [1952] 1 All ER 896.
[28] M Conaglen, 'The Enforceability of Arbitration Clauses in Trusts' (2015) 74 *CLJ* 450, 466.
[29] Holden (n 8) 547–48.
[30] *Schmidt v Rosewood Trust Ltd* [2003] UKPC 26, [2003] 2 AC 709 [36].

merely intended as an internal mechanism for allocating cases among domestic courts and was never meant to protect the collective jurisdiction of the courts against non-judicial forms of dispute resolution such as arbitration.[31] It is unfortunate that neither the courts, nor the UK Trust Law Committee which coined the second objection, explained in detail why it is that a court, as opposed to any other dispute resolution forum, might be better placed to supervise the administration of the trust. However, what is telling is the repeated references in the literature and case law to the need for supervision in aid of the beneficiaries. If the concern is that beneficiaries have recourse to an unbiased and neutral forum for the vindication of their rights, then it ought to be noted that at least in the context of commercial disputes, it has been widely accepted that arbitration can perform the requisite decision-making tasks and resolve disputes fairly and efficiently.[32] In fact, given parties' freedom to appoint arbitrators, one might say that a better panel of decision-makers drawn from trust specialists might potentially be fielded, as opposed to a hearing before a non-specialist judge.[33]

One principle at the irreducible core of the trust appears to be that the trustee must be accountable so that his status as the non-beneficial owner of the assets vested in him is not a sham.[34] If the beneficiaries have no rights enforceable against the trustee, there is no trust.[35] However, the recognition that beneficiaries must be allowed to call trustees to account does not necessarily mean that the contest has to be brought in the courts—logically, it only means that genuine contest by the beneficiary of a trustee's administration of the assets must be possible. Such a contest can be equally brought in arbitration as in litigation, save that the arbitration is usually confidential, whereas the litigation will be a matter of public record.

In any event, even taking on board the view that there 'is still a strong public policy in ensuring the action of the trustees remains susceptible to oversight by the courts',[36] there are at least three ways to manage the concern that beneficiaries must be able to have recourse to the courts. First, the settlor could choose to designate the location of the trust as the seat of the arbitration. This would expressly empower the court where the trust is located to supervise the procedural aspects of the arbitration, and to set aside the award in exceptional circumstances where, for example, it contravenes the public policy of the state vis-à-vis the trust. Second, as was done in clause 7 above, the settlor could always expressly provide that the

[31] Strong, 'Mandatory Arbitration of Internal Trust Disputes' (n 18) 617; Segesser (n 8) 45; and JH Langbein, 'The Contractarian Basis of the Law of Trusts' (1995) 105 *Yale Law Journal* 625, 627 (fn 20).

[32] Segesser (n 8) 45. While judges are public servants and arbitrators are privately appointed, it ought to be pointed out that the neutrality of the arbitrator is relatively rarely impugned, and judges are not without scandal either. The office alone does not confer a guarantee of neutrality or wisdom.

[33] Admittedly, there are currently very few trust specialists on the panels of arbitrators in most arbitration institutions.

[34] Strong, 'Mandatory Arbitration of Internal Trust Disputes' (n 18) 619; T Molloy and T Graham, 'Arbitration of Trust and Estate Disputes' (2012) 184 *Trusts & Trustees* 279, 287.

[35] *Armitage v Nurse* [1998] Ch 241, 253 (Millet LJ).

[36] Molloy and Graham (n 34) 288.

courts retain discretion to veto any submissions to arbitration as it sees fit. This would enable state courts to maintain oversight of the disputes that go to arbitration. Third, depending on the rules of the arbitral institution chosen, and the laws of the relevant jurisdictions, it may be possible for the settlor to provide that parties to the arbitration have a right of appeal to the state courts. The last option, however, is the least desirable, as only arbitral awards can benefit from the advantages of the enforcement procedures under the New York Convention, and a court order substituting or varying the award is unlikely to fall within that definition.[37]

Turning finally to the fourth objection, that an arbitral tribunal is ill-equipped to serve the usual functions that a court supervising a trust does, one criticism commonly levelled is that the arbitral tribunal cannot match the court's ability to grant the accounting and instructional reliefs often sought in respect of trust disputes. For instance, in *Rinehart v Welker*,[38] Young JA delivered a dissenting judgment on a dispute regarding the removal of the trustee from a family trust. The main thrust of his decision that such a dispute ought not to be arbitrated appeared to be that the arbitrator lacked the power to make the requisite orders that a court could grant to enforce its decision on the issue. If the court had decided to remove the trustee, it could make orders authorising a registrar to sign transfers on behalf of a former trustee and direct the registrar to register them; but an arbitrator could not. Similarly, while a court could imprison a trustee who refused to give a proper taking of accounts, that would not be available to an arbitrator.

It is acknowledged that the relief granted by an arbitral tribunal is most often in the form of monetary damages. However, an arbitral tribunal, through granting injunctive or declaratory relief, or through ordering a taking of accounts, should also be capable in theory of fashioning suitable remedies in performing the advisory function of a court supervising a trust.[39] Moreover, it is open to the tribunal to make the appropriate orders within its powers, following which, the parties can then seek enforcement before the courts where the appropriate supporting orders can be given.[40] Furthermore, as has been noted by the UK judiciary,

> the fact that an arbitrator cannot give all the remedies which a court could does not afford any reason for treating an arbitration as of no effect … [it] is just an incident of the agreement which the parties have made as to the method by which their disputes are to be resolved.[41]

Finally, it is submitted that if this criticism is to be taken on board at all, it would at best go towards the scope of trust disputes that are arbitrable. It cannot constitute a basis for the wholesale rejection of the arbitrability of trust disputes.

[37] New York Convention, Art III.

[38] Rinehart (n 3).

[39] *Roehl v Ritchie* 147 Cal App 4th 338; 54 Cal Rptr 3d 185 (2007).

[40] Conaglen (n 28) 457.

[41] *Fulham Football Club (1987) Ltd v Richards* [2011] EWCA Civ 855, [2012] 1 All ER 414 [103]. See also *Assaubayev v Michael Wilson and Partners Ltd* [2014] EWCA Civ 1491 [68]–[69].

Another criticism levelled under the fourth objection tends to be that the arbitral tribunal cannot match the court's ability to provide continuous supervision where the ongoing examination of accounting issues or the administration of a trust might so necessitate.[42] As Segesser notes, domestic courts may have a slight practical advantage to the extent that a trust dispute might require continuous supervision because initiating new arbitral proceedings and establishing an arbitral tribunal every time another dispute or disagreement arises may become burdensome. However, again, this criticism, if taken at its highest, only goes towards the scope of trust disputes that are arbitrable and does not form a valid basis for the wholesale rejection of the arbitrability of trusts. Moreover, it is not beyond the realm of the settlor's ability to provide for an ad hoc arbitration procedure that adapts from the processes common to large construction projects, where full-scale arbitration is only launched after parties fail to resolve their differences through an abbreviated hearing before a dispute resolution board.

IV. Enforceability

It is trite that the cornerstone of arbitration is party autonomy, and for that reason, without a valid agreement to arbitrate, the arbitral tribunal has no jurisdiction over the dispute. As such, the majority of the objections to the arbitration of trust disputes have focused on the difficulties inherent in enforcing the agreement to arbitrate against the relevant trustees and beneficiaries. In particular, it has been questioned whether the insertion of an arbitration clause can constitute a valid 'agreement in writing' as required under Article II(1) of the New York Convention,[43] and which has been defined in that provision to 'include an arbitral clause in a contract or an arbitration agreement, signed by the parties or contained in an exchange of letters or telegrams'. In particular, the Swiss[44] and American[45] judiciary, as well as commentators such as Christopher Koch,[46] have opined that given that a trust is not a contract, an arbitration agreement placed within the instrument in and of itself has no binding effect. Such views resonate with Lord Oliver's observation in *Marley v Mutual Security Merchant Bank* that 'the court is essentially engaged solely in determining what ought to be done in the best interest of the trust estate and not in determining the rights of adversarial parties'.[47]

[42] Segesser (n 8) 46.
[43] ibid 42.
[44] BJM 2007, 28 (Basel Court of Appeals).
[45] *Schonenberger v Oelze* 96 P 3d 1078 (2004) 208 Ariz 591; *Diaz v Bukey* 2d Civil No B225548 (Super Ct No PR90337A) (San Luis Obispo County); *In re Mary Calomiris*, 2 March 2006, 894A 2d 408, District of Columbia Court of Appeals; *William Lo v Aetna International Inc*, 29 March 2000, 2000 LEXIS 22531, US Federal District Court.
[46] Koch (n 3).
[47] *Marley v Mutual Security Merchant Bank* [1991] 3 All ER 198, 201.

Even though the basic elements of an express trust and a contract are not dissimilar insofar as their constitution is consensual and no individual can be compelled to be a trustee, it is accepted that a trust is not a contract, having different historical antecedents, and requiring different elements for valid constitution. To that extent, it is agreed that the insertion of an arbitration clause into the trust instrument alone is probably not sufficient to form a valid 'agreement in writing' or constitute 'an arbitral clause in a contract' for the purposes of Article II of the New York Convention. It also ought to be pointed out that it would be odd for the agreement to be perceived as being formed between the settlor, trustees and beneficiaries, given that the settlor drops out of the picture and has no enforceable rights under the trust once it is constituted.

However, it is submitted that there should be in principle no reason why a settlor cannot make it a condition of his appointment of the trustee as trustee, and a condition of his designating the beneficiary as the possessor of an interest under the trust, that they be required to enter into an agreement to arbitrate with *each other* (and not the settlor) on the terms stipulated in the arbitration clause inserted into the trust instrument. After all, even if 'beneficiaries' interests derive from equity fastening on the trustees' conscience',[48] as Danckwerts J explained in *Re Wynn*,

> they take purely by the bounty of the [settlor], and it might be said that, as they are not entitled to anything as of right apart from the provisions of the [trust], they must take their benefits subject to the conditions which are contained.[49]

That is why Andrew Holden, who strenuously argued that a beneficiary is not a party to the trust instrument or any arbitration agreement contained within it, nonetheless appeared prepared to accept that if the terms of the arbitration clause are crafted as a condition to the beneficiary's entitlement to an interest under the trust, that should be sufficient to bind beneficiaries who are of age and have legal capacity to act.[50] Similarly, the UK Trust Law Committee, though ultimately sceptical for other reasons that trust disputes could be arbitrated without the benefit of enabling legislation, conceded that

> it is feasible for any two or more persons of full capacity to enter into a valid standalone arbitration agreement … this can apply to a dispute between beneficiaries, or between beneficiaries and trustee, in regard to a trust in which they are interested.[51]

Viewed in this light, it is the trustees' and beneficiaries' respective *acceptance* of the positions conferred on them through the trust that can generate the requisite agreement to bind them to arbitration.[52] In that respect, the arbitration clause

[48] Molloy and Graham (n 34) 284.
[49] *Re Wynn* (n 26) 276.
[50] Holden (n 8) 547–48.
[51] Trust Law Committee (n 8) 297.
[52] In the instance where the settlor and trustee are one and the same, complications may arise generating the requisite acceptance by the trustee to arbitrate. However, it might still be said that that person,

in the trust instrument would become the 'agreement in writing' between the relevant trustees and beneficiaries provided they act to take up their respective appointments, even though the trust is in itself not a contract. The settlor's stipulations in the trust instrument may *facilitate* the making of the agreement to arbitrate between the trustees and beneficiaries but he does not himself become privy to that agreement.

In the relevant literature, there is a theory of 'deemed acquiescence' that has gained some traction in recent times. It amounts to the view that by accepting the settlor's bounty, the beneficiary is deemed to have also accepted the conditions under which the settlor is willing to have the beneficiaries profit from the settlor's bounty, which includes the agreement to arbitrate.[53] However, in those versions, the settlor continues to be seen as being privy to the agreement to arbitrate, although not having any enforceable rights under the trust itself. Critics have doubted whether acceptance of the arbitration agreement in this manner can constitute an 'agreement in writing' sufficient for the purposes of the New York Convention, because the acquiescence generated under that theory is deemed rather than actual.[54] By contrast, what is being suggested here is that where the settlor makes it an express condition of the appointment of the trustee and the conferring of interests on the beneficiary that they *enter into an agreement with each other* on the terms reflected in the arbitration clause in the trust instrument, two possible results can follow. Either, the parties fail to reach an actual agreement (whether because they were unaware of the condition or for some other reason), the appointments are not valid, and so the trust fails from the outset such that the parties have no standing to bring a trust claim before the courts. Or, the parties positively agree to the arbitration agreement as a condition of accepting the settlor's appointments, thus constituting actual acquiescence and not deemed acquiescence.

It is acknowledged that there is disagreement in the arbitration community[55] over whether Article II(2) of the New York Convention, which requires an 'agreement in writing' can be satisfied by the tacit acceptance of one party of a standard form arbitration clause in the other's communications. Specifically, some have interpreted the drafting history behind the provision's requirement for an 'exchange of letters or telegrams' as an intention to exclude tacit acceptances.[56]

whether in his capacity as settlor or not, offered to confer benefits on the beneficiary conditional upon the latter's acceptance of an obligation to arbitrate with him in his capacity as trustee. And the beneficiary, in seeking to enforce the terms of the trust, so accepted the condition.

[53] Koch (n 3) 190; Segesser (n 8) 42.

[54] eg M Hwang 'Arbitration of Trust Disputes' in *Selected Essays on International Arbitration* (SIAC Academy Publishing, 2013) 745.

[55] Countries such as Germany, France, Italy and Switzerland appear to have rejected the tacit acceptance doctrine, whereas England, the Netherlands, the United States, India and Canada have gone the other way.

[56] Born (n 12) 683.

However, it also ought to be noted that the references in Article II(2) to an 'arbitral clause in a contract' and 'an arbitration agreement, signed by the parties or contained in an exchange of letters or telegrams' are non-exhaustive examples of what would constitute an 'agreement in writing' and UNCITRAL has published recommendations emphasising that a strict literal application of the term 'agreement in writing' is not desirable.[57] Ultimately, the intent of the drafters of the New York Convention was to ensure that parties' consent to arbitration was obtained, the terms of which are to be sufficiently reflected in the written form to prevent uncertainty. Provided that the relevant trustees and beneficiaries were notified of the conditions stipulated by the settlor that they agree to arbitrate, the arbitration clause in the trust instrument ought to suffice as an 'agreement in writing' for the purposes of Article II of the New York Convention. This would be analogous to the existing cases interpreting the New York Convention, where it was held sufficient that a party which does not sign the contract or return a written confirmation but nonetheless performs its obligations may nonetheless be taken to have by conduct accepted the arbitration agreement.[58]

This chapter so far has been written on the basis that all the trustees and beneficiaries of the trust in dispute are readily ascertainable, of legal age, have legal capacity and collectively participate in any given arbitration arising out of the trust. However, that is obviously not the case in many trusts. But before moving away to consider other variations, it is apposite to consider the two other methods by which commentators have sought to generate the relevant agreement of a beneficiary to arbitrate. The theories have largely focused on the beneficiaries as it is generally accepted that a settlor can bind a trustee to arbitrate, if not under the terms of the appointment to the trust itself, then through a separate contract for service in the case of a professional trusteeship. The first is the idea of the 'conditional transfer'. It reasons that the binding effect of the arbitration agreement in the trust instrument stems from the understanding that the beneficiary's rights are '*wholly derivative*' from the settlor's wishes.[59] The settlor should be able to determine how the trust he or she establishes, and hence the property gifted, is to be administered.[60] The 'conditional transfer' is problematic in at least two respects: (i) it focuses on the intentions of the settlor in setting up the trust, rather than searching for evidence of the beneficiary's agreement to arbitrate as required under the New York Convention and just about every other variation on arbitration law; and (ii) like the 'deemed acquiescence' theory, it assumes that the settlor is privy to the arbitration agreement. The second method is specific to

[57] UNCITRAL, 2006: A/6/17, Recommendations Regarding the Interpretation of Article II, Paragraph 2, and Article IV, Paragraph I, of the Convention on the Recognition and Enforcement of Foreign Arbitral Awards.

[58] For a list of cases, see the commentary on Art II of the New York Convention: newyorkconvention1958.org/index.php?lvl=cmspage&pageid=11&provision=175#navig_art_181.

[59] Segesser (n 8) 42.

[60] ibid.

jurisdictions with the legislative equivalent of the UK's section 82(2) of the Arbitration Act 1966. That provision includes within the definition of a 'party' to arbitration any person claiming under or through a party to the agreement.[61] Based on the assumption that the beneficiary's interests have to derive from either the trustee's or settlor's title, certain commentators have attempted to argue that the beneficiary would be a person claiming 'through' a party to the agreement, namely either the settlor or the trustee. Andrew Holden doubts this and reasons that while it could be argued that a beneficiary's equitable title itself flows 'through' the settlor or trustee, in any event, beneficiaries are simply not parties to the trust instrument or any arbitration contained within it.[62] He also notes that section 82(2) of the Arbitration Act 1966 has not been interpreted in a manner consonant with the reading of a beneficiary as a person claiming 'through' a party to the arbitration agreement. This author agrees on both counts.

A. Minors, Legally Incompetent, Unborn and Unascertained

It has been mentioned that for the large part, this chapter has proceeded on the basis that the settlor, trustees and beneficiaries of the trust are of age and have legal capacity to act, as was stipulated in the scenario proposed at the beginning of the chapter. However, unlike most commercial arbitrations of contract matters, trust disputes often require the interests of minor or legally incompetent beneficiaries to be represented. Other problematic categories include unborn or unascertained beneficiaries. There has been criticism that the arbitration of trust disputes is lacking because, unlike a court that has the inherent jurisdiction to approve a compromise on behalf of minors or incapable beneficiaries, for example, by appointing a representative to safeguard their interests, an arbitral tribunal has no such power.[63] This is a particular problem within the context of the Model Law and the New York Convention as awards can be set aside on the basis that the party to the arbitration agreement suffered from incapacity.

To begin, this concern about representing minors, legally incompetents, the unborn and unascertained does not form a bar where the trust that a settlor wants arbitrated does not include any of these problematic categories of beneficiary, as would likely be the case where a commercial trust such as a Real Estate Investment Trust (REIT) is in question. Second, where such categories of beneficiary are likely to exist, it may be worthwhile for the settlor to insert a provision similar to clause 2 above, expressly acknowledging that the court can declare that the matter be litigated rather than arbitrated. This is to prevent allegations that the settlor has attempted to oust the supervisory jurisdiction of the court in respect of matters

[61] L Cohen and J Poole, 'Trust Arbitration—is it Desirable and does it Work?' (2012) 18 *Trusts & Trustees* 324.

[62] Holden (n 8) 549–50.

[63] *Chapman v Chapman* [1954] AC 429; see also Segesser (n 8) 43–44.

that are not arbitrable, or that a gift has been given to the beneficiary with one hand and taken away with the other. Third, potentially, the settlor could make the disposition to the beneficiary expressly contingent on there being a suitable representative, such as a parent or guardian, being willing to participate in arbitration if such need arises, failing which the gift will not vest. Another possibility is that the court's aid can be sought to appoint a representative for these problematic categories, who will then be empowered to act in the arbitration process. However, that then runs into the problem of whether the arbitral award thus rendered can be binding on these categories of person, given that arbitration is first and foremost a consensual process requiring the agreement of parties. Alternatively, the settlor might find it worthwhile to conclude from the outset that disputes arising out of such a trust would be better resolved through litigation, and do away with the idea of arbitration entirely. Finally, where not expressly prohibited by the laws of the relevant jurisdiction, it may be possible for the settlor to confer the power on the tribunal or a third party to appoint a representative to act on behalf of these problematic categories, and have the representation funded out of the trust assets.[64] However, given the sensitivities involved there remains a significant risk that a court called upon to recognise the arbitration agreement would decline to do so on the basis of public policy.

Matthew Conaglen has suggested that on the question of enforceability, there may be scope for the court to intervene on the basis of its inherent jurisdiction, to give effect to an arbitration clause, where it might otherwise fall outside the ambit of the arbitration statutes of the jurisdiction.[65] This might enable arbitration to occur where no formal agreement falling within the terms of the statutory provision may be found. However, where enforcement is likely to be sought in a foreign jurisdiction under the aegis of the New York Convention, problems may arise. Courts may refuse aid on the basis that the arbitration, not being founded on the consent of parties, was invalid. Similarly, complications may arise should the courts of the seat (if different from the one which exercised its inherent jurisdiction to compel arbitration) apply the rules of the Model Law.

In short, therefore, where minors, legally incompetent, unborn or unascertained persons may have an interest in the arbitration proceedings, the matter may be better off litigated rather than arbitrated. At the very least, it would be worthwhile to seek a court's declaration blessing the arbitration process and the proposed representatives of these problematic categories of beneficiary before embarking on what might ultimately prove to be a costly but fruitless expedition. Even then, where enforcement might be sought outside the jurisdiction that blessed the arbitration process, complications may arise. However, where the trust is constituted without the involvement of any such problematic beneficiaries, this objection should not form a bar to the general arbitrability of trust disputes.

[64] Holden (n 8) 551.
[65] Conaglen (n 28) 472.

B. Trustees, Beneficiaries and Third Parties Who Did Not Participate in Prior Proceedings

Another aspect of enforceability in which the suitability of arbitration as a dispute resolution process for trusts tends to be questioned is its ability, or lack thereof, to bind non-parties to the award rendered by the arbitral tribunal.[66] Unlike court judgments that can have third-party effects, an arbitral award is ordinarily binding only on those parties who had agreed to submit to the jurisdiction of the arbitral tribunal rendering it. This means that trustees and beneficiaries who came to the trust *after* the arbitral award has been rendered, as opposed to trustees or beneficiaries who had notice of the arbitral process but chose not to participate, could potentially bring up similar claims already resolved by one tribunal before another. Similarly, third parties who, for example, claim that the constitution of the trust was invalid, would also not be bound by any award rendered under an arbitration agreement in the trust instrument.

The ability of the settlor to require trustees and beneficiaries to arbitrate trust disputes, as explained above, stems from his making the agreement to arbitrate a condition on which he appoints the trustee as trustee and confers beneficial interests on the beneficiaries. Such would not apply to a third party of the trust, such as a forced heirship claimant seeking to have the trust declared invalid. Third parties bringing claims that the trust is invalidly constituted, or what has been termed 'rocket launcher disputes', would not be compellable to arbitration, which is ultimately a consensual process.[67] In disputes of this nature, as opposed to disputes wholly concerning the internal workings of the trust, the matter would be better settled via litigation rather than arbitration, unless the express consent of the third party to arbitrate can be obtained.

The situation is slightly different for a successor trustee who comes late to the trust. For him, the arbitral award would not be binding per se, given he had neither submitted to the jurisdiction of the tribunal nor had the opportunity to make representations. However, his commitment to stand by awards rendered prior to his assumption of office can nonetheless be secured if the settlor, in the trust instrument, expressly makes it a condition that the successor trustee takes his appointment subject to the awards rendered by arbitral tribunals in relation to the trust. In the same vein, for the beneficiary who comes late to the trust, for example, where the trustee exercises a power of appointment in his favour, similar conditions can be imposed via the trust instrument. However, as mentioned above, where trusts involve unascertained beneficiaries, on balance, one might be better off litigating rather than arbitrating, given the potential risk that such arbitrations may be

[66] Cohen and Poole (n 61) 327–28 and BC Janin, 'The Validity of Arbitration Provisions in Trust Instruments' (1967) 55 *California Law Review* 521, 553.

[67] Trust Law Committee (n 8) 300.

considered contrary to public policy if the interests of the unascertained beneficiaries are not adequately protected.

There is no question that settlors can attach conditions to their appointment of trustees and to the dispositions of trust that they make. Generally, these conditions are given effect by the courts save where they are contrary to public policy, such as in the case of *in terrorem* clauses.[68] It is submitted that both (i) the condition that trustees and beneficiaries agree to arbitrate on the terms stipulated in the trust instrument and (ii) the condition that trustees and beneficiaries agree to respect awards handed down by arbitral tribunals even prior to their having come to the trust, ought not to run afoul of public policy. This is because in both instances the settlor has a legitimate reason for imposing these conditions, namely, ensuring the efficient administration and dispute resolution of the trust.

One might argue that the first condition runs afoul of public policy insofar as it forces parties to agree to a dispute resolution mechanism where they might not otherwise consent, compromising party autonomy. In answer to this, it is worth pointing out that parties are not deprived of their autonomy as they always have the option of turning down the disposition or appointment that the settlor has made in their favour. If they make the choice to accept the settlor's appointments, they have to take the good with the bad. Furthermore, in the cases brought before the courts where a party has sought to enforce an arbitration agreement in a trust instrument, the focus of the objections made has typically been on the practical aspects of enforcing the agreement against the relevant parties, and securing the remedies required to do justice under the trust. It does not appear to have been within the contemplation of either the court or parties that party autonomy has been compromised by the settlor's attempts to have the trust disputes arbitrated rather than litigated.

One might also argue that the second condition runs afoul of public policy insofar as it deprives parties of their right to bring a contest in court where they would otherwise be entitled to do so, obstructing the access of the trustees and beneficiaries to justice. Such an objection would be circular, given that these parties would have had no rights to vindicate in court but for the fact that the settlor had seen fit to appoint the trustee as trustee and to confer on the beneficiaries the interests that they enjoy. In that sense, the condition that the trustees and beneficiaries, who come late to the trust, need to abide by earlier arbitral awards even though they were not represented at those proceedings is not repugnant to public policy provided the arbitral tribunal had given sufficient consideration to their interests prior to rendering the arbitral award.

[68] eg *AN v Barclays Private Bank & Trust (Cayman) Limited* [2007] WTLR 565.

V. Arbitration in a Jurisdiction with Existing Legislation

The argument has already been made that an arbitration clause inserted in a trust instrument ought to be enforceable provided (i) the settlor makes it a condition of participation in the trust that each trustee and beneficiary agrees to arbitrate with the other parties to the trust; (ii) that the scope of the arbitration agreement is limited to disputes arising out of the internal workings of the trust; and (iii) that all the parties to the trust are of age, of legal capacity and ascertainable at the date the arbitration is commenced, or alternatively, that a suitable mechanism is adopted to ensure the proper representation of minor, legally incompetent unborn and unascertained beneficiaries. Nonetheless, it is acknowledged that given the relative novelty of trust arbitration, the risk cannot be eliminated that an award on a trust dispute still runs the risk of set aside or refusal of enforcement by a state that exercises its prerogative to declare that the award is repugnant to its public policy. Yet, given the number of potential advantages that can be reaped from arbitrating rather than litigating trust matters, for a settlor the avenue remains one well worth considering.

It might be argued that given the number of difficulties in the way of a settlor who wishes to arbitrate a trust dispute in a jurisdiction that has not explicitly taken a stand, it might be easier all round for the settlor to choose to have the trust arbitrated in a jurisdiction which has enabling legislation. Given that the focus of this chapter is on whether arbitration is possible in a jurisdiction which does not have enabling legislation, an extensive discussion of the pros and cons of the legislation in each jurisdiction that has provided for such is simply not possible. However, it is argued, based on the limitations of what has been provided for in the respective legislations, as set out below, that none of the regimes provide a foolproof solution in any event to the questions plaguing the viability of arbitrating trust disputes.

Table 1: Main Limitations of Existing Legislation

	Main limitations
Florida	— Does not set out any method for appointing representatives for minors, legally incapable, unborn and unascertainable beneficiaries. — Excludes the question of validity of the trust from the scope of what is arbitrable.
Arizona	— Does not set out any method for appointing representatives for minors, legally incapable, unborn and unascertainable beneficiaries. — Limits the procedures that can be provided for to those which are 'reasonable' without explanation as to its meaning. — Does not make clear whether the reference to the binding effect on 'interested persons' extends to third parties to the trust who might seek to contest the trust's validity.

(continued)

Table 1: (***Continued***)

Uniform Trust Code	— Does not make clear which parties would qualify as 'interested persons' who may enter into arbitration on trust disputes, and specifically, whether third parties to the trust might be included within that definition. — Does not specify how parties may enter into agreements to resolve disputes other than by litigation, and specifically, whether an arbitration clause placed in the trust instrument can have effect.
Malta	— Does not set out any method for appointing representatives for minor, legally incapable, unborn and unascertainable beneficiaries. — Notwithstanding any clause in the trust instrument, the court retains discretion not to stay proceedings in favour of arbitration, creating uncertainty as to the proper forum in which claims should be brought.
Guernsey	— Does not specify method for appointing representatives for minors, legally incapable, unborn and unascertainable beneficiaries, although it is implied that the court could make the appointment. — Appears to limit the scope of what is arbitrable only to claims against trustees founded on breach of trust, and so excludes matters such as the variation of trust terms, or disputes on the reasonability of the trustee's fees.
Bahamas	— Despite the provisions laid out for appointing representatives to represent minors, legally incapable, unborn and unascertainable beneficiaries, the award may nonetheless risk being refused enforcement in New York Convention jurisdictions on the basis that the consent of these persons had not been obtained. — It appears to allow for the arbitration of questions as to the validity of the trust but does not set out how non-parties to the trust can be bound by the award rendered.

VI. Conclusion

Given the relative novelty of the subject area, it would be overreaching to say that the arbitration of trust disputes comes without risks, particularly when it is brought or an arbitral award is being sought to be enforced in a jurisdiction that has not expressly legislated in its favour. It is also not possible to say that all trust disputes can be conveniently arbitrated, particularly where the matter involves parties who are not able to represent themselves or for which there are interested parties who are not amenable and not compellable to arbitration. On the other side of the coin, however, given that there are various internal trust disputes that are suitable for arbitration, and it is in theory not impossible to see how the consent of the trustees, protectors and beneficiaries may be secured through the terms of the trust, as a whole arbitration provisions should not be regarded as unenforceable. To the contrary, the importance of the settlor's intentions to construing the ambit of the trust, and the potential advantages to be reaped from arbitration as a dispute resolution method for trust matters, provide every impetus for prima facie recognising the enforceability of arbitration provisions in trust instruments, save where specific circumstances render the opposite conclusion necessary. The matter turns ultimately on whether the settlor may transfer in part or in whole the supervisory jurisdiction of the courts to an extrajudicial body, and whether the settlor may impose conditions of arbitration on his appointments and gifts. And in both regards, it is submitted, as set out above, that the matter ought to be answered in the affirmative.

Annex

	Relevant provision	
Florida	(1) A provision in a will or trust requiring the arbitration of disputes, other than disputes of the validity of all or a part of a will or trust, between or among the beneficiaries and a fiduciary under the will or trust, or any combination of such persons or entities is enforceable. (2) Unless otherwise specified in the will or trust, a will or trust provision requiring arbitration shall be presumed to require binding arbitration under s 44.104.	Probate Code, s 731.401
Arizona	A trust instrument may provide mandatory, exclusive and reasonable procedures to resolve issues between the trustee and interested persons or among interested persons with regard to the administration or distribution of the trust.	Trust Code, §14-10205
Uniform Trust Code	(a) For purposes of this section, 'interested persons' means persons whose consent would be required in order to achieve a binding settlement were the settlement to be approved by the court. (b) Except as otherwise provided in subsection (c), interested persons may enter into a binding nonjudicial settlement agreement with respect to any matter involving a trust. (c) A nonjudicial settlement agreement is valid only to the extent it does not violate a material purpose of the trust and includes terms and conditions that could be properly approved by the court under this [Code] or other applicable law. (d) Matters that may be resolved by a nonjudicial settlement agreement include: (1) the interpretation or construction of the terms of the trust; (2) the approval of a trustee's report or accounting; (3) direction to a trustee to refrain from performing a particular act or the grant to a trustee of any necessary or desirable power; (4) the resignation or appointment of a trustee and the determination of a trustee's compensation; (5) transfer of a trust's principal place of administration; and (6) liability of a trustee for an action relating to the trust. (e) Any interested person may request the court to approve a nonjudicial settlement agreement, to determine whether the representation as provided in [Article] 3 was adequate, and to determine whether the agreement contains terms and conditions the court could have properly approved.	Section 111

(*continued*)

Malta	(1) It shall be lawful for a testator to insert an arbitration clause in a will. In such event such clause shall be binding on all persons claiming under such will in relation to all disputes relating to the interpretation of such will, including any claim that such will is not valid. (2) It shall be lawful for a settlor of a trust to insert an arbitration clause in a deed of trust and such clause shall be binding on all trustees, protectors and any beneficiaries under the trust in relation to matters arising under or in relation to the trust. (3) In the cases referred to in the preceding subarticles, the right of a party to seek directions of the Court of voluntary jurisdiction in terms of the jurisdiction in terms of the Trusts and Trustees Act shall not be limited by any such clause and notwithstanding the provisions of this Act, the said Court shall not be bound to stay proceedings in terms of article 15(5) or otherwise, but shall enjoy a discretion to do so until such time as it determines that the matter is of a contentious nature, in which case it shall stay the proceedings and shall refer the parties to arbitration.	Arbitration Act, Art 15A

(*continued*)

Guernsey	(1) Where— (a) the terms of a trust direct or authorise, or the Court so orders, that any claim against a trustee founded on breach of trust may be referred to alternative dispute resolution ('ADR'), (b) such a claim arises and, in accordance with the terms of the trust or the Court's order, is referred to ADR, and (c) the ADR results in a settlement of the claim which is recorded in a document signed by or on behalf of all parties, the settlement is binding on all beneficiaries of the trust, whether or not yet ascertained or in existence, and whether or not minors or persons under legal disability. (2) Subsection (1) applies in respect of a beneficiary only if— (a) he was represented in the ADR proceedings (whether personally, or by his guardian, or as the member of a class, or otherwise), or (b) if not so represented, he had notice of the ADR proceedings and a reasonable opportunity of being heard, and only if, in the case of a beneficiary who is not yet ascertained or in existence, or who is a minor or person under legal disability, the person conducting the ADR proceedings certifies that he was independently represented by a person appointed for the purpose by a court of law. (3) A person who represents a beneficiary in the ADR proceedings for the purpose of subsection (2)(a) is under a duty of care to the beneficiary. (4) For the avoidance of doubt, the ADR proceedings need not be conducted in Guernsey or in accordance with the procedural law of Guernsey. (5) In this section— 'ADR' includes conciliation, mediation, early neutral evaluation, adjudication, expert determination and arbitration, and 'proceedings' includes oral and written proceedings.	Trusts (Guernsey) Law 2007, s 63

(*continued*)

	Relevant provision	
Bahamas	91A. Arbitration of trust disputes. (1) The object of this section is to enable any dispute or administration question in relation to a trust to be determined by arbitration in accordance with the provisions of the trust instrument. (2) Where a written trust instrument provides that any dispute or administration question arising between any of the parties in relation to the trust shall be submitted to arbitration ('a trust arbitration'), that provision shall, for all purposes under the Arbitration Act, have effect as between those parties as if it were an arbitration agreement and as if those parties were parties to that agreement. (3) The Arbitration Act shall apply to a trust arbitration in accordance with the provisions of the Second Schedule to this Act. (4) The Minister may by order amend the Second Schedule. 91B. Powers of the arbitral tribunal. (1) This section shall apply except to the extent otherwise provided in the trust instrument. (2) The arbitral tribunal (hereinafter referred to as 'the tribunal') may, in addition to all other powers of the tribunal, at any stage in a trust arbitration, exercise all the powers of the Court (whether arising by statute (including this Act), under the inherent jurisdiction of the Court or otherwise) in relation to the administration, execution or variation of a trust or the exercise of any power arising under a trust. (3) Without prejudice to subsection (2), and to any provisions made pursuant to subsection (4), the tribunal has the same powers to appoint one or more persons to represent the interests of any person (including a person unborn or unascertained) or class in a trust arbitration as the court has under Order 15 rule 14 of the Rules of the Supreme Court in relation to proceedings before the Court. (4) The terms of a trust may provide for the appointment of one or more persons to represent the interests of any person (including a person unborn or unascertained) or class in a trust arbitration. (5) Where an appointment is made under subsection (3) or (4)— (a) the approval of the tribunal is required in relation to a settlement affecting the person or class represented; (b) the tribunal may approve a settlement where it is satisfied that the settlement is for the benefit of the person or class represented; (c) any award given in the trust arbitration shall be binding on the person or class represented by the person or persons appointed.	Trustee Act, ss 91A, 91B, 91C

(*continued*)

	(6) A person under a disability may not— (a) bring or make a claim in trust arbitration except by his next friend; (b) defend, make a counterclaim or intervene in a trust arbitration except by his guardian ad litem; or (c) take any step in a trust arbitration except by his next friend or guardian ad litem, unless otherwise ordered by the tribunal. (7) The terms of a trust may provide for the appointment of a next friend or guardian ad litem, for the cessation of an appointment and for the service of documents upon a person under a disability. (8) Subject to subsection (7), the tribunal may appoint a suitable person to be a next friend or guardian ad litem, may terminate an appointment, and may give directions for the service of documents upon a person under a disability. (9) Where a next friend or guardian ad litem has been appointed under subsection (7) or subsection (8), no settlement affecting the person under a disability shall be valid, without the approval of the tribunal. (10) Notwithstanding subsection (1), subsection (5), (6) and (9) shall apply irrespective of any provision in the trust instrument. (11) The Minister may make regulations to extend or clarify the powers of the tribunal in relation to trust arbitrations. 91C. Interpretation for sections 91A, 91B and the Second Schedule. For the purposes of sections 91A, 91B and the Second Schedule— '**administration question**' means any relief or question in respect of which an action, application or other reference to the court could, subject to section 91A and the Arbitration Act, be brought or made under Order 74 of the Rules of the Supreme Court under this Act or under the Purpose Trusts Act; '**beneficiary**' includes an object of a power, whether or not ascertained or in existence and a charity; '**dispute**' includes a difference; '**power holder**' means any person holding a power in relation to a trust (including any power of appointment, consent, direction, revocation, or variation, and any power to appoint or remove trustees or power holders) and includes a person in the position of a protector; '**the parties in relation to the trust**' means any trustee, beneficiary or power holder of or under the trust, in their capacity as such.	

10

Bribery

PAUL S DAVIES*

I. Introduction

Bribery is an important and difficult topic. In *FHR European Ventures LLP v Mankarious* (*FHR*), Lord Neuberger PSC said:

> As Lord Templeman said giving the decision of the Privy Council in *Attorney General for Hong Kong v Reid* [1994] 1 AC 324, 330H, 'bribery is an evil practice which threatens the foundations of any civilised society'. Secret commissions are also objectionable as they inevitably tend to undermine trust in the commercial world. That has always been true, but concern about bribery and corruption generally has never been greater than it is now: see for instance, internationally, the OECD Convention on Combating Bribery of Foreign Public Officials in International Business Transactions 1999 and the United Nations Convention against Corruption 2003, and, nationally, the Bribery Acts 2010 and 2012.[1]

It is obviously right that concerns about bribery are not new; in *Novoship (UK) Ltd v Mikhaylyuk*, Longmore LJ pointed out that problems of bribery are present as far back as Homer's *The Odyssey*.[2] Yet it is equally clear that in the modern world the law must operate effectively to combat bribery.

This chapter considers the role of equity in providing suitable remedies where bribery has occurred. Much has been written about the nature of the remedy available against a fiduciary who receives a bribe in breach of fiduciary duty, but this issue has been decisively resolved by the Supreme Court in *FHR*: the bribe is

* I am particularly grateful to Simon Douglas, Nick McBride, James Penner and Peter Watts for their comments on earlier versions of this chapter.

[1] *FHR European Ventures LLP v Mankarious* [2014] UKSC 45, [2015] AC 250 [42].

[2] *Novoship (UK) Ltd v Mikhaylyuk* [2014] EWCA Civ 908, [2015] QB 499 [2]: 'When Odysseus penetrated the underworld, he encountered, among many other ghosts, that of Eriphyle whom Homer (Od 11.326) calls "hateful" because she had been bribed by Polyneices with Aphrodite's golden necklace to reveal the whereabouts of her husband, so that he could be found and compelled to march on Thebes where he foresaw he would be killed. This may or may not be the first recorded instance of a successful bribe but, centuries later, bribery is still prevalent and pervasive however much legislators and judges try to stamp it out'.

held on constructive trust. It is now necessary to think harder about other problems that arise. There are some unresolved questions about the remedies available against the wrongdoing fiduciary, which will be addressed first, but the focus of this chapter is really upon the liability of the briber, a matter which has not received as much attention.[3] It is important to be clear both about the nature of the claims and remedies available against the briber, and about how the briber's liability fits with the liability of the fiduciary. It will be argued that the principal should be able to sue the briber either for the principal's loss or the briber's gain, regardless of whether or not the principal has set aside the transaction between it and the briber, and that such a claim can often succeed in addition to a claim against the wrongdoing fiduciary.

II. The Nature of Bribery

The criminal offence of bribery is established where a party offers a financial or other advantage to a person in order to induce the latter to perform his role improperly or to reward the improper performance of that role.[4] The recipient of the bribe also commits an offence if he intends to perform that role improperly.[5] A similar approach can be adopted in private law. If a person receives or is promised a benefit in order to act disloyally in the performance of his role, then he has been bribed. And the person who makes the payment is the briber.

This means that not all instances of inducing a breach of contract or inducing a breach of trust concern bribery. For example, *Lumley v Gye*[6] is not a bribery case. When Mr Gye offered Miss Wagner money to sing at his opera house, which required Miss Wagner to breach her contract to sing for Mr Lumley, Mr Gye did not bribe Miss Wagner. Miss Wagner did not perform her contract with Mr Lumley improperly. She did not deceive Mr Lumley. She simply did not perform her contract at all. Such cases should not be characterised as instances of bribery as a result.

It is undoubtedly true that in equity instances of bribery and secret commission have not been clearly distinguished and tend to be analysed together. *FHR* itself concerned a secret commission and not a bribe, but cases involving bribery were considered by the Supreme Court to be relevant and clearly influenced the decision reached. This is understandable. A fiduciary who takes a bribe or makes a secret commission will have breached his duty of loyalty by infringing the 'no-conflict' or 'no-profit' rule. And the briber or person who pays the secret commission will have committed the equitable wrong of dishonest assistance if he satisfies the

[3] In *Daraydan Holdings Ltd v Solland International Ltd* [2004] EWHC 622 (Ch), [2005] Ch 119 [1] Lawrence Collins J made it clear that bribery 'corrupts not only the recipient but the giver of the bribe'.

[4] Bribery Act 2010, s 1.

[5] ibid s 2.

[6] *Lumley v Gye* (1853) 2 E & B 216.

test of 'dishonesty'.[7] As regards both the fiduciary and dishonest assister there is little to be gained by trying to distinguish bribes and secret commissions. Cases on dishonest assistance can therefore help to shed light on the appropriate remedies available against the briber.

The focus of this chapter is upon the remedies available in equity. This reflects the reality of the case law in this area: claimants generally prefer to bring a claim in equity as a result of the more generous remedies available. The common law is more restrictive; there is no recognised tort of bribery,[8] and whilst gain-based relief is very difficult to obtain for breach of contract[9] or for the tort of deceit,[10] it is much more readily available in equity.[11] It may of course be questioned whether it is appropriate for the remedies at common law to be more confined that their equitable counterparts, but that lies beyond the scope of this chapter.

For present purposes, it is sufficient to note that the courts have been very flexible in finding a 'fiduciary relationship' in order to grant relief where a party has breached an obligation of loyalty, which clearly is a core concern of bribery. For example, in *Reading v Attorney General,*[12] an army sergeant used to ride on a lorry in full military uniform. The sergeant suspected that the lorries were used to transport drugs, and that his presence was designed to facilitate this. The sergeant accepted bribes to perform this role. It was held that the sergeant acted in breach of fiduciary duty and had to account for the profits he made. In the House of Lords, Lord Porter agreed[13] with Asquith LJ's observation in the Court of Appeal

> that the words 'fiduciary relationship' in this setting are used in a wide and loose sense and include, inter alia, a case where the servant gains from his employment a position of authority which enables him to obtain the sum which he receives.[14]

This is indeed a loose sense of 'fiduciary', but has effectively been adopted in subsequent cases.[15] Although space precludes a detailed analysis of this issue, it is

[7] See *Royal Brunei Airlines Sdn Bhd v Tan* [1995] 2 AC 378 (PC); see generally PS Davies, *Accessory Liability* (Oxford, Hart Publishing, 2015) ch 4.

[8] K Handley, 'Civil Liability for Bribery (No 2)' (2001) 117 *LQR* 536; *cf* C Mitchell, 'Civil Liability for Bribery' (2001) 117 *LQR* 207. It is sometimes said that the fraud claim for loss suffered by a bribe is *sui generis: Petrograde Inc v Smith* [2000] Lloyds Rep 486, 490 (Steel J).

[9] *Attorney-General v Blake* [2000] UKHL 45, [2001] 1 AC 268. Moreover, the remoteness rules for the recovery of loss caused by a breach of contract do not vary according to whether or not the breach of contract was deliberate and the result of a bribe; *cf* T Weir, 'The Staggering March of Negligence' in P Cane and J Stapleton (eds), *The Law of Obligations: Essays in Celebration of John Fleming* (Oxford, Clarendon Press, 1998) 126.

[10] See eg *Halifax Building Society v Thomas* [1996] Ch 217 (CA); *Devenish Nutrition Ltd v Sanofi-Aventis SA* [2008] EWCA Civ 1086, [2009] Bus LR 858. See further text to nn 115–18.

[11] It has been suggested that it would be preferable if 'the whole analysis of bribes would move into equity and abandon the common law claim of money had and received and the tort of deceit, with which it does not neatly fit': P McGrath, *Commercial Fraud in Civil Practice*, 2nd edn, (Oxford, OUP, 2014) para 10.54; see also P Watts and F Reynolds (eds), *Bowstead and Reynolds on Agency*, 20th edn (London, Sweet & Maxwell, 2014) para 8-224.

[12] *Reading v Attorney General* [1951] AC 507.

[13] ibid 517.

[14] [1949] 2 KB 232, 236 (Asquith LJ).

[15] See also *University of Nottingham v Fishel* [2000] ICR 1462.

suggested that it is not necessary invariably to characterise the employee–employer relationship as fiduciary for the range of equitable remedies to be available.[16] The key factor is that bribery necessarily entails a breach of a duty of loyalty—whether that be characterised as fiduciary or not—and equity is prepared to intervene because a person who has undertaken to serve another is not doing so faithfully.[17] This is often described as a breach of fiduciary duty, but there is no need to be distracted by analysing whether the employee really is a 'true' fiduciary: it is important to appreciate that equity will intervene because of a breach of a duty of loyalty. In any event, the paradigm cases of bribery do involve a dishonest assister who bribes a fiduciary, and that is the focus of this chapter.

III. Remedies Against the Recipient of the Bribe

A. Constructive Trust

In *FHR*, FHR European Ventures LLP purchased a long lease of the Monte Carlo Grand Hotel in Monaco for €211.5 million. The sellers agreed to pay €10 million to Cedar, an agent who was acting for the purchasers. This was a secret commission. The Supreme Court held that Cedar held the money on constructive trust for the purchasers. Lord Neuberger emphasised that '[c]larity and simplicity are highly desirable qualities in the law';[18] following *FHR*, it would seem that whenever a fiduciary makes a profit in breach of fiduciary duty he will hold those gains on trust for his principal.

One reason for the outcome in *FHR* is the need to combat bribery effectively.[19] For instance, if the fiduciary receives an Old Master painting as a bribe, then it is now clear that the principal can choose to claim that particular painting rather than simply the value of that painting. Of course, the principal might prefer to pursue a personal claim, but it is important that the choice belongs to him, rather than the wrongdoing fiduciary.[20] The fiduciary is simply not able to say that he should only have to give up the value of the bribe rather than the painting itself. This might well be considered to be sensible: any choice between remedies should be given to the innocent principal rather than the wrongdoing fiduciary.

The recognition of the constructive trust in *FHR* has a number of other significant consequences. Two were thought to be particularly noteworthy by the

[16] For discussion of this issue, compare R Flannigan, 'Employee Fiduciary Accountability' [2015] *Journal of Business Law* 189 and A Frazer, 'The Employee's Contractual Duty of Fidelity' (2015) 131 *LQR* 53.

[17] PD Finn, *Fiduciary Obligations* (Sydney, Law Book Company, 1977) 266–69.

[18] *FHR* (n 1) [35].

[19] ibid [42].

[20] ibid [7].

Supreme Court.[21] First, the availability of a proprietary claim under a constructive trust effectively gives the principal priority in insolvency over the fiduciary's other unsecured creditors.[22] Second, the principal's interest under a constructive trust gives him a proprietary base which allows him to trace into substitute assets.[23]

It is worth pointing out that there are two other potentially important ramifications of the constructive trust analysis in *FHR*. The first concerns limitation. It has been suggested that claims for personal remedies for breach of fiduciary duty are subject to a limitation period of six years, by applying the limitation period in tort by analogy to the equitable claim.[24] But no limitation period applies where a beneficiary seeks to recover from the trustee trust property or the proceeds of trust property.[25] Given that the bribe received should be considered to be trust property, principals might have longer to bring a proprietary claim than a personal claim, which could well prove to be useful. However, it is suggested that it is not entirely clear whether a limitation period can really apply by analogy to claims of breach of fiduciary duty. Claims for breach of the fiduciary obligation of loyalty, as illustrated in particular by the no-conflict and no-profit rules, are not analogous to any claim at common law, so no statutory limitation period should apply, even by analogy.[26] Whether the claim is for personal or proprietary relief, claims should be barred due to lapse of time only if laches is established.

Second, the prevalence of the constructive trust might create a tension between competing claims of the beneficiary and the state to the bribe, since the state might be able to confiscate the bribe. This issue arises where the criminal offence of bribery is established, and must now be considered more fully.[27]

i. Competing Claims under the Proceeds of Crime Act 2002

Section 2(2) of the Bribery Act 2010 provides that a criminal offence is committed when a person 'requests, agrees to receive or accepts a financial or other advantage intending that, in consequence, a relevant function or activity should be performed improperly'. Similarly, section 2(3) provides that an offence is committed when a person requests, agrees to receive or accepts a financial or other advantage, and the request, agreement or acceptance itself constitutes the improper

[21] ibid [1].

[22] And perhaps over secured creditors as well if they only took an equitable interest over the property, since equitable interests rank in order of time: see P Watts, 'Bribes and Constructive Trusts' (1994) 110 *LQR* 178.

[23] eg *Attorney General for Hong Kong v Reid* [1994] 1 AC 324 (PC).

[24] *Cia de Seguros Imperio v Heath (REBX) Ltd* [2000] EWCA Civ 219, [2001] 1 WLR 112.

[25] Limitation Act 1980, s 21(1)(b).

[26] *Tito v Waddell (No 2)* [1977] Ch 106, 248–50 (Megarry VC); *A-G v Cocke* [1988] Ch 414, 421 (Harman J).

[27] This issue is under-analysed; one leading book on remedies for fraud has said that the Bribery Act 2010 'is unlikely to have any significant bearing on the English civil law approach to liability for, and remedies arising from, bribery and so will not be considered in this book': McGrath (n 11) para 10.09.

performance by that person of a relevant function or activity. Relevant functions or activities are defined in section 3, and include any activity connected with a business,[28] or performed in the course of a business,[29] or performed by or on behalf of a body of persons,[30] and the 'person performing the function or activity is in a position of trust by virtue of performing it'.[31] This suggests that in many situations where a fiduciary receives a bribe, he will be committing a criminal offence.[32] Indeed, continuing to have possession of a bribe which is criminal property is also an offence.[33]

Where a criminal offence has been established, then it is possible for the state to bring a claim to confiscate the bribe.[34] An enforcement authority—generally the National Crime Agency[35]—is able to recover in civil proceedings property which is, or represents, property obtained through unlawful conduct.[36] The general rule is that '[i]f … the court is satisfied that any property is recoverable, the court must make a recovery order'.[37] This is mandatory: it follows that a confiscation order must be made when the trustee has committed the criminal offence of bribery under section 2 of the Bribery Act 2010. Prima facie, it therefore appears that the claim of the National Crime Agency to the property received as a bribe should trump that of the fiduciary's principal. However, it should be observed that the legislative scheme is somewhat messy and the drafters do not appear to have fully thought through what the interrelationship between public law and private law remedies should be.[38]

There are some exceptions to the strict approach under which the claims of the state must succeed,[39] but the most important for present purposes concerns section 281 of the Proceeds of Crime Act 2002:

> 281 Victims of theft, etc.
>
> (1) In proceedings for a recovery order, a person who claims that any property alleged to be recoverable property, or any part of the property, belongs to him may apply for a declaration under this section.
> (2) If the applicant appears to the court to meet the following condition, the court may make a declaration to that effect.
> (3) The condition is that—

[28] Bribery Act 2010, s 3(2)(b).
[29] ibid s 3(2)(c).
[30] ibid s 3(2)(d).
[31] ibid s 3(5).
[32] The briber is also likely to be committing an offence: see s 1.
[33] Proceeds of Crime Act 2002, s 329(1)(c) (Proceeds of Crime Act).
[34] ibid Part 5.
[35] ibid s 316(1).
[36] ibid s 240(1).
[37] ibid s 266(1).
[38] For instance, the legislation is somewhat awkward in that it seems to deprive private parties of private rights without expressly saying so.
[39] eg Proceeds of Crime Act, s 266(3)–(9) and ss 270–78.

(a) the person was deprived of the property he claims, or of property which it represents, by unlawful conduct,
(b) the property he was deprived of was not recoverable property immediately before he was deprived of it, and
(c) the property he claims belongs to him.

(4) Property to which a declaration under this section applies is not recoverable property.

This provision grants the court discretion not to make a confiscation order in favour of the enforcement authority. However, it is difficult to be sure whether the principal in the fiduciary relationship will be able to avail himself of this protection.[40] Of course, where the bribe itself comes from trust property then the beneficiary will be able to make out all three conditions easily.[41] But in most situations the bribe comes from the briber's property, and so it is difficult for the principal to claim that the requirement in (a) is satisfied, since he would not be deprived of property by unlawful conduct. For (a) to be satisfied, the principal would have to argue that the key moment is immediately after the bribe is paid and the constructive trust arises, but then requirement (b) poses a problem for the beneficiary, since the property of which he would be deprived *was* recoverable property immediately before he was deprived of it.

If the above analysis is correct, then there may still be a distinction between cases where the bribe was paid with property from the trust (where the principal takes the property) and cases where the bribe was paid with other property (where a confiscation order must be made). Yet the Supreme Court deprecated such a distinction in *FHR*, at least partly for the sake of clarity and simplicity.[42] In this context it might be argued that the distinction can be justified on the basis that the clear language of the legislation must be applied, but it is far from obvious that this sort of situation was envisaged by the legislators. Nevertheless, it is suggested that the distinction between the two situations can be defended: whilst a principal should not be deprived of his own property, in other circumstances it is arguable that nobody should be able to benefit from the criminal payment of a bribe and that confiscation should be ordered. In some situations there is no indication of whether a claim for confiscation should trump the claim of a private party,[43] but here it is made clear that in principle a confiscation order must be made. This seems acceptable, and it may even be the case that the principal will still have a personal remedy against the wrongdoing fiduciary.[44]

[40] See also L Tucker, N Le Poidevin and J Brightwell (eds), *Lewin on Trusts*, 18th edn (London, Sweet & Maxwell, 2014) paras 20-062–20-064.

[41] *cf Daraydan* (n 3) 119.

[42] *cf Sinclair Investments (UK) Ltd v Versailles Trade Finance Ltd* [2011] EWCA Civ 347, [2011] 3 WLR 1153.

[43] *cf Borders (UK) Ltd v Commissioner of Police of the Metropolis* [2005] EWCA Civ 197 [41].

[44] Although this might well be viewed as controversial if confiscation by the state is already thought to have achieved the purpose of deterrence, which is often thought to underpin gain-based relief.

It should also be noted that where the fiduciary has already paid the bribe to the principal, then the principal might try to rely upon section 308(3) of the Proceeds of Crime Act 2002 to resist a confiscation order:

> (3) If—
> (a) in pursuance of a judgment in civil proceedings (whether in the United Kingdom or elsewhere), the defendant makes a payment to the claimant or the claimant otherwise obtains property from the defendant,
> (b) the claimant's claim is based on the defendant's unlawful conduct, and
> (c) apart from this subsection, the sum received, or the property obtained, by the claimant would be recoverable property,
>
> the property ceases to be recoverable.

This is perhaps wider than section 281 since there is no requirement that the property is not recoverable property at the time of the payment. However, it is not at all clear that this section will protect the beneficiary. As the authors of *Lewin* observe, 'the court's judgment can do no more than give effect to a constructive trust which has already been constituted by the trustee's receipt of the bribe'.[45] Since the bribe was only obtained by unlawful conduct, and it was this which gave rise to the beneficiary's right, it is not unlikely that the court will insist upon the beneficiary's establishing a defence under section 281 in order to prevent a confiscation order being made.

B. Personal Remedies

The principal remains able to seek a personal remedy from the wrongdoing fiduciary who accepts a bribe: he can elect between the proprietary and personal remedy.[46] Although the principal cannot accumulate the personal remedy in addition to the proprietary remedy, it would appear that the principal's personal claim can be pursued on top of recovery proceedings instigated by the National Crime Agency. Even though the fiduciary may be mulcted twice over, it would seem that there is no inconsistency between the fiduciary having to give up the proceeds of crime, and also having to compensate the principal for any loss suffered.

The principal should be able to sue the fiduciary either for the loss the principal has suffered, or for the gains made by the fiduciary. Both the loss-based and gain-based claims are sometimes considered under the broad umbrella heading of 'equitable compensation',[47] which is used in this sense simply to denote a personal remedy. In some cases where the fiduciary has accepted a bribe, the principal's loss will be the same as the fiduciary's gain.[48] However, sometimes the value of the

[45] Tucker, Le Poidevin and Brightwell (n 40) para 120–066. On the other hand, it might be argued that if one had to go to judgment in order to get the payment then it is still paid 'in pursuance of a judgment'. This point is not entirely clear.

[46] *FHR* (n 1) [7].

[47] ibid [1].

[48] As was the case in *FHR* itself.

bribe paid will be greater than the loss suffered (since the briber has a particular need to enter into the transaction in order to make profits elsewhere or to defeat competitors, for example) and sometimes the fiduciary will accept a bribe which is less than the loss inflicted upon the principal.[49] The question of whether the principal can sue the fiduciary for both gain and loss is considered below.[50]

Is it possible to go beyond the profits made and award punitive damages against the wrongdoing fiduciary? After all, bribery can be a crime and, particularly where no criminal prosecution is brought and no confiscation order sought, the type of wrongdoing committed by the fiduciary might be thought suitable for a punitive remedy. However, equity has traditionally rejected any possibility of its being a penal jurisdiction.[51] This has been supported relatively recently by a majority decision of the New South Wales Court of Appeal.[52] Yet if punitive damages are appropriate at common law, it is difficult to explain why they are not similarly appropriate—in exceptional cases—where the defendant's liability is equitable.[53] Remedial coherence suggests that punitive damages should be available for equitable wrongs,[54] and if this step is taken then punitive awards may well be appropriate to help to deter and punish bribery.

IV. Remedies Available Against the Briber

A. Rescission

Where the principal enters into a transaction as a result of its agent taking a bribe, the principal is entitled to rescind the transaction *ab initio* or, if it is too late to rescind, then to bring the contract to an end for the future.[55] This was clearly reiterated by Millett J in *Logicrose Ltd v Southend United FC*.[56] In that case, the agent of Southend United FC entered into an agreement with a third party that the

[49] eg *Mahesan S/O Thambiah Appellant v Malaysia Government Officers' Co-Operative Housing Society Ltd* [1979] AC 374 (PC); considered at n 153.

[50] See section V below.

[51] eg *Vyse v Foster* (1872) LR 8 Ch App 309, 333 (James LJ).

[52] *Harris v Digital Pulse Pty Ltd* (2003) NSWCA 10, (2003) 197 ALR 626.

[53] See the judgment of Mason P (dissenting) in *Digital Pulse*, ibid. See also A Burrows, 'Remedial Coherence and Punitive Damages in Equity' in J Edelman and S Degeling (eds) *Equity in Commercial Law* (Sydney, Lawbook Co, 2005); *Cook v Evatt (No 2)* [1992] 1 NZLR 676.

[54] As was favoured by the Law Commission: Law Commission, *Aggravated, Exemplary and Restitutionary Damages* Report (Law Com No 247, 1997) paras 5.54–5.56.

[55] *Panama and South Pacific Telegraph Co v India Rubber, Gutta Percha, and Telegraph Works Co* (1875) LR 10 Ch App 515; *Armagas Ltd v Mundogas SA* [1986] AC 717, 742–43; *UBS AG (London Branch) v Kommunale Wasserwerke Leipzig GmbH* [2014] EWHC 3615 (Comm). In some situations, where the briber is the other party to the transaction and knows that the agent acts beyond his actual authority, then the transaction may even be void *ab initio* at common law: Watts and Reynolds (n 11) Art 73.

[56] *Logicrose Ltd v Southend United FC* [1988] 1 WLR 1256 (Ch), 1260–1262 (Millett J)

latter would pay the agent a bribe in order to arrange a licence, for the benefit of the briber, over land owned by Southend United FC. Millett J held that the principal could clearly choose to rescind the licence: '[t]he principal, having been deprived by the other party to the transaction of the disinterested advice of his agent, is entitled to a further opportunity to consider whether it is in his interests to affirm it'.[57]

It is important to note that if the third party was entirely innocent in paying the money over that constituted the bribe—for instance, if the third party did not appreciate that the fiduciary would keep the money for himself—then rescission should not be granted. But this is a rare case. Usually, the briber will know that the fiduciary is committing a breach of duty. In *Logicrose,* Millett J recognised that there is 'no direct authority on the degree of knowledge which he must possess of the existence of the agent's personal interest', but thought that actual knowledge or wilful blindness was necessary.[58] This is sensible, and indeed justified by Millett J partly because of 'a close parallel with the cases on knowing assistance in a breach of trust'.[59] This approach is helpful. Indeed, the judge went on to say:

> In my judgment, the difference between the two lines of authority (that is to say the 'bribery' cases and the 'knowing assistance' cases) lies not in the factual background but in the remedy sought; and the state of mind necessary to make the other party liable ought to be the same whether the claim is for an account of the money which he helped the agent to misappropriate or rescission of the transaction itself.[60]

This is a useful passage, which highlights that the liability of the briber, and the ability of the principal to set aside a transaction entered into with a briber, turns upon the knowledge of the briber.

B. Liability as a Dishonest Assister

It is important to recognise that the briber's liability is accessorial: it arises because of the briber's participation in the fiduciary's breach of duty. The language of 'knowing assistance' was generally employed at the time of *Logicrose*, but the phrase 'dishonest assistance' is now often preferred.[61] For present purposes, little depends upon the label attached to the mental element; it is clear that the defendant must be at fault, and that the approach identified in *Logicrose* remains apt: a briber should only be liable if he actually knew of the principal's rights, or deliberately turned a blind eye to facts he knew which would have led to that conclusion.[62] The focus here is upon the remedies available against the briber for dishonest assistance.

[57] ibid 1261.
[58] ibid.
[59] ibid.
[60] ibid.
[61] See *Royal Brunei* (n 7).
[62] See generally Davies (n 7) ch 4.

i. Loss-Based Claims

In *Royal Brunei Airlines Sdn Bhd v Tan*, Lord Nicholls said that '[a] liability in equity to make good resulting loss attaches to a person who dishonestly procures or assists in a breach of trust or fiduciary obligation'.[63] That an accessory has traditionally been said to be liable as a 'constructive trustee' has led to a general acceptance that an accessory can be liable to compensate the claimant.[64] In *Cowper v Stoneham*,[65] the court held that '[a]ll parties to a breach of trust are equally liable', and more recently in *Ultraframe (UK) Ltd v Fielding*, Lewison J could 'see that it makes sense for a dishonest assistant to be jointly and severally liable for any loss which the beneficiary suffers as a result of a breach of trust'.[66]

The language of 'trustee' in this context is clearly fictional and should be permanently jettisoned;[67] it may have been invoked in order to comply with a traditional rule of trust law that beneficiaries can only sue their trustees.[68] Nevertheless, because of the parasitic—but not necessarily duplicative—nature of accessory liability, the liability of the accessory and primary wrongdoer to compensate the claimant is often the same.[69] But this will not always be the case; since 'breach of trust and dishonest participation in a breach of trust are two species of equitable wrongs',[70] it might be expected that the briber and fiduciary will not always be liable to the same extent. The briber should only be liable for losses to which he has contributed;[71] the fiduciary may have contributed to even greater losses for which the briber does not bear responsibility.

Given the dishonest nature of the briber's wrong, the better view is that he should incur liability for all losses directly caused by the breach of fiduciary duty in which he participated. Arguing that the principal's loss was not 'reasonably foreseeable' is unlikely to avail a dishonest assister. However, the principles concerned with gain-based relief are more difficult.

ii. Gain-Based Claims

Gain-based claims against the briber are also possible. But this is controversial. Whereas a gain-based claim against the recipient of the bribe can readily be

63 *Royal Brunei* (n 7) 392.
64 eg *Casio Computer Ltd v Sayo (No 3)* [2001] EWCA Civ 661, [2001] All ER (D) 147.
65 *Cowper v Stoneham* (1893) 68 LT 18, 19.
66 *Ultraframe (UK) Ltd v Fielding* [2005] EWHC 1638 (Ch), [2006] FSR 17 [1600]; see also *Arab Monetary Fund v Hashim* (*The Times*, 11 October 1994) (Ch) (Chadwick J).
67 See *Williams v Central Bank of Nigeria* [2014] UKSC 10, [2014] AC 1189. Birks thought that the language of 'constructive trust' was 'surplusage': P Birks, 'Trusts in the Recovery of Misapplied Assets: Tracing, Trusts and Restitution' in E McKendrick (ed), *Commercial Aspects of Trusts and Fiduciary Obligations* (Oxford, Clarendon Press, 1992) 149.
68 L Smith, 'Constructive Trusts and Constructive Trustees' (1999) 58 *CLJ* 294, 300.
69 At least towards the claimant: for consideration of issues of contribution, see text to nn 165–70.
70 Lord Nicholls, 'Knowing Receipt: The Need for a New Landmark' in WR Cornish, R Nolan, J O'Sullivan and G Virgo (eds), *Restitution: Past, Present and Future* (Oxford, Hart Publishing, 1998) 244.
71 There is an irrebuttable presumption that the principal will have suffered loss at least equal to the value of the bribe: *Hovenden & Sons v Millhof* (1900) 83 LT 41.

justified on the basis that he is in a fiduciary position and therefore is not entitled to profit from his position,[72] it is clear that the briber does not owe any fiduciary obligations to the principal.[73] Fiduciaries and dishonest assisters should therefore be considered differently. It is suggested that it is right that a briber has to give up his gains, but the justification for that is not the same as that which applies to the wrongdoing fiduciary.

In *Novoship (UK) Ltd v Nikitin*,[74] Mr Mikhaylyuk was the general manager, commercial manager and later a director of the claimant, Novoship (UK) Ltd. Mr Mikhaylyuk was responsible for negotiating the charters of vessels owned by companies within the Novoship group. Mr Mikhaylyuk defrauded Novoship to the advantage of himself and others. As part of his dishonest scheme, Mr Mikhaylyuk breached his fiduciary duty in directing a third party to pay bribes to himself and Amon International Inc, a company owned and controlled by Mr Nikitin. Mr Mikhaylyuk also used his position to arrange charters of vessels ('the Henriot charters') to Henriot Finance Ltd, a British Virgin Islands company which was owned and controlled by Mr Nikitin. It was held that Mr Mikhaylyuk acted in breach of fiduciary duty due to the conflict between his personal interests and duty to his principal; since Mr Nikitin knew of this and nonetheless continued to participate in Mr Mikhaylyuk's schemes, Mr Nikitin was liable for dishonest assistance.[75]

The crux of the appeal in *Novoship* concerned the remedies available against a dishonest assister. The Court of Appeal recognised that, in principle, a gain-based measure of relief is available against the accessory. Longmore LJ, delivering the judgment of the Court, cited with approval[76] the following passage of Gibbs J in *Consul Development Pty Ltd v DPC Estates Pty Ltd*:

> If the maintenance of a very high standard of conduct on the part of fiduciaries is the purpose of the rule it would seem equally necessary to deter other persons from knowingly assisting those in a fiduciary position to violate their duties. If, on the other hand, the rule is to be explained simply because it would be contrary to equitable principles to allow a person to retain a benefit that he had gained from a breach of his fiduciary duty, it would appear equally inequitable that one who knowingly took part in the breach should retain a benefit that resulted therefrom. I therefore conclude, on principle, that a person who knowingly participates in a breach of fiduciary duty is liable to account to the person to whom the duty was owed for any benefit he has received as a result of such participation.[77]

[72] eg *Keech v Sandford* (1726) Sel Cas Ch 61; *Boardman v Phipps* [1967] 2 AC 46; *FHR* (n 1). See also L Smith, 'Fiduciary Relationships: Ensuring the Loyal Exercise of Judgement on Behalf of Another' (2014) 130 *LQR* 608.

[73] *Williams* (n 67).

[74] *Novoship* v *Nikitin* [2014] EWCA Civ 908, [2015] QB 499.

[75] Significantly, the Court of Appeal insisted that there is no need for the breach of fiduciary duty to relate to trust property for accessory liability to arise: ibid [93].

[76] ibid [76].

[77] *Consul Development Pty Ltd v DPC Estates Pty Ltd* (1975) 132 CLR 373, 397.

In *Novoship*, Longmore LJ went on to say that,

> [w]here, as here, the equitable wrong is itself linked with a breach of fiduciary duty we see no reason why a court of equity should not be able to order the wrongdoer to disgorge his profits in so far as they are derived from the wrongdoing.[78]

This decision is welcome. A party who is liable for dishonest assistance cannot sensibly demand that he keep the profits he makes. This is especially significant in the context of bribery: a briber has acted sufficiently badly that an account of profits should, in principle, be an available remedy to the principal who is a victim of the bribery.[79] However, although the remedy of an account of profits is potentially available, the Court of Appeal in *Novoship* held that such a remedy is discretionary, and will not be awarded where it would be 'disproportionate' with the wrongdoing.[80] The meaning of 'disproportionate' in this context is somewhat unclear, but it perhaps emphasises that, especially where the defendant is not a fiduciary, an account of profits is not available as of right. Nevertheless, where the defendant has dishonestly bribed a fiduciary it is difficult to imagine many cases where an account of profits would be 'disproportionate'.

In *Novoship*, the Court of Appeal also insisted that a causal link must be established between the bribery and the profit. On the facts of that case, the focus was on the gains made by Mr Nikitin. The key issue was the profit of almost $109 million that Mr Nikitin made from the Henriot charters. At first instance, Mr Nikitin was ordered to disgorge those profits to the claimant. The Court of Appeal allowed Mr Nikitin's appeal on this point since 'there was an insufficient direct causal connection between entry into the Henriot charters and the resulting profits'.[81] The Court of Appeal emphasised that the Henriot charters were entered into at market rates and were not disadvantageous to the claimant. The Court found that

> what Mr Nikitin acquired as a result of his dishonest assistance (and also as a result of Mr Mikhaylyuk's breach of fiduciary duty) was the use of the vessels at the market rate. That was merely the occasion for him to make a profit. The real or effective cause of the profits was the unexpected change in the market. As the judge recognised … Mr Nikitin made the profits 'because he judged the market well.[82]

The distinction between a breach of duty which causes a loss and one which simply provides the occasion for the loss to be suffered is well established at common law[83] and sensible to apply in this context.

Some sort of 'sufficiently direct' causal link between the accessory's participation in the primary wrong and resulting profits is required.[84] This explains the

[78] *Novoship* (n 74) [84].
[79] See also Law Commission, *Aggravated, Exemplary and Restitutionary Damages* (n 54) Part III.
[80] *Novoship* (n 74) [119]–[120].
[81] ibid [115].
[82] ibid [114].
[83] *Galoo Ltd v Bright Graham Murray* [1994] 1 WLR 1360.
[84] *Novoship* (n 74) [94]–[115] (Longmore LJ), citing J McGhee (ed), *Snell's Equity*, 32nd edn (London, Sweet & Maxwell, 2010) para 30-081.

result in *Fyffes Group Ltd v Templeman*.[85] On the facts of that case, Toulson J ultimately refused to order a defendant to account for the profits he made by bribing the claimant's agent: the claimant would have entered into the transaction with the briber even if the agent had not been bribed, so the briber's profit was not caused by the bribery of the agent.[86] This approach was criticised in *Murad v Al-Saraj*, but only because the liability of accessories was assimilated with the liability of fiduciaries. It is orthodox to conclude that if the conduct of the fiduciary falls within the scope of his fiduciary duty of loyalty, then no further enquiry into whether or not the profits would have been made anyway is appropriate.[87] But accessories are not fiduciaries. The comments of the Court of Appeal in *Murad* on this point were obiter since the claim in that case was brought against a primary wrongdoer and not an accessory; they were rightly disapproved by the Court of Appeal in *Novoship (UK) Ltd v Nikitin*.[88]

In *Novoship*, the Court of Appeal rejected a simple 'but for' test of causation, and instead demanded a 'sufficiently direct' causal connection. This latter concept requires further elucidation. In the context of bribery, it seems to be presumed that the briber will make a gain at least equal to the value of the bribe paid over, so the claim for the bribe itself should be considered to be 'sufficiently direct'. In some instances, the transaction entered into as a result of the bribe will produce further direct profits without the briber doing anything more. Such profits may well exceed the value of the bribe paid, but should nevertheless be recoverable. For example, a briber may pay £10,000 as a bribe to the claimant's agent to accept the briber's bid to carry out building works. It will then be irrebuttably presumed that the briber's profit is at least the amount of the bribe.[89] But the briber may well make more than £10,000 profit from performing such works, and in principle those profits might be disgorged to the claimant.[90]

In some situations, the briber might take profits made from the transaction which was induced by the bribe, and invest that money in shares which double in value. Should the principal be able to recover the uplift in value of the shares? In *Sinclair Investments (UK) Ltd v Versailles Trade Finance Ltd*, Lord Neuberger MR contemplated the possibility of 'extending, or adjusting, the rules relating to equitable compensation',[91] and such a flexible approach to 'equitable compensation' suggests that the answer should possibly be: 'yes'. But on balance that seems inappropriate.[92] The profits made from the shares is not 'sufficiently direct', given

[85] *Fyffes Group Ltd v Templeman* [2000] 2 Lloyd's Rep 643.

[86] The claim for damages was, however, successful. See also Mitchell (n 8).

[87] *Murad v Al-Saraj* [2005] EWCA Civ 959, [2005] WTLR 1573 [69] (Arden LJ), [120] (Jonathan Parker LJ).

[88] *Novoship* (n 74).

[89] *Hovenden & Sons* (n 71).

[90] *Fyffes Group Ltd* (n 85) 672 (Toulson J), citing C Needham, 'Recovering the Profits of Bribery' (1979) 95 *LQR* 536, 548.

[91] *Sinclair* (n 42) [90].

[92] If the opposite were true, then the briber (who of course is not a fiduciary) might nonetheless be entitled to an equitable allowance. Under the Proceeds of Crime Act, it may be possible to confiscate

the subsequent input of the briber to the profits, and the fact that it is further removed from the wrong itself.[93] The only way the principal should be able to trace into the shares is if he has a proprietary interest in the bribe at the outset. In *Novoship*, Mr Nikitin's gain was the opportunity to enter into the Henriot charters, but these were at market rates and not especially advantageous. The profit of $109 million was caused by market fluctuations, which were too remote from the breach of duty. The claimant would have had to establish a proprietary claim in order to strip Mr Nikitin of the uplift in value of the charters, but this was hopeless as the claimant had no proprietary interest in the charters.[94]

The decision in *Novoship* is helpful in making it clear that the remedies available against the fiduciary and the dishonest assister are not the same.[95] The case clearly rejects the view that the liability of the accessory is secondary in the sense of duplicative.[96] This seems entirely appropriate, but the Canadian court in *Canada Safeway Ltd v Thompson*[97] held that an accessory could be jointly and severally liable for the unauthorised profit made by a wrongdoing fiduciary. This result has been supported by Clapton, since '[e]ven if the assistant has not acquired a benefit from the breach, the need to safeguard the relationship of trust and confidence justifies this type of disgorgement award'.[98] But this begins to look like a punitive measure, since the accessory is made to disgorge profits he did not himself make. If such a punitive remedy is available against a briber, there is no reason why it should be assessed by reference to the gain made by the fiduciary. As Christopher Clarke J pointed out at first instance in *Novoship (UK) Ltd v Mikhaylyuk*:

> there is no equity to compel someone who has not made a profit from his breach, or dishonest assistance in that of another, to account for a profit which he has not made and which does not represent a loss which the principal has suffered.[99]

Similarly, the High Court of Australia in *Michael Wilson & Partners Ltd v Nicholls* has found that 'if an account of profits were to be sought against both the defaulting fiduciary and a knowing assistant, the two accounts would very likely differ'.[100]

gains if they constitute 'representative property' of the proceeds of crime (eg s 146(3); s 305), but this is because of wider concerns of public policy, and involves the transfer of gains from the wrongdoer to the state, rather than from the wrongdoer to the principal.

[93] This might be explained on the basis of remoteness of gain: G Virgo, 'Restitutionary Remedies for Wrongs: Causation and Remoteness' in C Rickett (ed), *Justifying Private Law Remedies* (Oxford, Hart Publishing, 2008).

[94] *Novoship* (n 74) [66].

[95] See also *Williams* (n 67).

[96] *cf* SB Elliott and C Mitchell, 'Remedies for Dishonest Assistance' (2004) 67 *MLR* 16.

[97] *Canada Safeway Ltd v Thompson* [1951] 3 DLR 295 (BCSC).

[98] MS Clapton, 'Gain-Based Remedies for Knowing Assistance: Ensuring Assistants do Not Profit from their Wrongs' (2008) 45 *Alberta Law Review* 989, 1010. See also Tucker, Le Poidevin and Brightwell (n 40) para 20-092.

[99] *Novoship* (n 74) [99] (this point was not expressly dealt with by the Court of Appeal, although see [77]).

[100] *Michael Wilson & Partners Ltd v Nicholls* [2011] HCA 48, (2011) 244 CLR 427 [106].

Nevertheless, the decision in *Novoship* has been criticised. For example, Devonshire has argued that gain-based relief should only be available against a defendant who procures or induces a breach of fiduciary duty, rather than a defendant who 'only' assists the breach of fiduciary duty.[101] Such a distinction is possible, and was for some time crucial to establishing accessory liability: the primary wrong of breach of trust needed to be dishonest for the third party to be liable as an assister,[102] but the third party could be liable as an inducer or procurer even if the primary wrong was not dishonest.[103] This distinction seems to continue to be important in Australia.[104]

However, the distinction between inducement and assistance is incredibly difficult to draw and it does not seem worth the effort.[105] Indeed, even in the context of bribery it is suggested that the complexities that would arise in trying to distinguish inducement from assistance are not worth it. Does it really matter whether the idea of the bribe originated with the fiduciary or with the briber? After all, even if the conduct of the briber constitutes assistance rather than inducement it may well be the case that there would not have been any breach of duty without that assistance.[106] It is suggested that Millett J was correct in *Logicrose* to insist that it is 'immaterial whether the initiative for the agent's taking an interest of his own came from the agent himself or from the other party to the transaction'.[107]

Devonshire argues that in instances of inducement or procurement an 'equitable wrong' is committed which 'engages the deterrent principle and lends weight to accountability for consequential gains'.[108] Yet it is not at all obvious why the same cannot be said about assistance. Devonshire writes that '[b]y instigating the breach, the third party is effectively a primary wrongdoer. In these circumstances, it is not anomalous to impose a full gamut of remedies for his or her participation in the substantive wrong'.[109] But it would appear that a dishonest assister is also a primary wrongdoer; the elements of the wrong are different from that of breach of fiduciary duty, which leads to different remedies. It is not clear why dishonest assisters should not similarly have to account for their profits.

One reason advanced by Devonshire is that an analogy should be made to the common law tort of fraud or deceit: as a common law wrong, the claimant should be limited to a claim for damages, and unable to disgorge the accessory's gains.

101 P Devonshire, 'Account of Profits for Dishonest Assistance' (2015) 74 *CLJ* 222.

102 *Barnes v Addy* (1874) LR 9 Ch App 244 (CA).

103 eg *Fyler v Fyler* (1841) 3 Beav 550; *Attorney-General v The Corporation of Leicester* (1844) 7 Beav 176.

104 *Farah Constructions Pty Ltd v Say-Dee Pty Ltd* [2007] HCA 222, (2007) 230 CLR 89.

105 P Sales, 'The Tort of Conspiracy and Civil Secondary Liability' (1990) 49 *CLJ* 491, 507–08; C Harpum, 'The Basis of Equitable Liability' in P Birks (ed), *The Frontiers of Liability*, vol 1 (Oxford, OUP, 1994); Davies (n 7) ch 4.

106 eg *JD Wetherspoon plc v Van de Berg & Co Ltd* [2009] EWHC 639 (Ch) [518] (Peter Smith J). See also the facts of *Mahesan*, considered in text to n 153.

107 *Logicrose* (n 56) 1261.

108 Devonshire (n 101) 232.

109 ibid.

But this is unconvincing. Although it is true that dishonest assistance has been described as an 'equitable tort',[110] attempts to impose common law liability upon a party who participates in an equitable wrong have consistently been rebuffed.[111] And even if that divide between common law and equitable wrongs is considered to be an accident of history that could be corrected, it is far from obvious that equity should adopt the approach of the common law rather than vice versa. Although current orthodoxy appears to be that restitutionary damages are not available for the tort of deceit,[112] this might be criticised. After all, punitive damages might be awarded in tort,[113] and why should a defendant who deliberately or recklessly commits a wrong *never* be subject to a restitutionary award of damages? Such an award would not be made automatically and in all instances, but seems to be an appropriate weapon in the judicial arsenal. The Law Commission thought that where the defendant's conduct showed a 'deliberate and outrageous disregard of the plaintiff's rights' restitutionary damages should be awarded',[114] which tends to indicate that the equitable position is preferable to that at common law.

Indeed, even at common law the position concerning deceit is difficult. That restitutionary damages are not available seems to be the result of *Halifax Building Society v Thomas*.[115] That case concerned a mortgage fraud by a borrower, which led to the lender choosing to sell the security. There was a surplus after the sale, which the lender claimed for itself. The Court of Appeal held that the claim should fail, apparently on the basis that gain-based awards are not available in the tort of deceit. But that was not necessary for the decision: the bank had actually affirmed the mortgage and obtained full satisfaction, and so did not choose to avoid the mortgage and rely upon the fraud. Interestingly, at first instance in *Murad v Al-Saraj*, Etherton J was prepared to grant restitutionary damages in the tort of deceit, and explicitly distinguished the *Halifax* case because there no loss was suffered and the lender had affirmed the contract.[116] This was branded a 'novel step' by Arden LJ in the Court of Appeal,[117] but in fact there was old authority in favour of such approach[118] and it does not seem inappropriate. At the very least, the position as regards restitutionary damages in tort is somewhat unclear and in many respects unsatisfactory,[119] and a shaky foundation from which to develop the law of accessory liability in equity.

From a very different angle, Gummow has argued that the result in *Novoship* was too generous to the dishonest accessory, and that the trial judge was correct

[110] *Abou-Rahmah v Abacha* [2006] EWCA Civ 1492, [2007] 1 Lloyd's Rep 115 [2] (Rix LJ).
[111] *Metall und Rohstoff AG v Donaldson Lufkin & Jenrette Inc* [1990] 1 QB 391 (CA), 481 (Slade LJ).
[112] *Devenish* (n 10).
[113] *Kuddus v Chief Constable of Leicestershire Constabulary* [2001] UKHL 29, [2002] 2 AC 122.
[114] Law Commission, *Aggravated, Exemplary and Restitutionary Damages* (n 54) para 3.49.
[115] *Halifax* (n 10) 229.
[116] *Murad v Al-Saraj* [2004] EWHC 1235 (Ch), [345]–[347] (Etherton J).
[117] *Murad* (n 87). The Court of Appeal did not need to decide on the common law claim.
[118] *Hill v Perrott* (1810) 3 Taunt 274.
[119] In particular, the Court of Appeal appears to restrict gain-based relief in tort to 'proprietary torts': eg, *Forsyth-Grant v Allen* [2008] EWCA Civ 505, [2008] 2 EGLR 16; *Devenish* (n 10). See also O Odudu and G Virgo, 'Inadequacy of Compensatory Damages' [2009] 17 *Restitution Law Review* 112.

to strip the defendant of his profits.[120] This is because 'the profit for which the account was sought was derived "by reason of" the dishonest assistance because that dishonesty at least materially contributed to, even if not immediately causing, the derivation of the profit on the Henriot charters'.[121] This takes a much more generous view (from the principal's perspective) of causation. On balance, it is suggested that such an approach is too harsh. In relying upon cases such as *Boardman v Phipps*, Gummow closely links the liability of the fiduciary and accessory in a way which threatens to blur the clear distinction that has recently been drawn between the liability incurred by a party as a result of the fiduciary obligations he owes, and the liability of another party who owes no fiduciary obligations at all. Given that the accessory has not voluntarily undertaken to act loyally as a fiduciary, a more stringent test of causation for gain-based remedies seems appropriate.

There is, however, a potential issue that arises when quantifying the profits made by the briber. A briber might pay £1,000 as a bribe, and consequently make profits of £4,000.[122] If an account of profits is ordered, should the briber have to pay £4,000 (the gross profits received by the briber) or £3,000 (the net profits received, once the money paid as a bribe is taken into account)? There is a general tendency only to order an account of the net profits made, and, since the claim itself is for bribery, courts may understandably incline towards ordering an account of £3,000 only. Without the bribe the claim does not get off the ground, so it might be consistent to take the bribe into account. Yet it is conceivable that the principal may contend that the briber should not be allowed to reduce the account of profits below £4,000 as this would involve the briber's relying upon his own illegal conduct in paying the bribe.[123] If such an argument were to succeed that may be thought to have a punitive effect, which, as has been seen,[124] is not generally favoured in equity. Given equity's traditional refusal to recognise a jurisdiction to punish, it seems unlikely that a punitive award would be made against a briber. Admittedly, in this context as well a refusal to award punitive remedies may appear unduly restrictive. Not all instances of bribery are the same, and so not all bribers should be made to pay punitive damages, but in some situations the briber will have deliberately set out to corrupt a beneficiary and cause harm to the principal. In such cases, the briber will have acted dishonestly and outrageously, which is surely when punitive damages are most appropriate. Indeed, a person who induces a tort or a breach of contract might be subject to a punitive award,[125] so it seems somewhat odd that a punitive award might never be made against a person who induces a breach of fiduciary duty.

[120] W Gummow, 'Dishonest Assistance and Account of Profits' (2015) 74 *CLJ* 405.

[121] ibid 409.

[122] See also *Mahesan*, considered in text to n 153.

[123] *cf Tinsley v Milligan* [1994] 1 AC 340; although see now *Patel v Mirza* [2016] UKSC 42, [2016] 3 WLR 399. In *Logicrose*, the principal was able to keep the bribe monies regardless of whether he elected to rescind or to affirm the transaction.

[124] See text to nn 51–54.

[125] This appears to have been assumed in *East England Schools CIC v Palmer* [2013] EWHC 4138 (QB), [2014] IRLR 191 [133]–[136] (Richard Salter QC); see also *HL Weiss Forwarding Ltd v Omnus* [1976] 1 SCR 776, (1976) 63 DLR (3d) 654 (SCC); *Texaco Inc v Pennzoil* 729 SW 2d 768 (Tex 1988).

Finally, it is appropriate to emphasise that the briber does not hold any of his profits on constructive trust in English law. Such a trust would be a remedial constructive trust, which has been clearly rejected in England and Wales.[126] The language of 'constructive trustee' to encompass the liability of the accessory does now seem to be fading away,[127] but references to the accessory incurring liability as if he were a trustee do sometimes linger on.[128] Such references should not be interpreted to mean that profits are held on trust, but rather that both loss-based and gain-based claims can be pursued against an accessory in the same way as is possible against a wrongdoing trustee.

V. Combining Remedies

Combining claims and remedies is a notoriously tricky topic. It is very difficult to be clear about when remedies can be awarded cumulatively or only as alternatives. This is hard when there is only one defendant; the problems multiply when additional defendants are factored in. Thus, where there is both a briber and bribee the law is far from easy. It is helpful first to start with the more straightforward case of only one defendant, before tackling the more complicated scenarios involving two defendants.

A. Situations Involving One Defendant: *Tang Man Sit v Capacious Investments Ltd*

Perhaps the leading decision on election between remedies in equity is now the decision of the Privy Council in *Tang Man Sit v Capacious Investments Ltd*.[129] This has been accepted as accurately stating English law.[130] Essentially, the case concerned a defendant who held houses on trust for the claimant. The defendant made profits from renting out the houses, and the claimant suffered losses from not being able to use the properties, and also from their diminution in value due to their wrongful use and occupation of the houses; the houses had badly deteriorated due to over-occupation by tenants. The Privy Council held that an account of the profits the trustee received from letting the houses was not cumulative with

[126] See Lord Neuberger in *FHR* (n 1) [47]. See also Lord Neuberger, 'The Remedial Constructive Trust—Fact or Fiction' (New Zealand Banking Services and Finance Law Association Conference, Queenstown, 10 August 2014): www.supremecourt.uk/docs/speech-140810.pdf.

[127] See n 67.

[128] eg *Novoship* (n 74) [75].

[129] *Tang Man Sit v Capacious Investments Ltd* [1996] 1 AC 514. The thrust of this judgment is consistent with the earlier decision of the House of Lords in *United Australia Ltd v Barclays Bank Ltd* [1941] AC 1.

[130] eg *Ramzan v Brookwide Ltd* [2011] EWCA Civ 985, [2012] 1 All ER 903.

but rather an alternative to damages for loss of use and occupation. The claimant had to make an election between the gain-based and loss-based remedies. However, that election was held not to be made simply because the claimant had accepted from the defendant some of the rents which had been paid. The claimant's right to elect between two measures is only lost once the claimant has all the information which enables him meaningfully to make an election; this may occur only after the process of discovery has finished.[131]

In giving the advice of the board, Lord Nicholls said:

> Sometimes the two remedies are alternative and inconsistent. The classic example, indeed, is (1) an account of profits made by a defendant in breach of his fiduciary obligations and (2) damages for the loss suffered by the plaintiff by reason of the same breach. The former is measured by the wrongdoer's gain, the latter by the injured party's loss. [...] Faced with alternative and inconsistent remedies a plaintiff must choose, or elect, between them. He cannot have both.[132]

It should nevertheless be observed that the two remedies will not inevitably be inconsistent. A principal may sue for an account of profits even when he suffers no loss. So if the principal has also suffered loss, it might seem logical for him to be able to sue for that loss as well as the fiduciary's gains, which would have been available in any event.[133] Claiming one should not necessarily preclude the other. As the Law Commission concluded:

> [U]ltimately the law is requiring an 'election' where it is not really necessary; the two remedies are not inevitably inconsistent. The 'principled' approach would be to recognize this, to remove any mandatory requirement of election, to allow a plaintiff to claim compensation and restitution, and for the court to resolve the problem of double recovery at the stage of assessing quantum.[134]

The question should therefore really be focused upon whether awarding both remedies would lead to 'excessive remedial cumulations'.[135] It may be that the deterrent function which would be fulfilled by a gain-based remedy, for example, would be adequately satisfied by a loss-based remedy, thereby eliminating the need for a gain-based award. But in principle the two are not inconsistent; it is simply a matter of determining whether the claimant would recover more than what is required in order to fulfil the goals to which the relevant remedies are directed.

Indeed, Tettenborn has argued that a principal should be able to recover both his loss and the agent's gain:

> [R]ecovery of the amount of a bribe from a dishonest agent is a recovery of a completely 'different kind' from recovery of the loss caused by his corrupt conduct. The former is

[131] See also *Island Records Ltd v Tring International Plc* [1996] 1 WLR 1256 (Lightman J).

[132] *Tang Man Sit* (n 129) 521.

[133] P Birks, 'Inconsistency Between Compensation and Restitution' (1996) 112 *LQR* 375. See also *Salford v Lever* [1891] 1 QB 168 (CA), considered in text to n 145.

[134] Law Commission, *Aggravated, Exemplary and Restitutionary Damages* (n 54) para 3.71; *cf* M Tilbury, *Civil Remedies: Volume 1* (Sydney, Butterworths, 1990) para 20–27.

[135] S Watterson, 'Alternative and Cumulative Remedies: What is the Difference?' (2003) 11 *Restitution Law Review* 7.

> basically penal (or at least deterrent), the latter compensatory; the measure of the former calculated on the bribe received, that of the latter on the loss suffered; the former is not dependent on wrongful or reprehensible conduct, the latter requires a wrongful act on the part of the defendant. In short, the measure the purpose and the prerequisites of such recovery are completely different.[136]

Moreover, the view that a claimant must elect between a compensatory and restitutionary measure, because every penny of gain given up by the defendant reduces the claimant's loss by a penny, and that every penny paid by the defendant as compensation reduces his gain by a penny, might be doubted. Personal gain-based claims are for value received, not value retained, so it generally does not matter if the defendant still has the gain or not. That the defendant has had to pay some money as compensation might therefore be considered not to affect the gain-based claim.[137]

On balance, though, since the gain and loss both flow from the same wrong, it seems natural to link the two.[138] This might help to justify why *Tang Man Sit* suggests that, as against the fiduciary (or briber), the principal should elect between pursuing a gain-based remedy or a loss-based remedy. This is a blunt approach to the issue, but it is generally satisfactory where only one defendant is concerned.[139] If the gain is greater than the loss, then the gain-based remedy will serve the dual functions of ensuring that the principal suffers no loss and deterring the breach of duty, since the fiduciary would not be left with any profits. Similarly, if the compensation claim is worth more than a gain-based claim, then the compensatory measure will still deter the breach of duty (since the fiduciary is left with no profits) and also satisfy the need to compensate the principal.

However, it should be observed that whilst this works satisfactorily where only one defendant and one wrong is at issue, it is not so clear whether this is appropriate

[136] A Tettenborn, 'Bribery, Corruption and Restitution: The Strange Case of Mr Mahesan' (1979) 95 *LQR* 68, 75. See also *Salford* (n 133), considered in text to n 145. In *Stevens v Premium Real Estate Ltd* [2009] NZSC 15, [2009] 2 NZLR 384 the Supreme Court of New Zealand allowed a principal to recover both its loss and the commission paid to the agent, but there the commission came from the principal and not a briber, and was recoverable on the basis of total failure of consideration: see also P Watts, 'Commercial Decisions in the Supreme Court of New Zealand: The Prominence of Agency Law in the First Ten Years' in A Stockley and M Littlewood (eds), *The New Zealand Supreme Court: The First Ten Years* (Auckland, LexisNexis, 2015) 195–97.

[137] Birks, 'Inconsistency Between Compensation and Restitution' (n 133) 378; Tettenborn insisted that there was no public policy reason against double recovery, and noted that '[i]n the field of personal injury, for instance, "collateral" payments made to the plaintiff are not deducted from damages received, even though as a matter of fact it is hard to escape the conclusion that the plaintiff's loss is reduced as a result of them': ibid.

[138] Watterson (n 135). Moreover, where the claim is brought against the briber rather than bribee, then it seems less satisfactory to sue the briber for both restitutionary and compensatory damages, since the briber never undertook to act loyally as a fiduciary; as the Court of Appeal emphasised in *Novoship* (n 74), the remedy of an account of profits is discretionary.

[139] D Hayton, P Matthews and C Mitchell, *Underhill and Hayton: Law of Trusts and Trustees*, 18th edn (London, LexisNexis, 2010) para 87.72: 'In respect of a particular breach of duty, it is not possible to approbate and to reprobate, to adopt and to disavow, to blow hot and to blow cold. Suing for profits adopts the trustee's conduct whilst claiming compensation rejects such conduct'.

where there are multiple claims and multiple defendants. For instance, it may be that the fiduciary accepts a bribe of £1,000, and this causes loss to the principal of £3,000. In that situation, it would seem that the principal could not recover any more than £3,000, since that would be excessive (unless a punitive award were made). An easy way for the principal to recover £3,000 would be to say that he elects to recover for his loss. But the £3,000 total might also be reached by asking for the full gain-based amount (£1,000) plus partial compensation (£2,000). This alternative might be particularly significant when seeking to combine the claim against the fiduciary with a claim against the accessory, and this issue must now be analysed.

B. Situations Involving Two Defendants

There are conflicting streams of authority surrounding the question of whether the principal can combine a loss-based claim against one defendant with a gain-based claim against another. The first suggests that the remedies available against the briber can be claimed in addition to those available against the recipient of the bribe. The second suggests that a claimant must choose to recover either his gain or his loss, and that 'double recovery' is not possible. This is a difficult issue, but on balance it is suggested that the first line of authority should be preferred.

It is important to note that the focus of present concern is upon whether a loss-based claim against one defendant can be combined with a gain-based claim against another. Once the claimant has recovered his loss from one defendant, he cannot then ask to recover his loss from the other. Instead, the loss might be apportioned between the two defendants in an action for contribution,[140] but this does not affect the claimant.[141] Moreover, the claimant may seek two independent accounts of profits from the briber and bribee. As the High Court of Australia observed in *Michael Wilson & Partners Ltd v Nicholls*, 'if an account of profits were to be sought against both the defaulting fiduciary and a knowing assistant, the two accounts would very likely differ'.[142] The remedy of an account of profits is personal to a particular defendant, and so should be assessed solely by reference to the gains made by that defendant. After all, on one view an account of profits gives a claimant something of a windfall,[143] and once this is accepted there seems little reason to limit the claimant to one windfall from one defendant rather than two windfalls from two defendants. In addition, it has been held that the principal can sue his agent for the value of the bribe, regardless of whether or not he chose to rescind the transaction entered into with the briber.[144] More serious problems are encountered when seeking to combine claims for both gain and loss.

[140] Considered in text to nn 165–70.
[141] eg J Beatson and F Reynolds, 'Bribery of Agent' (1978) 94 *LQR* 344, 346.
[142] *Michael Wilson* (n 100).
[143] eg *Halifax* (n 10) 229 (Glidewell LJ).
[144] *Logicrose* (n 56).

i. Cumulating Remedies

In order to understand why it is possible to argue that the remedies against the briber and recipient of the bribe can be cumulated it is important to appreciate that two wrongs are at issue. The liability of the recipient is for breach of fiduciary duty. The briber, on the other hand, commits no breach of fiduciary duty. The briber commits the distinct wrong of dishonestly assisting (or inducing) a breach of fiduciary duty. Of course, dishonest assistance is parasitic upon there being a primary breach of fiduciary duty, and to that extent the two wrongs are linked, but the liability of the accessory is for his own wrong, not the wrong committed by the fiduciary. This creates the conceptual space for the remedies available against the two defendants to differ. It also explains why remedies may be sought in addition to one another, rather than in the alternative.

In *The Mayor, Alderman, and Burgesses of the Borough of Salford v Lever*,[145] the Court of Appeal took the view that the claimants could recover the amount of the bribe received from their agent, and also sue the briber for losses sustained as a result of the agent's disloyalty. The claimants were proprietors of gasworks, and the defendant was a coal merchant who submitted tenders for the supply of coal. The defendant had previously agreed to pay to the claimants' manager a bribe of 1*s* per ton, and consequently increased the prices in his tenders by 1*s* per ton. The claimants' manager advised the claimant to accept the defendant's tender. The claimants later discovered that their manager had committed various corrupt acts of a similar nature, entered into an agreement with their manager that he would assist them in bringing claims against various contractors, including the defendant, and that he would guarantee that at least 10,000*l* would be recovered by depositing at a bank securities worth 10,000*l*. The claimants subsequently sued the defendant, and the defendant argued that it was a joint wrongdoer with the manager, and that as a result the agreement between the claimants and the manager—together with the deposit of the securities—amounted to a discharge of the manager and thereby also a discharge of the defendant.

The Court of Appeal rejected the defendant's argument. The defendant and the manager were not jointly liable for a single wrong. The payer of the bribe and recipient of the bribe are liable for two distinct wrongs, even if the liability of the briber is dependent upon the primary wrong committed by the bribee.[146] As Lord Esher MR remarked, the fraud of the agent was 'separate and distinct' from that of the briber.[147] This led his Lordship to conclude that the briber 'was bound to pay back the extra price which he had received, and he could not absolve himself or diminish the damages by reason of the principal having recovered from the agent

[145] *Salford* (n 133).

[146] It is suggested that this is generally true in all instances of accessory liability: see Davies (n 7) 83–85, 284–85.

[147] *Salford* (n 133) 176.

the bribe which he had received'.[148] Lindley LJ was similarly forthright, expressing the view that

> it does not lie in the mouth of the defendant, who is a wrongdoer, to say that his liability to account to the corporation for the money received by him is to be determined by the circumstance whether they have already recovered from [the manager] Hunter the money received by him.[149]

In taking this approach, the court in *Salford v Lever* followed the earlier decision of the Court of Appeal in *Bagnall v Carlton*.[150] In that case, the principal brought an action against the briber for rescission of the transaction entered into as a result of the bribery, and a separate action against the agent for recovery of the bribe. The action against the briber was compromised, on the basis that the briber paid a sum of money to the principal, and the contract remained on foot. The Court was clear that this did not affect the principal's cause of action against his agent. James LJ said that this claim 'was, in truth, a totally distinct and separate' claim from that against the briber.[151] As far as the agent was concerned, the settlement with the briber was *res inter alios acta*.

Salford v Lever and *Bagnall v Carlton* are consistent decisions that suggest that the principal is able to sue his agent for a gain-based remedy, regardless of any claims brought against the briber. The inverse proposition is also true: a gain-based claim can be brought against the briber, regardless of any remedy obtained from the agent. As the headnote to *Salford v Lever* observes, 'the principal has two distinct and cumulative remedies'.[152]

However, these decisions of the English Court of Appeal were both doubted by the Privy Council in *Mahesan S/O Thambiah Appellant v Malaysia Government Officers' Co-Operative Housing Society Ltd*.[153] The Board emphasised that in *Salford* the only issue was a claim against the briber, and not any claim against the agent; there was no issue of double recovery against the briber.[154] Similarly, in *Bagnall* there was no question of double recovery against the agent.[155] The Privy Council was very concerned not to allow the principal double recovery against the same defendant. Indeed, that was the issue in that case. The agent of a housing society dishonestly agreed with Mahesan that the latter would purchase land which was for sale at a low price, and then sell it to the housing society for a profit. As part of the agreement, Mahesan paid a bribe of $122,000, but went on to make a net profit of $443,000. The Malaysian Federal Court held that the housing society could sue the agent both for the amount of the bribes, and also damages for the whole of the

[148] ibid 177.
[149] ibid 180.
[150] *Bagnall v Carlton* (1877) LR 6 Ch D 371.
[151] ibid 399 (James LJ), 404 (Baggallay LJ).
[152] This headnote was recognised as accurate by Lord Diplock in *Mahesan* (n 49) 381.
[153] *Mahesan* (n 49).
[154] ibid 379.
[155] ibid 380.

loss suffered. The Privy Council overturned that decision: as against the agent, the principal had to elect between the loss-based and gain-based remedy.

Mahesan has been approved by the Privy Council in *Tang Man Sit*,[156] and is sometimes thought to represent a decisive departure from *Salford v Lever*.[157] But as a strict matter of precedent in English law that seems unlikely to be true,[158] and it is important to appreciate that the focus of the advice in *Mahesan* was really upon double recovery against a single defendant. The Privy Council was critical of *Lever* to the extent that no regard was taken of the fact that the loss sustained by the claimant was reduced by the amount of the bribe recovered from the agent.[159] *Mahesan* might therefore support the view that a claimant must make a general election between a compensatory and restitutionary measure that applies to all its claims. This seems unsatisfactory; it would be preferable to allow the principal to make a separate election as against each defendant for each wrong.[160]

Lever and *Mahesan* might be reconciled on the basis that, in *Lever*, distinct claims were pursued against two separate defendants, whereas in *Mahesan*, claims for two different remedies were brought against the same defendant.[161] But *Mahesan* was clearly critical of the reasoning in *Lever*. If a choice is to be made between the two decisions, it is suggested that *Lever* is to be preferred, at least where there are two defendants for two different wrongs; the remedies sought against the briber and bribee need not be the same and can feasibly be accumulated. As long as the claimant is not recovering twice over for the same loss, then it does not seem objectionable for him to recover his loss from one defendant and strip the gains made by another.

This approach raises difficult questions concerning precisely what the claimant is recovering. Take the example, given above, where the fiduciary accepts a bribe of £1,000, and this causes loss to the principal of £3,000. And then further imagine that the briber makes a profit of £5,000 from the transaction entered into as a result of the bribe. If the principal first sues the briber, then it would be sensible to seek a gain-based remedy (£5,000 is obviously greater than £3,000). On one view, this might mean that the principal is unable to sue the agent for anything, since by recovering £5,000 the principal's loss is wiped out and his grievance satisfied. However, it is suggested that such an outcome would be unsatisfactory: at the very least, the agent should not be left with a profit of £1,000. It would therefore seem

[156] *Tang Man Sit* (n 129) 524–25.

[157] Tucker, Le Poidevin and Brightwell (n 40) para 20-069; Watts and Reynolds (eds) (n 11) para 8-222; H Beale et al, *Chitty on Contracts*, 32nd edn (London, Sweet & Maxwell) para 31-132.

[158] Although the status of Privy Council decisions in English law seems to be changing: *Willers v Joyce* [2016] UKSC 44; [2016] 3 WLR 534.

[159] *Mahesan* (n 49) 381.

[160] *cf Spring Form Inc v Toy Brokers Ltd* [2002] FSR 276 (Ch D); criticised by L Bentley and C Mitchell, 'Combining Money Awards for Patent Infringement' (2003) 11 *Restitution Law Review* 79.

[161] In *Novoship (UK) Ltd v Mikhaylyuk* [2012] EWHC 3586 (Comm) [93], Christopher Clarke J at first instance said that a principal can seek an account of profits from a dishonest assister 'as an alternative to equitable compensation'; this is consistent with the judgment of the Court of Appeal (n 78). See also *Shell International Trading & Shipping Co Ltd v Tikhonov* [2010] EWHC 1399 (QB) [29] (Jack J); *Otkritie International Investment Management Ltd v Urumov* [2014] EWHC 191 (Comm) [71] (Eder J).

that the principal can obtain an account of profits from the fiduciary as well. But it is more difficult to determine whether the principal could choose to sue the agent for his loss of £3,000 rather than the £1,000 profit made by the agent, having already sued the briber.

In principle, this result seems possible. After all, if the agent was the only party sued, he could not complain about having to pay £3,000 as compensation. And if the briber was the only party sued, he could not complain about having to give up £5,000 profits. There is a strong argument that neither should be in a better position because there is an extra wrongdoer involved, and because the principal only elects to recover a compensatory remedy against one defendant (not both) there is no double recovery. If correct, the principal could recover £8,000 in total. However, although this might not constitute 'double recovery', it could possibly be thought to represent 'excessive recovery'. In order to reduce the recoverable amount, it might be preferable to consider that when the £5,000 was recovered from the briber, then £3,000 of that was compensation for loss, and £2,000 restitution of gain. That would mean that in a subsequent action against the agent, the principal could only recover the £1,000 profit made by the agent, since his loss has already been accounted for. On this approach, the briber might consequently be able to seek contribution from the fiduciary for the compensatory element of the monetary award made.[162]

This reasoning might further explain why the principal can cumulate remedies against the briber and bribee: one party should not be absolved from all liability just because a claim has already been brought or settled against another. Indeed, the logic of this analysis should apply equally to situations where the agent is sued first, rather than the briber; it should not matter which claim is brought first.[163] The major restriction concerns recovering twice over for the same loss, but the gains made by each defendant are personal to them and can be disgorged.

If it is correct in the above example that the £5,000 required to be paid by the briber can be broken down and analysed as £3,000 compensation and £2,000 restitution then this might indicate that the compensatory remedy takes some sort of priority. Indeed, it is said that the remedy of an account of profits is discretionary,[164] and in situations where there are claims for both gains and losses it may be that the restitutionary award is only necessary to the extent that a compensatory remedy would fail adequately to deter the defendant from committing the wrong. However, deciding how to apportion the money between gain and loss is not at all easy, and it is suggested that a 'compensation first' approach would be too simplistic. For instance, if the briber only made a profit of £500 rather than £5,000, then the principal would choose to recover £3,000 from the briber, since this is the value of the principal's loss. But even this award should perhaps be considered to be £500 restitution of gain and £2,500 compensation for loss, so that the principal can next

162 See text to nn 165–70.
163 See *Salford* (n 133) 176 (Lord Esher MR), 180 (Lindley LJ), 181–82 (Lopes LJ).
164 *Novoship* (n 74) [119]–[120].

sue the agent for £1,500: a gain of £1,000 and loss of £500. Although this may look like the principal is suing the same defendant for gain and loss—something which is contrary to *Tang Man Sit* and *Mahesan*—here that should be acceptable because the total amount awarded is less than a full compensatory award. This also indicates that where the gain exceeds the loss, the monetary award should represent first the full total of the loss and then a gain-based element, whereas where the loss exceeds the gain, the sum awarded should represent first the gain-based element and then compensation. In this way the principal is not prejudiced by bringing his claim against one defendant before the other.

It is important to be clear about the compensatory element of any monetary award because that might be significant for the purposes of any claim in contribution. The briber may seek contribution from the bribee regarding any compensation that has to be paid, and vice versa, but contribution should not be available for the personal gain-based claim, since the disgorgement of gains is personal to a particular defendant.[165] One potential difficulty with a claim in contribution was raised by Lindley LJ in *Salford v Lever*, when he said that 'the present action is, in reality though not in form, an action by one thief against another to recover part of the plunder'.[166] Where both the briber and bribee have committed a criminal offence then it may be that no claim in contribution should lie. However, the courts have generally been prepared to contemplate contribution in proceedings linked to fraud,[167] and the courts have shown themselves increasingly willing to consider disputes between parties tainted by illegality.[168] It is perhaps likely that in most instances—absent the most serious of bribes and frauds—the court would entertain a claim for contribution.[169]

Admittedly, it is not at all clear how the court would apportion the liability to pay compensation between the parties. Given the wide range of factual scenarios that may arise, it is impossible to provide concrete guidance. Indeed, section 2(1) of the Civil Liability (Contribution) Act 1978 provides that 'the amount of the contribution recoverable from any person shall be such as may be found by the court to be just and equitable having regard to the extent of that person's responsibility for the damage in question', which clearly gives the court much room for manoeuvre. Harpum has suggested that an inducer might bear greater responsibility for loss than the party who was induced, but this is only one factor to consider. In the context of bribery, the lack of clarity in this area might not cause too much concern: both the briber and bribee have acted reprehensibly, and perhaps some lack of clarity is a price to be paid for their conduct.

[165] *cf Charter plc v City Index Ltd* [2007] EWCA Civ 1382, [2008] Ch 313.

[166] *Salford* (n 133) 180; *cf Taylor v Bhail* [1996] CLC 377.

[167] eg *Dubai Aluminium Co Ltd v Salaam* [2002] UKHL 48, [2003] 2 AC 366.

[168] eg *Saunders v Edwards* [1987] 1 WLR 1116 (CA); *Townsend v Persistence Holdings* [2008] UKPC 15.

[169] This conclusion seems to be reinforced by the recent decision of the Supreme Court concerning the defence of illegality: *Patel v Mirza* [2016] UKSC 42, [2016] 3 WLR 399.

Finally, it should be noted that if punitive awards are possible, these should be considered to be personal to each particular defendant, so the imposition or not of a punitive award against one defendant should not affect the question of whether a punitive remedy should be awarded against another defendant. However, it has been suggested that in cases where there are multiple, joint defendants, then punitive damages should not exceed the lowest sum that any of the defendants ought to pay.[170] This seems inappropriate in its own terms: joint and several liability for punitive damages should not be accepted. Any punitive award should be assessed separately for each wrong and each wrongdoer, taking into account each individual defendant's conduct.[171] This would be important in the context of bribery, since the briber and bribee are liable for distinct wrongs.

VI. Conclusion

Equitable claims and remedies will undoubtedly remain significant in combating bribery. Understanding the key issues regarding equitable liability addressed in this chapter is therefore important. It is crucial to understand that the briber and recipient of the bribe commit distinct wrongs. As a result, the remedy against each may differ, but those remedies may also be combined. Recognition of the fact that two separate wrongs are at issue—one by the briber, one by the bribee—should help to lead to greater clarity when considering how the available remedies should be assessed.

[170] *Cassell & Co Ltd v Broome* [1972] AC 1027 (HL) 1063 (Lord Hailsham LC), 1090 (Lord Reid); *Francis v Brown* (1997) 30 HLR 143 (CA); *Rowlands v Chief Constable of Merseyside Police* [2006] EWCA Civ 1773, [2007] 1 WLR 1065 [38].

[171] See Law Commission, *Aggravated, Exemplary and Restitutionary Damages* (n 54) paras 5.186–5.208.

11

Accessory Disloyalty: Comparative Perspectives on Substantial Assistance to Fiduciary Breach

DEBORAH A DEMOTT*

I. Introduction

Culpable participation in another actor's wrongful conduct is an independent basis for liability, that of an accessory. Much about this contingent form of liability is open to dispute, including the operative definition of participation and other elements requisite to establishing liability, as well as whether criteria for liability should operate uniformly regardless of the field of substantive law that defines the primary wrong. Moreover, a primary wrongdoer's liability may be grounded in a type or degree of culpability that does not match the accessory's, leading to outcomes that may seem asymmetrical. To illuminate these questions and their consequences, this chapter draws contrasts between the law in the United States and the United Kingdom, focusing on accessory liability when the primary wrong constitutes a breach of fiduciary duty.

In both jurisdictions, accessory liability is controversial but for reasons distinctive to each. In the United States, well-established general doctrine defines the elements requisite to establishing accessory liability, whether stemming from breach of fiduciary duty or another wrongful act.[1] What prompts controversy is how the doctrine applies to categories of actors, most recently investment bankers who advise boards of target companies in merger-and-acquisition (M&A) transactions. When the Delaware Supreme Court upheld a $75.8 million judgment against an

* For comments on earlier drafts, I thank Jo Braithwaite, as well as Paul Davies, Richard Nolan and the other participants at the conference.

[1] Tortious interference with a contract has long been treated separately and is outside the scope of this chapter: see American Law Institute, *Restatement (Second) of Torts* (St Paul, MN, American Law Institute Publishers, 1979) §§ 766–67 (improper interference with contract; impropriety assessed through seven-factor test).

investment bank as an accessory to a board's breach of fiduciary duty,[2] accessory liability drew new interest from M&A lawyers and their clients. Although much attention focused on the bank's evident conflicts of interest in acting as an adviser to the target board, the Court's analysis of the bank's liability additionally stressed the elements requisite to liability, which in the United States sounds in tort. In contrast, in the United Kingdom, accessory liability in connection with breach of trust or fiduciary duty is controversial because the law is less clear, in part as a consequence of significant shifts in doctrinal basics within a relatively short period of time. Additionally, private law in the United Kingdom particularises accessory liability, defining its requisites differently depending on the nature of the primary wrong.

The chapter's central claim is that in both jurisdictions, how the law categorises a wrong matters for the elements of accessory liability. That is, breaching a fiduciary duty and culpably assisting a fiduciary's breach are both instances of wrongful conduct. Characterising both as tortious, as does US law, has consequences for the elements of accessory liability. In contrast, within UK law, equity houses both wrongs, while the requisites for accessory liability in connection with a tort are very different. The contrast suggests that fundamental taxonomic choices about doctrinal organisation can be consequential for doctrinal substance. Additionally, understood more functionally, accessory liability for breaches of fiduciary duty can operate interstitially to complement and supplement liability based on the primary wrong. Difficult though it would be to establish empirically, situating accessory liability in tort may facilitate its interstitial operation.

Section II introduces the doctrinal basics for the United States that specify when an actor's liability is contingent on another actor's breach of fiduciary duty. Section II also introduces the significance of factors distinct from private law that can shape the conduct of primary actors and those who advise or assist them, including formal regulation and extralegal constraints. Against this background, Section III draws contrasts with UK law, surveying doctrinal legacies as well as more recent shifts in doctrine. Section IV focuses on recent applications of accessory liability to investment bankers in high-stakes M&A litigation in Delaware courts. Section V concludes. An introductory word about terminology is warranted. Throughout, the chapter uses terminology that is consistent with the independent nature of accessory liability. This status is undercut when accessory liability is termed 'secondary',[3] 'derivative', or 'parasitic'.[4] Thus, although the chapter uses the term 'primary' wrong, its overall terminology presupposes that an accessory's liability, albeit contingent, stems from the accessory's own wrongful

[2] *RBC Capital Markets LLC v Jervis* 129 A 3d 816 (Del 2015).

[3] PS Davies, *Accessory Liability* (Oxford, Hart Publishing, 2015) 54: 'the language of "secondary liability" might … suggest that an accessory is secondarily liable for the same wrong as the primary wrongdoer'; J Dietrich and P Ridge, *Accessories in Private Law* (Cambridge, CUP, 2015) 7–8: 'secondary liability' is misleading if understood to mean an accessory must be liable for same wrong as a primary wrongdoer and subject to the same remedies.

[4] Davies, *Accessory Liability* (n 3) 54: 'the parasitic nature of accessory liability is crucial'.

conduct. Additionally, in no way is accessory liability an instance of vicarious liability, through which the law charges one actor with the legal consequences of another actor's conduct on the basis of the relationship between them.[5] Accessory liability is not an offshoot of agency doctrine but an instance of wrongful conduct that directly subjects an actor to liability.

II. United States: Basic Doctrine

A. Accessory Liability and Breach of Fiduciary Duty

In the United States, private law has long situated within tort the liabilities that stem from breach of fiduciary duty as well as accessory liability for participating in a fiduciary's breach. As stated in the *Restatement (Second) of Torts*, an actor who stands 'in a fiduciary relation with another is subject to liability to the other for harm resulting from a breach of duty imposed by the relation'.[6] The commentary to the *Restatement* recognises that a tort claim for breach of fiduciary duty may supplement other remedies available to a plaintiff that do not require showing harm.[7] The section's remedial focus anchors the availability of compensatory damages for breach of fiduciary duty but does not define the circumstances under which such a duty arises.[8] For this task other law—agency, trusts, corporate law and the like—supplies the substance. Indeed, an action in tort is often not a plaintiff's first resort in response to a breach of fiduciary duty. In some settings, non-tort remedies are exclusive, as when a trustee breaches a duty to a trust beneficiary. While the standard remedy—an equitable surcharge to restore trust assets—can resemble the monetary outcome of a tort claim, the procedure that leads to the exclusive remedy is equitable in character.[9] This eliminates the prospect of jury trial, which is a procedural backdrop to US tort litigation that arguably shapes tort doctrine in various ways.[10]

[5] The quintessential example is the vicarious liability of an employer or other principal for torts committed by a servant or other agent: see American Law Institute, *Restatement (Third) of Agency* (St Paul, MN, American Law Institute Publishers, 2006) § 7.03(2). When the principal's own fault subjects the principal to liability, the liability is direct, not vicarious: see cmt b.

[6] *Restatement (Second) of Torts* (n 1) § 874. The original *Restatement of Torts* contained a verbatim formulation: see American Law Institute, *Restatement of Torts* (St Paul, MN, American Law Institute Publishers, 1939) § 874.

[7] ibid cmt b.

[8] For further discussion, see DA DeMott, 'Breach of Fiduciary Duty: On Justifiable Expectations of Loyalty and their Consequences' (2006) 48 *Arizona Law Review* 925, 925–34.

[9] American Law Institute, *Restatement (Third) of Trusts* (St Paul, MN, American Law Institute Publishers, 2012) § 95.

[10] On the tort claim in settings without specialised remedies, see *Kann v Kann*, 690 A 2d 509 (Md 1997); *Bank One, NA v Borse*, 812 NE 2d 1021 (Ill App 2004). On the civil jury's significance for tort doctrine, see MD Green, 'The Impact of the Civil Jury on American Tort Law' (2011) 38 *Pepperdine Law Review* 337, 340–45.

Likewise, tort law has long encompassed accessory liability for participation in a fiduciary's breach of duty. As detailed further in section IV, this is so even in Delaware. Although law and equity have not been merged in Delaware, and equity jurisdiction resides in a separate court (the Court of Chancery, in which there are no jury trials), tort doctrine shapes significant aspects of fiduciary litigation. Moreover, across US jurisdictions, with the exception of tortious interference with contract,[11] the authoritative formulation of accessory liability is trans-substantive, that is, applicable across the board regardless of the nature of the primary wrong.[12] Some courts quote all or part of the relevant formulation in the *Restatement (Second) of Torts* § 876[13] as if it constituted primary statutory authority, not just persuasive secondary authority:

> For harm resulting to a third person from the tortious conduct of another, one is subject to liability if he
>
> (a) does a tortious act in concert with the other or pursuant to a common design with him, or
> (b) knows that the other's conduct constitutes a breach of duty and gives substantial assistance or encouragement to the other so to conduct himself, or
> (c) gives substantial assistance to the other in accomplishing a tortious result and his own conduct, separately considered, constitutes a breach of duty to the third person.

Although this section is entitled 'Persons Acting in Concert', only subsection (a) addresses conduct pursuant to a common design or otherwise in concert.[14] On equal footing is subsection (b), applicable to conduct that 'gives substantial assistance or encouragement' to another actor whose conduct is known to constitute a breach of duty. One who gives such assistance or encouragement is often termed an aider and abettor to the primary wrongdoer. Aiding-and-abetting liability is

[11] *Restatement (Second) of Torts* (n 1).

[12] In federal criminal law, the statutory formulation is also trans-substantive. A general statute provides that all actors who knowingly provide aid to persons committing federal crimes, with the intent of facilitating the crime, themselves commit a crime: see Act of Mar 4, 1909, ch 321, 35 Stat 1088, 1152, codified as 18 United States Code § 2.

[13] *Restatement (Second) of Torts* (n 1) § 876. The first *Restatement of Torts* did not include tortious action in concert or pursuant to a common design, as stated in the *Restatement (Second) of Torts* § 876(a). Instead, the first subsection subjected to liability an actor who 'orders or induces such [tortious] conduct, knowing that the conditions under which the act is done or intending the consequences which ensue': *Restatement (Second) of Torts* (n 1) § 876(a). More contemporary formulations relocate many instances of 'ordering' another's tortious act to agency law: see *Restatement (Third) of Agency* (n 5) § 7.03(1)(a) (principal subject to direct liability when agent acts with actual authority and agent's conduct is tortious). Inducing another actor's tortious conduct constitutes intentional action by the inducer: see American Law Institute, *Restatement (Third) of Torts: Liability for Physical and Emotional Harm* (St Paul, MN, American Law Institute Publishers, 2010) § 1.

[14] See *Heckmann v Ahmanson*, 168 Cal App 3d 119, 214 Cal Rptr 177 (1985): accessory defendants who purchased shares in target corporation agreed with directors to drop challenge to defensive acquisition in exchange for corporation's commitment to repurchase shares at above-market price, enabling target's directors to retain control; if directors breached fiduciary duty to corporation, accessory defendants subject to liability on the basis of action pursuant to common plan or design to commit a tort.

premised, not on an agreement with the primary wrongdoer, but on giving assistance, knowing of the primary wrongdoer's breach of duty.[15]

Claims based on aiding-and-abetting theories of liability are often asserted when the primary wrongdoer is insolvent and is alleged to have engaged in tortious conduct in a commercial setting.[16] A large majority of jurisdictions in the United States accept the premise of subsection (b) in some context, most typically when the primary wrong alleged is fraud or breach of fiduciary duty.[17] However, in 1994, the Supreme Court held in *Central Bank of Denver, NA v First Interstate Bank of Denver, NA*[18] that the general prohibition on fraud in the Securities Exchange Act of 1934 did not create or support a private cause of action based on aiding and abetting. Following *Central Bank*, the private law liability of actors who facilitate federal securities fraud must be premised on violations of state securities statutes or common law principles of accessory liability. Those principles, as stated above, operate generally, whether the primary wrong is fraud or breach of fiduciary duty.[19]

And now to return to questions of terminology. Section I characterised accessory liability as 'contingent'. Within tort doctrine, accessory liability is not a unique instance of contingent liability. For example, an actor who makes a material misrepresentation of fact, opinion, or law acts fraudulently when the maker knows that the representation is false.[20] But the maker is not subject to liability for the common law tort of fraud unless the misstatement is made to induce another to act or refrain from acting.[21] Additionally, when the maker intends to mislead, the maker is not subject to liability unless the person to whom the misrepresentation was made suffers economic loss caused by justifiable reliance on the misstatement.[22] Thus, one who knowingly makes a material misrepresentation of fact may meaningfully be said to act fraudulently,[23] but whether the actor is subject to

[15] RC Mason, 'Civil Liability for Aiding and Abetting' (2006) 61 *Business Lawyer* 1135, 1138; *cf Heckmann* (n 14) 183–84 (characterising acting pursuant to common design with primary wrongdoers as instance of aiding and abetting liability).

[16] Mason (n 15) 1135.

[17] ibid 1139–40. Accessory liability claims against lawyers may be subject to the assertion of privilege so long as the lawyer's action was on the client's behalf and within the scope of the attorney—client relationship. See HS Bryans, 'Claims Against Lawyers by Bankruptcy Trustees—A First Course on the *In Pari Delicto* Doctrine' (2011) 66 *Business Lawyer* 587, 594.

[18] *Central Bank of Denver, NA v First Interstate Bank of Denver, NA*, 511 US 164 (1994).

[19] Although most aiding-and-abetting claims concern fraud, 'breaches of fiduciary duty are close behind'. Mason (n 15) 1159.

[20] *Restatement (Third) of Torts: Liability for Economic Harm* § 10 (Tentative Draft No 2, 2014).

[21] ibid §§ 9, 11.

[22] ibid. On the significance of reliance as a distinct element, see *Rosen v Spanierman*, 894 F 2d 28 (2d Cir 1990); JCP Goldberg, AJ Sebok and BC Zipursky, 'The Place of Reliance in Fraud' (2006) *48 Arizona Law Review* 1001. A plaintiff may premise a claim on third-party reliance when misrepresentations are and are intended to be communicated to the plaintiff through a third party and thereby relied upon to the plaintiff's detriment: see *Mid Atlantic Framing, LLC v Varish Construction, Inc*, 117 F Supp 3d 145, 153 (SDNY 2015) (applying New York law).

[23] This is especially so when through the misrepresentation some other wrong is perpetrated: see Goldberg, Sebok and Zipursky (n 22) 1003. Relatedly, an actor who drives a car at high speed on a city

liability for the tort of common law fraud is contingent on the presence of additional elements that define the tort.[24] Accessory liability, likewise, is contingent on the presence of several distinct elements defining the wrong. One, of course, is the occurrence of a primary wrong. Thus, private law accessory liability, while not inchoate,[25] is nonetheless contingent.

B. Elements of Claim

Based on the reported cases, accessory liability claims in connection with breaches of fiduciary duty fall into clusters defined by typical types of defendants. Lawyers, directors and officers, and financial intermediaries of various sorts are frequent defendants, as they are in cases in which fraud constitutes the alleged primary wrong. An accessory claim requires that the plaintiff allege: (1) the existence of a fiduciary relationship; (2) a breach of duty by the fiduciary; (3) the accessory defendant's knowing participation in the breach; and (4) damages to the plaintiff as a result of the accessory defendant's participation and the fiduciary's breach. Thus, an aiding-and-abetting claim necessarily fails when no fiduciary relationship exists[26] or when no one has breached a fiduciary duty.[27]

Some cases restrict the availability of aiding-and-abetting claims to defendants who are not themselves fiduciaries.[28] But if an aiding-and-abetting claim fails against a defendant on this basis, the defendant's conduct might well have breached a fiduciary duty it owed to the plaintiff. In *Calesa Associates, LP v American Capital, Ltd*,[29] a recent Delaware case, minority shareholders alleged

street may meaningfully be said to act negligently, although no one (or thing) is hit. For the classic statement, see *Palsgraf v Long Island R Co*, 248 NY 339, 349 (1928) (Andrews J dissenting): 'Should we drive down Broadway at a reckless speed, we are negligent whether we strike an approaching car or miss it by an inch'. Under contemporary tort law, if the driver of the approaching car or her passenger suffers severe emotional harm resulting from the perception of imminent bodily harm from what appears to be an imminent collision, the harm may be compensable; see also, *Restatement (Third) of Torts: Liability for Physical and Emotional Harm* (n 13) § 47(a), cmt e, Illus 2, elaborating on 'zone of danger' principle.

[24] One might say the presence of these elements completes the tort. Alternatively, for Professor Goldberg and his co-authors, the fact that reliance is essential to the definition of common law fraud underscores the tort's relational quality: Goldberg, Sebok and Zipursky (n 22) 1026.

[25] Davies, *Accessory Liability* (n 3) 32. In criminal law, in contrast, inchoate liability is distinct from accomplice liability: MS Moore, *Causation and Responsibility* (Oxford, OUP, 2009) 284.

[26] For a recent example, see *Rocky Mountain Exploration, Inc v Davis Graham & Stubbs LLP*, 2016 WL 908640 (Colo Ct App 2016): a law firm represented an entity in connection with its purchase of oil and gas interests owned by the plaintiff. The purchasing entity acted as an unidentified principal represented by an agent, also represented by the law firm. The Court held that the agreements between the plaintiff and unidentified principal's agent did not create a fiduciary relationship. Thus, the plaintiff's aiding-and-abetting claim against the law firm 'necessarily fails'; see also text to n 7.

[27] See text to n 25 for a discussion of inchoate liability.

[28] See *Metro Life Insurance Co v Tremont Group Holdings, Inc*, 2012 WL 6632681 *18 (Del Ch Dec 20, 2012); the Delaware Supreme Court's own statements of the elements of the claim do not include this qualification: see *Malpiede v Towson*, 780 A 2d 1075, 1098 (Del 2001).

[29] *Calesa Associates, LP v American Capital, Ltd*, 2016 WL 770251 (Del Ch Feb 29, 2016).

breaches of fiduciary duty in connection with the corporation's dilutive issuance of new equity. The plaintiffs alleged that a substantial shareholder, a private equity firm, coerced members of the corporation's board of directors into authorising the issuance, which redounded to the private equity firm's distinct benefit. The court held that the minority shareholders' aiding-and-abetting claim against the private equity firm would fail were the court to find that the firm was a controlling stockholder at the time of the transaction because that status would, under Delaware law, itself impose fiduciary duties on the private equity firm owed to the other shareholders.[30] But, in the alternative, as a non-fiduciary, if the private equity firm aided and abetted breaches of fiduciary duty committed by the company's directors, it would be subject to liability.[31] More generally, the alternative claims elaborated in *Calesa* underscore the independent nature of accessory liability for breach of fiduciary duty. Albeit dependent on the commission of a primary wrong, the accessory claim does not duplicate its elements.[32]

Consistent with *Restatement (Second)* section 876(b), an accessory's liability requires that the accessory knows of the fiduciary's breach of duty. Most courts define 'knowledge' to mean actual knowledge of the fiduciary relationship and the breach,[33] rejecting a standard of constructive knowledge that charges a defendant with such knowledge as would have been obtained through the exercise of reasonable care.[34] Conscious avoidance—suspecting a fact, realising its probability and refraining from confirming the fact—implies a culpable state of mind, as opposed to the imputed state of mind that follows constructive knowledge on a negligence theory.[35] Regardless of the applicable standard, the analytic focus is the accessory's knowledge of the fiduciary relationship and its breach. Participation in the fiduciary's breach with knowledge of the fiduciary relationship and the breach establishes the accessory's culpability. These requisites have consequences for how the tort is characterised for some purposes under US law, including claims for contribution, discussed in section IV.

Conduct through which an actor participates in a primary wrong is susceptible to further parsing. 'Substantial assistance or encouragement', as in the *Restatement* formulation, may imply that accessory liability cannot stem from conduct that

[30] The criterion is whether the shareholder owns a majority interest in the corporation or exercises control over its business affairs: *Kahn v Lynch Communications Systems, Inc*, 638 A 2d 1110, 1113 (Del 1994). The Delaware corporation statute does not include oppression remedies. Delaware's functional alternative to a statutory oppression remedy to protect minority equity investors is the imposition of fiduciary duties on controlling shareholders.

[31] See also *Carsonaro v Bloodhound Technologies, Inc*, 65 A 3d 618, 658 (Del Ch 2013).

[32] For a rare example to the contrary that characterises aiding-and-abetting liability as superfluous and duplicative of elements of primary wrong, see *Sompo Japan Insurance, Inc v Deloitte & Touche, LLP*, 2005 WL 1412741 (NC Superior Ct June 10, 2005), discussed in Mason (n 15) 1163.

[33] Mason (n 15) 1160.

[34] *Invest Almaz v Temple Inland Forest Products Corp*, 243 F 3d 57, 83 (1st Cir 2001).

[35] *Fraternity Fund Ltd v Beacon Hill Asset Management, LLC*, 479 F Supp 2d 349, 368 (SDNY 2007). Some Delaware cases formulate the standard to encompass constructive knowledge as an alternative to actual knowledge but also require that the aider and abettor have acted with *scienter*: see section IV.

induces or otherwise initiates another actor's breach of duty. In Christopher Kutz's terminology, accessories are by definition never the exclusive authors of harm to the plaintiff; instead accessories would always be inclusive authors of harm-producing actions in which they culpably participate.[36] But knowingly to induce a breach of fiduciary duty is a significant basis for accessory liability, as is evident in section IV; one might view inducement as a form of 'encouragement' of an initiatory, not a tag-along sort, constituting both exclusive and inclusive authorship. However styled, an accessory's participation in a fiduciary's breach of duty is not a basis for liability unless it is connected to harm suffered by the plaintiff. The *Restatement* formulation requires that the assistance or encouragement be 'substantial', that is, 'a substantial factor in causing the resulting tort', which excludes minimal or slight conduct.[37]

More generally, as prior scholarship recognises, conventional but-for tests of causal connection do not work well when a series of multiple autonomous actors each engages in distinct conduct that results in an indivisible injury to a third party.[38] Positing, as did HLA Hart and Tony Honoré, a special form of causality for interpersonal situations, does not generate a causally-framed test for liability.[39] An alternative, championed by Michael Moore, recognises that harms may have co-causes and treats causation itself as a 'primitive', a 'factor' with a scalar quality that does not operate in binary fashion.[40] As Paul Davies proposes, it may be best to focus on participatory linkages through which an actor made more than a minimal contribution to the primary wrong.[41] More descriptively, one might acknowledge that situations in which multiple autonomous actors choose in various ways to contribute to a primary wrong are not the prototypes assumed by conventional formulations of causation.

Accessory liability requires culpable participation in the primary wrongdoer's breach of fiduciary duty. This requisite calls into question whether accessory liability might be premised on failure to act when the accessory knows that the primary culprit is engaged in wrongdoing but remains silent, resulting in loss for the plaintiff. Framing accessory liability within tort law makes salient a bedrock principle of common law tort: the absence of a duty to rescue when an actor has not created or increased the risk of harm and is outside the ambit of relationships in which such a duty is implied.[42] Undoubtedly, typical illustrations of the bite of the no-duty-to-rescue principle involve actors who know that they could easily save others from physical harm at no jeopardy to themselves. But the principle

[36] C Kutz, *Complicity* (Cambridge, CUP, 2000) 105–06.

[37] *Restatement (Second) of Torts* (n 1) § 876, cmt d.

[38] Davies, *Accessory Liability* (n 3) 33–40; Kutz (n 36) 169–70.

[39] Kutz (n 36) 170; see also HLA Hart and T Honoré, *Causation in the Law*, 2nd edn (Oxford, Clarendon Press, 1985) 388.

[40] Moore (n 25) 300.

[41] *Restatement (Third) of Torts* (n 13) § 26; Davies, *Accessory Liability* (n 3) 40.

[42] *Restatement (Third) of Torts: Liability for Physical and Emotional Harm* (n 13) § 40, cmt f.

operates more generally as a justification for non-intervention, just as duty serves as a central organising concept across tort law.[43]

Thus, banks and comparable institutions generally owe non-customers no duty to protect them from fraud perpetrated by bank customers.[44] However, once a bank has 'clear evidence' that trust funds on deposit in a fiduciary account have been misappropriated, the bank breaches its duty to safeguard the funds if it fails to investigate.[45] But a bank owes a duty to safeguard trust funds on deposit with it. The bank breaches its implied duty to prevent diversion through a passive failure to make reasonable enquiry once aware that improprieties may be occurring. In contrast, when a bank owes no duty to a plaintiff, the bank is not subject to liability when it fails to inform the plaintiff that a customer may be engaged in fraud.[46]

One practical generalisation is that substantial assistance may be easier to establish when the primary wrong is breach of fiduciary duty than when it is fraud. This may be due to 'the higher level of duty owed by the fiduciary', which may make more apparent the connection between the accessory's conduct and the harm to the plaintiff.[47] Alternatively, an accessory who knows that the primary wrongdoer is tied to the plaintiff by a fiduciary relationship may seem more readily to join in as a co-author of harm to the plaintiff than accessories who become aware of another actor's fraud.

C. Regulation and Environmental Circumstances

Private law doctrines do not operate in isolation as constraints against wrongful conduct, including breaches of fiduciary duty and conduct that knowingly assists such breaches. In some settings, the general law may operate to supplement requirements imposed by statutes and regulation. For example, broker-dealer firms that operate as clearing firms provide essential clearing services for accounts, including trading, settlement and delivery of securities. Clearing firms typically have no customer contact for accounts for which they perform these services. But regulation requires that clearing firms monitor accounts for illegal activity, including violations of trading and anti-money laundering rules.[48] Regulation positions such firms—which are few in number—as gatekeepers on behalf of investors and market integrity more broadly, distinct from the firms' relationships with their direct clients. Likewise, when a firm operates as a prime broker and learns that

[43] For the same principle, see *Fitzalan-Howard v Hibbert* [2009] EWHC 2855 [44].

[44] *MLSMK Investment Co v JP Morgan Chase & Co*, 431 Fed Appx 17, 20 (2d Cir 2011); T Frankel, *The Ponzi Scheme Puzzle* (New York, OUP, 2012) 180.

[45] *Lerner v Fleet Bank, NA*, 459 F 3d 273, 295 (2d Cir 2006).

[46] *In re Sharp International Corp*, 403 F 3d 43, 52 n 2 (2d Cir 2005).

[47] Mason (n 15) 1163–64.

[48] *Re Goldman Sachs Execution & Clearing, LP f/k/a Spear, Leeds & Kellogg LP*, Securities Exchange Act Release No 55,465 (14 March 2007).

a hedge fund client has over-valued investment portfolios, the prime broker's regulatory responsibilities include reporting the situation to the Securities and Exchange Commission (SEC).[49] In contrast, investment banks that serve as M&A advisers—the focus of section IV—are not positioned by regulation as gatekeepers comparable to the financial institutions discussed above. Nor does industry self-regulation define responsibilities for M&A advisers or sanction departures from defined responsibilities,[50] comparable to the ethical rules and professional disciplinary systems applicable to lawyers.[51] As a consequence, the significance of general legal doctrine and its enforcement may be amplified when specialised regulation does not constrain harmful conduct.[52]

Beyond the law and formal regulation as well as structured self-regulation, wrongful conduct may be constrained by an actor's concern to establish and maintain a good reputation. It is open to question whether reputational constraints now operate more weakly than in the past in some environments, including those populated by financial firms and professional services firms.[53] However, intense journalistic scrutiny may enhance what might otherwise seem weak incentives to avoid problematic conduct, in this context conduct that enters or closely skirts the boundaries of accessory liability. As section IV explores in greater detail, conflicted investment banks that serve as M&A advisers are potentially subject to accessory liability through conduct that places directors in jeopardy of breaching their fiduciary duties. These widely reported risks triggered quantifiable changes in how target boards choose their advisers. That many more targets now choose advisers free of potentially conflicting lines of business suggests the power of accessory liability to amplify the force of other constraints on conduct by inducing greater care in selecting an adviser.[54]

The advice lawyers give their clients can also strengthen incentives to steer away from legally problematic conduct. When legal doctrine is unclear or the consequences of breach uncertain, counsel may be less resolute or categorical in

[49] For an example, see *Fraternity Fund Ltd*, 479 F Supp 2d, 357 (prime broker precipitated collapse of fraudulent investment scheme when it refused to provide additional financing and reported over-valued investment portfolios to the SEC).

[50] See generally AF Tuch, 'The Self-Regulation of Investment Bankers' (2014) 83 *George Washington Law Review* 101.

[51] On debates concerning the adequacy of constraints on lawyers' conduct in financial transactions, see D Howarth, *Law as Engineering* (Cheltenham, Edward Elgar, 2013) 97–140; D Kershaw and R Moorhead, 'Consequential Responsibility for Client Wrongs: Lehman Brothers and the Regulation of the Legal Profession' (2013) 76 *MLR* 26.

[52] Admittedly, the interplay between courts and legislatures in this connection is complex, requiring close attention to the prototypical actor assumed by general legal principles: see S Gardner, 'Knowing Assistance and Knowing Receipt: Taking Stock' (1996) 112 *LQR* 56, 78–84 (distinguishing the situation of 'ordinary traders' from professional agents).

[53] See J Macey, *The Death of Corporate Reputation* (Upper Saddle River, NJ, FT Press, 2013).

[54] L Hoffman, 'Firms Ask: Are Our Bankers Conflicted' *Wall Street Journal* (3 March 2016) (reporting rise to 19% of M&A advisory revenue earned in 2015 by 'boutique' advisory firms that specialise in advisory services, up from 8% in 2008); for a broader account, see WW Bratton and ML Wachter, 'Bankers and Chancellors' (2014) 93 *Texas Law Review* 1.

advising clients. The reported reaction of English counsel is instructive. During a period recounted in section III, accessory liability for breach of trust turned on whether the accessory acted with a dishonest state of mind, not just on whether the accessory *was* dishonest (or acted with knowledge of the trustee's breach of duty, as US law formulates the counterpart of this element of liability). The Law Lord who dissented from this turn in doctrine explained extrajudicially:

> As the majority left it, the law was incoherent. The profession recognized this, and many members of the Bar whose opinions I respected told me that they were dismayed by the decision which they considered made it difficult to make directors and other liable when they behaved dishonestly.[55]

Later developments arguably shifted the law to conform to the dissenter's view, as discussed in section III. For present purposes, the point is that how lawyers understand legal doctrine and how they advise their clients are crucial to mechanisms of translation and transmission.[56]

III. The United Kingdom

A. Doctrinal Structure

To some readers, the generality of so much private law accessory doctrine in the United States may come as a surprise. For in the United Kingdom, just as tort and equity occupy distinct precincts in the overall taxonomy of private law, accessory liability is not generalised, and the substantive requisites for accessory liability differ based on the nature of the primary wrong. It may seem counterintuitive that generality and relative doctrinal certainty characterise the United States, a jurisdiction organised with multiple sovereign states that is also known for relatively high levels of litigation between private parties and jury trials in civil cases.

Two institutional factors concerning the United States are necessary preludes to further discussion of the United Kingdom. First, Delaware's Court of Chancery is the most prominent court in articulating and applying doctrines that define accessory liability for breach of fiduciary duty, at least in high-profile disputes grounded in corporate law. But as the Court's name suggests, it is—distinctively if not uniquely in the United States—a court of equity. As section IV elaborates, Delaware situates accessory liability in tort; indeed the Court characterises breach

[55] P Millett, *As In Memory Long* (London, Wildy, Simmonds & Hill Publishing, 2015) 176–77.

[56] Such anecdotes suggest that formally structured dialogues between court and counsel do not exhaust the possibilities for exchanges that may prove influential. On forms of judicial dialogue specific to the House of Lords and the UK Supreme Court, see A Paterson, *Final Judgment* (Oxford, Hart Publishing, 2013).

of fiduciary duty as an 'equitable tort'[57] and readily accommodates accessory liability within a framework structured within tort doctrine. Second, although the United States is a large and remarkably varied country in which basic areas of private law are within the province of each state, centripetal or centralising forces operate as well. Undoubtedly, unlike Canada, the United States has no national level corporations legislation, but in practice many publicly held corporations are incorporated in Delaware. De facto Delaware's corporation statute, plus the Court of Chancery and Supreme Court, all operate on a national plane. Additionally, over the twentieth century, courts in some states influenced sister states' courts, while the Restatements served to make decisional law more uniform, albeit not evenly so on all points within private law.[58]

B. Legacies and Evolution

i. Tort

As Paul Davies recounts the situation, accessory liability in tort, now subsumed into 'joint tortfeasance', is somewhat obscure and dominated by concepts of conspiracy.[59] No doubt history beyond the scope of this chapter explains much. In general, the conduct requisite to accessory liability consists of combination, authorisation or procurement.[60] Absent a common design, an actor who furnishes substantial assistance to another actor's tort is not subject to accessory liability.[61] When fraud is the primary or underlying wrong, the reasoning in prominent judgments excludes the possibility of imposing liability on an actor who assisted the primary fraudfeasor but was not party to a common design.[62]

One potential justification for defining accessory liability so narrowly is fear lest the requisite that assistance be 'knowing' be weakened by pressures to demand less

[57] *In re Rural/Metro Corp Stockholders Litigation*, 88 A 3d 54, 98 (Del Ch 2014), affd *sub nom RBC Capital* (n 2) ('a breach of fiduciary duty is an equitable tort') (*Rural/Metro I*). As the author of *Rural/Metro I* wrote extrajudicially, 'a breach of fiduciary duty is in fact a tort, although a unique species historically called an "equitable tort"'): JT Laster and MD Morris, 'Breaches of Fiduciary Duty and the Delaware Uniform Contribution Act' (2010) *Delaware Law Review* 71, 71; UK courts apply the term 'equitable tort' to characterise dishonest assistance (eg, bribery) to induce or assist a breach of fiduciary duty: see P Davies, 'Gain-Based Remedies for Dishonest Assistance' (2015) 131 *LQR* 173, 176.

[58] Likewise, the Uniform Commercial Code was a major force towards greater uniformity in contract law, even for portions not encompassed by the Code. See EA Farnsworth, *Contracts*, 4th edn (New York, Aspen, 2004) 40, 298–99, 596.

[59] Davies, *Accessory Liability* (n 3) 178–79. The UK Supreme Court expressly adopted the terminology of accessory liability in tort in *Fish & Fish Ltd v Sea Shepherd* [2015] AC 1229.

[60] ibid 188, adopting formulation in H Carty, 'Joint Tortfeasance and Assistance Liability' (1999) 19 *Legal Studies* 489.

[61] Davies, *Accessory Liability* (n 3) 195; see also PS Davies, 'Accessory Liability in Tort' (2016) 132 *LQR* 15. In general, accessory liability requires that an actor has assisted the commission of an act by the primary wrongdoer, that the assistance be pursuant to a common design, and that the primary wrongdoer's act constitutes a tort as against the claimant; *Fish & Fish* (n 59) 1248.

[62] Davies, *Accessory Liability* (n 3) 198, discussing the judgment in *Credit Bank Lyonnais NV v Export Credits Guarantee Department* [2000] AC 486 (HL).

than actual knowledge of the primary wrong.[63] The US experience suggests that judicial vigilance is necessary but achievable. That civil juries significantly feature in US tort cases (but not in the Delaware Court of Chancery) may help explain this stringency. Additionally, if the policy justifications for a narrow definition of accessory liability presuppose, as a prototypical tort, fraud or copyright infringement, the risk is that accessories to torts commonly viewed as working more fundamental harms—battery, for example—will be under-deterred and their victims under-acknowledged and under-compensated outside the ambit of criminal law and its administration.[64]

ii. Equity

A crucial starting point is the nature of duties characterised as 'fiduciary'. Famously, Millett LJ said in *Bristol & West Building Society v Mothew* that '[t]he expression "fiduciary duty" is properly confined to those duties which are peculiar to fiduciaries and the breach of which attracts legal consequences differing from those consequent upon the breach of other duties'.[65] As becomes evident in section IV, US terminology is not as sparing in using the term 'fiduciary'.[66] In particular, corporate directors who breach their duties of care, even in the absence of a conflicting interest, are viewed as having breached a fiduciary duty. But for present purposes this may not matter much because had US law confined the label of 'fiduciary' breach to directors' loyalty-related transgressions, directors' breaches of the duty of care would (one thinks) have been litigated as torts, and claims against accessories would have proceeded within the generalised framework elaborated in section II.[67]

Overall, in equity, accessory liability developed somewhat haltingly, from a long-lived legacy of restrictive definition towards relatively greater clarity and coherence.[68] In particular, the definition of the primary wrong requisite for accessory liability in connection with breach of fiduciary duty expanded. Nonetheless, the constitutive elements of accessory culpability may retain an overhang of precedent requiring not only that an accessory has acted dishonestly but that

[63] ibid 220.

[64] ibid 220 (criticising the implication that an expectation of loyalty from a fiduciary should rank higher than 'the right to bodily integrity and freedom').

[65] *Bristol & West Building Society v Mothew* [1998] Ch 1 (CA) 16, [1997] 2 WLR 436, 448.

[66] But some bodies of doctrine do not characterise as 'fiduciary' all duties that an actor might owe. Agency law, for example, differentiates an agent's duties of performance from duties of loyalty. See *Restatement (Third) of Agency* (n 5) Topic 1 (Agent's Duties to Principal).

[67] English law on the applicable framework is not clear. See Davies, *Accessory Liability* (n 3) 100.

[68] Davies, *Accessory Liability* (n 3) 88. For a detailed account, see EP Ellinger, E Lomnicka and CVM Hare, *Ellinger's Modern Banking Law*, 5th edn (Oxford, OUP, 2011) ch 7, pt 5. See also 289, as applied to banks; regulation may have substantially overtaken the potential risk of accessory liability under English law: 'a bank that has been used for the diversion of trust assets or as part of some other fraudulent or criminal scheme may well have other more pressing concerns'.

the accessory has been self-aware of acting dishonestly, a requisite focused on a defendant's conscience that owes much to criminal law.[69]

One legacy of the nineteenth-century precedent, *Barnes v Addy*,[70] was a two-limbed specification of accessory conduct derived from a case in which the accessory defendants acted as solicitors for an initial trustee and his (bankrupt) successor, who misappropriated trust property. The initial trustee's solicitor advised him of the risk that the successor might misappropriate trust property, but the initial trustee thought this unlikely. The successor trustee's solicitor, acting on his client's instructions, prepared the deeds requisite for the transfer. As Lord Selborne formulated the bases for liability, non-trustees could be subject to liability stemming from a trustee's breach when 'they are found making themselves trustees *de son tort*', or 'actually participating in any fraudulent conduct of the trustee to the injury of the *cestui que trust*'.[71] Separately, a non-trustee's receipt of trust property may subject the receiver to liability in restitution.[72] More generally, wrote Lord Selborne,

> strangers are not to be made constructive trustees merely because they act as the agents of trustees in transactions within their legal powers, transactions, perhaps of which a Court of Equity may disapprove … unless they assist with knowledge in a dishonest and fraudulent design on the part of the trustees.[73]

Thus, unless the accessory received trust property through the trustee's breach of trust, this precedent limited accessory liability to instances of fraudulent and dishonest misconduct by trustees in which the accessory 'actually' participated.

As Paul Davies suggests, the narrowness with which *Barnes v Addy* formulated requisites for accessory liability may reflect its time, in which trustees' liability encompassed 'innocent incompetence'.[74] Anachronistic though the comparison might seem, 'innocent incompetence' characterises some breaches of directors' duties under Delaware corporate law, as section IV explains. Additionally, it is worth noting that the facts of *Barnes v Addy* are unpromising as a basis for liability under US law, based on the *Restatement* formulation. The solicitors lacked anything approaching actual knowledge that the successor trustee planned to misappropriate trust property. And how did the solicitors 'encourage' the successor trustee's breach? Certainly, the breach was preceded by advice to the initial trustee from his solicitor and by drafting done by the successor trustee's solicitor, but these actions fall far short of culpability.

[69] Davies, *Accessory Liability* (n 3) 119. Whether dishonesty for civil law purposes should be defined differently from criminal law is open to dispute. See *Starglade Properties Ltd v Nash* [2010] EWCA Civ 1314 [42]–[44] (Lord Leveson).

[70] *Barnes v Addy* (1874) LR 9 Ch App 244 (CA). On the longevity of the two-limbed doctrine and the cases preceding *Barnes v Addy*, see W Gummow, 'Knowing Assistance' (2013) 87 *Australian Law Journal* 311.

[71] *Barnes* (n 70) 251–52.

[72] Unless the recipient has a defence, such as change of position.

[73] *Barnes* (n 70) 251–52.

[74] Davies, *Accessory Liability* (n 3) 94.

Over one hundred years later (1995), the Privy Council broadened the scope of accessory liability by rejecting the requirement that the primary wrong constitutes (as it did in *Barnes v Addy*) dishonesty.[75] In *Royal Brunei Airlines Sdn Bhd v Tan*,[76] an insolvent travel company defaulted on its debt to an airline. The airline sued the company's principal director and shareholder. Delivered by Lord Nicholls, the judgment jettisoned the requirement that the trustee's breach was dishonest and fraudulent; what mattered was the accessory's fault and its character, not the character of the trustee's fault. Indeed, explained Lord Nicholls, 'the case for liability of the dishonest [accessory] seems stronger when the trustee is innocent, because in such a case the [accessory] alone was dishonest and that was the cause of the subsequent misappropriation of trust property'.[77] Put differently, were the accessory honest, unless the accessory made an honest mistake, most likely the breach of trust would not have occurred. To define 'dishonesty', *Tan* adopted an objective standard that expected an individual 'to attain the standard which would be observed by an honest person placed in those circumstances'.[78] An honest person—a legal construction, like the reasonable person in tort law[79]—has regard to known circumstances, which may dictate what course of action to take, including asking questions and possibly declining to become involved.[80] Premised as it is on the accessory's knowledge, liability under *Tan* appears to follow consistently with US doctrine, albeit in equity not tort.

Seven years later (2002), the force and clarity of *Tan* were undercut by the House of Lords in *Twinsectra Ltd v Yardley*.[81] Four of five judgments rejected *Tan*'s objective standard grounded in the accessory defendant's knowledge for a more subjective and inward-looking test; as Lord Hutton wrote:

> [I]it would be less than just for the law to permit a finding that a defendant had been 'dishonest' in assisting a breach of trust where he knew of the facts which created the trust and its breach *but had not been aware that what he was doing would be regarded by honest men as being dishonest.*[82]

The accessory defendant in *Twinsectra* was a solicitor acting for a property entrepreneur. Acting on his client's instructions, he paid over borrowed money to his client knowing that it would not be used to acquire property although the solicitor knew that the money had been received from the lender with an undertaking

[75] For Australia, the scope of accessory liability retains the formulation in *Barnes v Addy*: see *Farah Constructions Pty Ltd v Say-Dee Pty Ltd* [2007] HCA 22 [161].

[76] *Royal Brunei Airlines Sdn Bhd v Tan* [1995] 2 AC 378.

[77] ibid 385.

[78] ibid 390.

[79] Of course, as legal standards, honesty and reasonableness make different demands on the actors subject to them.

[80] *Royal Brunei* (n 76) 390–91.

[81] *Twinsectra Ltd v Yardley* [2002] 2 AC 164. And to some observers, *Tan* itself 'left room for doubt and uncertainly as to the precise test' for dishonesty: Ellinger, Lomnicka and Hare (n 68) 282.

[82] *Twinsectra* (n 81) 174 (Lord Hutton) (emphasis added).

that it would be retained until applied to acquire property.[83] Cross-examined at trial about his state of mind, the solicitor testified he 'merely' followed his client's instructions and had no reason to disbelieve his client's statement that the money would be used to buy property. But the client used the money for other purposes and failed to repay the loan. In the assessment of Lord Millett, the dissenter, the solicitor was unaware of no relevant fact. Although he was not wilfully blind to the facts, he did close his eyes to their implications, 'that is to say the impropriety of putting the money at [his client's] disposal'.[84]

As Lord Millett wrote extrajudicially, *Twinsectra* weakened the force of the law and thus of the advice lawyers could give their clients, premised as accessory liability was on a defendant's own subjective appreciation of wrongfulness.[85] In fairness to the majority, a standard of culpability geared solely to an accessory defendant's knowledge catapults the court into a fraught body of English law defining 'knowledge', from which the majority sought to avert (as did Lord Nicholls in *Tan*). But the *Twinsectra* majority did not explain why the relevant standard should instead protect accessory defendants who—unlike the solicitor for the successor trustee in *Barnes v Addy*—know all relevant facts, fail to appreciate their consequences and act to facilitate breach of fiduciary duty.

Two years later (2004), the Privy Council appears to have agreed with Lord Nicholls and Lord Millett. In *Barlow Clowes International Ltd v Hamilton*,[86] the principal directors of a company providing offshore financial services facilitated the operation of a fraudulent investment scheme by transferring investors' funds as directed by the scheme's organiser into transactions with no apparent commercial purpose. And one director, fully aware of the nature of the organiser's business and how it sourced liquid funds, came to know enough to suspect misappropriation but nonetheless authorised transfers of investors' funds into accounts controlled by the organiser and his confederates. The *Barlow Clowes* judgment does not deal straightforwardly with *Twinsectra* and its implications. Instead, acknowledging 'an element of ambiguity' susceptible of being read to encompass the defendant's subjective views of honesty, *Barlow Clowes* claims to clarify that what was required was 'only that his knowledge of the transaction had to be such as to render his participation contrary to normally accepted standards of honest conduct'.[87] Given the facts, it is remarkable that the defendant's argument had any prospect of success, for unlike the other accessory defendants in this sequence of cases, the accessory knew his client was engaged in major criminal misconduct via out-and-out misappropriation of investors' money.

[83] ibid 168 (Lord Hoffman).
[84] ibid 203 (Lord Millett).
[85] Millett (n 55).
[86] *Barlow Clowes International Ltd v Hamilton* [2005] UKPC 37, [2006] 1 WLR 1476.
[87] ibid 1481.

IV. Investment Bankers as Accessories

Although the general structure of accessory liability is well established in the United States, its application to categories of actors can be controversial, most recently among investment banks and the lawyers who advise them. This section opens with a brief description of salient features of Delaware corporate law that shape liability in the M&A context. The section next reviews recent applications of accessory doctrine to investment bankers, focusing mostly on the best developed and most recent case, and then explores implications of accessory liability in this setting.

A. Duties, Liabilities and Roles

In contrast to the sparing definition of 'fiduciary' that typifies UK doctrine, Delaware law characterises directors' fiduciary duties as multifaceted, consisting of a duty of loyalty (which incorporates a duty of good faith) and a duty of care.[88] Cases fleshing out distinctive content for the duty of good faith cast it as a component of the duty of loyalty that prohibits knowing or reckless conduct detrimental to the corporation's interests.[89] When directors initiate or consider engaging in a M&A transaction that would end the company's separate existence or otherwise transfer control, the duties that directors owe to the target and its shareholders remain the fiduciary duties of loyalty (and good faith) and care; but the object towards which the duties should be exercised narrows to obtaining the best deal reasonably available for the target's shareholders.[90] To fulfil their duties, target directors often retain an expert adviser to assist in estimating the company's value relative to the price and other terms on which it might be sold.[91] Investment banks that perform this advisory service often serve an additional agency role on behalf of the target by contacting prospective bidders, conducting an auction or otherwise attempting to elicit the best price and executing the transaction.[92] As section II noted, some investment banks furnish only these services; others—typically larger banks—also furnish financing to enable purchasers to complete M&A deals, including those

[88] On the history of the duty of good faith as a component of the duty of loyalty, see AS Gold, 'The New Concept of Loyalty in Corporate Law' (2009) 43 *University of California, Davis Law Review* 457.

[89] ibid.

[90] The intricacies of a sizeable number of cases articulating the specifics are beyond the scope of this chapter. Conventionally, though, target directors are said to owe *Revlon* duties, a label derived from *Revlon Inc v Macandrews & Forbes Holdings Inc*, 506 A 2d 173 (Del 1986), which made clear that the court's review in this context is distinctively exacting.

[91] AW Tuch, 'Banker Loyalty in Mergers and Acquisitions' (2016) 94 *Texas Law Review* 1079, 1093–98.

[92] ibid 1093–95.

for which the same bank also serves as an adviser to the target company's board.[93] Providing financing for an acquisition generally commands much higher fees than advising the board of an acquisition target.

The Delaware corporation statute permits a company to include a provision in its charter—its 'certificate of incorporation'—that exculpates directors from monetary liability stemming from breaches of duty, except for breaches of the duties of loyalty and good faith.[94] Thus, in a typical company, directors who breach their duties of care do not confront a risk of monetary liability, whether or not the breach occurs in the M&A context. The protection afforded by an exculpatory provision extends only to directors and not to officers or third-party providers of professional services, like investment banks. As discussed more fully below, the terms on which a target's board retains an investment bank may attempt to address and mitigate liability risks for the bank, including those stemming from its provision of advisory services to a target and financing to a bidder linked by the same M&A deal. In general, Delaware cases do not give effect to provisions in engagement agreements that through general or unspecific terms purport to relieve the bank of liability.[95]

B. Accessory Doctrine Applied

The Delaware Supreme Court's 2015 opinion in *RBC Capital Markets LLC v Jervis*[96] is a legal landmark for many reasons. Indeed, *RBC Capital* was not the first acknowledgment from a Delaware court that investment banks could be subject to accessory liability when the bank's conflicting interests had a substantial connection to breaches of fiduciary duty by a target's directors.[97] The precedential gravity of *RBC Capital* stems in part from its procedural status. Unusually, the case 'went the distance' through a full trial before the Court of Chancery

[93] Bratton and Wachter (n 54) 24 (describing practice of 'stapled financing' and the conflicts it engenders).

[94] Del Code Ann tit 8, § 102(b)(7).

[95] *Rural/Metro I* (n 57). There is no clear English authority addressing the availability to an accessory of an exclusion clause that protects a primary wrongdoer. For discussion of exclusion clauses when the primary wrong is a breach of contract, see Davies, *Accessory Liability* (n 3) 145.

[96] *RBC Capital* (n 2).

[97] Noteworthy predecessors are *In re El Paso Corp Shareholder Litigation*, 41 A 3d 432 (Del Ch 2012) (directors relied on advice from M&A adviser that owned 19% equity interest in prospective buyer; bank's team led by banker with large personal shareholding in buyer); *In re Del Monte Co Shareholder Litigation*, 25 A 3d 813 (Del Ch 2011) (M&A adviser to target surreptitiously assisted potential bidders in structuring joint bid, among other instances of problematic conduct). An earlier precedent questioned the general propriety of 'stapled financing', ie, acquisition financing offered by target's M&A adviser to prospective bidders. See *In re Toys 'R' Us Shareholder Litigation*, 877 A 2d 975 (Del Ch 2005). Still earlier authority recognised a claim of accessory liability against an adviser retained by a management group taking a company private. See *In re Shoe-Town Inc Stockholders Litigation*, 1990 WL 13475 *7–8 (Del Ch Feb 12 1990).

and two lengthy opinions from that Court to an appeal decided by the Delaware Supreme Court.[98] Although the bank as appellant expressly made no arguments on appeal requiring review of any finding of fact, the Supreme Court examined the record in its entirety, documenting its effort in an opinion dominated as much by a detailed factual narrative as by legal analysis. This underscores the settled and straightforward basics of this accessory tort under Delaware law. It also underscores the character and degree of the bank's departures from legally tolerable conduct.

Engaged as its M&A adviser by the board of a long-time client, Rural/Metro Corp, the bank structured the sale process on an unusual two-track basis with the objective—not initially disclosed to its client—of enabling the bank to obtain a role in financing the sale and acquisition of another company. That this company was a direct competitor of Rural/Metro complicated the sale process and limited the number of bidders. The bank also, in the court's characterisation, engaged in 'illicit manipulation' of the directors' deliberative process by altering its valuation analyses to cast a better light on the bid favoured by the bank. As a consequence, Rural/Metro sold for substantially less than it was worth, injuring its shareholders;[99] Rural/Metro's directors breached their fiduciary duties of care through the underpriced sale, their acquiescence in a flawed process, plus false statements made to Rural's shareholders concerning the deal.

RBC Capital articulates the elements of accessory liability in familiar terms. Focusing in particular on the requirement that the accessory knowingly participated in the primary breach, the court endorsed the Court of Chancery's statement that accessory liability requires the accessory to have acted with *scienter*, that is with 'an illicit state of mind', meaning with 'actual or constructive knowledge that their conduct was improper'.[100] One might wonder how close the *scienter* standard comes to *Twinsectra*'s subjective requirement that an accessory proceeds with self-awareness of dishonesty, beyond knowledge that its conduct is dishonest. The 'manifest intentionality' of the bank's conduct, according to *RBC Capital*, 'is demonstrative of the advisor's knowledge of the reality that the Board was proceeding on the basis of fragmentary and misleading information'.[101] This formulation turns on an objective assessment of whether an accessory acted with knowledge of the primary wrong, not the more subjective focus required by *Twinsectra*.

[98] For this terminology, see *Amalgamated Bank v Yahoo! Inc*, 2016 WL 402540,*17 (Del Ch Feb 2, 2016) (discussing *In re The Walt Disney Co Derivative Litigation*, 907 A 2d 693 (Del 2006) as instance that 'went the distance').

[99] Delaware characterises such injuries as individual to shareholders, not injuries to the company that give rise to claims that must be brought in derivative suits.

[100] *RBC Capital* (n 2) 862, quoting *Wood v Baum*, 953 A 2d 136, 141 (Del 2008) (Del 2015) (internal quotation marks omitted). Although this language posits constructive knowledge as an alternative to actual knowledge, the *scienter* requirement seems to obviate its significance.

[101] *RBC Capital* (n 2).

C. Further Implications

RBC Capital emphasises the bank's authorship of breaches of duty committed by the target's directors: the bank 'knowingly induced' the breaches 'by exploiting its own conflicted interests to the detriment of Rural and by creating an informational vacuum'.[102] Undoubtedly, the directors failed to exercise adequate oversight of the bank once they knew that it had entanglements with prospective bidders, but the bank's own conduct initiated the cascade of woes that followed.[103] Given its emphasis on damning factual specifics, *RBC Capital* leaves open whether liability follows when an adviser is subject to an undisclosed conflict and aware of breaches of the duty of care by directors, but overall the adviser's conduct is less problematic.[104]

A separate question is how best to characterise the relationship between a target corporation (or its directors) and an investment bank retained to act as a M&A adviser. To the extent that the relationship—founded as it is in an engagement agreement—is contractual,[105] the bank's obligations might be delimited by agreement. *RBC Capital* explicitly rejected the Court of Chancery's description of these relationships that positions M&A advisers as 'gatekeepers'.[106] This characterisation, unmoored by any articulation of duty, lacks clarity and coherence with tort doctrine more generally. Additionally, *RBC Capital* does not explicitly characterise the relationship between target directors and their M&A adviser as fiduciary.[107] Instead, discussing the informational asymmetries that typify contracting between a bank and its client, the Court emphasised the significance of disclosure to 'level the field' but also concluded with an unqualified assertion of an obligation 'not to act in a manner that is contrary to the interests of the board of directors'.[108] This links the bank's liability back to basic tort doctrine by stressing the categorical obligation to refrain from intentionally wrongful conduct.

Finally, *RBC Capital* 'went the distance' in an additional and unusual respect. The bank, as the sole defendant not to settle prior to trial, confronted a judgment for $91,323,554.61, or $4.17/share, representing damages suffered by Rural's

[102] ibid.

[103] This calls to mind the argument in *Tan* that the justification for accessory liability is even stronger when the primary wrongdoer is only hapless or careless.

[104] Recent examples lack the full factual development of *RBC Capital*. See *Singh v Attenborough*, 137 A 3d 151, *2 n 7 (Del 2016) (characterising the bank's conduct in *RBC Capital* as duping the board into breach of duty of care for the bank's own motives; bank in instant case, in contrast, delayed its disclosure of prior pitch of advisory client to acquirer until the merger agreement was signed); *In re TIBCO Software Inc Shareholders Litigation*, 2015 WL 6155894 (Del Ch Oct 20, 2015) (denying motion to dismiss; not wanting to jeopardise $47.4 million fee, adviser concealed from target board information that shares had been miscounted and that acquirer had relied on miscount in calculating consideration, resulting in bargain price for acquirer).

[105] See Bratton and Wachter (n 54) 7–8.

[106] *Rural/Metro I* (n 57).

[107] On justifications for so characterising M&A advisers, see Tuch, 'Banker Loyalty in Mergers and Acquisitions' (n 91).

[108] *RBC Capital* (n 2) 865.

former shareholders. Relying on the Delaware statute governing contribution among tortfeasors,[109] the bank sought a credit against the judgment for settlement amounts paid by other defendants—$5 million by another bank that served in a secondary role, and $6.6 million by two conflicted directors who played significant roles in the sale process. Resolving questions of first impression, the Court of Chancery apportioned responsibility between the bank and the other defendants. To do so required assessing the character of the bank's tort.

Although Delaware's contribution statute does not explicitly bar contribution on behalf of intentional tortfeasors, the Court considered at length the type of intentional tort that accessory liability represents. The bank knowingly participated in (and to a considerable extent induced) the directors' breaches of duty, but its conduct was not criminal and was not intended to cause physical injury.[110] Its intentional tort thus lacked the moral gravity that should exclude the possibility of contribution. On the other hand, to the extent the bank misled its client's directors, it came to equity with unclean hands in its quest for contribution; to permit contribution (here in the form of settlement credit) would enable the bank to 'take advantage of the targets of its own misconduct'.[111] Calculating contribution in this light, the Court exercised its discretion to reduce the judgment against the bank to $75.8 million, having allocated some measure of fault to two directors who had distinct personal interests in the sale.

V. Conclusion

These contrasts help make the case for accessory liability a worthy subject for further academic scrutiny. The comparative account in this chapter also demonstrates the significance of taxonomic placement for substantive doctrine. The emphasis in US law on objective measures for accessory culpability fits well with tort law's general focus on legally constructed reasonable persons, not the inward-looking reflections of individual actors. As Justice Holmes wrote: 'The law takes no account of the infinite varieties of temperament, intellect, and education which make the internal character of a given act so different in different men. It does not attempt to see men as God sees them'.[112] The chapter's comparative account also highlights the interstitial function that accessory liability can serve, whether characterised as a tort or an equitable wrong. The prospect of accessory liability may deter conduct by actors situated to withhold facilitation necessary to the wrongdoing of others,

[109] Delaware Uniform Contribution Among Tortfeasors Act, Del Code tit 10 §§ 6301–08.

[110] *In re Rural/Metro Stockholders Litigation*, 102 A 3d 205, 237 (Del Ch 2014) (*Rural/ Metro II*), affd *sub nom RBC Capital* (n 2).

[111] *Rural/Metro II* (n 110). Thus, albeit the tortious character of the bank's wrong, equitable doctrine applied.

[112] OW Holmes, *The Common Law* (Boston, Little Brown & Co, 1881) 108.

especially when other constraints on problematic conduct are weak, as well as serving as an additional source of recovery for victims of wrongdoing. The comparative account also illustrates the independent character of accessory liability, which rationalises outcomes—as in *Tan* and *RBC Capital*—in which an accessory's culpability differs from that of the primary wrongdoer.

12

Equitable Liability of Corporate Accessories

JAMIE GLISTER*

I. Introduction

The purpose of this chapter is to discuss two different models of equitable liability that may apply to corporate accessories to a breach of trust or fiduciary duty. By 'corporate accessory' I simply mean a company that has become involved in a breach through receiving property,[1] or taking a diverted business opportunity, or somehow acting in a way that has assisted a fiduciary to breach his or her fiduciary duty.

These corporate accessories have distinct legal personality and so are strangers to the underlying relationship between fiduciary and principal. However, sometimes the connection between the wrongdoing fiduciary and the corporate accessory is so close that the courts have felt able to treat the two as relevantly the same actor. The corporate accessory may be termed the 'creature company' or 'alter ego' or 'cat's paw' of the fiduciary. In these cases the corporate accessory and its controller are viewed as one unit, rather than as separate parties, and the same orders are usually addressed to both.

Clearly, not all corporate accessories that become involved in breaches of fiduciary duty can properly be seen as creature companies of the wrongdoing fiduciaries. Where a corporate accessory cannot be characterised in this way, it will be treated as a separate actor—as a 'true' third party—in the normal way. That corporate accessory may or may not be liable for its involvement in the breach, but any liability will be on the conventional *Barnes v Addy* basis.[2]

* I would like to thank the participants at the conference, and the editors, for their helpful comments. I am also grateful to Newcastle Law School, UK, where I wrote this chapter as a visiting fellow in early 2016.

[1] I include knowing recipients as 'accessories', although I acknowledge that recipient liability itself might not properly be categorised as 'accessorial': see PS Davies, *Accessory Liability* (Oxford, Hart Publishing, 2015) 91–93.

[2] *Barnes v Addy* (1874) LR 9 Ch App 244 (CA).

I outline in section II these two different models of corporate liability: first, treating the wrongdoer and the company as the same actor; second, treating the company as a separate actor but with imputed knowledge so as to ground *Barnes v Addy* liability. As will be seen, there is doubt over the continued existence of the first model in England and Wales. It may be that corporate accessories in that jurisdiction can now *only* be treated as distinct actors, even where the creature company description does fit and where the accessory is simply being used by the wrongdoing fiduciary as a vehicle for his or her actions.

In section III, I explain the possible differences that may follow depending on whether a corporate accessory is treated as the same actor as the wrongdoing fiduciary, or as a separate actor. The most obvious involves liability for gains: under the first model, the fiduciary and the accessory are each liable for the total profits made by both; under the second model, liability for gains is several. But there may also be differences in respect of the calculation of compensation payable, and in respect of whether a claimant can seek gain-based and loss-based remedies against two separate wrongdoers.

II. Two Models of Corporate Liability

The concept of a corporate 'alter ego' can be used in two distinct senses here. The first is where the court effectively disregards a company's separate existence and treats actions by the company as actions by the controller of it. This has two results: first, it means that the company's controller (who is usually a wrongdoing fiduciary) can be personally liable for gains that are in fact made by the associated company; second, it means that the company can be liable to account to the fiduciary's principal even though the company did not owe any duty to that person. It should be noted that, although the company's separate existence is being ignored to a certain extent, these cases still generally involve orders being made against both the fiduciary and the company that he or she controls.[3]

This line of authority is considered in the section below. As will be seen, there is real doubt about its continued existence in England and Wales. Following *Prest v Petrodel Resources Ltd* in particular,[4] the courts may prefer to see companies associated with wrongdoing fiduciaries as true, separate third parties. These companies may have the fiduciary's knowledge attributed to them (and it is here that we see the second sense of 'alter ego'), and this imputed knowledge may ground *Barnes v Addy* liability to the fiduciary's principal. However, as will be discussed in

[3] This may not be the case if the company in question has already been dissolved, eg, Arcutes Holding Inc in *Otkritie International Investment Management Ltd v Urumov* [2014] EWHC 191 (Comm).

[4] *Prest v Petrodel Resources Ltd* [2013] UKSC 34, [2013] 2 AC 415. See also *VTB Capital Plc v Nutritek International Corp* [2013] UKSC 5, [2013] 2 AC 337 (company controllers not to be seen as liable under contracts made by their company).

section III, the nature and extent of liability imposed on a *Barnes v Addy* analysis will not necessarily be the same as that imposed when the company and its controller are seen as relevantly one person.

A. Model One: Wrongdoer and Company as the Same Actor

In *Gencor v Dalby*,[5] a fiduciary, Mr Dalby, channelled a secret profit to a company that he controlled in the British Virgin Islands, Burnstead Ltd. Orders to disgorge that profit were made against both the fiduciary and the company. Rimer J had no time for the argument that no order could be made against Mr Dalby because he had not actually made any profit, and no order could be made against Burnstead Ltd because it had not breached any fiduciary duty:

> I do not accept that argument which, if correct, would provide the easiest possible escape from the rigours of equity's strict principle of accountability. All that would be required would be for the profiting director to ensure that he diverts the profit into his own creature company. The facts of this case are that Burnstead was an offshore company which was wholly owned and controlled by Mr Dalby and in which nobody else had any beneficial interest. Everything it did was done on his directions and on his directions alone. It had no sales force, technical team or other employees capable of carrying on any business. Its only function was to make and receive payments. It was in substance little other than Mr Dalby's offshore bank account held in a nominee name. In my view this is the type of case in which the court ought to have no hesitation in regarding Burnstead simply as the alter ego through which Mr Dalby enjoyed the profit which he earned in breach of his fiduciary duty to ACP. If the arrival at this result requires a lifting of Burnstead's corporate veil, then I regard this as an appropriate case in which to do so. Burnstead is simply a creature company used for receiving profits for which equity holds Mr Dalby to be accountable to ACP. Its knowledge was in all respects the same as his knowledge. The introduction into the story of such a creature company is, in my view, insufficient to prevent equity's eye from identifying it with Mr Dalby … I hold that Mr Dalby and Burnstead are both accountable for the profit represented by this commission and I will make an order against them accordingly.[6]

Another example is *Trustor AB v Smallbone*.[7] In that case, Mr Smallbone caused payments to be made from Trustor, of which he was managing director, to another company that he controlled, Introcom. These payments were made in breach of his fiduciary duty owed to Trustor. Introcom then disbursed the funds, including paying some to Mr Smallbone personally. The case is discussed below on the point of the quantum of equitable compensation payable by a dishonest assistant.[8] It is

[5] *Gencor ACP Ltd v Dalby* [2000] EWHC 1560 (Ch), [2000] 2 BCLC 734.

[6] ibid [26]. Although Mr Dalby and Burnstead Ltd were liable on this basis, this would not have prevented Rimer J from finding another defendant, Mr Meehan, liable for dishonestly assisting Mr Dalby to divert the relevant opportunities to Burnstead. For other reasons, however, no order was made: ibid [83]–[88].

[7] *Trustor AB v Smallbone (No 2)* [2001] EWHC 703 (Ch), [2001] 1 WLR 1177.

[8] See text to n 79.

also relevant to the current discussion because Morritt VC decided that Trustor could pierce the corporate veil of Introcom, so as to make receipt by Introcom treated as receipt by Mr Smallbone personally.[9] Since an order had already been made against Introcom in earlier proceedings,[10] Morritt VC's order had the effect of making Introcom and Mr Smallbone jointly liable for the receipts of both.

Both *Gencor v Dalby* and *Trustor v Smallbone* were decided on a 'piercing the veil' basis, but a different approach was taken in *CMS Dolphin v Simonet.*[11] In that case, Mr Simonet diverted business opportunities away from CMS Dolphin, a company of which he was a director. The business was first given to a new partnership, referred to as Millennium, and then transferred to a new company that Mr Simonet formed, Blue Ltd. Although it operated for a time, Blue Ltd soon failed. The question was whether Mr Simonet was personally liable for the profits made by Blue Ltd. Lawrence Collins J concluded that both Mr Simonet and Blue were equally liable for those profits,[12] with the reason being that 'they have jointly participated in the breach of trust'.[13]

Cases in this line usually involve the same person being both a wrongdoing fiduciary and the controller of a corporate accessory. The point is to enlarge the personal liability of the fiduciary by making him or her liable for gains that were actually made by the accessory. However, it is not necessary for the defendant specifically to be a fiduciary; the important point is that he or she is a wrongdoer. At first instance in *Novoship*,[14] Christopher Clarke J had applied *Gencor v Dalby* and *Trustor v Smallbone* in treating dishonest assistants and their companies as the same actors. In relation to one of the assistants, Mr Nikitin, Christopher Clarke J held:

> The account must be against Henriot Finance, who were the immediate earners of the profit, and also against Mr Nikitin, who was the architect of the dishonest assistance effected through him and Henriot Finance, which was both his alter ego and the company which he chose as the immediate destination of the profits. It is not necessary to determine where, as between those two, the profits have ended up. That does not mean that the Claimants are entitled to recover twice: only that both are accounting parties.[15]

[9] *Trustor AB v Smallbone (No 2)* [2001] EWHC 703 (Ch), [2001] 1 WLR 1177 [23]–[25]; *cf Law Society of England & Wales v Isaac & Isaac International Holdings Ltd* [2010] EWHC 1670 (Ch) [40].

[10] For details of the earlier proceedings, see *Trustor AB v Smallbone* [2000] EWCA Civ 150 [8]–[18]. A brief summary is also given in *Trustor AB v Smallbone (No 2)* [2001] 1 WLR 1177 [1].

[11] *CMS Dolphin Ltd v Simonet* [2001] EWHC 415 (Ch).

[12] ibid [98]–[105] (in fact no final order was made against Blue as it was insolvent).

[13] ibid [103]; see criticism of this reasoning in *Ultraframe (UK) Ltd v Fielding* [2005] EWHC 1638 (Ch) [1574]–[1576]; *National Grid Electricity Transmission Plc v McKenzie Harbour Management Resources Ltd* [2009] EWHC 1817 (Ch) [117]; *VTB Capital Plc v Nutritek International Corp* [2012] EWCA Civ 808 [69]–[74] (appeal dismissed [2013] UKSC 5, [2013] 2 AC 337; only brief comment made on this point [136]).

[14] *Novoship (UK) Ltd v Mikhaylyuk* [2012] EWHC 3586 (Comm).

[15] ibid [529]; see also [413]–[414] re another defendant, Mr Ruperti, who settled and was not involved in the appeal: see *Novoship (UK) Ltd v Mikhaylyuk* [2015] EWHC 992 (Comm).

This point was not discussed in the Court of Appeal, where it was simply assumed that Mr Nikitin could be liable for profits made by companies that he controlled.[16] The issue in the Court of Appeal was the availability and calculation of accounts of profits against third parties, not how those third parties may be treated inter se.

Cook v Deeks may also be an example of this type of 'same actor' case.[17] Three directors of the Toronto Construction Company acquired a contract for their own benefit in breach of their fiduciary duty to the company. The directors formed a new company, the Dominion Construction Company, which took over the contract and made substantial profits. Finding in favour of the plaintiff, a shareholder in the original Toronto Construction Company, Lord Buckmaster LC said:

> Their Lordships have throughout referred to the claim as one against the defendants GS Deeks, GM Deeks, and TR Kinds [the three directors]. But it was not, and it could not be, disputed that the Dominion Construction Company acquired the rights of these defendants with full knowledge of all the facts, and the account must be directed in form as an account in favour of the Toronto Company against all the other defendants.[18]

There is, however, some doubt about what exactly *Cook v Deeks* decided on the liability point. Some later cases have treated it as establishing joint and several liability among the three directors and the Dominion Construction Company for the same global amount.[19] On this 'same actor' approach, each defendant would be liable for the profits made by themselves and the others: in effect, one account would be taken against all four defendants. But Lewison J took a different view in *Ultraframe (UK) Ltd v Fielding*.[20] He said that *Cook v Deeks*

> was a case in which the directors and the company were each ordered to account for profits. But there is no indication that the order for the account went further than ordering each of them to account for his (or its) own profits.[21]

Lewison J preferred to see the liability of third-party companies as independent *Barnes v Addy*-type liability (which he recognised could include a liability to account for profits).

[16] *Novoship (UK) Ltd v Mikhaylyuk* [2014] EWCA Civ 908, [2015] 1 QB 499 [62].

[17] *Cook v Deeks* [1916] 1 AC 554.

[18] ibid 565. The slightly odd phrasing is explained by the TCC itself being formally a defendant. The plaintiff was a TCC shareholder (and the fourth director) and the central question in the case was whether or not the three defendant directors could validly resolve that TCC had no interest in the impugned contract. That resolution was held ineffective. The outcome was that the account would be taken in favour of the TCC, against the three defendant directors and the DCC, but the plaintiff Cook 'must have the conduct of the proceedings'.

[19] Examples include *CMS Dolphin* (n 11) [104]; *Grimaldi v Chameleon Mining NL (No 2)* [2012] FCAFC 6, (2012) 200 FCR 296 [243]; *Cornerstone Property & Development Pty Ltd v Suellen Properties Pty Ltd* [2014] QSC 265, [2015] 1 Qd R 75 [98]; J McGhee (ed), *Snell's Equity*, 33rd edn (London, Sweet & Maxwell, 2015) para 7-055.

[20] *Ultraframe* (n 13).

[21] ibid [1574]. A point in favour of this view is that if *Cook v Deeks* did involve a form of joint liability for profits, then it apparently operated to make the three human defendants liable for profits made by each other too. The general rule of several liability for profits might be sidestepped by treating a fiduciary and company as relevantly the same actor, but applying that analysis among humans would be a much bolder step.

i. Basis of Liability

The liability imposed in these cases is easy to describe in general terms. The wrongdoing fiduciary and the company are treated as relevantly one actor, with each liable for the gains made by, and losses caused by, themselves and the other. But the proper basis of this liability is more difficult to pin down. In *Gencor v Dalby* and *Trustor v Smallbone*, we have seen that orders were made against both the wrongdoers and the companies that they controlled. The judges therefore saw no inconsistency in using a 'piercing the corporate veil' rationale to ground liability in the fiduciary, yet still making orders against the relevant companies.[22] Rather than piercing the veil, Lawrence Collins J in *CMS Dolphin v Simonet* preferred to explain this type of liability on a breach of trust in which the fiduciaries and their companies had 'jointly participated'. In *Cook v Deeks*, the Privy Council simply said that the Dominion Construction Company acquired the rights of the directors 'with full knowledge of all the facts'.[23]

In *Prest v Petrodel Resources Ltd*,[24] Lords Sumption and Neuberger sought to explain the results in these cases in a way that did not involve references to piercing the corporate veil or to a particular type of joint liability. In relation to *Gencor v Dalby*, Lord Sumption noted that the order against Mr Dalby could be justified because he had received the money through his agent, Burnstead Ltd; and the order against Burnstead could be justified because Mr Dalby's knowledge was imputed to Burnstead, which meant Burnstead was aware of the 'prior equitable interest' of the claimant. Some features of this explanation are worth noting. First, it involves Burnstead being Dalby's agent for the purposes of receipt, but Dalby being Burnstead's agent for the purposes of attribution of knowledge. Second, it also involves conceptualising the claimant's right to the secret profit as an equitable interest of which Burnstead could have knowledge.[25] Yet the claimant only ever sought an account of profits, and both *Gencor v Dalby* and *Prest v Petrodel* were decided before *FHR v Cedar Capital*[26] (although *Gencor* was decided at a time when *Reid*[27] may have been assumed to reflect the law in England). This equitable interest point is important because Lord Sumption went on to say that the result in *Gencor v Dalby* would have been the same if Burnstead was in fact a natural person through whom Dalby had channelled his profit. For that to be true, the money in the hands of the natural person must have been subject to a prior equitable interest. Seen as an agent of Mr Dalby, a natural person would only be

[22] This point admittedly ignores the litigation history in *Trustor*. The correctness of the order made against Introcom was not in issue before Morritt VC.

[23] *Cook* (n 17) 565.

[24] *Prest* (n 4) [31]–[33] (Lord Sumption), [68] (Lord Neuberger); see also CH Tan, 'Veil Piercing—A Fresh Start' [2015] *Journal of Business Law* 20.

[25] A similar analysis was used *Queensland Mines v Hudson* (1976) ACLC 28,658, although the claim in that case was time barred and the finding of underlying breach of fiduciary duty was overturned: (1978) 18 ALR 1.

[26] *FHR European Ventures LLP & Ors v Cedar Capital Partners LLC* [2014] UKSC 45, [2015] AC 250.

[27] *Attorney General for Hong Kong v Reid* [1994] 1 AC 324.

personally liable for inconsistent dealing (which requires a prior interest). Even seen as a wholly separate third party, with no imputation of knowledge, a natural person recipient would only be liable if she personally knew of an *interest* binding the money, not a claim in respect of it.[28]

Lord Sumption explained *Trustor v Smallbone* in a similar way: Introcom was Mr Smallbone's agent, so receipt by Introcom counted as receipt by Mr Smallbone. This analysis 'did not involve piercing the corporate veil, and did not depend on any finding of impropriety'.[29] His Lordship did not explain on what basis the order against Introcom (whose receipt on this analysis appears ministerial) could therefore have been made.[30]

Cook v Deeks was not mentioned in *Prest v Petrodel*, but we have seen that Lewison J in *Ultraframe* questioned whether it ever did involve joint liability among the defendants. *Cook* was also recently mentioned in *Novoship* in the Court of Appeal,[31] where it was seen as providing authority for the award of an account of profits against a *Barnes v Addy* third party. That interpretation is consistent with the view taken in *Ultraframe*. If, on the other hand, the three human defendants in *Cook v Deeks* were actually liable under the ordered account to disgorge profits made by the company, then the case provides no instruction on the liability of a *Barnes v Addy* third party.

Since *Prest v Petrodel*, only one case appears to have treated a corporate accessory as an alter ego in the sense used here. In *Otkritie International Investment Management Ltd v Urumov*,[32] Mr Urumov and Mr Pinaev were held liable for sums that were actually received by a company they owned and controlled (and that Eder J had 'no doubt … was their vehicle for receiving and distributing the fraud proceeds').[33] The company itself had since been dissolved and was not a defendant. *Trustor v Smallbone* and *Prest v Petrodel* were both cited. There were also alternative bases for the relief that was awarded, and, quite simply, the point was not seen as important in otherwise mammoth litigation.

The subsequent re-explanations of *Gencor* and *Trustor* in *Prest v Petrodel* do not fit those cases exactly. Of course this is not surprising; as a matter of history the cases were not actually decided on those grounds. But the important question is whether or not this re-explanation will actually mark a change in the English approach to cases of this type.[34] If even very closely connected corporate

[28] Knowledge of a claim can count as knowledge of an interest, but the interest itself still has to be there. It is not enough to have perfect knowledge of a personal claim: see *Papadimitriou v Crédit Agricole Corp and Investment Bank* [2015] UKPC 13, [2015] 1 WLR 4265 [12]–[21].

[29] *Prest* (n 4) [32].

[30] Lord Sumption recognised that the order against Introcom had been made at an earlier stage in proceedings, but was still operative: ibid [22]. Also see the different treatment of Lord Sumption and Lord Neuberger of the point of why in *Jones v Lipman* [1962] 1 WLR 832 the vendor's company, in addition to the vendor himself, was amenable to an order of specific performance: ibid [30] (Lord Sumption); [73] (Lord Neuberger).

[31] *Novoship* (n 16) [82]–[83].

[32] *Otkritie* (n 3) [371], [404]; see also [167], [397].

[33] ibid [309].

[34] This form of alter ego liability still seems to exist in Australia: see *Green v Bestobell Industries Pty Ltd (No 2)* [1984] WAR 32, 40; *Grimaldi* (n 19) [243]. In *Cornerstone* (n 19) [97]–[103], Jackson J was

accessories are always to be treated as *Barnes v Addy* third parties, rather than as alter egos of their wrongdoing fiduciary controllers, what does that mean? I will argue below that the consequences for a corporate accessory may be different depending on whether it is seen as (i) the alter ego of the fiduciary, and so in effect as another first-party wrongdoer; or as (ii) a true third party, liable for knowing receipt or dishonest assistance, albeit that this liability is imposed because the fiduciary's knowledge can be attributed to the company.

Finally, it may be noted that the cases in this line are generally concerned with making a natural person liable for some benefit or opportunity that was actually diverted to their company. Although orders can be made against the companies too, the point is really to enlarge the liability of the human controller. Whether or not this is objectionable, it would be quite another matter to make a company with other activities liable for a gain that was actually made personally by its controller. So far the courts have not struggled with this point simply because, in most of the cases, the associated companies can easily be seen as nothing more than pure vehicles for the impugned actions of their controllers. Where the companies do not have any other activities, the difficulty does not arise. However, in *CMS Dolphin*, Blue Ltd had operated successfully for a time and had presumably secured some contracts that were not tainted by Mr Simonet's original breach. (The point was still not live in that case because Blue was insolvent by the time of the hearing and was joined to the litigation as purely a formal matter.) The reason why the courts have not been troubled on this point is probably similar to the reason why they have not been troubled on the question of the necessary degree of control.[35] Cases where the degree of control is not obvious are (or were) probably not argued as alter ego or piercing the veil cases. Similarly, if a company has ongoing, independent activities it is less likely that it could be characterised as the alter ego of one of its controllers in the first place.

B. Model Two: Company as Separate Actor, with Imputed Knowledge

The second use of the phrase 'alter ego' involves a method of attributing knowledge to a company, usually for the purpose of making that company liable in some way. The same concept is seen when reference is made to a company's 'directing

critical of this type of liability, although he pointed out that *Farah Constructions Pty Ltd v Say-Dee Pty Ltd* [2007] HCA 22, (2007) 230 CLR 89 seems to assume it. See further J Glister, 'Diverting Fiduciary Gains to Companies' (2017) 40 *University of New South Wales Law Journal* (forthcoming).

[35] See *Gencor* (n 5) [19]; *Trustor AB v Smallbone* (n 10) [97] (Mr Smallbone thereafter conceded that he controlled Introcom: *Trustor AB v Smallbone (No 2)* [2001] 1 WLR 1177 [16]); *Antonio Gramsci Shipping Corp v Stepanovs* [2011] EWHC 333 (Comm), [2011] 1 Lloyd's Rep 647 [17] (on joint control; case since disapproved but not on this point: *VTB Capital* (n 4) [147]).

mind and will'.[36] But, unlike the *Gencor v Dalby* and *Trustor v Smallbone* line of cases discussed above, in this type of alter ego case the company is treated as a separate actor. It is liable as a third party for its own wrong, not for the fiduciary's wrong. In the current context, the relevant liability is normally knowing receipt or dishonest assistance, with the imputed knowledge being used to establish the mental fault elements in those claims. Unlike the cases in the previous section, the imputed knowledge here does not have to come from a wrongdoer. This is because it is not only knowledge of a person's *own* wrong that can be imputed to a company that he or she controls.

The most famous example of this type of imputation case is *El Ajou v Dollar Land Holdings plc*.[37] In that case, the defendant company, DLH, was held liable for knowing receipt based on the imputation of its chairman's knowledge that the funds received were the proceeds of fraud. The complication was that the chairman, Mr Ferdman, had not acquired his knowledge of the fraud while acting for DLH. For this reason, the Court of Appeal held that Mr Ferdman's knowledge could not be imputed on general agency principles. However, it could be imputed on the basis that Mr Ferdman was DLH's directing mind and will.[38]

The basis of imputation was not specifically addressed in *Aerostar Maintenance International Ltd v Wilson*,[39] although it seems also to have been a 'directing mind and will' case. Mr Wilson, a director of Aerostar Maintenance, diverted business to another company, Avman Ltd, in breach of his fiduciary duty to Aerostar. Morgan J declined to follow *CMS Dolphin v Simonet* and make Mr Wilson personally liable for profits that were actually made by Avman Ltd.[40] He also distinguished *Gencor v Dalby* and *Trustor v Smallbone*.[41] However, Morgan J did find Avman Ltd liable as a third party for knowing receipt and dishonest assistance. The necessary knowledge or dishonesty was easily imputed:

> As to Avman's knowledge, at the time that Avman entered into the contract with Romaero and Galaxy, the knowledge of Mr Wilson is to be imputed to Avman and, as so imputed, Avman knew that the benefits of the contracts it was making were property, or the traceable proceeds of property, held subject to fiduciary duties and that there had been a

[36] See generally E Ferran, 'Corporate Attribution and the Directing Mind and Will' (2011) 127 *LQR* 239.

[37] *El Ajou v Dollar Land Holdings plc* [1994] 2 All ER 685. In *Lebon v Aqua Salt Co Ltd (Mauritius)* [2009] UKPC 2 [24], Lord Hoffmann saw *El Ajou* as a forerunner of *Meridian Global Funds Management Asia Ltd v Securities Commission* [1995] 2 AC 500; see also *Bilta (UK) Ltd (in liq) v Nazir (No 2)* [2015] UKSC 23, [2016] AC 1 [68].

[38] Note that Mr Ferdman was not one of the original wrongdoers; he merely had knowledge of their wrongdoing.

[39] *Aerostar Maintenance International Ltd v Wilson* [2010] EWHC 2032 (Ch) (liability); [2012] EWHC 1353 (Ch) (quantum, after the claimants had elected for equitable compensation; see text to n 109).

[40] ibid [202]. Of course, a corporate accessory does not have to be a fiduciary's alter ego before it will be a breach of duty for the fiduciary to divert opportunities to it: *Pennyfeathers Ltd v Pennyfeathers Property Company Ltd* [2013] EWHC 3530 (Ch) [117].

[41] ibid [205].

> breach of fiduciary duty in allowing or causing Avman to enter into those contracts. In these circumstances, in my judgment, it was unconscionable for Avman to receive and retain the benefit of the contracts … The case for dishonesty on the part of Avman is that Mr Wilson was dishonest and his dishonesty is to be imputed to Avman. I find that Mr Wilson was dishonest.[42]

Another case where the wrongdoing fiduciary was also the accessory's directing mind and will is *Odyssey Entertainment Ltd v Kamp*.[43] Odyssey, a film sales agency, successfully sued its former chairman and chief executive, Mr Kamp, for breaching his fiduciary duty by pursuing opportunities on behalf of a new company, Timeless, that he owned with his wife. Mr Kamp secured a deal for the rights to *Space Chimps 2: Zartog Strikes Back* and also conducted a clandestine meeting with 'the creative mind behind Postman Pat'. Although Mr Kamp sought to resist the finding of a breach of fiduciary duty, he admitted to being Timeless's directing mind and will. Once an underlying breach of fiduciary duty had been found, it was therefore a short step to finding Timeless liable as an accessory.

The editors of *Bowstead & Reynolds* have questioned how far a 'directing mind and will' doctrine should operate generally, as opposed to in the specific contexts of the construction of statutes and contracts. In their view, general principles of agency should apply when the question is about fixing companies with *Barnes v Addy* liability, and they argue that that the mandate-confined rule of imputation does not operate as sharply as was thought in *El Ajou*.[44] For the most part I can bypass this issue, because the main point here is to distinguish between (i) treating the corporate accessory and the wrongdoer as the same actor, and (ii) treating the corporate accessory and the wrongdoer as separate actors. The way that knowledge is imputed in cases in the second category is therefore not of central importance. Even so, it is still worth making a brief digression.

i. Corporate Accessories and Human Accessories

Although the means by which knowledge is imputed is not relevant to the central distinction drawn in this chapter, it is worth noting that the availability of a 'directing mind and will' mode of imputation marks a difference between the

[42] ibid [195], [198]. Both knowledge and dishonesty can be imputed: *Roadchef (Employee Benefits Trustees) Ltd v Hill* [2014] EWHC 109 (Ch) [167]. But dishonesty cannot be aggregated, unlike (perhaps) knowledge: see P Watts, 'Imputed Knowledge in Agency Law—Excising the Fraud Exception' (2001) 117 *LQR* 300, 302; C Mitchell, 'Assistance' in P Birks and A Pretto (eds), *Breach of Trust* (Oxford, Hart Publishing, 2002) 139, 203–04; P Watts and F Reynolds (eds), *Bowstead and Reynolds on Agency*, 20th edn (London, Sweet & Maxwell, 2014) para 8-208(e).

[43] *Odyssey Entertainment Ltd v Kamp* [2012] EWHC 2316 (Ch). In fact the claimant apparently sought to ground liability on both models, though it is not clear if this was successful: see [228]–[229], [283], [287].

[44] Watts and Reynolds (n 42) paras 1-024, 8-209, 8-214; also P Watts. 'The Company's Alter Ego: An Imposter in Private Law' (2000) 116 *LQR* 525; P Watts, 'Imputed Knowledge in Restitutionary Claims: Rationales and Rationes' in S Degeling and J Edelman (eds), *Unjust Enrichment in Commercial Law* (Pyrmont, Thomson Reuters, 2008) 429. In *Bilta (No 2)* (n 37) [197], Lords Toulson and Hodge '[saw] the force in the suggestion' that an agency analysis would have worked in *El Ajou*.

treatment of corporate and human accessories.[45] In cases where natural persons receive property, the correct scope of the relevant agency principles then becomes particularly important. Those principles may be broader in scope than sometimes thought, but they are not wide enough to encompass a 'directing mind and will' concept that applies among natural persons.[46]

An example of the possible result of this difference in treatment can be seen in the recent Australian case of *Australasian Annuities v Rowley Super Fund*.[47] Mr Rowley, the sole director and one of two shareholders in Australasian Annuities Pty Ltd (AA), a financial planning business, arranged for the company to borrow $2.5 million from Macquarie Bank. With Macquarie's knowledge, that money was to be paid (and most of it was so paid) into the superannuation funds of Mr and Mrs Rowley so they could take advantage of certain tax concessions. When AA then failed during the global financial crisis, Macquarie Bank appointed receivers and managers and tried to recover the funds that had been paid out as superannuation contributions. The receivers argued that the payments had been arranged by Mr Rowley in breach of his fiduciary duty to the company, and this was accepted at trial and in the Court of Appeal. The receivers also argued that the superannuation trustee, Rowley Super Fund Pty Ltd (RSF), should be imputed with the knowledge of Mr Rowley, who was also a director of that company. That contention was rejected at trial but was accepted by a majority of the Court of Appeal. RSF was therefore liable in knowing receipt to repay the superannuation contributions to AA.

For our purposes, the case is interesting because of the status of the superannuation trustees. At first, the superannuation funds were held and managed by four family members: Mr and Mrs Rowley and their two children. The trustees were, therefore, four natural persons. Most of the superannuation payments paid by AA were made during this period. It was only later that the corporate trustee RSF was created, with the four family members as directors. The existing superannuation funds were then transferred to this new corporate trustee, with some fresh contributions also being made.

In Australia, superannuation trustees are not seen as volunteers. Instead, they give value.[48] This means that the equitable liability of such trustees, whether

[45] And, therefore, of incorporated and unincorporated businesses.

[46] Note Professor Watts's tentative suggestion that the rules of imputation of knowledge could apply outside agency relationships: 'familial relationships, natural and corporate, may provide a separate basis for imputation where the transaction is not, in substance, one at arm's length': Watts, 'Imputed Knowledge in Restitutionary Claims' (n 44) 436. There must indeed be cases where a wrongdoer has channelled funds to a wholly oblivious family member who has since spent them. But these would probably not be treated as knowing receipt cases, so the imputation point would not arise.

[47] *Australasian Annuities Pty Ltd (ACN 006 313 408) (in liq) (recs and mgrs apptd) v Rowley Super Fund Pty Ltd (ACN 129 688 455)* [2015] VSCA 9, (2015) 318 ALR 302. Disclosure: I was an academic consultant on RSF's unsuccessful application for special leave.

[48] *Cook v Benson* [2003] HCA 36, (2003) 214 CLR 370 (although one of the Court of Appeal judges in *Australasian Annuities*, Neave JA, doubted that *Cook* applied to a self-managed situation: *Australasian Annuities* (n 47) [144]–[150]).

natural or corporate, depends on knowledge at the time of receipt.[49] In *Australasian Annuities v Rowley Super Fund*, the Court of Appeal held that Mr Rowley's knowledge of his own breach could be imputed to the corporate trustee, RSF, because Mr Rowley could be seen as the company's directing mind and will.[50] The corporate trustee was therefore liable in knowing receipt for all of the funds it had received.[51] But Mrs Rowley and the two children were not liable in knowing receipt for the contributions that had earlier been paid to them. This was because they had no personal knowledge of the breach, and Mr Rowley's knowledge could not be imputed to them because there was no agency.[52] The difference between a situation involving natural trustees and one involving a corporate trustee is therefore stark.

ii. 'Fraud Exception'

It is also worth mentioning here the 'fraud exception' to the attribution of knowledge, although it may well be that the label should now be discarded.[53] This 'exception' operates to prevent knowledge of a director's fraud on his company from being attributed to that company. In most cases it prevents the wrongdoing director, or a third party whom the defrauded company is pursuing, from arguing as a defence that the claimant company had full knowledge of the wrongful conduct. Since the principle usually operates in this context, it does not normally appear in cases where it is the company itself that is being sued (and these are the cases that are relevant to the present discussion). Indeed, in England it can probably be said that the principle is simply inapplicable to such cases.[54] However, one of the corporate defendants in the Australian case of *Grimaldi v Chameleon Mining NL (No 2)* did escape liability through this use of the fraud exception.[55]

In that case, Chameleon was suing Murchison, a company controlled at the relevant time by Mr Grimaldi, for knowing receipt and assistance in respect of Mr Grimaldi's breach of fiduciary duty. Murchison accepted that its controlling

[49] *cf* the English case of *Clark v Cutland* [2003] EWCA Civ 810, [2004] 1 WLR 783, where knowledge could be given later because the pension fund trustees were volunteers.

[50] *Australasian Annuities* (n 47) [136]–[143] (Neave JA); [261]–[269] (Garde AJA, citing *El Ajou*).

[51] Including those funds that were transferred from the natural person trustees. It is arguable that, to a three-quarter extent, those funds had passed through the hands of bona fide purchasers for value. Peter Watts makes the same point in his chapter in this volume.

[52] On this point all four judges agreed: *Australasian Annuities Pty Ltd (in liq) v Rowley Super Fund Pty Ltd* [2013] VSC 543 [100]–[116] (Almond J); *Australasian Annuities* (n 47) [97]–[105] (Warren CJ), [135] (Neave JA), [303] (Garde AJA).

[53] See *Bilta (No 2)* (n 37) [9], [44], [191]: endorsing the view taken in Watts and Reynolds (n 42) para 8-213, that the exception simply describes situations where there is no need to impute knowledge to the company. See also Watts, 'Imputed Knowledge in Agency Law' (n 42).

[54] See *Morris v Bank of India* [2005] EWCA Civ 693, [2005] 2 BCLC 328 [114]; *Bilta (UK) Ltd (in liq) v Nazir (No 2)* [2013] EWCA Civ 968, [2014] Ch 52 [34]; [2015] UKSC 23, [2016] AC 1 [87]–[88]. Also see *Moulin Global Eyecare Trading Ltd (in liq) v CIR* [2014] HKCFA 22, (2014) 17 HKCFAR 218 [101], [131] (Lord Walker of Gestingthorpe NPJ); E Lim, 'Attribution in Company Law' (2014) 77 *MLR* 780, 800–02.

[55] *Grimaldi* (n 19).

mind was Mr Grimaldi and that his knowledge could be imputed to it, except where it involved knowledge of a fraud on Murchison. By characterising Mr Grimaldi's actions as a fraud on Murchison, rather than (or in addition to) a fraud on Chameleon, Murchison escaped liability to Chameleon.[56] The fraud exception was therefore applied to a case where the company was the defendant rather than the claimant, with the reason being that the director's scheme involved a fraud on the defendant company as well as a breach of duty in respect of the claimant company. It may be noted that a similar argument had been summarily rejected by the English Court of Appeal in *Morris v Bank of India*,[57] although in that case the 'fraud' perpetrated on the defendant company was argued to be exposing it to potential liability for fraudulent trading under the Insolvency Act 1986, section 213. As the Court held, a company could never be liable for fraudulent trading at all if that argument was valid.

Even if it is theoretically possible for a company to raise the fraud exception in the context of defending claims, which seems extremely doubtful in England, it should still be hard to characterise the fiduciary's actions as a fraud on the company if that company is simply being used to channel funds away from a principal. Merely exposing the company to liability in knowing receipt or assistance, and liability for costs, will not be sufficient.

III. Differences between the Two Models

Section II outlined two different models of corporate accessory liability. This section will discuss three areas where there is, or might be, a difference in outcome depending on which model is applied. The areas to be discussed involve gain-based liability (where liability among fiduciaries and third parties is several, and each is not liable for gains made by the other); loss-based liability (where the position is not entirely clear, but where the liability might differ between fiduciaries and third parties); and the question of whether a plaintiff can recover on different bases from the fiduciary and the third party, or whether to do so would be inconsistent.

A. Gain-Based Liability

An undoubted difference between treating a corporate accessory as an alter ego of the fiduciary and treating it as a separate third party concerns accountability for

[56] Murchison escaped liability in respect of some of Mr Grimaldi's breaches, but not all: ibid [285], [747].

[57] *Morris* (n 54). In the Court of Appeal in *Moore Stephens (A Firm) v Stone & Rolls Ltd (in liq)* [2008] EWCA Civ 644 [114], Mummery LJ commented with some geographical accuracy that such an argument 'turns the world upside down'.

gains. Under the alter ego model, the accessory would be liable for its gains and gains made by the fiduciary. Similarly, the fiduciary would be personally liable for gains actually made by the accessory. Under the second model, however, both the fiduciary and accessory would be liable only for gains that they individually made. To put it another way, liability for gains between fiduciaries and third parties is several.

This is the position in a nutshell, but some further points can briefly be made. First, the issue is not always recognised. In *Warman International Ltd v Dwyer*,[58] for example, accounts of profits were sought by Warman International against its former employee and fiduciary, Mr Dwyer, and against two businesses Dwyer controlled, BTA and ETA. The trial judge had made a single order, against all three of Dwyer, BTA and ETA, of the combined amount of the profits made by BTA and ETA. The structure of this order was not challenged in the High Court, where the Court noted:

> It is arguable that any order, such as that made by the trial judge, for payment of a sum determined by an account of BTA's and ETA's profits should be divided into two orders, one against BTA alone for the amount determined by reference to its profits and the other against ETA alone for the amount determined by reference to its profits … As has been mentioned, however, Dwyer, BTA and ETA did not argue in this Court or in the Court of Appeal that the respective orders made in the courts below should not have been made against the three of them jointly. In the absence of any such argument, it has effectively been common ground that any orders made should be against all three.[59]

Second, there is an argument that a dishonest assistant ought to be liable for profits actually made by the fiduciary. This does not depend on any alter ego argument; it is simply a question of the nature of the liability owed by someone who is genuinely a third party (and a similar issue is discussed in the next section in relation to an assistant's compensatory liability). The proposition derives support from a line of Canadian cases,[60] although it has been examined and rejected in recent years by courts in both Australia[61] and England.[62] While the proposition was rejected in *Grimaldi*, it was suggested that for reasons of legal policy a fiduciary and third party might be jointly and severally liable for profits if they acted in concert to secure a mutual benefit: it should not be for a plaintiff to 'untangle' such matters.[63]

[58] *Warman International Ltd v Dwyer* (1995) 182 CLR 544.

[59] ibid 569.

[60] *Canada Safety Ltd v Thompson* [1951] 3 DLR 295, 323; *D'Amore v MacDonald* (1973) 32 DLR (3d) 543, 549; *Abbey Glen Property Corp v Stumborg* (1976) 65 DLR (3d) 235, 282; *MacDonald v Hauer* (1976) 72 DLR (3d) 110, 130; *Hanson v Clifford* 1994 CanLII 2982 (BCSC); see also SB Elliott and C Mitchell, 'Remedies for Dishonest Assistance' (2004) 67 *MLR* 16, 40–41.

[61] *Glandon v Tilmunda* [2008] NSWSC 218 [108]; *Grimaldi* (n 19) [557]; *cf Hodgson v Amcor Ltd* [2012] VSC 94 [1718]–[1721]; see also *Agricultural Land Management Ltd v Jackson (No 2)* [2014] WASC 102 [480]; JD Heydon, MJ Leeming and PG Turner, *Meagher Gummow and Lehane's Equity: Doctrines and Remedies*, 5th edn (Chatswood, LexisNexis Butterworths, 2015) para 5-270.

[62] *Ultraframe* (n 13) [1595]–[1601]; *Electrosteel Castings (UK) Ltd v Metalpol Ltd* [2014] EWHC 2017 (Ch) [50]–[51].

[63] *Grimaldi* (n 19) [558].

Third, the calculation of an account of profits may differ if the accessory is considered a discrete third party. That is, the total amount of disgorgeable profit recoverable (severally) from the fiduciary and accessory may be lower if accessories are considered separately. This is because the accounts may be calculated differently when made in respect of a third-party accessory rather than a first-party fiduciary. The Court of Appeal in *Novoship* drew a distinction between true fiduciaries and third parties in this context, and also noted that the court has discretion to refuse an account sought from a third party.[64] I return to this point below.[65]

Fourth (and this is a minor point) there is an occasional judicial tendency in England to refer to equitable compensation as a remedy awarded pursuant to a liability to account for profits.[66] That is perhaps consistent with seeing equitable compensation as nothing more than the amount owing after an account has been taken, but it still sounds odd. It is worth mentioning because, as will be discussed in the next section, it is probably the case in England that a dishonest assistant is jointly and severally liable with the fiduciary for the principal's loss. If the fiduciary's liability to account for profits is referred to as a liability to pay equitable compensation calculated according to the amount of the profit, there is a risk that the assistant may be held jointly and severally liable for that amount.

B. Loss-Based Liability

The second area where treatment might differ involves the assessment of equitable compensation for the principal's loss.[67] The question here is whether a third-party accessory is liable to the same extent as the wrongdoing fiduciary, or whether the accessory is liable only for the consequences of his or her involvement in that breach. Is a dishonest assistant liable for losses flowing from the underlying breach in which he or she assists, or is the assistant liable only for the consequences of the assistance itself? This question is relevant to our discussion because, if the compensatory liability of third parties and fiduciaries is assessed differently, corporate accessories could then be in a different position depending on whether they are seen as separate third parties or as alter egos of the wrongdoing fiduciaries.

We should immediately note that the actions of an accessory may be so vital to the carrying out of the fiduciary's breach that it is appropriate to make the accessory liable for the whole loss flowing from that breach. In many cases, the point addressed here will therefore be hidden. But the important question is whether this equal liability *necessarily* applies: once a baseline finding of assistance has been

[64] *Novoship* (n 16) [94]–[115], [119]. The decision is criticised in W Gummow, 'Dishonest Assistance and Account of Profits' (2015) 74 *CLJ* 405.

[65] See Section IV.

[66] eg *FHR* (n 26) [6].

[67] Much of the material in this section is taken from the fuller discussion in J Glister, 'Knowing Assistance and Equitable Compensation' (2016) 42 *Australian Bar Review* 152.

made out,[68] along with the requisite mental element, is the accessory *necessarily* liable to the principal[69] for the consequences of the fiduciary's breach?

This is an area where the law is somewhat unsettled, or at least is not firmly entrenched. In England, the law appears to be that dishonest assistants will be liable to the same extent as the fiduciary; that is, liable for the consequences of the trustee's breach. Those assistants are therefore unable to reduce the award of equitable compensation made against them by showing, for example, that the trustee would have gone ahead regardless of their help. However, although this appears to be the position, it cannot be regarded as entirely settled. The point has only been part of the ratio in two decided cases; it was not closely argued in either case; and in one of the cases the Court of Appeal gave an alternative reason for the result. In addition, and while again the point cannot be regarded as settled, it may be that the law in Australia takes the opposite view. The area will therefore be discussed in some detail, although of course the material that follows does not apply only to corporate accessories.

i. English Authorities

It is difficult to find old authorities directly on the point. This is probably because the language of equitable compensation as a remedy for loss simply did not exist until recently. Instead, the question was whether or not a third party was to be made a 'constructive trustee' for the purposes of liability to restore the trust fund. Within such language it is implicit that, once a third party was found to be a constructive trustee, the attendant liability was the same as that owed by the true trustees.

In *Wilson v Moore*,[70] agents of executors helped the executors to misapply estate property. Today the case might be treated as one of inconsistent dealing or knowing assistance. Sir John Leach MR said:

> If [the agents] Messrs Marryat are chargeable, it is because, in the consideration of a Court of Equity, they, by being parties to a breach of trust, have themselves become trustees for the purposes of the testator's will … All parties to a breach of trust are equally liable; there is between them no primary liability.[71]

[68] A claimant 'must at least show that the defendant's actions have made the fiduciary's breach of duty easier than it would otherwise have been': D Hayton, P Matthews and C Mitchell, *Underhill and Hayton: Law of Trusts and Trustees*, 18th edn (London, LexisNexis, 2010) para 98.52; *Brink's Ltd v Abu-Saleh* [1999] CLC 133; *Brown v Bennett* [1999] 1 BCLC 649, 659.

[69] Regardless of the extent of the third party's liability to the principal, questions of contribution may arise between the third party and the fiduciary: see C Mitchell, 'Apportioning Liability for Trust Losses' in P Birks and F Rose (eds), *Restitution and Equity vol 1: Resulting Trusts and Equitable Compensation* (London, LLP, 2000) 211; A Gurr, 'Accessory Liability and Contribution, Release and Apportionment' (2010) 34 *Melbourne University Law Review* 410. An added Australian complication, which will not be discussed here, is the potential application of the Civil Liability Acts.

[70] *Wilson v Moore* (1833) 1 M & K 126.

[71] ibid 146.

Wilson v Moore was followed in *Cowper v Stoneham*,[72] where the question was whether solicitors of trustees had made themselves constructive trustees through intermeddling. Stirling J said that it was 'not a case of primary liability on the part of the trustees and secondary liability on the part of the solicitors, but that Messrs Stoneham and the trustees are all equally liable'.[73]

The point being made in both cases was that the defendant third parties were just as 'primarily' liable as the defaulting trustees themselves.[74] The liability of the third parties did not depend on the trustees being unable to satisfy a judgment, or indeed on the trustees being pursued at all. Essentially, the cases simply determined that the same liability was owed by the trustees and the relevant third parties. It is true that the cases did not explicitly address the point of the *quantum* of liability as between the trustees and the third parties, but it was implicit in each case that the full loss could be recovered from all defendants (subject to double recovery).

a. *Grupo Torras v Al-Sabah*

In terms of the modern law, the starting point for any discussion must be *Grupo Torras SA v Al-Sabah (No 5)*,[75] one of the two cases that actually decides or applies the point. The case concerned a Spanish company, Grupo Torras, and its parent, the Kuwait Investment Office, both of which were the victims of several large-scale frauds perpetrated by their directors. It was alleged that several third parties had dishonestly assisted these breaches. In response to the submission that a plaintiff must prove that the dishonest assistance has itself caused the loss suffered by the plaintiff, Mance LJ held:

> The starting point in my view is that the requirement of dishonest assistance relates not to any loss or damage which may be suffered, but to the breach of trust or fiduciary duty. The relevant enquiry is in my view what loss or damage resulted from the breach of trust or fiduciary duty which has been dishonestly assisted. In this context, as in conspiracy, it is inappropriate to become involved in attempts to assess the precise causative significance of the dishonest assistance in respect of either the breach of trust or fiduciary duty or the resulting loss.[76]

Mance LJ actually applied the law as postulated, because (following a baseline finding of the fact of assistance) he only considered whether defendants were

[72] *Cowper v Stoneham* (1893) 68 LT 18.

[73] ibid 19; see also *Blyth v Fladgate* [1891] 1 Ch 337, involving a solicitor-trustee who invested money in a poorly-performing security. The question was whether the solicitor's partners were also liable for the loss suffered. Stirling J held that they were, but this was either on the grounds of vicarious liability for the acts of a partner, or on the grounds that all three partners were co-trustees *de son tort*: see the discussion of the case in *Re Bell's Indenture* [1980] 1 WLR 1217, 1226–31.

[74] In this respect compare liability under *Lumley v Gye* (1853) 2 E & B 216; discussed in Davies (n 1) 258–60.

[75] *Grupo Torras SA v Al-Sabah (No 5)* [1999] CLC 1469.

[76] ibid 1667; (Mance J had been appointed to the Court of Appeal between the hearing and the decision).

dishonest in the *Royal Brunei Airlines v Tan* sense.[77] Ultimately, Mance LJ found that four assistants were not dishonest, and one, Mr Folchi, was dishonest. Mr Folchi was a lawyer who had assisted in some of the frauds by carrying out instructions that were obviously questionable. In respect of those frauds, Mr Folchi was liable for the same amounts as were the wrongdoing fiduciaries. An appeal by Mr Folchi failed, and the Court of Appeal expressly agreed with Mance LJ's analysis of the point. However, and perhaps unhelpfully, the Court of Appeal also added the following comment: 'In any case Mr Folchi was, as the judge found on ample grounds, a linchpin of the arrangements for all four transactions'.[78] This alternative reason for the result—that Mr Folchi's conduct was sufficient on any model to attract liability for the full amount—perhaps undermines to some degree the authority of Mance LJ's statement of principle.

b. *Trustor v Smallbone*

The essential facts of *Trustor v Smallbone* have already been given during the alter ego discussion.[79] The case is also relevant to the question of the extent of an assistant's liability because of a comment made by the Court of Appeal. The context was that Rimer J had made an interim payment order against Mr Smallbone in the amount of £1 million, and the Court of Appeal had to decide whether or not this order could be justified. Rimer J had made the order on the basis that Mr Smallbone would clearly be liable to Trustor for damages or compensation for breach of his directors' duties in an amount of at least £1 million. The order had not been made on the basis of obvious liability in dishonest assistance. Scott VC, with whom Buxton LJ and Gage J agreed, said:

> Introcom is liable, as constructive trustee, to account for and repay to Trustor the Trustor moneys that were paid to it. Hence the order for repayment to Trustor of the SEK 166.7 million, the £404,000 and the FIM 70.45 million (the whole totalling some £20 million in value). In respect of £426,439, the Trustor money received by Mr Smallbone from Introcom, Mr Smallbone, as well as Introcom is accountable. But what of the balance? Introcom was the creature of Mr Smallbone. He owned and controlled Introcom. The payments out by Introcom of Trustor money were payments made with the knowing assistance of Mr Smallbone. Rimer J, on several occasions in his judgment, characterised Mr Smallbone's participation in the steps taken to extract Trustor's money and pay it out to various recipients without the authority of Trustor's board as being dishonest … *It would follow, it seems to me, from the judge's finding of dishonesty on Mr Smallbone's part in respect of the payments out made by Introcom of Trustor's money, that Mr Smallbone would be liable jointly and severally with Introcom for the repayment of that money with interest thereon. Mr Smallbone's joint and several liability would not be confined to the part that he personally received.* In my judgment, the judge's order for an interim payment by Mr Smallbone of £1 million was not justified as an interim payment on account of

[77] *Royal Brunei Airlines Sdn Bhd v Tan* [1995] 2 AC 378.
[78] [2001] CLC 221, 255 (an appeal by another defendant was successful).
[79] *Trustor AB v Smallbone* (n 10); *Trustor AB v Smallbone (No 2)* [2001] 1 WLR 1177.

> damages or compensation for loss caused by breach of duty as a director. The amount of that loss is still too uncertain. But Mr Smallbone is, in my view, clearly liable, jointly and severally with Introcom, for the whole of the sums for which Introcom is accountable.[80]

In fact it is far from clear that Mr Smallbone could be characterised as a dishonest assistant, since what he was doing was causing Introcom, the first recipient of tainted funds, to squirrel those funds still further away from Trustor. But the relevant fiduciary breach was Mr Smallbone's own, as a director of Trustor; it was not that of Introcom. Putting that to one side, the paragraph does assume joint and several liability on the part of a dishonest assistant for the whole loss suffered.[81] But the point was merely assumed, and ultimately the Court of Appeal decided *not* to uphold the order anyway—precisely because Mr Smallbone had not had the opportunity to make submissions on the reasoning used in the passage quoted above.

c. *Casio Computer Co Ltd v Sayo*

The analysis in *Grupo Torras* was applied by the Court of Appeal in *Casio Computer Co Ltd v Sayo*,[82] the only other case where the point has been important. The case concerned the issue of whether, in an action for dishonest assistance, the act of assistance constitutes a harmful event 'relating to tort, delict or quasi delict' for the purposes of the Brussels Convention. The Court of Appeal held that it does. A further question then arose relating to causation, because liability in tort, delict or quasi delict 'can only arise provided that a causal connection can be established between the damage and the event in which that damage originates'.[83] Tuckey LJ referred to *Grupo Torras*:

> *Grupo Torras* also establishes that in a claim for dishonest assistance it is not necessary to show a precise causal link between the assistance and the loss. Loss caused by the breach of fiduciary duty is recoverable from the accessory. This is the relevant causal connection for this purpose. In the absence of such a connection the accessory would be under no liability. So this type of claim does depend on there being 'a causal connection between damage and the event in which the damage originates'.[84]

Again, the point was not the subject of argument and it seems fair to say that its correctness was assumed rather than decided. Having said that, in some ways *Casio v Sayo* is the strongest authority in favour of joint and several liability because it was necessary for the decision in the case and there was no alternative reason also suggested for that decision (as there was in *Grupo Torras*). It can also be noted that, although those two cases agree on the legal position in respect of the assistant's liability, they are not entirely consistent in their rationales. At least, there is a

[80] *Trustor AB v Smallbone* (n 10) [97]–[98] (emphasis added).

[81] Note the comment assumes liability for the whole loss on assistance grounds but only for the amount received on receipt grounds; *cf* the approach to *Trustor v Smallbone* taken in *Prest v Petrodel*.

[82] *Casio Computer Co Ltd v Sayo* [2001] EWCA Civ 661.

[83] *Handelskwekerij GJ Bier BV v Mines de Potassed'Alsace SA* [1976] ECR 1735, 1746.

[84] *Casio* (n 82) [15] (Tuckey LJ); see also [52]–[53] (Pill LJ).

difference of emphasis. In *Grupo Torras*, Mance LJ employed a legal policy argument: 'it is inappropriate to become involved in attempts to assess the precise causative significance of the dishonest assistance'.[85] In *Casio v Sayo*, on the other hand, it was treated as a causation point: as a matter of legal causation, assistance of more than a de minimis level *causes the whole loss* suffered as a result of the breach. (Of course, on this latter approach it is wrong to distinguish between liability 'for the breach' and liability 'for the assistance'.)

d. Other Cases

The point has been mentioned in a few other English cases, but very little seems to have turned on it and it has certainly not been explored. In *Ultraframe (UK) Ltd v Fielding*, Lewison J said that he could 'see that it makes sense for a dishonest assistant to be jointly and severally liable for any *loss* which the beneficiary suffers as a result of a breach of trust'.[86] But the two claims for dishonest assistance made in that case both failed: one for a lack of dishonesty, the other for a lack of relevant assistance. In *Madoff Securities International Ltd v Raven*, Popplewell J said that the 'liability of the assistant is for such loss as the party in breach of fiduciary duty would be liable for. It is not necessary to show that the assistance itself is causative of any loss'.[87] Again the point was not truly in issue, however: Popplewell J found no relevant breach of fiduciary duty, no dishonesty on the part of the third party, and said that in any case no loss was suffered. The point was also mentioned in *Novoship* at first instance and on appeal,[88] but that case was really about the calculation of accounts of profits.

In *Otkritie International Investment Management Ltd v Urumov*, Eder J said that 'liability is not limited to the loss caused by [the] assistance but extends to the loss resulting from the relevant breaches of fiduciary duty'.[89] The point might have had some relevance there because the relevant defendant, Mr Jemai, was clearly not one of the ringleaders in the fraud and he might otherwise have sought to reduce his liability. Having said that, Mr Jemai was found liable for the full loss anyway on the alternative grounds of deceit and conspiracy.[90] (It is also interesting

[85] *Grupo Torras* (n 75) 1667. This is also the reason given in Snell: 'Since the defendant's fault is serious, he cannot put the claimant to proof of the specific causal connection between the assistance he gave and the loss that ensued': McGhee (n 19) para 30-081.

[86] *Ultraframe* (n 13) [1600]. The original emphasis on 'loss' exists because Lewison J was really addressing the point about whether an assistant is liable for gains made by the trustee.

[87] *Madoff Securities International Ltd v Raven* [2013] EWHC 3147 (Comm) [339], cited in L Tucker, N Le Poidevin and J Brightwell (eds), *Lewin on Trusts*, 19th edn (London, Sweet & Maxwell, 2015) para 40-053.

[88] *Novoship* (n 14) [90]; *Novoship* (n 16) [103].

[89] *Otkritie* (n 3) [79], citing *Grupo Torras*.

[90] ibid [519]. Mr Jemai's sister, Ms Jemai, was also found liable for certain amounts on perhaps problematic bases (eg, she was found liable for dishonest assistance, or in the alternative knowing receipt, in respect of money that she had not received and when the company could not easily be said to be her alter ego: see [549]). Gloster LJ gave permission to appeal in [2015] EWCA Civ 766, not directly on this quantification point, but it may still be useful to observe any full appeal. Mr Jemai's application was refused: [2015] EWCA Civ 916.

to note that Eder J saw the liability to pay equitable compensation and the liability to account as separate—yet on a traditional analysis it was the liability to account that informed the nature and extent of the relief.)

ii. Australian Authorities

Several cases in Australia appear to take the view that an assistant is liable for the whole loss flowing from the breach. However, in none of these has the point been important. In *New Cap Reinsurance Corporation Ltd v General Cologne Re Australia Ltd*, Young CJ in Eq noted that 'the accessory is jointly and severally liable with the principal malefactor to pay the amount of equitable compensation required to restore the trust fund',[91] but nothing apparently turned on it. In *Re-Engine Pty Ltd (in liq) v Fergusson*, Dodds-Streeton J would have found a third party jointly and severally liable with the fiduciary for the 'total loss and damage to the plaintiffs sustained by reason of his breaches of fiduciary duty',[92] but the claim for knowing assistance failed due to a lack of relevant assistance. Ward J referred to Mance LJ's *Grupo Torras* formulation in *George v Webb*,[93] but the third party's conduct in that case was so egregious that he would undoubtedly have been made liable for the whole loss on any approach. Ward J's analysis of the area was then adopted in *Craigcare Group Pty Ltd v Superkite Pty Ltd.*[94] Hallen J did not find knowing assistance proved in that case, but would have found the assistant liable for the whole loss if he had done so.

The High Court case of *Michael Wilson & Partners Ltd v Nicholls*[95] may require a different answer, however. That case has a complicated history and it was not directly concerned with the point under discussion here. Nonetheless, at least one subsequent case has been decided on the basis that *Michael Wilson* mandates that a knowing assistant is liable only for the consequences of the assistance and not the consequences of the underlying fiduciary breach.

a. *Michael Wilson & Partners Ltd v Nicholls*

The case involved the plaintiff, Michael Wilson & Partners (MWP); Mr Emmott, a former director and shareholder of MWP; and the defendants Mr Nicholls and Mr Slater who were both former employees of MWP. The facts were relatively straightforward: Emmott, Nicholls and Slater left MWP to form their own company and took some of MWP's clients with them. MWP pursued various claims against Emmott in London, under an arbitration agreement contained in his

[91] *New Cap Reinsurance Corporation Ltd v General Cologne Re Australia Ltd* [2004] NSWSC 781 [34].

[92] *Re-Engine Pty Ltd (in liq) v Fergusson* [2007] VSC 57 [131], [158]. Dodds-Streeton J had liability for the breach, not the assistance, in mind.

[93] *George v Webb* [2011] NSWSC 1608 [262].

[94] *Craigcare Group Pty Ltd v Superkite Pty Ltd* [2014] NSWSC 326 [224], [267] (note this case came after *Michael Wilson*, discussed below).

[95] *Michael Wilson & Partners Ltd v Nicholls* [2011] HCA 48; (2011) 244 CLR 427.

contract, and pursued Nicholls and Slater in the Supreme Court of New South Wales. Relevantly, MWP claimed that Nicholls and Slater had knowingly assisted Emmott in the breach of his fiduciary duties to MWP.

To cut a very long story short,[96] Mr Nicholls and Mr Slater argued that their liability could not be determined until the final accounts had been struck between Mr Emmott and MWP in London. Those accounts would include compensation owed by Mr Emmott to MWP for losses caused by his breach of fiduciary duty. But the accounts would also include (and this would almost certainly be a greater amount) money due to Mr Emmott as a part owner of MWP. Mr Nicholls and Mr Slater argued that they would only be liable to MWP in the event that the accounts between Mr Emmott and MWP revealed an amount owing to MWP. In effect, Nicholls and Slater were trying to take advantage of Emmott's ability to bring into the account his shareholding in the MWP business.

The Nicholls and Slater argument took the form of seeking a stay of the New South Wales proceedings until the London arbitration had been concluded. They argued that it would be an abuse of process to allow MWP to continue. The New South Wales Court of Appeal had granted a stay, and MWP appealed to the High Court. In allowing MWP's appeal, Gummow ACJ, Hayne, Crennan and Bell JJ said:

> All of the arguments that asserted there was an abuse of process proceeded, explicitly or implicitly, from a common starting point—that any liability of the respondents to MWP for knowingly assisting Mr Emmott in the breach of his fiduciary duties was limited by the nature and extent of the relief MWP sought and obtained in the arbitration of its claims against Mr Emmott. That is, as Lindgren A-JA put the point, the liability of the respondents was no more than 'ancillary, or coordinate with', the liability of Mr Emmott. This understanding of the relationship between the liabilities of a defaulting fiduciary and a knowing assistant of the fiduciary's breach should not be accepted.[97]

Their Honours continued:

> No matter how the allegation of abuse of process was formulated, the allegation depended upon treating the liability of the respondents as necessarily confined by the extent of Mr Emmott's liability to MWP. This was said to be because the respondents' liability to MWP was no more than accessorial to the principal wrongdoing of Mr Emmott. That is not so. The claims against the respondents, as knowing assistants, were not dependent upon the claims made against Mr Emmott in the fashion asserted by the respondents.
>
> As MWP rightly pointed out, this Court has held that liability to account as a constructive trustee is imposed directly upon a person who knowingly assists in a breach of fiduciary duty. The reference to the liability of a knowing assistant as an 'accessorial' liability does no more than recognise that the assistant's liability depends upon establishing, among other things, that there has been a breach of fiduciary duty by another. It follows, as MWP submitted, that the relief that is awarded against a defaulting fiduciary and

[96] Fuller details can be found in Glister, 'Knowing Assistance' (n 67).
[97] *Michael Wilson* (n 95) [100].

> a knowing assistant will not necessarily coincide in either nature or quantum. So, for example, the claimant may seek compensation from the defaulting fiduciary (who made no profit from the default) and an account of profits from the knowing assistant (who profited from his or her own misconduct). And if an account of profits were to be sought against both the defaulting fiduciary and a knowing assistant, the two accounts would very likely differ. It follows that neither the nature nor the extent of any liability of the respondents to MWP for knowingly assisting Mr Emmott in a breach or breaches of his fiduciary obligations depends upon the nature or extent of the relief that MWP obtained in the arbitration against Mr Emmott.[98]

For present purposes, the question is whether the reasoning in these passages necessarily ousts or forbids a rule which provides that a knowing assistant is liable for the total loss suffered as a result of breach in which he or she assists. That is a difficult question and can probably only be answered by observing the way that later cases treat this aspect of *Michael Wilson*. But it can at least be said that *Michael Wilson* did not have to be decided in such a way. This is because it is quite possible to recognise that the quantum of equitable compensation owed by a fiduciary and two knowing assistants is the same, and even owed by them jointly and severally to the plaintiff, while still acknowledging that no defendant can take advantage of a right of set off held by another defendant. If a plaintiff 'recovers' the loss from the fiduciary through including the figure in an accounting exercise, the fiduciary may seek contribution from the assistants. Alternatively, the plaintiff may proceed against the assistants first, recover from them, and then the equity to prevent double satisfaction would mean that the liability could no longer be included in the account taken with the fiduciary. The assistants could then claim contribution from the fiduciary. It follows that it was not necessary, in rejecting the model of liability proposed by Mr Nicholls and Mr Slater, to decide that there was *no* link between the liability of a defaulting fiduciary and the liability of his knowing assistants.

Nonetheless, at least one subsequent Australian case has treated *Michael Wilson* as requiring fiduciaries and assistants to be treated separately as regards equitable compensation. *Singtel Optus v Almad*[99] involved a senior employee of Singtel Optus, Mr Curtis, who breached his fiduciary duties by placing Optus's business with third-party companies he controlled. An account of profits was sought from one of those companies, Sumo, while equitable compensation was sought from another, Electrosales. Optus tried to make Electrosales liable for the same amount of equitable compensation as was sought from Mr Curtis himself. But McDougall J held, relying on the *Michael Wilson* case:

> There is no principle that, where it has been shown that an 'assistant' has been knowingly involved in a breach of duty by a fiduciary, the liabilities of the fiduciary and the assistant must necessarily be the same. It is clear, for example, that one may be called upon to

[98] ibid [105]–[106] (references omitted).

[99] *Singtel Optus v Almad* [2013] NSWSC 1427 (point not considered on appeal: *Hasler v Singtel Optus Pty Ltd* [2014] NSWCA 266, (2014) 87 NSWLR 609).

make compensation, and the other to account for profits. And it is equally clear that the measure of loss recoverable from each may differ.[100]

It must immediately be noted that the point was not central to the case, and that McDougall J did not even have the benefit of submissions on it. The same outcome could also have been reached by noting that Electrosales did not relevantly assist in many of the breaches in respect of which compensation was sought from Mr Curtis.[101] Even so, McDougall J explicitly decided the case on the grounds that *Michael Wilson* stood as authority for the proposition that the measure of loss recoverable from a fiduciary and an assistant could differ. The authors of the latest edition of *Meagher Gummow and Lehane* agree. According to them, the Australian position was formerly that 'a knowing participant was joint and severally liable with the defaulting fiduciary for losses suffered by the principal as a result of the fiduciary's breach of duty'.[102] But the authors think that the law has now changed, and they cite *Michael Wilson & Partners Ltd v Nicholls* in support of that position.

For the reasons given above, the law on assessing the equitable compensation payable by a knowing or dishonest assistant is not entirely settled in either England or Australia. Academic opinion on what the position should be is also divided.[103] If assistants can reduce or eliminate their liability by showing that the fiduciary would have gone ahead anyway and the same loss would have been suffered, or by arguing that the assistance provided by other third parties had a greater causative effect, then this will mark another difference between treating corporate accessories as the alter egos or fiduciaries and treating them as discrete third parties.

C. Recovery on Different Bases from Fiduciary and Third Party

A claimant cannot recover both an account of profits and equitable compensation from the same defendant in respect of the same breach. He or she must elect between these inconsistent remedies.[104] The equity against double recovery, sometimes referred to as the principle of full satisfaction, also prevents a claimant

[100] ibid [280].

[101] ibid [284].

[102] Heydon, Leeming and Turner (n 61) para 23-555.

[103] See G Virgo, *The Principles of Equity and Trusts*, 2nd edn (Oxford, OUP, 2016) 735–37; Davies (n 1) 257; M Campbell, 'The Honest Truth about Dishonest Assistance' [2015] *Conveyancer and Property Lawyer* 159, 166–67; all taking the view that assistants are liable for the whole loss but criticising this position. By contrast, and in support of that position, see Elliott and Mitchell (n 60); C Mitchell and S Watterson, 'Remedies for Knowing Receipt' in C Mitchell (ed), *Constructive and Resulting Trusts* (Oxford, Hart Publishing, 2010) 115, 150–53; and for different reasons, P Ridge 'Justifying the Remedies for Dishonest Assistance' (2008) 124 *LQR* 445, 457–59; P Ridge, 'Monetary Remedies for Equitable Participatory Liability: General Principles and Current Questions' in S Degeling and J Varuhas (eds), *Equitable Compensation and Disgorgement of Profit* (Oxford, Hart Publishing, forthcoming).

[104] *Tang Man Sit v Capacious Investments Ltd* [1996] 1 AC 514, 521. It is not entirely clear why the remedies are inconsistent: see P Birks, 'Inconsistency Between Compensation and Restitution' (1996) 112 *LQR* 375; S Watterson, 'Alternative and Cumulative Remedies: What is the Difference?' (2003) 11 *Restitution Law Review* 7; A Burrows, *The Law of Restitution*, 3rd edn (Oxford, OUP, 2011) 628–29; and Paul Davies' chapter in this volume.

recovering compensation from several defendants in an amount greater than the actual loss suffered. But a claimant apparently can claim equitable compensation from the fiduciary and an account of profits against a third party: as we have seen, the plurality in *Michael Wilson* said 'the claimant may seek compensation from the defaulting fiduciary (who made no profit from the default) and an account of profits from the knowing assistant (who profited from his or her own misconduct)'.[105]

There do not appear to be many cases where this actually happens,[106] and in *Michael Wilson* no authority was cited on the exact point.[107] The plurality simply said it followed from the proposition that liability to account as a constructive trustee is imposed directly on a third party. In any event, there must be limits to the analysis. If a director causes £1 million to be paid away from the company to a third party, the claimant company surely cannot recover £1 million from the director as equitable compensation and an additional £1 million from the third party as an account of profits. In form that appears consistent but in substance it is double recovery for loss. Having said that, if the third party puts the money to gainful use and turns the £1 million into £2 million, it should be possible to recover these profits, and it should be possible to do so without being required to abandon the claim against the fiduciary. The position should be this: the fiduciary is liable for £1 million and the third party is liable for £2 million, but the claimant cannot recover more than £2 million in total.[108] That may be effected by ordering that both the fiduciary and third party are liable in respect of £1 million (joint and several liability for that sum), and ordering that the third party is liable for an additional £1 million.

A more difficult analytical question is whether a claimant can still claim equitable compensation from a third party after an account of profits has been secured against the fiduciary. It might be argued that an election for an account of profits against a fiduciary wrongdoer effectively ratifies the underlying breach, and means that no liability to pay equitable compensation can then be grounded on it.

Again, these considerations do not pertain only to corporate accessories. But they do provide another example of the possible difference in outcome between treating corporate accessories as alter egos and treating them as discrete third parties.

[105] *Michael Wilson* (n 95) [106].

[106] One is *Singtel Optus* (n 99), where compensation was sought from Mr Curtis and an account of profits from Sumo. The latter was eventually given effect through a declaration of constructive trust.

[107] The passage was adopted from the supplementary submissions of the appellant, and the only authority cited there was a 'cf' reference to a comment by McLelland J at trial in *United States Surgical Corp v Hospital Products International Pty Ltd* (1982) 2 NSWLR 766, 817. The correct interpretation of what McLelland J said there is a matter of debate: it has been questioned whether he meant to say that assistants are liable for gains made by the fiduciary (see Heydon, Leeming and Turner (n 61) para 5-270), and on one reading it also suggests that assistants can be liable *both* for their gains *and* losses suffered by the principal.

[108] *cf Charter plc v City Index Ltd* [2008] Ch 313 [64]–[71].

IV. Conclusion

The previous section III explained the possible differences between treating a corporate accessory as a discrete third party and treating it as the same actor as the wrongdoing fiduciary. It must be remembered, however, that the discussion in this chapter is focused specifically on corporate accessories that can (or could) be seen as alter egos. The question is really about the differences in treatment that may be seen here: would the outcome of a case be different if a corporate accessory *that could have been treated as an alter ego* is instead treated as a discrete third party?

Some cases would indeed have different outcomes. We have seen that, in *Aerostar Maintenance v Wilson*,[109] Morgan J refused to treat the corporate accessory, Avman Ltd, as the alter ego of its controller Mr Wilson. This meant Avman was liable to disgorge profits it had made, but Mr Wilson was not. In the event, Avman failed between the liability and quantum judgments. The fact that Mr Wilson could not be made personally liable for the original Avman profits influenced the claimant's decision to elect for equitable compensation against Mr Wilson. If Avman had been treated as an alter ego, the claimant would probably have elected for an account of profits against Mr Wilson, but calculated on the basis of profits actually made by Avman.

On the other hand, some of the distinctions identified in section III may not obtain when applied to third parties who are so closely connected to the wrongdoing fiduciaries that they may be seen as their alter egos. Take the specific point about the *calculation* of accounts of profits, for example. Although the Court of Appeal made it plain in *Novoship* that the assessment of accounts awarded against fiduciaries and third parties would differ, it is not easy to see how such a difference would work in a case where the third party was controlled by the wrongdoing fiduciary. That is, even if the corporate accessory is to be considered as a discrete third party, and not as the alter ego of the fiduciary, the fact that the third party is controlled by the fiduciary must tell on the calculation of the account taken against the accessory. It would seem wrong for equity to allow a fiduciary to limit the scope of the obligations owed to his or her principal by operating through a corporate vehicle and thereby putting gains that would otherwise have been disgorgeable beyond the reach of that principal.

In conclusion, the liability of a corporate accessory could conceivably differ depending on whether it is seen as the alter ego of its controller or as a separate actor. That said, the closer the relationship between a company and its controller, the less likely it will be that the company's treatment under a 'separate actor' model will be very different from its treatment under an 'alter ego' model. A company treated as an alter ego can in theory be made liable for profits actually received

[109] *Aerostar Maintenance* (n 39).

by its controller; however there do not appear to be any cases where this has been the point of the exercise. Instead, the point of an alter ego analysis is to enlarge the personal liability of the controller by including amounts that were actually attributable to the company.[110] Indeed, it is here where the distinction between the two models will be more clearly seen: the different models of corporate accessory liability may not significantly affect the liability of those accessories, but they will change the personal liability of the wrongdoing company controller.

[110] See Glister, 'Diverting Fiduciary Gains' (n 34).

13

The Nature of 'Knowing Receipt'

WILLIAM SWADLING

I. Introduction

Suppose a trustee holds a parcel of shares on trust for a class of objects. The trust might be fixed or discretionary. For the sake of argument, assume the simplest possible scenario, a fixed trust with one adult beneficiary. In breach of trust, the trustee transfers the shares to the defendant. There are two types of claim the beneficiary might bring against the defendant, one for the return of the shares themselves, which we will call the 'specific' claim, the other a monetary claim for their value, which we will call the 'personal' claim.

The specific claim is undoubtedly strict,[1] subject only to a defence of the recipient being 'equity's darling'. The personal claim, which is the subject matter of this chapter, is, by contrast, fault based, although, as will be seen, there is controversy over the exact level of fault required. For the moment, we will simply refer to the fault requirement as one of 'knowledge'. That 'knowledge' is of the rights having been dissipated in breach of trust. The defendant might have had that knowledge at the point of receipt, or have acquired it later, whilst the rights were still vested in him.[2]

The purpose of this chapter is to examine the various explanations of the personal claim. One is that there are in fact two potential personal claims, one in unjust enrichment, the other in wrongs. This is the view of Lord Nicholls, writing extrajudicially,[3] and Birks.[4] The unjust enrichment claim is strict, though yielding only the value of the rights received and subject to defences of change of position and bona fide purchase. The wrongs-based claim, by contrast, is fault

[1] Details of the specific claim are set out in section III below. It is often called 'proprietary', though this is a misnomer as the rights which the court orders to be returned may well be personal.

[2] *Agip (Africa) Ltd v Jackson* [1990] Ch 265, 291 (Millett J).

[3] Lord Nicholls, 'Knowing Receipt: The Need for a New Landmark' in WR Cornish, R Nolan, J O'Sullivan and G Virgo (eds), *Restitution: Past, Present and Future* (Oxford, Hart Publishing, 1998) 231.

[4] P Birks, 'Receipt' in P Birks and A Pretto (eds), *Breach of Trust* (Oxford, Hart Publishing, 2002) 213.

based, requiring dishonesty, with relief extending to the beneficiary's loss or the recipient's gains beyond the value of the rights themselves. The wrong, according to Lord Nicholls, is a species of the equitable wrong of dishonest participation in a breach of trust, akin to the common law wrong of inducing breach of contract.[5]

A second view holds that one who receives rights with knowledge of their dissipation in breach of trust becomes a genuine trustee of such rights. In one version of this thesis—that propounded by Mitchell and Watterson—such recipient will become immediately accountable to the beneficiary for what he does with the rights. Should he dissipate them in breach of trust, the beneficiary can falsify the recipient's account, thus rendering the recipient liable to be ordered by the court to reinstate the trust fund, either in the hands of the original trustee or in new trustees or in the beneficiary himself if he is of full age, sound mind and absolutely entitled. Although the payment away will be a breach of trust, the claim is for falsification and is not a claim in wrongdoing.[6] A simpler version of this thesis is put forward by both Gardner[7] and Chambers,[8] who likewise say that one who receives rights with knowledge of a dissipation in breach of trust becomes a trustee of such rights. They argue that the recipient will commit a breach of trust if such rights are transferred by him to someone other than the original trustee or to new trustees or to the beneficiary himself if of full age, sound mind and absolutely entitled. The claim in knowing receipt, they say, is simply the money claim for the wrong of breach of trust.

So far as the first view is concerned, the position adopted in this chapter is that although analysing knowing receipt as claim in wrongs is possible, though not the particular wrong of dishonest participation in a breach of trust, there can be no claim in unjust enrichment on the scenario set out above for the simple reason that the defendant's enrichment, the shares, comes not from the beneficiary claimant but from the trustee. The defendant's enrichment, in other words, is not at the beneficiary's expense. As to the second view, the argument will be made that the knowing recipient is not a trustee and is therefore under no duty to provide an account which can be falsified; nor can he be sued for breach of trust. As indicated above, the best account of the liability we call knowing receipt is that it is an equitable wrong. However, it is not the 'receipt' which is the gist of the action, but the later dealing with the rights in a way which is inconsistent with the terms of the trust on which they were originally held. 'Knowing receipt', therefore, is a misnomer—the liability is better seen as a species of the equitable wrong of 'inconsistent dealing'.

[5] Nicholls (n 3) 243–44. The other form of participatory liability according to Lord Nicholls is the dishonest assistance of a breach of trust.

[6] C Mitchell and S Watterson, 'Remedies for Knowing Receipt' in C Mitchell (ed), *Constructive and Resulting Trusts* (Oxford, Hart Publishing, 2010) 115.

[7] S Gardner, 'Moment of Truth for Knowing Receipt?' (2009) 125 *LQR* 20.

[8] R Chambers, 'The End of Knowing Receipt' (2016) 2 *Canadian Journal of Comparative and Contemporary Law* 1.

II. Two Possible Distractions

At the outset, we must notice two possible distractions. The first relates to rights held beneficially at the point of dissipation. The second concerns the equitable liability known as 'inconsistent dealing'. As already indicated, the second turns out not to be a distraction at all.

A. Rights Held Beneficially

This chapter is only concerned with rights previously held on trust, not those held beneficially at the point of wrongful dissipation. Unfortunately, the distinction between the two has not always been properly drawn. In the past, the specific and personal claims outlined above have also been available in cases concerning persons in fiduciary relations with companies, for example, directors, who cause through a breach of fiduciary duty on their part rights held outright by the corporation to be transferred away. Claims are then brought by the company against the recipient to recover either the rights themselves or their value.

An example is *Bank of Credit and Commerce International (Overseas) Ltd v Akindele*,[9] where the defendant, Akindele, entered into a contract with International Credit and Investment Co (Overseas) Co Ltd (ICIC), a company within the BCCI group, for the purchase of shares in the holding company of the group, BCCI Holdings, for US$10 million. The agreement provided that should Akindele wish to sell the shares within two years, ICIC would buy them back at 15 per cent compounded per annum more than he paid. Akindele exercised the option and ICIC repurchased the shares for US$16.679 million. The liquidators of the by now insolvent ICIC claimed the US$6.679 million profit from Akindele on the ground that the whole scheme had been fraudulently entered into by its directors to inflate the apparent worth of the BCCI group. This, they said, meant that the sum claimed had been transferred to Akindele in breach of fiduciary duty and that he was liable as a knowing recipient. At first instance, Carnwarth J rejected the claim, though only on the ground that Akindele had acted honestly throughout—a conclusion which the Court of Appeal refused to set aside, though at the same time taking the opportunity to frame the enquiry not in terms of dishonesty but of 'unconscionability'. Akindele's lack of knowledge of the directors' fraud, it was held, meant it was not 'unconscionable' for him to retain the profit.

This line of authority was, however, decisively rejected by the House of Lords in *Criterion Properties plc v Stratford UK Properties LLC*.[10] Two directors of the

[9] *Bank of Credit and Commerce International (Overseas) Ltd v Akindele* [2001] Ch 437 (CA); see also *Belmont Finance Corpn v Williams Furniture (No 2)* [1980] 1 All ER 393 (CA); *Eagle Trust v SBC Securities* [1993] 1 WLR 484; *Cowan de Groot Properties v Eagle Trust* [1992] 4 All ER 700; *El Ajou v Dollar Land Holdings* [1994] 2 All ER 685 (CA).

[10] *Criterion Properties plc v Stratford UK Properties LLC* [2004] UKHL 28, [2004] 1 WLR 1846 (HL).

claimant company purported to enter into a 'poison pill' agreement on its behalf with the defendant company. When the defendant company sought to enforce the poison pill agreement, the claimant sought to have it set aside as against the defendant company as having been procured by the directors of the claimant company in breach of their fiduciary duty. The claim was argued in terms of the defendant company being liable for the unconscionable receipt of rights from the claimant, *scil* the rights under the poison pill agreement. The House of Lords held that the claim was misconceived. Lord Nicholls said:

> If a company (A) enters into an agreement with B under which B acquires benefits from A, A's ability to recover these benefits from B depends essentially on whether the agreement is binding on A. If the directors of A were acting for an improper purpose when they entered into the agreement, A's ability to have the agreement set aside depends upon the application of familiar principles of agency and company law. If, applying these principles, the agreement is found to be valid and is therefore not set aside, questions of 'knowing receipt' by B do not arise. So far as B is concerned there can be no question of A's assets having been misapplied. B acquired the assets from A, the legal and beneficial owner of the assets, under a valid agreement made between him and A.[11]

Thus, the issue was seen not as one of the unconscionable receipt of rights but whether the claimant company gave authority for the signing of the poison pill agreement. If it gave actual authority for the signing of the agreement, then there was nothing wrong with the receipt of rights transferred under it. If there was no actual authority, then the question was whether there was apparent (ostensible) authority. However, even if apparent authority was present, it would not avail a counterparty who knew or ought to have known that there was no actual authority. According to Lord Scott:

> If a person dealing with an agent knows that the agent does not have actual authority to conclude the contract or transaction in question, the person cannot rely on apparent authority. Apparent authority can only be relied on by someone who does not know that the agent has no actual authority. And if a person dealing with an agent knows or has reason to believe that the contract or transaction is contrary to the commercial interests of the agent's principal, it is likely to be very difficult for the person to assert with any credibility that he believed the agent did have actual authority. Lack of such a belief would be fatal to a claim that the agent had apparent authority.[12]

In this respect, but in this respect alone, a test of constructive notice (which is what unconscionable receipt might possibly be)[13] would be relevant in a case where a company is caused by a fiduciary acting in breach of duty to transfer rights it holds beneficially to a third party. It is, however, crucial to understand that this issue does not go to any recipient liability. It is concerned instead with the logically prior question whether the contract, assuming there was such a contract, pursuant to

[11] ibid [4].
[12] ibid [31].
[13] See text to nn 37–44.

which rights were transferred was valid. If the contract was valid, then that would be the end of the matter.

What, however, of the situation where the contract is void on the ground that there was no actual or apparent authority, or there was apparent authority but the recipient knew or ought to have known of the lack of actual authority? Lord Nicholls said that in such cases a strict liability personal claim in unjust enrichment was available to the claimant company:

> If … the agreement is set aside, B will be accountable for any benefits he may have received from A under the agreement. A will have a proprietary claim, if B still has the assets. Additionally, and irrespective of whether B still has the assets in question, A will have a personal claim against B for unjust enrichment, subject always to a defence of change of position. B's personal accountability will not be dependent upon proof of fault or 'unconscionable' conduct on his part. B's accountability, in this regard, will be 'strict'.[14]

Although this statement was obiter dicta in *Criterion*, it was accepted by the New South Wales Court of Appeal in *Fistar v Riverwood Legion and Community Club Ltd*[15] and by the Full Court of the Federal Court of Australia in *Great Investments Ltd v Warner*.[16] We are not concerned in this chapter with whether such a proposition is correct, save to note that it is not free from criticism.[17] Crucially, however, the unjust enrichment claim in such cases is not caught by the objection made below in respect of rights held on trust immediately prior to their disposition: in cases like *Fistar* and *Great Investments*, the defendant's enrichment was clearly at the claimant's expense since it was the claimant itself which transferred the rights to the defendant, not a third party.

B. Liability for Inconsistent Dealing

The second point to note is the existence of a species of equitable liability known as 'inconsistent dealing'. The leading case is *Lee v Sankey*.[18] Here, a firm of solicitors was employed by will trustees to receive the proceeds of the testator's real estate, which had been compulsorily purchased by a railway company. The solicitors were to hold the money until a suitable investment became available. In breach of their instructions, the solicitors paid over the money to one of the trustees without the authority of the other. The money was then dissipated in breach of trust and, the trustee in breach having died insolvent, a claim was successfully made against

[14] *Akindele* (n 9) [4].
[15] *Fistar v Riverwood Legion and Community Club Ltd* [2016] NSWCA 81.
[16] *Great Investments Ltd v Warner* [2016] FCAFC 85.
[17] R Stevens 'The Proper Scope of Knowing Receipt' [2004] *Lloyd's Maritime and Commercial Law Quarterly* 421, 425.
[18] *Lee v Sankey* (1873) LR 15 Eq 204.

the solicitors for the loss by the surviving trustee and the trust beneficiaries. Bacon VC held that the solicitors were:

> liable to make good to the trust estate the amount of trust moneys which they received by the authority of the two trustees, and from which they have not been discharged by any act or authority of the same two trustees. It is well established by many decisions, that a mere agent of trustees is answerable only to his principal and not to cestuis que trust in respect of trust moneys coming to his hands merely in his character of agent. But it is also not less clearly established that a person who receives into his hands trust moneys, and who deals with them in a manner inconsistent with the performance of trusts of which he is cognizant, is personally liable for the consequences which may ensue upon his so dealing.[19]

Although for many years thought to be simply part of the liability known as knowing receipt, one difference to the scenario posited at the beginning of this chapter is that the receipt by the solicitors in *Lee v Sankey* was perfectly lawful and not a dissipation in breach of trust. This led Millett J (as he then was) in *Agip (Africa) Ltd v Jackson*[20] to state, contrary to the position adopted at the time by the practitioner text *Snell*,[21] that inconsistent dealing was a separate and distinct head of liability from knowing receipt, and that 'much confusion has been caused by treating [knowing receipt] as a single category and by failing to differentiate between a number of different situations'. In his Lordship's view, there were 'two main classes of case':

> The first is concerned with the person who receives for his own benefit trust property transferred to him in breach of trust. He is liable as a constructive trustee if he received it with notice, actual or constructive, that it was trust property and that the transfer to him was a breach of trust; or if he received it without such notice but subsequently discovered the facts. In either case he is liable to account for the property, in the first case as from the time he received the property, and in the second as from the time he acquired notice.
>
> The second and, in my judgment, distinct class of case is that of the person, usually an agent of the trustees, who receives the trust property lawfully and not for his own benefit but who then either misappropriates it or otherwise deals with it in a manner which is inconsistent with the trust. He is liable to account as a constructive trustee if he received the property knowing it to be such, though he will not necessarily be required in all circumstances to have known the exact terms of the trust.[22]

The conclusion this chapter will reach is that though it is right to question whether cases of inconsistent dealing can properly be analysed as a species of knowing

[19] ibid 211.

[20] *Agip (Africa) Ltd* (n 2); see also *Baden, Delvaux and Lecuit v Société General pour Favoriser le Développement du Commerce et de l'Industrie en France SA* (1983) [1993] 1 WLR 509, 571–72 (Peter Gibson J).

[21] PV Baker and P St J Langan, *Snell's Principles of Equity*, 28th edn (London, Sweet & Maxwell, 1982) 194, 195.

[22] *Agip (Africa) Ltd* (n 2) 291.

receipt, the best explanation of cases in Millett J's first category is that they are in fact a sub-category of the equitable wrong of inconsistent dealing.

III. The Specific Claim

We will now set out the nature of the specific claim. We do this because if the defendant is *ipso facto* a trustee of the rights he receives, this may go some way to explaining the personal claim as involving the duties of a trustee. The purpose of this section is accordingly to demonstrate that, though commonly described as such, the recipient is not a trustee of the rights he receives but simply liable to be ordered to return them at the suit of the beneficiary.

It is well settled that if in the example given at the beginning of this chapter the defendant still has the shares, he is liable at the suit of the trust beneficiary to be ordered by a court to reconvey them in specie to the original trustees, or to the solely-entitled adult beneficiary himself should he so choose. The same regime will apply to the traceable proceeds of the shares should they have been exchanged for other rights by the time of trial. This claim to the shares or their traceable proceeds will also apply to remote recipients, those who receive from the initial recipient, to those who receive from remote recipients, and so on. The specific claim is strict. In other words, it does not matter what the recipient knew or ought to have known when receiving the shares or their traceable proceeds.

The only defence to the specific claim is that the recipient was 'equity's darling', ie, that in good faith he gave value in exchange for a right recognised by the common law (and shares are such rights) and that he had no notice, actual, constructive, or imputed, that the original transfer was made in breach of trust.[23] It is important to stress that this must be a purchase[24] for value of a legal right; if equitable rights are transferred in breach of trust, for example, where the transferred rights were the subject matter of a sub-trust, bona fide purchase will not avail the recipient, no matter how much value he gave, how much bona fides he possessed, and how little notice he had.

What is the status of the person who still has the shares or their traceable proceeds but who is not equity's darling? It is often said that he is a trustee of such rights. But what sort of trust is this? Is the recipient a trustee of an express trust? Or is it a constructive trust? It is clearly not an express trust. Take the case of an innocent recipient who gives no value. No one would say that they had the same duties as the trustee from whom the rights were received. If, for example, the recipient gave away the shares whilst innocent, it is accepted on all sides that

[23] *Pilcher v Rawlins* (1872) 7 Ch App 259.

[24] Purchase in this context means consensual transfer rather than transfer by operation of law, eg, as on intestacy. Thus, a gift is a 'purchase', which explains the otherwise redundant requirement that the purchase be 'for value'.

he would not be personally liable for breach of trust. Nor would he be liable if he spent the dividends earned from the shares on a holiday for himself. Yet such acts by the original trustee would undoubtedly make him liable to be sued for breach. At best, therefore, the recipient can only be a constructive trustee of a constructive trust, though that still leaves open the question of the content of such constructive 'trust'. It is, however, submitted that the language of trusteeship is inapt even here. The description of the defendant as a trustee seems to be used only to indicate that he does not hold the rights beneficially, that they are encumbered by the ability of the beneficiary to obtain a retransfer.

The description of the recipient as a trustee in such a situation is probably due to a dictum of Lord Lindley in *Hardoon v Belilios*, where he said: 'All that is necessary to establish the relation of trustee and cestui que trust is to prove that the legal title was in the plaintiff and the equitable title in the defendant'.[25] Such thinking was, however, rightly rejected by Lord Browne-Wilkinson in *Westdeutsche Landesbank Girozentrale v Islington LBC*, where he described the proposition that 'where the legal title is in A but the equitable interest in B, A holds as trustee for B' as 'fallacious'.[26] His lordship said:

> There are many cases where B enjoys rights which, in equity, are enforceable against the legal owner, A, without A being a trustee, eg an equitable right to redeem a mortgage, equitable easements, restrictive covenants, the right to rectification, an insurer's right by subrogation to receive damages subsequently recovered by the assured ... Even in cases where the whole beneficial interest is vested in B and the bare legal interest is in A, A is not necessarily a trustee, eg where title to land is acquired by estoppel as against the legal owner; a mortgagee who has fully discharged his indebtedness enforces his right to recover the mortgaged property in a redemption action, not an action for breach of trust.[27]

Moreover, the statement in *Hardoon v Belilios* should not be taken out of context. That was a case of an express trust, with shares being vested in the claimant for a third party. The defendant was an assignee of the third-party beneficiary. The claimant trustee was held liable on calls made on the shares and sought an indemnity from the defendant, who sought to escape liability on the ground that he had made no promise to indemnify. The Privy Council held that it did not matter, that it was enough that there was a trustee/beneficiary relationship. The case therefore says nothing about the operation of constructive trusts.[28]

[25] *Hardoon v Belilios* [1901] AC 118, 123.

[26] *Westdeutsche Landesbank Girozentrale v Islington LBC* [1996] AC 669, 706.

[27] ibid 706–07.

[28] One decision which might be cited in support of the proposition Lord Browne-Wilkinson thought fallacious is the Court of Appeal case of *Independent Trustees Services Ltd v GP Noble Trustees Ltd* [2012] EWCA Civ 195, [2013] Ch 91 (CA), where at [79] doubt is thrown on his Lordship's reasoning by Lloyd LJ. However, this is immediately qualified at [83] by the statement that: 'It may not matter whether the holder of the legal title who is liable to be sued so as to enforce such rights is or is not to be categorised as a trustee. What does matter is the recognition of the right to sue and thereby to enforce those rights, in relevant circumstances'. Moreover, Lloyd LJ relied on an article by Sir Peter Millett

The upshot, therefore, is that there is no need to describe the recipient of rights dissipated in breach of trust as a trustee; it is enough to say that he takes subject to an encumbrance, viz the beneficiary's ability to obtain from the court an order that he reconvey the rights he received. We are perfectly happy to describe other encumbrances in such terms, for example, leases, easements and restrictive covenants over land, so it is difficult to see why the language of trusteeship is needed here.

IV. The Personal Claim

We now turn to the focus of this chapter, the personal claim. If by the time of trial the defendant no longer has the shares or their traceable proceeds, he will be liable at the suit of the beneficiary to be ordered by the court to pay a sum of money to the beneficiary representing the value of the shares if he had knowledge at the point of receipt that the shares were transferred to him in breach of trust and he received the shares beneficially. He will also incur such liability if, though innocent at the point of receipt, he acquired the knowledge later, before dissipating the shares. Like the specific claim, the only defence will be that the defendant was equity's darling, a bona fide purchaser of a legal right for value without notice, actual, constructive, or imputed.

A. Constituent Elements of 'Knowing Receipt'

i. Rights Transferred in Breach of Trust

The first requirement of the liability is that the rights received were originally transferred in breach of trust. As we have seen, rights held beneficially at the point of the impugned transfer are not the subject of this liability.

ii. Knowledge

The second requirement is that the recipient knew, either at the point of receipt, or later whilst they were still vested in him, that the rights received were previously held on trust for the claimant beneficiary and transferred away in breach. There is, however, no agreement on exactly what knowledge means in this context, which is undoubtedly a product of the failure of judges properly to analyse

(as he then was) entitled 'Restitution and Constructive Trusts' (1998) 114 *LQR* 399, where he said, at 404, that the issue was 'essentially a question of semantics' and that it 'probably does not matter if we say that the relationship is not a trust relationship, so long as we call it something else. The trouble is that we have no other name for it'.

the type of liability in question. In *re Montagu's Settlement Trusts*,[29] Megarry V-C, after a careful review of the authorities and much argument, held that knowledge meant exactly what it says, that the defendant must know of the dissipation in breach of trust, or have deliberately shut his eyes to the possibility. This was to be contrasted with 'notice', which included not only what the defendant knew (actual notice), but also what he would have discovered had he made reasonable enquiries and inspections (constructive notice), and the knowledge of his agent (imputed notice). In *re Montagu's Settlement Trusts* itself, the claimants were keen to attribute the knowledge of the defendant's solicitors to the defendant recipient, but Megarry V-C said that whilst that was the right test in relation to disqualifying the defendant from any defence of bona fide purchase for value without notice—which had no possible application on the facts as the recipient was a donee—only conduct amounting to a 'want of probity' would suffice for the personal claim, which required either knowledge or a deliberate closing of the eyes.[30]

On the other hand, many judges do talk in terms of notice. Thus, Millett J in *Agip* said that constructive notice was enough for the personal claim:

> [T]he person who receives for his own benefit trust property transferred to him in breach of trust … is liable as a constructive trustee if he received it with notice, actual or constructive, that it was trust property and that the transfer to him was a breach of trust, or if he received it without such notice but subsequently discovered the facts.[31]

This was also the view of the Supreme Court of Canada in *Citadel General Assurance Co v Lloyds Bank Canada*, where La Forest J said:

> Relief will be granted where a stranger to the trust, having received trust property for his or her own benefit and having knowledge of facts which would put a reasonable person on inquiry, actually fails to inquire as to the possible misapplication of trust property. It is this lack of inquiry that renders the recipient's enrichment unjust.[32]

The Canadian Supreme Court was there talking of the claim being in unjust enrichment, in which case, as we will see, a fault requirement makes no sense whatever.

Finally, in the recent decision of *Papadimitriou v Crédit Agricole Corp & Investment Bank*,[33] Lord Sumption did exactly what Megarry V-C said could not be done and equated the test for notice in the defence of bona fide purchase with that of knowledge in recipient liability, thus incorporating even imputed notice. He said:

> Whether a person claims to be a bona fide purchaser of assets without notice of a prior interest in them, or disputes a claim to make him accountable as a constructive trustee

[29] *Re Montagu's Settlement Trusts* [1987] Ch 264.

[30] ibid 285.

[31] *Agip (Africa) Ltd* (n 2). His Lordship took the same view in *El Ajou v Dollar Land Holdings plc* [1993] 3 All ER 717. The Court of Appeal also adopted a constructive notice approach in *Houghton v Fayers* (2000) 2 ITELR 512 (CA), where Nourse LJ said that the defendant will be personally liable for receipt if he knew or ought to have known that the money was paid in breach of fiduciary duty. It should, however, be noted that constructive notice may well be the correct test in such cases, which all involve rights being held outright before the impugned dissipation.

[32] *Citadel General Assurance Co v Lloyds Bank Canada* [1997] 3 SCR 805 [49].

[33] *Papadimitriou v Crédit Agricole Corp & Investment Bank* [2015] UKPC 13 (PC).

> on the footing of knowing receipt, the question what constitutes notice or knowledge is the same.[34]

The point, however, was unnecessary for the decision; moreover, the case was a Privy Council one on appeal from Gibraltar. It is, however, vital to understand that the facts which disqualify a defence of equity's darling and the level of knowledge required for liability for receipt have nothing whatever to do with each other. The first is concerned with the question whether an equitable interest survives a transfer of a legal right which it burdens, which legal right may or may not have been held on trust. Thus, prior to the enactment of the various registration regimes in land law,[35] it was the test used to decide whether titles to land were burdened by prior equitable[36] encumbrances such as restrictive covenants, equitable easements, options to purchase and so on. The latter, by contrast, is concerned with the question whether a court will order a defendant to put his hand in his pocket and pay a sum of money to a trust beneficiary. The confusion in this area is again symptomatic of the fact that no judge has stopped to examine the nature of the liability we call knowing receipt.

Finally, we have the hopeless formulation in the decision of the Court of Appeal in *BCCI v Akindele*,[37] where we are told that the test for recipient liability is whether it would be 'unconscionable for the defendant to retain what he has received'.[38] We have already seen how the House of Lords in *Critierion* held that the Court of Appeal in *Akindele* was wrong to see the case in terms of recipient liability. It is in any case odd for the Court to use the language of 'retention' in cases where the defendant no longer has the right in question. It is even odder, however, to talk about 'unconscionability', relying, as the Court did, on the Privy Council decision in *Royal Brunei Airlines Sdn Bhd v Tan*,[39] where that word was expressly said to be unworkable as a test in the context of assistance liability.[40] Predictably, no one knows what it means. Nor is it possible to know. As Birks pointed out:

> 'Unconscionable' gives no guidance. At one extreme it is unconscionable not to repay what you were not intended to receive. At the other extreme, it is unconscionable to be dishonest. 'Unconscionable', indicating unanalyzed disapprobation, thus embraces every position in the controversy.[41]

[34] ibid [33].

[35] Land Charges Act 1925; Land Registration Act 1925.

[36] Legal encumbrances bound without more.

[37] *Akindele* (n 9).

[38] ibid 455.

[39] *Royal Brunei Airlines Sdn Bhd v Tan* [1995] 2 AC 378 (PC).

[40] ibid 392 (Lord Nicholls): 'It is essential to be clear on what, *in this context*, unconscionable *means*. If unconscionable means no more than dishonesty, then dishonesty is the preferable label. If unconscionable means something different, it must be said that it is not clear what that something different is. Either way, therefore, the term is better avoided in this context' (emphasis in original).

[41] Birks, 'Receipt' (n 4) 226.

Looking to how the word is treated in the courts, unconscionability might be said to exclude constructive notice, and that was certainly the view of Judge Chambers QC in *Papamichael v National Westminster Bank plc*.[42] However, in *Akindele* itself, Nourse LJ said that unconscionability lay somewhere 'between actual and constructive knowledge' in the context of the particular case.[43] As we have seen, this may well be correct in a claim which turns on whether one contracting party can rely on the other's apparent authority. But in the context of recipient liability, the test of 'unconscionability' is best forgotten.[44]

iii. Beneficial Receipt

A lack of understanding of the nature of recipient liability also seems to explain the third requirement, that the defendant's receipt be 'beneficial'. In *Agip (Africa) Ltd v Jackson*,[45] the defendants escaped liability for receipt (but not assistance) because they received the rights as agents and passed them on to third parties according to instructions issued by their principal. Millett J said:

> The essential feature ... is that the recipient must have received the property for his own use and benefit. This is why neither the paying nor the collecting bank can normally be brought within it. In paying or collecting money for a customer the bank acts only as his agent. It is otherwise, however, if the collecting bank uses the money to reduce or discharge the customer's overdraft. In doing so it receives the money for its own benefit.[46]

According to Millett J, this was not 'a technical or fanciful requirement. It is essential if receipt-based liability is to be properly confined to those cases where the receipt is relevant to the loss'.[47]

A requirement of beneficial receipt is, however, decidedly odd since, *ex hypothesi*, the recipient will not take the rights beneficially unless he is equity's darling, in which case he will escape liability completely. What Millett J seems to be talking about, therefore, is how the defendant perceives himself to be taking the right.

The requirement can also lead to bizarre results. As *Agip* itself shows, if the defendant is an agent, he is free of recipient liability, no matter that he has actual knowledge that the dissipation is in breach. So, too, if he takes as trustee, another form of non-beneficial receipt. Suppose I hold shares on trust for a claimant. In breach of trust, I transfer those shares to the defendant to hold on trust for my son. The defendant will not, apparently, be liable to a personal receipt claim by the

[42] *Papamichael v National Westminster Bank plc* [2003] EWHC 164 (Comm) [247], [2003] 1 Lloyd's Rep 341.

[43] *Akindele* (n 9) 458.

[44] Unfortunately, despite *Criterion*, some cases still use unconscionability as a test of liability, one example being *Charter plc v City Index Ltd* [2007] EWCA Civ 1382, [2008] Ch 313 (CA).

[45] *Agip Africa Ltd* (n 2) aff'd [1991] Ch 547 (CA).

[46] ibid 292.

[47] ibid.

claimant even if he has actual knowledge of my breach.[48] There is no good reason for the defendant to escape liability here.[49] As seen above, the motivation of Millett J's rule in *Agip* was the protection of banks. However, banks always give value in exchange, so are potentially equity's darlings. It is also important to note that Lord Millett is a supporter of the unjust enrichment analysis of recipient liability,[50] where ministerial receipt is certainly a defence.[51] However, if, as will be argued below, recipient liability is not a species of unjust enrichment, then it may be that the requirement of beneficial receipt is misplaced.

V. Understanding the Liability

What then is it that triggers the liability in knowing receipt? Is it a species of wrongdoing? Is it unjust enrichment? Or is it something else altogether?

A. The Language of Awards

One thing obscuring analysis in this area is the language of the awards made by the courts. Orders to pay money at common law come in various guises: damages, debt, payment of the agreed sum, and money had and received. However, since this is a claim by a beneficiary of a trust, and the common law does not recognise trusts, it is of necessity a claim in equity. Here, money claims are couched in terms of the 'accountability of a trustee'.[52] The language is, however, fictitious. As Ungoed-Thomas J explained in *Selangor United Rubber Estates Ltd v Cradock (No 3)*, a case concerned with liability for assisting a breach of trust, such a defendant is not a trustee, merely 'liable to account *as though he were* a trustee'.[53] Unfortunately, many cases ignore the fiction and speak of the defendant being 'liable to account as a *constructive* trustee'. Indeed, in one of the leading cases of recipient liability, Hoffmann LJ unhelpfully described the claim as one 'to enforce a constructive trust on the basis of knowing receipt'.[54]

The language of accountability 'as if' or (worse) as a 'constructive trustee' poses a number of difficulties of analysis, most especially the fact that it is used to cover

[48] *El Ajou* (n 31) 738 (Millett J); *Savings & Investment Bank Ltd v Fryers* [1990–92] MLR 339, 362.

[49] He will not escape liability in New Zealand (*Gathergood v Blundell & Brown Ltd* [1992] 3 NZLR 643) or in Australia (*Quince v Varga* [2008] QCA 376).

[50] *El Ajou* (n 31) 738–40; *Twinsectra Ltd v Yardley* [2002] 2 AC 164, [105] (HL).

[51] A Burrows, *The Law of Restitution*, 3rd edn (Oxford, OUP, 2011) 558–68.

[52] More recently, there has also been a tendency to use the language of equitable compensation, even, bizarrely, for claims which have as their object the disgorgement of gains: *FHR European Ventures v Mankarious* [2014] UKSC 45 (SC) [1], [6], [7], [22], [33], [41], [42].

[53] *Selangor United Rubber Estates Ltd v Cradock (No 3)* [1968] 1 WLR 1555, 1583 (emphasis supplied).

[54] *El Ajou* (CA) (n 9) 700.

many sorts of different liabilities. Thus, compensation claims against those who commit the equitable wrong of dishonestly assisting a breach of trust are framed in such terms, as are claims made against those who make gains in breach of fiduciary duty.[55] It is even used in equitable unjust enrichment claims, for example, in cases of undue influence.[56]

At a general level, therefore, it is impossible to work backwards from the language of remedy to deduce what is going on. In this respect, knowing receipt might be a claim in unjust enrichment, a claim in wrongs, or something else altogether. It is like saying there is a money remedy at common law and trying to work out from that fact alone the nature of the cause of action. In our case, the only thing we know is that some sort of analogy is being drawn with the position of a trustee; what we do not know is whether this is at the substantive or remedial stage of the enquiry. In other words, we do not know whether some of the duties of the trustee are being exported to the recipient (substantive), or whether what is at stake is merely a liability to be ordered to do what trustees are sometimes ordered by courts to do, viz, put their hands in their pockets and pay over money to the claimant (remedial).

Of late, courts have eschewed the use of the language of accountability as a constructive trustee in money claims against non-trustees, saying that it has no substantive content and is purely remedial. Thus, in *Paragon Finance Plc v DB Thakerar & Co*, Millett LJ said:

> Equity has always given relief against fraud by making any person sufficiently implicated in the fraud accountable in equity. In such a case he is traditionally though I think unfortunately described as a constructive trustee and said to be 'liable to account as constructive trustee'. Such a person is not in fact a trustee at all, even though he may be liable to account as if he were. He never assumes the position of a trustee, and if he receives the trust property at all it is adversely to the plaintiff by an unlawful transaction which is impugned by the plaintiff. In such a case the expressions 'constructive trust' and 'constructive trustee' are misleading, for there is no trust and usually no possibility of a proprietary remedy; they are 'nothing more than a formula for equitable relief'.[57]

His lordship made similar remarks in *Dubai Aluminium Co Ltd v Salaam*, where he described the 'constructive trust' as 'merely the creation of the court … to meet the wrongdoing alleged: there is no real trust'.[58]

More recently, in *Williams v Central Bank of Nigeria*, Lord Sumption said that cases of assisting a breach of trust and the receipt of rights dissipated in breach involve:

> [P]ersons who never assumed and never intended to assume the status of a trustee, whether formally or informally, but have exposed themselves to equitable remedies by

[55] *Attorney General for Hong Kong v Reid* [1994] 1 AC 324 (PC).
[56] *Allcard v Skinner* (1887) 36 ChD 145 (CA).
[57] *Paragon Finance Plc v DB Thakerar & Co (A Firm)* [1994] 4 All ER 400, 409 (CA).
[58] *Dubai Aluminium Co Ltd v Salaam* [2003] 2 AC 366, 404 (HL).

> virtue of their participation in the unlawful misapplication of trust assets. Either they have dishonestly assisted in a misapplication of the funds by the trustee, or they have received trust assets knowing that the transfer to them was a breach of trust. In either case, they may be required by equity to account as if they were trustees or fiduciaries, although they are not … The intervention of equity in such cases does not reflect any pre-existing obligation but comes about solely because of the misapplication of the assets. It is purely remedial.[59]

However, despite the courts' recent preference for the language being purely remedial, one question addressed below is whether, in the particular instance of recipient liability, the language of constructive trusts is not a fiction but entirely appropriate, that there really is a trust and duties of trusteeship in such cases. However, we begin with unjust enrichment.

B. A Liability in Unjust Enrichment

Peter Birks originally explained the personal claim for the receipt of rights dissipated in breach of trust as one in unjust enrichment.[60] Liability in unjust enrichment is generally strict, which meant that the fault requirement in a case like *Re Montagu* was immediately out of place, but that was precisely the point of Birks' analysis. Drawing on standard cases of unjust enrichment, in particular, the strict liability of the recipient of a mistaken payment in a case like *Kelly v Solari*,[61] where the claimant insurance company allegedly paid out by mistake to the defendant on a policy which had lapsed, Birks argued that the same rationale applied to the recipient of rights dissipated in breach of trust. In the case of the mistaken payment, strict liability is explained by the law's focus on the lack of the claimant's consent to the transfer, more particularly, its vitiation (due to the mistake). The state of mind of the recipient is neither here nor there, at least when determining the constituent elements of the cause of action.[62] In the case we are discussing, the claimant beneficiary gave no consent whatever to the transfer; he was 'ignorant' of it. According to Birks, that made it an even stronger case for strict liability. Yet the case law requires fault, which, he said, must be a mistake.

Though never abandoning this thesis, Birks later changed his mind in one important respect. This was in his adoption[63] of the view of Lord Nicholls that there are two possible claims in such a scenario: a strict liability unjust enrichment claim and a fault-based claim in wrongs.[64] The claim in wrongs would be relevant

[59] *Williams v Central Bank of Nigeria* [2014] UKSC 10, [2014] AC 1189, [9].

[60] P Birks, 'Misdirected Funds: Restitution from the Recipient' [1989] *Lloyd's Maritime and Commercial Law Quarterly* 296.

[61] *Kelly v Solari* (1841) 9 M & W 54.

[62] The defendant's state of mind may, however, be relevant in the context of defences.

[63] Birks, 'Receipt' (n 4) 223.

[64] Nicholls (n 3) 244.

where what was sought was a sum greater than the amount by which the defendant was enriched. For example, the trustee might have lost valuable investment opportunities whilst the trust rights were in the hands of the defendant; the only way through to such losses would be via a claim in wrongs. So, too, with secondary gains.

Let us focus for now, however, on the unjust enrichment explanation of the receipt claim. It suffers from a number of difficulties. The first is that there is no recognised unjust factor. As just seen, Birks based his cause of action on the beneficiary's 'ignorance' of the transfer away of the trust rights, but ignorance has never been acknowledged as an unjust factor, even at common law.[65] At common law, Birks relied on cases such as *Holiday v Sigil*,[66] where the plaintiff dropped a £500 note which was then picked up by the defendant. The claimant brought a successful action for money had and received and the defendant was ordered to pay him £500. However, this is hardly authority for a ground of ignorance at common law. First, no argument was made in the case other than as to the type of evidence admissible to prove the alleged facts. Second, the long-abolished action for money had and received was multi-causal. Though it could be brought for certain cases of unjust enrichment, it was also available for wrongdoing, and even consensual debts. Third, the defendant's enrichment could not be said to be at the claimant's expense. There is no doubt that the defendant was enriched by his taking of the physical note itself, the 'thing', but what he did not receive was the claimant's right with respect to the thing. In this respect, it is different from the cases with which Birks makes a comparison where the claimant's right passes to the defendant. The point has been noted by Chambers. In speaking of the difference between a person to whom a title to a car was transferred as a result of a fraudulently induced mistake and one who received a title from someone who stole the car, he wrote:

> The real difference between us is the source of our enrichment. You received the previous owner's title, the transfer of which was flawed and therefore reversible. In contrast, the true owner of my stolen car retains a title which was never transferred to me. The thief who stole the car thereby obtained a new title (that is, a new right to possession created simply by taking possession). I acquired the thief's title, and my enrichment is not at the owner's expense. While the owner can sue me for wrongful interference with her or his right to possession, this is not a claim for restitution of unjust enrichment. The owner is enforcing a pre-existing right to possession (presumably acquired by consent) and not attempting to reverse the thief's transfer to me.[67]

The position in equity is no different. The precise problem was pointed out by Lionel Smith in 2000.[68] Once again, the defendant is enriched in the example

[65] See further WJ Swadling, 'Ignorance and Unjust Enrichment: The Problem of Title' (2008) 28 *OJLS* 627.

[66] *Holiday v Sigil* (1826) 2 Car & P 177.

[67] R Chambers, 'Two Kinds of Enrichment' in R Chambers, C Mitchell and J Penner (eds), *Philosophical Foundations of the Law of Unjust Enrichment* (Oxford, OUP, 2009) 242, 250.

[68] L Smith,' Unjust Enrichment, Property and the Structure of Trusts' (2000) 116 *LQR* 412.

posited at the beginning of this chapter; the receipt of the shares is undoubtedly an enrichment. But crucially those rights came not from the beneficiary himself, but from the trustee. As with the case of the thief at common law, it is completely different from *Kelly v Solari*, where the defendant's enrichment undoubtedly came from the claimant. The defendant's enrichment in our case is therefore at the trustee's expense, not that of the beneficiary. According to Smith:

> In the mistaken payment, the defendant is enriched by the receipt of value which the plaintiff used to have but no longer has … But what happens in the case of receipt of trust property? The defendant gets (we may assume) legal title to the trust property; that is something which the beneficiary never had. In some kinds of trust it may be that the trustee itself did not have legal title. But in any case the defendant acquires its interest from the trustee, and so gets something which the beneficiary never had.[69]

Despite this fatal criticism, Birks refused to concede the point,[70] dismissing it as 'technical', in the same way that he dismissed objections I had previously raised to his arguments for ignorance at common law.[71] The reason he thought it technical seems to have been that, for him, there was something called 'equitable title', which was to be contrasted with legal title. In the case of a trust, whilst the trustee had legal title, the beneficiary had equitable title. Thus, in the case posited at the outset of this chapter, there will be a legal title to the shares vested in the trustee, and an equitable title vested in the beneficiary. Moreover, for Birks, these were two versions of the same thing. It was this 'equitable title', which in ways that were never explained, which gave the beneficiary the ability to sue.

However, talk of equitable title behind a trust is mistaken. Although Birks did not fall into the trap of thinking that placing rights on trust involves a splitting of the subject-right into two parts —a legal part, and an equitable part—he misunderstood the nature of a trust, which is not to create an equitable analogue of the right held on trust.[72]

The most obvious illustration of this point is that, as Smith notes in the quotation above, equitable rights can also form the subject matter of a trust. In such a situation, it is impossible to say that the trustee holds the legal right and the beneficiary the equitable right. We would have to instead say that the trustee holds the equitable right and that the beneficiary also holds the equitable right—a clear impossibility.

Moreover, it is not the case that the beneficiary has an equitable version of the trustee's right, for this would mean that English law was in a perpetual state of conflict. Speaking of the rule found in section 25 of the Judicature Act 1873, that

[69] ibid 428–29.
[70] Birks, 'Receipt' (n 4) 233–39.
[71] Swadling (n 65).
[72] It is significant that Birks never thought in terms of rights as enrichment, but only value. It may be this failure on his part which explains his mistake in this area.

in the case of conflicts between law and equity, the rules of equity are to prevail, Maitland said of a trust of a title to land:

> Equity did not say that the *cestui que trust* was the owner of the land, it said that the trustee was the owner of the land, but added that he was bound to hold the land for the benefit of the *cestui que trust*. There was no conflict here. Had there been a conflict here [section 25] of the Judicature Act [1873] would have abolished the whole law of trusts. Common law says that A is the owner, equity says that B is the owner, but equity is to prevail, therefore B is the owner and A has no right or duty of any sort or kind in or about the land. Of course the Judicature Act has not acted in this way; it has left the law of trusts just where it stood, because it found no conflict, no variance even, between the rules of the common law and the rules of equity.[73]

In truth, the rights of the beneficiary of a trust are of a completely different order from those held by the trustee. The rights of the beneficiary are to an account of the exercise of the rights of the trustee and not some attenuated form of the subject-rights themselves. This is made clear by James LJ in *Smith v Anderson*, who defined a trustee as:

> a man who is the owner of the property and deals with it as principal, as owner, and as master, subject only to an equitable obligation to account to some persons to whom he stands in the relation of trustee, and who are his *cestuis que trust*.[74]

The fact that the beneficiary does not have an equitable version of the trustee's right is neatly illustrated by *Schalit v Joseph Nadler*,[75] where a lease of land was vested in trustees on trust for a beneficiary. The beneficiary sought to exercise the remedy of distraint, which was then available to trustees for non-payment of rent by the tenant.[76] The court held that she could not do so:

> The right of the cestui que trust whose trustee has demised property subject to the trust is, not to the rent, but to an account from the trustee of the profits received from the demise … The cestui que trust has no right to demand that the actual bank-notes received by the trustee shall be handed over to him or that a cheque for rent drawn to the trustee shall be indorsed over. What he can require is that the trustee shall account to him, after taking credit for any outgoings or other payments properly chargeable, for the profits received from the trust property.[77]

[73] FW Maitland (eds AH Chaytor and WJ Whittaker) *Equity: A Course of Lectures, revised by J Brunyate* (Cambridge, CUP, 1936) 17. When Maitland speaks of the trustee being the owner of the 'land', he of course means a right with respect to that land, such as a fee simple or a lease.

[74] *Smith v Anderson* (1880) 15 Ch D 247, 275: 'Property' is here used to describe the right held on trust, rather than any physical thing to which it might relate.

[75] *Schalit v Joseph Nadler* [1933] 2 KB 79.

[76] The landlord's right of distraint was abolished with effect from 6 April 2014 by Part 3 of the Tribunals, Courts and Enforcement Act 2007. However, a statutory scheme (Commercial Rent Arrears Recovery) was immediately enacted, though only for commercial premises.

[77] *Schalit* (n 75) 83 (Acton and Goddard JJ). Note that this has nothing to do with the distinction between law and equity, but with the fact that the right to rent is vested in the trustee, not the beneficiary, with the result that, viz a viz the beneficiary, no money is due. Thus, even if there was a 'fusion' of law and equity, the result in this case would have been no different. Another decision in the same vein is *Atlasview Ltd v Brightview Ltd* [2004] 2 BCLC 191, where beneficiaries of trust of shares sought to

Viscount Sumner spoke in similar terms in *Baker (Inspector of Taxes) v Archer Shee*:

> The trustee has the full ... property in the whole of the trust fund and the beneficiary has not. ... It is the trustee alone who can give a discharge for interest, rent or dividends to the parties who have to pay them in respect of the invested trust estate, nor need they know the beneficiary in the matter. All that the latter can do is to claim the assistance of [the court] to enforce the trust and to compel the trustee to discharge it.[78]

We see the same thinking in the decision of the Court of Appeal in *MCC Proceeds v Lehman Brothers*,[79] which involved bearer shares held on trust for the claimant. As shareholders, the trustees had a right to the exclusive possession forever of the share certificates. In breach of trust, they pledged the shares to the defendant as security for a loan by handing over the share certificates to the defendant. The claimant beneficiary brought an action against the defendant for conversion of the share certificates, a tort committed by those who interfere with another's right to the exclusive possession of tangible moveables. The beneficiary's claim was rejected by the Court of Appeal. It was the trustee who had a right to exclusive possession of the share certificates, not the claimant beneficiary, who could not therefore maintain conversion.[80] It is for the same reason that a beneficiary cannot sue a thief of the subject matter of rights held on trust; that is a job for the trustee, though in certain circumstances the trustee must lend his name to the beneficiary should he refuse to sue.[81]

Of course, this objection only holds true for rights previously held on trust. To be fair to Birks, many of the cases he was concerned with, cases such as *BCCI v Akindele*,[82] involved rights held outright, so that the enrichment of the defendant was undoubtedly at the claimant's expense.

Birks further spoke of having to see the package of protection as a whole. In his view, the beneficiary's right to bring an unjust enrichment claim against a recipient from the trustee was connected to the fact that claims in respect of traceable substitutes were only explicable as responding to unjust enrichment.[83] As to this latter proposition, he thought that wrongdoing as an explanation was ruled out following the Court of Appeal's decision in *Jones (FC) & Sons (a firm)*

bring an unfair prejudice action under s 459 of the Companies Act 1985. Such action is only available to the members of a company. The claim was dismissed on the ground, inter alia, that the claimants were not members of the company.

[78] *Baker (Inspector of Taxes) v Archer Shee* [1927] AC 844, 850 (PC).

[79] *MCC Proceeds Inc v Lehman Brothers International (Europe)* [1998] 4 All ER 675 (CA).

[80] The reason they did not bring a claim against the defendant in respect of their own right was that it was liable to be defeated by a plea of bona fide purchase for value without notice. No such defence, however, would have applied on the facts to the right to exclusive possession at law. The defendants, however, had not interfered with that particular right; indeed, they were transferees of it.

[81] These situations are limited. They are described in *Vandepitte v Preferred Accident Insurance Corpn of New York* [1933] AC 20 (PC). For full discussion, see L Tucker, N Le Poidevin and J Brightwell (eds), *Lewin on Trusts*, 19th edn (London, Sweet & Maxwell, 2015) paras 43–01–43-016.

[82] *Akindele* (n 9).

[83] Birks, 'Receipt' (n 4) 216–22.

Trustee v Jones,[84] and that an appeal to the miscellany beyond consent, wrongs and unjust enrichment could not work. That left only unjust enrichment as a plausible explanation.[85] The connection with the personal claim under consideration here was this. If, according to Birks, there had been a substitution by the recipient in our example of the shares, and that substitute was still in the recipient's hands, the claimant could bring a tracing claim, which was, in his view, a proprietary unjust enrichment claim. It would, argued Birks, be inconsistent in such circumstances to deny a personal unjust enrichment claim on our facts.[86]

This, however, is an extremely insecure foundation on which to rest an argument for unjust enrichment as an explanation of recipient liability in cases of breach of trust. The reason is that no one, Birks included, has ever come up with a satisfactory explanation why we allow claims to substitutes. Over a century ago, Maitland said it was excessively generous to trust beneficiaries,[87] and it still is.

Despite these difficulties, Lord Nicholls also argues for an unjust enrichment claim on the facts given above,[88] as does Burrows,[89] and the editors of *Goff and Jones*.[90] However, like Birks, none give a convincing reason why the defendant's enrichment in the case at hand can be seen as at the beneficiary's expense.

C. Knowing Recipient is a Genuine Trustee Who Owes a Duty to Account to His Beneficiary

We saw above that the language of awards that the defendant is liable to account as a constructive trustee is nowadays dismissed by most judges and commentators as pure fiction, designed only to bring the defendant within equity's jurisdiction. Although the defendant is liable to account 'as if he were' or 'as a constructive' trustee, it does not mean he really is a trustee; it is trusteeship by a metaphor. There is not the substance of a trust; the language is purely remedial, much like that of quasi-contract in unjust enrichment claims before the abolition of the forms of action in the mid-nineteenth century.

Mitchell and Watterson, however, argue that in this particular instance the knowing recipient is a genuine trustee of the rights he receives. They say:

> Liability for knowing receipt is a distinctive, primary, custodial liability, which closely resembles the liability of express trustees to account for the trust property with which they are charged. In short, when the courts say that a knowing recipient is 'personally

[84] *Jones (FC) & Sons (a firm) Trustee v Jones* [1997] Ch 159 (CA).
[85] *cf* the appeal to the reasoning of Sherlock Holmes by Lord Millett in *Twinsectra* (n 50) [100].
[86] Birks, 'Receipt' (n 4) 238.
[87] Maitland (n 73) 220.
[88] Nicholls (n 3) 236–39.
[89] Burrows (n 51) 416–31. The enrichment objection is discussed briefly at 428–29.
[90] C Mitchell, P Mitchell and S Watterson (eds), *Goff and Jones: The Law of Unjust Enrichment*, 9th edn (London, Sweet & Maxwell, 2016) paras 8–119 to 8–137.

> liable to account as a constructive trustee', they mean exactly what they say: because of the circumstances in which knowing recipients receive title to the misapplied property, Equity fixes them with custodial duties which are the same as some of the duties which are voluntarily assumed by express trustees.[91]

As a trustee, they argue, the knowing recipient is duty bound to account to his 'beneficiary' for his stewardship of the rights he holds for him on trust. This stewardship duty entails a duty to retransfer the right received to the trustee. If the recipient transfers away the right other than back to the trustee from whom it was received, or to the beneficiary if he or she is of full age, sound mind and absolutely entitled, the beneficiary can falsify the account and ask the court to enforce the trustee's primary duty to reinstate the trust fund. This would be done by an order that the defendant pay over the value of the right and it is this claim to pay money which Mitchell and Watterson argue is the one we call 'knowing receipt'.

The authors stress that this is not a claim for breach of duty; nor is it a claim for unjust enrichment, though they would also allow a strict liability claim for the latter. The difference between the two is that the unjust enrichment claim would be subject to a defence of change of position and would only yield the defendant's gain at the point of receipt. So, in the shares example, unjust enrichment would give the claimant the value of the shares at the date of receipt, whilst the account claim would give the value at the date of claim, which would be of importance where the shares had risen in value in the interim.

Mitchell and Watterson claim two advantages for their thesis. The first is that it is consistent with the language of the courts. The second is that it explains the requirement of knowledge, which in the authors' view is what turns the recipient into a trustee of the rights he receives. There are, however, at least five problems with their thesis.

The first is the paucity of authority for their theory.[92] Not a single decision cited by Mitchell and Watterson is directly on point which, given the number of recipient liability cases, is surprising. They also place much reliance on the strange Australian case of *Evans v European Bank Ltd*[93] where a company, Benford Ltd, which was used as a vehicle to channel fraudulently obtained funds, was held to be a constructive trustee of such funds for the victims of the fraud and thereby fixed with a duty to track down those victims and repay them from the funds it held, and in the meantime invest the funds for them. The case is, however, hardly a strong precedent. First, it relies on the Australian High Court decision in *Black v S Freedman & Co*,[94] which held that a thief holds his title to things he steals on trust

[91] Above n 6, 129–30.

[92] It was, however, adopted subsequently by Sir Terence Etherton, giving the advice of the Privy Council in *Arthur v A-G of the Turks & Caicos Islands* [2012] UKPC 30 (PC). However, the point was obiter. Moreover, the decision did not involve rights previously held on trust but outright. Finally, it also seems to have been decided in ignorance of *Criterion*.

[93] *Evans v European Bank Ltd* [2004] NSWCA 82 (NSWCA).

[94] *Black v S Freedman & Co* (1910) 12 CLR 105 (HCA).

for his victim. This is controversial in the extreme, not least because the victim's title to the stolen goods will be superior to that of his trustee/thief. For that reason alone, the case is unlikely to be followed in this jurisdiction. Second, a receiver had been appointed in respect of Benford, and it was the receiver who was making the argument—against Benford's own interests—that such duties were owed. This meant that the point that Benford was a trustee was hardly contested.

Other cases relied upon involve defendants inducing breaches of trust, which are clearly distinguishable from cases of receipt. Mitchell and Watterson also claim the support of Megarry VC in *re Montagu*, Millett J in *Agip (Africa) Ltd v Jackson*, and Lord Browne-Wilkinson in *Westdeutsche Landesbank Girozentrale v Islington LBC* for the proposition that, unless the recipient is equity's darling, he must restore the rights to their rightful owner if he still has them. However, not only are such statements obiter dicta, they are also ambiguous, for they could equally well be saying that the defendant is liable to be ordered by a court of competent jurisdiction to restore the rights, which is something less than there being an immediate duty to do so absent any court order.[95]

The second problem is that no explanation whatever is provided why a defendant who receives with 'knowledge' is turned by operation of law into a trustee. We might, with Lord Browne-Wilkinson in *Westdeutsche Landesbank Girozentrale v Islington LBC*,[96] say it is a necessary condition, for it would be unreasonable for a person with no knowledge that he had received rights held on trust for another or for a purpose to be fixed with trusteeship duties. However, it does not thereby follow that it is sufficient. The vast majority of trusts arise consensually, with right-holders being bound by the obligations of trusteeship precisely because they have been voluntarily assumed. That will not, of course, be the case here.[97] At the very least, it is incumbent on Mitchell and Watterson to explain why trusteeship duties are being imposed on such a person. At present, their argument does nothing more than imply an 'ought' from a 'can'.

Third, it is difficult to see how Mitchell and Watterson's thesis can be squared with the subsequent decision of the United Kingdom Supreme Court in *AIB Group (UK) Plc v Mark Redler & Co Solicitors*.[98] Even if there was a duty to account before payment away, does not payment away mean that the transaction is now 'complete', so that the only claim available is one for equitable compensation? It might be argued that the transaction would only be complete if the rights were returned to the original trustee/beneficiary, but in both the earlier case of *Target Holdings*

[95] Indeed, all Lord Browne-Wilkinson seems concerned with is the continuing enforceability of the right against a recipient who is not equity's darling.

[96] *Westdeutsche Landesbank Girozentrale* (n 26) 709 (HL).

[97] As Lord Sumption said in *Williams v Central Bank of Nigeria*: 'The essence of a liability to account on the footing of knowing receipt is that the defendant has accepted trust assets knowing that they were transferred to him in breach of trust and that he had no right to receive them. His possession is therefore at all times wrongful and adverse to the rights of both the true trustees and the beneficiaries. No trust has been reposed in him': [2014] UKSC 10 [31] (SC).

[98] *AIB Group (UK) Plc v Mark Redler & Co Solicitors* [2014] UKSC 58 (SC).

Ltd v Redferns,[99] and in *AIB* itself, the fact that the moneys were paid away to unauthorised persons did not stop the transactions being so adjudged. These, of course, were cases of express trusts, so the proposition should apply a fortiori to a trust which is the creation of the law. Thus, in a case like *re Montagu* where all that remained following the death of the life tenant was an absolutely entitled beneficiary, the Tenth Duke of Manchester, the payment away by the father of the rights he received in breach of trust meant that that transaction was also complete, with the result that the only possible claim against him would have been one for equitable compensation; no claim for falsification of an account would have been available.

Fourth, is it really true to say that there is a duty on the recipient to retransfer the right to the trustee at the point at which knowledge supervenes? A more viable explanation would be that there is at best only a liability to be so ordered, with no duty before judgment. What, for example, if difficult issues of fact were involved as in *BCCI v Akindele*,[100] where a trial was necessary to decide whether the defendant had notice of the dissipation in breach of duty? In such a case, can it really be said that there is a duty to repay before any adjudication on the state of the recipient's state of mind? Moreover, to say, as do Mitchell and Watterson, that there is a duty to restore because restoration will absolve the defendant from any claim in court[101] is nonsensical. Obviously, if a recipient voluntarily restores rights received in breach of trust, then the claimant beneficiary will have nothing left to complain about. But it does not thereby follow that there must have been a duty so to do. To take an example from the law of unjust enrichment, if title to a painting is transferred to me by mistake and I immediately and voluntarily reconvey that title, no claim in unjust enrichment will lie against me. But we cannot read into that fact the proposition that I was under some kind of duty to make specific restitution.

Fifth, and finally, even in the case of express trustees, is it correct to say that the beneficiary has a 'right' to an account without having to go anywhere near a court? Take the case of a beneficiary who alleges that the trustee negligently invested the trust fund and now seeks to surcharge the account with the shortfall. Is it really possible to say that the defendant trustee is immediately bound to pay what a court will only later find due after a trial? Are we seriously saying that all trustees have crystal balls? Whilst it may be true that there is a primary duty on a trustee to produce the trust accounts to certain beneficiaries,[102] falsification and surcharge do not involve the performance of primary duties; they are nothing

[99] *Target Holdings Ltd v Redferns* [1996] AC 421 (HL).

[100] *Akindele* (n 9).

[101] Mitchell and Watterson (n 6).

[102] Mitchell and Watterson say that a trustee is under a primary duty to produce accounts, though they present no proof. They simply point to fact that the trustee will be liable for costs of proceedings if he does not produce them and will have to pay costs of accounting too, as opposed to being able to charge it to trust fund: ibid 120, fn 22.

more than court ordered remedies for breach of trust. Indeed, Mitchell and Watterson give the game away when they say that in an action for a common account, the trustee has to justify his records.[103] But this can only mean justify *to the court*. This is clear from their statement that 'evidential presumptions are made against him if he fails to do so'.[104] Such language only makes sense if we are talking about court proceedings, not duties arising before trial. Indeed, Mitchell and Watterson go on to say that 'the accounting process is the conceptual mechanism through which beneficiaries can bring … different types of compensation claim against trustees',[105] which is hardly consistent with any pre-existing duty.

D. Knowing Recipient is a Trustee and Commits a Breach of Trust When He Dissipates the Rights; The Money Award Made Against Him is for Breach of Trust

A view similar to Mitchell and Watterson has been put forward separately by both Simon Gardner[106] and Robert Chambers,[107] save that they are not talking about the enforcement of any 'primary custodial duties' which, for the reasons explained above, is problematic, but instead a secondary duty to pay damages for breach of trust in transferring the rights away other than to the trustee/truly entitled beneficiary. According to Chambers:

> liability for knowing receipt is nothing other than liability for breach of trust. It arises because the recipient has obtained assets that are held in trust, and after becoming aware of the trust, has failed to perform the basic trust duties to preserve the trust assets and transfer them to either the beneficiaries or the proper trustees. This requires actual knowledge of the trust or the circumstances giving rise to it. Notice is insufficient. This is not a form of restitution of unjust or wrongful enrichment, so it should not matter whether the assets were received for the recipient's own benefit. The recipient is an actual trustee and not just being treated as if that was true. This is not a form of accessory or secondary liability. It is fundamentally different from liability for knowingly assisting a breach of trust or fiduciary duty.[108]

However, the question once again is why a knowing recipient is a trustee of the rights he receives. Gardner says that the defendant cannot be liable for failing to safeguard the rights he receives unless he knows that the rights he holds are trust rights. This, however, is no justification at all, for, like Mitchell and Watterson, it does no more than imply an 'ought' from a 'can'. Chambers puts forward a more sophisticated argument based on an analogy with the duties of a finder of goods,

[103] ibid 121.
[104] ibid.
[105] ibid 122.
[106] Gardner (n 7) 22.
[107] Chambers, 'The End of Knowing Receipt' (n 8).
[108] ibid 4.

who, he says, is just as much a bailee as one entrusted with their care.[109] But though it is true that a finder has been held to be a bailee and subject to the same duties to care for the goods as a gratuitous bailee,[110] this is an insecure foundation on which to build, for the notion of the finder as bailee was invented purely to allow losers of goods to bring detinue against finders. It is nothing more than a distortion of the forms of action, similar to the idea that claims in unjust enrichment and restitution for wrongs rested on an 'implied contract'; it should not be allowed to change the substance of the matter.[111]

E. A Liability in Wrongs

The best hope of explaining the liability we call knowing receipt is as a species of wrongdoing. However, for the reasons given immediately above the wrong cannot be said to be breach of trust, as the recipient is not a trustee. What other alternatives exist?

We saw above that Lord Nicholls advocated seeing knowing receipt, like assistance of a breach of trust, as a species of dishonest participation in a breach of trust.[112] It is, however, difficult to see how this can work, for the defendant's receipt need not be coterminous with the breach of trust; the rights may have been received many years later and need not have come from the trustee himself. Moreover, the receipt by the defendant may have been purely passive.

Lionel Smith has suggested that knowing receipt is equity's analogue to the common law tort of conversion.[113] His main argument is that both conversion and knowing receipt involve a wrongful interference with proprietary rights.[114] Moreover, such thinking, according to Smith, is consistent with the scenario whereby the recipient only later becomes aware that his receipt was of rights dissipated in breach of trust 'since it presupposes a continuing proprietary right in the plaintiff with which the defendant interferes'.[115] As to the fact that conversion is strict, whilst knowing receipt is fault based, this is explained by the fact the former has to be strict because the common law has no equivalent of the Roman *rei vindicatio* for goods. The only way the common law can enforce rights in respect of goods is through the law of wrongs, and their protection would be too weak with only a fault-based wrong. Equity, by contrast, has the specific claim, which means that it can be 'more sensitive about what counts as wrongful receipt'.[116]

[109] ibid 8–11.

[110] N Palmer, *Bailment*, 3rd edn (London, Sweet & Maxwell, 2009) ch 26.

[111] As witness the inapplicability of the rule that a bailee is estopped from denying his bailor's title in the context of so-called bailment by finding: *Biddle v Bond* (1865) 6 B & S 225.

[112] Nicholls (n 3) 243–44.

[113] L Smith, 'W(h)ither Knowing Receipt?' (1998) 114 *LQR* 394.

[114] ibid 395.

[115] ibid 396.

[116] ibid 397.

Is Smith's analogy with common law conversion convincing? A first difference is that the holder of title to goods needs only one right, whereas the trust beneficiary will need two. The right of a title-holder to goods to exclusive possession binds generally. However, it is not as simple as regards the position of a beneficiary of a trust. Such a person clearly has rights against his trustee, but these are to the due administration of the trust and it is not that right which a claim for knowing receipt can possibly be enforcing. We would therefore have to say that he has another right, viz, that third parties do not knowingly receive rights transferred to them in breach of trust. This is certainly possible, for it is already the case that a trust beneficiary has a right that others do not dishonestly assist the trustee to commit breaches of trust.[117] Moreover, there is likewise a right against third parties that they do not knowingly induce the trustee to commit a breach of trust.[118] And we have already seen how those who receive rights in an authorised fashion, but who then knowingly deal with them inconsistently with the terms of the trust, will be liable to make good losses to the beneficiaries.[119]

However, even if there were multiple rights, a further problem is that the defendant in a knowing receipt claim, as opposed to one who induces or assists breaches of trust, need not have done anything at all. Whilst conversion cannot be committed without some action on the part of the defendant, this is not the case with knowing receipt where, as we have just noted, the receipt can be purely passive. A wrong generally requires some action on the part of the defendant, as witness the common law's general reluctance to impose liability for mere omissions to act.

This raises the vital question whether receipt really is, as the Court of Appeal said in *Novoship (UK) Ltd v Mikhaylyuk*, 'the gist of the action'.[120] Such a proposition is already doubtful when it is remembered that, in the case of innocent receipt, liability may arise later, if and when knowledge supervenes. Might the essence of the liability instead be the subsequent dissipation of the rights with knowledge? Given the availability of a strict liability claim for the specific return of the rights, a claimant will only bring a knowing receipt claim where the rights have already been dissipated, a fact which renders the case law ambiguous, for whether it is receipt or dissipation which is the 'gist' will be hidden from view. However, if it was the dissipation, things become much simpler, for knowing 'receipt' would then be simply a species of inconsistent dealing.

[117] *Royal Brunei Airlines Sdn Bhd v Tan* [1995] 2 AC 378 (PC); *Twinsectra* (n 50); *Barlow Clowes International Ltd v Eurotrust International Ltd* [2006] 1 WLR 1476 (PC); *Abou-Rahmah v Abacha* [2006] EWCA Civ 1492 (CA).

[118] *Fyler v Fyler* (1841) 3 Beav 550; *Eaves v Hickson* (1861) 30 Beav 136; *re Midgely* [1893] 3 Ch 282.

[119] *Lee v Sankey* (n 18).

[120] *Novoship (UK) Ltd v Mikhaylyuk* [2014] EWCA Civ 908 [89]; see also *Agip (Africa) Ltd* (n 2) 291, where Millett J said that the knowing recipient was 'liable to account for the property … from the time he received the property'.

It should be stressed that we are not here saying that the recipient is subject to the same duties as the trustee. The trustee may, for example, have been under a duty to invest or to sell. The recipient will be under no similar duty. His duty is simply not to dissipate the rights in a way which is inconsistent with the terms of the trust. In this respect, the wrong is analogous to the common law tort of inducing breach of contract.[121] Strangers to a contract are never duty bound to perform the obligations of the contracting parties. They are, however, under a duty not to knowingly induce a contract party to breach his contract, such duty being owed to the counterparty to the contract. Likewise, one who knowingly receives rights which have been dissipated in breach of trust, or who later discovers they were so dissipated whilst the rights are still vested in them, comes under a duty not to further dissipate the rights in a way which is inconsistent with the original trusts on which they were held.

Such assimilation of knowing receipt within inconsistent dealing would have the advantage of catching the case where rights are received not because of a breach of trust, but equally not because of some authorised disposition by the trustees. Suppose a sole trustee dies intestate, as in *Paul v Constance*,[122] and the rights held on trust pass under the rules of intestacy to his widow. There is no doubt that the widow is liable to be ordered to give up the rights themselves if she still has them. One would have thought that she would be personally liable should she dissipate them with knowledge that they were held on trust, though this comes within neither knowing receipt—because the right was not received by virtue of a breach of trust—nor 'inconsistent dealing'—because the receipt was unauthorised.

Analysing knowing receipt as a species of inconsistent dealing would have a number of consequences. First, it would show that the difficult requirement of 'beneficial receipt' was misplaced. As we have seen, such a requirement only makes sense if knowing receipt is analysed as a species of unjust enrichment. Seeing it instead as a manifestation of the equitable wrong of inconsistent dealing means it has to be removed. Second, it would mean time running not from point of receipt but from the later dissipation. Third, it would mean that there was no claim if the rights were lost without fault on the part of the recipient.

We have already noted the uncertainty surrounding the correct level of fault necessary to trigger liability in knowing receipt. Does analysis as part of a wider wrong of inconsistent dealing help to resolve this issue? Although the case law is sparse, the rule in inconsistent dealing cases is that there must be actual knowledge that the dealing is inconsistent or a deliberate closing of the eyes to that fact. Thus, in *Williams-Ashman v Price & Williams*,[123] Bennett J refused to hold a solicitor liable for inconsistent dealing whose only sin was that he acted honestly but 'incautiously'.[124] The upshot, therefore, is that Megarry V-C was ultimately

[121] *Lumley v Gye* (1853) 2 E & B 216.
[122] *Paul v Constance* [1977] 1 WLR 527 (CA).
[123] *Williams-Ashman v Price & Williams* [1942] Ch 219.
[124] ibid 228.

right in *re Montagu's Settlement Trust* to insist on a high degree of fault, and that those cases which hold that constructive or even imputed notice is enough are wrongly decided.

VI. Conclusion

This chapter has examined the nature of the nature of the equitable liability we call 'knowing receipt'. It has rejected an explanation as one in unjust enrichment for a number of reasons, prime amongst them being that the defendant's enrichment—the receipt of the right dissipated in breach of trust—does not come from the beneficiary. The enrichment, in other words, is not at the claimant's expense. This is not, of course, an issue where rights which are held beneficially by a corporation are misapplied by a fiduciary, but as the House of Lords pointed out in *Criterion Properties plc v Stratford UK Properties LLC*,[125] such cases cannot be analysed in terms of knowing receipt. The notion that the knowing recipient is a genuine trustee of the rights he receives was also rejected for a number of reasons, the chief being that there is no satisfactory reason why he should be a trustee. The recipient is, of course, bound by the rights of the beneficiaries to obtain an order from the court for the return of such rights, but he does not have the custodial duties of a trustee and so is not liable to account to the 'beneficiary'; nor is he liable to pay money for breach of trust. The only viable explanation is a liability in wrongs, though not one of participating in a breach of trust, as the receipt might come after the breach and may well involve no action on the defendant's part. Instead, the liability should be seen as a species of a larger wrong called inconsistent dealing. Such wrong is committed when the recipient deals with the right in a way which he knows is inconsistent with the terms of the trust on which they were originally held, or to which fact he deliberately closes his eyes. It should be stressed that we are not saying that the recipient is a trustee of the rights received, merely that he will commit a wrong should he dissipate them in a way which is inconsistent with the trusts on which they were originally held. What this means, therefore, is that 'knowing receipt' is a misnomer. Receipt is not the gist of the action, but the later, inconsistent, dealing.

[125] *Criterion* (n 10).

14

Exposing Third-Party Liability in Equity: Lessons from the Limitation Rules

SARAH WORTHINGTON

I. Introduction

It is impossible to explain the law unless its foundations are clearly understood. This chapter owes its genesis to my inability to explain the law set out by the Supreme Court in *Williams v Central Bank of Nigeria*.[1] The headline finding in *Williams* is that dishonest assisters and knowing recipients[2] are not 'trustees', so they never run the risk of time running without limitation under the Limitation Act 1980, section 21(1). This might look unexceptional were it not that other parties who are also not express trustees, or even trustees at all, are not similarly protected. These less fortunate 'trustees' will be exposed to claims without limitation of time if the claim is for fraud or fraudulent breaches of trust, or for the recovery of trust property or its proceeds in these trustees' hands or converted to these trustees' use.

The law on limitation, especially limitation in equity, is typically considered difficult. But the decision in *Williams* cannot be confined to its limitation context. The Supreme Court made a number of crucial claims about the fundamental nature of dishonest assistance and knowing receipt, and it is these, not any particular limitation rules, which are the central concern of this chapter. The Court's final conclusions on limitation depend entirely on the accuracy of the initial characterisation of dishonest assisters and knowing recipients. This chapter seeks to unpick the logic. The result is to raise doubts about the majority's interpretation.

[1] *Williams v Central Bank of Nigeria* [2014] UKSC 10, [2014] AC 1189 (SC).

[2] 'Unconscionable recipients' may seem to be more appropriate modern terminology, but it has proved difficult to use in recent cases: see CE Webb and T Akkouh, *Trusts Law*, 4th edn (London, Palgrave Macmillan, 2015) 345–46 for a rather damning assessment. In *Williams* itself, a word search produces 117 hits for 'knowing' and only two for 'unconscionable'.

Based on the analysis here, a number of significant claims are advanced. In particular, and despite popular assertion to the contrary, it is suggested that knowing recipients and dishonest assisters are indeed fiduciaries. This conclusion has at least two obvious consequences. First, it clarifies the nature and quantum of the remedies available against these third parties, and the justification for them. It also distinguishes and illuminates the remedies available against innocent donees. Second, this novel recognition of the importance of fiduciary characterisation in applying the limitation rules, if correct, has the advantage of enabling straightforward negotiation of equitable liability under the Limitation Act 1980, and eliminating the current confusing complexity.[3]

The conclusion that these third parties are fiduciaries may appear dramatic, but the reality is that much of the case law before *Selangor United Rubber Estates Ltd v Cradock (No 3)*[4] and *Paragon Finance Plc v DB Thakerar & Co*[5]—two authorities relied upon by the majority in *Williams*—was precisely along these lines, and understood as such. What confounded straightforward analysis was use of the word 'constructive' without holding firmly to its roots. Courts imposing third-party liability sought to identify what level of knowledge would constitute a defendant a 'constructive trustee'. This way of posing the question—and its detours into notice, constructive notice, dishonesty and unconscionability—provides a veritable feast of often rather unfocused legal analysis. With the benefit of hindsight, this focus misunderstands the question to which knowledge, dishonesty or unconscionability might be the answer. The crucial question, in modern terminology, is simply whether the defendant is a fiduciary. This focus was always there, but hidden behind the word 'constructive'.

Moreover, the conclusion advanced here produces an outcome where there are strong and sound parallels between the position at common law and the position in equity in relation to property, fraudsters and other wrongdoers. That is not necessarily a good in itself. There may be sound policy reasons for treating common law and equitable rights differently, but where those reasons for difference are not obvious, analogies can be reassuring. This is so with the Limitation Act provisions.

Finally, these conclusions highlight a number of crucial features concerning trust and fiduciary law generally, and accessory liability in particular. The key insight is to notice that equity's unrelenting focus is on property holding and property management. In particular, equity's focus is on the property itself, and not on the parties with interests in the property or with claims in respect of its mismanagement. It is this property focus, rather than a claimant focus, which

[3] Contrast the current convoluted position: see L Tucker, N Le Poidevin and J Brightwell (eds), *Lewin on Trusts* 19th edn (London, Sweet & Maxwell, 2015) paras 44-049–44-078, especially the distinctions between corporate opportunities and bribes at paras 44-071–44-072, and theft at para 44-078.

[4] *Selangor United Rubber Estates Ltd v Cradock (No 3)* [1968] 1 WLR 1555 (Ch).

[5] *Paragon Finance Plc v DB Thakerar & Co (A Firm)* [1998] EWCA Civ 1249, [1999] 1 All ER 400 (CA).

marks a powerful divide between equity and the common law, with some striking consequences.[6]

In making out these claims, this chapter considers, in turn, the Supreme Court analysis and its basis; an alternative and preferred basis for drawing the relevant analytical distinctions; the route to finding that dishonest assistants and knowing recipients are fiduciaries; and finally, the general remedial and particular limitation consequences of this. The chapter includes a brief comparison of the resulting parallels between the equitable and common law limitation rules, and the appropriateness of this, and then sums up by exposing the crucial and distinctive characteristics of accessory liability in equity.

II. The Supreme Court Analysis in *Williams*

Williams v Central Bank of Nigeria[7]is the first decision at Supreme Court level on the Limitation Act 1980 as it applies to strangers to the trust.[8] The facts were simple. Williams was the victim of a sting operation perpetrated by the Nigerian Security Services. He deposited US$6.5 million with a solicitor in England in order

[6] See S Worthington, 'Revolutionary Breakthroughs in Personal Property Law: Redrawing the Conceptual Map' in S Worthington, A Robertson and G Virgo (eds), *Revolution and Evolution in Private Law* (Oxford, Hart Publishing, forthcoming 2017).

[7] *Williams* (n 1). See also the Singapore CA decision in *Yong Kheng Leong v Panweld Trading Pte Ltd* [2013] 1 SLR 173 [49]–[55], pre-dating *Williams*, but consistent with its conclusions in adopting the *Paragon Finance* distinction between Type I and Type II constructive trusts, and holding that the exclusion of limitation in their equivalent of the Limitation Act 1980 s 21(1) applies only to Type I. Here, a director-shareholder was held to be in that category, and to have behaved fraudulently, so no limitation applied.

[8] The decision has been subjected to extensive academic comment: see PS Davies, 'Limitation in Equity' [2014] *Lloyd's Maritime and Commercial Law Quarterly* 313; J Lee, 'Constructing and Limiting Liability in Equity' (2015) 131 *LQR* 39; Z Bryan, 'Limitation and Fraudulent Breaches of Trust' (2015) 21 *Trusts & Trustees* 405; M Carn, '*Williams v Central Bank of Nigeria*: Constructive Trusts and the Law of Limitation' (2014) 28 *Trust Law International* 3; C Hare, 'Trust Law's Limitations' [2014] *Restitution Law Review* 110; E Talbot Rice and A Holden, 'A Trustee by Any Other Name: Who is a "Trustee" for Limitation Purposes?' (2014) 7 *Journal of International Banking and Finance Law* 438; S Watterson, 'Limitation of Actions, Dishonest Assistance and Knowing Receipt' (2014) 73 *CLJ* 253. Also see J Dietrich and P Ridge, *Accessories in Private Law* (Cambridge, CUP, 2015) 284–86. More generally, see W Swadling, 'Limitation' in P Birks and A Pretto (eds), *Breach of Trust* (Oxford, Hart Publishing, 2002); S Gardner, 'Moment of Truth for Knowing Receipt' (2009) 125 *LQR* 20; R Walker, 'Dishonesty and Unconscionable Conduct in Commercial Life—Some Reflections on Accessory Liability and Knowing Receipt' (2005) 27 *Sydney Law Review* 187; C Mitchell, 'Dishonest Assistance, Knowing Receipt, and the Law of Limitation' [2008] *Conveyancer and Property Lawyer* 226, 229; D Sheehan, 'Disentangling Equitable Personal Liability for Receipt and Assistance' (2008) 16 *Restitution Law Review* 41; C Mitchell and S Watterson, 'Remedies for Knowing Receipt' in C Mitchell (ed), *Constructive and Resulting Trusts* (Oxford, Hart Publishing, 2010); J Palmer, 'Attempting Clarification of Constructive Trusts' (2010) 24 *New Zealand Universities Law Review* 113; L Smith, 'Fiduciary Relationships: Ensuring the Loyal Exercise of Judgement on Behalf of Another' (2014) 130 *LQR* 608; W Swadling, 'The Fiction of the Constructive Trust' (2011) 64 *Current Legal Problems* 399; D Whayman, 'Remodelling Knowing Receipt as a Gains-Based Wrong' (2016) *Journal of Business Law* 565.

to guarantee what turned out to be a bogus loan. The solicitor/trustee paid away US$6 million to the defendant's bank account in England, and kept US$500,000 for himself. More than 20 years later Williams launched proceedings, claiming in knowing receipt and dishonest assistance against the bank. The preliminary issue was whether his action was time barred. By majority the Supreme Court held it was.

Although the focus here is on the general issue of third-party liability in equity, the limitation context is salutary. It demands robust characterisation of claims.[9] Section 21(3) of the Limitation Act 1980 prescribes a six-year limitation period for any 'action by a beneficiary to recover trust property or in respect of any breach of trust' not otherwise covered by the Act. But a significant exception appears in section 21(1):

> No period of limitation prescribed by this Act shall apply to an action by a beneficiary under a trust, being an action—
>
> (a) in respect of any fraud or fraudulent breach of trust to which the trustee was a party or privy; or
>
> (b) to recover from the trustee trust property or the proceeds of trust property in the possession of the trustee, or previously received by the trustee and converted to his use.

On its face, this provision applies only to trusts and trustees. However, the Limitation Act provides, in section 38(1), that 'trust' and 'trustee' have the same meaning as in the Trustee Act 1925, which itself provides, in section 68:

> (1) In this Act, unless the context otherwise requires …
>
> (17) … the expressions 'trust' and 'trustee' extend to implied and constructive trusts, and to cases where the trustee has a beneficial interest in the trust property, and to the duties incident to the office of a personal representative.

From those seemingly slim pickings, and despite the express words in the Trustee Act 1925, the Supreme Court held that 'constructive trustees' who acquired that label by being knowing recipients or dishonest assistants were not themselves 'trustees' within the Limitation Act section 21(1), and neither were they defendants being sued 'in respect of any fraud or fraudulent breach of trust to which the [true] trustee was a party or privy'.[10] Accordingly, the Limitation Act 1980 section 21(1) did not disapply the six-year statutory limitation period. In short, the Central Bank of Nigeria could not be sued. Lord Mance delivered a robust dissent.

[9] The same is often said of the insolvency context, which demands accurate characterisation of proprietary and personal claims.

[10] On the first issue, the 4:1 majority was led by Lord Sumption and Lord Neuberger, each giving separate judgments, Lord Hughes signing up with the latter and Lord Clarke agreeing rather reluctantly with both. On the second issue, the Court split 3:2, Lord Mance and Lord Clarke dissenting. That second issue is not important here.

In reaching this conclusion, the distinction seen as critical by the majority was one identified by Millett LJ in *Paragon Finance Plc v DB Thakerar & Co*.[11] In that case, Millett LJ had distinguished between constructive trustees who are true trustees (now labelled Type I) and those simply exposed by their unlawful conduct to trustee-style remedies (Type II). Only the former category, so the majority held, were within the ambit of section 21(1) of the Limitation Act.[12] Millett LJ explained the differences:

> [Type I cases are those] where the defendant, though not expressly appointed as trustee, has assumed the duties of a trustee by a lawful transaction which was independent of and preceded the breach of trust and is not impeached by the plaintiff. The second [Type II] covers those cases where the trust obligation arises as a direct consequence of the unlawful transaction which is impeached by the plaintiff.
>
> … In the first class of case, however, the constructive trustee really is a trustee. He does not receive the trust property in his own right but by a transaction by which both parties intend to create a trust from the outset and which is not impugned by the plaintiff. His possession of the property is coloured from the first by the trust and confidence by means of which he obtained it, and his subsequent appropriation of the property to his own use is a breach of that trust … In these cases the plaintiff does not impugn the transaction by which the defendant obtained control of the property. He alleges that the circumstances in which the defendant obtained control make it unconscionable for him thereafter to assert a beneficial interest in the property.
>
> The second class of case is different. It arises when the defendant is implicated in a fraud. Equity has always given relief against fraud by making any person sufficiently implicated in the fraud accountable in equity. In such a case he is traditionally though I think unfortunately described as a constructive trustee and said to be 'liable to account as constructive trustee'. Such a person is not in fact a trustee at all, even though he may be liable to account as if he were. He never assumes the position of a trustee, and if he receives the trust property at all it is adversely to the plaintiff by an unlawful transaction which is impugned by the plaintiff. In such a case the expressions 'constructive trust' and 'constructive trustee' are misleading, for there is no trust and usually no possibility of a proprietary remedy; they are 'nothing more than a formula for equitable relief'.[13]

One might ask why, if equity saw fit to make all these parties liable precisely as if they were real trustees,[14] it should not also subject them to the same limitation rules.[15] Indeed, commentators had assumed this followed automatically from the

[11] *Paragon Finance* (n 5) 408–09, cited in *Williams* (n 1) [10]. Lord Millett reiterated these views in *Dubai Aluminium Co Ltd v Salaam* [2002] UKHL 48; [2003] 2 AC 366 [141]–[142]. See also Ungoed-Thomas J in *Selangor United Rubber Estates Ltd* (n 3) 1579, cited in *Williams* (n 1) [10].

[12] *Williams* (n 1) [4], [8]–[9], [12]–[13], [26]–[31], [49]–[57], [64]–[68], [90], [114], [165]. Perhaps rather inconsistently, these people were nevertheless sufficiently within the definition of 'trustee' to enable them to be given the protection of the six-year limitation period in the Limitation Act s 21(3).

[13] *Paragon Finance* (n 5) 408–09.

[14] The detail emerges in the discussion which follows.

[15] *Paragon Finance* (n 5) 414, a suggestion rejected by Lord Neuberger in *Williams* (n 1) [65].

revisions enacted in the Limitation Act 1939 which had adopted a wider definition of trusts and trustees, now repeated in the Limitation Act 1980.[16]

In rejecting this conclusion, the Supreme Court paid a great deal of attention to the findings of older cases and the development of the law on limitation in equity. The gulf between the majority and the minority in interpreting these materials is notable. In large measure it reflects quite different approaches to the relevant history. Originally, before any statutory intervention, it was only express trustees who were subjected to claims without limitation. The rules on limitation in equity have now changed dramatically, moving from no statutory prescription at all to rather detailed statutory coverage, and from no limitation for express trustees to six-year limitation periods for a broader class of defendants but subject to exceptions. In addition, the language of trusts (express or otherwise) and fiduciaries and all their various remedial consequences has tightened up significantly,[17] and the jurisdiction itself has expanded enormously.[18] In this new environment, it is impossible to find hard answers to current technical questions simply from the words used by judges in earlier times. It is essential that decisions are grounded in policy and principle.

The Supreme Court adopted the distinctions identified by Millett LJ in *Paragon Finance*. These may be exactly the right distinctions, but the judgments contain more by way of assertion than justification in explaining why this might be so, and in particular why a statute specifically worded to apply to 'constructive trusts' and 'constructive trustees' should apply only to a select subset of such trusts and trustees. If the Supreme Court's analysis is to be applied confidently in the future, its underpinnings need to be clearly understood.

III. Distinguishing between Types of Constructive Trustee

In identifying the types of 'trustee' exposed to liability without limitation, the Supreme Court drew distinctions between (i) those who had lawfully assumed fiduciary obligations from the outset (even without formal appointment) and those whose possession or interference was from the start wrongful and adverse to the rights of the beneficiaries; (ii) those who intended to act as trustees and those who did not; (iii) those in whom the beneficiaries reposed trust and confidence and those in whom no one ever placed trust and confidence; and finally

[16] Lord Mance provides some detail in *Williams* (n 1) [140]–[142], [144]–[145], [148].

[17] As is well illustrated by the wide-ranging categories of 'fiduciaries' analysed in PD Finn, *Fiduciary Obligations* (Sydney, Law Book Company, 1977). See also the discussion in S Worthington, 'Fiduciaries: Following Finn' in T Bonyhady (ed), *Finn's Law: An Australian Justice* (Sydney, Federation Press, 2016).

[18] Consider common intention constructive trusts, Quistclose trusts and proprietary estoppel claims.

(iv) those involved in an existing/institutional trust and those subject merely to a remedial formula.[19] Describing the distinctions in this way highlights a number of incongruities.

Take the first two differences: these seem to suggest limitation rules will punish trustees who begin life innocently but turn bad, while relieving those who are bad from the outset. On its own terms, this looks odd. Defendants who take it upon themselves to act as de facto trustees, acting properly at the outset, will be Type I constructive trustees and subject to the disadvantages in section 21(1); by contrast, defendants who behave dishonestly from the outset in assisting or interfering in the management of the trust assets and their distribution will escape, being subject merely to a six-year limitation period on the authority of *Williams*.[20] Moreover, clean and clear factual distinctions between the two classes may be impossible to determine. In short, enormously significant legal distinctions seem difficult to justify in principle or to draw in practice.

Alternatively, take the line between an institutional trust and a remedial formula. In England, all trusts are institutional.[21] Knowing recipients must therefore be individuals who once held assets on an institutional (albeit constructive) trust, and are now sued because they no longer have either the assets or their proceeds. By contrast, company directors do not hold property on trust, but are liable by analogy with express trustees; they are thus subject to what emerged, historically, as a 'remedial formula'. However, we know from *Williams* that the appropriate limitation categorisation falls precisely the opposite way: the section 21(1) limitation provisions apply to directors but not to knowing recipients. We return to this later,[22] but note for now that a classification based on contrasting an institutional trust with a 'remedial formula' may be difficult.

The difficulties go well beyond this. Take the line between lawful and adverse possession of property. If an express trustee absconds with trust assets, or takes an opportunity which ought to have been pursued for the trust, or takes a bribe, are these gains held on Type I or Type II constructive trusts? The difference matters. The analysis in *FHR European Ventures LLP & Ors v Cedar Capital Partners LLC* might suggest that all disloyal gains are held on the original trusts, and thus the Limitation Act section 21(1)(b) applies.[23] But it might equally be argued, particularly in relation to the opportunity and the bribe, that the beneficiary's interest in these assets is not 'independent of and preced[ing] the breach of trust

[19] *Williams* (n 1) [9]–[11], [31], [64], [165]. Lord Clarke seemed to think (iii) was decisive, whereas that might be thought of least significance. See the similar list advanced by P Smith and R Davern, 'I Want My (Equitable) Property Back: Time Limits on Recovering Trust Property from Innocent Volunteers' (2015) 21 *Trusts & Trustees* 1096, 1097–08.

[20] Although note that Millett LJ places *Pallant v Morgan* [1953] Ch 43 firmly in the Type I category: *Paragon Finance* (n 5) 409.

[21] *Westdeutsche Landesbank Girozentrale v Islington LBC* [1996] AC 669 (HL); *FHR European Ventures LLP & Ors v Cedar Capital Partners LLC* [2014] UKSC 45 (SC).

[22] See below, VI. 'Dishonest Assistants Are Fiduciaries'.

[23] *FHR* (n 21).

[but instead arises] as a direct consequence of the unlawful transaction'.[24] The complications multiply if the defendant is not a trustee but a company director. The problem is not academic.[25] This too is considered later, and a more direct approach suggested.[26]

IV. Language and Logic

We cannot think about legal concepts clearly unless we use language that is clear. The immediate trap is how we understand 'constructive'.

In equity, we typically use the expression 'constructive' to mean 'is not X, but because of the surrounding circumstances will be treated as if it were X'. On this basis we might unthinkingly say that a constructive trusts 'are not trusts, but because of the surrounding circumstances will be treated as if they were trusts'. This is flawed. Equity's historical starting point was the express trust. Accordingly, it would be more accurate to say that constructive trusts 'are not express trusts, but because of the surrounding circumstances will be treated as if they were express trusts'. Similarly, constructive trustees 'are not express trustees, but because of the surrounding circumstances will be treated as if they were express trustees'. This makes it plain that constructive trusts must indeed be trusts (ie, property splits), but by contrast constructive trustees need not be trustees at all (ie, they need not hold property on trust, although of course they may);[27] they are simply people owing trustee-like personal obligations in relation to the management of another's property. If this is the analogy, then they are, in short, fiduciaries, made so by virtue of the personal obligations to which they are subject.[28]

There is a further twist to this. Notice that not all trustees are fiduciaries. An ignorant donee who receives trust property holds that property on 'constructive trust', but owes no fiduciary or other personal obligations in respect of it. Notice too that not all fiduciaries hold assets on trust. A company director is a familiar example. We thus need words which separate the property-holding structure (here, trusts and trustees)[29] from the people subject to equity's distinctive

[24] *Paragon Finance* (n 5) 408.

[25] See above, n 3.

[26] See below, IX. 'Limitation and Fiduciary Disgorgement'.

[27] Hence de facto trustees and company directors can be 'constructive trustees', whether or not they hold legal title to the managed assets on trust.

[28] This terminology is only possible now that we use the term 'fiduciary' in a very much narrower sense than we once did: see above, n 17.

[29] And under that umbrella term, the trusts may be express, constructive, resulting, implied, or any other descriptive terminology thought appropriate to characterise the property split. 'Trust/trustee' is used here to indicate the property split only, and not to indicate any associated personal obligations, notwithstanding the analysis in *Westdeutsche Landesbank Girozentrale* (n 21) 705, and its controversial insistence that a trust only exists if there is both a property split and knowledge, with the latter justifying the imposition of the personal obligations essential to a trust.

property-management obligations (fiduciaries). Precise terminology is important, so note that this 'fiduciary' label is applied to the person, and is applied even though most of the property-management obligations owed are not fiduciary; but it is the fiduciary addition to the mix which makes the role distinctive and warrants labelling the person a 'fiduciary'. This labelling would avoid the current confusing use of 'constructive trustee' to refer to two types of people: those holding property on trust (whether or not there are associated fiduciary obligations); and those owing fiduciary obligations (whether or not there are associated trusts). Such breadth makes the 'constructive trustee' category analytically useless. By contrast, 'constructive trust' does not mislead in the same way; there is indeed a trust and a trustee (although the trustee may not be a fiduciary).

Digging further into the fundamentals, a 'trust' describes a property split between legal owner and beneficial owner.[30] The term itself does not identify how that split arose or the particular details of the arrangement. The broad distinction is between express trusts and trusts arising by operation of law. Express trustees are subject to duties of strict compliance with the terms of the trust (and a duty to discover what those are),[31] and corresponding duties of care and skill in managing the assets, and fiduciary duties. This is a unique package, made distinctive by equity's addition of fiduciary constraints to the more familiar package of compliance and care elements.[32]

Similarly, although this might seem a bold assertion, constructive trustees and resulting trustees are also subject to duties of strict compliance with the terms of the property split *as they know them*, and then to corresponding duties of care and skill, and fiduciary duties.[33] The qualifier is important. Individuals holding assets on constructive trust may be completely unaware of that fact (as with innocent donees), or they may know only that the assets do not belong beneficially to the constructive trustees themselves, or they may be fully aware of all the detail of an original express trust. Their duties of care and their fiduciary duties follow directly from their particular knowledge of the underlying property split. At one extreme, this means that a constructive trustee will owe no personal duties at all, whether of compliance, care, or fiduciary obligation, if the trustee is entirely ignorant of

[30] Sub-trusts follow analogous rules, although the detail is not noted in this chapter.

[31] With non-compliance here embracing both *excesses* of power and *abuses* of power, although the distinction between the two is important in assessing the respective remedies for breach.

[32] These 'fiduciary' constraints require self-denial, ie, putting the beneficiaries' interests ahead of the fiduciary's own, with disgorgement of gains as the remedy whenever this obligation is breached by the fiduciary entering into transactions where there is a conflict between duty and interest. This fiduciary duty is quite distinct from the duty to act in good faith in the beneficiaries' interests by exercising powers for proper purposes, which is a further duty owed by fiduciaries, but also by those who are not fiduciaries: see the development of the language of 'fiduciary' over time as detailed in Worthington, 'Fiduciaries: Following Finn' (n 17). Note too that the compliance and care elements are also distinctive in the context of property management, just more subtly so: see below, XI. 'Exposing Third-Party Liability in Equity'.

[33] See the detailed analysis in S Worthington, *Equity*, 2nd edn (Oxford, OUP, 2006) ch 6. More recently, see Mitchell and Watterson (n 8); R Chambers, 'The End of Knowing Receipt' (2016) 2 *Canadian Journal of Comparative and Contemporary Law* 1.

the property split. But otherwise, constructive trustees are liable for their own misapplication or mishandling of the trust property, and for disgorgement of personal gains derived from misuse of the trust property, with the extent of liability depending on the constructive trustee's knowledge of the particular terms of the original trust. If the constructive trustee has full knowledge of the investment or other management requirements of the trust, as is often the case with de facto trustees, then liability will follow accordingly, and will track the liability of the corresponding express trustees. The same is true where there is no property split, but the principal's assets are simply managed by fiduciaries without being held on trust: for example, the liability of de facto and de jure directors corresponds with the liability as discussed for de facto and express trustees. None of this is controversial, even if it has not been stated in quite this way before. Recall the familiar proprietary and personal consequences visited on de facto trustees, *Quistclose* trustees, knowing recipients and parties holding property on either vendor–purchaser constructive trusts or common intention constructive trusts.[34]

Exactly when these property-holding and property-management consequences arise is a further question, not addressed here.[35] Two points are noteworthy, however. Recall that in equity one party is considered to hold assets on trust for another whenever the circumstances are such that it would be unconscionable for the legal owner not to recognise the beneficial interest of the other.[36] Notice that the test does not require the legal owner to have knowledge of the beneficiary's proprietary interest in the underlying assets: a property split may arise by operation of law in any event.[37] By contrast, property-management obligations are only imposed when that knowledge is present, whatever other factors might also be deemed essential.[38] And once those property-management obligations are imposed, then the manager is subject to all the claims noted in the previous paragraph: ie, loss-based claims for failure to comply, or failure to comply with due care, with the known terms of the property split; and disgorgement remedies for personal gains made from self-serving management.[39]

If these proprietary and obligational concepts are not kept distinct, significant difficulties can arise. For example, if *every* trustee must necessarily owe duties of compliance, care and fiduciary obligations, then we will be moved irresistibly to

[34] Every textbook on trusts confirms this. Some of the detail appears in Worthington, *Equity* (n 33); and S Worthington, *Proprietary Interests in Commercial Transactions* (Oxford, OUP, 1996).

[35] All the main works on equity and trusts and a good number of specialist works cover the detail of trusts arising by operation of law and the incidence of fiduciary obligations.

[36] This means the line between express and other trusts can be seen as relatively thin: see S Gardner, 'Reliance-Based Constructive Trusts'; and B McFarlane, 'The Centrality of Constructive and Resulting Trusts' in C Mitchell (ed), *Constructive and Resulting Trusts* (Oxford, Hart Publishing, 2010). On the other hand, recall the endless debates in the lead-up to the decision in *FHR* (n 21).

[37] eg innocent donees of trust property, or legal owners subject to proprietary estoppel, vendor–purchaser or common intention constructive trust claims.

[38] *Westdeutsche Landesbank Girozentrale* (n 21) 705.

[39] Recall the endless debates on notice, knowledge, dishonesty and unconscionability in the context of knowing recipients and dishonest assistants, and then the loss and disgorgement remedies which follow.

concluding that there is no trust at all whenever the context will not support duties of compliance, care and fiduciary obligation. *Westdeutsche Landesbank Girozentrale v Islington LBC* itself,[40] and its comments on *Chase Manhattan*,[41] provide a well-known example; so too did *Lister v Stubbs*.[42] But we do not make the same mistake with innocent donees receiving unauthorised distributions of trust property.

The same is true of fiduciary obligations. It can be too easy to fall into the trap of asserting without pause for thought that because certain individuals are not trustees, they therefore do not owe fiduciary obligations. We typically do this with dishonest assisters, as was done in *Williams* itself. We do not make the same mistake with company directors or partners.

Finally, we can be seduced by language, and insist that certain parties cannot be fiduciaries because they have never undertaken to act in a loyal manner, or because nobody ever reposed trust in them: see *Williams* again.[43] But this is not, and has never been, the test of when fiduciary obligations arise.[44] Take express trustees: these individuals may indeed have accepted or undertaken to act in a loyal manner, and they may be trusted by their beneficiaries, but both points are irrelevant; fiduciary obligations will be imposed in any event. The same is true of fiduciaries outside status-based fiduciary relationships, as in joint venture relationships.[45] And it is equally true—if remedies are anything to go by—of any individuals who take it upon themselves to assume the care or management of property known to belong to others. In short, personal undertakings and reposed trust are immaterial. Instead, the law insists, by its remedial force, that anyone involved in the holding or management of property known to belong to others is obliged to respect that interest. This is considered in more detail below.[46]

V. Applying this Language to Limitation

All of this categorisation is material to limitation, and prompts a return to the list of distinguishing characteristics of constructive trustees favoured in *Williams*.[47] The very early non-statutory limitation rules differentiated between express

[40] *Westdeutsche Landesbank Girozentrale* (n 21).

[41] *Chase Manhattan Bank NA v Israel–British Bank (London) Ltd* [1981] Ch 105 (Ch).

[42] *Lister & Co v Stubbs* (1890) LR 45 Ch D 1 (CA). Although now see *FHR* (n 21).

[43] *Williams* (n 1) [31], [64], [165].

[44] See *Hospital Products Ltd v United States Surgical Corporation* [1984] HCA 64, (1984) 156 CLR 41 (HCA) 69 (Gibbs CJ): 'an actual relation of confidence—the fact one person trusted another—is neither necessary nor conclusive of the existence of a fiduciary relationship'.

[45] *Ross River Ltd v Waveley Commercial Ltd* [2013] EWCA Civ 910, [2014] 1 BCLC 545 (CA).

[46] See below, VI. 'Dishonest Assistants Are Fiduciaries' and VII. 'Knowing Recipients Are Both Trustees (on Receipt) and Fiduciaries (on Acquiring Knowledge)'.

[47] See above, III. 'Distinguishing between Types of Constructive Trustee'.

trustees (who could be sued without limitation) and others (who could not). This rule was slowly expanded by analogy. A search for analogies might seek alignment with the consensual nature of the express trust (its 'express' characteristics), or the trust's proprietary characteristics (the 'trust' element), or the trustee's personal characteristics (the 'fiduciary' element). Interestingly, and perhaps surprisingly, the list in *Williams* seems to focus on the first. Yet the language in *Williams* and earlier cases,[48] and the universal acknowledgement of the broader scope of the current statutory rules, suggest it is the last that is crucial. Put another way, some form of property holding or property management for another is crucial, but the managed property need not be held on trust,[49] and the property-holding/management obligations can be imposed by operation of law rather than by agreement.[50] What is crucial, however, is that the defendant is a fiduciary.

This fiduciary language was adopted by Lord Hoffmann NPJ in *Peconic Industrial Development Ltd v Lau Kwok Fai*.[51] It is obviously more informative than the 'constructive trustee' language used in *Williams* and *Paragon Finance*.[52] Nevertheless, Lord Hoffmann did not pursue the distinction from first principles, but simply adopted the classification proposed by Millett LJ in *Paragon Finance*. However, he then described Type I individuals as fiduciaries and Type II as non-fiduciaries. Accordingly, without more, he concluded that knowing recipients and dishonest assisters were not fiduciaries. This is doubted, and is considered in more detail in the next sections.

VI. Dishonest Assistants Are Fiduciaries

The overwhelming view of the courts is that dishonest assistants are neither fiduciaries[53] nor Type I trustees exposed to the risks of liability without time limitation,[54] but are simply accessories to the primary wrongdoers.[55] On closer examination, this may be flawed. There seems to be nothing material dividing dishonest assistants from either fiduciaries or Type I trustees, and the parallels

[48] See below, and note the number of references to fiduciary and fiduciaries in *Williams* (n 1).

[49] Directors confirm this: ibid [9], [28], 152].

[50] eg the illustrations in *Paragon Finance* (n 5) 408–09; *Williams* (n 1) [9]–[13].

[51] *Peconic Industrial Development Ltd v Lau Kwok Fai* [2009] HKCFA 16, (2008–09) 11 ITELR 844 [19].

[52] Although notice the explanation given by Lord Mance in *Williams* (n 1) [120]: the majority position in *Williams* is that 'the exception to the right to limit would be confined to trustees or those owing fiduciary duties'.

[53] *Novoship (UK) Ltd v Mikhaylyuk* [2014] EWCA Civ 908 (CA) [68]; *Williams* (n 1), by inference; *Paragon Finance* (n 5). See also *Peconic* (n 51).

[54] *Williams* (n 1).

[55] ibid [65], [99], [124], [127], [154], [180]. This is also the tenor of all the modern authorities and commentary on dishonest assistance.

between them are powerful. Moreover, although the courts say that dishonest assistants are accessories, not primary wrongdoers, and in particular not fiduciaries, what they do by way of analysing liability and delivering remedies suggests otherwise.

Start with the fiduciary parallels. Individuals who are fiduciaries are subjected to fiduciary duties of loyalty in the management of property for the benefit of their principals. And, in reverse, if individuals are subjected by the courts to fiduciary duties of loyalty, then they are fiduciaries.[56] The distinguishing characteristic of fiduciaries is the legal insistence on self-denial, and the corresponding disgorgement remedy for breach.[57] Disgorgement in other contexts is remarkably rare, and then demands careful justification.[58] So when dishonest assistants are compelled to disgorge the personal gains derived from non-compliance with particular property-management duties,[59] as they are,[60] then classification of these people as fiduciaries seems irresistible, notwithstanding the courts' explicit denial of that conclusion.

This notion that a dishonest assistant is a fiduciary is further reinforced by a comparison with Type I constructive trustees. Recall that these Type I individuals may not be trustees at all (as illustrated by company directors), but they are invariably fiduciaries. Consider first the roles of de facto trustees and de facto directors. These are people who involve themselves in the management of trust or corporate property, often without holding title to it. They are treated as if they were indeed what they purport to be: ie, express trustees or de jure directors (Type I).[61] The remedies available against them, and the limitation rules protecting them, are as for express trustees. These remedies are of course only available once the de facto misbehaves. Sometimes that can happen early in their management endeavours, sometimes later; the timing is immaterial.

Notice that precisely the same might be said of dishonest assistants. These individuals are also people who involve themselves in the management of trust or other property. They do so with other trustees or fiduciaries, as do most de facto trustees and directors. In addition, and barring the limitation rules, misbehaving

[56] See the pointed articulation of this in Finn (n 17) 2.

[57] S Worthington, 'Fiduciaries: When is Self-Denial Obligatory?' [1999] *CLJ* 500.

[58] For such an exception, see *Attorney-General v Blake* [2001] 1 AC 268 (HL); and *Esso Petroleum Co Ltd v Niad Ltd* [2001] EWHC 458 (Ch), one of very few cases applying it. Other jurisdictions have declined to follow the UK authorities: see P Devonshire, 'Account of Profits for Secondary Liability: How Far is Too Far?' (2015) 23 *Restitution Law Review* 59, 67. Note that common law cases awarding compensation measured by 'use value' or 'release value' are making awards measured on a different basis from disgorgement of personal gains: see *Wrotham Park Estate Co Ltd v Parkside Homes Ltd* [1974] 1 WLR 798.

[59] True, these duties are typically identified as the duties owed by the primary wrongdoer, but see the discussion which follows, suggesting the pre-requisite of 'dishonesty'—knowing contravention of these duties—is proxy for imposing the same duties on the assister.

[60] *Novoship* (n 53) [82]; see also [71], citing a large number of first instance decisions in support of the conclusion affirmed in this case that a dishonest assistant must account for its own profits. See too *Westdeutsche Landesbank Girozentrale* (n 21) 705.

[61] *Williams* (n 1) [9]–[11].

assistants are treated in exactly the same way as express trustees when determining the appropriate remedies. Again, these remedies are only available once the assistant misbehaves, and this may be early or late in the relationship. Although the Supreme Court in *Williams* appeared to assume that the assistant's behaviour was from the outset adverse to the beneficiary, this is often untrue. Banks and solicitors are common targets for such claims, yet in most cases their behaviour in dealing with the managed assets will be perfectly proper at the outset, only deviating at some later stage. In this regard too, the parallels with express and de facto trustees are obvious, despite the assertions to the contrary in *Paragon Finance* and the cases following it.[62] Moreover, the 'dishonesty' element with assistants is not a distinguishing characteristic of the type of wrongful activity, but of the actor's mental state. Its purpose is to confirm that the assistants are sufficiently aware that the managed property is not at their free disposal, but is held for other parties, and that their interference with it is contrary to that arrangement.[63] This makes sense as a prerequisite, just as it makes sense to have rules to ensure that express trustees know which property they hold on trust, and on what terms. In short, in the continuum of express trustees, de facto trustees and dishonest assistants, the last two seem to have key characteristics which are indistinguishable.[64]

Then there is the notion of accessory liability. The majority in *Williams* regarded the fact that liability was accessory (or ancillary) rather than primary as particularly persuasive in classifying dishonest assistants as Type II trustees. Accessory liability provides the prevailing explanation of the liability of dishonest assistants,[65] yet in equity the line between primary and accessory liability is particularly difficult to draw. For example, in establishing 'accessory' liability, the court's focus is exclusively on the accessory's awareness that the contemplated activities are inconsistent with the terms on which particular underlying assets should be managed for the principal;[66] there is no focus on the relative degree of the accessory's

[62] See the paragraph cited above at n 13, and the distinctions exposed above at III, 'Distinguishing between Types of Constructive Trustee'.

[63] See *Barlow Clowes International Ltd v Eurotrust International Ltd* [2005] UK PC 37, [2006] 1 WLR 1476 (PC) [28], where Lord Hoffmann held that the approach in *Brinks Ltd v Abu-Saleh (No 3)* [1996] CLC 133 was wrong: the point was not whether the defendant knew of the trust, but whether she knew or suspected that she was assisting in a misappropriation of someone's property.

[64] In *Williams*, Lord Mance similarly considered that dishonest assistants and Type I constructive trustees should be assimilated for the purpose of both liability and limitation. He did not comment on whether this assimilation would inevitably constitute them fiduciaries, and—contrary to the approach advocated here—he viewed them as accessories, but regarded that as an added reason for assimilation: *Williams* (n 1) [123]–[126], citing a number of older cases in support, and noting that of course the scope of the personal obligations in issue may be much more extensive in relation to somebody appointed as an express trustee.

[65] SB Elliott and C Mitchell, 'Remedies for Dishonest Assistance' (2004) 67 *MLR* 16; P Ridge, 'Participatory Liability for Breach of Trust or Fiduciary Duty' in J Glister and P Ridge (eds), *Fault Lines in Equity* (Oxford, Hart Publishing, 2012); PS Davies, *Accessory Liability* (Oxford, Hart Publishing, 2015); Dietrich and Ridge (n 8); Chambers, 'The End of Knowing Receipt' (n 33) 26–27. See also Devonshire (n 58) 67, who thus disagrees with any move to make dishonest assisters disgorge their own gains, since this is inappropriate for accessories. By contrast, see Whayman (n 8).

[66] See above, n 59.

involvement in the primary wrong such as to make the accessory equally responsible for that primary wrong. This suggests a focus on establishing the dishonest assistant's *own* duties, being duties as a fiduciary managing the principal's property, rather than potential liability for involvement in a separate and independent primary wrong committed by someone else. This initial intuition is further confirmed by the remedies then awarded. As noted earlier, these are unequivocally remedies which can only be generated by breach of the dishonest assistant's own obligations, and fiduciary obligations at that, requiring compensation for loss to the managed property fund and disgorgement of disloyal gains acquired personally by the dishonest assistant.[67]

On reflection—in my case a good deal of reflection—this says something very important about accessory liability. With contract, tort and crime, accessory liability focuses on a mental element and a conduct element, considering the details of the relationship between the accessory and the primary wrongdoer to establish whether the accessory, although not a principal wrongdoer, should nevertheless be made liable, and liable for the primary wrong not for some independently committed personal wrong. In equity, however, the relationship under the microscope is not that between the accessory and the primary wrongdoer; it is the relationship between the accessory and the managed property. This replicates the analysis applied directly to express trustees. The tag 'constructive' marks out those parties considered to have either property-holding or property-management obligations resulting from their analogous relationships with the managed property. These people do not have a liability which is accessory to, or ancillary to, the primary wrongdoer; they have a liability which is directly referable to the principal's property, and they are themselves therefore also primary wrongdoers, just as co-trustees or co-directors are. Thus, in a rather surprising way, equity's focus on property means that it determines the liability of strangers to an express trust, or strangers to the property-management relationship, very directly: it asks whether these people, too, are trustees or fiduciaries or both. It does not go through an additional loop, first asking the unnecessary question about whether they are accessories. This direct route to liability was the focus of the language of constructive trusts, discussed earlier, a language used long before accessory and ancillary liability became fashionable.

If further evidence were needed, consider the analysis applied to the liability of parties who induce or procure a trustee to commit a breach of trust. English law

[67] But see *Novoship* (n 53) [107]. Here it was suggested that since dishonest assistants are not fiduciaries, disgorgement gains (and query compensation claims) should be subjected to the common forms of causation, remoteness and quantification of damages. *Fyffes Group Ltd v Templeman* [2000] 2 Lloyd's Rep 643 (QB Comm) adopts the same causation test. Although there is no complaint with the outcome, the suggestion seems misconceived. Disgorgement claims face difficulty in identifying precisely the quantum of the defendant's profit made *as a result of the breach of duty* (on the argument here, necessarily breach of fiduciary duty). The goal is no different for express trustees, and it is the facts not the principle which typically create difficulty. The careful approach in the Australian case of *Warman International Ltd v Dwyer* (1995) 182 CLR 544 (HCA) provides a useful illustration.

often lumps these people together with dishonest assisters. However, that ignores one subtlety. Although these people will be liable in the same measure as dishonest assisters, it cannot be on the basis of dishonest assistance, since no question of honesty is ever asked, nor on the basis of accessory liability, since the 'primary' or instigating wrong is the inducer's, not the trustee's or fiduciary's.[68] With these people, too, the appropriate analogy would seem to be with Type I de facto trustees, who do owe fiduciary obligations. Reinforcing this by reverting to the limitation context, in policy terms it would seem odd to protect such people fully, applying the six-year limitation rule without exception, but not similarly protect de facto trustees.

In summary, the position with dishonest assisters in establishing breach and in quantifying liability follows the model for fiduciary liability, not the model for accessory liability; and on the facts it is frequently impossible to draw a clear line between breaches by dishonest assistants and breaches by de facto or even express trustees. That renders the *Paragon Finance* and *Williams* Type II classification of dishonest assistants for limitation purposes as suspect.[69] Instead, the analogies suggest the dishonest assister is a fiduciary, and is made liable in a direct manner, not an accessory manner, for any breaches.

VII. Knowing Recipients Are Both Trustees (on Receipt) and Fiduciaries (on Acquiring Knowledge)

Next consider knowing recipients. In *Williams*, as in many cases before it, dishonest assistants and knowing recipients are bundled together,[70] both regarded as instances of ancillary liability, and both therefore meriting equal treatment under the limitation rules.[71] Neither are regarded as fiduciaries.[72] By contrast, and following what was said about dishonest assistants in the previous section, an analogous treatment here would identify knowing recipients as trustees on receipt of the property (not being bona fide purchasers for value) and as fiduciaries on

[68] Even in jurisdictions such as Australia which still require a dishonest and fraudulent design on the part of the trustee as a prerequisite for liability of the dishonest assistant: *Farah Constructions Pty Ltd v Say-Dee Pty Ltd* (2007) 230 CLR 89 (HCA)[164]. See also *Novoship* (n 53) [161]. See generally C Harpum, 'The Stranger as Constructive Trustee: Part 1' (1986) 102 *LQR* 114, 144; M Leeming, 'The Comparative Distinctiveness of Equity' (2016) 2 *Canadian Journal of Comparative and Contemporary Law* 403, 412–13.

[69] Indeed, the usefulness of the Type I/Type II classification in any event is doubted. See below, XI. 'Exposing Third-Party Liability in Equity'.

[70] Contrast the commentators, who increasingly separate the two classes, regarding only assistants as accessories: see generally Davies, *Accessory Liability* (n 65); and Dietrich and Ridge (n 8). By contrast, the approach here is to regard both classes as primarily liable for their own wrongs, and neither as accessories: see above, VI. 'Dishonest Assistants Are Fiduciaries'.

[71] See *Williams* (n 1) [36].

[72] See above, n 53.

acquiring knowledge that any property still in their hands belonged beneficially to another. At that stage, the knowing recipient with both property and the relevant knowledge would be both a trustee and a fiduciary. Liability for mismanagement of the trust assets would follow accordingly, including limitation rules. Put another way, and using the language of *Paragon Finance* and *Williams*, knowing recipients would seem to be 'real trustees',[73] of Type I.

Williams was to the contrary, but that conclusion was not closely argued. It appears premised on the assumed identical classification of recipients and assistants, and ignored the detail of the classification advanced by Millett LJ in *Paragon Finance* and adopted by the Court in *Williams*. In particular, all the relevant distinguishing features of Type I trustees were simply assumed to run against the knowing recipient.

But the facts are often not amenable to such assumptions. The knowing recipient, typically a solicitor or a bank, will not usually take the trust assets adversely to the beneficiary from the outset, but will instead take them under an agreed mandate; the assets will be held on an institutional trust (whether express or constructive); and the recipient will have a formal often trusted management role. On these facts it is difficult to see what divides a knowing recipient from a de facto trustee, or sometimes an express trustee. The remedial consequences should therefore be the same, including the limitation consequences.

Of course, the facts may not be so kind. But whatever the factual scenario, knowing receipt inevitably requires a recipient to be holding trust property with knowledge that it is beneficially owned by others, and then subsequently to dispose of those assets in defiance of the beneficiary's interest. A person holding assets known to belong beneficially to others is, by definition, not just a trustee holding assets subject to a property split, but also a fiduciary[74]—or, as the majority in *Williams* would put it, a 'real trustee'.[75] When, in breach of that trust, the assets are disposed of and eventually a claim is made, it is impossible to see what classificatory steps justify a Type II conclusion rather than a Type I conclusion.

Moreover, and bar the limitation context, *all* the remedies available against knowing recipients conform to the model that these are individuals who hold assets on trust and then dispose of those assets in breach of their obligations as fiduciaries under that trust. The relevant responsibility is a responsibility not to deal with the assets inconsistently with the trust, with the recipient's knowledge of

[73] Adopting the form of language used generally in *Paragon Finance* (n 5) and *Williams* (n 1).

[74] See above, IV. 'Language and Logic'. Note that 'property' and 'knowledge' may not be acquired at the same time: the trust arises on receipt; but the fiduciary obligations owed in relation to it (or in relation to whatever remains of it in the recipient's hands) are imposed only when the relevant knowledge is acquired.

[75] Also see *Westdeutsche Landesbank Girozentrale* (n 21) 705. See also Chambers, 'The End of Knowing Receipt' (n 33) 10; Gardner, 'Moment of Truth for Knowing Receipt?' (n 8) 24; Finn (n 17) [205], citing *Reid-Newfoundland Co v Anglo-American Telegraph Co* [1912] AC 555, 559; P Jaffey, *Private Law and Property Claims* (Oxford, Hart Publishing, 2007) 190–91.

the particular third party's interests making that failure culpable.[76] These recipients are accordingly liable to make compensation for losses to the trust property, and to disgorge any personal gains derived from self-interested management.[77]

All of this accords with institutional trusts (constructive or otherwise), orthodox fiduciary obligations, and Type I trustee categorisation. In short, the knowing recipient on any of these measures is both a trustee and a fiduciary who, by the time the knowing receipt claim is advanced, has disposed of some or all of the assets in a knowingly unauthorised manner so that the only claim available is personal liability for equitable compensation, plus disgorgement of profits where that might be relevant.

This assertion that a knowing recipient is indeed a fiduciary holding assets on trust—ie, is a 'real trustee'—is not new. I made it in extended form over a decade ago, and will not repeat the arguments here.[78] The same claim has been advanced by others.[79] The arguments seem compelling, yet the cases remain to the contrary. They do not explain their contrary position, and convincing explanation seems well-nigh impossible.

One further comment might be made. The law on knowing recipients focuses on their personal liability, not on proprietary claims, but by definition these recipients must at some stage have received property on trust. At the time of receipt, when the claim may be purely proprietary, the issue might be seen simply as one of priorities.[80] In such a priority competition, a recipient who is not a bona fide purchaser for value without notice will take subject to the beneficiary's interests. The trust which arises will be constructive.[81] It has been suggested that in these circumstances, where the relief is proprietary, there is no difference between the limitation rules for express and constructive trusts,[82] since the difference explained by Millett LJ in *Paragon Finance* refers only to situations where the remedy is non-proprietary and the term 'constructive trustee' is then 'nothing more than a formula for equitable relief'. This is messy. It involves classifying recipient

[76] Worthington, *Equity* (n 33) 185–86; see also P Jaffey, *The Nature and Scope of Restitution* (Oxford, Hart Publishing, 2000) 329; *Re Montagu's Settlement Trusts* [1992] 4 All ER 308, 320.

[77] *Novoship* (n 53) [82]. See also Lord Sumption in *Williams* (n 1) [31]. On disgorgement, see in particular *Ultraframe (UK) Ltd v Fielding* [2005] EWHC 1638 (Ch) [1577]; *Sinclair Investments (UK) Ltd v Versailles Trade Finance Ltd (In Administration)* [2007] EWHC 915 (Ch) [125]; Walker (n 8) 202; Mitchell and Watterson (n 8) 142.

[78] Worthington, *Equity* (n 33) ch 6 (and in the same terms in the first edition in 2003).

[79] Chambers, 'The End of Knowing Receipt' (n 33); Gardner, 'Moment of Truth for Knowing Receipt?' (n 8); Mitchell and Watterson (n 8). See also M Bryan, 'Recipient Liability under the Torrens System: Some Category Errors' in C Rickett and R Grantham (eds), *Structure and Justification in Private Law: Essays for Peter Birks* (Oxford, Hart Publishing, 2008) 340, 342–44.

[80] *Agip (Africa) Ltd v Jackson* [1990] Ch 265, 292.

[81] P Matthews, 'The Words Which Are Not There: A Partial History of the Constructive Trust' in C Mitchell (ed), *Constructive and Resulting Trusts* (Oxford, Hart Publishing, 2010) 5, commenting on Lord Browne-Wilkinson in *Westdeutsche*, citing PJ Millett, 'Restitution and Constructive Trusts' (1998) 114 *LQR* 399, 403–04 and W Swadling, 'The Law of Property' in P Birks and F Rose (eds), *Lessons of the Swaps Litigation* (Oxford, Mansfield Press, 2000) 257–61.

[82] Matthews (n 81) 24, following a long citation from *Paragon Finance*.

'trustees' as caught and penalised by section 21(1) while property is still in their hands, but not on and after its disposal. Moreover, although the conclusion that time runs without limit in reclaiming the assets themselves may well be right, it is not self-evidently in line with the far broader analysis now advanced in *Williams*. The *Williams* analysis, by contrast, potentially raises the possibility of a six-year limitation period for *property* claims against recipients. This is considered in the next section.

VIII. Innocent Donees Are Trustees But Not Fiduciaries

Although the position of innocent donees was not relevant in *Williams*, its consideration completes the picture of third-party liability in equity. Much of the basic law is uncontroversial, bar the comments on tracing made at the end of this section. Yet applying the analysis in the context of limitation is difficult. The confusion suggests a lack of clarity concerning the types of claim being made against innocent donees, and the types of claim being limited by the Act.

Take the simplest case of a trustee making an unauthorised disposition of trust property (a Picasso painting, say) to an innocent donee. The beneficiary's title is not lost, but persists in the property in the donee's hands: the donee holds the property on trust (a constructive trust) for the beneficiary.[83] The same is true of a purchaser who is not a bona fide purchaser for value without notice of the beneficiary's prior equitable interest. The notice requirement is significant. Notice is relevant for the bona fide purchaser for value defence, but a person who holds assets on trust because of an inability to rely on that defence does not necessarily thereby become a fiduciary.[84] That requires something more, being knowledge that the transferred assets are not at the free disposal of the recipient,[85] or that the assets do not belong beneficially to the recipient.[86] This stricter knowledge test for fiduciaries (not mere notice) is the same knowledge test as is applied in considering whether a person can be sued personally as a knowing recipient if property either received or held with this knowledge is then used or disposed of contrary to the beneficiary's interest.

Also notice that innocent donees do not hold the property on the original trusts (except as they define the relative shares of the beneficiaries). These original trusts may well entail significant management obligations, and innocent

[83] This appears uncontroversial notwithstanding the analysis in *Westdeutsche Landesbank Girozentrale* (n 21) and its insistence that a trust only exists if there is both a property split and knowledge.

[84] R Chambers, 'Distrust: Our Fear of Trusts in the Commercial World' (2010) 63 *Current Legal Problems* 631, 645–49.

[85] As in Quistlose trusts.

[86] The arguments need not be rehearsed here, nor authorities cited. The detail appears in leading texts. Also see Chambers, 'The End of Knowing Receipt' (n 33) 11–16.

donees, having no relevant knowledge, owe no personal obligations at all in relation to the property they hold: they will not be personally liable for disposing of it or acting in ways which diminish its value. Their only liability is to respect the beneficiary's proprietary interests once notified of them. This idea of a property split without concomitant fiduciary obligations is widely recognised: 'fiduciary obligations do not derive from the trust but from the circumstances which give rise to it'.[87]

The consequences in relation to limitation merit thought. Assume the beneficiary does not discover the misapplication for over six years. Can the Picasso painting be reclaimed? The beneficiary's proprietary interest persists, but is action to enforce barred?

On one view, the beneficiary's claim is simply a priority claim. In the most straightforward case, the beneficiaries are doing no more than seeking to vindicate their own equitable title against the original trust property now in the innocent donee's hands. These beneficiaries do not need to assert a wrong by the donee as part of their claim, nor impugn the transfer; indeed, its occurrence is the very basis of their claim against the innocent donee. In these circumstances the Limitation Act 1980 may be irrelevant, and time simply will not run. This priorities approach looks sound, and the results are consistent with common assumptions about innocent donees, although robust precedent seems lacking.[88] In addition, the approach has attractive parallels with the common law concerning both thieves and recipients from thieves: there time runs without limit until the property is taken by a bona fide purchaser for value, and then time is limited: Limitation Act 1980 section 4. This is discussed in more detail below.[89] Notice that this priority approach means that the analysis for trustees misdirecting assets to innocent donees is different from that for directors, even though both are fiduciaries managing property for others.[90] This is not indicative of a flaw in the logic, however. The proprietary structure of trusts and companies differ fundamentally, so differences in proprietary consequences will follow inevitably.

Alternatively, it is also true that on a straightforward reading of the Limitation Act the beneficiary's claim against an innocent donee might be considered to fall within section 21(1)(b), being a claim 'to recover from the trustee trust property' [here the trustee is a non-fiduciary constructive trustee].[91] Just as time does not

[87] Millett (n 81) 406. The distinction was also appreciated by Megarry VC in *Re Montagu's Settlement Trusts* [1987] Ch 264, especially 272–73, 278, 285.

[88] See text to nn 80–82.

[89] See below, X. 'Parallels between the Equitable and Common Law Limitation Rules for Property'.

[90] Trusts are as described here. But in analogous corporate situations the company is unlikely to have a beneficiary's prior equitable interest. The company's purported disposition or contract with the counterparty may be fully effective, despite being unauthorised, or may be merely voidable against complicit recipients, with all the proprietary ramifications inherent in that analysis. See S Worthington, 'Corporate Attribution and Agency—Back to Basics' (2017) 133 *LQR* 118.

[91] Especially since 'trust' includes 'constructive trust'. Seemingly in agreement, see the dicta of Henderson J in *High Commissioner for Pakistan in the United Kingdom v National Westminster Bank* [2016] EWHC 1465 (Ch) [125], in relation to both resulting trusts and constructive trusts (citing *Williams*),

run against an express trustee who is considered to be holding without interruption for the beneficiary, so here too perhaps time simply runs without interruption against an innocent donee. If this is so, however, then it is not clear which *Williams* or *Paragon Finance* Type I and Type II analogies between the express trustee and the innocent donee justify their equal treatment. And the further oddity is that an innocent donee who later acquires knowledge then immediately becomes a knowing recipient and, on the analysis in *Williams*[92] (at least if the property is then knowingly dissipated), would then be protected by the six-year limitation period in section 21(3), and not exposed to *either* limb of section 21(1). If a *knowing* recipient (admittedly one sued personally) is not caught by section 21(1)(b), then there seems little reason to think that an innocent recipient should be caught.[93] This is the conclusion reached by Smith and Davern.[94] They advance a good argument, although one which highlights the problems with the analysis adopted in *Williams*. In short, as they implicitly point out, the simple suggestion here—that a straightforward reading of section 21(1) points to time running without limit against innocent donees still holding trust assets—rather goes against the tenor of the analysis in *Williams* with its Type I and Type II trustees. Nevertheless, the simple approach seems doctrinally more compelling.

The issue is clearly difficult, and any proposed doctrinal response might usefully be tested against questions of policy. On that basis, too, however, the same outcomes still seem appropriate—ie, time running without limit in property claims against an innocent donee. The Limitation Act is a statutory package designed to protect defendants from unlimited exposure to claims for wrongdoing. Section 21 is directed to wrongdoing fiduciaries as a special category, providing them with some protection against claims for breach of their property-holding and property-management obligations, but subject to exceptions to that protection in cases of fraud or where they have benefited personally. The fraud exception occurs frequently in the Limitation Act; the personal benefit exception is special, but is especially apt for fiduciaries given their fiduciary obligations. The implicit agenda of most of the judicial and academic discussion cited in this chapter accords with this, even if the precise detail varies. On this approach, section 21 provides protection to fiduciaries who hold or manage property for others: most claims will be barred after six years. But exceptions exist where the fiduciary has

although see also [130] and the possible distinction between constructive trusts of Type I and II based on knowledge. See also *Burnden Holdings (UK) Ltd v Fielding* [2016] EWCA Civ 557 (CA) in relation to assets received by directors (ie, fiduciaries) in breach of trust; *James v Williams* [2000] Ch 1 (no limitation *iro* executor/trustee *de son tort*). However, in all these cases, including the first, it might be possible to argue that there is sufficient knowledge of the context to make the defendant a *fiduciary* holding the assets on trust, and thus amenable to arguments which are tougher, but which may not necessarily apply to innocent donees. See also nn 81–82 above (Matthews).

92 An analysis not accepted here.

93 It might be different if s 21(1)(b) dealt only with the recovery of traceable proceeds, and required a continuing proprietary interest. But it does not.

94 Smith and Davern (n 19).

behaved fraudulently, or has benefited personally (no matter how innocently). Innocent donees subjected to proprietary claims for recovery of trust assets fall, in policy terms, within the class of trustees who have benefitted personally, albeit quite innocently.

If a choice has to be made, as it undoubtedly does, the priorities approach is favoured here. It seems to best reflect the claim in issue. But it is reassuring that both approaches would deliver the same outcome if section 21 were viewed in the way just suggested.

The problems do not stop there, however. Picasso paintings and family castles are perhaps the only types of asset where the illustrative scenario might indeed be played out. Otherwise it is almost inevitable that within six years the innocent donee will dispose of the property received in ignorance. Given the donee's innocence, there are no associated personal obligations. It follows that if no trust assets remain in the donee's hands, then the beneficiary will be left without proprietary or personal claims. But what if the disposition delivers traceable substitutes? Should the innocent donee be amenable to a tracing claim? By definition, the innocent donee was not a fiduciary when the substitutions were effected. This makes it crucial to know exactly what tracing is doing. *Foskett v McKeown*[95] does not directly address this scenario, but its foundational principle is that tracing into substitutes is part of English property law. If the beneficiary's initial claim was not subject to limitation, then it seems difficult to argue against the same outcome in relation to substitutes *if* they follow simply from the fact of English property law. In policy terms, however, this looks unattractive: it is one thing to vindicate existing rights in the original identifiable assets which have been passed to a donee; it is another to extend those rights into substitutes when the donee owed no personal obligations at all to the beneficiary. To do otherwise promotes exactly the consequences the limitation rules were designed to avoid. In earlier writing I suggested an alternative view of tracing: the detail is beyond summary here, but the result was to tie the relevant tracing analysis to wrongdoing; it is thus an approach which contradicts the analysis in *Foskett v McKeown*, although not the outcome on those facts, but has the advantage of delivering more palatable results in difficult non-fiduciary cases.[96]

[95] *Foskett v McKeown* [2001] 1 AC 102 (HL). See also Millett (n 81) 409.

[96] According to the House of Lords in *Foskett v McKeown* (n 95), a property right can simply be traced into its substitutes and preserved in that substituted form. The result is that a beneficiary may have a continuing property claim in substitutes even though the innocent donee no longer has the original property and even though the donee is not personally liable to her. On the other hand, if tracing merely secures the insolvency priority of an associated *personal* claim once the original property is gone, then the beneficiary would have *no claim at all* here. See Worthington, *Equity* (n 33) ch 4, where the latter approach is preferred. Also see S Worthington, 'Justifying Claims to Secondary Profits' in EJH Schrage (ed), *Unjust Enrichment and the Law of Contract* (The Hague, Kluwer Law International, 2001) 451.

IX. Limitation and Fiduciary Disgorgement

One of the less obvious consequences of the analysis in *Williams* is the doubt which it feeds in relation to applicable limitation periods in the recovery of disloyal gains from defaulting fiduciaries.[97] The simplest possible case is surely where an express trustee (unequivocally a Type I trustee/fiduciary) absconds with trust assets, or takes an opportunity which ought to have been pursued for the trust, or takes a bribe. As noted earlier,[98] the problem might be approached on the basis that all these disloyal gains are simply held by the trustee on the original trusts, adopting the most favourable interpretation of *FHR European Ventures LLP & Ors v Cedar Capital Partners LLC*.[99] But the limitation cases themselves paint a more convoluted picture, recognising the various Type I and Type II distinctions described in *Williams*, and pursuing them to their logical ends so as to hold that some of these assets are held on Type II trusts, with a consequential six-year limitation window and no possibility of time running indefinitely.

The leading cases in this area involve directors rather than trustees. A selection indicates that companies can recover without time limitation from directors taking unauthorised distributions from the company,[100] or making profits through self-dealing with the company[101] (a conclusion which seems doubtful, since these transactions are merely voidable), but that a six-year limitation applies in respect of gains from corporate opportunities[102] (perhaps now subject to reinterpretation following *FHR*).[103] The only escape from this analytical headache is to run an argument to postpone the commencement of the limitation period on the grounds of fraud, concealment or mistake, all rather widely defined: Limitation Act 1980 section 32.

This is again an area where the policy underpinning the Limitation Act is necessarily brought to the fore. If the purpose of the unlimited time provisions in section 21(1) is to protect the property of beneficiaries and principals against fraudulent losses or disloyal extractions by the managing fiduciaries themselves, then a principled distinction in relation to disloyal extractions might be based on whether their recovery would constitute an unexpected windfall to the beneficiary, or whether it would simply represent recovery of the very assets which should have

[97] See Talbot Rice and Holden (n 8).

[98] See above, III. 'Distinguishing between Types of Constructive Trustee'.

[99] *FHR* (n 21).

[100] *Tintin Exploration Syndicate Ltd v Sandys* (1947) 177 LT 412.

[101] *JJ Harrison (Properties) Ltd v Harrison* [2001] EWCA Civ 1467, [2002] 1 BCLC 162.

[102] *Gwembe Valley Development Co Ltd v Koshy* [2003] EWCA Civ 1048, [2004] 1 BCLC 131. Although here the claim was saved because the director's breach was considered to have been fraudulent and dishonest, and thus caught by s 21(1)(a) in any event.

[103] *FHR* (n 21).

been part of the managed fund if all had gone according to plan. But even if this difference appears compelling in theory, no case has ever relied on it, and in practice it is a distinction which disappears into non-existence.[104] Something more straightforward is clearly needed. The obvious candidate is to discard all Type I/Type II distinctions in favour of far more pointed fiduciary/non-fiduciary distinctions. This would capture all these disloyal gains on the same basis, with the sole exception of self-dealing claims.

More needs to be said about self-dealing. Ignoring the authority noted above, *should* section 21(1)(b) assist recovery without limitation of time? The answer ought to be no,[105] and without resort to Type I/Type II distinctions. What is crucial is that in a self-dealing transaction the purchasing fiduciary does not hold the received assets on constructive trust;[106] the contract is merely voidable at the option of the principal, and until the contract is avoided the fiduciary is the legal and beneficial owner of the assets. This means that on its face a claim cannot be brought under section 21(1)(b), since the fiduciary is not holding trust property but simply property which was once the trust's. The principal thus has six years, under section 21(3), to avoid the voidable contract and recover the property which originally belonged to the trust but has been lost by virtue of a self-dealing breach by the fiduciary. This limitation outcome can be avoided, but only if the claim can be brought under section 21(1)(a) as a fraudulent breach of trust.[107] If the goal is to treat all recoveries of disloyal gains alike, then the pressure to fit the disgorgement claim into this fraud box may seem irresistible. The pressure seems even greater given our familiar assertion that a beneficiary's proprietary interest is not overreached by a transfer to a purchaser who is not a bona fide purchaser for value: surely a self-dealing fiduciary must be regarded as having at least this degree of notice. But this maxim suffers from its own generalities: it indicates a priority outcome, not the steps or limitation impediments to reaching it; a claim to an interest in the original managed assets must be linked with rescission and *restitutio in integrum* of the corresponding benefits received by the principal.

[104] See an attempt in S Worthington, 'Fiduciary Duties and Proprietary Remedies: Addressing the Failure of Equitable Formulae' (2013) 1 *CLJ* 720. The *only* case thought to fall outside the class involving 'assets which should have been part of the managed fund if all had gone according to plan' was *Attorney General for Hong Kong v Reid* [1994] 1 AC 324 (PC).

[105] Other cases have reached this conclusion relying on Type I and Type II distinctions. See *Taylor v Davies* [1920] AC 636 (PC), concluding the self-dealing claim was Type II. *Beckford v Wade* (1805) 17 Ves 87 (PC) similarly relied on a 'not a real trustee' distinction on facts suggesting the need to unravel an allegedly unauthorised sale to the defendant before any property could be said to be held on trust for the claimant.

[106] Contrast *JJ Harrison (Properties) Ltd* (n 101).

[107] Fraud is equated with dishonesty: *Armitage v Nurse* [1998] Ch 241, 251, 261.

X. Parallels between the Equitable and Common Law Limitation Rules for Property

The majority in *Williams* felt confirmed in their adopted distinctions between Type I and Type II constructive trustees, and their characterisation of third parties as Type II, because the outcome ensured that equitable fraudsters were not treated more harshly than common law fraudsters, and were in a better position than defaulting trustees.[108]

Of course it is possible to draw analogies with fraudsters who at common law are protected by a six-year limitation rule.[109] But there is an alternative and seemingly more appropriate analogy. At common law, any fraudulent dealings with the *claimant* are protected by six-year limitation rules; but fraudulent dealings with the claimant's *property*—ie, theft—run without limitation against the thief, and against all those taking through the thief until the transactional chain reaches a bona fide purchaser for value: section 4. The provisions in section 21(1) can be seen as on all fours in relation to protecting equitable interests in managed property.

The assumed stark contrast with defaulting trustees is also fragile. The Limitation Act itself puts defaulting trustees in a special category, but then defines 'trustees' to include 'constructive trustees'. Thus, the important question is whether dishonest assisters and knowing recipients are constructive trustees. 'Constructive trustee' is the old-fashioned equivalent of 'fiduciary'.[110] The majority saw the fiduciary relationship between claimant and defendant as key as long as it was pre-existing.[111] On the analysis here the fiduciary relationship is seen as key whenever it provides the package of duties which is infringed. Functionally, surely this is the same thing. The hard question, then, is whether dishonest assisters and knowing recipients are fiduciaries breaching their duties. Here, contrary to *Williams*, it is suggested they are.

XI. Exposing Third-Party Liability in Equity

The principal conclusions on third-party liability in equity can be summarised relatively simply, but they, in turn, depend on a clear appreciation of the regime relating to primary liability. This is familiar territory, but sometimes we miss key

108 *Williams* (n 1) [118].
109 Subject to the possibility that time may not start to run immediately: s 32.
110 See above, IV. 'Language and Logic'.
111 See the earlier discussion of Type I and Type II constructive trustees: III 'Distinguishing between Types of Constructive Trustee'.

facets and idiosyncrasies. Trust law and fiduciary law both concern themselves with property holding and property management for others. Express trustees do both, but it is equally possible to do one without the other: innocent donees hold property without managing it; company directors manage property without holding it on trust.

The property-holding notion in equity is well understood. One person holds legal title; another the beneficial interest. This is a trust, regarded as a special invention of equity. So it is, but analogous sharing arrangements are equally well known to the common law, and are of older parentage. The common law version concerns possession: one person holds legal title, another the possessory interest. In both cases, the relevant detail behind intentionally sophisticated arrangements must be spelt out, but equally in both cases trivial and informal arrangements can also be accommodated; innocent donees in equity and finders at common law are illustrative.

The idea of personal obligations of property management for the benefit of others is trickier. There are two key strands. First, property managers (fiduciaries) must care for and administer the managed property in defined ways, but their liability is inevitably measured by loss to the managed property fund, not loss to the individuals with interests in the fund.[112] This seemingly unremarkable feature is what distinguishes prescriptive property management in equity from common law contractual obligations and duties owed in tort. Second, the activities of these property managers are constrained by fiduciary obligations. These provide 'do not' rules, rather than 'do' rules. Their purpose is not to incentivise property managers to deliver peak financial performance or avoid terrible disasters. Their purpose is simply to ensure that every benefit achieved, whether considerable or meagre, is delivered to the beneficiaries and not diverted to the property managers themselves. This is done by disgorgement remedies.[113] In total, therefore, the equitable property-management regime requires strict compliance with the management plan, appropriate care of the managed assets and fiduciary loyalty. The first two rules are remedied by reference to any loss in value of the economic interest in the managed assets; the last by disgorgement of gains. In all of this it is immaterial whether the managed assets are held on trust or not.

[112] Compare the assessment of liability for non-compliance with the strict terms of the trust deed, or for negligence in performance of the management role, with the assessment of liability in contract and tort. The former focuses on the lost value to the managed property: *AIB Group (UK) Plc v Mark Redler & Co Solicitors* [2014] UKSC 58 (SC). By contrast, contract and tort focus on the economic loss to the individual affected by the breach. Since the focus is on an individual, the particular economic loss caused by any breach can be somewhat at large. As a result, both contract law and tort law have developed rules on foreseeability and remoteness. There is no equivalent risk with property managers: the managed property is known, and the managers take responsibility for changes in its economic value caused by their breach. All regimes of course demand causation: defendants should only be liable for the damage caused by their wrongdoing, not damage caused otherwise.

[113] *FHR* (n 21); *Novoship* (n 53). See also *Consul Development Pty Ltd v DPC Estates Pty Ltd* (1975) 132 CLR 373.

The next issue is how these property-holding and property-management rules are attracted. They can arise consensually or by operation of law. In either case, the analogies are with express trust property holding regimes and express trustee management regimes. Consensually agreed express trusts are well known, but property holding also arises by operation of law when courts insist that one party must be recognised as holding an asset for the benefit of another, as with vendor–purchaser trusts, Quistclose trusts, proprietary estoppel, etc. Generically, these are all 'constructive trusts'—ie, 'not an express trust, but is treated as if it were an express trust', with analogous property-holding consequences. Similarly, consensually agreed express trusteeship is well known, but equally the law may insist that others behave as if they were subject to equitable controls on their management of property for others. These people are now called fiduciaries, with company directors, agents, solicitors, etc providing illustrations. Historically, however, these people were called 'constructive trustees'—ie, 'not express trustees but treated as if they were express trustees'.

That brings us to accessories.[114] Although we now talk a great deal about accessory or ancillary liability, equity historically dealt with these strangers to an express trust or consensual fiduciary relationship without going through a loop which sought to determine whether these people were accessories. Instead it moved directly to considering whether these people were either property holders or property managers for others. In making this move, equity's focus is squarely on the relationship between the stranger and the managed property (as it is with express trustees and fiduciaries), and not the relationship between the stranger and the beneficiary (as it would be in finding primary duty/liability relationships at common law), nor on the relationship between the stranger and wrongdoer (as it would be with common law accessories). Thus, in a rather surprising way equity's focus on property means that it determines the liability of strangers to an express trust, or strangers to the property-management relationship, very directly: it asks whether these people, too, are trustees or fiduciaries or both. It does not go through an additional loop, first asking the unnecessary question about whether they are accessories. This direct route to liability was the focus of the historical language of constructive trusts, discussed earlier, a language used long before accessory and ancillary liability became fashionable.[115]

Pursuing this line eliminates a good number of uncertainties. If strangers are to be made fiduciaries, then their knowledge that the managed assets belong in equity to others is crucial. This clarifies the focus of the current notice, knowledge, unconscionability and dishonesty debates. And if strangers are trustees or fiduciaries, then their liability follows accordingly: it is personal not secondary, and it

[114] Two important books have been written, both providing access to crucial secondary material: Davies, *Accessory Liability* (n 65); Dietrich and Ridge (n 8).

[115] Much of the modern commentary is critical of Lord Selborne LC in *Barnes v Addy* (1873–74) LR 9 Ch App 244, 251–52 (CA) but, in hindsight, he may have had it in a nutshell.

includes proprietary claims, compensation for loss and disgorgement of disloyal gains.

Pursuing this line will also necessarily include these strangers being subject to the same limitation rules as express trustees, and these rules themselves should be approached with a clearer and more useful focus on trusts and fiduciaries—ie, property holding and property management—not Type I and Type II constructive trustees.[116]

XII. Conclusion

The arguments advanced in this chapter are as follows:

1. The distinctions drawn by the Supreme Court in *Williams* are unduly complicated. The line between Type I and Type II constructive trustees is inadequately defined, probably inherently so, and its alignment with the characteristics that are material to the distinctions drawn by the Limitation Act 1980 is unclear.
2. The language of constructive trusts and constructive trustees is confusing. It disguises a relatively straightforward search for situations where there are property splits (trusts) or property management responsibilities (fiduciary responsibilities). These can exist independently of each other (innocent donees and directors illustrate the possibilities). We should use language which makes the specific details clear: ie, *trust* (referring to a property split only), *trustee* (referring to property holding only) and *fiduciary* (referring to personal property-management obligations whenever this parcel includes fiduciary duties which ban self-interested management).
3. Accessory liability in equity is something of a misnomer, since the drive is not to find individuals with particular associations with the wrongdoer and shared liability for the primary wrong, but instead to find individuals who are themselves trustees or fiduciaries because of their particular association with the original managed property. Liability follows accordingly. It is a primary liability not a secondary liability, notwithstanding that the characterisation of the stranger as trustee or fiduciary arises by operation of law rather than by consensual agreement.
4. Pursuing that line of analysis in the context of dishonest assistance and knowing receipt, dishonest assisters are seen to be fiduciaries, and knowing recipients to be trustees on receipt of the property and fiduciaries on acquisition knowledge. These parties are sued for breach of their property-holding or property-management duties. Innocent donees, by contrast, are trustees, but not fiduciaries. Claims against them are priority disputes, not breach of duty cases. Liability in each case follows accordingly.

116 See above, V. 'Applying this Language to Limitation'.

5. Where there are fiduciary responsibilities for property management, liability is in two forms: compensation for loss to the managed assets; and disgorgement of disloyal gains. The former is distinguishable from common law compensation in its focus on remedying loss to the property fund, not the loss to individuals interested in the fund.
6. Finally, and rather as a sideshow to these other important conclusions, all of this has obvious ramifications for the limitation rules. The preferable distinction is not between Type I and Type II constructive trustees, with only the former exposed to time running without limitation under section 21(1), but between fiduciaries and non-fiduciaries. Recognising this and bringing it front and centre would immediately eliminate an enormous number of practical difficulties which currently exist in applying the limitation rules, but would nevertheless accord with the outcomes in the majority of decisions, and with principle in the remainder.

INDEX

www.ingramcontent.com/pod-product-compliance
Ingram Content Group UK Ltd.
Pitfield, Milton Keynes, MK11 3LW, UK
UKHW020906190926
475560UK00010B/300

9 781509 907298